Praise for *Movement*

"In this meticulously researched opus, Nicole Gelinas shows us the underbelly of NY politics, the brinksmanship, the civic commitment, the short-sighted self-interest, and the long view. She shows us the heroes and the villains and the people who at different times wore both hats. As a New Yorker, I related (and sometimes laughed) to be reminded of the Guardian Angels, the token suckers, the dismal conditions of public transit. . . . I learned something in every chapter. Kudos to Nicole, I will refer to this book again and again."

—**Rachel Weinberger**, Regional Plan Association

"Why is America's urban landscape so car-centric? Nicole Gelinas exposes some universal dynamics in *Movement: New York's Long War to Take Back Its Streets from the Car*. While Robert Moses "has shouldered the blame," Gelinas shows that generations of politicians and planners have failed to right the wrongs. Advocating for people over cars is not easy. In one of many fascinating examples, Gelinas reveals that urbanist Jane Jacobs was ready to compromise in the battle to exclude cars from Washington Square Park. Another woman, Shirley Hayes, saved the day."

—**Richard K. Rein**, author of *American Urbanist: How William H. Whyte's Unconventional Wisdom Reshaped Public Life*

"You will never look at a city street in the same way again after reading Nicole Gelinas's magisterial and gripping history of the rise, and maybe decline, of urban car culture. Gelinas persuasively re-interprets 'The Power Broker' for the 21st century, showing how a cacophonous crowd of politicians, business elites, labor, newspapers, and others pulled New York City into a chokehold of cars. She also offers hope in her nuanced and captivating account of how a new mix of public servants, civic leaders, community groups, and determined New Yorkers have started on a path where car-clogged streets may well yield to pedestrians and mass transit, the bedrock of the thriving city."

—**Elizabeth Glazer**, founder of *Vital City*

"This is a story that needs to be understood by everyone with who cares about the urban realm. For a century or more, creating space for cars has been associated with improving the prosperity of cities when, as Gelinas shows in her comprehensive and engaging account of New York's history so cogently, they have done the opposite. Yet, even now as many cities are taking in the lessons, New York remains at a crossroads. Gelinas is in no doubt about which path it should take and this book is a powerful argument not just for Gotham city, but for politicians and planners everywhere."

—**Christian Wolmar,** author of *Are Trams Socialist? Why Britain Has No Transport Policy*

Movement

Movement

New York City's Long Battle to Take Back Its Streets from the Car

Nicole Gelinas

EMPIRE STATE EDITIONS

AN IMPRINT OF FORDHAM UNIVERSITY PRESS

NEW YORK 2025

Furthermore:
a program of the J.M. Kaplan Fund

Funding for this book was provided by
Furthermore: a program of the J. M. Kaplan Fund.

Small portions of chapters 10, 12, 13, 18, and 21 were originally published in *City Journal*.

Visit us online at www.fordhampress.com/empire-state-editions.

Library of Congress Cataloging-in-Publication Data available online at https://catalog.loc.gov.

Printed in the United States of America

26 25 24 5 4 3 2 1

To Nana and Grampy, who took us on the #72 trackless trolley

CONTENTS

Movement

INTRODUCTION

STARTING A CENTURY AGO, the automobile changed the world—and helped drive New York City (and other cities) to the brink of irrevocable urban decline. To many, the mass-market automobile seemed to make subways, buses, and commuter trains—and thus a city built around them—obsolete. This perception led city officials and planners to reimagine New York around the automobile. After World War II, this assault on urban viability accelerated, as cheaper and faster travel on new highways lured much of America's white middle class out of a crowded, dirty, and increasingly dangerous city to sprawling, leafy, modern suburbs. Through the mid-twentieth century, elected officials tried to reverse this exodus by attempting to make New York more hospitable to the car, gutting neighborhoods to build modern highways and in the process leaving subways to rot and pedestrians defenseless against traffic and pollution. Their efforts, however, only accelerated the exodus and left the city peopled by poorer residents, governed by officials who struggled to address growing unemployment, crime, drugs, and urban decay. By 1975, New York City had sunk to its lowest point. Violent crime was soaring, and tax revenues were sinking. The nation's largest city was losing the geographic war for people and jobs. Businesses were leaving Manhattan, taking their office workers first to nearby suburbs and then to western and southern regions of the country. Manufacturers took blue-collar jobs to the south and then abroad. Within a decade, one million people had fled New York.

One man has shouldered the blame for this urban plight and flight: New York's twentieth-century "master builder," Robert Moses. Since the 1974 publication of Robert A. Caro's *The Power Broker*, Moses has emerged as the convenient uber-villain, responsible for sacrificing the city to the automobile. During his decades-long reign, according to Caro, Moses diverted scarce finances to new roads rather than old subways; designed motor parkways to repel buses; cut off suburbs from poorer and minority families who didn't own cars; and displaced tens of thousands of New Yorkers so he could lay asphalt and pour cement over once thriving neighborhoods.

The problem with this enduring narrative is that it holds one man responsible for an entire city's collective sins. Moses, for much of his public life, served as the public face of policies New York's elected officials, technocratic planners, and business communities desired; toward the end of his career, he served as a scapegoat for elected officials and civic leaders avoiding their own accountability in decisions that shaped New York to accommodate the automobile. Even after he had left his last leadership position in 1968, elected officials found it easier to blame Moses for New York's urban woes rather than finding ways to ease, for example, the burden that the Cross-Bronx Expressway—indelibly associated with him—foists on hundreds of thousands of Bronx residents.

It is easier to blame one man for redesigning New York City around the automobile rather than generations of city officials, civic leaders, and businesspeople, including generations that have failed to right Moses's supposed wrongs in the decades since his death. From three New York mayors who ripped up the city's trolley tracks in the early twentieth century to Governor Nelson Rockefeller who, in the 1960s, promised to rebuild the transit system without offering fiscal resources to do so, successive generations of elected officials—supported by the big-business community, the *New York Times*, and even the public—made the decisions that shaped pre-millennial New York.

By the second half of the twentieth century, New Yorkers began to understand that the automobile had failed urbanism as an engine of growth. For New York to recover from its twentieth-century mistakes, it had to repudiate, at least partially, the auto age. In the 1950s, a band of Greenwich Village housewives—who had been told by Moses, elected officials, and civic groups to accept an open-cut road through Washington Square Park—mastered the political savvy and stamina needed to say "no" to power. A decade later, urbanist Jane Jacobs used that knowledge to defeat the Lower Manhattan Expressway, which would have thrust across SoHo—then a postindustrial wasteland in the view of city officials, today one of the city's most expensive neighborhoods. The decision ended the city's half-century of automobile expansion. New York thus safeguarded an asset that most American cities sacrificed: an intact urban center.

Killing mega-highways was only the start. In the 1970s, the city's subway, bus, and commuter-rail system barely functioned. After decades of neglect, breakdowns were so common that the transit authority gave commuters notes to excuse them from tardiness. To ride the subway after dark was to put oneself in peril of violent crime. By the 1980s, state, city, and business leaders emphasized that they would reembrace the city's subways, which, in turn, helped reverse the city's population decline.

New York also had to rethink the use of its existing streets, taking space away from cars and giving it to walkers, buses, and bicyclists. In the 1960s, only eccentrics rode bikes in the city; thanks to their efforts, by the early twenty-first century, pastel-shirted bankers pedaled up Midtown bike lanes on municipal bikes. In the 2000s, people laughed when the mayor converted much of Times Square into a pedestrian plaza; by 2019, that plaza was so crowded that it was difficult to walk around. Taking back public spaces for people not cocooned by automobiles was possible only because New York made public spaces safer: by 2019, homicides were nearly 90 percent below 1990 peaks.

In re-embracing transit and in repurposing streets, New York redefined what it meant to be a global city: not a place that is easy to drive through but a place where people can take transit, walk, and bike to work, to school, or just for fun. By early 2020, the city's population, subway ridership, and jobs were near record highs, with midnight trains as crowded as rush-hour trains had been decades earlier. New York's new pressing problem was that it had become so popular, even people with well-paying jobs could barely afford it.

However, even before March 2020, when the pandemic hit New York harder than any other American city, Gotham's transportation future—and its urban success—was not assured. Overcrowding and mismanagement overwhelmed transit. For all New York's progress since the 1960s, cars and trucks still dominated public space. The rise of ride-hailing services had added tens of thousands of cars to dense streets, a reminder of the persistent lure of a private ride over transit, even if that ride caused congestion and pollution. From children breathing in fumes from the Cross-Bronx Expressway to women on bikes dodging heavy truck traffic in Williamsburg, we still live in the world that, many insist, Moses had built.

The pandemic and its aftermath proved the gravest challenge to urban life since the Model T. By 2023, COVID-19 had killed more than forty thousand New Yorkers. A longer-term threat emerged, like the menace a century earlier, when cars had enabled the middle class to move to the suburbs. The work-from-home phenomenon among Manhattan's office workers, forced by the pandemic but persisting after the crisis, revived the perception that the city was obsolete. Manhattan's office buildings remained half-empty. Violent crime was up, underground and in the streets. The city was at risk of reversing decades of population and jobs growth.

These dislocations both caused and reflected New Yorkers' changed relationship to transit. Even by spring 2024, four years after the onset of the pandemic, subway ridership, once a part of day-to-day life across the income scale, had recovered only to three-quarters of pre-COVID levels. A surge in motor vehicle purchases showed that more New Yorkers considered a car a necessity. In turn, a retreat from energy-efficient urban density, density enabled by mass transit, reverberates beyond New York, and risks progress in America's battle against climate change.

Will COVID-19 soon be, in hindsight, a surmountable tragedy for the city, akin to the September 11, 2001, terror attacks? Or will 2020 have marked a turning from prosperity to decline—as traumatic as the 1970s? A survey of New York's modern transportation history—told from the sidewalk, the subway platform, the saddle of a bike, and, yes, from behind a windshield—shows that New York cannot recover its pre-pandemic success unless it protects its public transportation and streetscape from that century-old menace: automobile dependency. The key to New York's continued success as America's global city—and a destination of opportunity—is its re-embrace of subways and buses as well as a more ambitious repurposing of streets. It's time to stop blaming Moses, a man who has been dead for more than four decades, and look to our current generation of leaders to give us the city we need.

Part 1

DRIVING TO THE BRINK

Chapter 1

New York's Original Sin

Scrapping Street Transit

> We will tear up the unsightly and unwieldy trolley tracks . . . and put [them] in the . . . scrap heap.
>
> —Mayor John "Red Mike" Hylan, 1921

> There is danger of the opinion establishing itself that the surface [trolley] in Manhattan is an obsolescent institution.
>
> —*New York Times*, 1926

NEW YORK'S ORIGINAL BETRAYAL of transit was the destruction of its sturdiest, most efficient form of mass transit, second only to subways: streetcars. By the 1920s, as the automobile asserted its presence, the streetcar—despite carrying New Yorkers from one place to another more than a billion times a year—was reviled by the political class. Beginning more than a decade before Robert Moses had any city government power, three mayors—John Hylan, Jimmy Walker, and Fiorello LaGuardia—worked to see this priceless infrastructure destroyed. Obliterating trolley lines was New York's first failure in its stewardship of its mass transit system and its streets.

One Billion Electric-Powered Rides a Year

In the early twentieth century, when New Yorkers needed to get from one place to another, they had choices: descend underground to their fast-expanding subway, climb stairs to an elevated rail line, or take the streetcar, or trolley. By the turn of the century, omnibus operators had converted horse-drawn conveyances that had plied New York's avenues and cross streets since the 1830s into electrified trolley service. Trolleys—with multiple, wide doors for boarding and tracks straight down the middle of avenues and streets—were efficient and fast. Nearly a century before anyone thought about pollution, clean energy powered streetcars, with no direct emissions other than a spark. They were also cheap: trolley companies charged a nickel, just as subways did. By 1920, 1,800 miles of track crossed New York.[1] From Staten Island to the Bronx, Astoria to Harlem, Forty-Second Street to Brooklyn's Mermaid Avenue, streetcars, at their 1920s peak, carried more than one-third of the city's transit passengers.[2] The streetcar even gave Brooklyn's then–major league baseball team their nickname: "Trolley Dodgers."

But trolleys faced a threat from a supposed innovation: motor buses. New York got its first buses in 1907. That year, a private company called the Fifth Avenue Coach line replaced its "two-horse and three-horse hitch" carriages, which had carried passengers along the elegant avenue for decades, with London-style motor buses. Fifth Avenue Coach had chosen to motorize buses rather than replace its horse-drawn conveyances with trolleys because business interests along "that plushy thoroughfare" considered tracks unsightly.[3] The firm had a government franchise to charge a premium ten-cent fare—twice the regulated fare on the subway, which had opened in 1904—for customers to board its double-decker open-air buses, or "coaches."[4] A conductor went from seat to seat to collect the fare, holding "out a device into which the rider pushed the dime and was rewarded with the little sound of a bell." Teens paid to ride on the top deck and "spoon" as they took in the scene below; housewives paid the extra fare, relative to the subway, to bring parcels home in style.[5]

Excepting Fifth Avenue, New York was behind the times compared to London. In 1906, the *New York Times* had noted, "Visitors to London . . . are likely to be surprised at the change that has come over the omnibus traffic in that great city of fogs and blocks. . . . The emancipation of the equine seems to be rapidly approaching. Every third or fourth bus that goes through Fleet Street, the Strand, and Piccadilly is a motor. It . . . dodges in and out of the confusion of traffic with an ease and rapidity." Its only drawback: a "disagreeable odor of petrol."[6]

New York considered following London's example. With its population having grown from 3.4 million residents in 1900 to 4.8 million a decade later (and on its way to 5.6 million by 1920), the city was growing outward, beyond Manhattan tenements, across the rivers to Brooklyn, Queens, the Bronx, and even the farmland of Staten Island. As it expanded, New York grew less dense, with developers erecting smaller apartment buildings and single- to three-family houses. Building trolley tracks to serve these neighborhoods didn't seem cost-effective, as fewer passengers per mile would live along each line. In 1912, New York officials sent an engineer to London and Paris to learn about those cities' bus systems. The engineer agreed that building bus routes to areas of the city "not already supplied" with trolleys was a good idea, but he advised against replacing existing streetcars with buses. "There is no reason why a motor bus should be permitted on the same street as a trolley," as it would siphon customers from the trolley without creating any advantage over it.[7]

A Mayor Driven by Ideology

Nominally, Democratic mayor John "Red Mike" Hylan, who governed New York from 1918 to 1925, was a Tammany Hall man, supported by the backroom Manhattan machine whose bribery scandals dated to the nineteenth-century days of William "Boss" Tweed. Unlike most Tammany men, however, Hylan despised big business and finance. In one of his speeches, he compared the Rockefeller-controlled Standard Oil to the Ku Klux Klan, accusing both organizations of comprising "America's secret dynastic rulers." He often railed against capitalism—an "invisible power whose black and menacing form hovers over every fireside."[8]

To Hylan, the companies that ran New York's subways and streetcars were evil. It's not that Hylan favored the burgeoning auto industry. His sister, Mary, "was run down and killed by an automobile in Brooklyn, July 10, 1911," Hylan wrote, leaving him "without any close blood relative."[9] Hylan just hated railroad and transit companies with a monomania. He never missed an opportunity to castigate the "traction interests," as he labeled them, as "useless" or corrupt.

Part of the animosity was personal. A native of upstate New York, Hylan had moved to Brooklyn as a young man, where he took a job building a rail line; "a common railroad labor hand," as he put it, "driver of spikes." Hylan worked his way up to train engineer with an affiliate of the Brooklyn Rapid Transit (BRT) company, one of two major operators. But the company fired him after he took "a curve too fast, endangering a supervisor."[10]

More than a grudge, though, Hylan's dislike of the transit industry became a carefully honed aspect of his economic and political worldviews. Hylan saw rail companies as part of the crony-capitalist system. He accused firms of controlling elected officials, particularly Republican lawmakers and governors, by parceling out stock ownership interests and favors.

Indeed, subway and streetcar companies were monopolies. Rail transportation is not a naturally competitive industry. Interborough Rapid Transit (IRT) and the BRT's successor, Brooklyn-Manhattan Transit (BMT), controlled their respective subways and, through affiliates, trolleys. Unlike supermarkets that can vie for customers based on service and price on the same block, rail companies can't compete along the same passageways, and it would have been prohibitively expensive for companies to duplicate each other's physical infrastructure to compete for the same customers. Each company had a territory, determined by the government, and trolley companies purchased one another to expand their territories. As they did, they became more powerful. Then as now, government's power to award such franchises presented opportunity for corruption.

Hylan's solution: destroy the subway and trolley industry. His strategy, which also happened to be his major public policy: forever freezing the five-cent subway and trolley fare. At the turn of the century, subway and trolley lines had signed agreements with the city to maintain a nickel fare; the city would have to grant permission for any increase. Nobody likes price increases, and the nickel fare was popular with New Yorkers and thus among politicians. For Hylan, however, the fare was not just one among several populist positions calculated to win election and reelection; it was *the* position.

The mayor was not economically naïve. He knew that with inflation pushing up costs in the aftermath of World War I, keeping the nickel fare would put subway and trolley operators out of business. Hylan's plan was to bankrupt the subway operators so that, as he put it, "the private operators [would] turn the subways back to the city [to run]," even though this outcome meant that the city would have to pay their investors for the value of their assets and assume responsibility for their debt. These costs were unavoidable; for the city to expropriate subway assets without compensation would guarantee lawsuits.

For trolleys, Hylan envisioned a different fate. He viewed trolley assets—cars and tracks—as worthless, and any proposed purchase would have been tantamount to a bailout of politically connected companies. "In the mayor's opinion," the *Times* noted, "[trolleys] should have been relegated to the junk heap . . . [and] should not . . . be taken over."[11] His plan was to destroy not only the industry's ownership structure but also its physical infrastructure. But he did not want to wait until the nickel fare forced trolley companies to cut back on maintenance so severely that they could no longer provide service. Instead, he would compete against them, using buses, which, he insisted, could run profitably on a nickel fare.

In 1919, the mayor had an opportunity to put his plan in motion. That August, workers struck against the Brooklyn subway and streetcar systems, demanding better pay and hours. Hylan deployed "emergency buses," hiring private-sector drivers to replace suspended transit service.[12] After taking a ride on one "emergency bus" across Lower Manhattan, Hylan enthused that "the death knell of the traction ring and their agents . . . has been sounded."[13] (These "agents," Hylan never failed to remind the public, were often elected officials, part-time lawyers, or board members at transit firms.)

After the strike, Hylan continued to expand the city's bus service, often boasting that buses would kill trolleys. By 1920, the city was overseeing forty-six bus routes, carrying seventy-five million passengers a year.[14] As trolley companies struggled amid this competition and as their assets deteriorated for lack of reinvestment, Hylan claimed that the companies had "abandoned" their duties; indeed, in some cases, bankrupt firms walked away from their tracks.

Fixated on his goal, Hylan was flexible in his ancillary principles. The city didn't exactly run these "Hylanic jitneys," but contracted with owners of sixteen- or twenty-passenger conveyances.[15] Hylan was even flexible with the sacrosanct five-cent fare. During one strike, the Queens Chamber of Commerce protested that "buses that have been supplied to serve as a substitute have been permitted to charge a ten-cent fare when the trolley company was denied this privilege."[16] When Hylan directed Grover Whalen—a Tammany hand who was then commissioner of plant and structure—to prepare a citywide bus network, the plan that emerged would rely on private operators. In one bid, George Loft of the Loft Candy Company, for example, proposed "a system of electrically operated buses," offering "comfort and luxury."[17]

Trolley companies reacted aggressively. They alleged that Hylan's bus service was illegal under state franchise law, under state utilities regulation, and under the contracts that the city had signed. Law and contracts had promised exclusivity, without which trolley firms would not have made investments; it didn't make sense to install tracks to have buses compete along the same line. Trolley lines sued and won. "There is not the slightest excuse for this lawlessness," one judge excoriated Hylan.[18] Yet rulings made Hylan's point. "The traction ring went where corporations always go," said Whalen, "to a federal judge—and there they got what corporations always get."[19]

Hylan made buses the centerpiece of an unsuccessful 1922 gubernatorial campaign. "With the election of a progressive governor, one who is not tied to the traction corporations, . . . the people will then begin to ride in fine, commodious, city-owned buses, and the antiquated trolley cars will soon disappear."[20] Opening one "trackless trolley"—a bus powered by overhead wires—on Staten Island, the mayor inveighed against "the public utility corporations, who want to run the city; the underworld and gambling interests, who want to run the police; and . . . the Rockefeller Foundation, who want[s] to run the schools."[21]

The trolley companies outflanked him. They determined that if they couldn't stop the bus, they would run the buses. In 1922, the state-controlled transit commission, pressured by trolley firms, preempted Hylan, preparing a plan to replace 30 percent of Brooklyn trolleys with buses.[22] The companies not only had politicians as their allies. Hylan charged that the "traction-controlled newspapers" were pushing the state plan. Whereas once editorialists had opposed buses, now, they favored them. "The oscillations and gyrations of the editorial minds of the traction press surprise but do not confuse me."[23] But traction interests had beaten him. Hylan complained that the companies "have made a mental apportionment of the five boroughs" for bus franchises, so that they could maintain their monopolies by running buses instead of trolleys.[24]

For the remainder of his term, Hylan bickered with state officials over the bid process for buses to replace trolleys. Corruption charges flew. At one hearing, a motor-company president said that a man claiming to be close to Hylan had approached him about selling buses to the city, demanding ten thousand dollars a year. When a judge asked another witness about his "ability to sell buses to the city of New York," the witness forthrightly answered, "acquaintanceship for twenty years with . . . different commissioners."[25] At another hearing, a witness offered hearsay that would-be operators of one Bronx bus had provided a twenty-five-thousand-dollar bribe to Tammany Hall, earmarked for the "big chief." Whalen, allegedly the "big chief," interrupted: "Do not sneer, you dirty rat, you little liar."[26] Hylan left office in 1925—when he lost the Democratic nomination for mayor to Tammany-backed Jimmy Walker—without seeing his vision of a trolley-free New York realized. "I wanted to see buses running in every part of the city," he said. "I regret that I cannot see them."[27] But his departure wouldn't save the trolleys. After surveying "expert" opinion on buses' speed, reliability, and cost savings, the *Times* concluded that "trolleys are doomed."[28]

A Mayor Driven by Greed

Mayor Jimmy Walker was the opposite of Hylan. "Beau James" Walker was the dandy mayor for the pre-Depression Jazz Age. As a young man, Hylan had labored on the railroad to support his family; Walker, the Greenwich Village–born son of a politician, had written songs. Hylan wore baggy suits and combed his balding hair over one side; Walker had a slicked coif and fitted his suits to his physique, pocket square chosen to highlight his tie (and socks). Hylan retired to Queens; Walker spent months of his mayoralty on first-class trips to Italy, Florida, and Cuba. Walker, however, had one policy goal in common with his predecessor: to destroy the streetcars. Unlike Hylan, though, Walker was driven by greed, not ideology.

Walker didn't revile streetcars as thoroughly as Hylan had, but he saw opportunity in a bonanza of new franchising contracts. There was plenty of bribe money to be scooped up in awarding new bus contracts to replace existing streetcar contracts as companies scrambled for political advantage. Ironically, given his predecessor's hatred of monopoly, Walker tailored the bid process for bus franchises to favor monopoly streetcar companies, which had the deepest pockets with which to convince Tammany politicians. City hall designed contracts under which operators would bid for routes across entire boroughs.[29] One new company, Equitable Coach—a mysterious "unknown quantity," as the *Times* put it, incorporated one week after Walker won his campaign—was in the running.

Walker supported Equitable Coach for a Brooklyn, Manhattan, and Queens contract. He supported a subsidiary of the Third Avenue Railways company, a streetcar monopolist, for the Bronx.[30] Ignoring the fact that no one seemed to know who actually owned Equitable and that the Third Avenue Railway company was a monopoly, the mayor—having postponed a trip to Cuba to lobby the Board of Estimate, a powerful governing entity made up of the mayor, the comptroller, the president of the board of aldermen, and the five borough presidents—cynically argued that his chosen firms would break the monopolies: "Delay was merely playing into the hands of the existing transit companies."[31] Observers fell for this ruse: "One reason why the bid of the Equitable Coach Company had found favor in the eyes of the transit experts . . . was the fact that it would bring . . . new blood," the *Times* reported.[32] Over three years, Equitable wound its way through the convoluted process of securing city and state approval. By early 1929, the company had almost succeeded: the state transit commission offered "tentative" approval.[33] Having secured its franchises, the supposedly independent company announced plans to merge with the monopoly BMT.[34]

Yet the firm had declared victory too early. That winter, a former Hylan official, Cornelius Sheehan, during a Board of Estimate hearing came forth with an interesting observation: a half-a-million-dollar payment by Equitable to a third-party firm from what "looks suspiciously like a slush fund." Walker objected to this "insinuation." Sheehan replied, obliquely, "We know who the man is. I don't think, Mr. Mayor, that you would like me to . . . tell his name." "Stop that!" Walker answered sharply.[35] Walker arrogantly demanded an investigation. "If anyone can show that anyone talked to me about a slush fund," he said, "I'll resign."[36]

The city's deputy comptroller duly launched the requested investigation. But Equitable "flatly refused" to reveal whom the company had paid and for what.[37] Over another three years, the inquiry into "the fiasco of the Equitable Coach Company," as the *Times* put it, widened. One official at the winner of the Queens franchise had a power of attorney giving him access to a safety-deposit box half-owned by the mayor.[38] An Equitable associate had opened a ten-thousand-dollar line of credit for Walker. The Equitable bid was dead.[39]

The scandal didn't deter Walker from pursuing monopoly contracts; in fact, he became bolder. In 1931, he was back before the Board of Estimate. He argued openly this time that monopoly ownership would be a feature, not a bug: streetcar companies should win bus franchises, he argued, because they were more capable than "independents." The mayor also argued, correctly, that avoiding monopoly would be futile. The *Times* reported, "The history of the surface-car franchises has convinced him that awards to independent operators will inevitably be followed by the acquisition of the franchise by large operators."[40]

Walker couldn't escape the consequences of his transit and other corruption, however. That year, the state legislature, prompted by Governor Franklin Roosevelt, launched an investigation called the Seabury investigation after its chief counsel, former judge Samuel Seabury, to study the Walker era's odd practices. The "extremely bad impression . . . produced by the Mayor's maneuvering in connecting with bus franchises . . . played . . . a prominent part."[41] Unable to explain the irregularities that Seabury uncovered, Walker resigned in September 1932. The *Times* summed up the administration as "one of gay and cheerful muddling."[42]

Just as Hylan's departure hadn't saved streetcars, Walker's abrupt exit offered no reprieve. As streetcars still clanged the streets, two caretaker mayors completed the bid process. Fifth Avenue Coach—whose corporate relationships now included New York Railways, a longtime surface operator and affiliate of the Interborough subway, as well as General Motors[43]—was on its way to winning a "virtual monopoly" in Manhattan.[44] Third Avenue Railways would control the Bronx, and a BMT affiliate would control Brooklyn. On Staten Island, a company called Tompkins Bus Corporation ran service, having coincidentally decided around the same time to buy a money-losing newspaper from the borough president for an above-market price.[45] "Traction interests" had prevailed. It was traction itself—streetcars and tracks—that would vanish.

Doomed by the Folly of Technocrats

Hylan's and Walker's plots to destroy the streetcars did not take place in a vacuum. As ever shabbier trolleys clanged through New York's streets, still carrying hundreds of millions of annual passengers, conventional wisdom hardened against them. From business leaders to editorialists, prominent voices determined streetcars were not a solution but a problem, one that technology (that is, buses) would fix.

The reason ancient streetcars didn't belong on modern streets, the argument arose, was that most modern of problems: traffic. The motor vehicle had gone from curiosity to ubiquity. By 1926, New York City counted 421,000 automobiles, 107,000 trucks, and 34,000 buses and taxis. The number of vehicles in the broader region had risen to 1.3 million, or one vehicle per 7.6 residents (up from one vehicle per 35 people in 1916).

Unlike streetcars, private cars were an inefficient means of transportation—instead of dozens of people, they often carried one or two people per ride. Yet, in the eyes of a growing number of people, trolleys, not cars, were the cause of traffic. As early as 1922, one city official had said that "the removal of trolley car tracks . . . is a necessity because of . . . their stoppage of automobile traffic."[46] In 1929, Walker mused that the streetcar "is a great maker of traffic congestion."[47] The city and state purchased the streetcar right-of-way across the Manhattan Bridge from Brooklyn, so that "traffic lanes could be established on the site of the trolley tracks," making more room for cars.[48]

Another argument was safety. Streetcars were never perfectly safe: in 1911, 109 people, mostly pedestrians, died in trolley crashes, including 33 children. But early on, motor vehicles proved more perilous. The same year, even with few cars on the road, 142 people died in automobile crashes. ("Wagons" killed another 172 people, for a total of 423 victims.)[49] Unlike cars, trolleys glided predictably; drivers were professionals. Relative to people carried—still close to a billion a year in the late 1920s[50]—trolleys, along with subways, were New York's safest form of transportation. By 1929, as the number of cars had grown, fatalities had nearly quadrupled. Of the 1,521 people who died in car, truck, and trolley crashes in 1929, just 55 people died in a crash with a trolley.[51]

Yet cars made trolleys seem dangerous. Pedestrians were no longer dodging just trolleys; now, as they boarded and exited streetcars in the middle of avenues, passengers had to dodge automobiles. Though car and truck drivers were supposed to maintain an eight-foot buffer around trolley stops, many did not. People didn't blame the automobile but its victim—the trolley. "Since the advent of the automobile the operation of surface cars is a menace to life and limb," *Times* letter writer George Le Brun wrote in 1933. Le Brun thought that "buses are safer because they draw up to the curb," avoiding "pedestrians . . . struck by motorists who will not . . . obey the eight-foot law."[52]

Businesses and civic organizations fought trolleys. In 1921, Jesse Isidor Straus, president of Macy's department store, acknowledging that it was "unfashionable" for people of his class to support the anti-corporate mayor, called Hylan's plan to eradicate streetcars "one of the most constructive plans for relief of congestion."[53] Fifth and Park Avenues didn't have trolley tracks, but the Fifth Avenue and Park Avenue Associations supported destroying the streetcar infrastructure on nearby Madison Avenue. "The line is an obstruction to traffic, and . . . its removal would increase realty values," a Fifth Avenue Association representative told the Board of Estimate. (The Park Avenue Association didn't want buses, either. "We would suggest that this avenue be reserved for . . . private motor cars," its counsel said.)[54] The Broadway Association argued that trolleys posed congestion and danger; 77 percent of its members wanted the streetcars removed.[55] The Central Park West Association wanted tracks ripped up so that motor cars could better access Central Park. In fast-growing Queens, the Bayside Civic Association preferred buses. Insisting that trolleys "depreciate the value of their homes," five thousand residents petitioned that "there is an endless stream of motor cars whose usefulness as compared with that of the trolley is beyond measure."[56] Bus companies played into this argument. Fifth Avenue Coach, the eventual General Motors affiliate, was an aggressive promoter of buses as an antidote to traffic. Frederick Wood, the company's head, pushed buses' lower costs and faster movement because, unlike streetcars, they are "not subject to delays by others . . . getting in their path." Unlike trolleys, if a bus broke down, there "is no tie up," he argued, "as a second bus could maneuver around it."[57]

Contrary voices persisted. The *Times* was on the right side of history, for a while. In 1926, editorialists cautioned that "the whole question of the motor bus as a substitute for the trolley under Manhattan conditions must still be regarded as experimental."[58] The paper noted that though Manhattan surface-car passenger figures, at 354 million, were below their 427 million peak, "the trolley is about as important . . . as it has ever been."[59] The paper observed that buses might not be the panacea promoters were presenting. "Gasoline power threatens to become more and more costly with time, while electric power tends to develop in the opposite direction," the paper predicted. As for the idea that buses would be profitable on a nickel fare due to lower costs, Staten Island's buses lost money.[60]

A few business interests also resisted. The Merchants' Association tried to protect the streetcar lines. The group argued that "electric surface lines are a highly important transportation factor . . . penetrating all parts of the city and carrying 1,061,402,247 passengers in 1924"— two out of every five transit customers. "A large proportion of the population is and must long continue to be dependent upon these lines," the coalition warned. "Even the most comprehensive bus routes proposed could . . . carry only a small proportion."[61]

The trolley car manufacturing, electric-powering, and servicing industry, of course, cautioned against junking its technology. In 1924, a utility manager, B. C. Cobb, maintained, "Much relief could be given. . . if city authorities would see to it that street cars, on account of their carrying such a large number of people, had preference over every other form of street traffic."[62] In 1926, the American Electric Railway Association's Lucius Storrs warned too that a bus "cannot carry large numbers of persons as cheaply or as quickly . . . [and] adds to traffic congestion."[63] American Transit Association engineers found that a roadway shared between trolleys and cars had 40 percent greater capacity than the same roadway shared between buses and cars. Trolleys could seat fifty-five people, buses only forty-four.[64] For a while, even the BMT and the Third Avenue Railways pleaded to save streetcars. The BMT's Gerhard Dahl argued that three streetcars could carry the equivalent of five buses; he argued that congestion was due to surging numbers of taxicabs and parked automobiles and appealed to restrict Brooklyn parking to keep objects out of the way of tracks.

Some bus customers, too, preferred trolleys. When, in 1920, the Hylan administration had replaced a Staten Island trolley service with buses, Staten Islanders proclaimed themselves "tired" of the buses. They wanted streetcars back, even offering to pay more than the still politically sacred five-cent fare.[65] One Staten Island petitioner asked rhetorically: "Have you ever ridden in one of those buses? . . . They are awful. . . . Give us back our trolleys, and we'll gladly pay 10 cents," an offer the city ignored.[66] A pregnant woman, E. C. Morris, wrote to the *Times* in 1922 that as a "prospective mother," she much preferred to "strap-hang" than to be in a "jerking, jolting bus."[67] In a caustic reply to a letter-writer who predicted that buses would "roll along in practical silence,"[68] a W. D. Durkin countered that "trolleys . . . [are] commodious, clean, safe. . . . The people who are against them are the automobile hogs, who would rather see the streets empty of everything but their own selves and who [would] rather run down human beings than slow down." In 1926, the *Times* reported that bus patrons were "rather critical of such factors as speed, comfort and intervals between vehicles."[69]

By the 1930s, though—with the number of cars registered in the city having risen from 216,000 in 1920 to 764,000[70]—more people subscribed to the idea that streetcars impeded traffic. By 1932, the *Times* had changed its mind, frustrated with the delay in the switch to buses. "Trolley lines . . . have no place in the crowded avenues of Manhattan," the paper complained.[71] Trolley supporters appeared eccentric and nostalgic.[72]

A final factor militated against trolleys: self-fulfilling prophecy. In the 1920s, Hylan and Walker had used outdated equipment as a reason to jettison trolleys. "It is the junk of today," said state transit commissioner George McAneny of Manhattan's streetcar track in 1921.[73] By the 1930s, trolleys had been in limbo for more than a decade. The Depression pushed ridership down. Financially distressed trolley companies, facing competition from buses and dim prospects of a fare hike, had cut back on maintaining equipment.

As trolleys deteriorated, riders grew frustrated. Just like, nearly a century later, a surly yellow-cab driver could be threatened with competition from Uber, a discourteous streetcar conductor could be threatened with obsolescence. "Apparently the street car conductors and motormen in the Bronx feel quite secure," mused Emanuel Strum of the Bronx. "I wonder whether they have given thought to the possibilities of displacement by bus."[74] Broken rails and rusty trolleys were hardly an advertisement; auto drivers complained that "broken, bent and loose" rails punctured tires.[75]

A few voices noted that the true comparison wasn't old trolleys to new buses, but buses to new trolleys. In 1921, Clarence Shearn, the state transit commission's counsel, defended trolleys. "It does not follow [that] they are junk, because a great many of them were well maintained up to the war

. . . [and with catch-up investment could] give good service."[76] More than a decade later, James Clark of Brooklyn wrote that "modern trolleys" would "make less noise, travel faster . . . [and be] much more comfortable than a bus and leave no odorous fumes."[77]

City officials, however, were engaged in purposeful blight. Decades later, they would employ the same tactic to demolish neighborhoods. They would propose a highway or housing project, causing apartment building owners and homeowners in the targeted neighborhood—put off by the uncertainty the announcement created—to pull back from keeping up their properties. The city would use the ensuing dilapidation to argue that the neighborhood was too distressed to save. Similarly, trolleys became irredeemable scrap.

A Mayor Driven by Boosterism

When Fiorello LaGuardia took office in 1934, trolleys still had a chance to survive. In 1933, even as ridership had fallen because of the Depression, 731.9 million passengers had boarded New York's streetcars, more than one-fourth of the city's transit customers.[78] By mid-1934, transit ridership was increasing for the first time since the beginning of the Depression.[79] The new mayor could have saved the trolleys. However, instead of investing in streetcars—which he associated with New York's past—LaGuardia wanted to invest in the city's modernist future. He promised a "speedy motorization."[80]

The second half of the 1930s would be a well-publicized, well-celebrated auto-da-fe of the past—a bonfire of rails—as streetcars were sold as recyclable metal. Each trolley, "having cost from $7,000 to $10,000 to build, now brings . . . between $50 and $60 a ton as scrap," the *Times* informed readers.[81] The first high-profile destruction came in 1935. Effective February 1, at 5:00 a.m., Madison Avenue trolleys—the world's oldest streetcar service, which began as a horsecar service in 1832—would cease operations. The Fifth Avenue Association held a celebratory lunch at the Roosevelt Hotel.[82] LaGuardia declared, "The surface transportation problem in Manhattan is solved."[83] The *Times* enthused over the "long, sleek and powerful motor bus."[84] On the eve of the substitution, LaGuardia told a radio audience that trolleys were "as dead as sailing ships" and would be gone from Manhattan within a year.[85] On the day of the changeover, "the quiet rolling of rubber tires replaced the rattle of trolley wheels . . . one minute after midnight." The "last trolley . . . ended its run at Forty-Second Street and was then driven in defeat back to the car barn." New Deal workers ripped up tracks.[86] Madison was a "smooth and trackless oasis, . . . cleared of the relics of the trolley age."

Months later, the mayor repeated the feat in Queens. On Queens Boulevard, "before a cheering crowd of 1,000 persons, . . . Mayor La Guardia announced that the last barrier to the removal of the tracks . . . long an obstacle to . . . improvement [read: widening for cars] of that thoroughfare, had been disposed of." Modern, "up-to-date bus service" would serve eight thousand people daily along Queens's spine. "I look at this great highway and I see the ground . . . taken up by trolley tracks," the mayor said. "They have no business there."[87] A month later, back in Manhattan, the final trolleys down Eighth Avenue clanged their last trip, "reminders of a bygone era . . . decked in black crepe. A WPA band played a funeral dirge."[88] Manhattan's Broadway fell in February,[89] trolleys replaced by "commodious, speedy gasoline-propelled vehicles," the *Times* cheered.[90]

As the city subjected more people to buses, more customers complained. "For bumpiness, the new buses are as bad as the Coney Island 'Dodg'ems.' The overcrowding on the vehicle was a source of great irritation. . . . The discomfort caused by twenty people standing in space meant for ten was very great. . . . The people of New York City will be making a great mistake if they allow motorization of all street car lines," wrote one rider.[91] "The chief objection to buses is the awful fumes," agreed another. "If all of our trolley lines are to be replaced, . . . the inhabitants of this city will eventually be compelled to wear gas masks."[92] An elderly woman, Ellen Garrigues, said the mayor "was condemning those no longer strong," as buses were more crowded than trolleys and difficult to board.[93]

Three thousand people petitioned LaGuardia to reconsider.[94] Herman Rinke, a streetcar expert, noted that "traffic complainers" were "motorists; but . . . they cannot see that a slight sacrifice . . . is due from them for the general good, in exchange for the privilege and convenience of riding around in a car."[95] As Everett White, an ardent pro-trolley letter writer, pointed out, the Board of Estimate had never held hearings to consider technocratic arguments of trolleys versus streetcars.[96] Trolley enthusiasts, or mourners, spent a Brooklyn afternoon riding condemned rails, booing bus drivers.[97]

The remaining trolleys got a stay of execution during World War II.[98] The U.S. Office of Defense Transportation in 1943 informed officials that because of rubber and fuel shortages as well as the need to use buses for military transport, "substitution of buses for trolleys would be contrary to the public interest."[99] "It looks now as if we'll have to . . . go back to the old, dilapidated, noisy, rattling trolley cars," LaGuardia lamented.[100] In Manhattan, passengers on Forty-Second, Fifty-Ninth, and 125th Streets continued to ride the rails. As the federal government ordered fuel rationing, bus lines cut service—one of the first instances of a gas crisis.[101] People waited for "buses that did not come."[102]

In 1945, "antiquated, clangorous and slow" streetcars, as the *Times* continued to describe them, were back on the "way to oblivion." The trolley would be "as extinct in Manhattan as the horsecar."[103] That fall, a final trolley crossed Forty-Second Street. "Midtown strollers up early enough will see the last trolley make its Forty-Second Street crosstown run this morning when the new streamlined buses of the Third Avenue System replace surface cars that began operating in 1898."[104] The "death knell was sounded . . . when four decrepit trolley cars with 200 passengers," including "stars of stage and screen, creaked from Forty-Second Street and Fifth Avenue to The New York Times Tower." Hollywood star Janis Paige broke a Champagne bottle over the bus.[105] In May 1947, people dressed in "gay nineties" costumes marked the end of the Third Avenue service.[106] "That's progress for you," lamented Anthony Raftenberg of the Bronx, who hadn't realized he was on the last streetçar.[107] That June, "1,200 persons lined the streets" on 125th Street for a streetcar funeral.[108] "Manhattan will hear no more clanging, no more motor chugging."[109] In 1948, the last Bronx trolley sported a "rest in peace" bouquet, with an inspector saying the streetcar was his "sweetheart."[110]

The demise of the trolleys also meant that the city lost the most efficient form of street transportation between boroughs. In 1948, the last trolley ran over the Williamsburg Bridge between Manhattan and Brooklyn; Police Commissioner Arthur Wallander noted that the roadway could expand from six to eight car lanes, and "greatly relieve the traffic congestion."[111] In 1954, the city completed "modernization" of the Brooklyn Bridge, minus trolley lanes; four lanes for cars had become six lanes.[112] More room for cars, though, meant less room for people overall. In 1907, the Brooklyn Bridge carried 426,000 people daily. After "modernization," the number was 178,000. In the early twentieth century, as Sam Schwartz, former New York City traffic commissioner, later pointed out, the four East River bridges from Manhattan to Brooklyn carried 1.96 million people each day. After modernization, the figure was 1.03 million.[113]

By 1948, Brooklyn had the "dubious distinction" of being the only borough with multiple trolleys.[114] Equipment was "in too good condition" to junk.[115] But time was on the city's side. In 1951, "a sight as synonymous with Brooklyn as . . . Ebbets Field and the borough's numerous churches will become part of the past," when "the last of the Flatbush Avenue trolley cars will reach journey's end."[116] Five years later, on Church Avenue, thirty buses would replace thirty-four trolleys, not enough to maintain adequate service.[117] Ebbets Field itself shut down in 1958 as the Dodgers moved to car-centric Los Angeles, and wreckers demolished the ballpark in 1960.

Veteran transit officials remember the trolleys. Harris Schechtman spent his career managing buses for the New York City Transit Authority. "I was . . . a child at the end of the trolley age," he remembered. "I had an aunt who lived on Ocean Avenue," in Brooklyn. "I could remember going to bed . . . and hearing the trolley cars pass." His fond memories meld with professional judgment. "Justifications for getting rid of the streetcars were really poor," he says, "driven by the fact that suddenly the car was king. All people wanted to do was make room for the cars." He remembers seeing a document that was an "eye-opener," because, he estimates, "half of the streetcar routes were showing a profit, even at the nickel fare, which was incredible." It wouldn't have taken much—a higher fare and catch-up investment—for trolleys to return to good condition.

In 1957, New York's final trolley crossed the Queensboro Bridge at midnight.[118] "The trolley car era . . . will hear . . . the last clang," the *Times* said.[119] "Mostly teen-agers and trolley-car enthusiasts" were aboard. "The trolley car survived almost to the time when the first jet transports began to come into our airports."[120] New York's crudely de-railed streets—entirely the responsibility of elected city officials and not Robert Moses—belonged to cars, the buses stuck behind them. By then, New York was in the final throes of a parallel effort: because removing efficient transit from avenues and streets didn't make adequate room for clunky cars, the city was slicing through and around neighborhoods to build wide roads for motor traffic.

Chapter 2

The 1929 Regional Plan

Paving New York's Car Future

We are determined to make use of the indignation which has been aroused among the dwellers in this neighborhood to obtain the removal of the deadly tracks.

—Henry Schneider, Track Removal Association, 1908

The central area of congestion in New York . . . has become so large that any comprehensive system of express roads must cross that area.

—The Graphic Regional Plan, 1929

ASK EDUCATED URBANISTS WHO IS responsible for New York's twentieth-century trajectory, and most will tell you: Robert Moses. Since the publication of Robert Caro's *The Power Broker*, the accepted wisdom has been that we live in the city Moses built. "With his power," as Caro puts it, "Robert Moses shaped New York. Physically, any map of the city proves it." Whether building the Cross-Bronx Expressway across dense neighborhoods or decreeing that bridges on parkways would be so low that they would bar buses, "for forty years nothing could stand in Moses' way. No Mayor or Governor dared to try." Without Moses, Caro asserts: "It is impossible to say that New York would have been a better city if Robert Moses had never lived. It is possible to say only that it would have been a different city."[1]

Until the final years of his career, Moses never minded the illusory public perception that, starting in the late 1920s—over four decades of building beaches, playgrounds, parks, bridges, tunnels, parkways, expressways, and housing—he had had dictatorial powers, jackhammering democracy. Moses was not just the chairman of the city's Triborough Bridge and Tunnel Authority, builder of cash-generating tunnels and bridges connecting New York City's five boroughs. After World War II, he held eleven titles at once, from state parks chairman to city construction coordinator, in charge of highway and housing development.[2] He was accustomed to receiving letters from supplicants praising him for good deeds or begging him to stop a bad one, with petitioners taking for granted that he alone could help or harm them.

The reality was more mundane. Moses survived not through Machiavellian machinations to subvert political will but by smoothly delivering on political will—executing what the state and city's governing class, business leaders, and editorial boards wanted him to accomplish. Predating Moses, in the early twentieth century, New York's governing, business, and media classes wanted roads and highways for that new contraption, the motorcar. Starting in the 1930s—after he had made a name for himself with Jones Beach State Park on Long Island, opened in 1929, and New York City's Triborough Bridge, opened in 1936—Moses embodied this philosophy; but he was its creation, not its creator.

Death Avenue

For most of Robert Moses's adult life—the first half of the twentieth century—mass transit was seen as a necessary evil, not as the environmentally friendly, gridlock-busting blessing that future New Yorkers would perceive. Just as progressive politicians reviled trolleys, the public viewed trains as dangerous. Railroads cut through urban areas, in uncovered trenches and at street level. In addition to imperiling pedestrians, especially children, tracks bisected neighborhoods and severed residents from their waterfront. Though Moses found acclaim beginning in the late 1920s with the opening of Jones Beach and, the next decade, the Triborough Bridge, another project during the same era earned him political and public accolades, reducing the power of the reviled railroads to harm the citizenry.

Moses knew that the early twentieth-century public didn't view trains favorably. Decades later, when he testified before a hearing on New York transportation, Moses recalled that people, including his grandfather, used to refer to the roadway traversed by Lower Manhattan trains as "Death Avenue."[3] Indeed, tragedies were common. During the first decade of the twentieth century, 108 people, mostly children, had died under the wheels of West Side trains. According to one activist, the secretary of the Track Removal Association, "The children are usually carrying dinners to their fathers at work when the trains rush down."[4] A busy mother with no yard in which her children could play had no choice but to instruct her hard-to-see charges to watch out as they played on public streets.

Railroad and transit workers and passengers, too, were in peril. Train companies—then, like the trolleys, owned by private investors, not the government—considered workers expendable. In the two decades leading up to 1934, 490 workers died running New York's mass-transit network, averaging 24 deaths a year.[5] In 1902, 15 people perished when commuter trains crashed at Park Avenue in Manhattan. In 1918, 102 people died when a subway train—helmed by a strike-breaking worker replacing the motorman—crashed into a Brooklyn wall.

Cars were already beginning to pose a far greater danger to pedestrians than trains had, and car drivers showed an early, alarming tendency to fail not just to look out for walkers but for themselves. They crashed into trains, frequently. Just as automobile traffic did not mix well with trolleys and their passengers, autos did not mix well at the same physical surface level as fast-moving railroad cars. In 1926, C. E. Hill, New York Central Railroad's safety agent, argued correctly that motor vehicle drivers, not railroads, were responsible for an increasing number of crashes. "A large percentage of [auto] drivers are wholly incompetent, due to either mental or physical defects," Hill said. He further mused, "Before the coming of the automobile, when sixteen million horses and mules were the propelling power of vehicular traffic . . . they recognized the necessity of stopping at railroad crossings, . . . but with the coming of the automobile the responsibility which had been so nobly assumed by those animals was shifted to mere man and all of [his] elements of thoughtlessness and carelessness."[6]

But decades of fearing the trains—and of putting up with the subpar service the monopolies provided—cost public goodwill.[7] After decades of pedestrian carnage, people blamed the trains for crashes with cars, and so the trains would have to get out of the way of the cars. One of Moses's earliest public works projects aimed to reduce the peril rail posed to the people, whether in cars or on foot. Starting in the 1920s and continuing over a decade, Moses showed his ability to execute complex infrastructure projects as he separated 113 railroad crossings, many along various Brooklyn and Queens avenues, from being at the same physical surface level as motor vehicles and pedestrians. Moving railroad tracks to go under or over street traffic, instead of intersecting with it, eliminated a source of conflict and crashes. Part of his motive was to allow cars to move more quickly and safely. Nevertheless, Moses's grade-crossing elimination program enjoyed public support even among people who didn't own cars—most people—because of the danger trains posed to pedestrians.

Separating the railroad tracks from the street level wasn't straightforward. New York City launched a fifty-million-dollar project in the early 1920s, but city taxpayers couldn't afford it, nor did the city have the power to force railroads to pay a share. Working for Governor Al Smith as chairman of the state parks council in 1925, and, beginning in 1927 as secretary of state, Moses, by designing two amendments to the state constitution, gradually transformed the project into a three-hundred-million-dollar statewide initiative.[8] Yet the project remained stalled because the state, too, could not get the railroad companies to pay their share. To speed funding, Moses, in 1938, proposed to lawmakers that they put a third constitutional amendment on the ballot. The voters could authorize the state to borrow the money and recover a smaller portion from the railroad companies later.

The idea faced opposition. To lawmakers, Moses's proposal looked like a bailout of crony-capitalist railroads; others objected to the proposed closure of seven railway stations. One observer described Moses "feverishly pacing back and forth with a [metaphorical] shovel" as the state senate debated. Smith—Moses's "old friend" from his service to the governor in reorganizing state government a decade earlier—saved the bill. As Smith beseeched the legislature, "Was anyone killed at a grade crossing this month? You bet." The highly regarded former governor's "eloquence" convinced elected officials. Mayor Fiorello LaGuardia further moved lawmakers, imploring that "all interested in human lives" join him in concern for "children playing." The mayor likely meant well, but lawmakers were moved not by any newfound concern for children; rather, they sympathized with car drivers menaced by railroad crossings.

Moses prevailed. He knew, even as he assured elected officials that railroads would reimburse some of the cost involved, that because of the competition posed by the car, they would never again be financially strong enough to do so.[9] As the *New York Times* said, in endorsing Moses's compromise, the amendment is "a poor way of achieving a good end," but "lives may be saved."[10] In 1943, celebrating the near end of the project, "LaGuardia paid tribute to the energetic championship . . . by Robert Moses. . . . 'There was a time,' said the mayor, 'when the [constitutional] convention was evenly divided. Bob Moses was for it and the rest of the convention was against it.'"[11] For the rest of his life, when few others recalled when trains, not cars, had seemed the greater danger, Moses would voice pride in this accomplishment, eliminating "the prime cause of many deaths and accidents."[12]

Maps Full of Highways

As Moses grew in prominence, trains increasingly represented the past, whereas motor vehicles represented the future. In 1929, prominent New Yorkers released a 416-page manifesto whose dry title—"Regional Plan of New York and Its Environs," vol. 1, "The Graphic Regional Plan"—belied the role it would have in shaping the landscape of New York City and beyond, including Connecticut and New Jersey.

The document represented seven years of work, overseen by prominent citizens. The Regional Plan project's chair was Frederic Delano, a railroad executive and uncle of FDR, then governor of New York. The board included George McAneny, a progressive reformer who had served as Manhattan borough president, and Lawson Purdy, a tax expert who had helped devise New York's 1916 zoning resolution to protect light and air from tall buildings.

Thanks to a million-dollar grant from the Russell Sage Foundation, a progressive philanthropy ($18 million in modern dollars), this board could work independently as it pursued its goal: "an analysis of the physical needs of the New York region." The pressing task was to "furnish a general outline . . . in respect to circulation [read: traffic]" as the tri-state region's population surged from ten million to a projected twenty million.[13]

The Graphic Regional Plan—called such because of dozens of maps—explained the burgeoning dominance of the automobile. By 1926, New York City counted half a million vehicles, three-quarters of them cars. In the broader region, the number of vehicles per person had quintupled in a decade. The authors didn't render an opinion on this trend. Rather, the report observed that "the motor car is too recent as a form of transportation to enable any final judgment. . . . It has helped to add to the congestion of the street while greatly aiding the movement of people and goods" and brought "increased . . . dangers" and "problems."

Despite this neutrality, the report concluded that the city would have to accommodate cars. "The demands of mechanically propelled vehicles have grown so rapidly . . . that it has been an almost impossible task . . . to keep up with the growing needs for extended highway[s]," with congestion now "a widely spread evil." The report accepted as a "premise" that "it is essential for . . . business that movement should be fast, have the least possible degree of interruption, and have ample space for parking." Cars and trucks should have the run of the urban road.

The authors acknowledged that some road construction would not achieve the desired goal of less traffic. "Doubling the width of a street . . . will not lessen congestion if the traffic use is doubled"; the planners understood that roads would become clogged with traffic immediately. But the study attributed this phenomenon to "badly planned" streets, "combined with overbuilding and an ill-assorted arrangement of industry, business and residence." The highways the study suggested would be well-planned and therefore would not suffer from this problem.

The 1929 report's suggestion was to build 2,548 miles of roadways. Highways would be "complementary" to rail tracks, more of which the report also proposed. But "if a bold and comprehensive treatment of the highway system is pursued . . . a great deal of the expense in railroad and transit line construction may be avoided," the report promised. The planners proposed a "coordinated and classified system of highways" from New Jersey to the west, to Long Island to the east, to Connecticut to the north. The network would center around a "metropolitan highway loop," encircling Manhattan, Queens, Brooklyn, and northern New Jersey. From the loop would extend dozens of "major regional routes" and 107 "minor regional routes." Cutting through the loop would be eight "express" highways.

The expressway, a multilane speedway separate from local traffic, was a new concept. The report noted that it could be built above the street, via an elevated viaduct, through tunnels below it, or in "open cuts" that demolished the street. "Uninterrupted movement requires the separation of grades at all important highway crossings," the report said. "Through intensively built-up areas this can only be accomplished by placing the express route on a viaduct above the existing street system"—that is, cutting off light and air; "in tunnel," the seemingly victimless option that was often too expensive to pursue; or "open cut below the existing streets," blasting a path near occupied buildings and leaving the depressed roadway uncovered to bisect neighborhoods.

The Graphic Regional Plan acknowledged the human cost. The authors agreed that it was optimal to build roadways through undeveloped areas so as not to disturb residents and businesses. But the report was forthright that urban disruptions would occur. "The central area of congestion in New York . . . has become so large that any comprehensive system of express roads must cross that area."

To that end, three express highways should traverse the densest parts of New York City: one from New Jersey "across southern Manhattan," via downtown's Canal Street, through to Long Island; another from New Jersey "across midtown" to Queens, via a tunnel underneath Midtown; and one across northern Manhattan, through Washington Heights, east "across . . . the Bronx," connecting northward to New England. Buses, trucks, and cars could travel through New York City over expressways without getting stuck in traffic.

Parkways for Cars

Beyond expressways, the Graphic Regional Plan praised a different type of highway: the parkway. In contrast to an expressway, whose purpose was to bring car and truck drivers from point A to point B, a parkway followed a meandering path, giving drivers and passengers a bucolic view. A parkway featured areas for picnics, cycling, and horseback riding nearby. A parkway prohibited bus and truck traffic, allowing car occupants relief from larger crash threats.

In admiring parkways, the Regional Plan looked to a recent example: Westchester County, the rural-turning-suburban region north of New York City. Between 1900 and 1930, Westchester had watched its population triple, to more than half a million. Grand Central Terminal had opened in 1913, allowing people to commute into midtown Manhattan via rail from outside of the five boroughs. By the 1920s, however, affluent New Yorkers were purchasing cars, creating demand for roads.

Westchester County's officials had determined to meet that demand. The state legislature authorized the Bronx River Parkway Commission in 1893, predating the car, with "a view to purifying the river and acquiring sufficient land on both sides" for carriages and "a pleasant park."[14] By 1914, the state legislature had approved a fifteen-mile "wide parkway" from the Bronx, New York's northernmost borough, through Westchester.

Construction on the Bronx River Parkway suffered delay as county leaders ensured that the design was impeccably scenic. Bridges, in particular—necessary to separate through parkway traffic from local streets—were the "subjects of many conferences," with rendering after rendering. Architects revised proposed arches, fitting bridges with stonework, to "avoid marring natural features of the parkway."[15] By 1920, the road was nearly complete and would be, the *Times* predicted, "magnificent."[16] In 1924, with much of the road open, the *Herald Tribune* informed "automobilists" that the parkway was "free from heavy traffic," with "only cars allowed."[17] Westchester was so pleased that its commission planned an extension. Referring to the Bronx River Parkway, the *Times* noted again that "no commercial cars of any description are allowed . . . and the same will apply to the proposed Hutchinson River Parkway. . . . [The] absence of heavily laden and wide motor trucks will be a genuine relief."[18]

Nearly five years later, in their 1929 report, the Graphic Regional Plan's authors lauded this "economy of parkways," praising Westchester's example for "attractive park strips along each side of the road, outside of which great increases take place in the value of the land . . . the parkway is particularly appropriate for the kind of traffic that serves residential areas because it is confined to passenger automobiles." In addition to relieving traffic on truck thoroughfares, parkways also "serve a great variety of communication [commuting] and recreational uses which cannot be obtained in ordinary highways. . . . It is desirable to promote the planning of more highways or parkways that will permit of partial segregation of different kinds of vehicles."

City leaders applauded the Regional Plan. More than 1,500 people, representing 528 civic groups, attended the May 1929 Manhattan unveiling.[19] Among officials heaping praise were Mayor Jimmy Walker, Governor Franklin D. Roosevelt, and President Herbert Hoover. Labor unions and social-justice advocates approved of the plan as well, with Lillian Wald, head of the Henry Street Settlement, calling it a "milestone." "Congestion in the central parts of the metropolis will diminish or disappear," the *Times* reported. Almost as an afterthought, the paper mentioned the two highways that would "pass under Manhattan."[20] In fact, this reporting was incorrect; one expressway, following Canal Street, would cross above ground to the Manhattan Bridge.

Over three and a half decades, many of the colored maps featured in the Graphic Regional Plan jumped from paper to reality. They would become familiar to New Yorkers stuck in traffic or breathing in fumes the traffic generated: the Cross-Bronx Expressway and the Brooklyn-Queens Expressway among them. Decades after the report's release, Paul Windels—a former counselor to Mayor LaGuardia, who, in the middle of the century, served as president of the nonprofit group that the Regional Plan analysts had become, the Regional Plan Association—tallied successes: "four bridges, three tunnels, 11 parkways and expressways."[21]

Moses as Supplicant, not Power Broker

The one person whose marks were missing from these blueprints was the one who, for the next century, became identified with them: Robert

Moses. In their acknowledgments, the influential planners thank the Long Island State Park Commission—which Moses chaired beginning in 1924, a position he had earned from Governor Smith as a reward for his state-government service—and list dozens of advisers by name. But they omit Moses, who had not yet built his formidable reputation. The first section of the Southern State Parkway, Moses's first parkway, to the east of New York City across Long Island, opened in 1927, and Jones Beach opened in 1929, the year the report came out.

During the half-decade the planners were researching and preparing their report, Moses's relationship with the Regional Plan began as one of supplicating and not power brokering. In 1923, not yet an official state employee but working closely with Governor Smith as a government reformer, he had written to Delano, the project's chair, to ask the committee for "an appropriation of $750" to his own nonprofit group, the New York State Association, so that he could finish a survey on Staten Island, New York's least developed borough. Moses noted, "Our resources are altogether too slender to carry this work on alone. We had a considerable deficit . . . printing of our park report." Moses had to explain his importance: "We have established certain contacts," he wrote. By June, Moses, having been shunted to an underling, wrote again, this time to the Regional Plan's assistant secretary, asking for the $750. "I have your request for further information regarding the contribution," Moses pleaded. "The $750 which we requested constitutes merely a small but important part of the amount which has already been spent. . . . Matters of this kind require an enormous amount of work."[22] Moses grew in stature as the late 1920s progressed, but he was in no position to set the agenda of the Regional Plan. Moses may later have "built every one" of New York's roads, as Caro wrote, but he did not plan them.[23] Politicians, planners, business interests, and press all thought, independently of Moses, that building thousands of miles of highways through, around, above, and below a dense city was a good idea.

Despite Caro's assertion that "Robert Moses built every mile" of New York's parkways, Moses also did not receive—or deserve—credit in the Regional Plan for the car-only thoroughfare concept.[24] In 1914, when Westchester had been planning the state's first parkway, Moses had been a young man with a PhD at the Bureau of Municipal Research think tank, advising New York City on workforce reforms. The parkway innovator, as Moses and the Regional Plan separately acknowledged, was Jay Downer, chief engineer of the Westchester County Park Commission and Bronx Parkway Commission. "I have been building parkways for . . . twelve years," Downer testified before the state assembly in 1925, noting that he had used "not State money, but County money, our own money."[25]

Throughout the 1920s, Moses asked for and received the older Downer's support for his own projects as he followed Westchester's example, devising Long Island parkways to lure New Yorkers eastward, including to Jones Beach, instead of northward to Westchester, for recreation. Downer told the state assembly, for example, that he agreed that Moses, to build Long Island parkways, would have to condemn land, displacing private-sector owners, despite community objection. "It would be impracticable to try and build a parkway without some provision for vesting title in condemnation," he said. Downer, in helping convince lawmakers to approve Moses's parkways, further told them of his Westchester parkway that New York City residents "come out on Sunday, go back again, enjoy the country, and we have not been harmed." Of future construction, Downer counseled that "it is better to have ten thousand automobiles come up on a forty- or fifty-foot parkway than to have them come up on [narrow] eighteen-foot roads."

Moses also relied on Downer for civic support. In 1928, the Exchange Club, a civic group in Rockville Centre, a Long Island village, invited Downer to speak, in his capacity as experienced parkway builder. Downer wrote to Moses that he didn't feel like participating—"it will about kill the whole day"—but that he would make the trip, "if it would be of any material benefit." Moses wrote that it "would be very helpful" indeed if Downer made the trip to "explain to these people that our right of way for the Southern Parkway is too narrow." Downer encouraged Moses on other occasions, noting that autumn, "You have hurdled your biggest obstructions . . . [and with] a good section of the Parkway available to the public next summer, you will have established a reputation."[26]

Moses never took credit for inventing the parkway. In 1928, in discussing Long Island's partially built system, Moses praised Downer's standard. "The Westchester County Park Commission . . . park and parkway system, are outstanding examples," Moses said, noting a near-doubling of real estate values.[27] Around Christmas 1928, Walter Russell, president of the Society of Arts and Sciences, invited Moses to a 1929 dinner at the Hotel Astor honoring the Bronx Parkway designers, "the seventeen men who created that beautiful example of landscape architecture. . . . We hope by such public recognition that the attention of the country will be so drawn to this marvelous object lesson that other localities will be stimulated to emulate their example." Moses responded, "I shall be glad to attend," and he was informed that he could sit at a front table, "as guests of our honored guests."[28]

Over four decades, as Moses expanded Downer's prototype, building parkways throughout New York, he hewed to Downer's rules, prohibiting large vehicles with an enthusiasm bordering on the fanatic. In 1946, an official at the city's marine and aviation department wrote to Moses inquiring whether a bus operator could use the Moses-built, car-only Belt Parkway, recently built through Brooklyn and Queens, to transport people to the airport. "This is the second time Mr. Carey has tried to get his buses on the parkways," Moses fumed. "Use of the parkways by commercial vehicles is prohibited by law."

Moses's anti-bus argument was no different from that of the Graphic Regional Plan: small and large vehicles don't mix. Buses and trucks, Moses insisted, could travel on "new, modern mixed traffic express arteries like the new Brooklyn-Battery Tunnel, Brooklyn-Queens Expressway, Queens Midtown Expressway, Prospect Expressway," all of which the city was building or planning under his direction by the 1940s.

Moses did not confine parkway rules to buses. In 1946, one of Moses's deputies at the Triborough authority, George Spargo, sent a memo to an underling. "I think you ought to talk to the police about the Army and Navy trucks," Spargo instructed. "They still seem to be going strong" on parkways, despite the large-vehicle prohibition. In February, a city parks official working for Moses sent a letter to another deputy: "Herewith are reports of Bridge Officers on Army and Navy trucks turned back at Henry Hudson Bridge," which, as part of the parkway network, prohibited large vehicles. "These have been photostatted and sent to the Service Officers." In response to these complaints, Moses received a groveling letter from Colonel John S. Roosma of Army headquarters on Governors Island. "I regret very much that our Army vehicles continue to violate regulations on . . . parkways," Roosma, a World War II hero with combat experience in Japan and Germany, wrote. "We will notify all provost marshals. . . . We will do everything within our power to curb these violations."[29]

That Moses's deputies, always working under his close eye, were unafraid of taking on a decorated hero to regulate military transport six months after the end of World War II shows Moses's own ease with power by then. These incidents cast doubt on the idea, popularized in *The Power Broker*, that Moses disliked buses, rather than all large vehicles, because buses might bring poor people and minorities into suburban parks and neighborhoods.[30] Indeed, in 1950, Bill Levitt, builder of Levittown, Long Island's whites-only suburb, pronounced buses on parkways a "terrific" idea. He mused that "there is no question that real estate values would be enhanced."[31]

Yet elite wisdom agreed with Moses, not Levitt. "The mere thought of allowing . . . buses and trucks, to use the parkways . . . is enough to make the citizen shudder," editorialized the *Times* in 1960, in response to the Carey company's renewed request to run buses to the airport.[32]

Clearing a Path for the Triborough Bridge

Just like Moses did not conceive of the cars-only parkway or the city-slashing expressways that would define his legacy, he did not conceive of the Triborough Bridge, a mega-project to which he would be inextricably linked. This four-mile steel and cement structure connecting the Bronx, Manhattan, and Queens would become evidence of Moses's prowess as well as the base of the fiscal power that, according to Caro, made him independent of elected officials—the "capital" of Moses's "empire."[33]

Civic groups had first proposed the Triborough at the turn of the twentieth century. By 1917, business groups in Manhattan and Queens were clamoring for a motor vehicle connection. "The property owners and business men of Harlem believe that the completion of the bridge will be a great impetus to business," said Frank Bowers, a Republican leader.[34] "It would be easy of access for Long Island farmers who bring in their vegetables, fruits and dairy products to our great residential section." Walter Willis, of the Queens Chamber of Commerce, agreed with Bowers: "From an automobile standpoint both for pleasure cars and business trucks, an additional bridge across the East River . . . is becoming more necessary." Traffic on the nearby Queensborough Bridge, which the city had built in 1909, had risen from 1,810 vehicles a day in 1910 to 9,858 by 1916. A new bridge, surely, would ease traffic jams.[35]

For more than a decade after the city reached this consensus, New York City's government could neither finance nor build the Triborough bridge, just as it was not able to eliminate railroad crossings until Moses came along. Fitful attempts fell prey to the Great Depression as well as to the incompetence of the Walker era. By 1934, foundations were abandoned. At the behest of Mayor LaGuardia, Moses took responsibility for the sixty-million-dollar Triborough venture in the 1930s.

Moses solved the Triborough project's two problems: financing and execution. In 1933, he proposed to the state legislature that it create the Triborough Bridge Authority, a nonprofit "public benefit" corporation. Triborough could issue bonds, insulating itself from investors' (bondholders') fears over strained city finances. Bondholders would depend on repayment from tolls that drivers would pay, a more predictable source of revenue than taxes, which had to fund competing needs, from hospitals to schools. (Triborough's first bondholder was the federal government, thanks to Depression-era public works funding.) Moses didn't invent the public authority concept; he borrowed it from the Port of New York Authority (later the Port Authority of New York and New Jersey), which had already taken over the Holland Tunnel between Lower Manhattan and New Jersey under such a structure, as well as Great Britain's London Bridge Authority.

Triborough's bondholders could take comfort in the fact that the nonprofit corporate structure provided insulation from political venality. The authority's three board members were mayoral appointees. But they would serve six-year terms, longer than the mayoral term, to prevent them from being pressured to make short-term decisions, such as lowering tolls, to please voters just before a mayoral reelection. In 1934, a year after the Triborough Authority's creation, one of the board members was caught taking a bribe; Moses, appointed by LaGuardia, joined the authority and became its chair. In two years, Moses brought the bridge back on schedule. He followed the orders of the mayor, who directed the bridge "to be built in the shortest time."[36]

The human costs were substantial and no secret. In 1934, six hundred Queens families found themselves in danger of homelessness. More than 250 apartment buildings "are to be razed for approaches to the Triborough Bridge," the *Times* reported. "Eviction orders have brought a storm of protests from the tenants, who mostly are so poor that they . . . cannot obtain quarters elsewhere."[37] Two years later, as the bridge neared completion, the *Times* focused on the "plight" of 1,227 Bronx families, 285 of whom depended on Depression-era relief funds. Even though officials would help them to find housing elsewhere, "the families [were] reluctant to move out of the neighborhood in which many of them have spent most of their lives." Landlords, knowing buildings were condemned, had added to the distress, "shutting off heat, hot water, and other essential services."[38] New York was not stirred by these depredations. Subway construction, too, had obliterated hundreds of buildings between 1900 and 1940, as had the Pennsylvania Station rail terminal on Manhattan's west side.[39]

Tenants displaced for the Triborough didn't live in the river across which the bridge would span, of course. Evictions were necessary because drivers didn't materialize at one side of a bridge and dematerialize at another. An eight-lane bridge needed miles-long highways across three dense boroughs to bring people to and from the bridge. These approaches required the construction of the Interborough and Grand Central Parkways through Brooklyn and Queens to bring drivers to the approach roads. "Everyone who knows anything about the Triborough project knows that its success depends upon the parkway connections," Moses wrote.[40] The Triborough was fated from its construction to be a linchpin of hundreds of lanes of highways, in line with the Graphic Regional Plan.

The press praised Moses for meeting this need—not just in Brooklyn and Queens, but in Manhattan. "When Commissioner Moses took active charge of the [Triborough] project, he found that one of the most important, perhaps the most important, phases had been overlooked—namely, inducing Manhattan motorists to use the bridge," the *Times* wrote. That inducement required building what would become the FDR Drive, a highway paralleling the East River along Manhattan's coast. The city's Board of Estimate—peopled by New York's major elected officials, from the mayor to borough presidents—accepted this argument, approving condemnations.

When the Triborough opened in July 1936, the reception remained uncritical. The *Times* lauded it as "unlike any other bridge," representing "a new freedom from congestion." Parklands and playgrounds under the bridge, also designed by Moses, weren't afterthoughts meant to dress up a highway. Rather, "to children it means new local playgrounds and to sports lovers access to a new sports center on Randall's Island," a small spot nestled among the bridge's newly connected boroughs."[41] Triborough filled with cars—11.2 million in its first year. Traffic proved that people wanted more bridges, and it meant that Triborough had the revenue to finance them. In 1937, the *Times* reported that of the 2,548 miles of major route planned in the Graphic Regional Plan, 40 percent was complete or under construction.[42]

Just before Christmas 1936, Mayor Fiorello LaGuardia inaugurated the Henry Hudson Parkway, built by Moses through a then separate authority, to a similar reception. After decades of fitful planning by New York City, Moses had built the road in two years. The four-lane, four-mile highway from Manhattan's Upper West Side north through the Bronx included a toll bridge for cars. As Bronx borough president James Lyons said, for twenty-five years—since Moses had been a student—"the people of the Northwest Bronx, together with civic organizations from all parts of the Bronx, have consistently and constantly pleaded and hoped for the consummation of this project. The opening of this bridge enables all . . . to rejoice."

LaGuardia didn't focus on this convenience for drivers. Rather, he focused on the result for walkers. "All danger of crossing" at street level "has been eliminated," the mayor said. The project, along with the recently opened West Side Highway to the south, was part of an initiative spanning the length of Manhattan to cover the New York Central Railroad's tracks and build a highway separated from pedestrians. The initiative, as the *Times* put it in a 1937 special supplement, was "nothing less than a total recapture of almost the entire shore line of Manhattan; the surrounding of this recaptured shore line with a continuous highway; and the creation of new waterfront parks and pedestrian promenades which will be within easy access of every resident." The author cautioned, "Mr. Moses has not convinced one that it was wise to give over so much of the Hudson River to . . . automobile traffic," but concluded that it was "one of the most magnificent water-view promenades and drives on earth."[43]

As Caro wrote, the Hudson Parkway destroyed woodland ("eradicate[d] . . . unique, irreplaceable forest") and was yet another link in a web of parkways, expressways, highways, bridges, and tunnels that would choke New York in traffic and decimate neighborhoods.[44] But many New Yorkers preferred it, and its recreational land, to the rail-related eyesore and peril that had come before. The fact that the road filled with cars, exceeding its estimate of 3.6 million vehicles months early, was a triumph: Moses could use the toll money to build a second deck.[45]

A half-decade later, Moses was on the defense—in fending off criticism that the city was slow in finishing its expressway and parkway network. "Since 1934 more has actually been done to meet the motor-vehicle traffic problems of New York City than in any large city," Moses insisted in 1943. "The problem has not been completely solved, and never will be. . . . Peak load conditions [rush-hour traffic] can never be fully met" with adequate road space.[46] Toward the end of World War II, the *Herald Tribune* ran a piece titled "Motorists' Millennium." The piece noted that "before the war Park[s] Commissioner Robert Moses . . . had provided us with a magnificent set of parkways, express highways and traffic tunnels—in particular the nearly completed peripheral highway around Manhattan. . . . Now we have to undertake a few vital missing links."[47]

Through the mid-1960s, Moses used the surpluses Triborough's toll collections generated to build more crossings. Moses's Triborough Authority would eventually control four additional major bridges in five boroughs—in addition to the Henry Hudson, the Whitestone (1939) and Throgs Neck (1961) between the Bronx and Queens and the Verrazano-Narrows between Brooklyn and Staten Island (1964)—as well as the Queens-Midtown (1940) and Brooklyn-Battery (1950) tunnels into Manhattan. Moses's success, along with the popularity he earned building parks and playgrounds with New Deal money, won him his additional positions, including as builder of New York City's non-tolled highways, reporting to the mayor.

Despite near-unanimous support, Moses couldn't keep up the pace of construction and blamed car manufacturers as the press complained about delays. "What makes street congestion?," he griped. "A surfeit of cars rolled off assembly lines by hard-boiled manufacturers who disclaim all responsibility for the pavements and surfaces their products must run on."[48]

Clearing a Path between Bridges

Just as the Triborough Bridge had doomed Brooklyn, Queens, and Manhattan to miles of highways, the construction of the first deck of the Port Authority's George Washington Bridge in 1931—not a Moses project—doomed the Bronx to its own highway. Most New Jersey drivers on the GWB weren't aiming for the Bronx. They had to traverse the northern borough from the west only to take the Queensborough, Triborough, Whitestone, or Throgs Neck bridges further east and north of the city. Even before Congress approved the interstate highway program in 1956, these bridges and supporting highways were forming a high-capacity interstate—later called I-95—from Florida to Maine.

But there was a 6.5-mile gap within New York City. In 1942, the *Times* echoed the thirteen-year-old Graphic Region Plan, calling for "a direct cut across the Bronx."[49] In 1950, the newspaper again editorialized in favor of this "direct cut." With the New England Thruway to the northeast under construction, "with New York's traffic problem as serious as it is, the construction . . . would merely add to the city's grief if something were not done at this end."[50]

Despite political and press support, the Cross-Bronx posed headaches for Moses. No elected officials had worried about the Triborough Bridge's displacements of families a decade earlier. Now, they cared. By 1946, the city's elected officials, via the Board of Estimate, had approved the forty-seven-million-dollar project in concept. That year, though, 400 Bronx residents, representing some of the first of 3,000 families to face removal, crowded a board hearing necessary to approve land condemnations for the easternmost part of the Cross-Bronx. Backed by a City Council resolution, families demanded postponement unless the city could assure that 540 households would receive replacement housing.[51] Mayor William O'Dwyer, a Democrat, gave the assurance. In 1947, as a gesture of goodwill, Moses spent $54,620 to relocate a three-story apartment building, complete with new foundation and electrical, water, and sewer hookups, 130 feet north.[52] Construction began.

By 1953, as Moses prepared to ask the Board of Estimate for permission to acquire land for the central part of the road, opposition had hardened. Fourteen hundred families across a 1.25-mile segment, largely working-class Jews in Tremont, would have to leave. Bronx borough president James Lyons, who had once praised the Henry Hudson Bridge bringing more cars to his borough, offered a compromise, condemning a slice of parkland and a bus terminal instead of homes. Moses resisted. Relocating a bus terminal would increase costs.

In April, the Board of Estimate did what it often did when it couldn't decide: delay.[53] Moses threatened to abandon the half-built Cross-Bronx.[54] "The two ends of the artery are finished," the *Times* reported, "with only traffic-choked local streets in between."[55] Moses—or, rather, the elected officials who almost universally supported the Cross-Bronx—had cruelly outwitted mid-borough residents. By approving condemnation in separate phases, the city had effectively prevented one neighborhood in the Bronx from coordinating with another. As Lillian Edelstein, who lived in the path, told Caro, she and her neighbors were aware that a separate section of the highway was under construction years before it would displace them ("over in the East Bronx somewhere," as Caro paraphrased her words). But "it had gone on so long, and you keep hearing and hearing and nothing happens, and after a while it doesn't mean anything to you," she said. "It was in the wind for a long time that he was going to come through the apartment houses. But we just didn't believe it."[56] Bronxites were understandably too busy commuting, eking out a living, and caring for families to organize against a highway project that was then far away in both time and place. By the time they received their eviction notices for their section of the road and mobilized, the city was not going to leave two halves of the interstate connection with a gap in the middle.

Lyons backed down. The city council president, still on residents' side, accused Lyons of succumbing to "blackmail."[57] Robert Wagner, running to succeed Mayor O'Dwyer in 1953, promised residents he would consider the alternative route. But once in office, he did what LaGuardia had done a generation earlier to the people in the path of the Triborough: he ignored them. A year later, the Board of Estimate approved land acquisitions, overriding "vociferous and sustained efforts" sustained, by then, for over half a decade. Moses, knowing Bronx residents had proven themselves to be politically powerless, resumed ignoring their requests. When one Julius Raffelson, representing 3,371 petitioners, wrote to Governor Thomas Dewey requesting an additional pedestrian overpass over the Cross-Bronx—arguing that "the longer route means that the children will be subjected to the hazards of additional street crossings"—Moses replied to the missive forwarded to him by the governor that "engineering considerations make it impractical . . . no real purpose would be served."[58]

Correspondence from the public also reminded Moses that evictions were a fact of city life. As one Betty Mueller, removed from her West Side home for the Moses-built Coliseum convention center in Manhattan, wrote to Moses in 1954, "I have always been taught to show my gratitude to anyone who helped to add to my happiness. Mr. Moses, I know you have been bogged down and harassed by . . . people criticizing you because of the many improvements you have made. . . . I, too, was among those who did not think too well of you, especially when I was served with an order to Show Cause why I should not vacate my apartment by December 31, 1953. For a while I was panicky and terribly disturbed. . . . I am now living in Forest Hills, [Queens,] and am delightfully happy not only with my new apartment, but with the neighborhood. . . . My purpose in writing this letter is to thank you for getting me out of the 'rut' I now realize I was in."[59]

Moses understood, though, that sentiment was changing. Delay and money for land in built-up areas meant higher costs, even without acceding to elected officials' requests, such as moving the Bronx bus depot. The Cross-Bronx outlay had nearly doubled, to $86 million. In a 1956 letter to Chairman Charles Buckley of the House public works committee in Washington, asking Buckley to tweak the interstate highway bill to add funds to relocate tenants, Moses observed, "Relocation . . . is presently the major obstacle to construction of arterial highways in all built up urban areas." He also noted, "Since the end of World War II we have relocated over 9,000 families in New York City to make way for new expressways. We are in the process of relocating another 2,000, and in order to carry out the program . . . we will have to step this up to 9,000 more during the next three years. In other words, there are some 70,000 individuals who have been or will have to be moved. We must reduce their hardships."[60]

A year later, in a CBS radio interview, he was more blunt. "You are familiar with the Cross-Bronx Expressway," he said. "One section there cost up to $15,000,000 for one mile. One mile at $15,000,000! And if you go up there, you will see an apartment house that is fourteen stories high being vacated."[61] Separately, he wrote, "You can't take down a solid row of twenty or thirty-story buildings without an uproar. . . . When we get through with the present program . . . I think that's going to be the end of major arterial construction. . . . Nothing short of an earthquake or atomic attack would clear the path."[62]

Moses was less diplomatic in a brochure touting the Throgs Neck Bridge in 1957. "We now face enormous opposition . . . [with the press quick] to publish lurid pictures of dispossessed families on the sidewalks. The hard-hearted sheriff is pictured, the grandfather who has a bad heart and is leaning on a highboy or lowboy, granma who is bedridden, an exhausted mother herding a brood of small children. There's actually been none of that sort of thing, except in extreme cases, sometimes long on relief with no member interested in work."[63]

Moses had no powers to overturn political will as it turned against him. His litany of losses was already long. In the 1930s, he had lost the battle to build a bridge rather than a tunnel from Lower Manhattan to Brooklyn, despite having promised to build "the most beautiful architecture wrought by man."[64] Powerful real estate and civic groups had opposed the destruction of Battery Park, at the tip of the island, for the bridge's supports, as well as the elevated approach roads' overshadowing of historic buildings. After having exhausted local political options, the real estate and civic leaders had outwitted Moses by convincing FDR's White House to step in. In 1950, he faced delay in an early attempt to build an expressway over Midtown Manhattan; Mayor William O'Dwyer, again supported by real estate owners and civic groups, rejected the shadow-casting route in favor of a tunnel and would not be cowed by Moses's threat to build nothing.[65] Also after World War II, Moses had lost a fight for control of New York's airports against the Port Authority, and he had lost a battle to prevent the Port Authority from building a bus terminal on Manhattan's West Side. Though the specifics of each case differed, they had one thing in common: when a critical mass of elected officials and powerful business and civic interests strongly opposed a Moses plan, that plan withered.

Even on small things, Moses could lose. In 1956, he lost a battle with the Upper West Side mothers over a proposed parking lot in Central Park. In 1959, when, as city parks commissioner, he attempted to ban buses with advertisements on their sides from driving through parks, saying commercialism marred the scenery, Mayor Wagner commented that "I expect every commissioner to cooperate."[66] Within months, he was out as city parks commissioner, an appointed position in which he had served at the mayor's pleasure.[67] Moses also knew how far he could—and couldn't—go with land seizures. "It has been proposed that we build in the center of 57th or 59th Street," he said of the Mid-Manhattan Expressway, but "no one would ever let us run in the middle of those fine streets, because we would ruin all the abutting property."[68]

As he completed the Cross-Bronx Expressway, though, Moses's approach to the two unbuilt highways across Manhattan wasn't to slow down but to speed up, before costs and criticism increased. In 1956, his deputy, George Spargo, told him he was "rushing it a little bit" on the Mid-Manhattan Expressway, pointing out obstacles: "(1) Because we have previously asked the Board [of Estimate] to approve this project several years ago and were turned down. (2) We have no funds." Moses scrawled: "No. I don't expect to be around forever."[69] Moses would never build those Manhattan highways; a determined housewife would show intellectual Jane Jacobs how to defeat the powers behind him.

Chapter 3

Kids versus Cars

A Housewife's Fight to Save Washington Square Park

I expect more from girls than from boys and from women than from men. . . . They have a surer instinct for the right thing. . . . Moreover, most of you girls will have more leisure . . . to ponder over the imponderables.

—Robert Moses, Hewlett School commencement speech, East Islip, 1954

Mr. Moses must not be allowed to sell out Washington Square Park for a mess of motor potage. . . . There can be no compromise.

—Shirley Hayes, remarks to the City Planning Commission, 1958

THE THIRTY THOUSAND PEOPLE WHO visit Washington Square Park every day to sunbathe, play chess, listen to music, study for class, or watch their children splash in the fountain would find the idea of sharing this refuge with traffic to be laughable. Well into the second half of the twentieth century, the tens of thousands of New York children for whom the ten-acre expanse amid the apartments of Lower Manhattan's Greenwich Village and Lower East Side was their backyard had to share that refuge with cars and buses. Six hundred buses cut through Washington Square Park daily, to shorten the three-mile trip between Midtown and Lower Manhattan. Even after the death of a child—three-year-old Anna Pellone, in June 1942, after "she ran under the wheels of a Fifth Avenue bus"—the thought that heavy, high-speed vehicles don't belong in a park didn't cross most people's minds.[1]

A car-free park was not the course of history. It took one housewife most of the 1950s to get cars and buses out of Washington Square. She had to fight public figures such as Robert Moses as well as skirmish with people who were on her side, including urbanist Jane Jacobs. Without Shirley Hayes, New York would never have had its first victory over the car—a victory that, a decade later, created the blueprint for others to defeat expressways that would have obliterated Lower and Midtown Manhattan.

A Gash through the Park

In February 1952, mothers watched their children play in the chill of Washington Square Park. Shirley Hayes, a neighbor, approached the women, clutching a newspaper.[2] "Washington Square is due for a large measure of reconstruction," the *New York Times* informed readers. The park had always had a narrow road running through it. This drive—connecting Fifth Avenue to the north with West Broadway to the south—dated to the pre-car era, when horses had trotted through with their buggies. Moses, now parks commissioner under the mayor in addition to his other positions, and Manhattan borough president Robert Wagner Jr. had determined that to accommodate traffic, "the congested two-directional roadway [should be] replaced by two new roadways." The wider roadways would mean other transformations that park "habitués," as the *Times* called them, might notice. "One of the chief changes will be the disappearance of the old fountain." To ease traffic, "the new southbound roadway will cut through the western half of the fountain's space." In return, parkgoers would get a playground—wedged between roadways.[3]

The article was informative not just for what it included but also for what it omitted. The author did not interview planners who might question the determination that more road space would solve traffic congestion. Nor did the author interview a skeptic who might wonder at taking play space away from the "baby boom" generation. Also absent was community opinion. Washington Square Park was the center of Greenwich Village's small-town-within-a-city of nearly one hundred thousand people, including fifteen thousand children. The park had once been a potter's field. By the mid-1800s, as housing and factories built up, New Yorkers began using it for recreation. In 1892, architect Stanford White's white marble arch made the park a landmark. What did people who depended on the park think of "reconstruction"? Handing decisions from on high was how New York City's government did public projects.

If Moses had happened upon the women on the bench, he would not have thought he had much to fear. The forty-six-year-old Hayes was defined by her husband; she signed letters "Mrs. James Hayes." A Chicago native, she had moved to New York in 1932, at twenty, after graduating from Chicago's Goodman Theater school. A former actress who had wanted to make it on Broadway, she had served her country during World War II by broadcasting for the Voice of America. By the 1950s, she had settled in Greenwich Village to be wife to an advertising executive and mother to four boys. Hayes looked the part of a 1950s housewife, clothed in shell dresses and pearls, wearing gloves on fancy occasions, carefully made up, hair swept into an updo. One paper later described her as a "vivacious blonde." Hayes was educated; she had attended the University of Wisconsin before drama school. But she had never shown interest in urban policy, let alone the savvy and persistence she would need to best City Hall.

Gentrified Opposition

Hayes was an emblem of change in the Village—change that would topple Moses's way of doing things. The neighborhood—particularly around Washington Square Park—was no longer the Village of longshoremen, factory workers, and immigrants or children of immigrants, grateful for help from the Democratic Party with housing and jobs and willing to show gratitude with a vote. John LoCicero, who grew up in the East Village, witnessed the transformation. After World War II, he remembers, "The neighborhood was changing. Americans from different areas [including his wife, who came from Illinois] were changing the whole style." Longshoremen and metalworkers were giving way to "the artist, the entertainers, the clubs." Newcomers such as "beatniks, bohemians [brought] new ideas."[4]

Blue-collar parents with children were just as much pulled as pushed out, with many families thinking that car-centric suburban life, with multiple bedrooms and large yards, would be superior to apartment living. As they moved away, they left apartments available to be rented cheaply to childless adults attracted to the Village's arts and culture.

These bohemians brought cachet—one that attracted wealthier newcomers, including couples with children. The Village was increasingly home to people like Hayes: college-educated newcomers who had time and political independence to think about what they wanted their city to be. "Whole blocks have been infiltrated by solid citizens," the *Herald Tribune* reported in 1959. "It's no longer a cheap-rent paradise, and high rents mean tenants with substantial incomes," including "doctors, lawyers, professors, stockbrokers, bankers, and business executives, as well as people with good jobs in advertising, publishing, editing, or the art, music, television, and theater worlds."[5]

The Village gentrified. Between 1950 and 1960, it shrank from 90,500 people to 83,000 people. Developers, often operating under New York's federally subsidized "slum clearance" program, demolished tenements to build middle-class housing, resulting in fewer people with higher incomes living in higher-quality, more expensive apartments. The number of immigrants declined, from 20,000 Villagers to 17,500.[6] The Village grew educated, with 23 percent of adults having a college degree, up from 19 percent. The biggest change was in income. The median income increased by two-thirds (inflation, by contrast, was 26 percent). Households earning ten thousand dollars or more a year—the top category—increased 12 percent. Although thousands of blue-collar residents still worked in the neighborhood—in the shoe making, book binding, or metal fabrication trades—the Village increasingly had more advertising agencies and fewer craft workers. Newcomers would use their education, boldness, and organizing skills to fight for a higher quality of life outdoors to match the higher quality of life indoors, one that their predecessors may have desired but couldn't achieve for lack of resources, sophistication, and time.

Underestimating the Mothers

The women in the park reading the *New York Times* that day in February 1952 immediately "started being outraged," Hayes remembered, and "we started meeting at my house." Thus was born the Washington Square Park Committee.[7] A month after that first newspaper article, Hayes, under the group's masthead, wrote to Moses for details. His staff saw no reason to convince her of the park road's merits. His deputy noted, "I have your telegram . . . and enclose a print of our plan." After telephoning an assistant to Wagner, the borough president, to ask for a meeting, Hayes jotted a note to herself: "Mr. Moses said—'he is unlikely to sit down and discuss.'"[8]

That spring, the group grew from "six parents who were very upset," as Hayes put it, to thousands. Door knock by door knock, storefront to storefront, note by note given to children to share with fellow students at school to give to their parents, the mothers built a coalition. By March, four thousand residents had signed petitions.[9] The mothers gained support from business groups, hotels, and apartment buildings. George Sundel of the Eighth Street Business Men's Association wrote that his group was "in complete accord." The vicar of St. Luke's School noted that his institution "would like to protest the establishment of a playground between lanes of traffic in Washington Square."

Facing concentrated opposition, Wagner did something astute: he backed down. In March, he invited Hayes and two other women, a "Mrs.

Schafer and Mrs. Polacheck," for a meeting, three volunteer women against five professional men. The borough president pledged, in Hayes's telling, "if there was such opposition . . . for the present no further work would be done." After promising what Hayes termed a "temporary suspension," Wagner removed the road from the Board of Estimate's calendar, stating he "would not impose an undesirable project."[10]

For Hayes, Wagner's promise was not enough. She wanted the existing traffic out of Washington Square Park altogether. She grasped that this project would not disappear so easily: absent vigilance, the existing road would always be subject to widening, and history was on her side. Moses, as the public face of New York's pro-car bias, generally got his way, with elected officials who had the power to approve or disapprove any change in land use, via the Board of Estimate, deferring to the plans he drew up to accommodate the government and business goal of accommodating more traffic. But he didn't *always* succeed. His plans to remake Washington Square went back more than a decade. In 1939, Moses had launched a plan to "remodel" the square and build a road around it. In 1940, three hundred Village residents came to a community meeting to subject Moses's plan to "ridicule, sarcasm, civic wrath, neighborhood indignation and esthetic criticism."[11] Moses shelved that plan, but let the park deteriorate. The fountain no longer sprayed water.

In 1952, after Hayes's Washington Square Park Committee had convinced Wagner to stop the wider road, Villagers supposedly wiser than Hayes used this history to justify refraining from further action. "If you only knew how long and hard some of the rest of us have worked," Robert Weinberg, an architect and planner (and later preservationist) experienced in New York City politics, warned Hayes, "you would perhaps realize why some of us have learned that half a loaf is better than none."[12]

Hayes was determined to use local power not just to stop more traffic, though, but to eliminate existing traffic. Her Washington Square Park Committee devised a strategy it would employ for a decade. The handwritten minutes of an early meeting read, "Break down the wall of mystery" surrounding government, by "building up a feeling of the schools working together on a neighborly basis such as might be done in a small town."

The women laid out their reasoning. On May 1, 1952, the group mailed a letter to "friends and neighbors." In case Wagner's promise to suspend the project proved only temporary, the letter—after assuring readers that the group had "given much time and study" to the now-averted proposal—listed three reasons to remind readers why the road expansion project isn't warranted. First, current vehicle volume: "Present traffic through Washington Square Park is light . . . [and] does not warrant . . . new roadways." Second, area needs: referencing the Village's children, the letter cautioned that Moses's proposal would "destroy" play space and leave only "a small and dangerous playground caged in between two parkways." Third, cultural preservation: the neglected fountain could serve not only as a "badly needed wading pool for city-bound children" but was "a beloved landmark."

The letter, if confined to these points, would have been revolutionary. Stay-at-home mothers—amateurs—were asserting their right to engage in an expert bastion: urban planning. But Hayes's Washington Square Park Committee did something that was a departure from thirty years of traffic-planning policy. The committee's letter pointed out that even if traffic *were* a problem, building roads would not solve it. "New or improved roadways through the Park would only serve to attract additional traffic,"[13] a phenomenon known as "induced demand." This is why building an extra lane on an interstate seldom reduces traffic.

By the mid-1950s, New York was already experiencing induced demand. The region had built hundreds of miles of highways as well as bridges and tunnels into Manhattan, largely overseen by Moses carrying out the Graphic Regional Plan. These roads carried more traffic into the core. In 1924, two hundred thousand motor vehicles each day had entered the most crowded parts of Manhattan, below Sixtieth Street. By the mid-1950s, the figure was more than half a million.[14] After having removed the trolleys, mid-century Manhattan was doing everything it could to alleviate traffic by giving traffic space, from narrowing sidewalks to converting two-way avenues into one-way thoroughfares.

Nothing worked. Confronted with this crisis, New York professionalized the new field of traffic management. In 1950, Mayor William O'Dwyer had created a traffic department separate from the police. But the city's expert class remained bent on building roads. Officials had also recently condemned several apartment buildings near Washington Square Park, leaving tenants without heat and water, as New York prepared to build a "Verrazzano Street" to move traffic faster across downtown to bridges and tunnels. Officials even considered forcing Bleecker Street's fruit and vegetable pushcarts out to make way for cars—a battle fictionalized in the 1964 storybook *The Pushcart War*.

The next big step was highways across Manhattan. In that sense, Washington Square Park was a microcosm. Just as New York would destroy the park to allow Manhattan traffic to flow through it, the city would destroy Manhattan to allow regional traffic to flow across it. As highways across Manhattan would not benefit Manhattan, the Washington Square Park project would not benefit Villagers: Of 45,000 workers who lived in the area, only 2,000 took a car to work. Most (26,000) took public transportation, while 8,500 walked. Even in the postwar auto boom era, most Villagers did not own a car.

A Partial Victory

At Washington Square Park, the women would take the opposite tack from Moses and the conventional-wisdom planners: fix traffic by prohibiting traffic. They demanded in their neighborhood missive: "The only possible Alternate Plan is that of CLOSING THE PARK TO ALL VEHICULAR TRAFFIC." Hayes understood that facts and reason, though necessary, were insufficient in New York politics. The women would have to demonstrate that the coalition they had organized could maintain its attention span once the immediate threat of a wide park highway had stalled. One of Hayes's first stops in demonstrating this ability was the Village's "community planning council," a precursor to modern New York City community boards and one of twelve Manhattan advisory bodies created in 1951 by Wagner.

Wagner, though beholden to Tammany Hall, was experimenting with more open democracy in the spirit of "reform" politics. The first roster of the Greenwich Village community planning council's thirty-six members reflected the neighborhood. It included a police patrolman, the assistant to the chancellor of New York University, business leaders, a member of the longshoreman's union, and a school principal. It was also an early way in which women became involved in city government. The list included ten women, most without political background, including Hayes, who had desired to serve on the board to advocate for playgrounds.

Hayes, in convincing the council to recommend closing the park to traffic, faced a formidable task. Months before, the board, chaired by Weinberg, the architect and planner, had put itself on record as amenable to the wider park road. Hayes didn't just have to convince the council to support closing the existing road; she had to convince fellow members to reverse their recent decision.

Hayes used her stage experience. In a strategy she would employ repeatedly, she reminded everyone, including vote-hungry politicians, that she was not alone. "I'm representing over 4,000 parents and people," she told the council in April 1952. "This community of 100,000 people have insufficient play areas, schools without playgrounds, and but one park." Hayes presented four choices: plans A through D. Plan A called for removing the existing road crossing the park from Fifth Avenue to West Broadway. Plans

B through D offered a tunnel, a single roadway, and two one-way roads. She outlined the drawbacks to the latter three. The council reversed itself, adopting with "near unanimity" Plan A.[15]

After this endorsement from an advisory government body, the Washington Square Park Committee gained even more support. By June, petition signatures had reached six thousand.[16] Supporters included neighborhood anchors: the Greenwich Village Association, the Lower West Side Civic League, the First Presbyterian Church, the Protestant Episcopal Church, two public-school parent-teachers' associations, and the St. Joseph's Academy school. "[The] plan has the support of every church, parent, business and civic group," Hayes said.[17] Another stakeholder whose support Hayes courted: New York University. NYU had taught students in buildings neighboring Washington Square Park for more than a century, and a surge in postwar enrollment was turning the private university into a real estate and political powerhouse. It worked with slum-clearance officials, including Moses. Hayes wrote to Chancellor Henry Heald. He replied positively, saying that closing the park to buses and cars would be "satisfactory."

Her efforts came to nothing. Between 1952 and 1955, the government engaged in obfuscation and delay, with each bureaucracy foisting responsibility onto another. In September 1952, Wagner's office promised Hayes "some word." By December, the office had concluded, "[We have] very limited jurisdiction and the agreement of the Department of Parks, Department of Traffic and perhaps the Police and Fire Departments would be required. . . . The Board of Estimate itself has final say." Traffic commissioner T. T. Wiley noted that the park's 6,000 daily cars were "too much of a traffic volume" to detour elsewhere.

Another complication: at the time, politically connected private companies ran New York's buses, and one company, Fifth Avenue Coach, had not only a contract to use the park but also ties to Tammany Hall. City council president Stanley Isaacs warned that Hayes's proposal would depend on "the Fifth Avenue Company [being] willing to surrender that part of its franchise. . . . I have always been told that the solution was impossible." The *New York Herald Tribune* concluded that "Greenwich Village civic groups . . . have lost their fifteen-month-old fight."

A Renewed Battle

In 1955, the reason for delay became clear. City government had been regrouping. Wagner, formerly borough president, was now mayor of all five boroughs, and so less beholden to Manhattan mothers for votes. In March, Wagner's successor as borough president, Hulan Jack, announced a plan for a "submerged speedway" through the square, releasing details to "startled" members of the district planning council. The four-lane highway wouldn't just cut through Washington Square, as the plan that Hayes, Lyons, and fellow volunteers had killed off three years earlier had proposed.

The depressed roadway would obliterate the park, with a pedestrian overpass to connect the halves. Newspapers described it as an "open cut." The breadth of the destruction was obvious. "To protect everyone using the park from falling into the new speedway," the *Villager* related, "an eight-foot iron guard rail or fence is proposed. . . . For access from the eastern half to the western half of the park or vice versa, it is proposed that an ornamental footbridge be constructed. It will have a gradual incline so that baby carriages can be pushed across with moderate effort."[18]

If Moses's tactical approach to carrying out that city's strategy was to threaten a more destructive project to punish Villagers for their stubbornness and threaten them into compromise, it worked—at first. The Village Chamber of Commerce launched a contest for architects to propose an alternative road "acceptable to the city authorities."[19] Prominent groups—responsible, measured people, who understood when they had lost—surrendered. Anthony Dapolito, a baker known as the mayor of Greenwich Village, was an executive at the Downtown Community Association. Dapolito said that he'd "like to go along with the 'Bofat's (those advocating blocking off Fifth Avenue Traffic [through the park])," and "wouldn't mind avoiding traffic noise." But as a merchant, he understood "traffic flow needs too well. . . . Truck and auto use . . . will double by 1965! How will drivers like us get around if we start blockading main city boulevards?" Weinberg, now of the Washington Square Association, also pled reality. "A Washington Square freed of all north-south traffic appeals to the imagination and would be ideal if the Village were not in the heart of 20th Century New York City," he wrote.[20]

Establishment groups, in pushing compromise, held themselves out as neutral mediators. In mid-December 1955, the Downtown Community Association held a "mass meeting" of three hundred members, inviting the public to "the largest hall they could find," the Our Lady of Pompeii church on Bleecker Street.[21] The DCA would hear from the people: "three main speakers" would present choices, and "any speaker recognized from the floor [would] be allowed to present his or her views."

Hayes, experienced after three years, took control. She told attendees, "No tunnel or roadway through the park will solve the traffic problem."

Warning that a wider road would bring "constant heavy streams of fast-moving traffic," making the park "uninhabitable," she concluded to applause, "The few acres of Washington Square Park ought to be reserved for people." Her case won. "A noisy Village audience voted Monday against any superhighway through Washington Square Park," the *Village Voice* reported, with most voting to "block all traffic."

Moses's strategy was backfiring. The majority didn't embrace compromise, as "wise" men did. Instead, they entrenched. In preparing a longer fight, Hayes benefited from the presence of Greenwich Village's staid groups. The Village boasted so many organizations that they often competed against one other for attention. A savvy operator could play one off another. Weinberg, who privately continued to advise Hayes, even as he publicly pushed for compromise, observed to her that "the Greenwich Village Association and the Washington Square Association . . . cancel each other out," and "they (unfortunately) give too much consideration . . . to very large property owners." If these groups would not join the fight, they could be fought, as part of a rotting establishment.

As the Village marshaled, it had a potent weapon: the *Voice* itself. Published by Edwin Fancher, a psychologist, the *Voice* was an upstart. Its first issue was published in 1955 to meet demand created by the neighborhood's educated newcomers. Its founding editor, Dan Wolf, was a New York native with an eclectic background; he had written parts of the *Columbia Encyclopedia*. The *Voice* pronounced itself an entertaining alternative to the *Villager*, the boring weekly.[22] It distinguished itself by jumping into the argument over Washington Square. Its second edition, in November, devoted its front page to an oversized "FATE OF SQUARE" spread. Over the next near-decade, the park fight would define the *Voice* and vice versa.

Without the *Voice*, Hayes could not have attained prominence. In December 1955, in a full-page spread called "THE BATTLE OVER WASHINGTON SQUARE," the *Voice* demonstrated its failure to respect authority, presenting Hayes as a figure equal to the heads of three city departments as well as the Washington Square Association and the Downtown Community Association, all of whom wrote a piece presenting their views. Each person or entity, save Hayes, favored a wider road. In its section, Moses's parks department stuck to its "four-lane highway through the park, with pedestrian overpass," adding that "no other plan . . . would do the job." Weinberg and Dapolito called for a smaller surface road and a tunnel, respectively.

Hayes stood out. Pictured in the *Voice* in updo and pearls, lipstick showing in black newsprint, she did not shy from disagreeing with the men.

"Arguments for . . . highways on the assumption that they are the answer to city traffic problems, are sheer nonsense," she wrote. Villagers were proposing a "constructive" alternative: "closing-off of all vehicular traffic." She noted that her committee had coordinated the desires of property owners, civic organizations, parents and schools, churches, the local community board, and "hundreds of individuals, including well-known city planners and architects." The Village, notwithstanding a few timid groups, was united not just against the wider road in Washington Square Park but also against keeping any road.

A Notable Foot Soldier

Though Hayes's Washington Square Park Committee had spent four years trying to get traffic out of the park by 1956, the battle was only half over. The committee had to convince the Board of Estimate not only to vote down Moses's plan to expand the road but also to formally "de-map" the existing road. De-mapping a road was not something the city did casually, especially in that era, when the Board of Estimate's movement was in the other direction, approving mile after mile of highway.

The women turned petition-gathering skills into a full-time operation. Handwritten notes included such information as "sisters [nuns] cannot go out after 7:30 in [the] evening." The women distributed instructions to neighbors. "Write two of the following postcards . . . 'I am opposed to any roadway being built over, under or through Washington Square Park. I strongly urge that Washington Square Park, one of the City's most important historical and cultural landmarks, be closed to all vehicular traffic.'"

The women distributed sign-up sheets inviting people to explain how they could help. One respondent wrote, "[I] have a sporadic job, but when not working will give 4–5 hours a day." They divvied cards block by block, organizing supporters by "cleaners and tailors," "restaurants and hotels," "stationery, book stores, etc.," "food stores," "drug stores," "laundromats," and "hairdressers and barbers," directing signature-gatherers not to miss "Mrs. Mosso's brother's grocery store," the "Espositos," "the Village Bake Shop," and the "Village Fish Market." The women weren't above using gender. Edith Lyons remembered asking Eleanor Roosevelt's niece, who lived along the park and who was "a very top model," to "get half a dozen of your colleagues, beautiful models like you, to walk on a Sunday . . . and . . . get signatures."[23]

One volunteer was Mrs. R. H. Jacobs—a Hudson Street resident later known as Jane Jacobs. In sending her petition to Hayes in 1955, Jacobs wrote, "Thanks for your good work. I've written the Mayor + Borough President, each, the attached letter. Please keep me informed of any other effective action that can be taken." Identifying herself as a homeowner "in the heart of the city," Jacobs noted in her letter to City Hall, "I have learned of the Alternative Plan of the Washington Square Park Committee to close the Park to all vehicular traffic. Now that is the plan that the city officials, if they believe in New York as a decent place to live and not just to rush through, should be for."[24]

In 1957, in her own note to Hayes, a Mrs. Robert Brayton Nicols referred to Jacobs as a participant in this movement against the car. "Dear Shirley," Brayton dashed off in a note, "I'm sorry I didn't have time to send you these before. . . . Not a very big haul. . . . I asked Jane Jacobs to carry the torch (she took the rest of my boxes—but I hear she's short of cards.)" Jacobs collected petitions from the Candy Store, the Chung Laundry, the dry cleaner, the laundromat, the jewelry store, a *perfumerie*, and a pharmacy. A year later, the women had amassed thirty thousand signatures, one-third of the Village's population.

Hayes became a master at publicity. In 1957, a neighborhood group invited children to exhibit drawings of an imagined car-free park. "Please see that there are always enough blank [petition] cards on hand [at] the exhibit," a volunteer instructed. Hayes wrote to the sisters at St. Joseph's Academy that the exhibit was "extremely effective." Finally, she understood newspapers, penning press releases, writing to editors to correct inaccurate accounts, telephoning reporters, amassing clippings, and encouraging neighbors to write letters.

Revealing a Deal

As Hayes's group gained attention, one person who preferred to stay behind the scenes betrayed frustration by going public. In 1956, a Robert Moses deputy, Stuart Constable, paid the Washington Square Park Committee a compliment: Constable admitted that Moses could no longer ignore them. "They're a nuisance. They're an awful bunch of artists," Constable said.[25]

As Hayes built her coalition, Moses built *his* coalition. The Fifth Avenue Association—peopled by officials from banks ranging from Chase Manhattan to First National City, real estate interests including Rockefeller Center, the electricity provider Con Ed, and department stores—wasn't easy to convince. In September 1956, Moses had complained in a private letter, "As to the Fifth Avenue Association, . . . they have not been helpful. . . . They have ducked or opposed the depressed extension of Fifth

Avenue South through Washington Square. . . . Why . . . should I appear at one of their dinners?" A week later, though, he was directing a deputy to "get a table for the Fifth Avenue Association" dinner—generally meaning a big donation.[26]

A month later, the Fifth Avenue Association made up its mind. Michael Grosso, its president, wrote to Moses, "Our Board of Directors at a meeting held on Wednesday, October 10, 1956, unanimously went on record approving the plan linking Fifth Avenue to West Broadway by means of a depressed four-lane highway running through the park in an open cut from Fifth Avenue under Washington Arch. . . . I have also written to Borough President Jack today . . . with the request that the plan be acted upon by the Board of Estimate."[27] In November, Moses added to the pressure on Jack and the Democratic Party. In a memo to one of his lawyers on his slum clearance office's stationery, Moses directed, "Won't you talk to Carmine De Sapio [Manhattan's party boss] and Hulan Jack about the extension of Fifth Avenue through Washington Square. We have a contract commitment with the Federal Government to put these street changes through and this should not wait."[28]

Yet Moses's usual pressure tactics were failing. Beginning to feel pressure of his own, he made a tactical blunder. On Christmas Eve 1957, Moses himself issued not private directions but a public statement, part decree, part threat. "What a splendid opportunity presents itself to those more interested in controversy than progress," he wrote. "Here are the cold facts. . . . Fifth Avenue now splits, runs around, and on a narrow roadway bisects Washington Square. . . . Closing the Square to all through traffic is completely unworkable. . . . Forcing traffic into already overburdened side streets is an absurdity, cannot be done legally anyway, and is contrary to established agreements and common sense. . . . One of these agreements is with the developers of the Washington Square South apartments who were formally, officially, and reliably promised under the Slum Clearance Act a Fifth Avenue address."[29]

Moses's mention of this hitherto secret agreement was meant to settle the matter. Instead, it proved a blunder. Moses had accidentally revealed the city as not just pushing an unwanted road but engaging in a coverup. Now, the question of traffic through the park wouldn't be just a question of technocratic street management; it would become part of a conspiracy of evictions and teardowns to serve a real estate developer who wanted to sell his customers a Fifth Avenue calling card and a university that wanted to amass private property with government help. Already, Villagers opposed slum clearance, the nearly decade-old federal program that rewarded cities for razing apartments housing poorer people and handing the property to developers. Under the proposed Washington Square South project, the city would raze nine blocks south of the park. A developer would build apartment towers on six blocks; NYU would get three. The Village had already fought this plan—and lost; the Board of Estimate had approved it.

Here in Moses's holiday letter was a new weapon that opponents of the Washington Square Park road could wield: Hayes had caught the city in a lie. In 1954, Jack, the borough president, had written to Hayes to disavow connection between the slum clearance project and the road. "When the Washington Square . . . Title I project was adopted by the Board of Estimate, I made it quite clear . . . that the approval . . . would have no bearing whatsoever on any future development of Washington Square Park."[30] Now, Moses, out of growing panic at another year of delay, had contradicted Jack's assurance, making a connection between the slum clearance and road projects. NYU, a beneficiary of the slum clearance, in the five years since Heald's 1952 response to Hayes agreeing that closing the square to traffic would be "satisfactory," had changed its mind. By 1958, Heald's successor, Carroll Newsom, dismissing "idealism," said that the park needed a "somewhat wider" road.

Sensing a Trap

Moses and elected officials weren't Hayes's sole adversaries. She would have to fight some on her own side as well. The hurdle, as ever, was compromise. Rather than the forty-eight-foot road Moses proposed, the Village's moderates were stepping in with a reasonable-sounding compromise: a narrow "emergency road" for fire engines, police cars, and ambulances.

Ray Rubinow, a civic leader who, as head of the J.M. Kaplan Fund, would later shape the city's philanthropic landscape, was determined to broker a truce. Theoretically, he was on the right side of history: "New York has got to settle the question of automobiles versus people," he said. "All of our official planning seems to have acquiesced to the proposition that more and more traffic is inevitable. . . . We think the time has come to reverse this kind of thinking, and Washington Square seems a good place to begin."[31] Like other measured people, though, when challenging powerful people, he fell short in practice. Rubinow didn't think the city could get full closure but that an "emergency" road would win official support.

One urbanist added her voice to the compromisers: Jacobs, who, thanks to her urban-planning writing in *Architectural Forum* and elsewhere, was growing in prominence. Unlike Hayes, she blinked. In a 1958 speech to the New School, the progressive Manhattan college, Jacobs promised the crowd, "We are going to defeat that piece of vandalism and get Washington Square Park closed to all but emergency traffic. . . . This is a chips-down test of the whole question of whether human values can survive in the city."[32]

Superficially, Jacobs's rhetoric was sound; but in changing her language from her 1955 letter to City Hall, in which she had called for a road closure to embrace the "emergency traffic" option, she made a major tactical error. Hayes understood, as Jacobs didn't, that the emergency road was a ruse. "In all my Park sitting days, I have never seen a fire engine go thr[ough] the Park," Hayes wrote. "The emergency road . . . is just another name for a regular . . . road. . . . If the Borough President has control . . . he can turn it into a normal traffic lane."[33]

Like much activism, this battle grew acrimonious. In choosing the "emergency road" compromise, Jacobs supported what amounted to a neutralizing of Hayes's half-decade-old committee. Jacobs joined Rubinow to form the Joint Emergency Committee to Close Washington Square to Traffic. In 1958, this rival group met with city officials and newspaper editors, who found its members to be more reasonable than Hayes's group. Hayes was frozen out. Carol Greitzer, then a local activist on her way to the city council, recalls the dispute. "Shirley Hayes and Edith Lyons, they started it," Greitzer said, "and when it gained steam, they tried to throw them out. They thought she was not sophisticated, too strident. She was strident. But you had to be strident."[34]

The rupture became clear in a letter Hayes penned to Rubinow—"My dear Raymond." In the letter, Hayes referred to a meeting at which Rubinow and Jacobs had argued for the narrow road. The new group claimed to have community support—but in doing so, it cited the petitions Hayes had collected for a full road closure. "Jane Jacobs screaming '30,000 people' over + over again hysterically at my question 'what org do you represent' was not worthy of an editor of Ar[chitectural] Forum," Hayes wrote. "I refresh your memory or Jane's, the petition campaign was launched by the WSPC [Washington Square Park Committee] . . . and petitions mimeographed by us. . . . It has been so obvious from the beginning that it was the intention of you and several others to take over the WSPC under a new name." Hayes informed Rubinow that "this is to notify the [Joint Emergency Committee] formally that it or its representatives"—including

Jacobs—"cannot represent [the Washington Square Park Committee]."[35] The moderates did not speak for the Village.

Finding a Counterweight to Moses

If Hayes couldn't beat Moses, Wagner, and Jack, she would appeal to a person who had power over them. In 1958, Carmine De Sapio was at the pinnacle of New York politics. He was New York's "boss," having rebuilt Tammany Hall from the ignominy of bribery scandals. From his Village headquarters, the fifty-year-old De Sapio had made Mayor Wagner's career five years earlier; he had helped get Wagner elected mayor by identifying issues on which Wagner should run: keeping subway fares and apartment rents from rising. Nothing important happened in New York without De Sapio's approval.[36] De Sapio, like anyone who gets anywhere in the New York political world, was familiar with corruption. (In a separate incident in 1957, he disavowed having anything to do with $11,200 in cash lost in a taxicab when the driver tried to return it to him and, eventually, would go to prison on an unrelated matter.) But De Sapio prided himself on long-term strategy and understood voters' hopes and anxieties. In understanding Village voters' desires, De Sapio was driven by self-interest. His power base was his elected position as Greenwich Village's "district leader." Each district had two leaders, a man and a woman. De Sapio looked down upon politicians who clung to backroom party power despite not being able to retain their districts and had promised that if he ever lost his district vote, he would step down at Tammany Hall.[37]

Every two years, De Sapio thus had to go before these voters. De Sapio knew that his district was changing and that voters increasingly cared about Washington Square Park. In 1956, Hayes had written to him. Citing her petitions, she told him, "You must be concerned."[38] De Sapio knew too that the Village's transformation made it harder to do business the old-fashioned way, with secret deals. By 1957, a dissident political clubhouse, the Village Independent Democrats, had emerged to challenge De Sapio and Tammany Hall. The two VID candidates for the positions of male and female district leader—Herman Greitzer, Carol's husband, and Gwenn Worth, an attorney and a sales executive, respectively—campaigned on the Washington Square Park issue, blasting Parks Commissioner Moses and reiterating that the VID wanted the park closed. Before the September primary, the VID ran a *Voice* ad. After touting free polio vaccines, the challengers noted that the VID had "voted to close Washington Square to traffic." These "unknown candidates" then "managed to collect a surprising 36 percent of the Democratic vote against Carmine G. De Sapio," the *Voice* reported. The area's "changing character" had shaken the election.[39]

De Sapio heeded the warning. Just before Christmas, the week Moses issued his screed revealing the deal with the developers desiring a Fifth Avenue address, the party chief ended his silence. De Sapio telegrammed the Lion's Clubs Committee to Save Washington Square Park to "heartily endorse the sentiment of the vast majority of my neighbors for the closing of Washington Square Park to all through traffic." De Sapio cited the only fact he needed: "Congratulations to your membership," he said, "for their assistance in obtaining . . . signatures, all demanding the preservation of the park."[40]

A Deceptive Victory

By 1958, Hayes had to demonstrate political savvy before powerful officials—and navigate new traps. In May, as a precursor to the decisive Board of Estimate vote, the City Planning Commission, made up of city appointees, had to approve the wider road. Turnout at the hearing was high, and the "overwhelming array of witnesses . . . favored closing the square to all vehicles," the *Times* reported. Hayes reminded officials that Villagers are voters, listing, one more time, the number of parent-teacher organizations and local groups who supported her cause. Reminding the crowd of the children's art exhibit, she said, "They painted what they preferred to have in the center of the park instead of roadways."

The hearing had a star: Eleanor Roosevelt, who kept a home near the park. Roosevelt had devoted her column in the *New York Post* to the topic, noting that "it would be far better to close the Square to traffic . . . than to accept the reasons given by Robert Moses." Now, to a standing ovation, the former First Lady said, "Desecration of the square by putting a large artery for traffic through it would harm not only the square itself but, really, the city."

The crowd derided attendees who favored the road. Newsom, the NYU president, "was hissed." He faced student opposition. Preceding the era of university protest by a decade, NYU student Robert A. Meister presented one thousand student signatures in favor of closing the road. The project divided families. "Whitney North Seymour, president of the Municipal Art Society, testified that the society doubted the feasibility and safety of eliminating traffic. . . . His son, Whitney North Seymour Jr. . . . showed up . . .

as a representative of 'the enlightened generation' and supported closing the square."[41]

The marathon hearing ended in anti-climax. Everyone—Hayes and Moses alike—would have to wait three more months. In September, the Board of Estimate would hold its own hearing. At a rally beforehand, the women deployed a hand-painted banner, with red and black lettering exhorting neighbors to use their "last chance." The goal, unlike that of the faction pushing for a compromise, was clear. "We are opposed to highways through Washington Square Park," the banner read.[42]

This time, the speaker who garnered attention was De Sapio. He would make his first appearance before the Board of Estimate. De Sapio promised protesters, "we will beseech the city fathers to grant our request. We hope and pray they will listen." The party boss presented the signatures to the Board of Estimate, with 150 or so "determined" Villagers ignoring Wagner's "frantic attempts to gavel them quiet." Wagner, too, understood the political gravity; he skipped the state party's annual dinner to attend the hearing.[43]

As the Village awaited decision, the *Voice* remained clear about who would take the blame for the wrong choice. "Those wise in . . . politics have always assumed that the decision over Washington Square rests ultimately with Carmine De Sapio," it editorialized. "He is the LAST WORD in Greenwich Village. Only the totally naïve can believe that an appeal by the leader of a Tammany Hall for a specific action within his own bailiwick would be pushed aside. . . . Mr. De Sapio, the Village should know then whether the secret interests outweigh the public interest."[44]

The decision was a thunderclap: the Board of Estimate would ban cars from Washington Square Park—immediately—for a trial period. Every advocate in the six-year battle declared victory. Said the *Voice*, "Washington Square will be closed to traffic on Saturday. The event will be treated with the elaborate ceremony it deserves, for it is one of those significant victories that can mark the reversal of a trend. In this rare instance, the auto has given way to the people. . . . We learned the lesson Mrs. Hayes taught us. We were not the brightest pupils."[45]

It was time to celebrate. Rubinow's Joint Emergency Committee feted Wagner, De Sapio, and Jack. The "Joint" produced fliers announcing the festivities: "GRAND CLOSING!! Of Washington Square. Come and help tie up the Square with *ribbons—not cars*!" Decades later, Jacobs remembered the temporary closure to be final victory. "That supposedly temporary thing had really settled the issue," she said. "The battle was won. . . . At some point it was just regarded as a fait accompli. . . . There was never any campaign to remove the temporary thing and there didn't have to be."[46]

Everyone celebrated—except Hayes. She studied the fine print—and didn't like what she read. The park would remain open not just to "emergency equipment" but to "buses"—a loophole that would allow hundreds of vehicles each day not only to traverse the park but to idle. By early 1959, the *Voice* was backtracking from its victory declaration, noting, "If you think those are buses you see, you're correct! . . . The buses have preempted the Square as far as the fountain." One mother told the *Voice* that "no parent can feel secure as long as there is traffic." Added a father, watching his children, "There are three buses sitting in the park . . . fouling the air."

It was becoming clear too that the city may have had less than pristine motives for closing the park for a trial period to see if traffic elsewhere in the area worsened or not: it was one last shot at exhausting Villagers into giving up before the next election. The traffic commissioner, T. T. Wiley, told officials that the closing, after four months, was "inconclusive." The Joint Emergency Committee was still talking with officials about building a wider "emergency" road.

A Data-Driven Victory

In preparing for one last showdown, Hayes had a new weapon: data. As the city balked at doing a traffic study to determine whether the temporary road closure was successful, her committee did its own. Christopher Hayes, Shirley Hayes's son, recalls being deputized with other children to count cars in the days before and the weeks after the trial closure.

The women and children had to act fast in fall 1958, before the city closed off the route, to amass data for a before-and-after comparison. They stood in pairs, counting vehicles. The volunteers, including writer Grace Paley, crossed off stick-line tallies. The women transformed their counts into spreadsheets, handmade with pencils and rulers. The women conducted this census over two days, three times each day, and asked a professional planner to certify the process. The result, in red handwriting: "DECREASE OF 15% . . . ON 5TH AVE. BELOW 8TH ST."[47]

By summer 1959, the city did something unexpected: it surrendered. DeSapio—facing yet another electoral challenge from the VID and a four-part public-television series, reported by Mike Wallace, called "Revolt Against De Sapio," finally achieved a permanent decision.[48] The Board of Estimate would "de-map" the existing road altogether, forever precluding the possibility of the city gradually transforming an "emergency road," over the years, into an everyday road.[49]

Notable at the hearing was a new voice: John V. Lindsay. A young freshman in Congress, Lindsay represented not just Manhattan's "silk stocking" Upper East Side but also the Village. He had learned about the controversy during his campaign, talking to "mothers in the playground" to "try to persuade them that it was all right to vote Republican." He telegrammed from Washington, "The experiment which the Board of Estimate adopted at the urging of thousands of New Yorkers has proved to be an overwhelming success. This was one of the few times that people have won out over automobiles."[50] In August, the *Voice* reported in a front-page banner, "City Shifts to Hayes Plan—Car, Buses, Everything Out!" The "surprise move" did not include an emergency road.

Hayes's verdict: it "seems perfect." It would take another four years, though, for the law of the land to become reality on the ground, as Fifth Avenue Coach balked at change. These years would further transform city and Village politics. De Sapio had chosen the right side, but only under intense political pressure, and he was acting far too slowly, in voters' view, in forcing the city to remove the buses from the park after the Board of Estimate's vote. That year De Sapio kept his seat, but so narrowly—by six hundred out of nine thousand votes—that the *Voice* decreed the outcome a "death blow."[51] In 1961, voters completed their execution of the Tammany boss. De Sapio faced another primary fight against VID challengers, this time James Lanigan and Carol Greitzer. Greitzer charged that the park was still a "private garage" for buses. "VID has insisted and will continue to insist that the park must be permanently closed to traffic." This time, they won the election. The vote was lopsided by neighborhood: Lanigan and Greitzer got 71 percent of the vote around Washington Square.

Two years later, in 1963, De Sapio made a comeback attempt for his old seat against new opponents: Greitzer and her new district-leader election partner, a young attorney named Edward I. Koch, who joined the call to remove the buses. Frustration at the Democratic machine's still-glacial pace of getting buses out of the park was peaking. Suddenly, just before the election, the buses were gone. In September 1963, the "11-Year Fight Ends," reported the *Voice*. "No More Buses in Washington Sq"—in practice as well as on paper.

De Sapio attempted to take credit. "The question of which political leader led the fight against the buses is a matter of heated dispute," the *Times* reported. The *Voice*, though, reminded its readers how slowly

De Sapio had acted. "Beginning in 1952," the *Voice* editorialized, "park mothers, organized by Shirley Hayes, valiantly, single-handedly fought off Robert Moses and his road-builders. They were shunned, . . . called 'crackpots,' by the politicians. ATTEMPTS TO WIN DESAPIO'S SUPPORT ALWAYS MET WITH THE SAME RESPONSE; 'DESAPIO DOESN'T GET INTO LOCAL FIGHTS.' But [as] he faced a major primary challenge from the Village Independent Democrats, who were long on record against the roadway—De Sapio spoke. He said he opposed traffic through the Square. . . . It was only this week, . . . under the persistent urging of the Village Independent Democrats, that the buses were finally cleared. . . . Mrs. Greitzer, Koch, and the VID . . . had a major part." At a pre-election rally, one sign read, "THANK YOU Ed & Carol for giving us back our park!"[52] Koch and Greitzer won the election, with their biggest margin around Washington Square. Recalled LoCicero, voters saw that Koch supported "keeping the traffic out, . . . and said, maybe we should go with the reformers."

Hayes never met Moses. "I saw him once, peeking in, at a Board of Estimate meeting," she recalled. "I'd been making enough noise to warrant his peeking in."[53] In 1959, Hayes received a letter of surrender. Constable, Moses's parks deputy, who years earlier had dismissed her group as a "nuisance," was back in touch. "Dear Mrs. Hayes," Constable's letter read. "We shall be happy to receive suggestions from your Committee concerning reconstruction of Washington Square." As the Washington Square road was de-mapped, Hayes proved to understand the on-the-ground landscape one more time. Jane Jacobs counseled against putting water in the Washington Square fountain. But others, including Hayes, "contended a water fountain was the original use."[54] Today, the water flows.

Two Full-Time Jobs

The mothers who won the more than decade-long battle for Washington Square Park had to master New York's political machinery—understanding, as Hayes did and Jacobs didn't—that an "emergency road" would be a defeat, not a victory, and that de-mapping the road from the city's official map was the only guarantee of success. They had to apply skepticism to how traffic worked—understanding that a wider road would attract more vehicles—long before city officials did so. In teaching herself about traffic, Hayes clipped articles far beyond Washington Square, ranging from how Italy was introducing the "startling concept that pedestrians have precedence" to pieces on "park-like" pedestrian "malls" in Toledo and Kalamazoo.

At the same time Jacobs and urban thinkers were grappling with cities on an intellectual level, Hayes applied theorizing to the real world. "Two daring women, Mrs. Shirley Hayes and Mrs. Edith Lyons . . . took the remarkable intellectual step of envisioning improvement for certain city uses, such as children's play . . . at the expense of vehicular traffic. They advocated eliminating the existing road, that is, closing the park to all automobile traffic," Jacobs wrote in *The Death and Life of Great American Cities* in 1961. In Hayes's copy, Jacobs inscribed, "For Shirley Hayes, who taught me so much and influenced me more than she will ever guess."[55]

Hayes understood before few others did that Moses did not have the power to slip the bonds of democracy. Moses's power came from the fact that usually, the political class desired his projects. When one faction of the public proved that it could present a sustained threat to Tammany Democrats, the real power brokers, such as De Sapio, reined in Moses's supposed sovereignty.

Defeating the roadway was an intense vocation that demanded the skills of women who, in a later era, might have been doctors, bankers, or lawyers. Also, in the 1950s, keeping house and raising children was more demanding than it is today. "We were too busy with babies and kids," Hayes remembered. "There were no . . . paper disposable diapers. . . . You boil[ed] the baby's glass bottles and nipples . . . it took a lot of time."[56]

By the end of this battle, Hayes was no longer known by her husband's name. A notice of James Hayes's ad-agency promotion described him as "the husband of Mrs. Shirley Hayes who led the . . . campaign to close Washington Square Park to traffic." After "retiring" from civic life, Hayes resumed her paid career, broadcasting for New York's public-radio station. She also advised Lindsay, who won the mayoralty in 1965, on how the city could court the entertainment industry, including promoting streets and parks as movie backdrops. Hayes died in 2002, at eighty-nine.

Hayes and her Washington Square Park Committee helped change New York's attitude toward cars. Political newcomers, including Greitzer and Koch, would defeat other car-centric infrastructure projects in the Village, from saving Bleecker Street's pushcarts to killing the project to ram Verrazzano Street through apartment buildings. Hayes's success also inspired residents' organized resistance to one of Moses's major crosstown highway projects: the Lower Manhattan Expressway, a ten-lane elevated highway designed to run across SoHo and Little Italy.

Chapter 4

Changing Times (and Minds)

Defeating the Lower Manhattan Expressway

There is something very sad about the professional athlete who hangs on too long.

—Robert Moses, 1954

We will wait for groundbreaking before we uncross fingers. . . . There is still time for the Board of Estimate to get cold feet.

—*New York Times*, 1962

ROBERT MOSES WAS PAST retirement age, having turned seventy-two in 1960. He had seen the motorcar era eclipse the transit era. He was intent on finishing New York's expressways. The Regional Plan Association was pushing the "next step": the "elevated express route near Canal Street [across Lower Manhattan] to tie the Holland Tunnel and West Side traffic to the Manhattan and Williamsburg bridges."[1]

Yet the expressway would never make the leap from paper to concrete. It would remain but an urban legend: symbol of a near-miss disaster for New York, the city that came close to bulldozing neighborhoods so that cars and trucks could treat Lower Manhattan as a bypass. Starting in the mid-1960s, politicians and the press, faced with the results of their decades-old planning strategy, collectively changed their minds. Highways were bad for cities and the people who lived in them. By the end of the 1960s, activists had succeeded in using Hayes's tactics to kill the illusion that Moses had unlimited power—and by doing so, killed the Lower Manhattan Expressway (Lomex) and its devastating effect on the city's core.

Expensive Asphalt

That Moses hadn't already built the Lomex and its companion, the Midtown Manhattan Expressway, was part plan, part accident. Through the 1930s, it had made sense to first knit Manhattan to other boroughs via bridges and tunnels. Drivers could inch across Manhattan's streets, but they couldn't float across water (except on inefficient ferries). In the 1940s, World War II stalled public works. After the war, the Cross-Bronx Expressway consumed Moses's attention, giving Manhattan a reprieve.

Financially, building highways across dense neighborhoods was difficult, as the Cross-Bronx had proven. As Moses said, [Lomex] "does not lend itself [to] a separate toll . . . the only place where you can get money of this kind is in Washington." Part of the challenge was tollbooths, straightforward to place on a bridge with a few entrance points, but hard to do on an elevated highway with multiple entrances across the island of Manhattan. Politically, too, it would be difficult to ask people to pay one Port Authority toll for using the Holland Tunnel from New Jersey only to ask them for another toll, collected by a separate authority, once they entered Manhattan. In 1956, after stating that the city has "no choice except to provide adequate highways for those who from compulsion, preference or convenience use an automobile," Moses observed before a state commission, "Why has it taken so long to build the Cross-Bronx Expressway, the Brooklyn-Queens Expressway . . . ? Why have we not started the Lower Manhattan Expressway, construction of the Sheridan Expressway [in the Bronx]? Because we have limited funds."[2]

That year, Moses secured funds through President Dwight Eisenhower's interstate highway bill. The country had determined that highways, including highways through cities, were the future. Moses promised to finish "the great ring which before long will encircle our entire metropolis, separate the main thoroughfares from city streets and pave the way for smooth regional and transcontinental travel." He expected to start construction on the Lower Manhattan highway—followed by the Mid-Manhattan and the Bushwick Expressways across Brooklyn, the Clearview Expressway extension across Queens, and the Richmond Parkway across Staten Island.

Moses thought the outcome on the Lower Manhattan and Mid-Manhattan Expressways would be the same as the Cross-Bronx: a battle, but one in which the highways would prevail. "The opposition . . . seems to have died down," he said in 1957 regarding Lomex. He dismissed the furrier trade, whose businesses were in the path of the Mid-Manhattan Expressway, as "marginal."

His confidence seemed justified. Just like the Cross-Bronx Expressway, the Lower and the Mid-Manhattan Expressways were missing links in interstate networks. It made no sense to build tunnels, bridges, and connecting highways and leave Manhattan inaccessible, just as it would not have made sense to build the George Washington Bridge and the Whitestone Bridge and leave a gap in the Bronx. "All bridges and tunnels lead to Manhattan," Moses wrote in 1957. As Moses embarked on this project he was at the crest of his purported powers. In 1960, he held ten posts.

Lomex, the first cross-Manhattan project scheduled for construction, enjoyed political support. The City Planning Commission had approved it in 1941 and reapproved it in 1960.[3] The commission had noted on the latter occasion that "the pressures generated by . . . congestion are slowly but surely strangling the economic life of this section of the city and unless drastic remedial action is taken soon the condition will become insupportable."[4] The project was supported by the business community, including the Downtown Lower Manhattan Association, headed by Chase Bank chief David Rockefeller (brother of Nelson Rockefeller, the Republican who became governor in 1959) as well as the Real Estate Board of New York and, of course, the Regional Plan Association. Mayor Wagner, who took office in 1954, also supported the project; in 1960, through an aide, he pronounced that he was satisfied with "safeguards, services and benefits for persons and businesses to be uprooted," just as O'Dwyer had been satisfied with the Cross-Bronx plans.[5] Finally, Lomex enjoyed press backing. "The new highway," the *New York Times* reported, "will remove about 75,000 vehicle trips a day from the city streets, . . . [and thus] relieve congestion."[6]

As with every highway project, though, Lomex also faced opposition. Some of the 1,972 households and 804 businesses in the path, employing 10,000 people, didn't want to leave. But people's wishes and fates had never stopped a project before. SoHo, the neighborhood south of Greenwich Village, was a "deteriorating area with low property values," Moses argued, with "buildings . . . at least sixty years old . . . in poor condition . . . [and] numerous violations." The highway would "relieve traffic . . . and allow this locality to develop in a normal manner that will encourage improved housing, increased business activity, higher property values, . . . and an increase in . . . real estate tax revenues."[7]

As David Rockefeller and others had concluded, white-collar work was the future of New York, and therefore factories and warehouses were obsolete. Some residents of Little Italy and Chinatown, to the east of SoHo, would have to move, too, just as the working-class Jews of the Bronx had had to move for the Cross-Bronx. In 1960, Moses made these moves less painful. The city would raise the payment to tenants—people who, unlike building owners, wouldn't be compensated in condemnation—from $500 to $1,000, about $8,900 today.[8]

In 1960, Moses's self-assurance appeared justified. The Board of Estimate—again, representing every city- or borough-wide official in New York, including Wagner—approved the project, with construction to start the following year.[9] People in the path resigned themselves. "I'll be glad to get away," said jewelry repairman Phil Pasuk, 72. "I've been here long enough." Mike Squecciarine, 65, a retired iceman, told a reporter, "[He] feels no nostalgia for the neighborhood. He would like to have moved to Brooklyn or Staten Island many years ago."[10] Like Betty Mueller, these residents had come to accept that they no longer had control over one of the dignities of life: freedom in where to live.

Reexamining the Urban Expressway

One reason the fates of the people in the path of the Cross-Bronx in the 1950s were different from the fates of the people in the path of Lomex in the 1960s was Jane Jacobs. She had published *The Death and Life of Great American Cities* in 1961, as New York was set to build Lomex. *Death and Life* inspired an intellectual movement to underpin people's growing instinct that highways weren't good for cities. As the book put it, "This is not the rebuilding of cities. This is the sacking of cities."[11] Jacobs personally fought Lomex at the request of the reverend of the Church of the Most Holy Crucifix on Broome Street. "It would wipe out his street, church, parishioners, shops," she recalled.[12]

Jacobs, heading the Stop the Lower Manhattan Expressway Committee, became the symbol of the anti-highway movement by brooking no compromise; she had learned that lesson from the Washington Square Park battle the previous decade. She used her fame to help kill Lomex, which made her even more famous. As the *Village Voice* reported in 1962, "Jane Jacobs marched triumphantly through several Village organizations last week, all the way from right wing to liberal left, garnering support."[13] That December, at a "sometimes-stormy six-hour public hearing"—one of several the Board of Estimate held, part of elected officials' stalling tactics—forty-four people spoke against the highway, and only five spoke in favor. Jacobs called it a "monstrous and useless folly." Two years later, another hearing stretched fifteen hours.

The social and political infrastructure Hayes had built up a decade earlier in the Washington Square Park fight held. Back then, Moses had wanted to destroy a park to let traffic pass through downtown; now he wanted to destroy downtown to let traffic pass through Manhattan. But the same principles of opposition, too, scaled up. Jacobs used them to fight a bigger project over as long a time frame and with a larger coalition. She connected Lomex to the earlier Washington Square Park road to the north. In her appearance before the Board of Estimate in December 1962—described as a "knock-out . . . last stand" by the *Voice*—she called the arguments in favor of the elevated highway "the same . . . piffle" as in the earlier case.[14]

Hayes-style coalitions held, as well. Just as the Village had transformed itself a decade before into a haven for creative newcomers, SoHo too was undergoing change. Artists were repurposing lofts and warehouses. In 1969, toward the end of the decade-long battle, a group called Artists Against the Expressway, supported by painter Barnett Newman, held a 250-person benefit at the Whitney Museum, charging that the road would "destroy the downtown artists' community."[15] Anthony Dapolito, the bakery owner who had once called for compromise in Washington Square, helped found the Citywide Organizations Against the Lower Manhattan Expressway. He was in no mood for compromise this time, calling the expressway "a death blow to Little Italy."

The Village Independent Democrats, a new force in the earlier Washington Square fight, was more established. Led by Edward Koch in 1963, it remained on the side of the activists. Congressman John Lindsay opposed Lomex, just as he had opposed Washington Square's roadway. In 1962, eyeing the mayor's race three years away, Lindsay said that it was "hardly consistent with modern city planning to dump countless numbers of tons of automobiles and trucks into the middle of Manhattan." He and William Fitts Ryan, his counterpart on the Upper West Side, threatened to hold up federal funds.[16] As the Washington Square fight had proven, opposing a highway was a launching ground for higher office representing Manhattan: city councilmen Ted Kupferman and Ted Weiss would be elected to Congress after opposing Lomex.

The *Voice*, a fledgling outlet in the Washington Square fight, was more powerful. It ran front page after front page of advocacy journalism, a counterpoint to the *Times*'s support for the project. David Gurin, a Harvard graduate and Brooklyn native, was a lead reporter. Gurin had cultivated his revulsion to urban highways on a bicycle tour to Boston as a teenager. He had seen the deep cuts that the state of Massachusetts made through the city for the Massachusetts Turnpike highway, then under construction. That image "stayed with me," he says. He met Jacobs when she gave a speech at Harvard, and she had welcomed him as a protégé. In a 1965 piece in the *Voice* called "Last Exit to Lower Manhattan," he wrote, "Ten smooth lanes of elevated concrete and steel are proposed to entomb old Broome Street for its final sacrifice as the connecting link between the Holland Tunnel and the Williamsburg and Manhattan Bridges. Designed in Los Angeles to the latest open-country autobahn standards, the Lower Manhattan Expressway would create a Chinese Wall above Chinatown, wipe out little Italy, and bisect the Lower East Side."[17]

Jacobs and fellow activists made Lomex into an issue bigger than Lower Manhattan. Just as Hayes had warned that Moses's Washington Square road was the start of a transformation of the neighborhood, Gurin warned in the *Voice*, "If Robert Moses succeeds in forcing the Lower Manhattan Expressway upon us, he may succeed with a 30th Street expressway and a Bushwick expressway and the complete destruction of Ocean Parkway in Brooklyn (already the first few blocks of this beautiful boulevard have been bulldozed and 'improved' into an expressway)." After the 1963 destruction of Penn Station, preservation had become a cause of its own.

As destructive projects multiplied, and as residents could see the impact of previous roads, including the Cross-Bronx, the anti-highway coalition diversified beyond mostly white Manhattan residents. Lomex would impact black and Hispanic voters, a growing presence in the city. "Scarcely represented [are] 10,000 workers, . . . mainly [black people] and Puerto Ricans who work in manufacturing," who would have to make way for "lily-white" construction workers, Gurin wrote. NAACP and Congress of Racial Equality members spoke at hearings against Lomex.

In Queens, a new force emerged to fight the extension of the Clearview Expressway: the black middle class. As firefighter Samuel Murray and his wife, Eugenie, one of a thousand families to be moved for the extension, told the *Long Island Press* in 1966, "Because they are Negroes, they will have difficulty in purchasing a nice home in a nice neighborhood [if displaced]."[18] Samuel Murray, ninety-two in 2021, remembered the battle. Originally from South Carolina, Murray was orphaned at fifteen, at which time he moved to New York to live with his uncle. "I had only a fifth-grade education," he says. "I didn't go to kindergarten until I was nine years old. . . . [After tutoring,] I was able to get into Chelsea vocational high school . . . [and Queens College]." He joined the fire department in 1958. In 1963, he had saved enough money to move with his wife from "the projects" in Coney Island to a "brand-new house" in St. Albans, Queens.

That year, Murray recalls, "someone in the neighborhood who knew someone who worked in city planning . . . got the news that these houses would be torn down because the Clearview Expressway was coming through. . . . [Through church] we organized. We started having meetings." Like many anti-highway activists, Murray hadn't been political before. "I wasn't fighting for [racial] integration. I just wanted a place where I settle down with my family, get my kids a good education. I just wanted to be left alone."[19] Assemblyman Kenneth N. Browne of Hollis, Queens, one of an emerging class of black leaders who would go on to become a state judge, gained attention and support charging that the project threatened black families.[20]

Real-Life Lessons

As important as the activists' intellectual and political arguments was practical evidence that highways didn't ease congestion. As early as the mid-1950s, urbanist Lewis Mumford, writing in the *New Yorker*, questioned the "sacred right" of the driver of the "private motor car" to "go anywhere" in a city.[21] In response to one such article, Moses lamented in a private letter, "Look . . . at the pieces Lewis Mumford writes . . . which are always unfair and never factual."[22]

In the decade since then, it had become obvious that the planners had built a traffic jam. Since 1930, the number of motor vehicles had increased five times as fast as the population.[23] In 1924, 2.3 million people had descended upon Manhattan below Sixtieth Street each day to work, to play, or to run errands. By 1960, the number had increased to 3.3 million. People still mostly relied on transit: the number of daily subway commuters to Manhattan increased throughout that period, from 1.5 million to 1.9 million.

Yet the number and share of people coming by motor vehicle had soared. In 1924, fewer than 300,000 people traveled by car or taxi daily to the most congested part of the city, just 10.6 percent of the travelers making such a journey to core Manhattan. By 1932, the number had increased to 430,000, or 15.9 percent. By 1956, it was 736,000, or 22.2 percent, and by 1960, it was 886,000, or 25.9 percent. By then, streets were so saturated that people decided, via their behavior, that Manhattan couldn't fit another car. From 1960 to 1963, auto and taxi trips to core Manhattan dropped to

752,000, or 22.9 percent of the total, and transit ridership increased. Yet the city proposed Lomex to make life easier for drivers.[24]

The turning point was the Long Island Expressway. In 1963, the *Times* ran a front-page spread titled, "L.I. EXPRESSWAY: A DILEMMA." "A road prescribed less than 10 years ago as a specific remedy for the post-war traffic ills . . . has become part and parcel of the ailment." Wags called the Long Island Expressway "the world's longest parking lot." In Queens, "mile-long traffic jams are commonplace." A map depicted a tangle of Moses-created highways; a photo showed a confection of interchanges. Moses—who, the article reminded readers, "has dominated New York's highway scene for the last 40 years"—had a solution: "building a third tube for the Queens-Midtown tunnel; an elevated mid-Manhattan expressway . . . and a new (Bushwick) Expressway."[25]

Suddenly, the *Times* was no longer citing as fact Moses's contention that a new highway would alleviate traffic. "The road-builders have thrown mile after mile of new roads across the metropolitan area in all directions, only to see their projects inundated." That year, the editorial board affirmed that while "we stand by that earlier endorsement" of crosstown Manhattan expressways, "we must admit to a growing disenchantment."[26] By the late 1960s, Bill Ronan, a top aide to Governor Rockefeller, was warning that by 1985, "population growth would require 50 lanes in one direction" between Long Island and Manhattan.[27] For the rich and the brave, helicopters buzzed from Midtown's Pan Am Building to Kennedy airport, inaugurated in 1965. (They stopped in 1977, after a crash killed five people.) Auto-dystopia essays were common: "[On the] planet Motorious, . . . the car-riding population starves to death because of a flat tire," one author satirized.[28] Even Moses's car-only parkways were no longer a miracle, as columnist John Crosby wrote in the *Herald Tribune* in 1962. Calling Moses "dead wrong" in his continued resistance to buses, he reported, "The enormously complicated and ingenious parkways system built by Mr. Moses doesn't work the way he planned at all. These parkways were built for pleasure driving, . . . but . . . there's not much pleasure."

Finally, the myth of Moses's supposedly autocratic power was falling—ironically, in part because Moses and his deputies, finding themselves under new pressure, were beginning to dispute the legend that Moses could act unilaterally. Elected officials had liked to hide behind the fiction that Moses had unlimited power, because it deflected growing criticism over mass dislocations for highway and housing projects from them, a fantasy Moses was happy to go along with until the mid-1960s. In a 1966 city council meeting, for example, Councilman Dominick Corso, who had represented Brooklyn's Bushwick since 1960, observed to former Governor Charles Poletti, who had come to testify in support of Moses's proposed highways, "If the [Triborough Authority] desires to have an expressway going through let's say, Bushwick—where I'm opposed to it . . . they don't need any council authority." Poletti, though, refused to go along with this long-standing fiction. He revealed, correctly, "You can't have any capital funds [which were needed for any non-toll road, as an expressway was] without going through the [City] Council." Corso persisted in trying to hide behind the myth that he himself was powerless to stop an undesired project: "I wish you did heed us, because we would stop the Triborough Bridge and Tunnel Authority." In reply, Poletti insisted that New York City's elected government could stop Triborough from building an expressway through Bushwick. Backing him up, William Lebwohl, a Moses deputy, reiterated that "Triborough must coordinate its activities with the City, and cannot and has not built a single project . . . without the consent and approval of the City," generally through the Board of Estimate.[29] New Yorkers were figuring out, as Hayes had a decade earlier, that to stop a Moses project, one didn't fight Moses; one fought the elected officials who could stop Moses.

Moses himself began to undermine his own myth. In 1966, he wrote a letter to Rube Goldberg, the cartoonist.

> This is a Macedonian cry for help. . . . I am anxious to show graphically how many official agencies have to be consulted before any major public works. . . . The notion that we who are commissioned to build are off on our own without consulting elected and other officials is malarkey. We are almost overwhelmed by hearings, approvals and faultfinding by agencies which seem, most of the time, to be determined that their ideas shall prevail and that if they can agitate enough, nothing shall happen. . . . All of which is a roundabout way of asking if you will make us a cartoon or two showing the horned cattle which are involved in any big public enterprise in the construction, and especially transportation, fields. . . . If you will come to Randall's Island [Moses's headquarters beneath the Triborough Bridge], we will show you some exhibits, maps, models, renderings, etc. . . . and then you can demonstrate with some of your machinery what we are up against.[30]

The cartoonist obliged, creating a black-and-white drawing depicting the project approval process in seventeen satirical steps.

> Highway coordinator's tasty proposal for new project (A) is digested by state and city administrative goat (B) which happily wags tail activating legislative machinery (C) unwinding red tape (D) to obtain federal approval and opening bureau of public roads' shovel (E) which dumps nuggets (F) on truck alerting state supt. of public works (G) who starts crane yanking in consulting engineer (H) who . . . drops into coordinator's balloon (I) blast from balloon activates city agencies' apparatus (J) which approves plans making pencil (K) write advertisement of public hearings and causing hand of city planning commission to push report (L) into Board of Estimate hearing aid (M) which funnels approval into ear of mayor causing legal broom (N) to sweep condemnation awards and relocation bonuses (O) into stewing kettle (P) of tenants in right of way. As kettle drops out of sight it unveils hand of mayor (Q) which directs construction to proceed.[31]

Moses responded to Goldberg, "Just what I hoped for," and he invited the artist to visit his "shack" on Jones Beach.

Firing Moses

This time, the unwieldy approval process that Moses had asked Rube Goldberg to illustrate in his cartoon drawing would not yield the outcome it had yielded for the Cross-Bronx: approval. Wagner, in office from 1954 to 1965, did what many elected officials had done when pressured by irreconcilable yet increasingly matched sides and what he had done, as borough president, in the fight over Washington Square Park: vacillate and stall. Contemplating a 1965 run for reelection, Wagner couldn't outright cancel Lomex without suffering politically; he needed the support of the construction unions and the business establishment.

But he didn't begin building the highway, either. He announced delay after delay, always asking for one more study. In 1962, the mayor approved land condemnations, but somehow, the land acquisitions didn't happen. The *Times* was prescient to worry, after years of delay, that the Board of Estimate could get "cold feet."[32] That December, the mayor did find that his feet were chilly, and he promised not to break ground. In 1965, he reversed himself again, promising that work would begin in 1966. Wagner's stalling tactic worked in favor of anti-highway forces, who knew, from the earlier Washington Square fight, that stamina mattered. The mayor decided against running for another reelection, and by 1966, when Moses, supposedly, could finally start work on the project, New York would have a new mayor.

One mayoral candidate, Lindsay, ran against highways. In a 1965 nineteen-page manifesto titled "a modern transportation system for New York City," Lindsay set down a motto: "Cities are for people and for living." Noting that officials had to observe the "human costs" of highway construction, he said, "Our City can choke itself to death" and pledged:

> I would reverse Mayor Wagner's decision to proceed with the construction of the Lower Manhattan Expressway as presently designed. This 10-lane elevated structure would blight and disrupt an entire neighborhood. It must be rejected. . . . I would reject the proposed elevated Mid-Manhattan Expressway across 30th Street, a new tube for the Queens Midtown tunnel and the Bushwick Expressway through Brooklyn. These proposals would attract more traffic into the core, bulldoze substantial residential areas, cut a swathe through some of the most valuable commercial real estate in the world, and cost much more than they would be worth.[33]

Once in office, though, Lindsay did what his predecessor had done: play for time. Lindsay learned, as Wagner had known, it was not easy to defy business, real estate, and construction union coalitions. As the General Contractors Association warned members in a 1966 bulletin, "Why is Mayor Lindsay discarding the opportunity of providing a very much needed crosstown artery as well as jobs for literally thousands of people? . . . 'Cities are for people and for living and not for automobiles.' What kind of reasoning is that?" As David Rockefeller put it, he wanted Lomex, whether "above ground, below ground, or on the ground," in his plan to revitalize Lower Manhattan, which also included the World Trade Center's Twin Towers.[34]

The press, too, was hardly on Lindsay's side. In an appearance on a 1966 *Searchlight* program, a *Meet the Press* for local politics, Arthur Palmer, Lindsay's transportation coordinator, defended the Lomex delay. WNBC reporter Gabe Pressman charged, "[There is] a deplorable lack of continuity between administrations here. This is a problem that obviously has been studied for about a decade or more . . . one of the worst instances of traffic congestion in the whole United States." Agreed Joe Ingraham, *Times* reporter, "If you keep studying and studying and do nothing, all this federal money that's available is just going to evaporate. . . . How long can you keep studying something that Gabe and I both agree has been studied for almost 20 years?" Palmer calmly observed, "There has been no serious effort to find an appropriate solution other than to put in a ten-lane expressway across the island."[35]

Weeks after Lindsay's election, the *Times*, three years after its editorialists had pledged to "wait for groundbreaking [on the Lomex] before we uncross fingers,"[36] realized that "a huge, elevated structure that cuts off light and air is not likely to improve [SoHo]" and decided Lindsay's delay was "reasonable."[37] Yet the paper too couldn't let go of decades of highway support. In March, the paper was back to editorializing: "If the Lindsay administration has made a final decision to kill the Lower Manhattan expressway, it owes the city a much fuller explanation. . . . The expressway is far too important to the city to be subjected to such cavalier treatment."[38]

Lindsay couldn't convince the *Times*. But he didn't have to convince Moses; he could fire him. On July 11, 1966, the mayor drily informed him that "the continued designation of an arterial highway coordinator [a mayoral appointment that Moses had held (previously under a slightly different title) since 1946] is no longer necessary."[39] Moses surrendered: "It would be futile to argue again the errors of your logic."[40] Any mayor could have done it. No mayor had wanted to. At the time, Moses was also losing much of his state-level power, as Rockefeller asserted control. "Moses's 11 titles [were] now down to one," the *Times* observed—Triborough Bridge & Tunnel Authority chairman.[41]

Confronted with the same problem that had dogged Wagner—he couldn't irrevocably antagonize either side—Lindsay commissioned a study to see if an alternative, tunneling under Manhattan, was feasible. "There's no question that a high-speed multilane highway across Lower Manhattan is necessary," he said in 1967. "A tunnel would offer the best possibility."[42] Unsurprisingly, it wouldn't. Moses had said more than a decade before, correctly, "the cost of constructing . . . tunnel traffic across Manhattan is so excessive that it rules out any logical argument."[43] In the meantime, a decade's delay had pushed Lomex's cost from $50 million to $250 million or, critics warned, $500 million.

Lindsay couldn't run out the clock as Wagner had. In 1969, he faced reelection. After a first term marked by labor strikes, tax increases, crime, and unrest, Lindsay needed his original voters, including the growing and increasingly diverse anti-highway contingent. Jacobs, who had kept up her years-long fight, was arrested for disorderly conduct at a Lomex hearing in 1968; she was protesting Lindsay, not Moses, who was gone.[44] In July 1969, four months before the election, Lindsay picked a side. At an unrelated press conference, standing with Harlem's Charles Rangel, then a state assemblyman, exhaustion rather than strategy may have propelled the mayor, in answer to a question, to pronounce the Lomex highway "dead . . . for all time."[45] Nearly a decade after the new congressman had telegrammed from Washington to petition Wagner to close Washington Square Park to traffic, Lindsay, as Wagner's successor, killed a far more damaging Manhattan highway. He did so not out of idealism, but, as Carmine De Sapio had acted during the earlier decade, because of intense political pressure.

More parochially and prosaically, two months after his 1969 announcement, Lindsay's traffic commissioner decided that Moses's ban of buses on parkways wasn't ironclad. The city approved the Carey Transportation Company's request to run buses to the airport across the Grand Central Parkway, two decades after the company had originally asked.[46] As for the Church of the Most Holy Crucifix on Broome Street, saved by Jacobs from Lomex's path: in 2017, a developer bought the "defunct" church for $7.4 million.[47] By 2024, the builder was selling multi-million-dollar apartments on the site of the demolished church, now the site of a brand-new "architectural masterpiece" with "oversized windows . . . echoing the neighborhood's historic charm."[48]

Dead Ends

New York's era of expanding automobile infrastructure was over. The end of Lomex was also the end of the Bushwick Expressway, the Clearview Expressway extension, the Mid-Manhattan Expressway—all dead. As Samuel Murray, who protested the Clearview Expressway extension, recalled, after months of meetings with politicians, including a meeting that the government shut down because officials could not be heard over protestors, "They just backed down. . . . We would like to think that we fought so strongly [that the politicians thought,] maybe [the project] wasn't worth it." Fifty-eight years later, he lived in the same home. In the Bronx, the city halted the Sheridan Expressway miles short of its planned end point. Even on Staten Island, which, without a subway line, was the most car-dependent borough, Lindsay truncated the Richmond Parkway to avoid a repeat of the environmental destruction in Manhattan for the Henry Hudson Parkway three decades earlier.

Around the country and the world, mayors, governors, and presidents realized: highways wouldn't save cities. In 1970, the *Times* reported, "Interstate 95 [the interstate that included the Cross-Bronx] was designed a decade and a half ago as an 1,866-mile-long 'Main Street' of the East

Coast from Maine to Florida. But . . . it looks like a mortally wounded snake, severed in such places as Boston, Philadelphia, Baltimore and Washington," as activists had gained traction. Boston, New Orleans, San Francisco—all shrunk Moses-style highway projects, often too late to avoid partial destruction.[49] In London, the government had lopped off a slice of Hyde Park in one of the city's richest neighborhoods, creating a chunk of multi-lane highway steps from Mayfair. In Paris, activists forced the city to back away from its plan to fill in Canal Saint-Martin for a motorway.

More than five decades after Moses lost the battle to build the Lower Manhattan Expressway, and more than four decades after his death, the "power broker" remains stranded in the auto era, shouldering popular blame for the expressways and parkways that crisscross New York. It is less painful to cast Moses as eternal enemy than to confront the truth. For decades, New York's elite citizenry—from Democrats to Republicans, from the *Times* to the Rockefellers, from labor bosses to business executives—were oblivious to the possibility that they might be wrong. It is easier to stick with the narrative that one man had tricked them all. Even after New York's elite jettisoned Moses, though, they clung to the philosophy he had embodied: they would try to build one last Manhattan highway.

Chapter 5

No Way on Westway

A Watery Grave for Manhattan's Last Highway

> The automobile . . . has wrecked the twentieth-century American city.
> —Daniel Patrick Moynihan, "The Soulless City," 1969

> It is hard to think of a federal project which promises a better return.
> —Daniel Patrick Moynihan, 1976 Senate-campaign statement on Westway

AUGUST 17, 1974, HAD BEEN AN 88-degree day. Edward Abramowitz, 14, from Bath Beach, Brooklyn, seeking nighttime adventure, rode his bike ten miles across the borough and over the Brooklyn Bridge. The teen made his way to Manhattan's elevated West Side Highway, the pre-Moses span from the lower tip of the island along the Hudson River to Seventy-Second Street. Along the Greenwich Village portion, after midnight, Abramowitz fell through a months-old "gaping hole," dying of injuries.[1] The previous December, in the final days of the Lindsay administration, a truck had broken through the highway and created the chasm. Its driver (who survived) had ignored the route's weight restriction, ironically, to deliver materials for repairs.[2]

The collapse was an ignoble end for one of New York's earliest highways. Four decades earlier, in 1930, Manhattan borough president Julius Miller—for whom the roadway was named, although nobody called it "Miller Highway"—had proclaimed that it "foreshadowed a new era of speed." Yet within weeks, "the new speedway often became clogged with cars." Overuse and neglect during New York's burgeoning 1970s fiscal crisis had rusted it away.[3] After the 1973 collapse, the city closed the road for four miles, and much of the previous traffic didn't clog up nearby streets—it disappeared. The ghost highway became the city's largest informal bicycle path. Families picnicked as dogs frolicked. "No fumes," marveled one jogger.[4] Yet visitors stayed away from the collapsed area. Abramowitz hadn't known. "The boy's white bike left tracks on the roadway's accumulated dust."[5]

That New York had adjusted so well to the loss of a major highway—and even adapted the ruins to a badly needed, albeit dangerous, recreational use—demonstrated the opportunity that the fall of the West Side Highway posed for a post-Moses New York: to reverse its twentieth-century mistakes. Instead, New York State and City seized this final chance to build Manhattan its unwanted interstate. The New Yorkers who spent more than a decade rescuing the city from this "Westway" highway future created the conditions for a revitalized West Side.

A New Planning Approach

Even before the West Side Highway fell, New York was planning to replace it with a broader, eight-lane thoroughfare that would meet postwar interstate standards of straightness and width. State and city leaders during the early years of such planning, Governor Nelson Rockefeller and Mayor John Lindsay, however, maintained that they were determined to avoid the mistakes of the recent past: they wouldn't ram this interstate through a neighborhood against a community's will.

Elected officials were partly acknowledging community power flexed during the recent Lomex fight. In 1971, Lindsay and Rockefeller signed a memorandum to avoid "the frequent crises that have arisen" when government ignored local concerns. The project's director insisted that he wanted to work with the West Side community so that they would "desire" the highway. Five community boards—the successors to the neighborhood community planning councils on which Shirley Hayes had sat—would have input. Officials promised not to build "at all social, economic and other costs."[6] By 1973, they had met with more than two hundred groups. "A new approach to urban planning has evolved," the *New York Times* wrote.[7]

This supposedly enlightened attitude was also partly forced. Thanks in part to national anger over urban highways, New York officials had to abide by three new federal laws. First, the National Environmental Policy Act—passed by Congress in 1969 and signed into law by President

Richard Nixon on January 1, 1970—required that for any large project receiving federal money, a state had to publish an "environmental impact statement" to assess positive and negative effects, from expected traffic impact to businesses displaced. Via hearings and in writing, any person could comment on that expected environmental impact. The law also required states to consider alternatives and not just one plan. If Moses had built the Cross-Bronx Expressway after 1969, he would have had to explain why building across a route that residents preferred—cutting through parkland and condemning a bus depot rather than obliterating apartments—was impossible. Second, the modern Clean Air Act, signed by Nixon in 1970, forbade states from worsening pollution; the state and city had to send the federal government binding steps they would take to reduce auto use. Finally, in 1972, Congress passed the Clean Water Act. For the state to impact the Hudson River, as its proposed West Side Highway replacement would, New York would need a permit from the U.S. Army Corps of Engineers. If the Army found that the project would have a significant effect on the river's navigation, flooding, or fisheries, or if a reasonable alternative existed, the Army would have to deny the permit.

A New Marketing Approach

The state and city went far beyond navigating new federal laws and newfound anti-highway vigor, though. It changed the branding of highways altogether. The previous decade, the overriding purpose of a highway had been traffic flow: a growing postwar city needed to accommodate more cars. This argument was no longer as potent: Manhattan's population had fallen 20 percent between 1950 and 1970; now, the city was shrinking, and employers were shuttering local factories.

The new argument was "economic development." Manufacturing decline as well as shipping automation had left West Side piers in decay. In contrast to upper Manhattan, which featured the Moses-era Hudson River Parkway and Riverside Park, the Lower and Midtown Manhattan stretch of the river was devoid of recreation. To enjoy the river, the tens of thousands of people who lived nearby had to cross under the busy elevated highway, navigating abandoned cars, shuttered warehouses, prostitution, and drug dealing.

In 1970, the *Times* described how a new state-city plan for the river would "reverse history": "Miles of West Side waterfront would be reclaimed from well over a century of industry, and a stretch of the steel girdle of highway that encircled the city [the West Side Highway] would be replaced with virgin land that would reach out into the river to provide parks and housing and jobs."

The highway part of this project was presented as almost an afterthought. Underneath the two hundred acres of new land in the Hudson—"landfill," the sanitized term for acres of often contaminated dry-land dirt dumped into the riverbed—would be the new interstate, stretching from Lower Manhattan to just west of Times Square. "If the vehicle to achieve this [redevelopment] goal had to be a new highway [to replace the West Side span,] bury the road underground and let people live and work and play above," the state and city proposed.[8] Nobody would mind the new highway, because it would be in the river itself. John Zuccotti, city planning commissioner, christened the project "Westway."

New Arguments, Old Arguers

Despite this revamped approach, support and opposition to Westway broke down along lines that had defined the Lomex fight. The *Times* was an ardent supporter. Westway was "a priceless opportunity to transform a neglected decaying waterfront into an urban jewel . . . at no cost to the city."[9] Chase Manhattan chairman David Rockefeller's business and real estate coalition supported the project, as it had supported Lomex. "Westway will bring: a state-maintained park for an area that has the least parkland of any city neighborhood; a modern incinerator . . . and even a bus garage," wrote John Keith, the Regional Plan Association president.[10] Others in favor of Westway were the construction unions and contractors, as well as the United Federation of Teachers, a vote-producing union whose leaders argued that Westway would generate tax dollars needed for education spending.[11]

West Side residents quickly organized in opposition. Bill Bowser, head of the West Village Committee, launched the Ad Hoc Committee Against the Interstate Highway, a reprise of Jane Jacobs's anti-Lomex coalition. Opponents filled the pages of the *Village Voice*. *Voice* contributor David Gurin recalled, "I got my first inkling [of Westway] from the ever-watchful Greenwich Village community activists I met through Jane Jacobs. Jane had left the Village for Toronto [by the 1970s, but] it was natural for me to be attuned to the dangers of yet another highway."[12] In 1972, Gurin castigated Westway in print as a "six-or-eight-lane cement manufacturer's dream."[13] Another author, Frederic Morton, got to the point, presciently, considering the collapse that would come a year later: "Let the [elevated] West Side Highway crumble" and "rot" rather than replace it with a wider road.

Community members had honed their craft after decades of fighting highways. The Ad-Hoc Committee's newsletters were fun: pre-internet mashups of mimeographed clippings, appeals to small-scale donors, and jokes. "Help the neediest," one edition said, mischievously needling the *Times* by borrowing from its annual "neediest cases" charity drive. They had also absorbed the lesson that compromise equaled loss. "Our enemies . . . have long urged that we come forward with a detailed alternative to Westway. . . . We know of no instance in which interstate fighters have come up with a detailed alternative . . . where eventually the superhighway forces have not prevailed."[14]

By 1973, three of the community boards Rockefeller and Lindsay had attempted to co-opt had instead combined forces. They used a $100,000 government grant, "designed to increase community participation," to hire a consultancy that had killed a highway in Cambridge, Massachusetts. The consultants concluded that a wider West Side Highway would attract more out-of-state trucks passing through Manhattan.[15] "This plan induces new traffic," said the "combo" boards' Robert Kagan, of the Upper West Side, in 1974.[16] Westway wouldn't even extend as far north as Kagan's neighborhood—state and city officials had announced that early on, to head off wider opposition—but Kagan and his neighbors realized that a wide highway south of them would mean traffic with nowhere to go as it reached upper Manhattan.

This time, though, activists had broader concerns, beyond a wide road's physical impact upon its immediate landscape, that rendered the fact that the highway would be buried underwater irrelevant. Groups such as Friends of the Earth and the Sierra Club, part of the nation's burgeoning environmental movement, were worried about pollution; a wider highway funneling more cars through Manhattan would further foul the air.[17]

A related concern was the state of the city's mass transit system, long neglected in favor of highways. To improve the city's air quality, New York would have to get more people into its transit system; a wider highway, however, would get more people to drive. In the *Voice*, Gurin observed that "in a full day, the West Side Highway actually transports just a few more people than the Eighth Avenue subway does . . . for the one hour between 8 and 9 in the morning." It would be more sensible "not to respond to the ever-increasing demands of the automobile." Instead, he suggested, the city should repair and strengthen the existing highway and use the rest of the money for transit.

This argument was not just academic, because Westway and mass transit dollars became intertwined. In 1973, as cities soured on highways,

Congress gave states the option of "trading in" federal highway dollars for transit money, what Gurin had suggested in the *Voice*. Westway proponents could no longer credibly argue that when it came to money from Washington, it was Westway or nothing.[18]

Area city council members, state lawmakers, and congressional representatives followed constituents' leads. Miriam Bockman, the head of Manhattan's Democratic Party, pointed up the absurdity of the economic argument: "If someone offers you a billion dollars to cut your throat, do you?"[19] Congresswoman Bella Abzug, who sponsored the transit "trade in" bill, called the pollution Westway would generate a "severe health hazard."

As in the 1950s and 1960s, politicians coveting higher statewide or citywide office gained hyperlocal support by opposing Westway. In 1974, Brooklyn Congressman Hugh Carey, running for governor, observed at a hearing that "someone decides that the most important thing to be done is pave over another part of our lives with a bigger highway—as though the automobile, and not human beings, were the constituents." Carey replied to a questionnaire, calling "the concept of a huge truck-laden Interstate highway on the West Side Highway route a planning and ecological disaster."[20] Congressman Ed Koch of the Village, running for mayor in 1977, stood on the House floor to call Westway a "fiasco."

One Woman's Fight

Westway's most tenacious opponent wasn't an elected official or a well-funded group but a private citizen. Over more than a decade, Marcy Benstock—quiet, persistent, and logical, with her thick, dark bangs and unselfconsciously chic crisp shirts and skirts—would become Westway's formidable foe. A Buffalo native and Harvard literature graduate, Benstock had moved to Manhattan's Upper West Side in 1963. She had fallen for New York City as a child, when, "every year," her mother and father, the latter once a "starving actor" aspiring to Broadway, took the family to the city, "so that all of us could go to plays," Benstock says. "We would have cheesecake at the old Lindy's in Times Square. New York was my mecca." Benstock was self-sufficient, in part because of transit in Buffalo. "I took the bus or walked or bicycled everywhere" as a child, she recalled.

In New York City, Benstock became concerned about poverty and inequality. After earning a graduate degree in economics at the progressive New School, in 1969 she took a job in Washington at Ralph Nader's Center for Study of Responsive Law, where she became an environmental expert. She coauthored *Water Wasteland*, an appraisal of pre–Clean Water Act antipollution programs.[21] She thought not just about water but air. "I kept my apartment in New York [while in Washington] and visited . . . as often as I could—and found the windowsills coated with oily black soot," she said.

Back in New York in 1971, she launched the Upper West Side Air Pollution Campaign. The goal was to help enforce the city's air quality code against stationary sources of pollution, such as apartment-building incinerators. The campaign was so successful in getting building managers and residents to understand and comply with antipollution laws that workers at the city's environmental agency "begged" her to ensure that the city comply with the federal Clean Air Act. "They said, it is just going to die if there's no citizen uproar." She renamed the group the Clean Air Campaign.

Benstock became Westway's "clearinghouse for information . . . [and kept] a close watch on . . . the many government agencies."[22] One week, she might be calling Massachusetts officials to inquire about their experience in trading in highway money for transit. Another week, she might be writing in the Clean Air Campaign's newsletter to encourage recipients to testify. Benstock didn't fill her missives with invective, but facts and instructions. Benstock's lifestyle was as simple as her methods: with a rent-regulated apartment, she lived on eighteen thousand dollars a year. "I rarely had the time to do things that cost very much," she says.[23]

In addition to cementing opposition, the hundreds of meetings Benstock attended yielded ideas. At one Upper West Side meeting, she learned of a new strategy. "A boy in the audience said, 'you're all talking about money for mass transit. But what about the Hudson River? The river itself . . . ?' His name was Tom Stokes [a former merchant seaman]. A light bulb went off in my brain. . . . Tom Stokes later took me for a walk across the George Washington Bridge to look at the river," says Benstock. It was the first time she saw the river as a river.

Using Data as a Weapon

Thanks to the National Environmental Policy Act, Westway's opponents had a weapon that Lomex's opponents didn't have: thousands of pages of information from the state. In the mid-1970s, Westway began releasing its environmental impact statement and related documents, confirming what opponents had long charged.

Westway's design report confirmed the traffic absurdity of building an eight-lane underground highway only up to Forty-Second Street, where it would dump vehicles onto local roads. "There would be congestion and delay on the unimproved roadway [to the] north," the report acknowledged. The state projected that the road would carry 12 percent more traffic than the old highway, or 130,000 daily cars and trucks: a bad outcome for a traffic-choked city. But the same report noted that since 1973, traffic had declined, reversing decades of growth.

Traffic had fallen not only because of population and job loss, as well as the Arab oil embargo (when Middle Eastern nations cut off the nation's oil supply, which quadrupled gas prices), but also because of the collapse of the West Side Highway itself. City officials had been terrified that the closure of the region's second-busiest thoroughfare would cause chaos, just as the transit strike had eight years before. But the West Side Highway proved that the city didn't even need the road capacity it had. After the collapse, sixty-two thousand cars and trucks—10 percent of the vehicles that previously used the West Side Highway or a competing route—disappeared, and transit ridership rose. The experiment was "the earliest demonstration" of the inverse of induced demand, says Sam Schwartz, who then was a young city traffic engineer. Just as new highways attracted new trips, shuttering old highways—or letting them crumble—caused some existing trips to vanish. "The loss of a major highway shifted travel patterns so that two years later, while more people entered Manhattan's [central business district], they travelled in far fewer vehicles."[24]

The state's Westway filings also revealed that Westway would not be some magical highway, hidden underground. Of the new land to be dumped in the river, thirty-one acres would "be utilized for interchanges and ramps," the environmental-impact statement noted, and only 55 percent of the highway would be covered. "Open sections will occur," including at Canal Street and in Midtown, and ramps would connect the project to Lower Manhattan, Canal Street, Fourteenth Street, and Midtown.[25] The supposedly hidden highway would require acre upon acre of above-ground interchanges to connect to existing roads, interchanges that would make it dangerous for pedestrians to get to the water. Moreover, the highway would feature a surface road atop it, wider than the road beneath the old West Side Highway, meaning the benefit of burying the road would be lost.

The environmental impact statement demonstrated the folly of Westway's economic-development goals. Of the landfill, 110 acres would "be available for new development," the document said. To make way for interchanges, though, 109 people in forty-four apartments would have to move, as would ninety-two businesses, from picture frame manufacturers to a garment factory and fabric and envelope manufacturers to meat and fish purveyors, employing 577 people. To save New York City's overall economy, the state was bent on destroying its neighborhood economies. Only 93 landfill acres would be parkland, and renderings showed fragments, not an oasis akin to Central Park, to which Westway's supporters compared it.

The state admitted another deficiency: Westway would pollute. On whether the project would prevent New York from complying with the Clean Air Act, the environmental impact statement answered with a tautology. "Mid-70s deadlines for implementation of [pollution control] strategies will not be met," the report said. "However, . . . since the construction period . . . will be approximately ten years, operations of a new West Side Highway facility would not begin until 1987. Therefore, the new facility could not affect the achievement of air quality standards in the 1970s and early 1980s." In other words: *we'll figure it out later*. The highway would exhale exhaust via shafts, including at the edge of the Village. The state's contention that it could mitigate this pollution by planting thorny bushes to keep people away was laughable.

Public Trust Betrayed

Beyond data, federal environmental laws created a new avenue for opposition: the lawsuit. Perusing Westway's environmental statement, William Hoppen, a World War II veteran and former Manhattan assistant district attorney, determined that Westway would indeed violate New York's mandate to comply with the Clean Air Act. In 1974, on behalf of Action for Rational Transit, a collection of neighborhood groups, Hoppen sued in federal court.[26] Hoppen, though, could not make an engineering argument. He needed a professional. Hoppen approached Brian Ketcham—a man who knew more than anyone else about the city's legal commitment to comply with the Clean Air Act.

Brian Ketcham was an engineer before he was an environmentalist. He had loved engines, and, with three years of grad-school work at MIT behind him, had made a living designing them, first for General Motors and then for Curtiss-Wright, the arms contractor. In 1968, though, "my ex-wife's niece gave me a book on what we were doing to the environment." A newcomer to New York, observing the streets, he determined, "the city had to get rid of the car."[27]

Ketcham went to City Hall to see how best to accomplish this goal. Because of his knowledge of motor vehicles, officials sent him to the city's Department of Air Resources. The commissioner, Austin Heller, soon offered Ketcham a job, contingent on passing an engineering licensing exam. The working environment was dreary, "an old desk in a basement," Ketcham remembers.[28] "An elderly gentleman with a passion for porno sat next to [him]. . . . Little wonder New York City was making little progress [on air quality]."

Ketcham would change that. At the air resources department, Ketcham set out to prove Detroit carmakers wrong on a critical antipollution technology: catalytic converters. Carmakers opposed Environmental Protection Agency mandates requiring converters, saying that it wasn't clear that the technology would work and that lead in gasoline would damage the equipment. Securing a $1 million federal grant, Ketcham outfitted a Brooklyn lab and recruited suppliers to provide test converters. "Before the end of the year, we had test cars on the street, including a catalyst installed on the mayor's Cadillac." The catalyzers worked without reducing mileage, as the industry contended.

In 1972, New York had to prepare a mandated "implementation plan" to reduce pollution under the Clean Air Act. The state and city picked Ketcham to write it. In the plan, the city committed to doing everything from restricting parking to investing in transit. After writing the plan, though, Ketcham grew frustrated at hints that the city and state would delay executing it, or worse. In one 1972 meeting, Lindsay's deputy mayor said that "New York City had no intention of implementing anything that might hurt business," in Ketcham's telling. After the city demoted him, Ketcham left to join Citizens for Clean Air, a nonprofit advocacy group.

Now, joining Hoppen's Westway suit, Ketcham could use his knowledge of the plan he had written for the government, against the government. "Without funding, [we] spent a year building our case. I was the only engineer, indeed the *only person*, to testify against the formidable technical team assembled by the city, state, and federal government," he recalls. The contention was that the state's environmental impact statement didn't adequately describe Westway's projected traffic impact on the air. In 1975, Judge Thomas Griesa agreed. Griesa told the state to "reanalyze" its data. Westway had suffered its first legal setback—and New York's newspapers ignored it.

The professional expertise that Ketcham provided made him uniquely vulnerable to retaliation. Though Westway's supporters could dismiss civilian activists as do-gooders, they couldn't do that with Ketcham, because he had what no other opponent had: accreditation. "Technicians prudently consider their careers," Ketcham said in a 1978 Harvard speech.[29] For someone with his credentials, the money was on the other side, in government contracts. As the 1970s turned into the 1980s, with Westway unable to gain the public consensus Rockefeller and Lindsay (both by then out of office) had promised, pro-Westway politicians became "furious," Ketcham remembers.

One source of retaliation was New York Senator Daniel Patrick Moynihan. In 1969, Moynihan had written an essay against urban highways, called "Soulless City." Now, though, he saw Westway as a test of whether a struggling New York could still think big. In 1976, Moynihan, in running for Senate, had promised to accelerate Westway's federal approval.[30] In office, Moynihan exulted that Westway's new land in the river would "give us back the waterfront."[31]

In 1980, Moynihan found an opportunity to intimidate opponents. Ketcham's Citizens for Clean Air applied for a federal EPA grant to revive interest in the state's transportation-pollution control plan. Moynihan, on the Senate floor, demanded an investigation into the "politicized" relationship between the EPA and anti-Westway forces.[32] Though the inquiry concluded that Ketcham hadn't acted improperly, "[Citizens for Clean Air was] forced out of business. It was a very effective assassination." Ketcham needed a living. In 1982, to secure a state contract to investigate taxicab inefficiencies, he surrendered. "I was forced to sign an agreement that I would never again fight against Westway," he says. Later, *Times* columnist Sydney Schanberg called the episode "a serious violation of the public trust."[33]

Power Brokers, Right and Wrong

Westway's political support seemed impermeable. Once in office, in 1975 and 1978, respectively, Governor Carey and Mayor Ed Koch, having run against Westway, changed their minds. Koch betrayed his Village base—his old club, the Village Independent Democrats—for a straightforward reason: economics. After nearing bankruptcy in 1975, New York's finances were under the control of a post-bailout board of businessmen and bankers; the city was desperate to recover. Having lost six hundred thousand jobs between 1969 and 1977 and facing the prospect of seeing its population fall below seven million, New York seemed too weak to view the concerns of people who remained as outweighing real estate, financial, and business investors who might create jobs. "When he became mayor, he couldn't do anything," John LoCicero, a Koch adviser, says. "Any time anyone asked us for something, we had to say no. . . . Things were terrible, . . . so many teachers were laid off. Once he saw how much money we could get from the federal government," Koch supported Westway.[34]

Outside of elective office, though, a few prominent individuals bucked the wisdom of their rarefied world. Robert Moses came out against Westway, calling it "a spectacle of bamboozlement." Another was Seymour Durst, a developer. "Seymour was wonderful and a real maverick, a billionaire, but who didn't take government subsidies. . . . The basis for the family's fortune was on dry land. I assume he didn't want massive public subsidies building competing real estate in the Hudson River," says Benstock. The project "will probably take far longer than was anticipated and cost many times as much," Durst told a real estate publication. "They're wasting a billion dollars by putting a landfill into the river when it should go into the transit system."[35]

Nothing but a Pipe Dream

As Westway reconsidered its air quality data to satisfy Judge Griesa, the project faced more litigation. New York had a budding expert, Al Butzel, on another federal law: the Clean Water Act. Butzel would join Westway slayers who had not started out as environmentalists. A decade earlier, in 1965, he was "just out of law school," he recalled, working at the Paul, Weiss corporate firm. "By chance," an early environmental case came into the office: the case against Con Edison's project to build a hydroelectric plant into Storm King Mountain, part of the scenic Hudson Highlands north of New York City. A coalition sued, alleging that the project would damage the mountain and the river. "There were no litigators available," so he got the case.[36]

Storm King predated the 1972 Clean Water Act. But the case went on so long that the Clean Water Act killed it. The federal judge did not deny Con Ed a permit, just as Griesa hadn't decreed that Westway would violate clean-air standards. Rather, the time required to study data—including how Storm King would affect striped-bass fish in the Hudson—caused delay. Delay entrenched opposition. In 1974, Con Ed suspended the project, forever.

Butzel wasn't paying attention to Westway. "I thought it was a pipe dream to . . . stop the highway," he said. But Benstock knew him from her antipollution work and asked him to represent her group in opposing Westway's air quality permit from New York. He declined, but told her, "If you get [the] EPA to come out against it," he'd represent her. And she did. In 1977, the federal EPA's regional office declared the pollution that Westway would create to be "inconsistent" with New York's commitment, under the Clean Air Act, to reduce traffic. Again, in 1980, the EPA recommended disapproval of the state's air-quality permit for the project, saying that New York wasn't doing enough to support mass transit, a far cleaner method of travel.[37] In opposing Westway, then regional administrator Charles Warren says, he "was denounced by editorials in the *Daily News*, . . . even the *Times*."[38]

Butzel kept his word to Benstock, representing the Clean Air Campaign in the state air-permit hearing. A "critical factor [was] who carried the burden of proof," recalled Butzel. The state was so confident that it said, "'we do.' That turned out to be very important." Butzel argued that the state hadn't proven that Westway wouldn't make the air dirtier. "To everyone's astonishment, the hearing officer agreed." Once again, this decision, like the EPA's recommendation, wasn't final, but it cost time—"two years," said Butzel. "It slowed things down."

Butzel used that time wisely. Thanks to Storm King, he knew that the Army Corps would have to approve a separate permit under the Clean Water Act. Already, the National Marine Fisheries Service and the Fish and Wildlife Service, both natural-resources agencies, had warned the Corps that Westway could threaten one species, the striped bass. During the young fishes' first two years, bass migrated to the Hudson's "inter-pier" areas—the area to be buried under landfill—for protection from cold and currents, the agencies said. The Hudson refuge was important, since the river was second only to the Chesapeake Bay in striped-bass stocks, and the latter was in decline.

"No one had paid any attention to the national fisheries data," said Butzel. Warren, of the EPA, tipped him off. The EPA faced pressure for opposition to Westway. In 1978, Carey called Warren's predecessor a "lunkhead."[39] Knowing that the EPA could not hold out forever, Warren told Butzel, "This Clean Air Act stuff was not going to carry the day." But the Clean Water Act might. "I said to Al, 'there's a much better situation with regard to the striped bass.' . . . It was really dynamite," Butzel remembered.

As the Army Corps considered Westway's water permit, Butzel warned the Army Corps and the state that they would need to update the state's environmental impact statement to account for the fisheries. Yet the Corps "didn't take it seriously," relying on the state's determination in its final 1977 environmental-impact statement that the Hudson was a "biological wasteland." So, in 1979, Butzel, on behalf of Benstock's Clean Air Campaign, the Sierra Club, and the Hudson River Fishermen's Association, among other plaintiffs, filed a new federal suit, charging that the Army Corp's process for deciding Westway's river permit was deficient.

Westway's supporters pressed on. Warren, by then the EPA's top New York official, says that in 1980, an election year, with President Jimmy Carter under pressure, "I was forced to do conditional approval." As the Carter era gave way to the Reagan era, the fisheries services dropped its objections.[40] In 1981, the Army Corps issued its permit, the final hurdle.

That Labor Day, Ronald Reagan, in his first year as president, came to New York to present an oversized check for Westway to Koch at Gracie Mansion, with Moynihan and Republican Senator Al D'Amato looking on. New York was a swing state, and, a year earlier, it had swung for Reagan. The president enjoyed New York's construction union support. Westway was also a way to demonstrate how he would not let the nation be wrapped in red tape. Reagan boasted, "We have silenced the bureaucrats."

With federal, state, and city agreements in place, the landfill permit issued by the Army, and Reagan's check in hand, elites dismissed remaining obstacles to the now $2.3 billion project. "Although several court cases . . . remain, none are taken seriously," the *Times* noted.[41] In 1981, Judge Griesa dismissed several suits, including the air quality case Hoppen had launched seven years earlier.

Every case—"except for the fisheries," said Butzel.

Fixed Predetermination

Powerful interests, from the Rockefellers to the *Times*, had spent a decade insisting that Westway was a sure thing; only gadflies were in its way. Because of this narrative, the trial—*Sierra Club, Benstock's Clean Air Campaign, et al., Plaintiffs, v. United States Army Corps of Engineers, et al., Defendants*—gained little attention. "Westway Is on Trial Over . . . Striped Bass," the *Times* reported on page 35. Westway's opponents did something that Westway's supporters did not: take federal law seriously.

Though the trial didn't garner headlines, the verdict did. Nothing in Judge Thomas Griesa's background indicated environmental ardor. A former corporate lawyer, he was a Nixon appointee. He simply applied the law as Congress had written it. On the last day of March 1982, Judge Griesa determined that the Army Corps' landfill permit "violated the National Environmental Policy Act [and] the Clean Water Act." Griesa voided the permit, sending the matter back to the Corps to start over.

The ruling was scathing. It wasn't just that the Army Corps and New York's state government had ignored the striped bass; worse was their dishonesty. In 1979, a Westway consultant had found "an astonishing amount of fish life," leading the consultant to tell the state that the fish "demonstrated a statistically significant preference for the inter-pier zone." The state had suppressed this information. When the Corps had asked for this study, the state demurred. "The reason given . . . was that data in the hands of the Corps would be subject to disclosure under the Freedom of Information Act," Griesa wrote. The public did not see this fish-counting document until Butzel's lawsuit. "The information previously furnished . . . on the crucial question of fisheries was the complete opposite of the true facts," Griesa concluded.

The Corps had had "an almost fixed predetermination to grant the Westway landfill permit" and had "acquiesced in the urgings of the Federal Highway Administration and the New York State Department of Transportation that the facts and issues about fishery resources be withheld," even though federal law mandated disclosure. "The issues here do not involve a minor technicality," Griesa continued. "Millions" of people depended on fish for a balanced diet, and Congress had directed the Army Corps to consider fisheries. Thwarting Congress is "not some minor detail." Griesa further accused the project's sponsors of "collusion," "manipulation," even "perjury." He had "sentenced people to prison" for lesser violations.[42]

Westway's champions didn't grasp these words' import. Carey dismissed the loss as a "procedural error."[43] The *Times* chose sarcasm. "It's important that the Corps waste no time in going back to the trawl nets for a serious determination of what will happen to the bass if another piece of the Hudson disappears, as it has been doing . . . since the 18th century," editorialists snarked. They concluded, "Westway is blocked now only by a fin."[44]

Striped Bass Professors

Colonel Fletcher "Bud" Griffis of the Army Corps of Engineers was in charge of studying that fin. Griffis, a Florida native, had grown up watching his father build power plants. A football star, he earned a West Point nomination. He had never evinced concern about the environment, having slashed a highway through Vietnam.[45] "I like to build," he said.[46] Griffis was a model leader, respectful of his command. By 1983, he was the district engineer for New York after the Army pushed his predecessor out over his attempt to land a job with Westway's contractor.

Griffis determined that the logical step was "to learn something about those fish," he remembered. "I asked to get the best striped bass experts in the world. All had their PhDs in striped bass," he says. "These guys didn't know a darned thing," he learned. "Of my twenty-two PhDs, said one, 'anything you do, could kill striped bass.' Others said, 'hardy species.'

. . . They said they would need twenty years" to decide. Pressed, "they said they could probably draw statistical inferences after two years." Griffis decided: "If they said they had to have at least two years, then I had to have two years."[47]

He proposed a two-winter study—not received well by New York. When Griffis informed New York's new governor, Mario Cuomo, who had succeeded Carey in 1983, Cuomo petitioned the secretary of the Army. "The governor and mayor went to Washington and said, 'get the crazy colonel out of here,'" Griffis says. His superiors decided that Griffis could spend one winter doing one study. "I said, I don't like it, but we'll see what we can do," Griffis remembered. "It just didn't fly," he thought at the time. "I didn't think that was fair"—but he followed instructions.

From December 1983 to April 1984, scientists counted Hudson bass. That spring, the Army issued its draft environmental impact statement, and the result was clear: Westway would be bad. "The project site represents a significant portion of that habitat," the report said, with as much as one-third of regional stocks, and its loss would have a "significant adverse impact."

In November, the Army released its final environmental impact statement. The data were the same as in the earlier document: up to one-third of striped bass used the Westway habitat. Yet the conclusion the Corps drew was different. The habitat loss would no longer be "significant" but "inconsequential." The Army no longer thought the fish spent the winter in the inter-pier area; rather, one of its scientists, Bill Dovel, thought the young fish used the area only as a "staging area," moving in and out. "Juvenile striped bass do not overwinter in or near the Westway area," the report noted. The Army asserted, "Westway is a substantial portion of a striped bass habitat, but not the only such habitat."

Griffis had a weighty task: to use this contradictory report to decide whether to grant a permit. Griffis "read every one" of an avalanche of comments, 1,200 pages. "I studied the statistics," said Griffis. "I tried to stay out of politics and tried to focus on the decision." The report's expert comments were pointed. As for whether young fish moved back and forth between the piers and the ocean during winter, federal fisheries analysts maintained, "It is difficult to imagine that these fish would undertake the physiological stresses inherent in migrating to oceanic water and returning to fresh water. . . . Our skepticism . . . is further supported by sampling efforts spanning more than thirty years."

Though Dovel had no evidence to back his theory that fish didn't stay in the pier area, Butzel had gathered data to strengthen the opposite theory.

A member of the Hudson River Fishermen's Association had tagged forty juvenile bass in December 1983, and two tagged fish emerged come spring in the same area, "quite a significant return" for fish that had supposedly left, Butzel submitted in his comments. The "Dovel theory is really not supported by . . . the data; rather, the data seem to have been squeezed to try to fit the theory." One commenter pointed out that the Army had misspelled the Latin name for striped bass.

Over two years, Griffis missed deadline after deadline for permit issuance.[48] By 1985, Westway was a decade and a half old. He faced pressure. "Moynihan barged into my door," he says. "I thought I was going to have a heart attack. He said, 'grant the permit.'" Griffis thereafter made sure to have a stenographer present when a politician wanted to meet.

Despite that incident, Griffis said he made the decision on the merits. He had staff write two drafts—one to deny the permit, one to approve it. On January 24, 1985, after a weekend's consideration, Griffis issued his decision: approval. "Westway is not an overwintering area for the juvenile striped bass," he said publicly. "I believe that the interpretation of the statement that 25 or 30 percent of the bass would be denied the use of Westway has a much different meaning than it would have had in 1983. At the time, it was hypothesized that the fish spent the entire winter in one place. Had that hypothesis been true, the loss of such a critical habitat could possibly have been catastrophic." But under the new hypothesis, "the worst case . . . is that some portion of the 25 to 30 percent of the striped bass that will be displaced will be destroyed. . . . I honestly believe there will be little or no impact."

Weighed against Westway's benefits, the path forward, to Griffis, was clear. It wasn't that Westway would alleviate traffic. Rather, "Westway will have a major economic impact," Griffis continued in his approval. "The project will produce 86,000 man-years of employment and will benefit minority employment." For those reasons, "I have decided . . . to issue a permit."[49] Koch was cheery. "I am happy for the people," the mayor said. "I am happy for the striped bass."[50] Butzel's clients challenged the decision in court.

As the city awaited a second trial, Cuomo made a misstep that revealed arrogance or fear, or both: he directed the state-run transit authority to erect a Westway model within Grand Central Terminal. The marketing backfired. The Straphangers Campaign, a transit advocacy group, distributed anti-Westway leaflets near the model, only to have transit police tell them to desist; Gene Russianoff, its staff attorney, prepared a First Amendment court argument that transit authority was devoting public space to only one side of a political argument. The authority allowed leafletting to resume, and the exhibit disappeared.

A Final Injunction

By spring, the Sierra Club, Benstock's Clean Air Campaign, and co-plaintiffs returned to court before an increasingly annoyed judge. Griesa "was incredibly hostile," says Randy Mastro, who, as a "newbie assistant" under U.S. Attorney Rudolph Giuliani, defended the Army. "He hated the case."[51] Westway had gone on for so long that the opposition attorney, Butzel, had quit practicing law. Mitch Bernard, his protégé, took over.

The main issue was simple: why had the Corps changed its mind? "The judge wanted to know . . . you said one thing. Four months later, no new data, you just reversed it," says Bernard. "It's not that they couldn't make a change. They could. He just wanted [the Army] to say what the basis was."[52] In spring, the impact on the bass was "significant"; by fall, it was "minor." Yet, despite a court order to keep records, the Corps could not explain how it had changed its mind. The main explanation for the change was that Dovel's theory—that the young fish didn't stay in the area during the winter—had morphed from an idea to a conclusion.

Other documents prepared by Dovel emerged, contrary to his novel theory. These documents said the bass *did* winter in the area. Upon receiving that material during the trial, Bernard says, "I read it that night. . . . I was incredulous. If we could have convened court at 2 a.m., I would have been as happy as can be." The next day, "on cross examination, . . . I took him through his report. What he said was, 'I don't believe that anymore, what I wrote, is not what I think.' . . . He completely surrendered his credibility."

Griesa agreed. "Dovel's testimony is a collection of assertions so irresponsible that it is shocking that the Government ever tendered him," he said. Moreover, Corps witnesses—Griffis and two others—had said in court that they *hadn't* changed their mind, a position Griesa said was "bizarre" and "fiction." The Corps had failed to do its single task: study striped bass. "Griffis testified that he himself believed that he was being ordered to prepare a supplemental environmental impact statement without the studies which he deemed . . . necessary," Griesa noted.

Griesa considered one last question: Was Westway a highway or an economic development project? Federal highway dollars couldn't fund anything but highways. Yet in his Hudson permit approval, Griffis had said that Westway was a development project. The distinction mattered. "By his own admission," under the Clean Water Act, "if Griffis had characterized Westway as a highway, he could not have granted the landfill permit," the judge said, because less damaging road options—including repairing the existing West Side Highway—were available.

Westway's sponsors had already committed "serious misconduct" in awarding the original permit, the judge reminded the court. "Two failures . . . should bring the matter to an end."[53] On August 7, 1985, a decade after Griesa had told Westway sponsors, under Ketcham's challenge, to recheck their air quality facts, Griesa killed the permit, federal funding, and the project.

One Skirt and One Sweater

As Westway had plodded through the legal system, Benstock had used her time wisely. She focused decisionmakers on a parallel track: trading in federal funding for transit dollars. In its environmental documents, the state said that a trade-in would yield less money—first, because the federal government's required state matching funds for transit was 15 percent, not 10 percent as on highway projects, and second, because the city would be competing with dozens of trade-in projects around the country rather than receiving money from the highway trust fund.[54]

Benstock argued that highway funding wasn't a sure thing. In 1981, Benstock, accompanied by Durst, the Manhattan developer, flew to Albany to convince legislators that there was no such thing as "free" federal money. First, Westway's costs were rising, with the estimate having nearly doubled to $2.3 billion. The federal government had not guaranteed to cover overruns. As Westway consumed money, other state highways would suffer. Second, the state was already spending federal money on the project. But its fate remained uncertain: should any lawsuit succeed in stopping Westway, the state would have to repay those dollars. For Benstock, travel was a chore. "She had one skirt and one sweater for three days," a *New York Post* reporter said. "She had almost no money, so I took her to lunch."[55]

Benstock made a related case in Washington. After having combed "through all of those horrible cost-estimate books" of incomplete federal highways, she convinced lawmakers: Westway would consume a disproportionate share of federal dollars, harming other states. Benstock stayed with friends to avoid hotel expenses. "It was torture. . . . I like being in my own New York apartment."

But her gambit worked, as her argument appealed to fiscal conservatives. In 1981, Wisconsin Senator William Proxmire, a Democrat who had made a name fighting wasteful spending, awarded Westway a "Golden Fleece Award" for frivolity. The project would be "inch for inch the most expensive highway ever built," he said.[56] The National Taxpayers Union came out against Westway. Benstock's argument appealed to lawmakers who wanted to be *seen* as fiscal conservatives, as well. Most Washington Republicans didn't want to cut outlays; neither did the president. Despite rhetoric, spending was soaring. Yet the superficial nature of Washington made it important for lawmakers to cut *one* project.

Another Power Broker Intervenes

As the 1980s wore on, Reagan officials quietly made clear that the administration would be generous to New York in a transit trade-in, deflating the argument that the state would risk federal funds in canceling Westway. Reagan's decreasing enthusiasm for Westway had a source: Richard Ravitch. Ravitch, a real estate developer, had become chairman of the Metropolitan Transportation Authority (MTA), the state entity in charge of transit, in 1979. The governor who had appointed Ravitch was the Westway-boosting Carey.

Nevertheless, Ravitch worked behind the scenes to thwart the project. The reason was straightforward: the MTA needed the money. "It was obvious to any serious person, to spend all that money on a highway made no sense," Ravitch remembered. "New York was going to be a hell of a lot better off" were it to trade Westway for transit. "It would be malpractice for the MTA chairman not to be for the trade-in," recalled Steven Polan, a top Ravitch aide. Yet Ravitch "had to retain the support of Koch and Carey," according to Polan.[57] So Ravitch focused not on the governor and the mayor but on Washington.

Ravitch recalled an occasion when Reagan visited New York, his first stop, the *Daily News*. The paper's editor, Mike O'Neill, was a Westway supporter. "Mike's first question was, 'are you going to fund Westway?' [Reagan] said yes," and "the *News*" [then a first read for blue-collar New Yorkers] came out with a major, major headline, Reagan reinforces his support of Westway," Ravitch remembered. Unread, in Reagan's briefing documents, was a memo that Ravitch had helped prepare, advocating trading in Westway for transit. "I convinced the [federal] secretary of transportation, Drew Lewis, that it was not in the interest of the federal government to spend money on Westway," Ravitch said. "I persuaded David Stockman," Reagan's budget director. "It wasn't difficult to do, because the facts were self-evident."

The president's Westway support grew muted. As disputes wore on, Reagan called it "bureaucracy strangling in its own regulations." He ignored a missive signed by the city's great and good—David Rockefeller, as well as both senators, Moynihan and D'Amato, and Edward Cleary, president of the state's AFL-CIO umbrella—to use his bully pulpit to push the project.[58]

Ravitch's quiet work also nudged New York society. "I would not . . . underestimate the value of peers talking to peers," Benstock recalled. Of wealthy New Yorkers, "Ravitch was a peer . . . both in terms of his official position as head of the MTA, and because he was wealthy and because he was smart." Ravitch's dinner-party Westway opposition signaled to wealthy New Yorkers that they could question the project. This cover was important because fighting Westway wasn't free. The movement depended on wealthy supporters. Joan Davidson, heir to the grape-juice fortune that powered the J.M. Kaplan Fund, a charitable trust that also supported Carnegie Hall and the New School, was a donor.

Ravitch said his advocacy against Westway wasn't a secret to the governor or mayor. "I told him," he said later of Carey. "Carey didn't really have a strong conviction" on Westway. Asked whether Koch cared about the project, Ravitch says, "No. I don't think so." In Ravitch's view, New York's leaders supported Westway only because bankers, developers, and businesses—who controlled New York's recovery from fiscal crisis—supported it.

Tenacious Journalists

Throughout the Westway battle, a few press organs offered skepticism. At the *Voice*, Jack Newfield was a "drumbeat," says Benstock, and the *Wall Street Journal* opposed Westway on fiscal grounds. Even as the *Times* supported the project, it did what a paper should do: open its opinion page to other voices. Benstock earned space in this important real estate to make her case. In a 1980 op-ed, she wrote, "A trade-in . . . would be the single most significant step to reverse the terrible decline in New York transit." The trade-in was not as risky as Westway proponents insisted. "Eighteen cities in 15 states would not have opted for trade-in if it didn't work."[59]

Beyond guest essays, two columnists marshaled facts and invective. John Oakes got his credibility first through lineage: he was the nephew of publisher Adolph Ochs, who was *Times* royalty. Second, he was a World War II veteran, having served in Europe in the Office of Strategic Services, the CIA precursor. In 1978, the second week of the Koch administration, Oakes wrote, "No matter how disguised, Westway is . . . a superhighway project. It is, paradoxically, a retrogressive step. . . . Rejuvenation of the waterfront . . . can be accomplished . . . with virtually none of the environmental and neighborhood destruction Westway would bring," via a ground-level road and park.[60]

Oakes focused on corruption and cost. In 1983, calling the project "Westwaygate," he wrote, "So much dirty work involving Westway has already been uncovered in the federal courts . . . conflict of interest, bad faith, governmental cover-up, outright deception."[61] There was also the money. "Westway's cost overruns . . . will eventually create a gap estimated at anywhere from several hundred million to $2 billion."[62]

Complementing Oakes at the *Times* was Sydney Schanberg. Where Oakes got credibility from war service, Schanberg got gravitas from combat-zone reporting. Schanberg had spent the 1970s covering Cambodia's genocide, for which he won a Pulitzer Prize, before settling down as columnist. In 1981, he compared Westway to Vietnam, in that supporters refused to admit they had lost. "I don't think we can afford Westway," he wrote. "Privately, transportation officials say that because it would take the better part of a decade to build, the eventual cost . . . could reach $4 billion," money needed for "crumbling mass transit."[63] He made his readers aware of an "alternative": "A more modest surface boulevard with a promenade. . . . The difference in cost is striking [$500 million versus $4 billion]."[64] Schanberg also compared Westway to Watergate. The case had moved beyond striped bass to "grave violations of the public trust."[65]

Not Really the Best Way

Benstock's travel "torture" paid off—with exquisite timing. A month after Griesa's decision, an appeals court ruled that New York could reapply for a permit, with the Army Corps counting fish all over again. Yet the state faced another uncertainty. On September 11, 1985, by a 287 to 132 margin, the House of Representatives voted to kill Westway.[66] Every faction had its reason, but the outcome was the same. The New Jersey delegation resented subsidized competition to their own real estate, a short commute from Manhattan.[67] For conservatives, such as Wyoming Republican Dick Cheney, a vote against Westway was a vote for austerity.[68] Proponents tried to keep up swagger. Koch proclaimed, "Westway is still the best way," and said that absent Senate action, the House vote wasn't "a body blow."

Yet another factor was. After a decade and a half, Westway was up against a deadline. The federal law that allowed states to trade in highway money for transit would expire September 30. Koch became realistic. "You can hear the death rattle," he said.[69] Cuomo and Koch could try for a new Army permit—but if the third time failed, New York would lose $1.7 billion in funding.[70]

On September 26, 1985, Cuomo and Koch wrote to Elizabeth Dole, federal transportation secretary, asking for "withdrawal of your approval of the interstate system segment consisting of the 4.2-mile section of Interstate Route 478."[71] Nine hours before the deadline, Dole approved the trade-in.[72] She gave the pens to Moynihan and D'Amato. "I don't know why they thought this was an occasion for giving out pens," Moynihan said.[73]

Cuomo showed grace. To Benstock, he wrote, "Congratulations! I commend your commitment, your courage and your competence. I hope next time we will be on the same side."[74] The *Times* canceled Schanberg's column.[75]

The Best Way

The popular notion is that the striped bass killed Westway—and Benstock enabled the death. That was David Rockefeller's view. In his memoir, he wrote, "Extremists had defeated a project that was in the best interest of all New York's citizens." He singled out "Marcy Bienstock," misspelling her name. Correct spelling or not, ask politically aware New Yorkers about the saga, and they remember the fish, and they remember Benstock.

Yet she resists this mythology. "The idea that I was alone is . . . part of the fiction on the other side, which is useful, if it's just one woman, it's easy to write her off. . . . A staggering amount of work was done by dozens of leaders and large numbers of groups," says Benstock. "If any of those elements had not been present, then Westway would probably have been built."

The fish played a role—only because Congress intended it. Congress created laws to protect the environment. Activists, bureaucrats, and one judge took those laws seriously. "Without the federal framework," concurred Butzel, "the highway would have been built. . . . It was not the political opposition, at least not until the very end, that defeated Westway. It was the litigation." Bernard agreed: "[The outcome was] vindication for the primacy of the law. . . . No matter what the political power is behind something, . . . there's still a law." Federal courts had proved impervious to New York's power brokers.

But the law needed assistance. Griffis, like Benstock, thought opposition mattered. "You're never gonna build a project when it's 55 to 45," he said, referring to public opinion. "If you have 90 to 10, you could probably [have gotten] it," regardless of environmental laws. New York was too divided. "When you get a project that close, you're not gonna build it."[76]

In the 1950s and 1960s, New Yorkers had been able to convince local officials to stop the Washington Square Park road and the Lower Manhattan Expressway. By the 1970s and 1980s, with the city's economy weakened, local democracy had eroded. New Yorkers had to rely on Washington.

From Stagnation to Revival

It's possible that Westway would have been a boon. It's more conceivable that Westway would have been a boondoggle, akin to Boston's Big Dig highway burial, planned at the same time. In 1983, the Big Dig had a price tag of $2.6 billion; it eventually cost $14.8 billion.[77] As costs escalated, the federal government stopped paying, so the Big Dig diverted billions in state money from Boston transit. The Big Dig has made traffic flow more smoothly, but a six-lane road sits atop it.

What did New York get, instead? It wasn't until 1994 that New York, during the Mario Cuomo and Rudolph Giuliani gubernatorial and mayoral administrations, respectively, approved a West Side Highway replacement: a six-lane ground-level "boulevard," costing $380 million. Between the road and river, connected by crosswalks and red lights for pedestrians, is the Hudson River Park, peppered with dog runs, grass, and restaurants. The Hudson's bike path is the nation's busiest, serving both recreational and transportation needs. When the boulevard and the first park sections opened, in August 2001, New York got what Gurin, Ketcham, and others had proposed decades earlier.

The Hudson River Park did what Moynihan, Carey, Cuomo, Lindsay, Koch, and Rockefeller had desired: revive the West Side. Developers—including the Dursts—have built thousands of apartments near the river. Between 1990 and 2018, the West Side added 22 percent to its population, outpacing 15 percent city growth. The West Side's new problem was that it was so popular that it was out of reach for newcomers save for the affluent. "One of the keys," in granting the Army Corps permit, Griffis recalled in 2019, "was that I thought it would give the people . . . access to the water"—access the people eventually got, but without having to accept an underground highway where part of their river had been.

Part 2

GETTING BACK ON TRACK

Chapter 6

Struck City

The Shutdown That Stressed the Value of Transit

It's very difficult for a man, when he is shaving in the morning, to look at himself and say, "I'm not really essential."

—Mayor John Lindsay, January 3, 1966

The experiences of the strike period prove the folly of funneling more and more private cars into midtown and lower Manhattan.

—*New York Times*, January 20, 1966

MAYOR JOHN LINDSAY TOOK OFFICE ON January 1, 1966, full of ideas about how to fix New York's crime, poverty, and transportation problems. But before the young, blond Republican could tackle policies, he faced indignity: he had to cancel all but one of his inaugural parties because of traffic. Subway and bus workers had called a strike—the first citywide walkout—and New York was choked with cars. "With thousands expected at each reception, it was thought the travel to these events would aggravate what would become serious traffic snarls."[1]

Instead of galas, Lindsay got an introduction to one brutal fact of New York life: if the trains don't move, nobody moves. New York's subways and buses don't just move transit riders; they move everyone else by keeping millions of people out of cars. On an average day, 752,000 people took a car from elsewhere in the city or region to work, play, or run an errand in Manhattan's dense business districts (an additional 94,000 people arrived in trucks). Despite two decades of declining ridership, however, nearly

2.3 million people took the train or bus. City officials' great fear was that, during the strike, people who normally took the trains would attempt to drive into Manhattan; the streets could not absorb this traffic.[2] The immediate shock of the transit strike was devastating. Without transit, the city's economy largely shut down for nearly two weeks, costing New York $800 million in business (about $7.9 billion in 2024 dollars).

The longer-lasting consequence was salutary. Just as New York was canceling the Lower Manhattan Expressway, the strike demonstrated that New York, with its concentration of people in tall buildings, could never depend on roads to move most people around. After decades of neglecting subways and buses, the strike's legacy was to make New York understand that unless its future was transit, that future would be bleak.

Political Theater

As fall turned to winter in 1965, nobody believed there would be a strike. For a decade, the city-run transit authority's labor contract with the Transport Workers Union (TWU) expired every other year on December 31. Just as regularly, Mike Quill, TWU Local 100 leader, would threaten to take 33,000 men off the job. Each time, "New York City residents were treated to . . . nerve-tingling news reports of a threatened transit strike at dawn on New Year's Day. . . . The TWU postured, threatened to strike, and made outrageous-sounding public demands." Then, somehow, sequestered in a Midtown hotel, both sides would come to an agreement just as time ran out.[3] One newspaper dismissed this ceremony as a boondoggle via which management and labor got fancy meals and hotel rooms for a "New Year's Eve transit gala" on the farepayer's dime. "All that is needed is paper hats."[4]

For each previous deal, Robert Wagner Jr. had been the city's mayor. Wagner had favored organized labor since he took office in 1954. During his first mayoral campaign, he had pledged to recognize city employees' right to join unions and bargain for wages and benefits: "I and the cause I represent are right if organized labor stands behind us."[5] The TWU's bargaining rights dated back to the early 1930s, when New York's subway and bus systems were largely privately owned and operated, and the union began organizing workers before the city took over the distressed firms.

Wagner's pro-union bent was astute politics. City government workers were growing disillusioned with depending on favoritism from Tammany Hall for job placement and advancement, and sought to bargain for consistent standards for job titles and pay as well as for pensions and other benefits. From a politician's perspective, unions created a power base to rival Tammany.

Despite Wagner's pro-union stance, negotiations with the TWU were fraught. The union was the creation of Mike Quill. The seventh child (of eight) of an Irish potato farmer, Quill hadn't made it to the top of the nation's labor union movement by respecting authority. At twenty-one, he had emigrated to New York, where he found work building the city's third subway and, later, making change for passengers in a Queens subway station. During the Depression, one of the companies that then ran the subways, the Interborough Rapid Transit company, was struggling with deficits and wanted workers to take a pay cut. Quill began organizing fellow workers in a fiercely anti-union national environment; in 1937, on the day he won recognition for New York members, Ford Motor Company guards were beating union leaders in Detroit. In the late 1930s, Quill won a forty-eight-hour work week plus vacation, a precedent-setting victory; transit workers had worked seven twelve-hour days.[6] Quill prevailed not only against the government but against factions of his own union, ranging from Communist hardliners to conservatives.

Quill prevailed because of his personality. New York has always been an attention economy, and florid language held attention. "He began using his acid Irish tongue as a weapon in the nineteen-thirties, when his infant . . . union had nothing else." His method was to make outrageous demands and settle for a fraction at the last minute. Whenever he threatened to strike, "the men who faced him in negotiating sessions . . . never knew when he meant it," so the city transit authority erred on the side of a raise.[7] In the three decades since TWU's first Depression-era contract, he had won a forty-hour work week and benefits.

Two years before the 1965 contract talks, this method had worked. In 1963, Quill had demanded a thirty-two-hour, four-day week, better benefits, and a 15 percent pay hike over two years. A judge, following state law that prohibited strikes by government workers, issued a prohibition against a walkout. Quill called him a "lunatic" and a "senile old fuddy-duddy." He warned New Yorkers to find another way to get around. But behind the rhetoric, he extended a nonnegotiable 5:00 a.m. deadline New Year's Day to 7:00 a.m.[8] By mid-day on the first day of 1964, Quill had agreed to an eleven-cent raise for that year, or 4 percent, and a twenty-four-cent raise and better benefits for 1965. According to the *New York Times*, "Quill's usual bad behavior was, as usual, handsomely rewarded."[9]

In 1965, this *pas de deux* needed a new partner. Wagner was leaving office, to be succeeded by Lindsay as the clock chimed 1966. As the forty-four-year-old mayor-elect prepared to take over, he had no intention of repeating Wagner's grubby dance. A Manhattan Republican, Lindsay had won on a mandate for change. One of his advertisements quoted journalist Murray Kempton: "He is fresh and everyone else is tired."

The city wanted a fresh approach to managing wrenching adjustments. New York was on its way to a then-record population (7.9 million in 1969) and a then-record number of jobs (at nearly 3.8 million). Yet growth masked troubles. The city was shedding manufacturing jobs, which peaked in 1947. In lieu of jobs for people with little education, it was gaining financial jobs as well as other jobs requiring a college credential; such jobs wouldn't crest until 1969, when white-collar jobs, too, began to decline.

Replacing blue-collar jobs with jobs requiring a college degree didn't help most of the black and Hispanic migrants who were coming to New York. In 1950, fewer than 10 percent of city residents were non-white; by 1970, this percentage would more than double. In response to a growing population as well as concern about slum conditions, New York—after World War II and under Robert Moses's direction—had destroyed apartment buildings and brownstone blocks in favor of high rises, both middle-class resident-owned complexes and low-income public-housing developments. One result was dislocation and crowding of poor newcomers into remaining tenements, as middle-class residents left for the new suburbs. The cumulative effect was trauma. Alienation on the part of young male newcomers pushed up crime; the murder level had risen by 16 percent in the four years before Lindsay's election, topping six hundred annually. Spending on social services left the city with budget deficits, which Wagner had papered over with borrowing.

Voters were looking for an enlightened approach, one that would move New York away from the Democratic backroom, as exemplified by the city's kowtowing to the TWU. In the cycle of machine politicians succeeding reform politicians, Lindsay was a reformer. As such, even though Wagner hadn't been on the ballot, Lindsay had run against the incumbent, promising to stop the "decline and fall of New York" by sweeping out "tired management." Lindsay would govern idealistically and openly, not by bowing down to shadowy forces he castigated as "power brokers."[10] New York would once again be "the Empire City," he pledged.

Ironically, Lindsay would be the first leader to embrace transit in more than half a century, since the car had gradually captured elected officials' attention as the engine of growth. He proposed to solve New York's transportation crisis by reinvesting in subways and buses. The "survival of this City," as he put it in one of nine policy "white papers" published by his campaign, would depend on addressing the subway system's "sorry plight" of "ill-equipped and ill-maintained" and "sardine-packed" trains. He promised an "attractive, comfortable, convenient and speedy mass transit system," with the goal to "attract persons who presently use private automobiles."[11]

None of his lofty planning considered labor, though. Quill's threats were but a distraction to Lindsay. Days after winning the election, Mayor-elect Lindsay "ruled out" a strike, saying he would not "permit" one. In remarks before a good-government group, he called the collective-bargaining process an "archaic machine." Instead of the mayor and the union sparring, Lindsay suggested that "professors with tenure and no ax to grind would be a better form."[12] History backed the mayor's complacency: "In his 30 years as head of the Transport Workers Union, Mr. Quill has never called a subway strike," the *Times* reminded readers.[13] As usual, "the TWU boss will settle."[14] Only the *Journal-American* was skeptical: "Lindsay cannot be serious in declining to participate in negotiations. . . . What he doesn't do now may well compound what he'll have to do later," editorialists warned.[15]

Lindsay, advocating bloodless labor relations, forgot feelings. Wagner, attacked for months as a corrupt dinosaur during the campaign, had no incentive to assure a smooth transition and ink one final deal with Quill. More importantly, Lindsay had misread Quill. For all his bluster, Quill was a serious man who ran a serious union that had improved hundreds of thousands of families' lives. He wanted to be taken seriously. Moreover, at sixty, he was suffering heart problems and wanted to ensure that his union survived the modernization of New York's government.

On election night, Quill had telegrammed Lindsay with congratulations. He further noted that "our Union has a longstanding commitment with the membership of 'no contract, no work' . . . with no extensions whatsoever." In other words, Quill was warning Lindsay that the union would strike immediately when the contract expired come New Year's, unless a new contract were in place. Nearly a month later, the union head, still ignored, asked the mayor-elect to meet "at whatever time and place you designate."[16] Quill outlined sixty-seven demands, again including a thirty-two-hour work week, a 30 percent wage hike, and an extra week's vacation, for a total of six weeks. The package would cost $680 million over two years, doubling the transit authority's budget.[17]

Lindsay refused to play his part in this performance: "I'm not mayor until Jan. 1," he said. Later, he added that he wasn't sure both sides were negotiating in "good faith," even as Quill's language grew more incendiary and as Quill had taken to mispronouncing "Lindsay" as "Lindsley," his way of returning the disrespect that Lindsay was showing. By December, Quill had changed his tone, calling Lindsay a "coward" and an "ungracious sourpuss." He warned, "Let him run the trains and buses."[18] Lindsay waited until after Christmas, days before his inauguration, to meet Quill.

The mayor-elect remained aloof. "I am not an expert on labor matters," he said. "There are involved human problems."[19] On New Year's Eve, the day the contract expired, Quill, flouting another court injunction, issued his ultimatum, directed to the man who "sits and stares and looks over my head." If Lindsay didn't negotiate personally, "the whole thing would be decided on the streets."[20] As the sun rose on New Year's Day 1966, Quill directed members to walk off, refusing to relent under the threat of incarceration for breaking the anti-strike law. "The judge can drop dead in his black robes," he intoned. Trains and buses stopped, and Quill went to jail.

Stay Home—and Prove Yourself Irrelevant

The mayor who had tried not to sully his reputation with labor relations had to devote his inaugural speech not to hopes and aspirations for New York, but to condemning an "unlawful strike against the public interests."[21] Lindsay spent his first night as mayor awake at City Hall. Looking "haggard and shaken" the next morning, he gamely cracked a joke— "the hours are a little long," he said of his new job—as he called New York a "struck city."[22] The only consolation: January 1 was a holiday and a Saturday, meaning not many people would be getting around town.

The administration had two days before the work week to devise a plan for the biggest crisis since World War II. Though subway and bus usage had peaked just after the war, in 1948, nearly three-quarters of Manhattan's 3.3 million daily visitors—people coming to work, to shop, or to visit doctors or friends—still arrived via public transportation.[23] The centerpiece of the plan, then, would be to convince people to sit tight. "Only 25 percent of those who normally come to Manhattan will be able to do so," the mayor warned, telling "not really essential" workers to stay home. "It is vital that the flow of people . . . be reduced to a minimum," he said.[24] "If you're on your way to Manhattan by car, turn around and go home." He exhorted drivers who wouldn't stay home to "fill up the cars" with passengers.

On Monday, it appeared the plan would work. People listened to the instruction to stay home, with Manhattan receiving half of a normal day's cars. With the mayor having ordered schools closed, and with Christmas just passed, people were in a "holiday mood," with white-collar workers not minding an extra day off.[25] The New Yorkers who didn't stay home were creative in demonstrating to their employers—or to themselves—that they were essential workers, people who couldn't miss even one day at the office, the store, or the factory. The mayor demonstrated grit, walking seventy blocks for the cameras before switching to his limo and picking up commuters along the way to set an example for carpooling. A "partly blind news dealer trudged about four miles" to the Brooklyn Bridge, where he hitched a ride to Manhattan. A maintenance man from Astoria roller-skated across the Queensboro Bridge, "wheezing," but saying he "wanted to see if I could do it." One executive took his eleven-year-old daughter's bike to Wall Street.[26]

Yet by mid-week, the good mood had worn off. Despite Lindsay's entreaties to employers to pay absent employees, workers could not be productive at home. One executive said paying people to stay home would "subsidize the strike."[27] Lindsay's separation of workers between "essential" and "nonessential" failed. In a competitive city, lost time at work, even if one weren't paid by the hour, meant lost prestige. To stay home was to declare oneself unnecessary.

As the week wore on, roads into Manhattan were jammed with traffic, with 30 percent more cars and trucks "squeezed into Manhattan and then squeezed out again" on the second workday. "Bumper-to-bumper traffic twice as heavy as yesterday choked every major artery," with roads clogged by 4:45 a.m.[28] More than sixty thousand vehicles crossed the city's East River and Harlem River bridges from Brooklyn, Queens, and the Bronx into Manhattan, compared to a normal forty-nine thousand, between 6:00 and 10:00 a.m. Cars carried an average of two and a half passengers each, compared to the normal one and a half, but it wasn't enough. Lindsay, in a helicopter to survey traffic, warned, "There're too many cars . . . with just a driver."[29] He implored people to pick up passengers, but resisted mandatory restrictions in favor of "voluntary" cooperation. His traffic commissioner, Henry Barnes, said, "Things will get better [as] people will learn of the trouble spots." They didn't; sixty-four-year-old Sylvester Dalton of Brooklyn died of a heart attack in the clogged Brooklyn Battery Tunnel.

New Yorkers who heeded the mayor's call to leave the car at home—or who didn't have a car, which was most of the city—became "tired, sore-footed, and ill-tempered." One cyclist complained that there were so many walkers on the Brooklyn Bridge that he had to walk his bike. Commuter rail lines from the suburbs were running, but lines to enter Pennsylvania Station and Grand Central Terminal were hours long.[30] Patience waned: "I'm not really charmed by the fact that Lindsay walks downtown every day," said a commuter having an after-work drink in a Madison Avenue bar.[31]

Business grew fed up. Lindsay and Barnes devised a complicated system for "staggered" hours. They split Manhattan into four sectors, whose respective workers were supposed to commute at different times. White-collar firms such as Chase Bank, with eighteen thousand employees, Standard Oil, with three thousand employees, and Seagram, with eight hundred workers, said they would comply. But most employers showed a "staggering indifference" to the staggering plan. Dolores Opiolo, in charge of eight hundred employees at Cosmopolitan Mutual Insurance Co. at Columbus Circle at the northwestern tip of Midtown Manhattan, showed contempt. "Are you kidding?" she asked a reporter. "When they get here, they get here." An Equitable insurance spokesman said, "We are not complying with this pattern." A New York Stock Exchange official professed not to know his quadrant.[32] The mayor had lost control before he had gained it—and New York experienced the longest rush hour in its history, six and a half hours.[33]

Frayed Industries and Businesses

The nearly two-week-long strike demonstrated that to shut down New York's transit system was to shut down its economy. Business groups told Governor Nelson Rockefeller that the strike was "the most seriously damaging blow" since the Depression. With half of Manhattan workers out, fifty million hours of labor, or $125 million in wages, were lost the first week.[34] Businesses were losing as much as $100 million per day in productivity. Rockefeller requested federal aid, telling President Lyndon Johnson that the strike was "calamitous." Johnson responded with small-business loans—the first time the White House had approved such aid outside of a natural disaster.

No industry escaped. Department stores were nearly empty, with Macy's seeing one-third of its average 150,000 daily shoppers. The Metropolitan Museum saw only 1,250 daily visitors, compared to the normal 6,000 to 7,000. Though the arts industry had supported Lindsay's election, the cultural world's patience frayed. Theater producer David Merrick said the mayor had gone from "fatuity to banality" and added that his exhorting New Yorkers to stay home was harming theaters. Two Broadway shows closed. Newspapers suffered a slump, with revenue down by half, as retailers, theaters, and other buyers saw no reason to advertise if customers couldn't travel.

The economic impact was uneven—and hurt blue-collar industries that were already struggling. White-collar employers such as financial and law firms, with higher profit margins and better-paid employees, could withstand duress. They blocked off hotel rooms for top-paid workers, ensuring continuity. But retailers and manufacturers could not afford to pay absent workers.

The garment industry was the worst hit. "How can you pay a piece worker who's not here?" asked one clothing maker.[35] Only 35 percent of apparel workers showed up, compared with 70 percent of bankers. Apparel makers—concentrated in factories, warehouses, and showrooms west of Midtown—were critical to New York's economy. At the industry's peak employment, in 1948, the rag trade had employed 354,000 New Yorkers, or nearly 10 percent of the labor force, and one-third of the manufacturing base. But clothes makers already faced competition from lower-cost regions of the country; the local industry had shed tens of thousands of jobs over nearly two decades and had fallen to 175,000 workers, 100,000 of them in Manhattan.

Now they faced deadlines to fulfill spring orders. The mayor appeared oblivious. The first Sunday of the strike, touring the city's call-in center, Lindsay had advised a telephoning garment worker, buyer's assistant Jack Friedman, to stay home.[36] "If the strike goes another week, we would be severely injured," said the chief executive of the Arkin Organization, a dress company, at the end of the first week.[37]

Even in the garment industry, workers didn't share the burden equally.[38] Some 75 to 80 percent of "elite" cutters and designers made it to work, with haute-couture houses hiring cars to transport employees. But lower-paid machine workers, black and Puerto Rican, were not. These workers, disproportionately women, lived in what the *Times* called the "distant slums" of Brooklyn and Upper Manhattan.[39] Without cars and living too far to walk or cycle, they could no longer commute. As week two of the strike began, Lindsay made what the *Times* termed a "hurried tour," led by a "red fire chief's car," of three neighborhoods: Brooklyn's Bedford-Stuyvesant, the South Bronx, and Harlem. "I haven't been able to work," one woman told him.

Direct impacts cascaded into indirect ones. Without wages, "slum" dwellers couldn't spend money in local shops. Patrons cut back on purchasing goods in Puerto Rican–owned bodegas, with supermarket sales off by half or more.[40] A linen store owner on Dekalb Avenue in Brooklyn told the mayor that business was "very bad." Likewise, in Harlem, shoe store owner Oscar Hauben told the mayor, "I can't stand it." The mayor's response was, "I'm sorry." On his visit—faced with hecklers who told him, "you have the power"—"the mayor got into a car and drove off."[41]

By the twelfth day, the mayor had had enough. The strike could not persist a third week. Lindsay did what he had vowed not to do: get involved. "The mayor . . . took a more active part in negotiations," working with TWU officials in an "all-night round."[42] The city and the union settled a deal that included two annual 4 percent raises and a final 7 percent raise as well as a $500 pension bonus.[43] The deal would grant workers $60 million in new pay and benefits over two years, falling short of what Quill had asked for but in line with previous agreements. The settlement was not different from what a more astute mayor could have achieved on New Year's Eve. On January 13, "New York began to pull itself back to normalcy." A "handful of men," Lindsay said, had "consigned a city of eight million people to paralysis."

A Glimpse of 1970s Decay . . .

One party emerged victorious from the strike: the Transport Workers Union. The union victory, in turn, strengthened public-sector labor unionism in general.

"Messages of solidarity" came to Quill via telegram from rail unions as far away as Milan, Paris, and London. (The mail wasn't unanimous: "Gentlemen, please, my feet hurt," one commuter beseeched him.) The outcome was not just a wage and benefit gain—the "highest pay increase in [the] U.S.," it told its members—but a broader economic, cultural, and social triumph. "Your greatest victory," the union termed it.[44] The TWU had demonstrated that unionized government laborers would not surrender to bloodless economic and political technocrats. For the nearly six decades that have followed, organized public-sector labor, and not elected officials counseled by management and productivity consultants, has controlled how, and at what fiscal cost, New York City's government agencies deliver public services, a dynamic only briefly suspended during the 1970s fiscal crisis. Quill had won Lindsay's attention the hard way—and his words resonated across the generations. As John Samuelsen, president of the TWU Local 100 from 2009 to 2017, notes, Quill's rejoinder to the judge to drop dead in his robes "has been a driving force for waves of TWU leaders" and "still unites us all," setting the transit union "apart as fighters rather than cookie-cutter cooperators."[45]

Nobody else won, but Quill had suffered most. Quill "was on the verge of collapse" when he uttered his famous "drop dead" words; the phrase became his "final act of defiance," says Samuelsen. Hours after the judge jailed him, he suffered a heart attack and would spend most of his ten days in custody inside Bellevue Hospital. By the end of January, he was dead. Four years later, a judge ruled that his widow was eligible for workman's compensation, as the strain of the strike had made his heart disease fatal.[46]

The strike harmed public and political support for unions. Just a decade before President Jimmy Carter deregulated the airlines, the trucking industry, and the federal railroads against well-founded objections by labor unions that unfettered competition would lower wages, and a decade and a half before President Ronald Reagan broke the national air traffic controllers' strike, the walkout hardened burgeoning neoliberal sentiment against working-class assertion. Castigating "silent men" of other unions whose leaders failed to criticize the TWU during the walkout, the then-liberal *New York Post* editorialized, "If there are labor leaders who fought vainly against Lindsay's election now seeking to exert a measure of revenge . . . let them recognize that their own members are the daily victims of this unnecessary, unwarranted strike."[47] New York Senator Robert F. Kennedy said the strike had been "very, very harmful to . . . organized labor."[48] Public-sector labor would largely retain its power, as government service jobs were less vulnerable to automation, outsourcing, and offshoring than were manufacturing jobs, but private-sector union power steadily eroded.

The strike also damaged Lindsay. "[It] confirmed Lindsay's belief that there was a group of people who controlled the city, in the case of the subway workers, the leadership of the union," said Jay Kriegel, at the time Lindsay's twenty-five-year-old chief of staff.[49] Just before the settlement, Lindsay lashed out against unnamed "power brokers," who, he said, had attempted to "intimidate" New York. (Kriegel claimed that Lindsay, a Protestant, included the Catholic Church, whom many Irish American subway workers looked to for guidance, in this "power broker" category.) "This city will not capitulate before the lawless demands of a single power group," Lindsay had vowed. Yet the strike had made it obvious that New York depended on public sector workers—making this faction of power brokers more powerful. For the rest of his eight years in office, Lindsay would be plagued by labor unrest. The strike presaged "a whole series of labor disruptions," including the 1968 teachers' strike and the 1969 sanitation strike, said Kriegel.

The biggest damage was to the city's psyche. Lindsay argued that the strike had showcased New York's strengths, praising "good humor and toughness," and saying that by overcoming the emergency, "we shall have gained some future hope . . . [during this] test of a proud city." Yet the city wasn't proud; it was depressed. The Fifth Avenue Association business group declared that they would "never recover." Board of Trade chief Neil Anderson concluded that much business was "gone for good."[50] The *New York World-Telegram* asked, "How many New York City businessmen are thinking of moving out so that what happened Jan. 1–13 can never happen again?"[51]

Indeed, the strike was "the beginning of the decay of the city," said Kriegel. Job losses accelerated through the 1970s; the city eventually lost more than half of its nearly 1.1 million manufacturing jobs, including most apparel jobs. The number of white-collar jobs, too, stopped growing and contracted during the 1970s as corporations left the chaotic city.[52] Crime accelerated: the murder toll doubled, from 654 in 1966 to 1,466 by 1971.[53]

The city seemed ungovernable, and Lindsay's transformation from photogenic tonic into haggard man over two weeks did not change this perception. On the strike's final day, the *Times*'s A. M. Rosenthal encapsulated the mood. "If they were angry, New Yorkers are too tired to show it," he wrote. "All the taxes and all the city aggravations turned out to be just not enough to guarantee the woman from Harlem her right [to get to work.] . . . The fatigue in the city has been cumulative. . . . It was too much of a struggle. . . . New York had been stripped of its 'worthwhile things.'" The city was "just plain tired," he concluded—two months after Lindsay had won office on that slogan, "He is fresh, and everyone else is tired."[54]

. . . and a Glimpse of Recovery

During the strike, the New York State legislature held a prescheduled transportation hearing. Lindsay was to have been the first witness. Owing to the emergency, the mayor was absent. Robert Moses, still the Triborough Authority chairman, went first. State Senator Paul Bookson, who represented Lower Manhattan, observed, "We have a transit strike . . . this week. Obviously, if this kept going, it would reach a point where your [bridge and tunnel authority], the facility to move these automobiles, would break down. Without mass transit, these other authorities are not of real value. . . . Unless we have an effective transit system, your bridges, your highways, don't function properly." "I don't agree," Moses responded. "I don't follow your line of reasoning." Bookson persisted: "Supposing there were no mass transit system . . . how well would your highways, bridges or tunnels function?" Moses's reply: "I can't answer that."[55]

The rest of New York, though, had discovered that without mass transit, there was no effective urban transportation. Even though the strike had weakened Lindsay, it demonstrated that on transportation theory, if not execution, the mayor, in campaigning favoring transit over roads, was right. Lindsay had understood what most people needed the subway strike to grasp: without transit, the city didn't work.

Officials who preferred highway building argued the opposite. Lindsay's traffic commissioner, Barnes, a Wagner holdover, said the strike was "poetic justice" and had proven wrong "ivory-tower planners who believe the way to solve New York's traffic problem is to make it so difficult that no one will want to drive into the city . . . you have got to have autos as an alternate means."[56] Moses, too, insisted that his Triborough authority's motor vehicle crossings had "functioned smoothly throughout the subway strike."[57]

Yet everyone else could see: the lesson of the "ordeal" was that "the subways must continue to carry at least two thirds of the three million daily travelers into and out of the central business district," the *Times* noted.[58] In February, Lindsay told the press that "the transportation problems of the city . . . are of the utmost immediate concern. . . . This fact was dramatically demonstrated when our city was crippled."[59] From bank CEOs to garment workers, the mayor to the governor, New Yorkers now understood, in a way they hadn't for more than half a century, that the car could never replace the subway as the city's dominant form of transportation. The question now became: how to rebuild the subways after decades of neglecting them in favor of the car?

Chapter 7

Skull Practice at Triborough

Confronting Decades of Mass-Transit Deficits

> The five-cent fare was a sure-fire political contrivance. . . . Costs rose, equipment deteriorated, and the crisis came later.
>
> —Robert Moses, *New York Daily News*, Oct. 17, 1953

> The 15-cent fare should be maintained.
>
> —Mayor-elect John Lindsay, Dec. 7, 1965

IN THE LATE 1960S, humbled by the subway strike, New York crawled back toward mass transit—but it would not easily reverse the mistakes of the first two-thirds of the twentieth century. The city and state chose superficial battles concerning personality and power, rather than devising policies to ensure rational priorities and fiscal soundness, such as what to build and how to fund it. In stripping Robert Moses of power, real and imagined, elected officials would ignore the fact that Moses, who had embodied their misguided approach to transportation for four decades, was correct about one thing: contrary to a generation of elected officials' and transit advocates' insistence, toll surpluses from his Triborough Bridge and Tunnel Authority would never save subways and buses. By the end of the 1960s, Moses was gone, and New York had a state-run public authority to rebuild transit—but still lacked the fiscal resources to do so.

Inflation's Ravages

By the 1960s, New York's subways and buses as well as its two commuter rail systems from the suburbs were in trouble. The problem was partly ridership. New York wasn't yet losing population, but it was losing transit patrons. As wealthier New Yorkers and suburbanites chose cars, subway ridership had fallen from a peak of 2.4 million riders a day into core Manhattan in 1948, a postwar record, to slightly less than two million by 1956, where it remained through the following decade. Commuter rail ridership fell more precipitously, from 283,000 riders a day to fewer than 200,000.

The drops in ridership exacerbated problems that had persisted for decades, even when ridership had been at records. The biggest obstacle to robust transit was tension between social and political goals versus fiscal reality. Beginning in 1904, when the city's first subway—the Interborough Rapid Transit (IRT) line from downtown's City Hall to northern Manhattan—opened, the city required its private-sector operator, the IRT, which had built the system with city funds, to maintain the fare at a nickel. The Brooklyn Rapid Transit (BRT) company (later the Brooklyn-Manhattan Rapid Transit Company), which built the next line, agreed to the same contract.

Politicians never came to terms with the fact that subway fares—like the price of food, clothing, and other staples—would have to go up to cover costs of providing service, which rose with inflation. After World War I, as the cost of living surged, the city refused to revisit these contracts. No mayor wanted a fare hike. In addition to understanding that a fare hike would mean political death, many politicians cared about the plight of cash-strapped workers. It wasn't fair to ask workers, even middle-income earners, to pay the full cost of a subway fare when the subway system benefited businesses and real estate owners, as well.

But the city and state did not want to provide a tax subsidy to the transit system to make up for the difference between low-price fares and rising costs of providing the service. By 1918, the Brooklyn Rapid Transit company, one of two private subway firms, alone had racked up a $6.1 million deficit. With subways insolvent, the municipal government, starting in the 1930s, moved to take them over, consolidating them with the newer, city-built Independent line in 1940. The idea was to save money by streamlining costs.

The expected savings never materialized, as public transportation cost far more than city officials had anticipated. In addition to inflation, which would push prices up 150 percent between the pre–World War I era and World War II, a new force pushed up costs. The Transport Workers Union (TWU) was winning better compensation. Between 1940 and 1946, transit-labor costs rose 40 percent, to $86 million annually; they consumed 72 percent of fare collections, up from 54 percent. The city also had to spend $57 million a year to repay (or at least pay interest on) $1.5 billion in transit debt, incurred over nearly half a century, both to build the system and purchase the assets of the bankrupt lines. For every fare, the city lost two cents.[1] The *Herald Tribune* called the subways "the billion-dollar problem child of all New York mayors" and "the city's biggest headache."[2]

To make up for growing deficits, the city diverted scarce dollars—needed for schools, hospitals, sanitation, and parks—to transit. But there wasn't enough. By the late 1940s, in a city with an annual budget of $1.1 billion, payments of $40 million for transit deficits were not overwhelming; in 1948, for example, a $37 million payment for a "transit operating deficiency" (not a one-year operating deficit but, under a convoluted procedure, an annual payment on debt incurred for accumulated operating deficits) was lower than spending on general debt service ($222 million) and education ($210 million). But transit rivaled spending on sanitation ($42 million) and dwarfed spending on parks ($15 million) and public works maintenance ($11 million).[3] New York City was also hampered by subservience to the state. The main local revenue was a property tax because the city could not levy other taxes, such as income or sales taxes, without the permission of the more conservative state government.

Worse, the half-century-old subway was deteriorating. By the 1950s, half of transit cars were three decades old and due for replacement. In addition, the city wanted to expand transit. Thanks to federal subsidies for home mortgages and highways, it was competing against suburbs that could offer tenement dwellers spacious bedrooms and yards in which children could play. Less built-up parts of the city—such as eastern Queens, south Brooklyn, the east Bronx, and Staten Island—featured housing plots large enough for yards, a middle-ground alternative to car-dependent suburbs. But such areas, many an hour's commute from Manhattan, lacked subway lines. The city had planned several subways over decades, such as the long-delayed Second Avenue Subway to carry people from the east Bronx to Lower Manhattan, and a tunnel under the East River to carry more people from Queens to Manhattan. But work on Second Avenue had halted after the stock market crash of 1929, and work on other lines either stopped short of completion or never started.

When the city did finally raise the fare, it was too little, too late. In 1948, Mayor William O'Dwyer, after having pledged to "exhaust every other means of raising funds," capitulated and doubled the fare to 10 cents, representing the city's first-ever fare hike after forty-four years.[4] In 1953, Mayor Vincent Impellitteri hiked the fare again, to 15 cents. The previous year, he had vacillated to such an extent that he even proposed a 12.5-cent fare, making it impossible for any rider to buy one ride.[5] These moves, though belated, took courage, especially for two mayors running for reelection (O'Dwyer won; Impellitteri lost). They allowed the transit system to make investments during the 1950s, such as expanding platforms in older stations, so that longer trains could carry more passengers.[6]

Finances deteriorated sharply between the mid-1950s and mid-1960s. In 1953, the state legislature created the New York City Transit Authority. The idea was that the authority would be self-sustaining, separating transit revenues and expenses from the city budget. It would also be insulated from politics, with the mayor and the governor each appointing two board members, who would in turn select a fifth. This strategy didn't work, partly because neither the state nor the city offered consistent subsidies to support the authority and partly because the public and the city's special interests knew that the mayor could pressure the authority's supposedly independent board members regarding their decisions on fares and labor agreements; the state, despite its equal representation on the board, was content to let the city remain in charge of most decisions. Beginning in 1954, Wagner consistently awarded raises to the TWU, with no tax revenues to meet higher costs.[7] By 1965, on the eve of Lindsay's election, fares were falling short even of payroll costs, with the authority collecting $283 million but disbursing $285 million in wages and benefits.[8] Accounting for the union settlement after the 1966 transit strike, the authority would face an $80 million deficit on a $350 million budget, not including expenditures to replace assets or expand service.[9]

Moses's Advice, Ignored

Moses had no role in transit, but he offered advice. He had long said that subway revenues needed to keep up with inflation. "A higher fare seems the only answer," he had said in 1946. He also knew, though, that regular hikes to keep up with costs were a lost cause. The same year, he observed that "nobody can afford to favor a higher fare except those who don't have to . . . risk their political necks."[10] In 1952, Moses noted that, with costs rising, "even if fares were doubled there would still be a substantial deficit." In the *Daily News* in 1953, Moses wrote that "the 15-cent fare . . . has been overdue" for an increase "at least three years. . . . The candidate who promises the voters to reduce the 15-cent fare is a faker. Even this fare does not make the system self-supporting."[11]

Moses understood, too, that fares didn't have to cover costs. In 1966, he observed, "It's a sociological question . . . as to whether people in the city of New York can afford to pay . . . more. I don't know the answer to that. . . . if you were to raise it to what would be really self-supporting, say 25 cents [from the then-fifteen-cent fare.] . . . I'm not sure that would be just or proper."[12]

But he grasped that if fares didn't cover costs, the city needed to make up for the shortfall. To that end, he also advocated that the state and city should approve supplementary, dedicated taxes to cover transit deficits rather than diverting money from other government needs and still falling short. Decades before, in 1945, he had advocated for a doubling of the city sales tax to 2 percent, with the proceeds to go to transit, calling it "the easiest way" to finance subway rehabilitation. "There's no point in going into the question of a higher fare," he said at a budget hearing, nodding to political reality. "The easiest way would be to put the extra cent back on the sales tax and earmark the money for transit."[13]

Moses came under criticism for building roads, the job with which elected officials had tasked him, at the expense of transit. He didn't bother himself with what transit planners desired, because neither they nor he had a way to pay for those desires. In 1956, when Moses was about to spend three hundred million dollars building the Verrazano-Narrows Bridge between Brooklyn and Staten Island, transit planners and the press wanted him to spend extra money to make the bridge heavy enough to carry rail. Moses called the idea "preposterous."[14] He pointed out that thirty years previously, the Port Authority of New York and New Jersey had fortified the George Washington Bridge, but that no rail agency had taken advantage of this potential. He argued, too, that a rail link from Staten Island to Brooklyn would dump travelers onto Brooklyn's Fourth Avenue subway, running at capacity even as ridership was falling.

Just as Moses understood that engineers could not build a motor vehicle bridge in a vacuum—it required massive approach roads—he understood that they could not build a train line over a bridge in a vacuum. It would cost half a billion dollars, he estimated, to build enough rail capacity in Brooklyn to receive Staten Island passengers. Once the bridge with train tracks was built, the city's transit authority would have no money with which to operate more trains.

These were not insurmountable arguments. "This may be the last, as well as the first, bridge [to Staten Island]," the *New York Times* opined, so it was important to get it right.[15] With the economy booming, it was a good time for elected state and city officials to assess priorities and determine, for example, whether it was time for a dedicated tax, perhaps one related to real estate values, to pay for transit operation and expansion, including to Staten Island.

Instead, the city left matters in Moses's hands. Editorialists said of the Verrazano, "We continue to hope that Mr. Moses, with his genius for doing the impossible, will later find a way to tell us how it can be . . . built." Moses had no genius for doing the impossible. He built projects planned and financed by elected officials. Tolls from bridge and tunnel drivers were not unlimited and could not open-endedly subsidize transit, which was more expensive than roads to build and operate. Operating bridges and tunnels carried lower labor costs than running trains and buses. Triborough had 951 employees, as compared to the transit system's more than 33,000. (Transit was more efficient at carrying passengers, to be sure, but this thirty-five-to-one employee ratio far outweighed the three-to-one ratio of subway and bus commuters into Manhattan compared to car commuters.)

Mayor Wagner and the city's other elected officials, through the Board of Estimate, approved the Verrazano with no rail line and no funding for one. City officials weren't even serious about maintaining the existing rail service. The city, under Wagner, kept the subway fare flat for thirteen years, until 1966. The money the city *did* raise for transit—$500 million in bonds in 1951 to build the Second Avenue Subway—it diverted to maintenance of the existing system, work that was necessary but fell short of what elected officials had promised.

Mayor Lindsay, who took office in January 1966, was no more interested in raising the fare than his predecessors. "The subway fare must not be increased," he had said during the campaign. Yet he had no resources for subway deficits, let alone subways he wanted to build. The city budget was in deficit, thanks to Wagner-era spending. During Lindsay's first month in office, *Barron's*, the newspaper for Wall Street investors, ran a front-page article titled "Poor Credit Risk: New York City Has Yet to Balance Ends and Means." Lindsay's own spending proposals, on everything from social welfare to anti-narcotics police, required the state to approve sales and income taxes on businesses and residents; nothing would remain for trains.

The Enemy

What was needed was a pot of money, lying around for the taking—and Moses involuntarily provided one. The Verrazano-Narrows Bridge between Staten Island and Brooklyn, at a final cost of $350 million, was the last bridge that New York would complete. After Moses inaugurated the first deck in 1964, his Triborough Bridge and Tunnel Authority, which controlled seven major tolled crossings, was collecting a record amount of revenue—but had no more megaprojects to build. As a result, Triborough, by the mid-1960s, was banking a significant surplus. In 1966, after funding operations, maintenance, and debt, the authority would earn twenty-nine million dollars in excess of costs on sixty-three million in revenues.[16]

The new political guard's solution was simple: use these surpluses, generated by car and truck drivers, to ease deficits at the subway and bus system. In 1965, candidate Lindsay made this proposal a cornerstone of his campaign. In his nineteen-page "modern transportation system for New York City" blueprint, he proposed to increase subway capacity and comfort. To lure riders back and reduce car traffic, Lindsay would build the Second Avenue Subway as well as an east-west subway line across Manhattan's Forty-Eighth Street to encourage office development. He focused not just on long-term megaprojects, but on short-term amenities: he also wanted to install air-conditioning in train cars.

To fund these improvements, Lindsay proposed to unify Moses's Triborough authority with the city's transit authority. That is, Triborough's "consistent surpluses would help to bail the Transit Authority out."[17] The mayor, through his own "transportation coordinator," a mild-mannered investment banker named Arthur Palmer, would control both agencies. "Fares, toll rates and taxes must serve the city's overall objectives rather than those of . . . one particular mode of transportation," Lindsay concluded.

The idea of using Triborough surpluses for other purposes was not new. In the mid-1950s, a young New York University civics professor named Bill Ronan had spent three years preparing reports for state lawmakers, illustrating a problem and solution in one: as public authorities ran out of projects to build, they would accumulate resources. "Were an authority to continue to charge tolls . . . after its bonds have been retired, it would build up a surplus," one Ronan report noted, estimating a future Triborough surplus of thirty-five million dollars annually, not far from the mark. Ronan suggested merging Triborough's tolled facilities with free roads so that Triborough surpluses could maintain the entire road system.

As elected officials and advisers grew concerned at the amount of money Moses was starting to control, they grew concerned about Moses himself. Moses was chairman of Triborough but, by then, also in charge of the Bethpage (Long Island) State Park Authority, the Jones Beach Parkway Authority, and the New York State Power Authority, in addition to several city positions. Ronan suggested in 1957 that the state amend its public authority law so that no one chairperson could run more than one authority, a suggestion that the *Herald Tribune* called waving a "red flag at Robert Moses and . . . dar[ing] him to charge."[18]

The idea of using Triborough surpluses for other purposes had never been entirely technocratic and was less so by the Lindsay era. Lindsay knew that his proposal was rough justice. He ran his 1965 campaign as a disruption of politics as usual: the sclerotic machine man, Wagner, was out, and the young mayor with his young family was in. The old guard included Triborough, whose chairman, Moses, had been a public figure for decades. "You have to remember who Moses was," remembered Jay Kriegel, a top Lindsay aide. "He was the enemy. [Merging transit] wasn't about the trains."[19]

Lindsay's transportation unification idea was not just a fiscal device but theater: ruthless versus the idealistic, old versus young. Moses played his new role as the villain rather than the hero perfectly, moving ahead with contracts and land purchases for major road projects, including the two Manhattan expressways, even as Lindsay—first as mayor-elect, then as mayor—said that his government, which controlled the streets, would determine whether such projects would go forward. The *Daily News* tabloid, a Moses champion, ran a front-page banner: "MOSES DEFIES MAYOR."

Lindsay matched Moses's arrogance with insolence. As Lindsay was recovering from the transit strike, a reporter asked him, "Do you agree with the remark . . . that 'Mr. Moses is an eighteenth-century man?' . . . The mayor grinned and answered: 'you said that.'"[20] To Moses, accustomed to respect, mockery stung. "Less than two years after the opening of the Verrazano-Narrows Bridge, the greatest crossing of its kind in the world, the mayor announced publicly that those who built it . . . had no further usefulness," he complained.

The press, after decades of supporting Moses, collectively began to change their minds. The *Times* couldn't wriggle overnight from its decades-long support for Moses's highway projects. But the paper was repositioning. Days before Lindsay took office, it praised the idea of transferring Triborough surpluses, saying that "geography dictates that mass transit . . . must be the city's main reliance."[21] The *Herald Tribune* called Moses "obdurate" and wrote, "If there has to be a test of power, it seems certain the public interest will be served by Mayor Lindsay."[22]

Moses's Advice, Still Ignored

Moses was ready for the assault on Triborough. Over a decade, whenever anyone—from Ronan to good-government groups to even, briefly, Mayor Wagner—had suggested a merger of toll crossings and transit, he had quashed the idea. As he had told his staffers in response to the mid-1950s Ronan report, "These attacks must be answered once for all, because otherwise, they will be made year after year."[23] They were. In 1960, he publicly dismissed Triborough surpluses as "not the treasure of the Count of Monte Cristo."[24]

In 1966, as Lindsay posed a more credible threat, Moses made customary blunt attacks. In January, he called unity between Triborough and transit "hogwash." For good measure, he said the idea springs "from panic and not logic," further called it "illegal and fantastic," and said that Lindsay's Triborough appointees, unlike him, would be "complete stooges" with no independence from politics.[25]

Behind the bluster were technocratic arguments, honed over the years by Triborough's lawyers, bankers, investors, financial experts, and public relations men. The merger bills that Lindsay proposed would need the approval of both the state legislature, which had created Triborough and would need to amend it, and the city council, which generally initiated all significant changes in state law impacting the city, although it could not enact such changes itself.

Moses made three arguments. His first argument was constitutional and legal. In the 1930s, in creating the public authority, the legislature had given Triborough the power to enter private contracts with the bondholders who lent money for bridges and tunnels. Through such contracts, Triborough had pledged future revenues to bondholders, either to repay bonds or to reserve for specific, future projects that would generate even more revenues for bondholders. The legislature could not require Triborough to renege on those contracts and divert money to transit without violating the U.S. Constitution's contracts clause.

His second argument was managerial. Running Triborough and running the subways were two different businesses. Labor relations were different. Triborough's tollbooth clerks could never threaten to shut down bridges and tunnels during a strike. The bridges and tunnels would operate, just with revenue collection suspended or with managers filling in for strikers; unlike train operators and conductors, tollbooth clerks performed no navigation duties. Managing subways and buses, by contrast, meant managing tens of thousands of unionized workers who could shut down the transit system and thus shut down the city.

Finally, Moses made fiscal arguments. Triborough's surpluses would not cover transit deficits. Triborough surpluses in the tens of millions of dollars annually could not cover transit deficits that were forecast to climb from the tens of millions into the hundreds of millions. "The latest figures I've got on the [transit] deficit in operation, is 74 million dollars," Moses told lawmakers in 1966, as the transit strike raged. "Assuming . . . that [TWU president Mike] Quill gets around 37, 38, 39, 40 million dollars, the deficit, not including any capital improvements, then would be 115 million dollars . . . even a ten-cent increase in fare in the rapid transit system wouldn't give you that kind of money. . . . Now that's your picture. And it will have to be faced. Just looking around for some Santa Claus isn't any good. . . . Triborough is no Santa Claus."[26] The fiscal arguments could not be separated from the political arguments, as reluctance to raising the fare had proven. As Triborough officials had said a decade before, "no authority in the State of New York would be given by legislation a free hand to raise [subway and bus] fares at will."

Moses had facts on his side, but just in case, he directed staff to cook the books ahead of public hearings. Eyeing surpluses, he wrote internally, "There seems to be a serious misunderstanding as to our table indicating Triborough revenues and requirements in the next five years. Apparently, the table tentatively prepared does not distinguish as it should between repairs and improvements properly charged to surplus and impossible or impractical to finance in any other way, on the one hand, and major improvements to be financed by separate bond issues on the other." There did not appear to be enough of the former, Moses implied, and thus the surplus that Lindsay was eyeing appeared high. "I don't want to issue a list of demands on the surplus which is not absolutely and strictly honest. I don't want to show the exhaustion of the surplus merely for the sake of wiping it out. I want a statement which will stand any kind of fair analysis."[27]

Three months later, frustrated with his staff's failure to heed this message, Moses demanded from Triborough's finance people "up to date surplus estimates" through 1969, asking for a list "of possible, incidental, related City improvements which might legitimately and without endangering our solvency, be paid for out of the so-called Triborough surpluses in the next six years. . . . You will note my guess at amounts," penned into the margins. The staff obliged with these "guesses."[28] Coincidentally, the small projects Moses announced—including twenty parks calculated to win public support—would consume Triborough surpluses well past Lindsay's term.

Moses bolstered such machinations with his formidable coalition. Moses left nothing to chance as he prepared for legislative hearings. Twice that spring, in March and in May, before state and city lawmaking bodies, Moses amassed dozens of speakers—from construction contractors to labor unions, banks, investor groups, and law firms—to argue against Lindsay's merger of Triborough with the transit system. Samuel Rosenman, former FDR fixer and longtime Moses adviser, testified, as did former mayor Wagner. Some speakers, such as construction-union chiefs, advocated for their members' interests. As Moses had directed his staff in February, in rounding up contractors and union leaders, "there won't be any Triborough construction program for the building trades and employers and practically no federal-state aid program. They ought to wake up to this fact."[29]

New York's Automobile Club, with nearly half a million members, was another force arguing in self-interest—with prodding and help. As Moses directed his staff, "Be sure that the top Auto Club representative refers to: (1) [Lindsay transportation official Arthur] Palmer's absence and obscurity; (2) the announced purpose of the Mayor to stop all major arterial improvements and to abandon federal aid projects in order to keep cars out of Manhattan." And as one of Moses's PR hands, Murray Davis, assured him, "The A.A.A."—of which the Auto Club was a member—"is on our side completely. . . . For the first time in the history of the New York edition of MOTORIST, they are running an article with a coupon and asking their 400,000 members to fill it out for . . . their representatives in Albany."[30]

The club produced a twenty-page brochure, fighting "propaganda against the motor vehicle." The pamphlet included a section on the "economic impact of the automobile." As it informed members—using statistics Moses had compiled—"thousands of businesses in New York City are totally dependent on the motor vehicle," from auto dealers to highway construction (16,100 workers) to automobile credit to auto insurance to "eating and drinking places" to "magazine and newspaper automobile advertising." Overall, the industry provided direct employment for 51,000 people, or "one out of every 13 persons working in New York City," and paid "wages . . . of $416 million a year. . . . IT WOULD BE AN UNWISE AND RECKLESS GAMBLE TO MAKE THE AUTOMOBILE THE PERMANENT ORPHAN IN THE CITY'S TRANSPORTATION COMPLEX." As the brochure explained, conspiracy was afoot: "The party line has charged that cars are strangling cities and that building freeways and parking facilities is self-defeating, since such action only attracts more cars." The club's chief, Gilbert Phillips, told the legislature and city council that 80 percent of members were against using tolls to subsidize transit.

Some pro-Moses speakers made well-considered arguments. Joseph E. O'Grady, head of the city's transit authority, said that Triborough's surpluses would not solve the problem, because the problem was political: "The steady post-war deterioration of the system . . . was partly the result of the history of the private lines prior to unification, and manpower and material shortages during World War II," he acknowledged. "But mainly it resulted from the politically motivated decisions . . . to hold the five-cent and ten-cent fares long after they made economic sense." Merging Triborough and transit under the control of the mayor, O'Grady said, wouldn't solve these issues. Instead, "the authority would become a political authority, incapable of independent action."

Other speakers on Moses's side just wanted to be paid. As Lindsay's counsel, Lee Rankin, pointed out, "Almost every witness was either on the payroll of one of the authorities, or derives substantial benefits from one of them." Rankin didn't know how right he was. Former governor Charles Poletti, for example, made two obvious if accurate statements at both hearings: "Triborough cannot carry out one project without the approval of the City Planning Commission, the approval of the Mayor and others on the Board of Estimate," and "this Triborough legislation . . . is intended primarily to get rid of Bob Moses."[31] He then submitted a bill to Moses for services rendered. Moses had told his staff to pay people "reasonably" for taking the time to prepare statements.

But Moses had limits. He replied to Poletti, "Mr. DeLigio," the Triborough comptroller, "tells me you telephoned that you proposed to submit a bill of $25,000 [$250,000 in 2024 dollars] for Triborough services. Frankly, I am astonished. . . . Judge Rosenman on behalf of his entire firm only charged $7,500 and [attorney Franklin] Wood's bill for his entire firm was $17,000. I think you should cut yours to a maximum of $7,500." Poletti answered that "Triborough can pay me what it desires and I'll be satisfied. . . . I miss seeing you."[32]

Despite posturing and preparing, Moses betrayed signs of losing confidence. In a February internal memo, he noted, "I am disgusted with delays in getting out material [that would bolster the argument against the merger.] . . . I can't understand neglect of this and at a time when we badly need . . . all hands."[33]

The material Moses wanted was a response to an urban beautification conference, sponsored by Rockefeller money. At the conference, Triborough planning director David Caplan informed Moses, "One speaker offered the opinion that future highways, parking areas and other related facilities be built below ground. He stated that motor vehicles now dominate our cities, and something must be done to 'bring back the city to the people.'" Moses called this a "bum idea." That spring, he prepared his own "beauty" brochure, called "Public Works and Beauty: The Philosophy of

Triborough." He wrote to a deputy's draft that it was "a very sloppy looking dummy. I want to see it again in better shape. I'll go along with black and white to meet the April 4th date. . . . Put in overtime."[34]

The brochure was eccentric, even for Moses, who, like Quill, used baroque language to command attention. The brochure praised the ventilator shaft for the Brooklyn Battery Tunnel downtown, a hulk disguised with Art Deco flourishes, as "not [a] utilitarian silo" but "the finest building on the bay, combining beauty and use as Keats combined truth and beauty." Of the Verrazano-Narrows crossing, the leaflet said that the "greatest sculptural beauty man has created is the spiderlike, brave, unencrusted, urornamented suspension bridge." The brochure was defensive, repeating an old Moses line, that "we do not build gasoline gullies and mere utilitarian culverts. We do not deprive neighbors of light and air. We give them recreation and play facilities."[35]

Moses needn't have worried, not yet. At the March hearing, Lindsay displayed naivety about state and local politics, even after the transit strike's lesson months earlier. He appealed to public interest. "The members of the Triborough Authority have power to perpetuate the authority indefinitely, and keep its surplus funds permanently locked up by the simple expedient of issuing new bonds," he told state lawmakers. By contrast, his program was "for the welfare of all the people." It would allow New York to "balance . . . the competing demands of subway, bus and other mass transit operations, with those of the private automobile."

This lecture left legislators unmoved, as did his appeal to honesty. In May, Lindsay testified before the city council. The council, peopled with Democratic politicians who owed their careers to Tammany Hall, wasn't predisposed to cooperate with Lindsay, a Republican, who had run against that machine. The mayor accused the council of being corrupt, asking "whether the city council is to permit itself to be used by the interests representing the status quo" and "lobbyists and lawyers" working for construction contractors, unions, and investment banks, all with lucrative Moses business. He warned the body not to make a "cynical bargain."

Nobody likes being called corrupt, and Majority Leader David Ross, of the Bronx machine, bristled.[36] "This council has always been known as one place where lobbyists don't do very well," Ross said. Joseph Ruggieri, a Brooklyn councilman, said the mayor was trying to "intimidate" the body. To Poletti, the former governor who would demand a five-figure payout for his testimony, Brooklyn's Corso said, "I appreciate some of the remarks that you expressed about the members of this council. Nobody intimidates this council."

Lindsay misunderstood politics in another way. In wanting to consolidate all city transportation—toll roads and transit—under one person, his own transportation coordinator, he overreached. Lawmakers worried that he would vest too much power in one person. Ironically, notwithstanding Moses's perceived power, the press had begun to refer to Lindsay's proposed transportation and transit chief, Palmer, as a "czar." Palmer didn't help himself when, in a radio interview, he characterized himself as a "new boy learning a new job," walking into Moses's argument that he was "obscure." If Moses was a "czar," lawmakers seemed to think, at least he was experienced.

Moses's coalition held. By June, Bill Lebwohl, a Moses deputy, could report of the merger bills that "they seem dead." Moses's verdict was that the hearings had been "a rather stupid business but good practice in view of further pursuit of the same subject by brighter people."[37] The defeat, coming after the subway strike, represented another loss to Lindsay's reputation, even as his administration was just six months old. In July, after promising during the campaign not to do so, he was forced to raise the subway fare from fifteen to twenty cents. That month, the WINS news-radio station concluded that Lindsay had "failed" and that "the transit system is still losing money."

Lindsay had blundered, but his loss was inevitable. The state had been happy to let New York City run the subways, as they were a money-losing annoyance and labor relations headache. But it would not give city officials control of Triborough, an authority that made money rather than losing money, so easily. If Moses wasn't going to control Triborough's surpluses as well as its power over construction contractors and unions anymore, neither was a mayor of New York, especially one vying with a governor for a national profile. Lawmakers gave "no serious consideration" to Lindsay's proposal, Ronan said much later, because of the "rivalry" between Governor Rockefeller and the mayor.[38] Rockefeller would reserve power for himself. "With Mayor Lindsay's transit reorganization plan gasping its last," the *Long Island Press* reported, "Gov. [Nelson] Rockefeller is quietly working out his own."[39]

The State Steps In—and Takes Over

In 1967, New York saw a replay of the merger drama. This time, Moses faced a more formidable force. The third-generation heir to the John D. Rockefeller oil fortune, Rockefeller, like Lindsay, was a liberal Republican. Like most governors, he didn't care about transit. By 1966, into his second term, he had long dismissed transit as a "city problem. . . . Rockefeller . . . would prefer not to have any hand in the New York City transit picture," one paper had reported.[40]

Now, though, the governor was under pressure to care. The transit strike was fresh in people's minds. Two months after the walkout, a poll showed that 70 percent of voters across the state—including majorities of all parties, incomes, and regions—said that Rockefeller "could have done more" about the disruption.[41] For a governor facing reelection in 1967, these frustrations were worrisome.

Rockefeller also had a more perilous transit headache: the Long Island Rail Road (LIRR). In 1965, the state government had purchased the railroad out of receivership. Albany had spent $65 million to buy a dud: the once thriving private railroad, after a decade in bankruptcy, was a shell. (Here, too, Moses's critics would later say that he had failed by not building rail tracks down the middle of the Long Island Expressway in building that roadway a decade earlier—but the LIRR provided Long Island's narrow spine with ample rail trackage to Manhattan. Any new line down the expressway would have needed money for equipment and crew—money the state hadn't offered.)

Rockefeller knew, though, that he needed Long Island voters to win reelection. But those voters were upset at the railroad's unreliable and dangerous service. Now, the governor needed funds to operate the LIRR—so, like Lindsay, he cast his eye on Triborough surpluses. In his 1967 message to lawmakers, Rockefeller said that "in the great cities, life is drab, depressing and dangerous." To improve livability, "good transportation" was the second item on his list, between housing and crime. He then stole Lindsay's idea. Via legislation, he would take Triborough and merge it into the three-year-old Metropolitan Commuter Transportation Authority, the entity that controlled the LIRR. He would then take the subway and bus agency from the city's de-facto control and put it under the same umbrella. Triborough, as an independent entity, would disappear, effective the next year, in March 1968. The governor, through appointing a majority of board members, would control the public authority, whose name would be shortened to Metropolitan Transportation Authority, or MTA. Within the MTA, Triborough surpluses would fund transit.

Rockefeller coupled the MTA plan he presented to the legislature with a $2.5 billion "transportation bond act." The act, if voters were to approve it that November, would fund transit and highway improvements, not just in and around the city but across the state. New York would get its Second Avenue Subway, an East Midtown terminal for the LIRR, and a rail connection from Manhattan to John F. Kennedy Airport. Other regions would get sturdier roads. Beyond bailing out New York's mass transit system, this act was in keeping with Rockefeller's philosophy, as a liberal Republican, and with his future ambition to be president: that is, to build public works. The governor billed his bond act as "the greatest transportation advance . . . since the Erie Canal."[42]

To stop this plan, Moses followed the playbook he had used the previous year, calling the plan "absurd" and "grotesque." Within a month, though, he changed his mind. In February, he wrote to Rockefeller, "No one else seems to have a better idea."[43] By March, Moses publicly declared himself on the governor's side. "The Governor's program is indispensable," Moses said. "We believe the Governor is on the right track, that only a bold approach can succeed," and "for our part [we] shall cooperate."[44]

What happened to turn Moses around? One ostensible reason is that the governor added a paragraph to his legislation to protect Triborough bondholders, requiring debt payments and replenishment of reserves before any surplus transfers to transit could occur. As Moses said in supporting the governor's plan that March, "After considerable discussion, a paragraph protecting the rights of Triborough bondholders has been included by the Governor."[45]

Moses also likely understood that compared to the year before, fighting Lindsay, he would fight Rockefeller from a weak position. Moses, adept at politics for a third of a century, knew that any governor had more power than any mayor. The governor could do something Lindsay couldn't: offer an entirely new pot of money to complement Triborough surpluses. The $2.5 billion via the proposed bond act was a counterweight to Moses. The bond act's proceeds would exceed the money that Moses's Triborough, with tens of millions in annual surpluses, could raise. Based on projections of future surpluses, at low interest rates, Triborough could likely raise about $1 billion. A big part of the coalition that Moses had amassed to defeat Lindsay's proposal the year before—construction labor unions and construction contractors—could depend on Rockefeller's bond money for public works employment, instead of on Moses's Triborough money, and thus support Rockefeller.

Though any governor would have been a more formidable opponent than a mayor, this governor was a particular threat. Rockefeller, by virtue of family wealth, had more power than the average governor. His brother David was the chairman of Chase Bank. David was spearheading public and private developments, including the Lower Manhattan Expressway and the World Trade Center, to revitalize downtown Manhattan, Chase's headquarters. The Rockefellers's philanthropy made waverers or adversaries on any topic easy to convince. Rockefeller, like many people born into a dynasty, was accustomed to getting his way. To him, Moses wasn't the all-powerful Triborough chairman but just another employee.

Moses knew that the Rockefellers weren't dependent on him—and didn't like him. He had misjudged his power against this powerful family previously. In 1956, David Rockefeller had written to him asking for advice on Lower Manhattan redevelopment. Moses did not show himself awed by this request. His minions did a cursory job; David expressed himself "frankly disappointed." Moses replied that his staff had not been commissioned by him "in any capacity whatsoever on Downtown Manhattan problems and planning." He continued, "At my request, and I thought yours, he presented a rough memorandum for consideration when you got around to deciding what you wanted to do. . . . there are times when I get a little weary of doing good."[46] This dismissal was a high-handed way of treating the richest man in the land. In 1962, in a separate misjudgment, Moses had resigned five of his state posts in protest of the governor's lack of deference.[47] Moses may have expected Nelson Rockefeller to beg him to reconsider, but the governor accepted the resignations, cutting Moses's state power three years after he had already resigned four city posts, including parks commissioner.[48]

Moses had a similarly fraught history with Bill Ronan, the Rockefeller aide who was devising Rockefeller's transportation and transit unification plan. When Moses had dismissed Ronan's public-authority reports a decade before, he had done so in personal terms: in 1955, Moses had publicly called Ronan "perfectly ridiculous."[49] Two years before, Moses had made it clear that Ronan, then merely a professor, wasn't worth the time of day. When Ronan had inquired if Moses could meet with NYU researchers, Moses replied, "We simply do not have the time."[50]

One last reason existed for Moses's change of heart besides the realization that Rockefeller would get his way, whether Moses supported him or not. The previous year, Lindsay, in fighting his battle of good versus evil, had, in political ignorance, offered him nothing. In 1967, by contrast, Rockefeller was willing to trade. The *World-Journal Telegram* wrote, "Robert Moses is expected to cap his public service career as a chief architect of Gov. Rockefeller's Metropolitan Commuter Transportation Agency."[51] In March, a leak confirmed that Moses would have a role at the new MTA. "Rockefeller and Ronan prevailed on Moses to endorse the merger plan, telling him they wanted him to serve on the board," the *Daily News* reported.

Moses's Attempted Sabotage

A different reason exists, though, for Moses's support of Rockefeller's takeover of Triborough. Moses may have believed he could still win on his own terms—that is, outwit the governor and his brother.

A superficial reading of 1967 shows that Moses played nice. Moses appeared an enthusiastic marketer for Rockefeller's bond issue, which voters would have to approve. In *Newsday* in late October, appealing to Long Islander swing voters a week before the vote, he wrote an article titled, "Why NY Needs the Transportation Bond Issue." Moses wasn't subtle: "Every thinking voter should support the transportation bond issue. It authorizes large, properly spaced investments by the state in at least the beginning of a unified, coordinated rubber, rail, and air travel system relieving present congestion and anticipating growth."[52]

That fall, too, to the dismay of good-government groups concerned about the politicization of a nonprofit entity, Triborough spent $9,300 to post sixteen "vote yes" signs near bridges and tunnels for drivers to read, made a 12.5-minute film, and paid $30,108 for radio ads, with Moses saying in one, "We must put up with some congestion but need not be strangled." Triborough ran ads in newspapers, too: "Traffic-commuter-transit delays got your goat? Don't sit and grumble, go out and vote!"

Yet behind the op-eds and advertising, Moses spent the spring and summer sabotaging Rockefeller. First, he hoped the bond act would fail. "I would like to have a little skull practice with our top consultants and our staff on the transportation program," he wrote internally in March, "assuming that the public has yet to be persuaded." The bond issue might fall victim to "opposition and apathy," and without it, "the whole thing is a hollow shell." Moses's PR man, O'Brien, though, was privately confirming with public-opinion sources that voters "could well pass the bond act."[53]

Moses, then, tried to *make* it fail, using Triborough as a weapon. Even as he supported Rockefeller in public, he was telling private audiences that the merger would fail because Triborough had negligible surpluses. In April, Moses asked his staff for an "independent" third-party projection of the authority's revenues, an analysis that "of course, we would pay for."[54] The "independent" analysis showed that surpluses were mysteriously tied up not just until 1969, as had coincidentally happened the previous year, in beating Lindsay, but until 1986.

Moses also made it clear that Triborough surpluses would not exist for transit unless he continued to control them. He told the public that Triborough's surpluses "might under the most favorable circumstances be capitalized [that is, borrowed against] and contributed to a new . . . facility like the projected . . . rapid transit and commuter rail tunnel under the East River."[55] This statement marked the first time Moses had expressed interest in building transit. (Lindsay, from the sidelines, pronounced himself "surprised.")

Moses's obsession over control of Triborough surpluses and future projects made it clear to Rockefeller and Ronan that he had no intention of using a post as an MTA board member to wind down his career, ceding power to Ronan. He remained intent on building one last bridge, the Oyster Bay crossing between Long Island and Westchester. But Long Island and Westchester voters, whose support Rockefeller needed, were not in favor of the project, objecting to approach roads that would cut through their neighborhoods.

As Moses advocated for the bridge in spring 1967, Rockefeller, frustrated, wrote to him, "It is of the utmost importance that nothing be done which will in any way embarrass the bond issue. . . . I ask that you take no further steps nor progress any additional work."[56] Rockefeller, with an eye to future elections, wanted to judge the prospects of the sensitive project on his own time. Ultimately, he never built it.

Most threateningly, Moses spent months leading up to the public's bond issue vote instigating a poison-pill lawsuit: he wanted Chase Manhattan Bank to sue Triborough. Chase, the bank overseen by the governor's brother, was the trustee retained to look out for the independent interests of Triborough's bondholders, a feature of bond issuances. Moses had said publicly that Rockefeller's state law creating the MTA adequately protected the bondholders. But the suit Moses encouraged behind the scenes would charge that the MTA had no right to Triborough's surpluses. To take them from bondholder control, in violation of contracts between investors and Triborough, would violate the United States constitution's protection of private contracts, he continued to argue privately. In April, even as he was publicly supporting the creation of the MTA and the governor's bond act, he wrote to former governor Thomas Dewey, the lawyer for Chase, "I would like to have a short talk with you about the Metropolitan Transportation program, Triborough, and Triborough bondholders."[57]

A month later, Moses penned another private letter to "Nelson": "I am sending you a confidential memo of Triborough and bond counsel [the authority's own bond-underwriting counsel, not the same as Chase, the trustee for the bondholders] on the so-called Triborough surplus and the rights of our bondholders. . . . if this problem is not intelligently approached, it may jeopardize the entire program."[58] That is, if the MTA's right to Triborough's surpluses was unconstitutional, there was no reason to create the MTA and no reason for urban voters to vote for the bond act, as part of the purpose of the bond act was to enable the MTA to build big projects.

The bond counsel's opinion, procured by Moses, read, "If . . . the new added S569d [the paragraph protecting bondholders] is to be regarded as meaningful, it is clear that so long as present bonds are outstanding, that no surplus funds can exist for transfer by Triborough to M.T.A. or the Transit Authority. . . . Any attempt to cause Triborough to utilize these excess revenues for any purpose . . . would constitute a violation and impairment of the obligation of Triborough's contract with its bondholders."[59] That month, Moses also wrote to construction labor leaders, reminding them that "the small Triborough surplus which belongs to the bondholders can't be diverted. . . . Such a promise will inevitably compel the bondholders and their trustee and attorney to initiate all-out litigation which will hurt the [bond-act] campaign."[60] Construction labor leaders, Moses knew, were in contact with Governor Rockefeller.

Through these back-channel messages, Moses was attempting blackmail: unless Rockefeller agreed privately with Moses, despite the new legislation to the contrary, to leave Triborough surpluses alone, a lawsuit filed before the election would endanger the governor's bond issue. John Gilhooley, a commissioner to the city transit authority and a confidante of Rockefeller, warned Moses, telling him in a May letter, "I cannot tell you how strongly I feel that the whole effort to win the referendum must be a closely coordinated one under the Governor's leadership. We will all have important roles to play . . . but unless he and his people call the signals, the whole effort could be massively fouled up."

Nevertheless, Moses persisted. On June 9, he sent another memo to "Nelson" of a "suggested agenda" for a meeting with the governor and Ronan. On the agenda was "1. Triborough surplus. Opinion of our Counsel. Position of Governor Dewey . . . Prospective litigation. . . . 2. Campaign for Transportation Proposition. Special problems in certain areas. . . . Possible approved movie on safe, comfortable metropolitan travel offered by Triborough. . . . 4. Organization of MTA Membership."[61]

This missive did not yield results. A week later, Moses warned publicly, "Any effort to pledge our large, nonexistent, theoretical surplus will have to be met in court by our trustees."[62] On June 22, Moses wrote to his counsel, "I gather from a casual remark of Governor Dewey that Chase will shortly go into court to protect the Triborough bondholders. Please talk to Frank Wood [another outside counsel for Triborough] and ask him to see [former] Governor Dewey and find out when the move will be made. I got a definite impression it will be pretty soon and that they will not delay until after the vote."

On the last day of June, Moses was rewarded: Chase, represented by Dewey, sued on behalf of the investors of nearly four hundred million dollars in bonds. A court ruling in favor of Chase and against Rockefeller's law creating the MTA could undo all the campaigning Rockefeller was doing. The governor was barnstorming the state, making speeches calling his proposed bond issue "among the most significant measures ever enacted," which "can set the pace of progress and property in New York State for a generation."

The Triborough lawsuit Moses had instigated did not work. Delay pushed any ruling to 1968, after the public had voted to pass Rockefeller's bond proposal. In February 1968, three months after the successful bond vote, Chase settled the Triborough suit it had initiated the summer before. The bank dropped its complaint, in return for an extra payment by Triborough to investors. That month, the *Times* wrote, "The Chase suit on behalf of the bondholders pitted David Rockefeller, president of Chase, against his brother, the Governor, who fostered the transit consolidation program."[63]

This reading of brother against brother was not correct. Chase, as trustee, had had to sue, considering the Triborough chairman's opining—and procuring of legal opinion—that diversion of surpluses to the MTA would be unconstitutional. Otherwise, Chase, as trustee, would have been vulnerable to being sued itself, as not protecting the interests of Triborough bondholders. In the settlement that Chase achieved, those bondholders got something for nothing. After the merger with the MTA, Triborough's bonds were no riskier than they had been before; the new bond documents and the new law spelled out that the public authority had to repay Triborough bondholders and reserve funds multiple times over for that purpose before it could divert money to transit.

Yet in settling the suit, bondholders got a higher return. In March 1968, after this deal was agreed, Moses asked his comptroller what the financial result would be. The comptroller answered, "An increase of ¼ of 1% in interest to each holder . . . would mean that he receives an additional $2.50 per annum. . . . If the interest rate on a bond is increased, it also increases the market value of the bond. For example, our 4% bonds due January 1, 1985, are selling at 93 in the present market which is the equivalent of a 4.60 effective interest rate. If the coupon was increased to 4–1/4, the bond would be worth 96." This gain was important, because at the time, market interest rates were falling. Investors made a million dollars for free.[64]

Transit at the Breaking Point

In March 1968, the MTA subsumed Triborough, and Moses was offered only a consultancy at the authority. For observers not privy to how frustrating Moses's sabotage campaign must have been to the governor, Rockefeller appeared to go back on his word. Moses may not have been surprised, though. A year before, he had written to Franklin Little, publisher of the upstate *Ogdensburg Journal*, "I have a hunch that Bill Ronan [the erstwhile professor whom Moses had once dismissed] wants to run the whole show."[65]

Ronan did want to run the show. He became the MTA's chairman and gloried in announcement after announcement of grand projects. On the MTA's inaugural day, Ronan announced $2.9 billion in investments over two decades. The MTA's first annual report promised an expansion of New York City subways, which "for decades had been unable to meet the needs of the changing city." The MTA outlined these ambitions: "A new Second Avenue Subway will be built. . . . A new midtown Manhattan route will be built across 48th Street. . . . It will distribute passengers from the new East Side LIRR terminal." There was a buried warning, though: these projects would "be funded when other monies become available."[66]

The money would never be available. Ronan appeared powerful, to be sure. In 1967, after the passage of the law creating the MTA, one source told the *Times* that the authority's structure—with control over vehicular bridges and tunnels as well as subways, buses, and commuter rail—would make "Moses look like a schoolboy with a small allowance."[67] In 1970, the *Times* used the moniker "wholly Ronan empire" to describe the MTA.[68] These readings were naïve. As Moses had known, the only guarantee of power—and not ironclad, as events had proven—was a quasi-independent source of funds.

The MTA had no such funds. The state's merger of transportation and transit offered only Triborough surpluses, nothing more—no taxes dedicated to transit. The transit system's deficits overwhelmed Triborough's surpluses, as Moses had predicted. The MTA, with Rockefeller facing reelection, remained under pressure to increase workforce compensation and thus increase costs. In 1968, the MTA's first year, the authority awarded a new benefit to the Transport Workers Union, half-pay retirement, at age fifty, after twenty years. A year later, the subway and bus portion of the MTA had a $120 million deficit, but only a $45 million Triborough surplus.

The new retirement benefit affected subway operations, as well, and for years to come, "as large numbers of skilled and knowledgeable employees left."[69] After the creation of this retroactive benefit, workforce turnover grew to above 10 percent, up from 3 percent.[70] With fewer skilled workers, maintenance deteriorated, harming ridership and further cutting revenue.

Another factor worked against a balanced MTA budget and against money for big projects. During the 1967 bond-act campaign, Ronan had promised to keep the subway fare low—just as many mayors had done. All through 1967, Rockefeller, Ronan, and the press—but not Moses—had characterized the creation of the MTA as a way of saving the by then-twenty-cent fare. The *New York Post* had called it "Rocky's Save-the-Fare Plan." Repeatedly, Ronan had gone on radio and television to say that the new law "offers assurance that the 20-cent fare can be maintained for a very considerable time, because . . . the surpluses from the Triborough Bridge & Tunnel Authority will become available."[71]

It was not to be. In the 1970s, the fare would rise to thirty cents, then thirty-five cents, then fifty cents. As with earlier hikes, they were too little, too late. In 1970, a third-party report said that the MTA's "costs are accelerating faster than the combined net rate of productivity and inflation. . . . The picture looks dismal." Absent promised progress—no Second Avenue Subway, no new LIRR terminal—voters no longer believed grand plans peddled by Rockefeller. They rejected a bond issue in 1971 and another in 1973. By 1974, the cost of Ronan's subway program had ballooned to $4.7 billion, four times the 1968 figure. The airport link to JFK Airport was delayed, as was the LIRR's East Midtown Terminal and the Second Avenue Subway.[72] Half a decade after the Triborough transit merger had supposedly saved transit, the MTA faced a nearly half-billion dollar deficit. A new mayor, Democrat Abe Beame, warned that "transit . . . is at the breaking point."[73]

Rather than serving as a vehicle for renewal, the MTA was a vehicle to deflect blame—from elected officials. "They put together the MTA to avoid responsibility," observes Andrew Cuomo, who served as New York's governor from 2011 to 2021. "We can blame anybody but nobody. . . . The trains suck, and they're always gonna be late. Let's come up with a political system where the MTA is to blame. Who is the MTA? Nobody is the MTA. Most people think it is the mayor."[74] Bill de Blasio, New York's mayor from 2014 to 2021, concurs: "The MTA was built as a subterfuge to get people from blaming the elected officials."[75]

Despite this political reality, the transit merger yielded early benefits. The MTA, with money from the bond act, refurbished the Long Island Rail Road, purchasing railcars and rebuilding track. These improvements prevented more suburban commuters from defecting to automobiles. The MTA started work on the East River tunnel to increase capacity for both subways and commuter rail—although the first connection enabled by that tunnel wasn't complete until the late 1980s. (The second connection, for commuter rail, opened in 2023, along with the east side terminal for the LIRR.)

In the 1970s, though, as derailments became common and trains were scarred with graffiti, transit ridership plummeted. Between 1971 and 1977, the number of people commuting daily to Manhattan by subway fell from nearly 1.8 million to 1.5 million. Though overall travel by any mode into Manhattan had peaked at a high of nearly 3.7 million daily in 1948 and fallen to 3.3 million by the mid-Sixties, some of the people deserting mass transit in the Fifties and Sixties had switched to private cars, with the number of people arriving by car, taxi, or truck instead of transit rising from 657,000 in 1948 to 941,000 by 1973. Even as it was emptier, Manhattan was also dirtier, thanks to this movement to inefficient vehicles spewing leaden emissions.

As the 1970s wore on, though, people stopped switching from transit to cars, in part because the streets could not fit more vehicles; the number of people entering Manhattan by motor vehicle stagnated at around 900,000.[76] By 1973, the number of people coming to Manhattan each day—whether by car, train, or bus—was barely three million; by 1977, it had fallen to 2.9 million, close to the Depression-era level.[77]

Saturated roads and barely functioning transit were other reasons to leave the city altogether. From 1970 to 1980, New York City would lose 800,000 residents, or 10 percent of its population. Between 1969 and 1976, New York would lose nearly 600,000 jobs, from peak twentieth-century employment of 3.8 million to 3.2 million.[78]

A Small Comfort

Lindsay, though he lost the fight to wrest control of Moses's Triborough and lost city control over subways to the state's MTA, did have one triumph: air-conditioned subways. Transit bureaucrats told him that it couldn't be done: the electricity needs were too great, the maintenance costs too high. Using remnants of the city's fiscal leverage over subways just before the creation of the MTA, though, Lindsay stuck to his campaign pledge and refused to approve city purchases of railcars without air conditioning. In September 1967, six months before the MTA took over, the city ran an air-conditioned train along the F line; as one passenger said, "Bless John Lindsay."[79] The *Daily News* noted that the air-conditioned cars would be "hugely expensive" but "worth it," as they would "make New York far more of a Fun City than silly 'happenings' in parks."[80] A more comfortable commute was the foundation of future decades of improvement to quality of life on transit and in the city. Lindsay knew that to compete with suburbs, New York had to offer not only commuting utility, but this tiniest of amenities.

In the Triborough Bridge and Tunnel Authority's final annual report, for 1967, Moses included a warning. He worked on it carefully: "Note also my closing paragraph," he directed staffers in one hand-marked draft. That paragraph read, "Triborough was reconstituted by Mayor LaGuardia in 1934 on the wreckage of ambitious plans of incompetent officials. . . . Triborough is a special, limited ad hoc agency under government auspices, financed by prudent private investors, thus far nonpolitical, a sound business run wholly in the public interest. It would be a great pity to undermine, destroy or tarnish these principles, obligations and traditions and entirely unnecessary in achieving more effective metropolitan transportation, an objective which we heartily endorse."[81] It would take nearly another decade and a half for New York to start recapitalizing transit.

Chapter 8

Nixon's Nudge

The Federal Laws That Forced a New Direction

It will be necessary to upgrade the existing transit system if that proportion of drivers who cannot tolerate that system today is to be made amenable.
—New York City Metropolitan Area Air Quality Implementation Plan, 1973

The transit system could be rebuilt into a modern metro that is safe, attractive, and comfortable. This, however, requires significantly increased funding.
—*A New Direction in Transit,* New York City Department of City Planning, 1978

THANKSGIVING 1966 BROUGHT to New York's streets Donald Duck, Elsie the Cow, Bullwinkle Moose, Smokey the Bear—and "a pall of smog." The temperature was an unseasonable sixty-five degrees, and "the hazy blanket" coated the million people who came to see Macy's parade.[1] With warm air rising, trapping cooler air, "chimneys from the [electricity] plants that . . . power . . . the products of urban society along with the exhaust from all the trucks, buses and automobiles that keep society moving began pouring their wastes into the unmoving air"—a "poison balloon."[2]

Three days of foul air trapped "lethal gases and smoke," including contaminants from leaded gasoline. Eyes stung and heads ached.[3] Mayor Lindsay's advice to New Yorkers during the smog emergency echoed what he had told the public during the transit strike eleven months earlier: people shouldn't drive unless "absolutely necessary."[4] Twice in Lindsay's first year, autos had proven an urban plague. Cold air pushed smog away, but the impact remained. A study found that 168 people had died.[5] The federal government ranked New York's air the nation's worst, and the *New York Times* called fixing it "a question of survival."[6]

New York eventually cleaned its air, but it didn't do so voluntarily. It took a federal law, the Clean Air Act, and a decade of creative wrangling on the part of more than half a dozen individuals from wildly different backgrounds to get New York to do the obvious, long after the creation of the MTA: stop ignoring the most efficient way for millions of people to move in a packed city: mass transit.

Doing Better

Once again, New Yorkers mobilized against the impact of cars and trucks on the quality of life in their city. Before, led by Jane Jacobs and her coalition, they had an intellectual underpinning for growing concerns about highways; this time, they had concerns about the environment.[7] In 1962, science writer Rachel Carson had published *Silent Spring*, which, describing wilderness bereft of birdsong, attuned the public to environmental distress.

Activists mobilized to save the urban environment. In the 1960s, Carolyn Konheim and Hazel Henderson were two young mothers on the Upper West Side. Konheim worked for her then-husband's garment company; Henderson was an emigrant from Britain, which had "a tradition that young people go on a trip around the world." After completing her journey, including a year in Bermuda, working at travel industry gigs all along the way, she landed in New York as a ticket agent for American Airlines. That work allowed her free flights, whereby she saw "all of the U.S.A." before marrying a U.S. citizen and settling in Manhattan.

Henderson and her husband had a daughter, and the urban family depended on parks. "The play park . . . would have soot all over it," she recalled. The soot reminded her of a similar problem that plagued her home country. "I have a clear memory of the great smog in London in 1952," she says, "where 4,000 people died unexpectedly in one week." Though Henderson grew up in Bristol, "[her] parents happened to be in London . . . and . . . couldn't even see across their hotel room." Henderson, an "autodidact" who had never gone to college, learned that New York's pollution came from three sources: coal-fired power plants; cars and trucks; and, finally, "every little brownstone house had its own incinerator, which kind of cooked the garbage."[8]

Just as Shirley Hayes and fellow mothers had once discussed a highway through the park while minding their children, Henderson and Konheim discussed soot. They, too, decided to act. They talked with their city councilman, Robert Low, who gave them a corner in his office to start a citizens' organization. "Quite quickly, we ended up with block captains in all five boroughs [of New York]."[9]

In 1964, Konheim and Henderson called their outfit Citizens for Clean Air (CCA), spearheading a movement to get people and government to think about pollution as an everyday problem. People watched the weather report on television; pollution should be part of the report, they determined. "I spent time mostly typing out stuff on my typewriter in my bedroom," says Henderson, to convince television networks to publish a new index: air quality. At the time, reporting on air quality was "primitive." Meteorologists would put a piece of gauze up and see how much soot it had collected. "We should be able to do better," Henderson thought. "We might . . . get people to pay attention."

Henderson wrote a letter to Newton Minow, recently retired chair of the Federal Communications Commission and the networks' regulator, famous for having called television a "vast wasteland." Henderson wondered about reporting on air quality: "Isn't it in the public interest?" Minow agreed. She wrote to television stations. In 1964, Theodore H. Walworth Jr., vice president of WNBC, a New York local outlet, responded to "Mrs. Carter F. Henderson," the name she used in correspondence, to say he was taking up her idea. "We will shortly begin to include daily air pollution reports."[10] Other networks followed. Starting in the late 1960s, pollution became an everyday concern for television viewers.

As early antipollution activists, CCA's leaders became useful to government officials. Shortly after they began their work, Lindsay won the mayoralty, in part on an environmental platform. "Our polluted air is making New York an increasingly ugly, expensive, unhealthy, and depressing place," Lindsay had said during the 1965 campaign.[11] In office, he contacted Norman Cousins, editor of the *Saturday Review* magazine, and asked him to set up an air-pollution task force. Upon hearing of the appointment, says Henderson, "I immediately contacted Norman Cousins, and said, 'we at Citizens for Clean Air have done much of this.'"

Buoyed by city interest, CCA launched an advertising campaign. "I remember going up and down Madison Avenue, being thrown out of the offices [after asking advertising creators to work for free]," Henderson recalls. She'd almost given up when she reached a Third Avenue agency run by Carl Ally, whose ads had helped make start-up companies challenging incumbent corporations, such as package courier Federal Express and long-distance telephone provider MCI, into well-known brands.[12] Ally worked on the seventeenth floor. From his window, Henderson pointed out smokestacks emitting coal waste. Ally had a chronic sinus condition, and Henderson recalls him saying, "Oh my God, I had no idea [that it could be related to pollution]." His firm created five sixty-second television spots, as well as five radio spots and five print ads. They were trademark Ally advertising, featuring sarcastic humor. "Tomorrow morning when you get up," read one, "take a nice deep breath. It'll make you feel rotten." The photo was of a woman opening her apartment window, engulfed in a black cloud.

Henderson and Ally brought mock-ups to Cousins. Henderson recalls, "[Cousins] picks up the phone, calls up the biggest advertising mogul, Bill Bernbach . . . [and] says, 'can you make time for me to bring over a couple of people?'" The group trooped over and convinced Bernbach. "It would really help us," Henderson suggested, "[to] ask the *New York Times*, next time they run a Volkswagen ad, run one of our ads." Using the same pitch on other executives, "[Henderson and Konheim] got about five million dollars of free advertising." In 1966, the publicity attracted NBC's national *Today* show, whose cohost, Hugh Downs, gave Henderson nine minutes, including airing all five commercials.

Partly because New York was the nation's media capital, protecting the environment became a national issue. In a 1967 address, President Lyndon B. Johnson cited New York: "Two months ago, a mass of heavily polluted air—filled with poisons from incinerators, industrial furnaces, power plants, car, bus and truck engines—settled down upon the 16 million people of Greater New York. For four days, anyone going out on the streets inhaled chemical compounds." The return to "ordinary air" was no cure, the president added: "'Ordinary' air in New York . . . is filled with tons of pollutants." Johnson had strengthened an early version of the Clean Air Act to regulate pollution four years earlier, in 1963, a month after he took office upon JFK's assassination. Yet the public saw few results.[13]

Alarm grew. In summer 1967, black clouds obscured the river views from Robert Moses's Henry Hudson Bridge.[14] In 1969, oil gushed off California's Santa Barbara coast, slicking birds and seals. Air-quality alerts became frequent—as did the citizenry's noting of real-life detritus. "I remember . . . the window sills would be white in the morning . . . [but] you would come back at the end of the day, they would be gray," remembers David Schoenbrod, who was a young lawyer living, like Henderson, on Manhattan's Upper West Side.[15]

A Law with a Difference

New York got an unlikely savior: President Richard M. Nixon. On the first day of 1970, the president gave a speech from the western White House, in San Clemente, three hours south of Santa Barbara's oil spill. "The 1970s absolutely must be the years when America pays its debt to the past by reclaiming the purity of its air, its waters and our living environment," he told the public.[16] Three months later, he and the First Lady, Pat, planted a tree on the White House lawn to celebrate the nation's first Earth Day. That summer, Nixon created the Environmental Protection Agency (EPA). On New Year's Eve, the Republican signed into law the updated Clean Air Act. "The problem of automobile pollution," he said, "is one that not only now plagues my native area of southern California but all the great cities." Praising the bipartisan congressional vote, the president vowed, "Now comes the enforcement."[17]

What set the Clean Air Act apart from predecessor laws was compliance. The EPA would set limits on emissions from sources such as cars and trucks. The EPA also would set air quality standards for states. But Washington would not dictate how states would achieve the standards. Instead, states would prepare "implementation plans" setting out steps, such as discouraging auto use, for Washington's approval. Each state would execute the plan it had designed, meeting a 1975 deadline.[18]

The most important provision was private civil action. That is, the federal government was not the only entity that could push states to comply. As the EPA explained, "Any person may file a civil action against any person . . . for violations of emission standards."[19] If the EPA didn't do its job, people could sue. This provision would usher in an era of environmental entrepreneurism altering New York transportation history.

A White Paper with Teeth

Few New Yorkers would have considered 1973 salutary. After eight years, John Lindsay would leave office that December. Gone was his 1965 optimism and his campaign ads that promised "a new kind of hope." New York elected Abe Beame, previously the city's chief accountant. Beame had no vision; his campaign slogan, amid worries about New York's budget, was that he "knows the buck."

Lindsay had tried, but he hadn't fixed New York. The murder level stalled near the previous year's then-record high—1,680 killings, triple the 548 in 1963.[20] After the 1960s boom, the economy had stalled out: New

York lost 258,000 of its nearly 3.8 million jobs between 1969 and 1974, with both Manhattan and the outer boroughs suffering decline. Hundreds of thousands of people with skills, experience, education, or ambition followed jobs out of town.

Lindsay's final days were marked by irony to bookmark the transit crisis that had marked his first days: the Arab oil embargo. To conserve energy, Lindsay cut the top speed on city highways from fifty-five to fifty miles an hour and asked office-building managers to set winter temperatures at sixty-eight degrees. He implored drivers to take public transportation.[21] Lindsay's administration was going out the way it came in: whether because of a local transit strike, regional smog, or a global energy crisis, the urban answer was never the automobile.

In spring 1973, though, New York would do something that would set the course of four decades of transportation history. That April, to comply with the three-year-old Clean Air Act, Governor Nelson Rockefeller, with Lindsay's cooperation, sent to the federal government's EPA a dense, 352-page document titled, "New York City Metropolitan Air Quality Implementation Plan Transportation Controls." The document was too technical—its subtitle was "carbon monoxide, hydrocarbons, oxidants, nitrogen dioxide"—to garner attention. The *Times* offered it two columns of coverage—on page ninety-four. "Rockefeller sent the Federal Government yesterday a plan for meeting clean-air standards in New York City by 1975, but he said he did not intend to implement one of the key tactics," the paper reported, not explaining this contradiction.[22] "Nobody looked at it," says the report's author, Brian Ketcham, the anti-car fanatic.[23] That disinterest was because few people understood that the report's measures weren't suggestions. The report was a binding contract for New York's future.

In preparing the report, Ketcham held back nothing. "The legal basis of this plan is quite clear," the report said. "It is directed to carrying out the Congressional mandate of the Clean Air Act—to achieve and maintain air quality standards . . . no later than May 31, 1975." One of the biggest culprits of bad air was carbon monoxide. Cars and trucks emitted 95 percent of the city's carbon monoxide, and that problem was concentrated in Manhattan. Manhattan's narrow streets trapped the poison. Slow-moving traffic made the problem worse, as engines were less efficient at slower speeds. New federal rules on vehicle emissions, implemented in part as a result of Ketcham's earlier work with the catalytic converter, would improve air quality. Yet technology wouldn't be enough. Many older cars would remain on the roads.

The city thus would have to reduce driving. But it couldn't do much about trucks in the short term. With West Side dock activity moving to New Jersey, shippers had to move cargo into Manhattan. Moreover, trucks were only 12 percent of traffic. With the city losing manufacturing jobs, the number of trucks entering Manhattan had fallen by 21 percent between 1963 and 1971.

The problem was cars. "It will be necessary to restrict the entry and operation of vehicles on the island of Manhattan," Ketcham's report found. New York would have to reduce the supply of streets, either by prohibiting people from driving or parking or by charging drivers to do so—that is, "physical or extreme economic constraints, or both."[24]

The report laid out half a dozen strategies. Because drivers wouldn't come to Manhattan if they had no place to park, the report prescribed enforcing laws against parking—40 percent of vehicles were parked illegally—and reducing the number of legal spaces. The city would have to reduce Manhattan parking spaces by 30 to 40 percent, including a "complete ban on on-street parking south of 60th Street . . . during the business day." Since "the solitary automobile driver occupies far more of the public road than does his fellow taxpayer in the bus," the city should build bus-only lanes, the report counseled. Finally, the city should reduce the supply of free road space into Manhattan. It could do so by charging a toll on major bridges such as the Brooklyn Bridge and other spans leading over the East River from Brooklyn and Queens into Manhattan. These bridges, because they predated the era of the toll-funded public authority, were free.

The other strategy was to reduce demand for roads by rebuilding subways and buses. "The roads would be intolerably congested if not for . . . mass transit." A subway could carry nearly 2,000 people; forty automobiles could carry just 200 people, but they didn't, as most cars carried just the driver. "A relatively small percentage of transit ridership lost to automobiles translates into an inordinately large amount of additional vehicular congestion."

Rebuilding transit, after decades of neglect, would cost money beyond the toll subsidies that Triborough's bridges and tunnels were providing. Ketcham's report estimated—presciently—that the cost would be $16.4 billion over two decades, "substantially above past levels." But this investment was unavoidable. "The state of the municipal subways is a disgrace," the *Times* had concluded in 1970 after a train crash had killed two people, the first fatal incident since 1928.[25] None of the efforts to reduce traffic would work, unless the state and city gave commuters an alternative, the report said: "Make the subways attractive enough to induce people out of cars."

The prescriptions became law. When the governor, with the mayor's agreement, sent the report to the EPA for acceptance, the state and city would have the duty to implement them. Were these strategies to fail, the report offered one "contingency" strategy: "the banning of private automobiles in the central business district," even though it would be "very costly," the report concluded. (The paper also had nonbinding, fanciful ideas. It suggested that the city create "auto-free pedestrian zones," as well as "perhaps even bike lanes," something that wouldn't happen on a large scale until after 2000. It also suggested using "communications systems as a total substitute for transportation," thereby "enabling a significant number of white-collar workers to work at home," something that wouldn't happen until half a century later, during the 2020 pandemic.)

Ketcham knew that many of these strategies would antagonize powerful interests—including "the very powerful New York Automobile Club," which had backed Moses less than a decade earlier in his fight to keep Triborough—as well as taxi medallion and truck owners, drivers, and factories and stores. To neutralize criticism, he had made sure that everyone had input into the report. "We started with a major survey of anyone who might be affected," Ketcham recalled. "Every ox got gored." State and city government's approach to avoiding antagonism was different: delay implementation as long as possible.

Citizen Groups Are Not Nuisances

Exit Ketcham, the engineer; enter the lawyers. David Schoenbrod, Chicago native and recent Yale Law School graduate, had moved to New York City to do what many such young people wanted to do: use their education to help the less fortunate. Initially, he worked at the Bedford-Stuyvesant Restoration Corporation, an initiative of Senator Robert F. Kennedy and Mayor Lindsay to revive the distressed Brooklyn neighborhood. Schoenbrod was studying how "the government provided services in ways that were unfair to minorities and the poor," he says.[26]

Schoenbrod saw the subway as one of those services. As the middle class left, poorer minorities "had a worse time on the subway," hostage to worsening service. As the state-controlled MTA scrimped on maintenance, one affliction was noise—deafening screeches. The problem was dented wheels and wouldn't cost much to fix—a "trivial" expenditure compared to the damage that wheels were doing to tracks.

Schoenbrod could soon do something. In 1972, he took a job at the Natural Resources Defense Council (NRDC), founded by recent Yale Law School grads to use the legal system to protect the environment. "I was elated," he says. "I could sue the government." The first attempt was a legal failure. In 1974, Schoenbrod represented citizens harmed by subway noise as well as Bronx borough president Robert Abrams in their lawsuit against the MTA, charging that the state should reduce the noise.[27] The state's high court dismissed the suit, saying that the courts should leave fiscal decisions to elected officials.[28] Yet the case got attention, and after the MTA won, it secured a federal grant to reduce noise.

By then, Schoenbrod had a new colleague, Ross Sandler. Sandler had started his environmental law career at the United States Attorney's office in New York, where he resurrected an 1899 criminal statute prohibiting the discharge of pollutants into the Hudson River without a permit. The prosecutions Sandler launched were successful, but in 1972, Congress passed a new law, the Clean Water Act, giving responsibility for water discharge to the EPA. Now, he wanted to pursue a new field, one that he would help invent, "urban environmental litigation." Schoenbrod and Sandler fixated on poor transit as behind New York's auto-pollution woes. "The city couldn't survive unless the transit system was fixed," Schoenbrod says.

On the second try, the NRDC found footing: the Clean Air Act and its provision for private action. In 1975, the deadline by which the state and city were supposed to have implemented Ketcham's plan would pass. Rather than proving the state should spend money to reduce subway noise, the NRDC could make a straightforward case: alleging that the state had not done what it had legally promised to do to meet federal air quality standards. The NRDC sued to force the EPA to compel the state to implement its plan. "If we waited," says Schoenbrod, "that would have suggested to the courts and public opinion that we didn't think it was very important."

It had become clear that the city would not fulfill its Clean Air Act obligations voluntarily. Beame became a one-man obfuscation front, refusing to implement the compliance plan his predecessor had approved. To Beame, it was another headache among many, from the city's fiscal crisis to crime. By 1975, New York City was close to bankrupt, as tax revenues couldn't keep up with spending; it would spend that year seeking—ultimately successfully—a state and federal bailout.

As he grappled with insolvency, Beame said the transportation control plan would do "serious harm to the city's economy."[29] Daytime restrictions on Manhattan parking, for example, "would adversely affect every kind of business."[30] Tolls, taxi-cruising limits, and delivery restrictions would harm a city "struggling for economic survival."[31] Well past deadlines, he kept revising the plan. The modest steps Beame did take to reduce car usage encountered opposition. In April, the city attempted to put a bus-only lane along Queens Boulevard. Businesses complained, saying it would "cripple sales."

In delaying Clean Air Act measures, the mayor did not initially have elite opinion on his side. In October, the *Times*—having finally forsaken its support of highways—called Beame's complaints "fallacious, based on a misconception of the role of the automobile in a congested modern metropolis."[32] Complainers, the paper noted, were not the majority, and most patrons of local businesses arrived via transit. "The private car is not—and could not possibly become—the principal mode of conveyance in New York."

The *Times* was also advancing the issue beyond pollution to quality of life, something pioneers such as Hayes had understood two decades before. In May, the paper pointed out that "motor vehicles—some 25,000 per square mile in downtown Manhattan during peak hours—are responsible for one-half of all street noise and usurp 37 per cent of the land area of the central business district." A year later, the paper urged Beame and Governor Hugh Carey, who had succeeded Rockefeller, to stop fighting the federal government and "move forward."[33]

They would have to, it seemed—as Schoenbrod and Sandler triumphed in court. Although a district court ruled against them, the appeals court handed down a "stunning victory" in April 1976. Judge Walter Mansfield ruled that the Clean Air Act was working as intended. In devising the act, "Congress made clear that citizen groups are not to be treated as nuisances or troublemakers, but rather as welcomed participants," Mansfield wrote.[34] Schoenbrod and Sandler told the press, "This decision is of national importance because it recognizes that citizens can take legal action to force government officials to protect their health." By summer 1977, even as he looked to the Supreme Court for a rescue, Beame had no choice but to implement the Lindsay-era plan. The federal district judge said that further delay would put a "premium on inaction."[35]

Beame had lost in court—but hadn't wasted his time. He had turned public opinion to his side, not on the merits but out of exhaustion. Summer 1977 wasn't a good one for New York. That July, a two-day blackout spurred looting, with fifty-five fires in Bed-Stuy alone, a contrast from a similar blackout a decade before, during which New Yorkers had come together. The same month, the "Son of Sam" killer, a Yonkers man who targeted young women in Queens and Brooklyn, would kill his sixth and final victim.

Beame added to the aura of ungovernable chaos. That June, he had said, in trying to avoid implementing the Manhattan parking restrictions called for in the Clean Air Act plan, "we have a plan that will accomplish the same objective." His environmental administrator contradicted him, saying, "I don't have a plan." As Beame began enforcing parking restrictions, he did so only under protest, a self-proclaimed "reluctant" participant, and predicted that the restraints would turn New York into a "ghost town."

Beame interpreted the need to restrict parking under the city's Clean Air Act agreement in the most onerous light, hooding 206 parking meters in Midtown for twenty-four hours a day rather than just during the rush-hour times the plan had required. "A motorist coming into Manhattan now won't find a legal parking space," a city spokesperson warned[36]—although, with double-parking and other violations rampant, that was true before the new rules. "About 99 percent of the parking in the affected area was already illegal," Schoenbrod said at the time. Beame had "distort[ed] the meaning of the parking-limitation program," wrote *Times* columnist John Oakes, to scare New Yorkers rather than help them accept change. It was everything that was wrong with Beame's administration: "failure to move innovatively if at all; unwillingness to discommode a few New Yorkers for the benefit of the many; and refusal to take any political risk." The editorial board concurred, noting that "just as Mayor Beame planned it, merchants are angry and the public is disoriented."[37] Beame's strategy of disorder was working.

As if the situation weren't tumultuous enough, Congress reinvolved itself. State and local politicians weren't the only elected officials suddenly surprised at the scope of the Clean Air Act when it came time for action, not rhetoric. So were the city's representatives. The city, under Lindsay, had committed to tolling the free East River bridges—and now the federal judge was going to force Beame to do it. Two members of the city's Congressional delegation, Senator Daniel Patrick Moynihan and Congresswoman Elizabeth Holtzman of Brooklyn, were self-professedly stunned to learn that the federal government could force New York City to impose tolls. At their request, in amending the Clean Air Act that year to extend some deadlines by a decade, Congress passed bills to forbid the EPA from requiring bridge tolls—as long as the state found an alternative source of transit funds.

Holtzman says that she acted not under pressure from Beame, but independently, according to constituents' wishes and with the support of the Queens and Brooklyn congressional delegation. Indeed, after the judge had issued his February order, fifteen congressional representatives from the Bronx, Brooklyn, and Queens had stood on the Brooklyn Bridge, issuing a statement that tolls would "divide the city . . . middle-income families from the Bronx, Queens and Brooklyn would be discouraged from coming to Manhattan."[38] "It wasn't just bad for Brooklyn," Holtzman recalls. "It was bad for [all] the outer boroughs. It would have created a pollution problem wherever they put the toll booths, with more traffic backed up."[39]

From Litigants to Allies

The NRDC lawyers kept winning in court. In October 1977, the U.S. Supreme Court refused to consider the case.[40] Yet the lawyers might lose on the ground, as Congress's amendment abolishing the bridge toll agreement made clear. Sandler and Schoenbrod understood that managing traffic and rebuilding New York's transit system by federal court order was untenable. "The Clean Air Act is a very flawed law," says Sandler. "The federal government orders you to meet our standards, but you have to figure out how to do it. The grand principle of the Clean Air Act was the federal government gets all the credit and the states get all the blame." Another half-decade of forcing the mayor of a near-bankrupt city to carry out a predecessor's traffic-management plan under constant protest was unlikely to yield results.

It was time for collaboration. "We don't want to sit around and fight," Schoenbrod told the press.[41] In late August, as the city emerged from that worst summer in memory and prepared to elect a new mayor, the NRDC and New York compromised. "The governor's and mayor's people told Ross Sandler and me . . . 'you won, so tell us what we have to do,'" recalled Schoenbrod. To drivers' relief, "hoods will be removed from 206 parking meters in midtown, and parking will be permitted there after 6 P.M. Parking at 871 downtown meters will be banned only between 8 and 9 A.M.," the *Times* reported.[42] Instead of removing legal parking, the city would create bus lanes and crack down on illegal parking. The *Times* pronounced it an "encouraging armistice," noting that the "Natural Resources Defense Council, distressed at the Mayor's success in portraying them as environmental madmen bent on wrecking the economy, gave the package their blessing."[43]

The most important provision was transit. "Our real interest was the public transit system," says Sandler. "The system was really falling apart . . . [with] doors failing, lights out."[44] Since the state had created the MTA in 1968, it had never enacted revenue sources for it. The transit system had deteriorated just since Schoenbrod and Sandler had begun their quest. To paper over city deficits, Beame had borrowed $300 million in funds that were supposed to go to the subway and bus system. During the city fiscal crisis, which reached its nadir in 1975, the MTA had cut inspections of subway cars from every three months to four. More doors were breaking. The MTA had reduced picking up litter, inviting track fires that delayed trains. Transit managers had cut cleaners and painters, allowing graffiti to pile on graffiti.[45]

As part of the new agreement among the state, the city, and NRDC, the MTA agreed to accelerate modest improvements. It would speed up contracts for its ten-year, $62.5 million noise reduction program, spending seven years' worth of money in four years. As the entrepreneurial lawyers looked toward longer-term goals, New York's congressional delegation had given them a new tool: the requirement, in their 1977 amendment of the Clean Air Act removing bridge tolls, that the state must find other money for transit.

Averting New York's Doom

By 1978, New York had a new mayor. Edward I. Koch ran on a platform of undiplomatic change. "After eight years of charisma," he said, referring to Lindsay, and "four years of the clubhouse," referring to Beame's tenure in Democratic politics, "why not try competence?" Koch was an effective cheerleader, his "how my doin'?" street presence buoying depressed residents.

Koch knew, too, that for New York to flourish, it would need to rebuild transit. A resident of Greenwich Village and supporter of Shirley Hayes's quest to get vehicles out of Washington Square, he understood that New York could never become a car-dependent city. In 1971, as a Manhattan congressman, he had surveyed Fortune 500 companies to find out why executives were leaving; inadequate transit was one of the three top reasons (along with crime and costs).[46] Like Lindsay, he took a keen interest in the transit system. But unlike Lindsay, who had wanted to re-envision transit, Koch's goal was to achieve progress within the confines of New York politics.

Koch could do little directly. The city, because of its fiscal difficulties, remained under state receivership, with an unelected board of financiers signing off on budget decisions, as the price of its 1975 bailout. The city couldn't raise taxes; only the state legislature could approve most levies. New York City, then, had no money to contribute to the state-run MTA.

Koch was a shrewd politician, though—and one of his first acts was to withhold his support for Westway, the ill-fated underground West Side highway, in return for a pledge from the governor, Carey, to avoid yet another subway-fare hike. Although New York had refused to raise the subway fare for the first half century, it had more than made up for it by the late 1970s. The fare, by then fifty cents, had more than doubled over a decade. If the fare had kept up with inflation since the early 1900s, it would have reached only thirty-three cents. Every time the MTA raised the fare, it lost riders.

Koch took an equally shrewd step during his early months: commission a report. Unlike the old Triborough Authority, the MTA, because it could not fund itself out of its own fare and toll revenues, was not independent enough to advocate for itself; it needed elected officials to do so. After Koch took office, Sandler and Schoenbrod went to the head of the city's planning commission, Bobby Wagner. A lifelong New Yorker, son of a mayor and grandson of a senator, Wagner, a student of urban density, knew that density wouldn't work without transit.

The Koch administration and the environmental lawyers made a deal: "The city and state would supply the real facts about the transit system, and we would supply the rhetorical skills that we had previously used against them," said Schoenbrod. "Working with the city and state traffic and transit officials rather than against them . . . created mutual respect." The *Times* noted the dual role, reporting that "two lawyers are helping to prepare a study of mass transit" for the city. "In another role, they [have sued] the city over clean-air standards."[47] Though MTA leadership was wary of publicly advocating for more funding, mid-level experts within the transit authority were eager for improvement and provided information behind the scenes.

The result: a mod-looking silver-and-blue glossy report, "A New Direction in Transit," released in December 1978. As the report noted, "never before had the city . . . made a comprehensive, in-depth assessment of the condition of the existing transit system and prescribed the work necessary for its rehabilitation." The report made a doomsday case: cities without transit were unlivable. "Cities around the world are increasing their reliance upon transit because the automobile detracts from rather than supports the density needed to encourage economic and cultural diversity and growth . . . deterioration of transit implies a deterioration of the city," it said. "A collapse of rail transit would spell New York's doom." Yet "the system is depreciating nearly three times faster than it is being restored."

The report also presented an optimistic case. Even in its straitened state, the nearly eighty-year-old subway was something to be proud of. Subways carried 3.5 million people daily, ten times as high as any other American city, surpassed only by Moscow and Tokyo. Transit was not a lost cause; migration to cars could be reversed. Contrary to the myth that "nothing can be done to increase transit ridership," riders would respond to "quality, convenience, and cost." Better service would attract users and increase fare revenues. A new pedestrian tunnel connecting two subway lines under Bryant Park, one of the only improvements in years, had attracted customers.

The report made practical suggestions. It inventoried the state of buses, train cars, tracks, tunnels, ventilation, power systems, stations, signals, and the like. It also listed priorities, something the MTA had never done. Improving the existing system should take precedence over building train lines, contrary to Rockefeller-era grand plans. The MTA should change fare policies, too, allowing for transfers between subways and buses. It should raise the fare with inflation rather than in double-digit amounts after long freezes.

One priority was cleanliness. Trains covered in graffiti gave the impression that "no one cares," making people nervous. People were deterred, according to a 1978 poll, by "dirty conditions, overcrowding, fear of crime, and the overall appearance." Warned the report, "Filth, litter, breakage, graffiti, and noise combine to produce an atmosphere of degradation and fear."

The conclusion: the MTA needed $523 million a year, over ten years, for a total of $5.2 billion. With fares covering only $700 million of the MTA's $1.4 billion in operating costs and the Triborough Bridge and Tunnel Authority surplus providing only $70 million, the MTA needed a predictable source of revenue rather than watching the state and city promise money but diverting these funds to the city's day-to-day budget.

New Directions was "the first attempt to actually have a capital plan," says Schoenbrod: a long-term schedule, rather than panics and short-term fixes. Koch ensured that it got attention. The mayor, "in shirtsleeves, stood in the Blue Room at City Hall" pointing at the report's charts.[48] Editorial boards endorsed it. Sandler and Schoenbrod wrote an op-ed to remind *Times* readers that "inadequate transit has played a substantial role in the exodus of jobs. . . . [The] transit system can spur an economic revival."[49] The transit system now had a federal court order requiring the state and city to fund it—and a plan for that funding. The task was to secure money.

Chapter 9

The Lion of the MTA

The Push to Rebuild New York's Transit

Frosted commuters are stomping around packed platforms in anger and despair at what was once the greatest mass-transit system in the world.

—Robert Rickles and Harold Holzer, *New York Magazine*, February 1, 1982

I did what any rational human being would do.

—Richard Ravitch, former MTA chairman, 2020

AT 4:30 A.M. ONE SUMMER MORNING IN 1981, Alan Greenberg, chief executive of the Bear Stearns investment bank, Dick Shinn, chairman of MetLife insurance, and Bill Ellinghaus, president of AT&T, gathered on a subway platform for a VIP tour of the sweltering, decrepit New York transit system. Richard Ravitch, a titan of the city's residential real estate industry and the chairman of the thirteen-year-old Metropolitan Transportation Authority (MTA), had summoned the executives. "None of them, I suspected, had ridden a New York City subway recently," Ravitch recalled.[1] Ravitch realized that the chauffeured class had to see for themselves the conditions that their employees, vendors, and customers endured so that they would support the necessary government reinvestment in subways and buses to secure New York's future. By the end of the next year, New York's legislature and governor had approved a slew of taxes to fund what became a multi-billion-dollar, multi-decade project to repair and replace the subway tracks, trains, and signals, buy new buses, and get New York moving again.

New York's decision to reinvigorate the public-sector infrastructure that underpins its private-sector economy is one of the most successful government and business stories of the late twentieth and early twenty-first centuries. Comparatively few billions of dollars helped the city thrive, reemerging from the failures of the automobile age. Over nearly four decades, beginning in the 1980s, functional subways became the foundation of a record number of private-sector jobs without an attendant increase in traffic—and later gave New York City the flexibility it needed to convert hundreds of miles of street space for buses, bicycles, and pedestrians.

A Political Junkie

Ravitch was a rare creature for the 1970s: a businessman bullish about the future of his hometown. Born and raised on the Upper West Side—on the block where the Macy's Thanksgiving Day Parade blows up its balloons—he had left the city for one year, attending college in Ohio to "meet real people." He preferred New Yorkers and returned home to Columbia University. At his family construction business, undeterred by the fact that middle-class New Yorkers were fleeing the urban hub, he spent the early 1970s building thousands of apartments for such New Yorkers, from Waterside Plaza on Manhattan's East Side to Manhattan Plaza west of Times Square, helping preserve the city's population. Such construction depended on tax credits, so Ravitch was familiar with how New York State and New York City governments worked.

In 1975, the new governor, Hugh Carey, was in his fourteenth week in office, and he had a crisis: a state entity had defaulted on one hundred million dollars in bonds. The Urban Development Corporation (UDC), like the MTA, was a creation of Nelson Rockefeller; after the 1968 murder of Dr. Martin Luther King Jr., Rockefeller had created the UDC to make two billion dollars in low-income housing investments. Ravitch was familiar with the UDC, as he had considered working alongside it on one project but determined that its numbers were "fraudulent."

Carey, like Ravitch, was an unusual being: a politician who didn't owe much to interest groups. A Brooklyn native and heir to a modest oil fortune, Carey had earned a Bronze Star in Europe in World War II. He had grown bored with the family business and ran for Congress in 1960 in a "hopeless" campaign against an incumbent Republican. He won—and didn't have political debts, as few established Democrats had supported him. The next decade, he was to see tragedy: two sons died in a car crash, and shortly thereafter, his wife died. Months after his wife passed away, he ran for the governorship. With voters upset about Nixon's scandals, he won. He inherited a mess, with New York City threatening to follow the UDC into default. Without owing favors to anyone and "free of egotism," he turned to experts.[2]

Carey asked Ravitch to sort out the UDC mess. Ravitch was a natural fixer. He understood not just numbers but people. In the days before cell phones, he would sit at his desk and juggle phone calls, importuning in-person visitors to wait. In between calls, he would conduct conversations in his gravelly voice, interspersing observations about the Metropolitan Opera's latest performance with gossip about who might win which election and which government budget was the most in distress. "I love politics," he said.[3] Ravitch talked to everyone and listened to everyone. He always had a "huge team" of advisers, recalled attorney Steven Polan, a longtime aide, and "all of those people had other jobs."[4] Ravitch had a knack for identifying key elected officials and picking one of those elected officials' staffers to talk to, starting at the bottom to earn trust at the top. "Dick was a force of nature," Polan said. Taking over the UDC chairmanship, Ravitch staved off the agency's lenders as he restructured its finances.

Thanks to this work, Carey knew whom to call when, in 1979, the chairman of the MTA, Harold Fisher, resigned. Only the MTA's second chairman after Ronan, Fisher was a pragmatic Democrat, a lawyer who served as counsel to the assembly speaker in the 1960s. But he had no power base to achieve much for the MTA. "Fisher's unwritten first year assignment from the governor was to keep the MTA out of the news," Andrew Sidamon-Eristoff, a public-finance expert, wrote.[5]

Ravitch would take over. "I agonized over whether or not I should—I knew being chairman of the MTA . . . was incompatible with continuing to run my business," Ravitch remembered. "Business was lousy in '79. I decided that being chairman of the MTA would be more rewarding. . . . So, I made a deal to sell my business."[6] At a news conference in mid-October, preteen son in tow, the forty-six-year-old Ravitch said he'd take the job. "I take the subway at least twice a day," he said, something the *New York Times* observed made him "rare" among government officials.

An Independent Man

Ravitch represented a departure from MTA practice on the day of his appointment. A reporter asked Ravitch the perennial question: would he raise the fare? "I can't give you an answer to that question until I understand what the projected deficit will be," he said.[7] To emphasize the point, Ravitch asked one of his Democratic friends to ask at his state senate confirmation hearing whether the fare would go up. His friend responded, "Dick, we wouldn't want to embarrass you." But Ravitch insisted. The lawmaker asked at the hearing, "Are there any circumstances under which you would raise the fare?" And Ravitch responded, "of course, if I didn't have enough money."[8]

For the MTA, Ravitch's answer was a revolution. The MTA chairperson was supposed to be independent of the governor who appointed him. Under the 1967 law creating the authority, the chair held a six-year term, just as Moses had done at the Triborough Authority. That way, a governor couldn't fire an MTA chairperson who went against his wishes. But what was straightforward on paper was difficult in practice. "The MTA is not a textbook example of an autonomous public authority formed to combine the advantages of private management structures and revenue-based financing with the power of regular government agencies," writes Sidamon-Eristoff, because, unlike Triborough under Moses, it does not earn a surplus out of its revenues and thus depends on government subsidy and the favor of elected officials.

Previous MTA chairmen had been reluctant to antagonize a governor—and Ravitch's move might antagonize Carey. Carey had already pledged to Koch to freeze the fare and had reaffirmed the promise in 1979.[9] Ravitch, in saying that the MTA might not let the governor keep that pledge, was saying that he would be an independent chairperson, advocating for transit, not for any political patron. "A couple of days later," Ravitch recalled, "Carey calls me, says, 'come over to the mansion for a drink.' He said, 'thank God you bailed me out.'" Ravitch had wanted the question asked so that he could make it clear: the MTA board, not the governor, was responsible for fare increases. Ravitch also said that he would work for free, another signal. If he didn't have the freedom to carry out his mission, he could leave. "Carey didn't interfere," said Ravitch.

Ravitch signaled that his priorities would be different. Unlike his predecessors, he would not ignore the decline of the MTA's assets. At that same 1979 news conference, he noted that "the immediate problem is obviously the financial problem. The long-term problem is . . . to improve the physical infrastructure."[10] No more ribbon cuttings for projects that the MTA would never finish, such as the Second Avenue Subway, to please an elected official who wanted voters to identify him with a flashy new but never opened line. "Nelson [Rockefeller] spent money building [or not building] the Second Avenue Subway rather than fixing what was there," recalled Ravitch.[11]

A month after taking over, Ravitch leveled with the public: against an operating budget of $1.8 billion, more than double the budget of less than a decade earlier, the MTA would face a $200 million deficit, even before a round of labor negotiations. Voters had just approved a $500 million bond issue for transit, a signal that they wanted better subways and buses, but it would not be enough.

The answer Ravitch suggested: rather than depend on inconsistent subsidies from state and city government and rather than raise fares so high that they would drive away more riders, the MTA should receive its own tax revenues. That is, the state legislature should enact taxes that would consistently go to the MTA each year.[12] This idea was not new, but no appointee had laid it out publicly. For his bluntness, he won praise: The *Times* marveled, "Ravitch is taking full advantage of his honeymoon in office by asking himself and the public the right question: How shall the authority's perennial, growing operating deficit be eliminated?"[13]

Global events bolstered Ravitch's argument. New York grappled with a new oil crisis, a repeat of 1973. This time, revolutionary Iran had cut off supplies. The oil price nearly tripled, and consumer distress pointed up Americans' dependence on the automobile. Motorists had to wait a day to purchase gas according to whether their license plate ended in an odd or even number.[14] For the first time in two decades, New York's transit ridership stabilized and even grew slightly.

In February 1980, Carey unveiled his proposal to the legislature, upon Ravitch's advice: three gas-related levies, including a tax on petroleum companies' sales and a two-cents-a-gallon surcharge at the pump. The third tax was novel: a tax that would be a percentage of the price per gallon of gasoline, rather than a flat tax, thus having a natural index to inflation. (As the price of gas rose, the tax would rise.) The proposals continued the philosophy behind the creation of the MTA and its diversion of Triborough toll revenue to subways and buses: cars, the less efficient form of transportation, should subsidize transit.[15]

Yet Ravitch's plan was not fail-safe. These taxes would raise only $200 million—and the MTA's deficit had risen to $331 million.[16] Moreover, Warren Anderson, the Republican leader of the state senate, said he wouldn't support a higher gas tax. Hailing from the rural Binghamton area, a four-hour drive from New York City, he had little interest in transit; rumor had it that the state had constructed a highway, I-88, the state's least-used thoroughfare, to ease his drive to Albany. The business community was not enthusiastic. The Chamber of Commerce and Industry said taxes would harm the economy.[17] Another complication: 1980 was a legislative election year, and even lawmakers disposed to taxes didn't think the timing was right.[18] Stanley Fink, the Democratic leader of the state assembly, agreed with Anderson in preferring a stopgap: that is, subsidies to tide the MTA over another year.

Ravitch condemned this inaction, calling it "a hell of a way to run a railroad."[19] Carey, who wasn't up for reelection for two years, said he wanted a "full solution," not a "procrastinating legislature."[20] The legislature complained, in turn, that if Carey had been serious about passing the plan, he would have asked for their input before submitting it for a vote. By mid-March, the plan appeared dead.[21]

Ravitch made clear that he wasn't bluffing. If lawmakers wouldn't act, the MTA would take politically painful action. "No more waiting for the tooth fairy," said board member Stephen Berger, a veteran of New York's fiscal woes. Ravitch's board would not continue to starve the transit system of maintenance work because of the legislature's inaction. The MTA accelerated one hundred million dollars in bus maintenance that it had postponed for five years. To pay for a portion of this new investment, the board voted to curtail half-price fares for the elderly and said that it would hold hearings on potential toll and fare hikes. "We mean what we say, and we say what we mean," said Ravitch, noting that "the problems of the MTA system are real and have been ducked for too long."[22] Ravitch was a master at getting attention, and these moves were designed for public outcry. Raising fares on the elderly, a move ultimately reversed, wouldn't generate much money—only about forty million dollars—but it would outrage reliable voters.[23]

During this showdown, Ravitch was interrupted by an April 1980 transit strike, the second in history. In settling the eleven-day walkout, the MTA faced the same crisis the rest of the country faced after a decade of deficits to fund the Vietnam War and social spending: double-digit inflation. Transit workers demanded raises to fund their higher cost of living. To end the strike, the MTA obliged, with 21.5 percent raises over two years. It had made its deficit bigger: more than four hundred million dollars.[24] Now, Ravitch needed more money, and the legislature showed no signs of acting. In late April, Ravitch scheduled hearings to consider a fare hike of as much as twenty-five cents, or 50 percent.[25] He warned that it might not be enough: the fare might have to double and cross the psychological one-dollar threshold.[26]

Drastic hikes would not only harm ridership; they would contribute to the inflationary wage-price spiral. Private-sector workers commuting via subways would demand higher pay to make up for the higher cost. In May, the MTA continued this spiral, hiking tolls on Triborough bridges and tunnels by one-third, to one dollar.[27] By June, the MTA was modifying subway turnstiles to accept a different token, making it clear to the legislature that the massive fare hike, too, would be real.[28] Carey dug at the legislature, saying of Anderson's recalcitrance that Republicans were "behaving like traditional Republicans [with] no dedication to mass transit."[29]

By mid-June, though, lawmakers had changed their minds—halfway. Anderson's Republicans agreed to raise $235 million via one of Carey's proposed petroleum-sales taxes, despite objections from industry, including oil giant Mobil's threat to move bank deposits out of state-headquartered banks. "We're still left with a whopping deficit," Ravitch warned—but to reward the legislature, he kept his fare hike to ten cents, for a sixty-cent fare.[30] In July 1980, the Environmental Protection Agency reminded the state that under its revised Clean Air Act commitment, under which it was supposed to fund mass transit in lieu of tolling free East River bridges, the funding remained inadequate. In October, even the modest step the legislature had taken came to naught. A federal court said the tax was unconstitutional, as the state didn't have the authority to tell companies not to pass it down to consumers.[31]

Ravitch was a year into his tenure, and his proposals were failing. With no improvements, riders continued to flee, undoing gains made during the oil crisis. In November 1980, ridership was 79.2 million, the lowest in three years.[32] By December, new buses the MTA had ordered with the little money it had were cracking open; the manufacturer (falsely) blamed potholes. As the MTA removed the buses from service, delays ensued. After years of maintenance deferrals, one-quarter of subway cars were out of service. The MTA received 17,200 requests for employer "tardy slips" in 1980, up from 4,600 in 1976, as people couldn't get to work. "Riders now see themselves as reaching the limit of inconvenience and dislocation," the *Times* said.

Fewer riders did not mean less crowded trains. Train operators took trains out of service mid-route because of broken doors, leaving commuters stranded. Susan Pertell, waiting at Roosevelt Avenue in Queens to commute to her Wall Street secretarial job, said, "It's so crowded here you can't come down the stairs."[33] "Safe and convenient public transportation in New York is in danger," the *Times* wrote.[34] As 1980 turned into 1981, service reached a nadir. Only 70 percent of trains arrived on time.

MTA Saved, Not Fixed

A less confident chairman might have deflected attention from this year of disappointments or determined that the MTA's woes were insoluble and resigned. Instead, Ravitch—at the risk that riders and politicians would blame him—determined to show that things were not better under his watch but worse. To celebrate his anniversary, Ravitch did a four-hour subway tour, joined by a *Times* crew. "Obviously, there is something wrong," he said about the ten-minute delay for a train. A banker commuting to Wall Street stopped Ravitch to say, "I've been riding this line 14 years. I've never seen it so bad."[35]

Having met with little success with the legislature, a less self-assured chairman might have also reduced expectations. Instead, Ravitch raised them. At the end of 1980, he released a report cataloguing the MTA's needs. Nodding to the "New Direction" report of 1978, Ravitch said, "There is little quarrel with the requirements. We are not reinventing the wheel." The MTA's assets—710 miles of track and 460 stations, 6,500 subway cars and 4,500 buses—were worth $50 billion. But they were deteriorating quickly. Nearly six hundred subway cars were over thirty years old; more than 1,000 buses were over twelve years old. Nearly two dozen maintenance shops were over fifty years old, and tunnels were "badly" leaking. "It was sort of frightening," remembers David Plavin, then a top MTA official, "the magnitude."[36]

Upon releasing the report, said Ravitch, "I need not dwell on the present condition of the system. Everyone who uses it can see that it is deteriorating at an accelerating rate. We have one simple objective: to restore the system to a state of good repair," a new concept for the MTA, which had neglected existing assets in favor of never-attained expansion projects. The "bottom-line projection": "What is needed to restore this system to a state of good repair is $14 billion over . . . 10 years," he said. "I understand very well the feeling that people have about not wanting to pay more for a service that is not improving—in fact is probably getting worse."[37] The MTA would use any "first available funds" to purchase rail cars—1,000 for the subway, 400 for commuter rail.[38]

To make these investments, Ravitch proposed a more complex plan, an addition, not an alternative, to the new slew of taxes. To pay for infrastructure, the MTA would issue bonds backed by fare revenues. The MTA was making a bet that improvements it made with this debt would attract riders, thus increasing the fare revenues needed to repay the borrowing. The legislature would have to approve this plan, as well. In March, Carey unveiled a five-billion-dollar, five-year program of MTA improvements, paid for, in part, with two billion dollars in bonds backed by subway fares and five hundred million dollars in bonds backed by bridge tolls.

Part of Ravitch's doubled-down strategy was to court the business community. Business didn't want higher taxes, but neither could it survive with workers and customers immobilized. By April, the *Times* warned, "Delayed subway trips, commuter-train breakdowns and no-show buses are straining the commercial links that have made New York City, with its high density, a singular attraction. . . . While business was once helped by companies' ease of access to their bankers, their lawyers, their advertising agencies and their work force, a wild card has now entered the game: unreliable public transportation that executives say delays meetings and production schedules . . . and threatens the crest of guarded optimism." A director at the McKinsey consultancy, a white-collar employer, said that the firm was expanding in Connecticut, rather than New York, because "people . . . got sick of putting up with the commute."[39]

Independent studies tied transit to growth. Two agencies that rated New York City's bonds, Moody's and Standard & Poor's, said that New York's economy would not improve if transit didn't improve. Moody's called the issue of "grave concern" to recovery. The Federal Reserve Board of New York detailed New York's dependence on transit. It presented the results in April 1981, at a hearing convened by U.S. Senator Al D'Amato: subway "erosion" was costing the city $165 million to $330 million a year in economic activity. "It's critical for department stores, for service industries, for the general business climate, to get this mass transit system running," said developer Lew Rudin, powerful real estate developer and cofounder of the Association for a Better New York, a business-backed group.

In May, Ravitch wrote a public letter to Carey, Koch, and the legislature, releasing it at a press conference. He reiterated his call for fourteen billion dollars over a decade. "Failure to act will result in the continuing physical collapse of our system, catastrophic fare increases, and ultimately, economic strangulation," he warned. "During . . . the city's fiscal crisis, everyone demonstrated an ability to confront and resolve apocalyptic problems. The transit situation, though lacking the drama of imminent bankruptcy, represents an equally grave threat to . . . the survival of the greatest city in the world."[40]

In June 1981, Ravitch's campaign reached its apex. "[He] went on a PR campaign to . . . the heads of the banks in New York. Their success was dependent on New York," said Polan. With the support of Chase chairman David Rockefeller, Ravitch approached business leaders.[41] That month,

Ravitch summoned the five men to accompany him on his 4:30 a.m. subway tour. The men were the cross-section of New York's business and union elite: Richard Shinn, head of MetLife insurance; David Margolis of Colt Industries; Sol Chaikin, chief of the Garment Workers' Union; William Ellinghaus, head of AT&T; and finally, Alan Greenberg, at the Bear Stearns helm. After spending four hours on graffiti-scarred trains and in a repair barn with falling-down walls, "it is easy to understand now why trains are too . . . crowded, why they are too hot or too cold," Margolis told the press. "We are financial people and we are out to see what needs to be done," said Shinn. "At least 85 percent of the people who work for me ride the subways every day and we've known from television about how bad the situation is."[42]

Ravitch had another ally: Koch. The mayor did not always speak in unison with the MTA chairman. When Koch called subway workers loafers, Ravitch responded, "'The mayor's attack is totally inappropriate.' That was a big headline," he remembered four decades on. Koch apologized—"KOCH EATS CROW" was another headline—and Ravitch's wife, not wanting to see the mayor humiliated, invited him to "come have Chinese food with us," Ravitch recalled.[43] When the transit authority proposed in May 1981 to switch off air-conditioning on buses if the outside temperature was below ninety degrees, Koch responded, "We may have to get a new president of the TA. Not because I would remove him—I don't have the power. But he might suffocate."[44]

Koch wanted more state funding for the MTA, though, and he continued to use one weakness against Carey: the governor's desire to see the Westway highway built. Koch, by then, nominally supported Westway, but he continued holding it hostage to transit. Without state taxes for the MTA, Koch said, "we will opt for the boulevard"—that is, a wide surface road rather than the underground highway—"and take about a billion dollars and put it into the transit system."[45] Koch, a moderate Democrat who didn't generally favor higher taxes, also backed Ravitch in saying that "I am for taxes."

Ravitch had a final ally, appealing not to business or fiscal concerns but tying support for transit to future votes. A scrappy group, the Straphangers Campaign, was not a group of experts; it was New Yorkers tired of bad transit, organized by the New York Public Interest Research Group in the late 1970s. Gene Russianoff, a native Brooklynite and Harvard Law grad, was never the official president of Straphangers; he used the title of "staff attorney." For more than three decades, though, he would be the city's enduring transit advocate. (Russianoff wasn't the city's original transit advocate; that title belongs to Steve Dubrow, a mechanical engineer from Queens, who, driven by "extreme transit aggravation," earlier built up a mailing list through his tightly packed zine, the Committee for Better Transit newsletter.) Russianoff began work in 1978, answering an ad for an $8,300-a-year job; "that it meant so much for people's lives" attracted him.[46]

In March 1981, Straphangers organized a "speakout" at an Upper West Side school. Such events "gave people a chance to use their anger," says Russianoff. Ravitch attended, accepting criticism, but he was firm: "Unless we get the necessary funds . . . I can't give you any guarantees."[47] Russianoff developed a knack for sound bites. Lobbying in Albany, Russianoff said, lawmakers "shouldn't be jumping over the turnstiles"—that is, evading payment for the subways. Volunteers sported buttons that looked like subway tokens.[48] In June 1981, Carey proposed a revision of the oil tax, this time to be passed through to consumers to avoid a new constitutional challenge, a 0.5 percent increase in the regional sales tax, and a tax on commercial property in the city.

Yet all this lobbying was insufficient. Fink opposed the sales-tax hike, saying it would fall on poorer New Yorkers.[49] "I'm constantly being visited by delegations of tycoons telling me how important mass transit is," said Fink, saying he preferred a "direct tax on business."[50] Anderson remained against the oil tax, and even Koch called the proposed real estate levy "a sock to the city." Preparing to leave Albany for the summer, lawmakers approved the $5.6 billion capital plan—but no funding.[51] Meanwhile, the MTA's deficit had widened to $600 million, and the Reagan-era federal government was phasing out operating aid to large transit systems, costing New York $123 million by 1985.[52] Ravitch ratcheted up pressure. In July, the legislature out of session, he said that the fare would go to one dollar "in two weeks."[53] The MTA board approved a two-phase fare hike—75 cents immediately and, were the legislature to fail to act, crossing the dollar mark.[54]

Suddenly, lawmakers were scared. They agreed on five taxes to raise nearly eight hundred million dollars annually, including the oil tax, a 0.25 percent hike in the regional sales tax, and a 10 percent tax on real estate transfers over one million dollars in New York City. They passed the tax, despite Mobil spending eighty thousand dollars on full-page newspaper ads threatening jobs "in your district."[55] Ravitch was filled with praise: "It takes a lot of courage to enact taxes in the United States in

1981," the height of Reaganomics.[56] The oil tax passed the senate by three votes and the assembly by one. Brooklyn Republican Florence Sullivan, the final vote, said a fare hike to one dollar would harm her consituents more than the gas-tax hike would. Abraham Bernstein, senator from the Bronx, said that his vote would give the city "one last chance." Koch said that people could call the levies "the Koch tax."

The MTA was saved. As Ravitch told a Rockefeller-backed business group, the Partnership for New York City, in November, the push to overturn "massive physical deterioration, rising costs and declining service" had worked. "We have developed a $7.2 billion capital program [soon raised to $7.8 billion] the first systemwide capital reinvestment effort since the system moved from private to public hands," a half-century before.[57] Ravitch called the package an example of the state bearing a burden of a "new federalism," with Reagan cutting funding.[58] Koch, too, said the tax made "mass transit a responsibility of the MTA region and the state" rather than dependent on fares and inconsistent subsidies,"a major breakthrough," more than a decade after Rockefeller had created the state-controlled MTA but never funded it.[59] Russianoff's Straphangers promised to track progress with data. In fall 1981, its inaugural state-of-the trains survey, conducted by sixty volunteers, found that one out of five trains cars had broken doors; one out of ten had broken lights.[60] "We're going to hold him to it," said Russianoff of Ravitch's promises.[61]

The MTA's new capital review board approved the $7.8 billion plan, including $3.5 billion in bonds to be backed by fares and tolls. But first, the MTA would have to convince investors to buy the bonds. The next summer, Standard & Poor's awarded the bonds an investment-grade rating, meaning the MTA could borrow at reasonable rates. "The legislature had proven that it would take seriously its "responsibility to provide an adequate, reliable source of subsidy."[62]

Moody's, on the other hand, balked. "Moody's, who's sort of the stodgy rating agency," recalled Mort Downey, then the MTA budget director, said, "'We don't see it. It's a junk bond.' So we said, 'all right, we just won't ask you. Who needs you. We've got two ratings'"—the other was from a new agency, Fitch. "And they took great offense at that and they said, 'But we're Moody's.'" After Moody's threatened to rate the bonds anyway, even without the MTA asking, Downey negotiated with them. The MTA added a "maintenance pledge" to the bonds, saying that the authority would commit to maintaining the infrastructure that, in turn, enabled the fare collections that backed the bonds.[63]

MTA Still Not Fixed

The MTA nearly snatched defeat from the jaws of victory. In 1982, Ravitch was back begging. He now had money for the MTA's infrastructure. But, with some fare revenue needed to pay the interest costs on the new bonds, he lacked money to balance the day-to-day budget. He warned of a $400 million deficit on the $2.3 billion budget for 1983. The MTA was settling a labor contract that would cost $500 million over three years.[64] Just like the previous year, if the legislature didn't act, again, riders would face a 40 percent fare hike.

The legislature was sick of the Ravitch act. They had taken a risk with tax hikes the previous summer, yet riders weren't seeing better service. Ridership had fallen 6 percent in 1981, with passengers driven away by higher fares and recession as well as worse service.[65] The number of subway patrons was below one billion passengers a year for the first time since 1917—less than half its 1947 peak. The *Times* called it a "depressing milestone." Tax revenues were falling short (in part because the legislature, heeding Koch's complaining, repealed the real estate tax portion of the MTA bailout as quickly as it had enacted it). "This is a rotten time for a fare increase," said Ravitch in November—yet threatened that the fare would go from seventy-five cents to one dollar before Christmas unless Albany acted again.

It did. Carey was a lame duck, about to vacate the governor's mansion to make way for Mario Cuomo. He did one last deed: he called a session of the legislature weeks before leaving. Ravitch was concilitiatory: "I am confident they will do something. The legislature . . . has been of extraordinary help."[66] Nevertheless, the MTA board held an "all-night vigil" to see if it would have to hike fares.[67] Days before Cuomo took office, lawmakers approved a corporate-profit surcharge on companies within the MTA region—Fink's preferred tax—to raise $270 million a year.[68] "The fare is saved," declared Ravitch.[69]

As chairman, Ravitch couldn't focus just on Albany. He needed help from Washington—even Republican Washington. A Democrat, he would have to make friends with Republicans. In policy, Ravitch was fiercely liberal; in personality, he was not just willing to have long lunches with people on the other side, but enjoyed the debate. In 1980, Al D'Amato, newly elected Republican senator, called Ravitch, inviting him to breakfast. The first thing D'Amato said at breakfast, Ravitch recalled, was, "'did you vote for me?' I said, 'no.' He said, 'Can you arrange for me to meet the heads of the Jewish community?' He said, 'I'll get you more money that you can ever spend on mass transit, I'm gonna get on the mass transit appropriations committee.'" Just before D'Amato was sworn in, he told Ravitch, as the latter recalled, "If you see I'm doing anything stupid, call me."[70]

Ravitch used his connections to call in favors. First, the federal government could help by allowing transit agencies to take advantage of tax credits for private investment. That is, transit agencies, exempt from taxes, could sell assets, such as subways and buses, to private-sector companies, which would benefit from tax credits. Then, transit agencies could lease the assets back. This creativity allowed the MTA to save 20 percent on rail cars, getting one railcar free for every four that it purchased.[71] Bob Dole, the Republican senator from Kansas, frowned upon this creativity. Ravitch, who had raised money for Senator Moynihan, went to Moynihan, who said changing Dole's mind was key. Ravitch's staff "pulled the [campaign-donation] contribution reports for Dole and other key members" to find out what they *did* think was important and how fellow New York elected officials and donors could help with those issues.[72]

Ravitch and D'Amato also ensured that during the Reagan era, Congress might change its transit priorities, but would not neglect them. The Reagan administration did not want to subsidize transit agencies' operating expenses, reasoning (not inaccurately) that such subsidies encouraged inefficiencies. But the administration did support infrastructure. It raised the gas tax by a nickel a gallon in 1982. Thanks to D'Amato's efforts, one penny of that nickel went toward transit, the first time the federal government offered dedicated revenues to transit rather than roads.

Ravitch was not shy about praising Republicans—and D'Amato wasn't shy about asking. In one meeting with D'Amato, Polan remembers explaining how transit investments would benefit Long Islanders, helping the senator's constituents. "His response to me was, 'I don't give a flying fuck about them. What's in it for me?' Gave me my lesson in raw politics." Upon being told "he would get a lot of credit," D'Amato agreed.[73] In 1983, praising D'Amato for bringing home $1 billion over four years for transit, Ravitch publicly called him "a tiger"— improving his standing with swing voters.[74]

By 1983, New York's new governor, Mario Cuomo, was wary of a public official who could command as much attention and respect as Ravitch could. On his fifth day in office, Cuomo attempted to seize more control over the MTA, first considering abolishing it, folding it into New York State. Upon learning that such a move would require the state to assume the MTA's new debt, which, in turn, would require voter approval, Cuomo asked the legislature to enact a "reform" whereby the chair would serve at the pleasure of the governor. The *Times* called Cuomo's plan "pointless" and praised Ravitch as "wholesomely independent"—justifying Cuomo's fears, as he would always be competing for attention with the media-friendly MTA chairman.[75] The legislature repelled Cuomo's power grab, with Ravitch openly counseling against changes. "Cuomo was humiliated. We never spoke another word," Ravitch said.[76]

Ravitch left soon thereafter to "resume a more normal life."[77] He gave one last speech to the Association for a Better New York, a business-backed group. City council member Carol Bellamy had often told him that the MTA could achieve higher ridership "by providing monthly passes . . . but other problems . . . seemed to take precedence. We want to eliminate the token. We want to substitute a reusable ticket with a magnetic strip." (Bellamy got the idea from travels in Europe.) That month, in April 1983, the MTA allocated $100 million to study fare cards. A decade and a half later, monthly passes—unlimited ridership for a fixed fee—would become reality.

Independent, but Not Alone

How had Ravitch convinced New York's legislature to levy taxes not once, but repeatedly, in the 1980s anti-tax environment? According to Ravitch, lawmakers hadn't acted before because "nobody had ever suggested it." Things had to hit bottom. "The whole premise [to get the legislature to agree] was the absolute necessity," agreed Downey. "Dick [Ravitch] had convinced the business community, the editorial boards, that this was an absolute requirement."

Part of the secret was bipartisanship. Leaders had found common ground. Assembly leader Fink was a "gruff and intimidating" Brooklyn Democrat.[78] Anderson, Republican senate leader, was a lawyer, "reserved and businesslike"[79]—a "gentle leader" who "ruled by consensus." Yet they tried to understand each other. "Fink used to go upstate, visit dairy farms. Anderson would come down to different parts of the city," said Jerry Kremer, a former assemblyman.[80]

Bipartisanship was rooted in common interests. Republican senators from Long Island voted for MTA taxes because their voters were worried about the Long Island Rail Road (LIRR) service, just as they had been during Rockefeller's time. "They got arguably somewhat more than what might be their reasonable share," says Downey. John D. Cammerer, Long Island senator, wanted investment in the LIRR's Manhattan railyards so that commuters wouldn't have to wait for trains at Penn Station. (Ravitch named these railyards after Cammerer.) Senators further afield could benefit from MTA spending. Though the Ravitch-era MTA received criticism for contracting with Japanese and Canadian contractors to build subway cars, the companies would build the cars within New York State. Turning old factories into train facilities upstate, a struggling postindustrial area, "was of great interest to Warren Anderson," says Downey.

What lawmakers and Carey also had in common was the fiscal crisis. They had watched New York City nearly go bankrupt in 1975, roiling not just the city but the nation and the world. They knew what happened after elected officials left a problem to a future generation; they had been the future generation. "As an upstate Republican, [Anderson] could easily have used the crisis to his own political advantage by portraying downstate Democrats as fiscally irresponsible. Instead, he worked with his Democratic colleagues," said the Albany *Times-Union* about Anderson's role in the mid-1970s rescue of New York City.

Ravitch benefited from Carey's unusual approach to government, as well. Neither Carey nor his state transportation commmissioner negotiated with the legislature during this years-long process; Ravitch did it. "By not acting as the governor's agent in this matter, by not dealing through [the state transportation commissioner], I was able to establish a credibility with the legislature that made them view these issues not as partisan ones," Ravitch remembered.[81]

Part of this arrangement was luck. Carey "was busy with personal issues" of a happy nature, said Downey. "He had a new girlfriend," who later became his wife, after the losses that had marred his life. Yet Carey, too, had shown self-confidence in deferring authority to an independent actor. "Not everybody can tolerate a Ravitch," says Sandler. "Richard Ravitch [was] a force. . . . It's rare in politics that someone can take on someone as strong as Ravitch and then support him."

Ravitch made the most of circumstances. He had "institutional loyalty" toward the MTA, says Sandler, rather than toward the politician who had appointed him. In that sense, he was similar to Moses, who had had institutional loyalty toward Triborough. "Dick was in everyone's face every day in Albany, was fanning the flames in the papers, the editorials," said Polan. "When you were on the receiving end of a phone call from Dick Ravitch, you got an intensity coming at you about why you, the legislature, or why you, a member of the administration, why you needed to agree to do this." "He was politically shrewd," says Sandler. "He was bureaucratically shrewd. His strategy was, he looked at the budget. He said, you have to have a balanced budget, they were deferring maintenance. He said, 'I'm going to produce an honest budget.' When you do that—and don't defer maintenance spending—you have an enormous budget gap." To deal with this budget gap, adds Sandler, "He said, 'we're gonna raise the fare.' The legislature went nuts. He won the battle by just battling them down."

But Ravitch could not have done what he did without the Clean Air Act—and the lawsuit to enforce it. Pressure from Ketcham's nearly decade-old transportation control plan was ever present. In 1978, the year before Carey appointed Ravitch, the EPA rejected the state's transportation plan, part of its Clean Air Act requirement to fund subways and buses, as the plan had failed to present sufficient funding for transit. Again, in 1980, the EPA rejected the state's plan, saying it wasn't doing enough to support transit. "Nowhere else would even a slight shift from subways . . . into private cars have such a dramatic effect on air pollution," the EPA's regional administrator said. In its 1980 rejection, the EPA used the Koch administration's 1978 "New Direction" report for its cost estimates of mass transit need.[82] The Carey administration later cited new MTA taxes as proof that it was meeting its obligation—evidence that the taxes were the result, in part, of EPA pressure.

Asked whether the NRDC could have gotten leverage another way, Schoenbrod answers, "No. . . . Ravitch deserves 100 percent of the credit," but, without the Clean Air Act and the legal obligation it created for New York to fund transit and the attendant "New Direction" report, Schoenbrod says, "Ravitch or somebody like him might have said, you know, 'I ain't taking the job unless I get the money to do it right.' . . . A governor might have said, 'well, don't take the job.'"[83]

The Long Game

It took years for riders to see results. At the Straphangers Campaign, Russianoff ensured that after Ravitch, the transit authority's new management, chairman Robert Kiley and transit president David Gunn, stuck to promises grand and small. The Straphangers Campaign wasn't satisfied with rebuilt track and new subway cars; Russianoff advocated for modest improvements, too, such as audible announcements, a faster pace in fixing lights and doors, and things as basic as maps. "If you go in the subway and there is no announcement, broken doors," it was equivalent to the MTA saying, "screw you," recalled Russianoff. As riders waited for big investments, they needed small-scale "evidence that somebody cared." In reports detailing shortfalls, Russianoff annoyed Gunn and Kiley, who wanted to tell an uncomplicated tale of progress. "The thing we had going for us was our credibility," says Russianoff. "I can't tell you how many times we got a call" (from Gunn).

By 1984, subway on-time performance had climbed to 85 percent. By 1986, "straphangers are actually seeing new subway cars." Riders could "step into a new, air-conditioned car [and experience] something new . . . happening in a city that, throughout its fiscal crisis and for years thereafter, symbolized impoverished disrepair."[84] In the early 1980s, a subway car traveled just 8,000 miles before "failing," with operators taking it out of service, inconveniencing passengers mid-ride. By the mid-2000s, the figure was 125,000 miles. Many millennial riders, over entire careers, never had to step off a train because of a mechanical problem.

The Ravitch-era MTA supported four decades of New York's success. Over the thirty years after Ravitch's first 1981 capital plan, which eventually invested $14.4 billion, the MTA invested $140 billion in physical infrastructure, including building a one-stop extension of the 7 Subway to the far west side of Manhattan, opened in 2015, and the first three stops of the Second Avenue Subway, opened in 2016. From 1980 to 2017, the city's population grew by more than 20 percent, to a record 8.6 million, surpassing postwar highs. By 2019, New York had nearly 4.2 million private-sector jobs—up from fewer than 2.8 million in 1980, a 50 percent increase.[85]

New York could not have grown without a vastly improved transit system. In 1981, nearly 3.1 million people traveled to the island of Manhattan each day. By 2019, the figure was nearly 3.9 million. Yet the number of people coming in via car or truck fell—from 970,000 to 910,000, from 32 to 24 percent of the total, below early 1970s levels. The number of people coming in via subway rose by 40 percent, from 1.6 million to more than 2.2 million. By 2015, the modern record high, subway ridership citywide had nearly doubled from the early 1980s, to nearly two billion rides per year. Some weekdays, ridership of nearly six million smashed post–World War II records. Those 600,000 extra people each day could never have fitted in cars in the available street space. If Ravitch hadn't succeeded, hundreds of thousands of people would not have been able to live and work in New York; there would not have been room.

Subway ridership growth aided residents of poor neighborhoods. During the 1970s, "as neighborhoods crumbled in the South Bronx, central Harlem and large areas of Brooklyn, a number of stations along these and other lines had a 50- to 87 percent decline at the turnstiles," outpacing the city's fall in ridership of 26 percent.[86] Between 1990 and 2016, as New York revived, commuting by public transit more than doubled in what had been the South Bronx's poorest, most depopulated areas—Melrose, Hunts

Point, and Mott Haven—a period during which overall transit commuting in New York rose 30 percent. Subways were the foundation of the repopulation of the South Bronx as well as the means by which poorer people found work. In Mott Haven, Melrose, and Hunts Point, the percentage of people participating in the workforce rose by 72 percent between 1990 and 2016, versus 26 percent citywide.[87] People did not need to buy a car to land their first job.

The Very Long Game

Hidden in successes were future challenges. Although it was good that Ravitch gained authority for the MTA to borrow against future revenues, future governors and lawmakers would rely on this tactic to a dangerous extent (as Russianoff had prophesied early on, in another instance of earning the ire of transit officials). The MTA would never quite get its assets into a state of good repair, as Ravitch had promised; it would need capital investments indefinitely. "Ten years into the process, we began to realize this was a never-ending effort," said Downey. In four decades, the MTA's debt grew from nil to $45.8 billion, with debt costs consuming 16 percent of the MTA's day-to-day operating revenues, taking money needed for service. In the early 2000s, Republican governor George Pataki relied on debt whose payments wouldn't come due until years into the future to finance the MTA's capital investments.

The MTA's expenses grew beyond inflation. Future legislatures and governors would add tax upon tax to the Ravitch-era MTA. If it had risen only with inflation, the $2.3 billion MTA budget of 1983 would have reached $5.9 billion by 2019. Instead, the budget was $16.7 billion. By 2019, taxes brought in nearly $6 billion annually to the MTA by 2019, nearly three times the original Ravitch-era package when adjusted for inflation.[88] But it was never enough.

Moreover, the state continued to allocate transit resources unevenly, driven by politics, not planning. Just as Ravitch had given LIRR riders new railyards in return for support for his plan, the state continued to favor the suburbs' swing voters over reliable urban Democratic votes. Ever after, the LIRR would get a disproportionate share of transit funding—including, in 2023, the long-delayed $12 billion East Side Access terminal on the East Side of Manhattan.

One group of New Yorkers never fully benefited from the Ravitch-era renewal. The MTA has failed to make subways accessible to people with disabilities under the three-decade-old Americans with Disabilities Act, citing cost. Only one-fourth of subway stations have elevators, often broken. Without subway access, wheelchair users and other people who can't navigate stairs depend on slower buses and the even slower Access-A-Ride van service.

Beyond poorly distributed resources is a bigger problem: once the state and city rescued the transit system from crisis, they did not keep pace with other global cities, such as London and Paris, in expanding and modernizing it. Against New York's four new subway stations, London has built an entire subway line. Andrew Cuomo, governor from 2011 to 2021, explains political antipathy. "On transportation," the former governor says, "no elected official wants to do it. . . . because it is a disruptive task." Construction "is disruptive. It is fraught with risk and peril. And there is no upside."

Among risks, he notes, is the near certainty a project can't be completed within a political time frame, meaning that a current officeholder must take blame for disruption to see his successor take credit. Elected officials who want to appear to be concerned about infrastructure without having to incur voter wrath over disruptive projects have a refuge. They can announce something big, then hide behind federal and state environmental review processes until a successor inherits the project. The environmental review process, Cuomo says, is "an elegant procrastinating device. . . . If you don't force it, it will never happen." Another risk is corruption. "I'm gonna upset a community" with construction, "then . . . the [construction] contractor's gonna wind up being corrupt," he says.[89]

Finally, from the perspective of an elected official, MTA bureaucracy and contractors' incentive to stretch a project out as long as possible can seem impenetrable. Cuomo ensured that the first three stations of the Second Avenue Subway opened on time in 2016—only because, he says, he threatened to disbar contractors from future state work when they asked for yet another delay. "They come back, they say, 'we will get it done on time.' I say, 'at no additional cost.' I'm gonna go there three times a week at random times," to ensure crews are working.

Another project illustrates the opacity of infrastructure. In 2019, the MTA, after years of planning, was about to close the L train tunnel between Manhattan and Williamsburg, Brooklyn, for fifteen months to rebuild infrastructure, including "bench walls" in the tunnel containing electrical and communication cables, after damage from Hurricane Sandy in 2012. Cuomo, after consulting with engineering professors, canceled the closure, preserving commutes for hundreds of thousands of New Yorkers. Instead of replacing bench walls, the MTA would hang the cables in the tunnel. "I'm looking [online] at tunnels in Europe that they build in like

20 minutes," Cuomo remembered. "The MTA doesn't tell me any of this." Cuomo's directive saved Williamsburg more than a year of disruption because, without the governor's intervention, he says, "there was no incentive to do it cheaper and faster." MTA officials, though, claimed the shortcut delayed major work to future decades and heightens the risk of fire damage. An average voter can't assess these arguments; only time will tell.

Yet despite continued shortcomings, Ravitch—and Carey and Koch, Sandler and Schoenbrod, and Ketcham and Polan—won four decades of success for New York. "I was credible," said Ravitch. "They believed me. I said, 'New York City couldn't survive without transit.' Everybody knew, I was a businessman, a lawyer, and independent human being."[90]

Chapter 10

From Fear Train to Packed Train

Securing New York's Subways

> There has been an alarming and continuing increase in felonies, climaxed . . . by a brutal, senseless murder.
>
> —*New York Times*, April 5, 1965

> My son died, but the city is so much safer.
>
> —Karen Watkins, mother of Brian Watkins, 2005

BY THE MID-1980S, New York's subway system was sturdier; new trains ran on rebuilt tracks. But another crisis raged: violence. For two decades, city government had considered crime—including random murders—inevitable. In 1985, the *New York Times* ran an op-ed arguing that subways were safe "for those who avoided the most dangerous stations . . . in Midtown."[1] Despite such minimization, relentless violence, including twenty-six people killed underground in 1990 alone, repelled people from the subways and the city. People who realized that they were unlikely to be killed were put off by ceaseless disorder.

The transit leaders who succeeded Richard Ravitch—Robert Kiley and David Gunn—determined to fix what everyone accepted as unfixable. They turned to outside experts, who said that more than a dozen transit riders didn't have to lose their lives to murder each year. Elected officials, including David Dinkins, a mayor elected in 1989 on a tough-on-crime platform, reinforced their ideas. New York's population had stabilized, and a growing tax base provided resources for public safety. New York's subways became fear-free, with one or two murders annually by the late 1990s. Ridership—and New York's recovery—surged.

From Misdemeanor to Murder

From 1904 until the mid-1960s, New Yorkers rode without fear. At worst, "lush workers" relieved drunk riders of property,[2] and women suffered groping by "mashers."[3] Violence was rare. In 1949, the subway carried nearly two billion riders. Just 354 police officers patrolled 468 stations and thousands of train cars, open twenty-four hours a day. The subways saw no homicides, as it had seen no homicides the previous year. Fewer than four passengers were robbed each month.[4] "When I was eight years old [in 1949]," says Ray Kelly, who served as city police commissioner during the David Dinkins mayoralty in the 1990s and again during the Michael Bloomberg era of the 2000s, "I used to ride the subway by myself."[5]

Starting in the 1960s, crime soared. In 1964, riders and workers fell victim to 1,707 major crimes, compared to 1,119 in 1963 and 923 in 1959.[6] "New York's boast that its subways offer the safest transportation in the world needs revision," the *Times* observed. "Accidents are not the problem; crime is."[7] Bands of "youth"—teenagers—were "invading" trains, sometimes brandishing guns (including toy guns) or knives, sometimes using no weapon, to rob passengers.[8]

Transit crime couldn't be isolated from anxieties above ground. The number of murders citywide had increased from 548 in 1963 to 636 in 1964.[9] It wasn't just numbers, but the feeling of an uncaring city. One crime became an enduring motif—if an inaccurate one, it turned out—of a city where people didn't care about one another. In March 1964, twenty-eight-year-old Kitty Genovese was walking home in leafy Kew Gardens, Queens, when a stranger repeatedly stabbed her. Genovese screamed, and dozens of people came to their apartment windows. Yet thirty-seven witnesses failed to call police, a disclosure that caused "shock and perplexity."[10]

The age of many criminals was disconcerting. The word "baby-faced" appeared in the papers, as teens with unstable family lives, many of them migrants from the south, escalated from small thefts to murder. Teens arrested for violence often had juvenile records, showing the city's inability to grapple with delinquency before teens committed bigger crimes.

New Yorkers called for more police. Transport Workers Union chief Mike Quill wanted an officer on every train.[11] "The strongest weapon against [subway] crime is a strong, alert, well-trained police force," the *Times* agreed. In 1964, Mayor Robert Wagner said he would increase transit-police ranks—already at 984 officers, up from 603 in 195—to 1,146.[12]

In March 1965, a single subway horror intensified the response. After midnight on a Friday, Andrew Mormile, a slender seventeen-year-old who loved animals, was dozing on a Brooklyn A train.[13] Miscreants made their way through, shouting obscenities as they accosted passengers and groped girls. They shoved Mormile. Awakened, he walked away; cornered, he pushed back. One assailant repeatedly stabbed Mormile. As Mormile lay dying, the attackers fled.

The soon-apprehended killer, Christopher Lynch, was, like the victim, seventeen. The "product of a broken home," he had a record for knife possession and assault. His accomplice, another "baby-faced" teen with an assault history, lived with his mother in Brooklyn; his father lived in North Carolina.[14] The killing was "without reason"—the two hadn't robbed Mormile. A judge sentenced Lynch to life (he won release in 1985) but said that "this case cries out for the return of capital punishment," reflecting a hardening public stance.[15] Two months after Mormile's murder, a twelve-year-old girl stabbed sixty-year-old Zena Messina to death at the Queens Plaza station, "for no apparent reason."[16]

Stalling Crime

Mormile's murder shocked New York into action on subway "terror."[17] Wagner vowed to protect riders from "the mugger, the hoodlum, and the young punk."[18] He ordered a patrolman on every station and train between 8:00 p.m. and 4:00 a.m. He more than doubled the transit-police force, to 2,722. The city pioneered another tactic: retreat. The transit authority closed 175 subway entrances at night, inconveniencing commuters.[19]

Policing worked. By September, patrols had resulted in a "stunning" 58 percent fall in nighttime felonies.[20] By mid-1966, the *Times* reported that "murder, robbery, assault and other major crimes have been reduced nearly 60 percent."[21] Harvard government professor James Q. Wilson termed the program a "remarkable success."[22]

The victory was short-lived. By 1969, subway crime was up 29 percent over the previous year. Crime still fell at night—but daytime crime increased 40 percent.[23] That left overall subway crime up 20 percent since 1965.[24] Transit police, by then 3,200 strong, didn't have enough personnel to put a cop on every train during the day.[25] Coverage fell further in 1970, when a transit officer, Michael Melchiona, stopped a man smoking on a Times Square platform. The smoker shot and killed him. Police thereafter worked in pairs.[26]

Kelly, future police commissioner, remembers the "feeling of danger and disorder" during the 1970s. Crimes were random. In 1971, an attacker firebombed a Midtown train, burning three passengers.[27] In 1974, four youth killed a fifty-three-year-old hospital cook, Anibal Fernandez, on a Brooklyn train, as he reached for his wallet, despite his wife's pleas for mercy.[28] Mayor Abe Beame ordered the transit authority to lock rear train-car doors at night, crowding passengers into front cars for safety. In 1972, two women were raped; by 1973, the figure was ten, and by 1979, twenty-four.[29] The biggest category of crimes had an economic purpose: robbery. Parents feared the trip to school. "Gangs of youths have systematically attacked, threatened and robbed students."[30]

One killer was emblematic of New York's failure to control wayward youth. In 1978, fifteen-year-old Willie Bosket and his seventeen-year-old cousin shot and killed Noel Perez, a man on an Upper Manhattan train, emptying his pockets.[31] Days later, they murdered Moises Perez, "at the same place and in almost the same way as Noel Perez, to whom he was not related." Over weeks, Bosket shot and wounded a motorman as well as a passenger.[32] Bosket had spent time in a juvenile facility, whose social workers had protested his release. His murders spurred Governor Carey to sign a law allowing teens to face adult sentences.[33]

By the mid-1970s, the fiscal crisis was cutting into policing. In 1975, transit police, funded by city government, even though the state-run Metropolitan Transportation Authority (MTA) supervised them, fell from 3,600 officers to 3,100.[34] The city ended full-coverage nighttime patrols. That December, when robbers "terrorized" Harlem passengers with shotguns, the *Times* observed that no cop was aboard, "because that 10-year patrol policy was curtailed."[35]

Crime soared. In 1974, 7,626 riders fell victim to felonies. In 1978, the figure was 12,906.[36] Homicide was no longer rare. In 1972, six people were killed; in 1973, the figure was nine. In 1975, the number reached seventeen.[37] In 1977, eleven New Yorkers were murdered underground, ranging from a thirty-four-year-old teacher waiting on a Lincoln Center platform after purchasing "Mostly Mozart" tickets to Renzo Previdi, a bank clerk with cerebral palsy, killed in the Bronx.[38] In 1979, sixteen New Yorkers were killed.[39] Nearly all were stranger-on-stranger killings, the most-feared urban crime.

Gruesome Ends

It wasn't just that you might be murdered, but how. Fatal shovings in front of trains became regular news items in the 1970s. Two women were pulled to the tracks in separate incidents as robbers grabbed for their purses.[40] A woman and a man were crushed separately, for no reason.[41] In 1979, Renee Katz, seventeen, a prodigy flutist, was pushed under a Midtown train, losing her hand (surgeons reattached it). "At least . . . she was alive," the motorman said.[42] That year, a thirty-nine-year-old man, recently released from a mental facility, fatally shoved thirty-nine-year-old Yong Su in front of a Greenwich Village train after Su intervened to rescue a woman from harassment.[43]

Transit workers were trapped. In the late 1960s, subway-worker holdups numbered in the low hundreds each year; by 1971, they had reached 771. Subways had 829 token booths, meaning that nearly all were robbed yearly. In 1973, clerk Maurice Foley, thirty-six, died in Brooklyn during a robbery that netted $138.[44] Cops frequently "staked out" and shot such robbers.[45] Wilson, the Harvard professor, questioned this strategy. "Stake-out squads . . . may produce dead criminals rather than arrests," he observed.[46]

The transit authority responded with a design change. Until 1972, Jim Dwyer wrote in *Subway Lives*, "clerks sat in wooden kiosks, behind . . . barred windows." The MTA fortified the booths. "By 1978, every clerk had been shoved into baby-blue fiberglass and steel fortresses" behind "five layers of bullet-resistant glass," where they couldn't hear or be heard by their customers.

Criminals devised a way through. Each booth had a slot for passengers to push money. Robbers could push lighter fluid and a lit match through, as well. In 1977, token-booth clerk Oscar Williams burned to death in Brooklyn.[47] In 1979, three Queens teenagers, upset about having received a turnstile-jumping summons, torched the Broad Channel booth in Queens. Two clerks, Regina Reicherter, fifty-six, and Venezea Pendergast, fifty-two, suffered fatal burns.[48] "I have never seen anything like what I am seeing," a judge observed.[49]

Blaming Victims

Even police weren't safe. In 1972, a police officer died in a Bronx subway shootout.[50] In 1973, Kevin McDow, sixteen, robbed and stabbed to death a retired officer at a Times Square station.[51] Months later, another officer, Sidney Thompson, became "the fourth transit patrolmen shot since last Saturday and the second to be killed." At Thompson's funeral, Mayor Lindsay pleaded that "we're doing the best we can." In 1980, Seraphin Calabrese was killed stopping a turnstile-jumper at Columbus Circle; months later, another transit cop, Joseph Keegan, died the same way.[52] Police casualties further unnerved the public.

Police added to fear by burdening the victim. "Hello," read one card officers handed out. "The NYC Transit Police Dept. needs your help in preventing CRIME by not becoming a VICTIM." Tips included sitting in the conductor's car and securing a purse over the neck.[53] The MTA painted zones in the middle of platforms and counseled passengers to stand together. The effect was to reiterate that the platform was dangerous.[54]

New Yorkers felt brave to step down subway stairs. "When I get home," a retired teacher said, "I say, 'Thank God I made it.'"[55] In 1975, the state's Court of Appeals put a stamp of officiality on fear. Ellen Aronson had quit her job because she feared taking the subway after an assault. The government denied her unemployment fund application, saying she had left voluntarily. She appealed and won.[56]

As in the 1960s, subway anxiety reflected and magnified fear aboveground. Between 1965 and 1970, New York's annual murders doubled, from 634 to 1,117. By 1974, the figure was 1,554. In January 1974, Mayor Abe Beame's first month, "an overwhelming majority of New Yorkers—rich and poor, black and white, conservative and liberal—regard crime as the worst problem," the *Times* reported.[57]

A Great Scandal

New Yorkers turned to self-defense. In 1971, real estate agent John Britz, fifty-eight, shot and wounded two people robbing him on a Manhattan train. "The police said it was a mistake for Mr. Britz to sit in the rear car," the *Times* observed.[58] In 1979, on an East Side train, "threatened by a man with knife, a middle-aged subway passenger suddenly drew a gun and opened fire."[59] In 1979, a sixty-three-year-old man stabbed and killed a twenty-three-year-old who, he said, had tried to rob him. Newspapers tucked these accounts into middle sections.

One group of New Yorkers took an organized approach. In 1979, unarmed volunteers calling themselves the "Magnificent 13" started patrolling Bronx subways.[60] Two years later, the group, having attracted 700 members, renamed itself the Guardian Angels, known for satiny red hats. Curtis Sliwa was the group's coordinator. "We're willing to put ourselves on the line by making a citizen's arrest when we encounter a crime," he said.[61]

A Brooklyn native, Sliwa had moved to the Bronx after losing his supermarket job; he ran the night shift at a McDonald's. Running a McDonald's on a major Bronx thoroughfare (Fordham Road) in the 1970s wasn't for the easily scared; Sliwa's first "Angels" were his hardy McDonald's colleagues, whom he—or, rather, an oblivious McDonald's—paid extra hours to patrol the 4 train, the "mugger's express."[62]

The Guardian Angels began patrolling because of the "cumulative effect," Sliwa says, of the end of the full-coverage nighttime police patrols, just as gang activity was surging on trains. The idea of patrolling subways without weapons was considered "crazy"; Guardians searched each other to ensure that they weren't breaking their own rules out of fear. Police worried that the Guardian Angels would be easy for criminals to impersonate, lulling passengers into complacency. They also worried that Guardians would instigate fights.

The *Times*, though, approved. "The Guardian Angels are, plainly, popular. . . . It's a great scandal that the city should have to rely on such adolescent protectors." Yet "mostly black and Puerto Rican, they appear earnest, quiet, law-abiding and proud. . . . So we salute the red berets—warily."[63] But Mayor Ed Koch, who succeeded Beame in 1978, resented the Guardians, and police arrested Sliwa and colleagues multiple times; the mayor, Sliwa says, saw them as "an affront" to the city's failure to keep the public safe.

Scrawls of Danger

Passengers were not only fearful but depressed. Graffiti had once been so rare that, until 1967, the transit authority didn't have a punishment for it. In the early 1970s, a Greek American courier from Washington Heights started scrawling his tag, "TAKI 183," becoming "an underground mystery," Dwyer wrote. TAKI was joined by "Julio 204." Over the next two decades, hundreds of graffiti writers marked trains, planning their handiwork beforehand in sketchbooks and photographing it afterward rolling by. By the mid-1970s, "huge multi-colored designs" extended "the full length of the cars, including the windows."[64]

Graffiti writers were mostly young men and boys.[65] Middle-class and wealthier teens joined poorer adventurers as street culture grew trendy. Graffiti writers committed low-scale crimes beyond property defacement. The writers' code was to steal paint and to defend turf. A city report found that of fifteen-year-olds arrested for graffiti writing in 1973 and 1974, 42 and 28 percent, respectively, were arrested for serious crimes. Taggers also faced risks from the law and from the trains themselves. In 1983, police arrested Michael Stewart, twenty-five, in Manhattan for scrawling graffiti. Hours later, he was dead, a possible victim of police brutality. A jury acquitted three officers.[66] In 1989, two taggers, Daniel Gomez, "SONI," and Rubin Fernandez, "SLICK," were run over and killed by a train.

Graffiti-scrawled subways sent a message that no one was in charge. The Koch administration's 1978 report, "New Directions in Transit," listed "filth, litter, breakage, graffiti and noise" as producing an "atmosphere of degradation and fear." The Natural Resources Defense Council, as it tried to convince New Yorkers to take trains, knew New York had to improve the transit environment. "Graffiti, vandalism and farebeating . . . convey the message that the transit system can protect neither itself nor its passengers," the group reported in 1979.[67]

The MTA and the city remained hapless. As the authority's 1970s fiscal woes mounted along with the city's, it slashed cleaning staff. Efforts to force vandals to wash off graffiti "produced little deterrence," the city found, and "helped educate violators on Transit Authority procedures." In 1973, transit police devoted ten officers to graffiti, but gave up as violent crime rose. In 1982, the city stepped up restitution, forcing more teens and young adults to scrub trains. "We're making our mark in society instead of on society," said nineteen-year-old Larry Carson, parroting the city's public service announcement as he did his community service.[68] But trains stayed dirty. Koch wanted dogs to secure train yards. "If I had my way, I wouldn't put in dogs, but wolves," he said. In 1981, the MTA *did* dispatch dogs, Suzy and Red, to secure a yard, but this isolated step did little to deter large-scale defacement.[69]

Besides graffiti, vandalism was wanton. Teens smashed windows. Thieves smashed turnstiles or used their mouths to "suck" tokens out, ruining machines and contributing to farebeating. By the 1980s, 250,000 riders a day were beating the fare, and most people given a civil summons or a misdemeanor notice for doing so ignored them, leading police to call these "desk-appearance" tickets "disappearance" tickets.

Crime and disorder repelled passengers. The city's failure to assure safety fed on the state-run transit authority's failure to maintain infrastructure and vice versa; as unreliable trains pushed people off subways, sparser crowds contributed to a feeling of danger, which, in turn, meant sparser crowds. In 1962, nearly 1.4 billion people rode the trains every year; by 1972, 1.1 billion did.[70] "People cite fear of crime," the 1978 "New

Direction" report said. "The feeling of being trapped is reinforced by decrepit, dirty conditions." During the 1973 oil embargo and the 1979 oil price spike, some drivers ditched cars for transit. But they didn't stay.[71]

The *Times*, no longer alarmed as it had been in the 1960s, searched for justifications for why New Yorkers shouldn't be scared. In 1979, an "editorial notebook" argued that "risks are less than people have been led to believe." Counting "nine murders, 32 committed or attempted rapes, 262 assaults and 3,562 robberies in the subways" for 1978, the essay concluded that "subways appear . . . safe."[72] Safety was relative in a city whose above-ground murder total pierced ceiling after ceiling: in 1980, the city suffered a then-record 1,814 homicides.

Crime was a regressive tax. "Lorraine Ramsey . . . said she had gotten into the 'crazy' habit of taking a taxi at midnight from her job at a McDonald's restaurant at 103rd Street and Third Avenue to her home at 112th and Lexington Avenue, even though it was practically a direct trip on the IRT Lexington Avenue line. 'But I had gotten too afraid,'" Ramsey, nineteen, said.[73]

New People, New Victims

In the 1980s, violence reached a nadir. The decade began with thirty subway felonies in eight hours.[74] As Koch promised to be tougher, budget woes hindered his efforts. New York scrambled to rehire police officers it had laid off. It had only 2,253 transit officers to deal with violence that Wagner, fifteen years earlier, could never have anticipated.[75] In 1980, transit police put twelve German shepherds on patrol.[76] But this was show, not strategy. "We are strained at this moment in how to pay for essential services," Koch said in 1984, noting that to hire cops, he'd have to lay off teachers.[77] The transit authority surrendered more public space, shuttering more passageways and entrances.[78]

This approach ensured that statistics remained grim. In 1980, twenty New Yorkers were killed in transit. In 1981, the figure was thirteen; in 1982, seventeen.[79] In 1980, serious transit crime had reached 13,675 felonies—nearly 300 per week. By 1986, transit felonies totaled 14,018. Two decades earlier, in 1967, for the entire year, the subways had experienced 1,599 felonies—one month's worth by the 1980s.[80] In 1989, the subways saw 16,906 felonies. Horrific crime followed horrific crime. In 1982, Steven Crosland, seventeen, accepted at Howard University, was clubbed to death on a Harlem platform.[81] In 1988, Mona Pierre, thirty-nine, was killed when a robber firebombed her Brooklyn token booth.[82]

Transit crime was impervious to modest economic and population growth. During the 1980s, the population rose from 7.1 to 7.3 million. After years of decline, New York gained 420,300 jobs, or 13 percent. Yet a modest uptick in people riding the subways to Manhattan daily—from 1.6 million in 1981 to nearly 1.8 million by 1988—didn't reverse crime.

New arrivals could stand only so much. "Every time I went down in the subway, I felt I was taking my life in my hands," explained Kate Delano Condax, a West Sider. People sought refuge in automobiles. "The number of autos . . . is headed for a record this year," David Gurin, deputy transportation commissioner, said in 1980. Drivers were "people who used to ride the subways."[83] Three years later, the number of people taking motor vehicles into Manhattan reached nearly 1.2 million, up from 970,000 in 1981, reversing 1970s stabilization.

Vigilantism or Self-Defense?

After a decade of little-noticed self-defense actions, a bespectacled man named Bernie Goetz became New York's subway "vigilante." Three days before Christmas, 1984, Goetz, thirty-seven, an NYU grad and electrical supplier who lived in the Village, was riding through Union Square. Four teens, with records ranging from robbery to burglary and three with a history of farebeating, surrounded him, one asking for money.[84] He shot them, paralyzing one.[85] The gangly, shy Goetz was an odd hero. His gun was illegal; he said he had brought it from Florida after having been beaten on the subway in 1981. After the shooting, he fled, surrendering in New Hampshire.

Yet public opinion flocked to Goetz. A jury acquitted him of attempted murder, convicting him on a weapons charge. The *Times* editorialized, "Mayor Koch and Governor [Mario] Cuomo are right to speak out against vigilantism, but until they accept their duty to the public . . . , their ringing denunciations miss the point."[86] David Dinkins, Manhattan borough president, wrote that "subway crime is a terrible reality of life . . . and it justifiably inspires fear. But the verdict . . . may open the door for people to act on these fears." He feared vigilantes would act out of racism.[87]

Goetz's travails did not deter others. In 1986, a Williamsburg token clerk shot one of four robbers.[88] In January 1990, a man claiming self-defense killed a beggar at Columbus Circle.[89] That April, a robbery victim fatally shot one of four assailants on a Brooklyn train. The case merited a page-twenty-two story; the media had moved on.[90] A new decade and new mayor seemed to offer no relief. That year, 18,324 New Yorkers, including twenty-six murder victims, became felony targets.[91]

From Clean Trains to Safe Trains

Yet riders were becoming primed to demand a safer environment. Even as violence rose during the 1980s, riders had seen evidence that disorder could be tamed. In 1983, after Ravitch left the MTA, Robert Kiley took over; in 1984, he hired David Gunn to run subways. Neither Kiley nor Gunn respected authority—even when they *were* authority. A former CIA operative, Kiley had become Massachusetts governor Michael Dukakis's transportation chief. He had previously overseen Boston's school desegregation in the 1970s as a deputy mayor. Kiley knew the cost of bad transportation design: he had lost his wife and two children in a car crash on the Bronx's I-95.[92] Gunn, a Boston native, had a background managing transit, including in Philadelphia.[93]

In New York, Kiley and Gunn developed an obsession: graffiti. Ravitch's infrastructure refurbishment meant that delays were falling, and they could focus on other problems. Kiley and Gunn were skeptical of the MTA's efforts to stop graffiti, whether through policing or dogs. The MTA had even painted train cars white, remembers Gunn, but "it was a stupid idea." Transit bosses would mix "clean cars" with "dirty cars" on a train; said Gunn, "[The idea was to] have a pair of clean cars in the middle. You might as well have a sign that says, paint me next." Now, the MTA was getting new cars. Kiley was "beside himself," as "they were just going to send the new fleet out and it would be covered with graffiti."[94]

Kiley and Gunn began their anti-graffiti drive in 1984. Their strategy wasn't policing. The answer was "tight security" in train yards "and routine cleaning." The MTA started with the 4 and 7 subway lines. Once a car was clean, the MTA coupled it with other clean cars until it had a clean train. Once a train was clean, MTA workers kept it clean, erasing graffiti at the ends of each route. New stainless-steel cars were easier to clean. Thanks to the tax revenues Ravitch had spurred the legislature to enact, the MTA doubled the number of cleaners.

To deter vandals from repainting cars, the MTA delayed service, inconveniencing passengers as workers cleaned freshly painted cars. "Rub it out right away," Kiley said.[95] By holding clean cars as a priority above service, the MTA made a point to graffitists: spraying trains wouldn't be worth the effort. "It took 40 cans of paint and as much as 12 hours to complete a mural," the *Times* reported a graffiti expert as saying. "Now it is hard even to snap a photograph before the work is cleaned."[96] More than half of trains were clean by 1986. Russianoff, of the Straphangers Campaign, pronounced the progress "a miracle."[97] In 1989, the MTA removed its last graffitied train.

Listening to Fear

Kiley and Gunn saw disorder besides graffiti. Five thousand homeless people lived in the subways. Most were harmless. But suffering from mental illness or addiction, they were dangers to themselves, run over and killed in tunnels. Hundreds, too, took up multiple seats or aggressively panhandled, creating an inhospitable environment. Kiley and Gunn were also disturbed by the high number of farebeaters.

The MTA managers badgered transit police to fix these problems, but for years, they heard that nothing could be done. To get a fresh perspective, in 1985, they hired George Kelling, another outsider, as a consultant. Kelling, previously a social worker and probation officer, had observed what was wrong with policing. In 1982, with Wilson, the Harvard professor, he had coauthored an article for *The Atlantic*: "Broken Windows." Kelling and Wilson argued that low-level disorder, ignored by government, begot more disorder. "If a window in a building is broken and is left unrepaired, all the rest of the windows will soon be broken," they wrote. "One unrepaired broken window is a signal that no one cares." About low-level misconduct, they said, "we tend to overlook [a] source of fear" keeping people away from public spaces: "fear of being bothered by disorderly people. Not violent people, nor, necessarily, criminals, but . . . panhandlers, drunks, addicts, rowdy teenagers."[98]

The logic of stopping small crimes before they escalated, and even just to stop small crimes, appealed to Kiley and Gunn, who knew that riders were uncomfortable. "Fear and intimidation are at the heart of the subway crime problem," the 1979 NRDC report said. "Threatening situations which may be minor or avoidable on the streets . . . create a uniquely frightening situation for the passenger who feels trapped." Even smoking or "radio playing must also be put in the category of threat because they are often done with the stance to other passengers of 'I dare you to stop me.'"

Kelling suggested a new transit-police leader: Bill Bratton, forty-two, whom he had known in Boston, and who was open to new ideas. Bratton had served for four years as superintendent of Massachusetts's Metropolitan Police Department, which provided policing for public spaces such as parks. "He has never directed a police force of the size and complexity of the New York Transit Authority police," the *Times* wrote. "People have a sense that the subways are not safe, and I hope to change that," Bratton told the paper in April 1990.[99] But he kept expectations low. "The numbers . . . will probably not go down for a while," he said.[100]

The Right Mayor at the Right Moment

At 10:20 p.m. on Sunday, September 2, 1990, Brian Watkins, visiting from Utah, entered a Midtown subway with his parents, brother, and sister-in-law. Watkins, twenty-two, was a former high-school tennis star, in town to attend the U.S. Open. Several teenagers, having entered without paying fares, surrounded the family on the subway platform.[101] When Brian defended his parents, one mugger drove a knife into his chest. The killers went to the Roseland Ballroom nearby, buying tickets with the Watkinses' money. Watkins's killing represented New York's nadir, spurring *Time* to devote its cover to "The Rotting of the Big Apple." The killing provided another element of pressure to buttress Bratton: outrage. Watkins's "stabbing underlined the doubts, fears and frustrations that many people have," said the *Times*. "It underscored a sense of randomness."[102]

This perception had long been reality. But something was different. The year 1990 was an *annus horribilis*. After having hovered around 1,500 a year for nearly two decades, the city would top 2,245 killings. Several killings commanded attention before Watkins's death. In March, Julio González, thirty-seven, lined the entrance to the illegal Bronx nightclub where his ex-girlfriend worked with gasoline and set it alight. Eighty-seven people perished. Papers ran photos of bodies on the sidewalk for days. A killer styling himself the "Zodiac" targeted random New Yorkers, a gunshot for each astrology sign. Finally, New York had spent the summer mourning children. In one week, four children under ten were killed by stray bullets.[103]

The timing of Watkins's murder was politically fortuitous. The city had a new mayor, Democrat David Dinkins, in his ninth month. The previous fall, Dinkins had run against Rudolph Giuliani, a former federal prosecutor who had made his name fighting corruption. Dinkins ran on an anti-crime platform. Vowing to do "anything right that works" to rescue a city "under siege," he promised law and order. "Every crime must be punished," he said. "I don't care if you 'just' stole a car for the night, or if you 'just' took a few dollars."[104]

Before Watkins's killing, Dinkins had taken steps to improve safety. Three months before, the mayor had negotiated the budget with the city council. Despite a recession, the city added 3,234 officers. Recruits, after accounting for retirements, would leave ranks 1,000 higher, at about 27,000, still below the pre-1975 peak of nearly 32,000.[105] To pay for the initiative, the council and the mayor did something politically brave: enact the biggest tax hike in history, $800 million. Property taxes rose by an average of $50 per homeowner.[106]

That Watkins had been in town for the U.S. Open gutted Dinkins. The mayor was a tennis superfan, and the U.S. Open "was the biggest thing for him," recalls his first deputy mayor, Norman Steisel.[107] He regularly took vacation to attend the tournament. Indeed, he cared so much that he prevailed upon the Federal Aviation Administration to reroute planes around the stadium.[108]

The mayor also wanted the tournament to renew its lease, as the game brought in tourist dollars. "The timing, the U.S. Open, David Dinkins, the new elected mayor, this was going to be his signature event," remembers Bratton. "It attracted international attention. . . . The city was encouraging people to take the subway to the U.S. Open." Watkins's killing turned the event into a public-relations disaster. The family had been "perfect New York tourists" who came to the city even when friends had said it was dangerous.[109] It happened "just as we were coming into a big tourist season, the [Christmas] holidays," says Bratton.[110]

The Watkinses were gracious in grief. Devout Mormons, the family never lashed out. "New York City is sometimes depicted as a cold and heartless city, but we have found the opposite," they wrote in the *Times*.[111] Watkins's family came to New York to testify on subway safety, speaking in favor of more police.[112]

New York looked to Dinkins to do more than he had done in the summer budget. The mayor called the death an "atrocity."[113] Police caught Watkins's alleged killers, charging eight young men with murder. But the public wanted an immediate decline in crime. Transit advocates made the urgency clear. "We write to urge you to move now to combat the subway's growing crisis," implored the Straphangers' Russianoff, "an increase in crime that may mean as many as 20,000 reported felonies this year. . . . The tragic murder of Brian Watkins . . . was not an isolated incident. . . . Riders . . . are at risk as never before. . . . You must . . . get the transit police force up."[114] City council Speaker Peter Vallone, a centrist Democrat, called for 5,000 more officers citywide. To pay for the plan, remembers Vallone, "we said, we're going to add another $50 each [tax] to people making $50,000 or more."

Dinkins wanted to wait for earlier reforms to show results, but the pressure was relentless. The *New York Post* ran its front-page plea: "Dave, Do Something!" The *Times* expressed frustration. "Why does Mayor David Dinkins remain so quiet?" the *Times* wondered.[115] "Dinkins's call for patience seems weak."[116]

The business community, too, pressured Dinkins. Executives signaled that they would accept higher taxes, as they had done a decade earlier with Ravitch's MTA proposals. "The Rudins were really the leaders," says Steisel, referring to Lew Rudin, the real estate developer. "ABNY [the Association for a Better New York, a business coalition] was a very powerful voice." They were telling Dinkins that he could ask the governor for state tax funding, with business support.

Dinkins responded. "We must stop the drug runners, the child killers and the muggers, but we must also refuse to tolerate the subway farebeaters," he wrote a week after Watkins died, in a *Times* op-ed illustrated with a desiccated apple.[117] Governor Cuomo, in a Manhattan speech, concurred. "Either we respond," the governor said—referring to a "great wave of fear"—"[or] we admit to the most fundamental failure."[118] A month later, Dinkins unveiled his plan.[119] Under the umbrella "Safe Streets, Safe City," he proposed a record city police force, 31,944 officers.

By February 1991, the city council as well as Cuomo and the legislature had passed Dinkins's proposal. The plan required another property tax increase, of about $10 per homeowner, the extension of an income-tax surcharge, and expanded lottery revenues.[120] "The money . . . provided the real tipping point to turning around the crime and disorder in the subway," says Bratton. "[Watkins's] death was the beginning of the turnaround of twenty-some-odd years of crime."[121]

Fixing Broken Windows

Bratton now had the resources to implement the broken-windows plan he and Kelling already had been devising: reduce disorder, farebeating, and robbery, and thus reduce violence. A reinvigorated transit police department had advantages that police above ground did not. The subway isn't private property, but it isn't quite public space. It has its own rules. By entering, passengers agreed not to lie across benches, panhandle, or walk between cars. Kelling and Bratton focused on behavior, not on status. Looking disheveled was not a crime. But jumping over a turnstile was a crime. This strategy didn't involve imprisoning the vulnerable, however. Four months before the Watkins murder, in May 1990, Bratton had said that rather than arrest or ticket subway panhandlers, police would eject them.[122]

A month later, in June, Bratton attacked farebeating. The quarter-million people entering the system daily without paying comprised 6 percent of riders. Before stepping up enforcement, police warned the public. "There were not 250,000 criminals," Kelling said. "People got into bad habits." Passengers thought the ride was unreliable and not worth the money, or they saw other people beating the fare, and didn't want to be chumps. Part of the problem was broken equipment.[123] As the MTA repaired turnstiles, people who had once leaped over had no excuse. The MTA launched a campaign to "warn people, educate people," Kelling remembered. To show the public that farebeating was no longer accepted behavior, police were consistent. Transit police made sure the program was citywide, not targeting poor neighborhoods. "Lucrative places [to catch people jumping turnstiles and committing robberies, or gumming up machines and stealing fares from riders] were Times Square, Union Square, Wall Street," says Bratton.

Notwithstanding promised officers, Bratton was stymied by a manpower problem. "[A] phenomenal disincentive to making evasion arrests," he said, "[was that] one arrest could tie up an officer" as police transported arrestees to precincts or to court. Bratton perfected a "bust-to-the-bus" system: detain farebeaters and have them wait on a bus aboveground, outfitted with a fax machine. Most received only a civil summons, as they had no arrest history. These fare thieves were deterred from doing it again, though: they did not like being held on a bus for hours with hardened criminals.

Repeat fare evaders, or people who wanted to avoid the then-fifty-dollar fine, could sign up for community service, and it was a well-publicized event, part of the deterrence strategy. "Thousands of riders—including insurance salesmen, artists, messengers, college students and even grandmothers—are being . . . sentenced to painting Transit Authority buildings, scraping gum from station floors or scrubbing toilets as punishment for fare beating," the *Times* wrote in February 1991.[124] The shaming reiterated that, after decades of laxity, stealing the fare carried a penalty.

These actions quickly illustrated how Bratton's strategy would work: stopping small crimes did prevent larger crimes. Fare evaders, relative to the population, were more likely to be carrying a weapon, have an outstanding warrant for a felony, or have a history of ignoring farebeating summonses.[125] "One out of twenty-two was carrying a weapon," says

Bratton. "We . . . [stopped] serious criminals carrying weapons at the turnstiles before they [got] on the subways," says Bratton. "It became not a boring assignment, but an exciting one," improving police morale.

Repeat offenders who didn't show up in court faced a penalty, converting long-useless "disappearance tickets" into sanctions. "If you didn't show up for a transit warrant, we would be banging on your door," says Bratton. Finally, police pioneered another tactic. When a violent transit offender was about to get out of prison, detectives showed up to his probation meeting. The message was, "We know you're back," says Bratton.

Broken-windows policing yielded immediate results. In October 1990, a month after Watkins's killing, transit police ejected 10,994 people, compared to 2,309 people in October 1989.[126] Summonses that December nearly doubled, to 25,650; misdemeanor arrests nearly tripled, to 2,108. Felony arrests rose almost 13 percent, to 547. For the full year of 1990—driven by the post-Watkins final quarter—misdemeanor arrests were up 80 percent, to 18,268. That October, subway crime fell. The month's 1,607 felonies were 5 percent below the previous October's.[127] By 1991, transit police—their ranks boosted to 3,800—made 17,492 arrests for farebeating between January and November of 1991, compared to 8,679 in the same period of 1990.[128] Serious crime fell 15 percent.[129]

Crimes didn't vanish. Twenty people lost their lives in 1991.[130] Yet the downward trend held. In the first three months of 1992, transit police, ranks up to 4,300, arrested 6,601 people for farebeating, double the 1990 figure. That quarter, felonies fell 14 percent and robberies 32 percent.[131] By mid-1992, "[the farebeating sweep had] nabbed large numbers of people who are wanted on warrants for other crimes. And they have enabled the police to stop hundreds of people . . . from entering the subway armed with everything from small handguns to sawed-off shotguns."[132]

Bratton left in 1992 (returning as city police commissioner under mayors Rudy Giuliani in 1994 and, two decades later, Bill de Blasio), but Kelling's philosophy kept trains safe. By 1993, subway crime was down more than one-third since 1990.[133] In 1994, transit crime fell 22 percent, robberies 28 percent. Eight people were killed in 1993, eleven in 1994—less than half the 1990 total.[134] The NYPD took over transit police in 1995 but maintained the same strategy.

By 1997, fewer than 1 percent of riders, 35,000 a day, beat the fare.[135] Subway felonies were 70 percent lower than in 1990.[136] That year, 4 people were killed on the subway and 6,218 fell victims to felonies—one-third of the 1990 total. By 2005, felonies had fallen by half, again, to 3,100. From then on, one or two people became murder victims each year. By 2017, felonies, at 2,474, were down to 7 per day, from a high of 50. That year, no rider or worker lost his or her life to murder.[137] By the twenty-first century, it took eleven years for twenty-six people to become murder victims in the transit system, the number killed in 1990. Safety held, even as transit police ranks fell to 2,730 officers. Safe subways were part of a safe city: in the late 2010s, thanks in part to preventative policing, New York's murder level hovered at about 300 a year, nearly 90 percent below the 1990 figure.

Stopped and Frisked

Policing was one of several factors in the crime decline that continued until 2019. Investment in education under mayors Bloomberg and de Blasio pushed graduation rates up, giving young adults employable skills. A record number of residents and visitors created entry-level jobs. Cameras aided in catching suspects, preventing repeat crimes. Reduced use of cash and elimination of cash-like tokens reduced temptation.

Policing levies a cost. Although the subway is not an appropriate place for homeless and mentally ill individuals, ejection does not fix the underlying problem: federal, state, and local governments offer inadequate care. Bad policing and prosecution practices harm the innocent. One of the eight people arrested for killing Brian Watkins, and one of seven people convicted, was Johnny Hincapie. Eighteen when arrested, he spent twenty-four years in prison based on a coerced confession. He eventually saw his conviction overturned, as there was no evidence that he was at the crime scene.

For decades, New Yorkers have worried about racial disparities in crime and policing. In 1964, Martin Luther King Jr. said that subway crime was caused by "individuals who are victims of chronic poverty."[138] David Jones, an MTA board member and president of the Community Service Society, an anti-poverty group, worries about enforcement disparities. "Having grown up in Crown Heights [Brooklyn] in the 1950s and 1960s," says Jones, "I think every one of my generation has been stopped and frisked . . . [It's] a question of equity. It's not that you shouldn't stop farebeating, but you should be equitable."

Michael O'Connor, transit police chief from 1992 to 1994, differentiates the transit system's broken-windows policing from the broader above-ground tactic of stop, question, and frisk. "It was never part of the strategy," he says. "It's not appropriate on a mass scale. . . . It's designed for a specific situation." Transit police didn't target people for suspicious behavior, but those who were breaking a law or rule.

Still, Jones worries that enforcement punishes poverty. New York has ended its practice of the first half of the twentieth century and now raises the fare regularly. Most poor people pay their fares, and Jones spearheaded New York's "fair fares" program, launched in 2019, which offers a half-price fare to poor people. But police now conduct stings in poor neighborhoods, Jones says. "If you couldn't afford to pay $2.75, to get a fine, that's $100 [the current penalty,] the likelihood of affording $100 is not going to happen. People who don't show up to pay their fine, when they're caught again, they can get a misdemeanor," and have a criminal record. Yet to acknowledge that policing has disparate results doesn't solve how to prevent violence without policing.

Broken-windows policing, by preventing crime, reduced incarceration. In 1991, the population at the city's Rikers Island jails was 21,674; by 2019, even before a state law to reduce pretrial detainment took effect, it was 7,000. A lower crime rate meant fewer people behind bars in state prison, as well. If police had caught Watkins's would-be killers beating the fare that 1990 Labor Day weekend, they would have not only saved a man's life; they would have saved seven men from prison.

Safer subways resulted, eventually, in less policing—a phenomenon that Bratton, in 2015, called a "peace dividend."[139] In December 1990, transit police issued 28,304 arrests or summonses. By December 2019, the figure was 6,748. Yet no one was killed or raped in the subway that month, and just sixty people were robbed—a fraction of the nearly eight hundred monthly robberies nearly thirty years previously.[140] In 2019, most enforcement in the subway was civil, not criminal, with 89,181 civil tickets out of 99,688 total tickets and arrests. Yet this continued enforcement helped keep crime near record lows. In 2015, the NYPD removed forty handguns and six hundred knives from people beating the fare. They also caught fugitives. In 2016, Anibal Vargas, wanted for attempted murder in Massachusetts in 1990, jumped the fare in Greenwich Village and was apprehended.

In 2017, the Manhattan district attorney said that he would stop prosecuting the few farebeaters who, usually because they were recidivists, faced arrest rather than a civil summons. Crime didn't immediately rise. Police continued to write civil tickets and continued to find lawbreakers carrying weapons: 20 guns and 479 knives in 2019. Behavior learned over decades, coupled with deterrence created by crowds and a booming economy, held—for a while.

Women Alone

Bratton, Cuomo, Dinkins, Gunn, Kelling, Kiley, O'Connor, and Vallone helped avert some 450 murders over three decades. They also helped secure New York's future. Subways were the underpinning beneath New York's reversal of 1970s declines. In 1981, 1.6 million people took a subway into Manhattan daily; by 1990, the figure was 1.7 million; by 2000, it was 2 million; and by 2015, it was 2.3 million. By 2015, subways carried nearly 1.8 billion people citywide a year—nearly twice the 1990 figure. Midnight trains were as crowded as rush-hour trains three decades before.

By 2019, New York had a record population, above 8.5 million people, and a near-record 4.7 million jobs. New York welcomed 67 million tourists in 2019, almost triple the 1990 figure.[141] Population, jobs, and visitor numbers grew without adding a single commuting car to Manhattan. In 2019, 910,000 people came to Manhattan each day by motor vehicle, lower than the 970,000 in 1981.[142] Because New York accomplished the government's core jobs—providing public infrastructure and public safety—people felt confident in an enclosed space with strangers.

Not long before his 2019 death, Kelling took a late-night subway, noticing people "going over their iPhones, women alone. You would never have done that," he said. "They would have been targets."

Part 3

BEYOND TRANSIT

Wrestling with New York's Asphalt Legacy

Chapter 11

Splitting Lanes

From Bike Nuts to Bike Share

Bike riders will find their victory is short-lived.

—Mayor Ed Koch, 1987

We don't have as many bicycle lanes as we need.

—Mayor Michael R. Bloomberg, 2007

IN 1987, MAYOR ED KOCH SUMMONED REPORTERS to City Hall to announce a crackdown on bicyclists. The city would ban bikes from Manhattan avenues—Fifth, Madison, and Park—on weekdays between 10:00 a.m. and 4:00 p.m. Riders were "scaring the public to death," said police commissioner Benjamin Ward.[1] The banishment of an environmentally and physically healthy—as well as fast and cheap—way of getting around Midtown was a reversal of twenty years of progress for cyclists, beginning in the Lindsay era two decades earlier. But Koch's attempted ban had the opposite effect of what the mayor intended. He unwittingly united cyclists from disparate backgrounds—hirsute environmentalists or document-toting messengers; exercising, commuting, or working on the job—to create a bike lobby, determined to change who had a right to the streets.

It took another two decades and another mayor, though—one who didn't heed short-term criticism—to transform cycling from a fringe issue for people too weird or too poor to find another way to get around into everyday transportation. By the new millennium's second decade, thanks to Michael Bloomberg, bankers and lawyers in suits and skirts pedaling bright blue municipal bikes had become a common sight.

Car-Free Sunday Mornings

Before cars and trucks dominated New York's streets, bicycling was common. Children biked unsupervised. "I was an avid cyclist," recalls David Gurin, future journalist and transportation official, who grew up in Brooklyn in the 1940s and 1950s. But traffic grew. "When I was a boy, . . . there were probably a third to half of the cars as there are now. It kept on growing. . . . I couldn't help but feel attacked."[2] Sam Schwartz, Koch-era traffic commissioner, agrees. A fellow Brooklynite, he cycled to the new Verrazano-Narrows Bridge as a teen, in 1964, to find that the Moses-built span prohibited bikes. As cars took over, cyclists stuck to dedicated paths, such as along Ocean Parkway in south Brooklyn, New York's first bike lane, built in 1895. Space for cyclists was rare. "We were wonders and oddities," wrote Charlie McCorkell, an engineer who rode to college in Manhattan from his parents' home in Brooklyn, because of his "intense dislike . . . of the subway."[3]

As John Lindsay took office in 1966, a small band of New Yorkers determined to change the odd into the everyday. That spring, the Century Road Club Association, a cycling group, approached Lindsay's parks commissioner, Thomas Hoving, and his traffic commissioner, Henry Barnes, with a request: close Central Park's drives—four-lane shortcuts for autos traveling from upper Manhattan to Midtown—on three May Sundays for amateur bike races.

Barnes, a holdover from the Wagner era, opposed the closure. A veteran of traffic-management jobs in Flint, Michigan, the General Motors hub, and in Baltimore, a city then with no subways, he thought that the more space cars had on streets the more smoothly their occupants would flow.[4] It wasn't that Sunday traffic would be unmanageable without the Central Park drives. Rather, Barnes argued, a "serious consequence" would be that people would like the road closures so much that they would demand more closures, including, someday, on Fifth Avenue.

Hoving, a thirty-four-year-old former Metropolitan Museum curator, favored keeping the park open to cyclists for the rest of the day after the race was over. He recommended repeating the closures throughout summer to restore a "leisurely aspect" to what had become "menacing speedways." Central Park's nineteenth-century creators, architects Frederick Law Olmsted and Calvert Vaux, had designed the 843-acre Manhattan oasis's thoroughfares for slow-paced horse carriages, not for motor vehicles.

Hoving had the social and political capital needed to stand up to Barnes. His father, Walter, had been chairman of the Tiffany jeweler, president of the Lord & Taylor department store, and head of the Fifth Avenue

Association, the business coalition. The commissioners compromised, closing the road until 11:00 a.m. on the proposed three Sundays.[5] But "talk of experiments, automobile bans, and leisurely Sunday mornings" beyond the races was gone.[6]

This warning didn't deter anti-car activists. "We thought that something should be done," says Barry Benepe, an architect for the city, who, on his own time, was cochair of the traffic committee for the community board on the Upper West Side, near Central Park. Benepe was initially interested in pedestrians, not cyclists. "My involvement in pedestrian safety goes back to when I was a child," he said. "When I was walking with my father, I might have been six or seven, I used to walk with him to Gramercy Park at his office. . . . As we were approaching Madison Square, I heard the screech of brakes. I saw a taxi run into a pedestrian. I saw them lifting this man off the pavement." As an adult, Benepe was incensed by efforts by Barnes to narrow sidewalks.[7]

Benepe thought helping cyclists would help walkers, as they both faced the same threat—cars. On that first May Sunday, Benepe made sure racers were followed by a protest ride. An "amiable carriage horse named Sunshine led 60 cyclists, politicians, and other assorted humans" in an "anti-automobile" march, the *New York Times* wrote, bicycles festooned with "colored balloons." The group wanted the drive closed to cars and open to cyclists and walkers every summer Sunday. The protesters were recreational cyclists, a growing constituency. Child cyclists such as Gurin had grown up to be members of American Youth Hostels, a group that organized rides around the northeast, cementing ties useful for political organization. The "thicket of gleaming bicycle chrome" stopped traffic after the race. The group was haphazard; Benepe had organized riders to wear letters on their backs spelling out "SUNDAY CAR BAN/PEOPLE NOT CARS," but they disarranged themselves, so that the letters read as "NO SUNDAY CAR BAN/LEOEPPRACST." One driver, thinking cyclists were protesting the Vietnam War, called them "cowards."[8] But the group attracted support. One attendee was Ed Koch, then–Greenwich Village Democratic coleader and aspiring city councilman, riding in the carriage.

Cyclists got their wish. During the third closure, the mayor joined the group. With his wife and three young children, demonstrating "slow and steady pedaling" on his two-dollar rental bike, Lindsay pronounced himself in favor of Sunday closures until 3 p.m., all summer. The mayor was easygoing, pausing to let his six-year-old son catch up.[9]

Lindsay was publicly conciliatory toward Barnes, who was in the hospital, suffering from the heart ailment that would kill him two years later. When a reporter informed the mayor that the traffic commissioner opposed closures, he responded that "we'll work this out." Behind the scenes, though, the mayor had been firm. "Barnes was violently opposed," remembered Jay Kriegel, a top aide. "He told the mayor that he controlled the roads. The mayor, though, backed Hoving, and said, 'I make the decisions.'"[10] New York needed decisiveness: that pre-summer day, the temperature reached ninety-five degrees, and melting asphalt left the minority of New Yorkers who relied on cars stuck in traffic, sweltering with windows open.

Park closures—openings, from cyclists' viewpoint—were popular. By September, Lindsay had extended them to 4 p.m. and had added Brooklyn's Prospect Park as well as a park each in Staten Island and Queens.[11] The next year, the mayor added Saturdays and Tuesday nights. Soon after, he continued weekend closures all year.[12] Robert Abrams, Bronx borough president, said the "brilliant, provocative step" inspired him to convince the borough police commander to close the Grand Concourse, a major thoroughfare, on Sundays. "My office received a death threat," he remembered. "The Police Department wanted to cancel."[13]

Car-free parks became an unmissable feature of the hot city summer. Central Park was "jammed" with ten thousand cyclists. "East Side matrons in pants suits, East Village hippies and Puerto Ricans from East Harlem join others to stand in line for up to two hours to pay $1.25 to rent a bicycle," the *Times* reported. Cyclists were a who's who: Harry Belafonte, Kirk Douglas, Douglas Fairbanks Jr., Cary Grant—"the actual, real Cary Grant," one woman enthused—Sidney Poitier, Sandy Dennis, and Senator Jacob Javits. It was a pick-up scene. "There are so many men," marveled a twenty-one-year-old nurse.[14] In 1971, socialites organized a "bicycle bash" for the New York Eye and Ear Infirmary, paying forty-five dollars to ride through the park. "Mrs. Don Durgin" rode tandem with her husband, the NBC network president.

Antipollution activists saw the closures as an opportunity to collect data. Hoving asked Citizens for Clean Air to publicize the difference in noise and air. Carolyn Konheim, CCA's chairman, backed up public experience with statistics. On Friday, when traffic was normal, she and a member of the city's air pollution control board tested carbon monoxide levels. When the park was closed to traffic, the rate fell by two-thirds.

The festive air represented a win for the mayor. After the subway strike, and as he lost his battle for control of subways against Rockefeller, he needed some good PR. "It was a really nasty time," remembered Ted Mastroianni, another administration official. "People were very angry." Bicycling in the park, by contrast, was "really magical."[15] When so much wasn't working, park closures were, finally, a successful Lindsay program. "Lindsay would try things, and see how it worked," said Kriegel. "In . . . Central Park, it was clear that it worked well."

Cycling weekends were part of Lindsay's strategy of providing a better quality of life to retain affluent New Yorkers, akin to his push for air-conditioned subways. "Lindsay believed you had to make cities more livable," said Kriegel. More than three decades later, just after Lindsay's death in 2000, *Times* letter-writer Gerald Scorse said that though the former mayor would be judged on "large issues" such as crime, "the best thing he did was one of the smallest: closing Central Park to vehicular traffic on weekends."[16]

The coup reverberated. It wasn't the first defeat of cars: less than half a decade earlier, Hayes had paved the way in Washington Square. But Central Park was the backyard of Manhattan power, with media, corporate, financial, and government executives living on the adjacent Upper East Side. It was also a public space for all New Yorkers. Harlem bordered the north, and Hispanic migrants were moving to the northern edges of the Upper West Side. Because of this prominence, "psychologically," said Kriegel, "that was pretty much the first thing to say, this ratio between the cars and the people isn't foreordained."

No Weekday Commutes

Since recreational cyclists could become commuting cyclists, advocates reasoned, the next push would be to demand room on roads. To advocate for bike lanes, two Upper West Siders, Harriet Green and her husband, Port Authority architect Barry Fishman, cofounded Bike for a Better City. Taking advantage of Central Park cycling days, Fishman and Green designed buttons with a mod logo and sold them to riders. They amassed a mailing list. In 1970, they printed posters and mailings inviting people to join a "Bike to Work" ride.[17]

The initiative gained the mayor's attention as he tried, in his second term, to revive his freshness. In September, Lindsay proclaimed "Bike for a Better City Day," noting that riding was "a non-polluting mode of transportation." He and other luminaries, such as Charles Luce, chairman of electricity provider Con Ed, under fire for pollution, and David Dubinsky, cocreator of the Congress of Industrial Organizations labor coalition, joined one thousand musicians, artists, and regular people Fishman and Green had gathered to commute from Central Park five miles to Wall Street. Police cordoned a lane of Fifth Avenue and Broadway, the first time since automobile ascendancy that cyclists had enjoyed car-free space on Manhattan streets.[18] The *Times*, around the same time it was giving up on elevated urban highways, approved. "A reversal is beginning to assert itself as citizens take stock of the cost in debasement of the atmosphere" and "do something to keep their city livable."[19]

Lindsay promised to turn the event into change. "High officials" said that a permanent "special lane [for bicyclists was] very, very likely." "People want to travel around the city by bicycle," affirmed Lindsay's transportation administrator, Constantine Sidamon-Eristoff. "If setting aside a special lane on one of the avenues doesn't discombobulate too many motorists, why not?" In 1971, cyclists won easier access to the Brooklyn Bridge, with ramps and stripes to separate cyclists from walkers on the pedestrian level. Since nearly 80 percent of New Yorkers didn't live in Manhattan, the center of the city's jobs, access over crossings was important.[20]

Cyclists were soon disappointed, though. By 1971, Lindsay had "cooled" to bicycle commuting. The second bike-to-work day fizzled. Advocates, "disappointed" and "angry," found no city officials to accompany them. One official, Edward Skloot, warned riders, "There was no provision for special bicycle lanes," unlike the year before. When cyclists made it to City Hall, they had to navigate government workers' triple-parked cars. Skloot told cyclists that the city would issue a handbook on safety. "The new feeling was that setting aside special bicycle lanes would add more congestion, because bike riders would normally take public transportation." Skloot observed to the *Times* that Lindsay favored "recreational biking," as in Central Park, which was "easier politically."[21]

Special interests had objected. "The oil and gas lobby, the Auto Club, the trucks, they all said, 'no, no, don't do it,'" remembered Mastroianni. "Every commercial group, all the department stores, said, they didn't want any of that." Fifth Avenue Association retail interests scoffed at bicycle lanes encroaching upon parking and taxi space. Michael Grosso, head of the association, mocked the prospect of "matronly women" visiting Bergdorf Goodman, the high-end emporium, on two wheels. Unconvinced that cycle lanes would attract customers, executives thought the removal of car space would send customers to suburban malls. Lindsay's political calculus was cynical but correct. Cyclists were not powerful enough to outweigh corporate taxpayers. It was one thing to give cyclists room in Central Park. It was another thing to take space on traffic-clogged avenues.

Stung by criticism, though, Lindsay announced a half-measure in October. He would create bikeways in Manhattan. But the bikeways wouldn't be dedicated lanes, only signs informing drivers that they should share the route with bicycles. Cyclists reacted with derision. Cataloguing recent deaths, Bike for a Better City's Green asked, "How many more bikers do we have to lose?" Cyclists stood with political allies, few but staunch. Koch, now a congressman, criticized the mayor. "The only way to ensure safety for the many thousands of New Yorkers who want to bicycle is to designate official and exclusive bike lanes," he said. Eldon Clingan, the liberal minority leader of the city council, branded Lindsay's sign-only bikeways as a "deadly hoax," adding, "If biking were safe, we'd have 100,000 New Yorkers [cycling regularly]." Yet neither official had any local power.[22]

A Band of Bicyclists

The advocates who had gotten Central Park closed to cars on weekends honed their technique: the protest ride. This period was the era in which New Yorkers, like urban residents from Paris to Cairo, were taking to the streets, demanding everything from an end to the Vietnam War to rights for minorities, women, and gay people. Cycling advocates pedaled into streets to demand access to streets themselves.

Advocates found inspiration in Europe. With its lack of cheap oil, denser, smaller homes connected to transit, and a conservation legacy from World War II, Europe was ahead of New York. In 1966, Gurin informed *Voice* readers of the "white bike scheme," a project by a group of Dutch anarchists called Provo who were fighting both capitalism (soulless automation) and communism (soulless bureaucracy); their goal was to post seventy thousand free white bikes around Amsterdam. The dozens of bikes Provo put out as a pilot failed—police confiscated them, and people stole them—but it was an early attempt at the eventual Dutch success at getting its urban population to switch from cars.[23]

Bike advocates were also influenced by and influencers of the environmental movement. In 1968, Gurin, calling himself a "dissident city planner," organized a few "Urban Underground Friends" to picket the brand-new fifty-story General Motors skyscrapers on Fifth Avenue near Central Park. A more momentous event, two years later, was Earth Day, in April 1970. Lindsay—overruling police—shut down both Fifth Avenue and Fourteenth Street to cars. This "holiday" wasn't a practical day for bike riding because of the human mass that crammed streets. But with cleaner air and the atmosphere relaxed, it was a boon for the *idea* of riding. Gurin's front-page Earth Day article for the *Voice* was headlined, "The Everyday"—jams, noise, and pollution—"Never Seemed So Obscene."[24]

Two years after the inaugural Earth Day, a small group of protestors agitated against cars. The group—styling itself "Action Against Automobiles," to borrow the initials of the American Automobile Association—printed fliers to picket the annual auto show. "WE DEMAND: NO PRIVATE CARS IN MANHATTAN (then rearrange the system of buses, cabs, and trucks), MILLIONS FOR PUBLIC TRANSIT, NO MORE MONEY FOR HIGHWAYS (stop the spending of $2 BILLION on rebuilding the West Side Highway). Rebuild subways instead. FREE BICYCLES," exhorted a poster.

Gurin and fellow advocates—Benepe, McCorkell, Ketcham, urban planner and "gadfly" Roger Herz, and open-space advocate Fred Kent—decided that it would be wiser to be not against but for something, and to be, as Gurin puts it, "less extreme." Thus was born, in 1973, Transportation Alternatives (TA), "a more appealing title" than Action Against Automobiles. TA's first ride, in 1973, received good press, thanks to Gurin convincing a *Times* friend to come: "400 fresh-air enthusiasts bicycled through the perfect spring afternoon," accompanied by "six dogs on foot and two cats carried on children's tricycles." Cyclists made their way down Fifth Avenue to Washington Square, slowing traffic.

TA pursued the same goal as Bike for a Better City had, notwithstanding Lindsay's apathy. As the *Times* put it, "The group's principal demand is that city and state officials add the concept of exclusive bike lanes to strategies that they have devised [under the Clean Air Act] to reduce auto pollution." As Gurin told the paper, such lanes would correct an imbalance, as one-third of the city's land was devoted to traffic or "storage," otherwise known as parking.[25] In less than half a decade, the movement had evolved beyond weekend space for recreation, which implied that cycling was for fun, to insisting that the city treat cycling as commuting. Still, Gurin says, "we were on the fringes."

TA reprised the protest ride in 1974, joined by Congressman Koch. ("He barely knew how to ride a bike," says Gurin.) The fuel crisis had spurred hopes of an urban renaissance—if not car-free, cities not defined by cars. At a Washington conference, Edward K. Hamilton, a deputy mayor, said that skyrocketing energy prices would mean "you won't mobilize 300 horsepower to go to the drugstore for a pack of cigarettes."[26]

A parallel urban-livability argument was prescient. In 1974, Simon Breines, a preservation architect, and William J. Dean, a public interest attorney, published *The Pedestrian Revolution: Streets without Cars*. "In . . . built-up cities, the automobile simply leaves no room for the bicycle," Breines and Dean wrote. "Without the physical separation of bicycles from vehicular traffic, the bicycle will never be able to fulfill its potential role."

Noting that "bicycles are the fastest form of urban transport for trips up to three miles," the authors wrote that "urban bikeways are like highways: a good system will generate increased use."

The authors noted Amsterdam's successes over the previous decade in increasing cycling to 60 percent of central-city trips. They proposed a seemingly utopian idea. "Suppose it were possible to pick up a rental bike at convenient depots . . . , ride it to work, and leave it at another depot," under a paid subscription in return for unlimited rides. "Four hundred depots . . . in Manhattan" could generate ninety thousand subscribers, the authors predicted.

But present-day dystopia persisted. New York did not get its bike lane, never mind a shared-bike program. Gas prices fell. Under Mayor Beame, who succeeded Lindsay in 1974, the city's near bankruptcy and social woes eclipsed other priorities. When "whole neighborhoods were being emptied and burned—political space [as well as physical space] for bicycling was scarce," wrote Charles Komanoff, transportation and energy economist.[27]

A Willingness to Bike

In the 1977 mayoral election, cycling advocates had a stroke of luck. Koch, who had never owned a car, would succeed Beame. He had ridden—unsteadily—through Central Park with Transportation Alternatives. He had pushed for bike lanes. Gurin, who had been open about his anti-car and pro-bike stance, became a transportation deputy.

The era started promisingly. In 1978, the city unveiled Midtown bike lanes on Broadway and Sixth Avenue. The lanes hardly represented a transformation. The mayor didn't show up to inaugurate them. The city hadn't taken away driving lanes; rather, it had narrowed parking lanes. Cyclists didn't enjoy protection from faster, heavier vehicles via a physical barrier; rather, transportation workers had painted diamonds, "the international symbol of a bicycle lane." Drivers, unfazed by this symbol, double-parked. Still, one count showed bicycle traffic more than tripling, from 31 to 101 bikes an hour.[28] In 1979, Koch reserved a lane on the Queensboro Bridge for cyclists and pedestrians, "the first full-time [bicycle] link between Queens and the Central Business District," fulfilling a TA goal.[29]

Two years later, in 1980, Koch visited Peking. In the Chinese capital (now Beijing), "he saw all these bikes and he was very impressed," recalls Gurin. Another piece of happenstance fortified Koch. In March, the Transport Workers Union threatened a transit strike. Koch, "smiling," told the press that in a shutdown, "we'd like to see New York City look like Peking. . . . There are over one million bicycles used there every morning."[30]

On April Fool's Day, the transit union walked off the job for the second time. This eleven-day strike would be nothing like the walkout that had damaged Lindsay fourteen years earlier. Koch was in his third year in office, not on his first day, and his administration had planned for a strike. Koch understood better than Lindsay how organized labor worked and that it was important to be optimistic and organized, to show that the union couldn't paralyze the city. Finally, April is warmer than January.

Koch managed the strike so that it was a triumph, not a disaster. On day one, Koch greeted crowds walking over the Brooklyn Bridge. "There is never a boring day!" he exulted. Lindsay had begged people not to come to work; Koch said they *must* come. Wall Street banks hired boats to get workers from Brooklyn; when someone commented that "it looks like Dunkirk," the mayor "beamed" a rejoinder: "It looks like Nantucket." Koch stayed in the streets, keeping up spirits. "The worst fear is fear itself," he added, admitting that "Roosevelt said that better."

Behind the rhetoric, Koch had a contingency plan. A decade and a half earlier, traffic had overwhelmed the city; the city's goal this time was to keep the increase to 30 percent, without shutting commerce and leisure. "[In] the early months of 1980," says Schwartz, "we studied the 1966 strike, knowing an April strike was likely. We learned not to repeat . . . mistakes." The city had trained traffic agents in emergency measures. Lindsay had once unsuccessfully asked people to carpool; Koch, with "sharp restrictions," forced them, deploying police to enforce a three-person minimum per car. This time, 236,000 cars—26 percent more than usual—carried nearly eight hundred thousand people into the city at rush hour. Car volume was less than during the 1966 strike, when it had reached 260,000 cars, despite Lindsay's plea to stay home. The number of one-person cars entering central Manhattan fell from 60 to 3 percent. Half of cars carried four people. The city's emergency measures were a "traffic-engineering marvel," because, unlike in 1966, the goal was "moving people rather than vehicles," a study concluded. Eighty-six percent of workers made it in.[31]

The strike, like its predecessor, was painful. People reduced leisure visits; stores sales fell 30 percent. Tax revenue fell by two million dollars a day, even as the city had to spend one million dollars on police overtime. As in the 1966 walkout, the strike hit poor people hardest. Speaking to transit workers, the mayor said, "You are hurting the poorest of the poor, the Blacks, the Hispanics, the poor whites, the people living in Bedford-Stuyvesant and the South Bronx."

Yet the strike had two salutary effects. It demonstrated that the city *was* optimistic. The strike coincided with New York's population turnaround. Bankers and lawyers, artists, and African, Hispanic, Caribbean, and eastern European immigrants were refilling the city, with people from Harlem to Brooklyn's Park Slope rebuilding brownstones. Having no trains was part of the adventure. New Yorkers' success generated something else the city hadn't seen in a long time: governability. One *Times* letter writer said that "the transit strike is pulling New York City together."

The strike was manageable in part because of its second legacy: willingness to bicycle. Part of Koch's plan was "coned-off bicycle lanes," and people used them. More than two hundred thousand cyclists rode to work each day, including seventy-five thousand who cycled into Manhattan, compared to five thousand on a normal day. Many liked it. "It's kind of fun," said Dan Strick Berger, commuting across the Brooklyn Bridge. "It's faster than the subway." As trains rumbled again, people continued the practice. As TA's *City Cyclist* magazine said, "Many [cyclists] took their bikes out of the closet during the 1980 transit strike, and never put them back."[32] Cyclists revived their call for room on the streets. As one *Times* letter-writer noted, "Mayor Koch urged New Yorkers to ride . . . like the residents of Peking, and many of us did." But the cyclist added, "We want an avenue!"

A Short Bike Lane Experiment

The city was still under the now nearly decade-old federal mandate to improve its air, and Koch promised to make permanent the example residents had set. He promised "bike lanes in all five boroughs." He built a real bike lane, protected by barriers, in Midtown's heart. In October 1980, Koch, in a Dayglo vest painted with his name and sporting a helmet, glided down Manhattan's first protected bike lane. Across six feet of asphalt, bikers were protected from motor vehicles via concrete barriers. Within the half hour, "27 bicycles glided by, unimpeded by cars."[33]

Yet ominous signs intruded. At the unveiling, Koch himself was hardly a cheerleader. He had arrived in a car. He offered not encouragement but a warning. "It's an experiment," he said. If a "larger" number of cyclists did not use the infrastructure, "we're going to pull these lanes up again and give them back to the cars."

Koch was having second thoughts. The summer between the April transit strike and the October bike-lane debut had not been good for relations between cyclists and pedestrians, creating New York's first "bikelash." That

June, a cyclist hit Mary Ellinger, 43, in Lower Manhattan as she walked "a few yards from her home"; she died of head injuries.[34] In July, a wrong-way cyclist on the Upper East Side hit Virginia Ranney, 31, and fled the scene as she lay "bleeding profusely"; she died of a skull fracture. Days after Ranney's death, a hit-and-run cyclist hit Minnie Schoenholtz, 77, a retired teacher, in Central Park; she died two days later. The same week, another Central Park cyclist left Maria Traphan, 74, in critical condition. Manhattan councilwoman Carol Greitzer, who held Koch's old seat, called the crashes—all the victims women, all the known culprits men—an "epidemic of lawless cycling."[35] "New York is not quite ready" for "pedal power," the *Times* said.[36] TA pleaded with members to behave courteously.

Koch came under political pressure, just as Lindsay had.[37] Governor Hugh Carey dismissed the lanes as a "fetish" with a three-hundred-thousand-dollar price tag that the city, emerging from fiscal crisis, couldn't afford; the governor added that he had just missed being "totaled" by a "whistling" cyclist.[38] "There's another story which might be totally apocryphal," Gurin says. When President Jimmy Carter came to town, the mayor and governor picked him up. In the car, Carey told Koch, "If you don't get rid of these fucking bike lanes, I'm going to send the state police in to get rid of them." In a milder telling, Carey, pointing at the lanes through the car window, told Carter, "Ed is wasting your money."[39] Koch cared what the governor thought, as the city, having accepted a federal and state bailout, remained under the financial supervision of the state government.

Elected officials, corporate leaders, and journalists lacked peers who commuted via bicycle. "People were not used to riding," says George Arzt, a top Koch aide. An exception was Murray Kempton, the tabloid columnist. "There would be Murray blithely going down the street. It was an amazing sight." Remembers Steve Stollman, an alternative newspaper distributor and cyclist supporter, "Kempton would ride his bike and smoke his pipe," wearing a suit. This outlier—and two people's remembering the oddity decades later—proved the rule. To government officials, businessmen, and reporters, braving city traffic on two wheels as opposed to riding Sunday through Central Park remained alien.

Gurin pleaded with Koch for time, noting that there is a "learning process."[40] But one Sunday, Koch stood in Midtown, observing as just two cyclists passed in the bike lane. "They're not working," the mayor said. "I was swept away at the thought of what could be when I saw a million bikes in Peking," he added. Before Thanksgiving, ahead of holiday traffic, the city ripped the lanes out, spending one hundred thousand dollars to destroy fresh cement. Cyclists, including Benepe, protested the bulldozers.

Koch's lanes had lasted a month. The loss stung. A month when the temperature was dropping had not been long enough to judge success. "The experiment was going in the right direction," protested Elliot Winick of American Youth Hostels. Commuter Peter Samton philosophized that "bold new ideas do not always get immediate acclaim."[41]

Koch's abandonment was as much a marker, in the inverse, as Lindsay's having opened Central Park on weekends fourteen years earlier. Elite consensus was that the experiment wasn't just a waste of money but a joke. If Koch had gone to Cairo instead of Beijing, one wag said, he would have suggested New Yorkers ride camels. In 1983, the *Times* editorialized that "the most irresponsible drivers on New York streets are the bicyclists who ignore red lights, blindside motorists, ride the wrong way on one-way streets and, whistles blowing, threaten pedestrians." The paper bolstered this broadside by deriding Koch as someone who had "confused cycling in New York with cycling in Peking."

Despite their jilting, cyclists stuck to the streets. Twenty to twenty-five thousand people cycled regularly in Manhattan during the 1980s. But they themselves weren't safe. Joel Friedman, a city transportation official, said that cyclists and pedestrians were vying for "leftover space" dominated by motor vehicles.[42] Each year, between eleven and eighteen cyclists died under the wheels of cars and trucks. Cyclists, unprotected by a motor vehicle, suffered from crime, as well. In 1980, muggers blocked the Brooklyn Bridge's cycling path, beating one person unconscious and holding three others "hostage" for money. With multiple crimes on the bridge each month, Leonard Toga, Federation of New York Bicycle Clubs president, termed the situation "barbarism."

Blaming the Messengers

The low point came in 1987. "[There] are still too many bicyclists who just do not obey the law," Koch said outside City Hall, announcing his ban on daytime cycling in much of Midtown, as Greitzer, the Manhattan councilwoman, and David Dinkins, Manhattan's borough president and aspiring mayor, watched approvingly.

Koch was wrong to imply that the danger posed by bikes was larger than the danger posed by cars and trucks. Even as cycling had grown, of the 623 people who would die in traffic crashes that year, whether in cars, on bicycles, or on foot, nearly all perished at the hands of drivers, not cyclists.[43] As TA pointed out, pedestrian deaths from cars and trucks outnumbered pedestrian deaths from cyclists 150 to 1. Cyclists comprised 5 to 6 percent of Midtown traffic but did not cause a commensurate percentage of deaths.

Yet the deaths caused by cyclists got more attention than did the 320 pedestrians run over and killed by cars citywide—nearly one each day. The number of crashes between cyclists and pedestrians may have been low, but it was nearly double the 399 recorded in 1981. Most New Yorkers didn't bike in the city, and the public's perception of people who did was of aggressive men ignoring signals. Pedestrians perceived cars and trucks as objects, whereas they saw cyclists as people—rude ones.

This perception was bolstered by a newly ubiquitous cyclist: the messenger. The bike messenger was a sign of the improving economy and its dependence on white-collar work. Wall Street firms as well as counterparts in law, advertising, typesetting, art, and fashion paid messengers to deliver documents and samples. Messengers were vital to the city's information industry.

This industry created opportunities for New Yorkers who couldn't or didn't want to find a nine-to-five job. Robert Wyatt, a musician, moved to New York in the early 1980s. "Musicians and artists were bike messengers," he says. "If you couldn't come to work one day, it didn't matter." The work wasn't low paid: "You made a lot of money. . . . Bikers were taking home $500, $600, $700 a week"— six figures annually in 2024 dollars for full-time work (which many messengers, pursuing other opportunities, didn't do). "We're the last free spirits," one messenger, Steve Athineos, observed. Athineos, a former pot dealer, had turned to the messenger business in 1983. He had previously worked as a performer for Chippendales, "a strip club for ladies only," where he had earned well, "until [he] . . . was losing [his] mind."[44] A friend pointed out that since he liked riding his bike to work, he should ride *for* work.

Messengering was a job for people who faced employment barriers. "I've done so many [job] interviews," says Kurt Boone, a Queens native. Boone, a longtime foot messenger, has documented the bike messenger world as a photographer and filmmaker. "So many of my friends never made it to corporate jobs." Messengering, on the other hand, "was a job set up easily for a Black man to get, especially if you had a criminal record or came from a poor community."[45]

Messengers were not low-skill laborers. They were fit. They had a map of the streets in their heads. They were trustworthy, carrying artwork and confidential documents. Despite self-confidence—Wyatt cracks that his secret to safe riding was that, unlike fellow couriers, "I didn't smoke pot"—they were in danger, even when obeying the law. In 1986, cycling deaths reached twenty-four. Two messengers were killed annually.[46]

Messengers were demonized. "Like the Jews of medieval Europe, messengers make an objective contribution to the local economy but are viewed as utterly foreign," wrote one letter-writer in 1985 in response to a disparaging *Times* article.[47] TA's magazine ran one letter by a messenger, Bob McGlynn, that the *Times* had rejected: "Nobody talks . . . about messengers getting hurt and killed. . . . If we don't kill ourselves . . . we'll make no money. . . . The messenger business is the purist Capitalism."[48]

Part of the problem was economic. Messengers earned by the package. "This business arrangement greatly encourages . . . dangerous riding habits which threaten the safety of any New Yorker who is not blessed with eyes in the back of his or her head," Koch said. Messengers *did* run lights. Throughout summer 1987, leading up to Koch's ban, the *Times* focused on clashes. The paper observed one messenger "zipping the wrong way . . . hurtling through a red light, then pumping past pedestrians as he rode down the sidewalk. 'I don't want to hurt anybody, [the messenger said.] But . . . to get the job done, you have to take your chances.'"[49]

Animosity was, once again, spurred by pedestrian deaths. The previous October, a red-light-running messenger had hit Peggy Ryan, a Midtown worker. Ryan was one of three pedestrians to be killed that year; two had died in 1985. A new group, Pedestrians First!, had popped up; its mission was the opposite of TA's mission: reduce cycling. The theme at one rally was "stop killer bikes."[50] As *Crain's New York Business*, the business newspaper, editorialized, "Koch's plan to ban bikes from three major midtown avenues merely is a first step, and the city should go further."[51]

The conflict had another root: more people. As the 1970s exodus from the city reversed in the 1980s, the city would add 200,000 residents between 1980 and 1990. Yet with trains still unreliable for the first half of the decade and rife with crime, a record number of drivers and taxi passengers crammed the streets. In 1981, 970,000 people came to Manhattan each day by car or truck; by the mid-1980s, the total had reached 1.2 million.

Messengers Save Themselves

Instead of retreating from Midtown's marquee avenues, messengers transformed Koch's attempted defeat of their livelihoods into a historic and trend-changing victory for cyclists. A lawsuit by Transportation Alternatives bought them time; a judge paused the ban on its first day, ruling that the city hadn't provided notice.

Over the next few months, Koch lost not just in court but on the streets. The mayor didn't anticipate what became, in Charles Komanoff's phrase, a "bicycle uprising." The force behind the anti-ban protests wasn't Transportation Alternatives, though, whose members were largely middle-class commuters. Nor was it the environmental movement, also middle class. "None of the prominent environmental organizations were willing to petition City Hall," Komanoff wrote. Rather, it was "the ranks of those whose livelihood was . . . threatened." Athineos, thirty-one, was the leader. "People don't think of bike messengers as being able to organize," he said. Until, that is, "they tried to close off streets." With his waist-length black hair, sculpted body, and deep voice, he became the camera-friendly face of the protests. "He was our Greek god," recalled Mary Frances Dunham, one of TA's earliest members.

The protest rides Athineos spearheaded captured public attention. "Once or twice each week at around 5:30 p.m., the end of the messengers' workday, masses of cyclists, usually half a thousand and occasionally more, spread across Sixth Avenue and paraded the three miles from Houston Street to Central Park South," Komanoff wrote. The cyclists, joined by TA advocates, moved "slow[ly] enough that passersby could look past our bikes and see our bodies and faces. . . . We . . . did stop at red lights," demonstrating that cyclists were not the enemy. New Yorkers were not used to seeing cyclists take over an avenue, nor were they used to seeing muscled men riding slowly. Before and after the march, cyclists would raise their bikes above their heads, in a physical show of political strength. Passersby gaped.

Athineos got support from Stollman, the newspaper distributor. Stollman was not a cyclist, because, he says, "it was very dangerous." Yet he supported non-car transportation. Annoyed with TA, after having attended meetings and determining that "they had no ideas," his contribution was to allow advocates to use his Houston Street building downtown, which he had bought for thirty thousand dollars in 1974 as a place to build newsstands, as an organizing space. Messengers met to print fliers and plan strategies. Athineos also got support from McCorkell, by then the owner of a bike shop, Bicycle Habitat. Athineos, recalls McCorkell, "was hampered in his organizing by having a job. I decided to cover half his pay."[52]

TA, despite its middle-class membership's misgivings about messengers, stuck with them. "The message is clear: if you are Black and ride a bike you are not welcome on the most affluent streets of New York City," *City*

Cyclist told members. Dunham, a member, joined the rides. She later wrote, "As an older woman among mostly young people, I was a conspicuous participant." She was angered not just on behalf of messengers, but because, she says, "cyclists as a group were being punished for the sins of individuals. We were scapegoats for the chronic failure of the city . . . to control its rampant traffic disorder."[53]

TA buttressed messenger protests with a letter-writing campaign to rebalance Koch's correspondence, which was generally anti-bicycle. City Hall received 547 missives against the ban and 37 in favor. "Your absurd 'experiment' of banning bicycle traffic in midtown Manhattan is a discriminatory and exploitative policy that singles out bicyclists as a scapegoat for your administration's utter lack of vision in dealing with the city's perennial vehicular [and] pedestrian problems," wrote Ramon Fernan II of the Bronx.

Messengers turned public opinion, and with public opinion came political turning. Dinkins backed away from support of the ban. Greitzer conceded that the ban "would merely move the problem to other streets." All Manhattan city council members eventually opposed the ban.[54]

By 1988, Koch conceded. "The mayor asked for a meeting with myself, Charlie Komanoff, and Roger Herz," remembers McCorkell. "Koch made a very halfhearted attempt to get us to accept some small compromise. We were not buying, and the tone changed to, 'let's forget it and move on.' And as simple as that, it was over." The administration tried to save face; Sandler said that the reason the mayor had changed his mind was that bicycle-pedestrian crashes had fallen from 640 in 1986 to 510 in 1987. Greater attention, as well as more tickets—25,982 to cyclists, up from 19,148 the previous year—had worked.[55]

Well into his third term, with a year left until the 1989 election he would lose to Dinkins, the mayor's instincts were not what they had been. Koch had suffered a stroke in 1987 and had seen the previous few years wracked by scandal. Much of his transportation department had resigned in 1986 over corruption. Belatedly, though, Koch got it right. "We fought City Hall and won," Athineos said. The mayor was gracious, complimenting advocates on their "persistence."[56]

In the 1990s, technology and economics curtailed messengers. The culprit wasn't the fax machine, says Wyatt, as is the popular belief. Rather, it was the color printer (and e-mail). Further, the state and city cracked down on payroll fraud, charging that courier companies had falsely said their workers were independent contractors, not employees. The enforcement forced messenger services to pay for workers' compensation insurance.

By 1988, crashes between pedestrians and cyclists had declined for three years, from 707 in 1985 to 430 in 1988; no pedestrian that year died in a crash with a biker. By 1992, the number of crashes was 298, and no pedestrian had died in a crash with a cyclist since 1987.

Taking Cycling Seriously

The averted ban had a lasting impact. The mayor had unintentionally created a more cohesive pro-cycling network than the loose collection that had existed when, a decade and a half before, he had stood with Harriet Green to advocate for protected lanes. Part of the challenge in organizing cyclists was that unlike the residents of any neighborhood fighting highways, cyclists were dispersed. Harlemites might want to commute to Midtown; Bed-Stuy dwellers might want to commute to downtown Brooklyn. Cyclists were also culturally dispersed. Some cyclists were bankers; some were security guards. Some cycled for exercise and confined themselves to the park; some wanted transportation. Beyond motivating residents of one neighborhood, a formidable job, cycling advocates had to motivate people across the city who had little in common.

Moreover, the fact that cyclists were *for* something, not against, was an impediment. New Yorkers who had fought a wider road through Washington Square Park, a highway through SoHo, and the filling in of the Hudson for Westway had a discrete goal: halt a bad idea. Delay worked in their favor. The pro-cycling movement, by contrast, until the Koch ban, hadn't been a push to *stop* something, but a push to enable something—bike lanes. With his proposed Midtown bike ban, Koch had given cyclists something to stop, immediately, and factions finally had something in common: identity as scapegoats.

TA became a permanent part of New York's policy world. "You could speak up for cycling at a public forum and not be hooted down," Komanoff wrote. Komanoff, by then, was TA's new, unpaid president. A Long Island native, Komanoff had studied at Harvard in the 1960s. He grew interested in the environment after hiking out west during the summer of 1969. After teaching math at a suburban New York school to avoid the draft, he had taken a job, in Lindsay's second term, at the city's environmental protection department. Komanoff came late to cycling. In 1973, a colleague had taken him to rent a bike to ride in Central Park during one of Lindsay's weekend closures. A convert, he participated in pro-bike protests, enjoying "the liberating energy." By 1986, after having worked as a consultant after leaving government, Komanoff was ready for something new and had enough savings to devote time to "re-founding" TA, whose membership had dwindled.

The group used the ban to raise money and attract volunteers—the number tripled because of the publicity—and members. In the 1970s, TA had had dozens of active members; by the late 1980s, the membership numbered in the high hundreds. The organization hired its first full-time paid staffer in over a decade. Jon Orcutt, an economics and history student at Benstock's alma mater, the New School, had moved to New York from Massachusetts in 1987. Komanoff had met him when they had both traveled to a political meeting via bicycle. "I was disenchanted with academia and wanted to do things, not study them," says Orcutt of how he began codirecting TA.[57]

Komanoff and Orcutt solidified TA's post–bike ban energy. First, though policy-focused, it was a social organization. TA organized the five-borough bike tour, previously a Hostels project. The annual event, with tens of thousands of participants, was the largest ride in the world. TA also tried to show that cycling was inclusive of women, minorities, and poorer people, even if its leaders didn't quite succeed; only 4 percent of street cyclists were women. Its magazine featured commuters ranging from a sixty-one-year-old dental assistant, who said that other cyclists called her "grandma," to a mechanic who observed that "cycling is my way of making up for [working] in an industry that's not exactly good for the environment."

Dunham, one of TA's few women leaders, showed the importance of such diversity. A Radcliffe graduate and former classics teacher, she had lived with her husband, a U.S. foreign-aid official, in bicycle-rich Asia, taking her fold-up Dahon bicycle everywhere from Bangladesh to China to India. Though many cyclists, particularly male ones, saw cycling as a form of exercise, requiring special clothes, Dunham thought that people should integrate cycling into their normal lives. She wanted to show, "This is how you can get around; you don't have to take a shower [or] wear the Lycra." A mother, she understood that children needed to learn how to bicycle in a city. She ran a "bike rodeo," sponsored by the Girl Scouts, at which girls learned skills such as moving around parked cars.

TA was practical. It created a bike map and peppered its magazines with bike-store reviews and reports of "hot ticketing spots." The oppressive presence of the era's crime shows itself in tips on how cyclists could avoid becoming victims. *City Cyclist* counseled readers how to avoid muggings. "Be alert for the possibility of an ambush," warned one writer. TA exhorted members to fight nonviolent crime, as well. "Never buy a used bike on the street," its writers counseled, noting that twelve thousand bikes were stolen a year, many sold by drug addicts at St. Mark's Place downtown, offering deals that "would make [discount-store chain] Crazy Eddie's head spin." One tip was to avoid "crack confetti," scraps of tire-puncturing glass left on streets by car burglars.

TA advanced intellectual arguments. In 1988, it began hosting Auto-Free New York. The conference helped New Yorkers learn from what other cities were doing. TA's magazine ran stories about global practices. Where Koch had seen Beijing's throngs as a model, Dunham saw a bad omen: wealthier China's interest in cars. "China's days as a bicycle country are numbered," she wrote.

TA's *City Cyclist* had a grimmer task: obituaries. "In one week in January 1989, three bicyclists died in Manhattan." They were as diverse as New York. Randall Postell was a messenger. "Randy . . . was a proud parent and breadwinner who loved his five children," read TA's memorial. "He was a black man who managed to survive in a country where homicide is the leading cause of death in young black men. . . . He made it past his thirty-first birthday—only to die in the line of duty . . . on Sixth Avenue," hit by a truck.[58] Ten minutes later, Jay Rosenblum, an abstract painter, was killed, struck near his home on the Lower East Side. His wife had stopped riding the year before, after a limo had "doored" her. The same week, Julia Collier, a doll scholar at Christie's auction house, "died instantly under a truck's wheels on the Upper East Side." Collier, thirty-eight years old and about to have her first book published, had ridden for a decade. "I and thousands of others ride our bicycles to and from work, conscientiously obeying the laws . . . not a day goes by that I don't narrowly avoid a collision," she had written to *Our Town*, the Upper East Side's community newspaper.

Most important, TA honed policy. In 1993, the nonprofit released its "bicycle blueprint," a 170-page book covering every facet of integrating cyclists into the streetscape. TA predicted "pent-up demand" of seven hundred thousand cyclists if people could perceive cycling as safer. Goals were grand: a ban on street parking; a ten-dollar fee to enter congested areas of the city in a car; auto-free zones with pedicab service; and "barriered bus and bike lanes." The blueprint included access to all bridges. New York could not achieve these goals unless officials "take cycling seriously." Nationally, TA wanted Congress to allocate money for bike lanes as part of transportation infrastructure, to change the perception, highlighted by the Carter-Carey-Koch discussion in 1980, that cycling lanes were a waste of money. "We harnessed . . . bike-friendly New York to doable steps," says Orcutt.

TA continued street-level activism. In 1990, six cyclists, five of them TA members, rode across the Queensboro Bridge in defiance of a ban on bikes during reconstruction. The "Queensboro Six" won a landmark acquittal on ensuing misdemeanor charges. The judge ruled that "the death and illness of New Yorkers from air pollution and vehicles are far greater harms than that created by disorderly conduct," in the first state exoneration based on a "necessity defense."

But the group aspired to respectability, not radicalism. Cycling was no longer anti-capitalist, as it had been in the GM protest days: TA praised J. P. Morgan bank for its "guarded, secure, indoor bicycle parking" for employees.[59] "T.A. is at home in the corridors of power," it told members.[60] TA never irrevocably alienated government officials. It sent questionnaires to candidates for office, from governor to councilmember, so that members could vote accordingly. As membership grew—to 1,300 in 1990 and to 2,000 by 1991—city government had to take TA ideas seriously.

The group racked up successes. The Port Authority gave cyclists easier access to the George Washington Bridge, and the MTA allowed people to take bicycles on subways and off-peak commuter trains. The city built a lane for cyclists and joggers along the South Street Seaport in lower Manhattan in 1990 (although, as Benepe wrote, being "situated between a parking lot and a heavily traveled road under an elevated highway hardly qualifies it be called a 'greenway'"). The next year, TA "scored a major victory" by convincing the mayor to build a bikeway along the Williamsburg Bridge to Brooklyn, and the group made sure that Manhattan and Brooklyn Bridge renovations considered cyclists.

Most important, nearly two decades after the West Side Highway had collapsed, TA helped Manhattan get its Hudson River bike path. By the late 1980s, the state and city had formed a commission to determine what would replace the West Side Highway. Some officials saw a bike path there as recreational and unaffordable; Governor Mario Cuomo called it an "extravagance." But TA grasped how important a path would be for commuting. Noting that during the 1970s, cyclists had enjoyed "free space" atop the shuttered road, TA wrote that a north-south path would "transcend Manhattan boundaries," from residential areas uptown to Midtown and downtown workplaces.

Dinkins, as borough president in the late 1980s and then as mayor, supported the idea, prevailing against real estate developers. Developers "understood that a public esplanade, that opened the waterfront . . . for the first time in 200 years, would seriously reduce the probability of future real estate development on landfill . . . out in the Hudson," wrote Tom Fox, a member of the post-Westway task force. Dinkins sided with park proponents; later, in City Hall, he approved one hundred million dollars for construction.[61] Governor George Pataki, a Republican, and Mayor Rudolph W. Giuliani, who succeeded Dinkins in 1994, continued funding the Hudson greenway—the latter in part for a personal reason.[62] In the 1970s, as assistant U.S. attorney, "I used to ride to work on a bike . . . from 83rd [Street] and West End Avenue to Foley Square [downtown]," Giuliani says, "when the West Side Highway was closed down. I did it because it was fun, and exercise."[63]

The Hudson River path took shape, with a link between the Upper West Side and Midtown opening in March 2001. "The choice is simple," the *Times* wrote, "a sweaty, crowded subway commute, or cool breezes and the soothing sound of a river." After the city built safer infrastructure, customers came, just as TA had predicted. "It gets you out of the buses and cars," said one commuting lawyer.[64]

Progress was halting. Mayors resisted closing Central Park drives to cars entirely. Notwithstanding the Hudson River greenway, the city's position on Manhattan bike lanes hadn't changed since Lindsay and Koch: not enough people would use them. As transportation expert Michael Replogle said, this logic was akin "to determining the need for a . . . bridge based on the number of people . . . swimming." Though elected officials couldn't ignore a group whose members numbered in the thousands—some elections were close—cycling wasn't important enough for most New Yorkers to think about regularly, let alone vote for candidates based on positions on the issue. In any conflict, it was easier for officials to do what Lindsay and Koch had done and sacrifice cyclists.

Cyclists weren't safer in numbers. In 1997, twenty-two cyclists died, the highest in a decade.[65] In 1999, cycling had its "deadliest year ever," as TA said in a flyer for a "die-in" protest, with thirty-four killed.[66] Car and truck driver error contributed to 80 percent of fatalities.[67] But police blamed cyclists. Even as Dinkins and Giuliani cut murders—from 2,245 in 1990 to 649 in 2001 (not including the 9/11 attack)—cyclists were on their own.

The Right Mayor and Commissioner

When Michael Bloomberg took office on January 1, 2002, there was little reason to think that New York would become more hospitable to cyclists. Bloomberg, a billionaire who had made his fortune selling information infrastructure to Wall Street firms, took the subway to City Hall from his

Upper East Side home. But he wasn't a cyclist. After 9/11, two months before the election, his campaign focused on how to rebuild New York. "He was just this complete wild card," says Orcutt, who had moved on to the Tri-State Transportation Campaign, a transit-advocacy group. As mayor, Bloomberg kept in place as Department of Transportation (DOT) commissioner Iris Weinshall, a Giuliani appointee.

Inauspiciously, Bloomberg's introduction to cyclists was not via a moderate group such as TA, but a scrappy upstart: Time's Up! The group used Stollman's storefront as a base and organized protest rides through Manhattan, called "Critical Mass." Participants found Critical Mass rides fun; nighttime riders reclaimed streets from autos, riding fearlessly rather than cramped near parked cars. But pedestrians found the rides a nuisance. Critical Mass violated the tenet of cycling PR: be kind to walkers. The riders blew red lights. "Any chance of crossing the street tonight?" one woman yelled in 2004.

That summer, Time's Up! politicized the rides. When the Republican National Convention came to town, one gathering turned into a 5,000-strong anti-Bush protest against the Iraq War, which had started the year before. When the NYPD cracked down, Critical Mass gained sympathy: "Not the best use of New York's finest," said the *Times* after police arrested 250 people, knocking cyclists to the ground. But advocates feared that the rides' tenor alienated supporters. "I love riding my bike, but it is not a political thing," said one rider, Laurie Williams. TA was ambivalent. "Critical Mass is a two-edged sword," said one TA official. "It potentially paints bike riding in a very confrontational, not mainstream, sort of fringe light."[68]

This risk was troubling for a movement that needed the mayor's support. Bloomberg was a Republican, and he had lobbied the GOP to hold its 2004 convention in Manhattan. He spoke at Madison Square Garden in favor of Bush.[69] The Critical Mass protesters, in a way, were thus protesting Bloomberg himself. Bloomberg's position on Critical Mass was that the rides hadn't obtained permits, and their participants were therefore subject to arrest.[70]

Three years later, on a trip to Paris, Bloomberg wasn't more enthusiastic. In 2007, Paris had begun a bike-share program called Velib. Through the program— as Dean and Breines had suggested thirty-three years earlier, in *The Pedestrian Revolution*—cyclists could pick up a bike at one station and deposit it after riding to a different station. Bloomberg was skeptical that New York could imitate Velib. "New York is different," the mayor said, and the roads "tend to be much rougher."[71]

Five and a half years later, New York's cyclists—and anti-cyclists—considered Bloomberg the best bicycling mayor New York had ever had. Bloomberg's sudden enthusiasm was partly based on his increased focus on public safety, health, and the environment. The mayor was intent on cutting the murder rate, the obesity rate, and the city's climate change–inducing emissions, and he succeeded: murders fell from 649 in 2001, the year before he succeeded Giuliani, to 332 in 2013, his final year.[72] Initiatives to cut smoking—including banning smoking in bars, an unheard-of policy in 2003 imitated around the world—and reduce the consumption of fat, salt, and sugar cut heart and lung disease. Across race and gender, life expectancy rose.[73]

The mayor's bike turnabout had additional reasons. As Bloomberg started his second term in 2006, he faced a problem that predecessors could not have dreamed of. New York was a victim of success. Low crime and a booming financial, tech, and tourist economy were luring residents. Domestic migrants, having grown up watching *Seinfeld*, *Friends*, and *Sex and the City*, saw New York as a playground; immigrants saw the city as a place to escape poverty and danger. Projections were that by 2030, New York's population would reach nine million people. How could New York do so—and improve quality of life? Passengers were overcrowding subways, and pedestrians could barely make their way through crowds.

The answer was "PlaNYC: A Greener, Greater New York," a 158-page blueprint the mayor rolled out in April 2007, coinciding with Earth Day. "Our economy is humming, our fiscal house is in order," Bloomberg told a crowd at the American Museum of Natural History. "If we don't act now, when?"[74] The city would charge drivers a toll to enter core Manhattan by car or truck, a policy London had implemented four years previously. New York would tighten fuel standards for buildings, seed oyster beds, and plant a million trees. One more thing: On page 88, the plan promised, "New Yorkers should be given the option of reaching their jobs and major city destinations through cycling."[75] New York, though it had opened the Hudson River greenway and painted unprotected bike lanes, remained a perilous, inhospitable place for cyclists. Between 2000 and 2006, between thirteen and twenty-four cyclists had died each year, and cycling growth had stalled.[76]

As he prepared his Earth Day speech, Bloomberg was hiring a new transportation commissioner. One candidate was Janette Sadik-Khan, a native New Yorker and Columbia Law School grad with experience in transportation. A Dinkins campaign worker, she had gone to work for the new administration when the former mayor won in 1989. "When I talked to my mom" (Jane McCarthy, a former *New York Post* reporter), "after David Dinkins had won his election, . . . I told her, I wanted to do something that touched people's lives." She said, "sanitation or transportation." After the Dinkins years, Sadik-Khan had been deputy administrator of the Federal Transit Administration and was, by 2007, senior vice president at engineering giant Parsons Brinckerhoff. Sadik-Khan also rode a bike.

Sadik-Khan's interview with Bloomberg went poorly. Bloomberg asked her why she wanted to be "traffic commissioner." She answered that she *didn't*, as the position was transportation commissioner. "That was not the best starting-off point," she recalled. Sadik-Khan plunged into her spiel, telling the mayor that "we needed to redesign our streets and make it easier to walk" as well as make room for cyclists. She talked, too, about congestion pricing. But she saw "grim faces around the table."[77] Unbeknownst to her, the goals she brought up in her interview fit City Hall's yet to be released PlaNYC. "I, from the very beginning, was a huge advocate for bike lanes," says Dan Doctoroff, deputy mayor from 2002 to 2007 and PlaNYC architect. "I would ride my bike at 5:30 in the morning to City Hall."[78] Thanks in part to Doctoroff's support, Bloomberg picked Sadik-Khan, with his usual advice: "Don't fuck it up." The city came to know her—and love her or hate her—as JSK.

The commissioner was fast-moving. She hired Jon Orcutt, the former TA leader—a sign that DOT would listen to cyclists. She cut back hours during which drivers could use Central and Prospect Parks. For forty years, traffic had ebbed and flowed in Central Park as an indicator of the current mayor's attitude toward cars. Now, drivers could use the parks only during rush hours. The reduction made the right to drive through Manhattan's green space the exception.[79]

Months after taking office, the commissioner debuted something that the city hadn't seen in twenty-seven years: a protected Manhattan bike lane. This peculiar addition to the street wasn't just new—or, after the short-lived Koch experiment, new again—for the city, but for the nation.[80] The bike lane didn't protect riders via cement barrier. Rather, it protected them via immobile cars. The DOT had redesigned seven blocks along a one-third-of-a-mile stretch of Ninth Avenue in Chelsea, so that the left-most lane near the curb was for cyclists. The lane next to them was for parallel-parked cars, protecting cyclists from moving cars further to the right. The city buffered the parking lane with a striped no-man's zone, so that drivers and passengers opening doors from parking spaces couldn't hit cyclists gliding by.

Despite the speed with which Sadik-Khan's DOT deployed this infrastructure, it was the product of planning and not, as the Koch lanes had been, thrown up with little thought. Earlier that summer, Sadik-Khan and planning commissioner Amanda Burden—along with a top DOT official, Deputy Commissioner for Traffic Operations Michael Primeggia—had taken an unusual trip: a visit to Copenhagen to meet with public space architect Jan Gehl and to tour European innovations.[81] Walking around Copenhagen, Sadik-Khan, Burden, and Primeggia had seen this strange bike-lane design. To DOT staff, tasked with rethinking the streets but not wanting to clog scarce space with clunky Koch-style barriers or to embark on multi-million-dollar projects, the solution was perfect.

The Ninth Avenue bike lane was different from Koch's experiment in another way: Sadik-Khan didn't plunk her bike lanes in the heart of Midtown. "We were aware of the history of bike lanes," says Sadik-Khan. "We knew that they could disappear. . . . We wanted to stress-test a new design to see if it scaled on busy complicated streets." For this pilot, Ninth Avenue "was kind of like straight from central transportation casting, a very wide one-way street, low volumes compared to other avenues," says Sadik-Khan. Its six lanes of traffic and parking, more than most interstate highways (in one direction), were underused most of the day. The major intersection, at Fourteenth Street, was an obsolete tangle, with two-way traffic on Ninth Avenue for two blocks to provide access to a defunct postal facility, meaning redesigning it would benefit drivers.

Further, the area was near the Hudson River bike path, which had accustomed Greenwich Village and Chelsea residents to cycling. It gave thousands of people already on bikes a lane to try if they wanted to venture closer to the core city in the last few blocks of their commute. Finally, the project, though a strange specimen to visitors, wasn't sprung with no warning on people in the neighborhood. The DOT had met with the local community board, tweaking the project according to members' suggestions. The lane saw immediate success. Daily traffic increased from 782 to 1,291 cyclists, a 65 percent growth. Crashes with injuries fell 48 percent.[82]

Over two and a half years, Sadik-Khan expanded the concept. The DOT extended the lane further up and down Ninth Avenue and added space on nearby Eighth Avenue, thus giving West Side cyclists north-south travel room. On the East Side, First and Second Avenues got the same treatment, as did parts of Broadway in the middle of Manhattan and, north of Midtown, the Upper West Side's Columbus Avenue. Slowly, Manhattan was getting a network of protected bike lanes. Cycling increased by 59 percent, to 12,226, in these six lanes daily, while crashes with injuries fell 17 percent. "I wasn't nervous it wouldn't work," says Orcutt. "My whole time I've lived here, since the 1980s, people have flocked to new bike infrastructure."

Bike lanes, though they took space from cars, did not slow cars, as measured by taxi GPS monitors. Though on Second Avenue, for example, the volume of motor vehicles fell by 12 to 15 percent, as drivers lost a lane, traffic did not show up elsewhere. Instead, bus ridership along the corridor rose by 9 percent, as buses, too, increased speed in a new bus lane. Shirley Hayes's dictum was holding: Take away space from cars, and many would disappear.

Another Cyclist Dies

Sadik-Khan benefited from something that previous pro-cycling officials hadn't enjoyed: a mature advocacy community. TA was, by then, a well-staffed nonprofit. Its chief throughout much of the Bloomberg era was Paul Steely White, who—with button-down shirts and blazers, trim haircut, moderate tone, and easy smile—courted donors such as bankers, hedge-fund managers, and business leaders.[83]

Steely White had never meant to become an advocate. In grad school in Montana in the mid-1990s "to study grizzly-bear habitat," he was paying his bills by teaching English and working as a receptionist for a bike association. He was "opening the mail" when he came across a magazine called *Sustainable Transport*. Seeing that the sponsor, the Institute for Transportation and Development Policy, was an "amazing organization," he got in touch and landed a job, based in New York, to study cargo bikes in South Africa. "I never wanted to be here," he says of New York, but here he was, sharing an office with TA and reading Jane Jacobs. Living in a colleague's Brooklyn basement, he drove a truck to "collect used bikes" to send abroad. He left for South Africa but returned by 1997. That year, Rachel Fruchter, a health researcher, died in Prospect Park, killed on her bike by a van driver. Steely White was incensed that New York had "fucking cars in our crown-jewel parks and this woman dies."[84] He started volunteering for TA.

In 2004, TA needed a new director. John Kaehny, departing chief, was leaving. Kaehny "thought my naivete was useful," Steely White says. One colleague, after observing him at a meeting, noted to him, "You're really playing the hayseed routine." Steely White wasn't playing: He often felt out of his element. But, said the colleague, "you can get a lot done if you're not trying to be that urbane person everybody else is trying to be." Steely White navigated TA as it became a greater political force, growing from a half-million budget to $4.5 million. "Bicycling was very much in vogue with the Wall Street set," Steely White observes. To "win the respect and confidence [of donors]," Steely White says, "they want to know that you're serious, you're a player," that you can "keep the lights on." At fundraisers at multi-million-dollar mansions and hobnobbing with bankers, Steely White knew, it was "time to put our big-boy pants on."

One donor he courted was Tom Kempner, founder of an investment-management firm. A native New Yorker, Kempner remembers that "riding in NYC back in sixth or seventh grade, we used to ride around the loop in Central Park. . . . I always felt strongly that cycling was the most efficient mode of transportation." He was "familiar with the hazards of cycling, how it can be improved." Of his support for TA, he says, "We're trying to make the city safer for people who aren't in giant steel boxes." He observes that many philanthropists "only want to give money to 'Treasury bills'"—that is, safe bets, including donations to well-endowed institutions such as universities, where the donor knows the outcome of the gift. "These kinds of things," by contrast, he says, "you could lose all your money," if a push for cycling infrastructure fails. "Janette [Sadik-Khan] was really good. She's a strategic thinker."

Steely White understood coalition-building, even if it sometimes alienated veteran advocates and gave critics fodder against the "bike lobby." "We already had the ragtag bike people," he says, without dismissing their importance. "What put us over the top was getting the reasonable folks, the business community . . . real estate." Steely White also remained nonpolitical. "You're gonna get asked to endorse all kinds of crazy stuff," he remembers Kaehny telling him. "You just can't do it." (The exception was the Black Lives Matter movement in 2017.)

By demeanor and strategy, Steely White was an apt foil for critics. "TA has contributed to the demonization of cars," said Louise Hainline, a Park Slope resident who sued to stop a neighborhood bike lane. He (almost) never took the bait. "It's easy to focus on . . . conflict and friction," he told the *Times*. "But that's always going to happen when you're changing the geometry of something as dear as the asphalt." He never dismissed pedestrians' concerns, calling for riders to obey the law.

Advocates had become disciplined at the right time. Their job became something to which they were unaccustomed: supporting a mayor rather than criticizing him. "I called the bike advocates into a meeting at City Hall," says Howard Wolfson, a deputy mayor and a cyclist himself, "and I said, you know, guys, . . . you have in Mike Bloomberg and Janette the most pro-bike administration you will ever have. Unless we all work together, it will be the last pro-bike administration." When people protested bike lanes, advocates were there to outnumber them, sometimes two to one.[85]

Claiming an Avenue

Lindsay had once considered it radically innovative to give cyclists a portion of Central Park on a weekend day; now, on a few summer Sundays, Sadik-Khan gave cyclists and walkers an entire Manhattan thoroughfare. In 2008, on three August Saturdays, the city shut Park Avenue to traffic, allowing cyclists and walkers to parade through Midtown. "Cars are important, but streets are there for everybody," Bloomberg said. "We're going . . . to see if the public wants to go out in the streets."[86]

Dani Simons was the DOT official who spearheaded these "Summer Streets." She remembers watching a presentation by Jan Gehl, the Copenhagen planner. "I have a drawing still that he did, which was basically mapping out three phases of the public realm, starting with temporary interventions, pilot programs, then permanent programs." Summer Streets was a temporary intervention, an experiment to find out if it was possible to "repurpose street space, for a very time-limited event . . . something that was easily reversible, . . . if it didn't work." Simons prepared businesses and residents. "I walked a million miles, went business to business, to explain." At the Waldorf-Astoria hotel, she explained to managers "how they could make sure that the tourists would have ways to get a taxi on a side street, what they would do if there was an emergency." Before the first August day, she told her boss, "You can have my letter of resignation, if no one shows up, if someone gets hurt."

On the first day, she says, "I thought, now I really hope that people will show up." After fifteen minutes, "there were so many people biking, walking with their kids, and it was just like the most beautiful love letter to New York. . . . It was so amazing to see so many people, people were just connected to their city in this whole different . . . way." With fifty thousand people promenading or cycling each Saturday, the atmosphere was "giddy" and the fulfillment of Barnes's long-ago prophesy: people liked having the streets to themselves so much that they had demanded more.[87] Summer Streets became an annual event.

Minor Changes, Major Impact

What Sadik-Khan had done was not that radical. Prior to her installation of protected Manhattan bike lanes, drivers across these six north-south corridors had collectively enjoyed thirty-three lanes of moving or parking space. After the "road diet," as cycling advocates called it, they still enjoyed twenty-seven lanes, or most road space bisecting the dense island. A visitor to Ninth Avenue who had never viewed the thoroughfare before its makeover would still see plenty of room for cars, in motion and parked. During peak hours, twenty-seven lanes of traffic across six avenues wasn't sufficient capacity to move people quickly in the most inefficient form of transportation—ever-larger cars and SUVs with one occupant. As Moses had said, the city could never build enough driving space to meet peak demand. But as thirty-three lanes hadn't previously been enough, nor would fifty have been. Traffic existed before Sadik-Khan snatched room from motorists, and it existed afterward.

In the scheme of New York's political and media landscape, however, Sadik-Khan had launched a drastic transformation. Supporters greeted the Ninth Avenue bike lane in 2007 with breathlessness. At *Streetsblog*, a one-year-old website that was becoming what the *Village Voice* had been to the fights over Washington Square Park and the Lower Manhattan Expressway, editor Aaron Naparstek called it "The Street of the Future." "For years, Livable Streets advocates have pleaded with New York City . . . to just *try new things*. Finally," he wrote, "innovation is happening."[88] Another observer agreed. "What we did was on such a small scale," said Ed Koch. "What's being done now is on such a large scale."[89] As Bloomberg began his third term in 2010, having convinced the city council to suspend New York's two-term limit to keep a businessman in charge as the city recovered from the 2008 financial crisis, the pace continued.

Detractors were as ardent. Steve Cuozzo, *Post* real estate and restaurant columnist, was a persistent critic. In a 2008 column, called "Idiot DOT Takes a Walk on the Wild Side," Cuozzo warned, "Upper West Siders should be afraid, very afraid, of the Department of Transportation brainstorm to make their neighborhood more friendly [to cyclists]. . . . The bubble-brained traffic-busting scheme [is] to make drivers miserable."[90] In 2009, Cuozzo wrote of Sadik-Khan, "Her little-used bike lanes have forced cars to park in the middle of streets."[91] In 2011, "the city Department of Transportation [was] lying through its teeth about an alleged biker boom."[92] Manhattan businesses, guarding parking and loading space, also complained.[93]

Fellow politicos also pressured Bloomberg. Bloomberg faced the argument his predecessors had: bike lanes were a waste of money and space. In 2010, Anthony Weiner, Brooklyn and Queens Congressman and aspiring mayor, was a man with outer-borough name recognition that gave weight to his pronouncements. Weiner told Bloomberg at a private dinner, "When I become mayor, you know what I'm going to spend my first year doing? I'm going to have a bunch of ribbon-cuttings tearing out your fucking bike lanes."[94]

Much animosity was fear of change. Cars parked in the middle of the street *did* look weird, although they were no more an eyesore than cars parked on the side. Pedestrians had to look down a bike lane for oncoming traffic, as well as looking down car-traffic lanes. Older pedestrians relied on the noise cars and trucks made before they crossed the street; bicycles were silent. Many cyclists continued to ride the wrong way, still causing more of a nuisance than a danger, but a nuisance all the same. Jammed drivers often looked longingly at an "empty" bike lane—not grasping that, with bikes moving more efficiently through crowded spaces, a successful bike lane, like a successful bus lane, looked empty.

Some New Yorkers saw bike lanes as gentrification. The city had started its bike-lane buildout in Manhattan and northern Brooklyn. Manhattan was the densest part of the city, and thousands of people already bicycled in Manhattan and nearby Brooklyn, thanks to the West Side bike path and bike lanes along the East River bridges. Longtime residents were suspicious, fearing changes taking place in the city and fearing, too, if they were market-rate renters, that they and their favorite stores and restaurants might be priced out. In *Vanishing New York*, his 2017 jeremiad against affluent new residents, Lower East Side psychoanalyst Jeremiah Moss, who had moved to a rent-regulated apartment in 1993, eviscerated bike lanes as "green veins that stream gentrifiers into . . . neighborhoods." He did not address whether parked cars also belonged to, as he called cyclists, "a certain class of people." Some animosity was New York quirkiness. In Williamsburg, Orthodox Jewish residents complained that cyclists wore skimpy clothes, while other Orthodox believers hopped on bikes in their black suits.

Making It Personal

What began as "bikelash" went beyond absurdity in 2010. The previous year, DOT had unveiled a plan for Prospect Park West, the thoroughfare parallel to Brooklyn's 526-acre green oasis. Prospect Park West was a typical car-centric New York road: five lanes of one-way traffic, three for moving and two for parking, and no room for anyone else. The road, like Ninth Avenue, had extra capacity. Its average peak-hour traffic was 1,149 vehicles, but each lane could accommodate 700 vehicles per hour. Drivers used the extra room to speed, with three-quarters going more than the thirty-miles-per-hour limit. Speeding meant crashes, with fifty-eight collisions, many with injuries, along the two-mile stretch over three years.

DOT's proposal was similar to what it had done in Manhattan. It would take a lane from cars and create a parking-protected, two-way bike lane. The project fit into a broader makeover. Sadik-Khan was moving beyond waterfront Brooklyn deeper into the borough so that commuters who lived farther from Manhattan would have a safer route.[95] The community board had requested a bike lane. Sadik-Khan inaugurated the two-way Prospect Park West bike lane in October.

A small group of residents along Prospect Park freaked out. "Don't be conned by Sadik-Khan," one protest sign read. "Changing our lanes is risking our lives," read another.[96] Opponents were powerful. Park Slope was one of New York's wealthiest neighborhoods. Many residents of its two- and three-family homes and small apartment buildings hadn't moved there to try new things. The neighborhood was also home to current, former, and future politicians and government officials. In addition to the soon-to-be-mayor, Bill de Blasio, Senator Charles Schumer and his wife, former DOT commissioner Iris Weinshall, called Park Slope home, as did former Dinkins-era deputy mayor Norman Steisel.

They did not like a change in traffic patterns. The well-connected attempted to get their way through back channels, the kind that had worked with Lindsay and Koch. "Can't you get rid of that lane?" Schumer asked Bloomberg at a private dinner. Bloomberg was unfazed. "[If] you don't like it," he responded, "I'm going to make it twice as wide."[97]

Prospect Park West opponents went public. Weinshall, Steisel, and neighbor Hainline, a Brooklyn College professor, wrote a letter to the *Times*. "When new bike lanes force the same volume of cars and trucks into fewer and narrower traffic lanes, the potential for accidents between cars, trucks and pedestrians goes up rather than down," they argued.[98] (Serious crashes were more likely to occur on wide-open roads, allowing drivers to speed.) When neither private pleas nor public arguments worked, opponents sued, claiming the bike lane was arbitrary and that the city was massaging data.[99] Months later, a judge dismissed the suit on a technicality; though the opponents won reinstatement, five years later, they dropped the case.[100] (Of her involvement, Weinshall says, "I do regret it.")[101]

Opponents lost, but they gained attention. The "bikelash" had made "JSK" into a public figure, unusual for any New York City department head, save for police commissioner. It helped—or hurt—that like Marcy Benstock, Sadik-Khan had a striking presence. Her fringed shoulder-length hair, well-tailored suits, chunky jewelry, high heels, and blunt-toned voice made her stand out, usually in a crowd of men.[102] A 2011 *Times* profile found that she had "become notorious for a brusque, I-know-best style and a reluctance to compromise." Letitia James, then a Brooklyn city councilwoman, called the commissioner a "friend" but said that "she was pretty much despised by my colleagues."[103] De Blasio said that her approach was "alienating." Cuozzo accused her of a "reign of terror."[104] Cindy Adams, *Post* gossip columnist, called Sadik-Khan "the wacko nutso bike commissioner." More unusual were regular New Yorkers who recognized Sadik-Khan or her name and blamed her for traffic woes. On Ninth Avenue one afternoon in 2013, the family owner of a nearly one-hundred-year-old Greek pastry shop gestured at Friday-night rush-hour traffic, stalled and honking, as it had been for decades. "The commissioner with the three names," the bakery owner said, "she does what she wants."[105]

Much criticism was based on misperception. Critics said Sadik-Khan was impervious to debate. In fact, she or her top staffers participated in forum after forum, interview after interview, fielding questions on everything from lighting and potholes to bike racks and pedestrian crowding.[106] DOT had informed community boards of every project, and often incorporated board members' suggestions. Someone, though, in the end, had to decide to do something different—and not everybody would agree with that decision. If people ranging from a senior senator to a bakery owner would object so vociferously, any commissioner intent on change would *have* to be sharp. "Things we did, people said were impossible," she says. "People told me to my face." Sadik-Khan also had to be firm with staff. "Janette is a huge outlier," says Orcutt. "You need to tell your lawyers and your engineers, 'yes, we are going to do new things,'" even if they resist.

It was one thing to voice concerns about parking spaces; it was another to make personal attacks, ranging from criticism of Sadik-Khan's hairstyle to her name. Part of her confidence in the face of such antipathy came from her upbringing. "I had a father, [an investment banker,] who was a big believer in me. Women in our family, throughout the years, were celebrated." Sadik-Khan's background also made her aware of the high stakes and long game of New York City activism. Sadik-Khan's mother, McCarthy, was one of the founders of the Citizens for Clean Air. Hazel Henderson, another CCA pioneer, remembers her daughter playing with

Sadik-Khan as a child. Sadik-Khan grew up knowing "how difficult it is, to fix it to make it better."

The Arrival of the Blue Bikes

Sadik-Khan had one last task: bike share. New York would fulfill the dream laid out in the 1974 book *The Pedestrian Revolution*: a system by which New Yorkers could rent a bike at one "dock," take a ride, and return the bike to a different kiosk. Stakes were not low. "Any stumbles could call into question the wisdom not only of bike share itself but of its underlying premise: that bicycles are a key part of the city's transit system," the *Times* warned.

Sadik-Khan said that bike-share would start in 2012, one year before Bloomberg left office. The program, run by a private firm under a city franchise, would start with 330 docking stations and 6,000 bicycles. As with bike lanes, the city would start with Manhattan, as well as a slice of northern Brooklyn, and work its way out. That way, bikeshare customers—many inexperienced—could depend on a network of relatively safe lanes as they tried two wheels in the city and relied on Manhattan's density to keep car speeds slow.

Sadik-Khan's DOT didn't plunk docks down without warning. In 2011, the city pledged to participate in public hearings as it decided on placement of docks.[107] The city invited people to submit requests for stations, and officials received 10,000 submissions. New Yorkers came to meetings to complain about everything from the logo on the bikes—Citibank would be the sponsor, thus the name, Citi Bike—to the loss of parking.

Rollout ran into problem after problem. The contractor struggled with technology. The company stored bikes and docks in a warehouse on the Brooklyn waterfront, where flooding from Hurricane Sandy in 2012 ruined equipment. The *Times* called the program "star-crossed."[108] Critics derided the idea that riders would generate demand for thousands of bikes.

Bikeshare debuted Memorial Day 2013, a year late. Sadik-Khan and Bloomberg had seven months left in City Hall to make it succeed. Even Bloomberg hedged his bets, sounding an echo of Koch, thirty-three years earlier. "If people want to use them, they'll use them. If people don't, they don't," the mayor said.[109] Memorial Day Monday, he stood next to a bike—but didn't ride. "Are we ready?" he asked. Citi Bike smashed expectations, with 6,050 people taking the bikes out for a spin on that Monday; 772 people bought memberships. "By midafternoon, the passing flickers of blue were already ubiquitous," the *Times* wrote.[110] In two weeks, 170,000 riders used the bikes.[111] In June, monthly ridership was 618,572;[112] by July, it topped one million.[113]

Most riders were annual members using the bikes not for recreation but for trips to work, to school, or to run errands. The system's busiest stations were near Midtown and downtown transit, indicating that people used the bikes to replace subway rides, making room for commuters on packed trains. Citi Bikers also used bikes instead of cabs, lessening traffic. The operator's problem was that the company couldn't keep docks stocked. "Truckloads of bikes not enough to meet Citi Bike demand," read one headline.[114]

As important as numbers was something less definable: the clunky blue bikes had become cool. Cary Grant and Sidney Poitier had pedaled through Central Park in 1966; now a new generation of tastemakers embraced Citi Bike. Bill Cunningham, *Times* fashion photographer, offered an instant endorsement. In a video, Cunningham, calling Citi Bike "rent a bicycle," pronounced it "absolutely wonderful." People "on wheels in their business suits" in each other's way were "endlessly funny."[115] Leonardo DiCaprio, aging millennial New Yorkers' teen idol, adopted the bikes, sometimes alone, sometimes with a model girlfriend.[116] Kevin Bacon and Macklemore rode the bikes. When Paul McCartney appeared on *Saturday Night Live*, Jimmy Fallon asked him how he had managed traffic. "I took a Citi Bike," he said.[117] The *Times* Style section advised on wearing heels ("high heels are built like cycling shoes").[118] Newlyweds rode from ceremony to reception.[119]

As important as the people liking the bikes were the people who *didn't*. The bikelash became so ludicrous that it burned out. The *Wall Street Journal* used the image of people rolling about on Citi Bikes as background for a video with an attention-catching title: "Death by Bicycle." (Of 447 pedestrians killed in three years, none had been killed by a bicyclist.)[120] Editorial board member Dorothy Rabinowitz said bikeshare was a product of "the totalitarian running this government." Claiming she represented "the majority," she pronounced herself "appalled" at the "dreadful program." Lamenting that the "best neighborhoods are absolutely begrimed . . . by these blazing blue Citibank bikes," she concluded, this is "what happens when you get . . . an autocratic mayor" supported by an "all-powerful" bike "lobby."[121]

Citi Bike cemented cycling. No mayor would dare take it away or take away lanes new cyclists needed. "It made all the difference," says Wolfson.

"It mainstreamed that activity in a way that I don't think anything else would have. It created both supply and demand. The more people wanted it the more it got rolled out, the more it got rolled out the more people wanted it. I cannot tell you the number of people I have talked to [who said,] 'I want to bike more in the city but I'm not going to do it unless I feel safe.'" Citi Bike made more people feel safe. "I don't think there's any question that Citi Bike has exceeded certainly mine and everyone's expectations," says Sadik-Khan. "They could see themselves riding," she says of regular New Yorkers, just as in Dunham's vision. In July, the city closed most Central Park drives to cars until Labor Day, "the first long-term closing that the city has tried," as opposed to limited-hours and weekend closures, and Citi Bikers joined the throng.[122] As the system expanded to more than eight thousand bikes, ridership nearly doubled in four years, to 62,605 each day by September 2017.[123]

Kempner, the TA donor, says that supporting Citi Bike was his "big one." Of his peers, he says, "Everybody laughed. My friends said, the parking space in front of my house [is a Citi Bike stand,] I can't park there." As TA officials, including White, note, Kempner's support was not just financial. Like Ravitch's opposition to Westway a generation earlier, it was a signal to his social group, including Bloomberg's circle. As Kempner says, "The idea of Citi Bikes was widely thought to be a disaster, and I haven't heard that in several years. On the contrary, real estate people say it's far from a disaster, it's become an amenity." Among executives, he says, "senior people in finance have stopped complaining, [because] those same people now commute to work on Citi Bikes."

Impervious Leadership

Sadik-Khan had enjoyed advantages that predecessors did not. The city—for the first time in generations—was no longer in permanent crisis. Living in New York was no longer a fight to survive, as it had been in 1990 and 1970. The city had recovered after 9/11 and, with 3.5 million jobs by Bloomberg's last year, was a beacon for people across skill levels. By Bloomberg's second term, removing a rider from a cramped L train from Williamsburg to Manhattan, or from an overpacked-beyond-capacity #4 train from the Upper East Side to Midtown, by luring her to a Citi Bike, was a benefit to other subway riders. All forms of transportation were jammed beyond comfort, giving the city a motive to tap demand for an efficient form of moving around. Encouraging cycling was an answer to, "How are we going to accommodate moving nine million people?" says Doctoroff.[124]

Functional, albeit crowded, subways also left more room on streets for cyclists. A "key to actually getting the bike lanes done was getting rid of some of the traffic," observes Barry Fishman, who, so long ago, had led his Bike for a Better City commute-to-work protest. Because subways, rebuilt beginning under Richard Ravitch in the 1980s, brought so many people to Manhattan, the number of cars and trucks on the streets was lower than it had been in the Koch era. By the end of the Bloomberg era, only 934,000 people took a car or truck into core Manhattan on an average day, 29 percent below the high of 1.3 million in 1998.

Sadik-Khan benefited from something else, as well. It wasn't financial resources. Bike lanes were cheap. It was mayoral fortitude. "It wouldn't have happened without a mayor like Michael Bloomberg," says Sadik-Khan. Most mayors don't give commissioners autonomy; decisions become hostage to interests from real estate developers to swing-vote city council members to pique. Bloomberg, by contrast, "didn't care about the short-term politics . . . and was willing to look beyond a six-month time horizon," says Wolfson. "Mike's . . . view of management is you hire smart people with experience. Your job is to provide them with cover."

Bloomberg didn't give commissioners absolute freedom. "It wasn't a blank check," says Sadik-Khan. "There were times when I was definitely worried. . . . You don't just stand by and say, 'oh well, there's some backlash.' It's an exaggeration to say that Mike didn't care." He listened to criticism. But, Sadik-Khan remembers, when confronted with arguments against cycling lanes or bikeshare, he would come to City Hall with questions. "He wanted to know the stats, wanted to know what the stories were going to be."[125]

Bloomberg also supported the issue because, attuned to global competition, he didn't want his city to be left behind. After voicing skepticism of Paris's Velib program in 2007, Bloomberg, through frequent trips to London, saw a similar program, Barclays Bikes, launched in 2010, succeed. In the mid-twentieth century, cycling had been eccentric; by the twenty-first century, no global city could offer residents quality of life without encouraging cycling. "Some of it was . . . seeing how it worked in London," says Wolfson. "He believed that New York was constantly competing . . . to attract and retain talent and capital. That London could do this, and we couldn't, was not something that would sit well." Anarchists had once deployed whimsical bikeshare in Amsterdam to protest capitalism; bikeshare came to New York partly because of capitalism's pressures.

Koch, three decades earlier, had backed down from his lanes. He didn't trust staffers' insistence that the infrastructure could succeed over time.

Koch had also faced pressure from Carey. Further, he was tired of being mocked, with his Peking on the Hudson. Bloomberg remained sanguine. Says Bloomberg a decade later, "Back away from bike lanes . . . ? Never even entertained the idea. Carping in the press only made us more determined, especially as we saw the data on safety—and as we saw people flock to them."[126]

Normal Cycling

By the end of the Bloomberg administration, people couldn't argue with the numbers. By 2013, cyclists were making 75,200 daily trips to work and 380,000 daily trips overall, 58 percent higher than in 2008. Each day, 21,105 cyclists were crossing Fiftieth Street in Manhattan, a barometer of Midtown cycling—up from 5,310 in 1980. More than 20,000 cyclists daily were crossing East River bridges, compared to 1,635 hardy souls in 1980.[127] Deaths had not increased, remaining between 12 and 22 annually during Bloomberg's third term. With cycling rising, deaths per ten million trips had fallen from 83.7 in 2000 to 30.3.[128] Anti-cyclists were a minority. In 2013, a *Times* poll showed that 64 percent of New Yorkers approved of bike lanes, and 73 percent approved of bike-sharing.[129] No Citi Bike rider died in traffic until 2017—on a street without a protected lane.

By 2019, cycling was a workaday part of New York. Cyclists made 105,400 daily trips to work and 530,000 daily trips overall, 40 percent higher than in the final Bloomberg year; 30,511 cyclists crossed Fiftieth Street in Midtown each day, and traffic over bridges was steady (growth curtailed because of a new ferry); and 28 percent of commuting cyclists were women, a record. In September, the bikeshare program, with more than 12,000 bikes, attracted 80,475 people each day; on September 21, 100,373 people rode one of the blue bikes, breaking the six-figure mark.[130] Citi Bike had more than 150,000 members, exceeding projections in *The Pedestrian Revolution*. Over a decade, cyclists (none on Citi Bikes) had killed five pedestrians.[131] By contrast, car and truck drivers killed between 107 and 183 pedestrians each year.[132] Elected officials' complaint was that Citi Bike hadn't expanded sufficiently.

It took another mayor, Bill de Blasio, who took office in 2014, to do what even Bloomberg hadn't done: in 2018, close Central Park—and Brooklyn's Prospect Park—to cars, all the time. "That a park was somehow doubling up as a highway," de Blasio remembered, "we were all used to it, but it made no sense whatsoever. The notion, cars, bikes, all in super close proximity, wait a minute . . . it all sort of started to crystallize." Safety was the biggest factor; de Blasio, who lives near Prospect Park, recalled Fruchter's death, the death that had spurred Steely White's activism. De Blasio also had a "growing consciousness of, . . . we need more parks. The parks we have, should be used as parks." When he asked officials what the traffic impact would be, he remembers, "Even the people really focused on traffic flow acknowledged . . . , it just didn't have a massive impact."[133] In Prospect Park, walkers and cyclists outnumbered vehicles three to one.

That June, TA's Paul Steely White drove the symbolic final car through Central Park. Advocates sang, "This is the last car." Watching were veterans of Lindsay-era weekend closures a half-century before: Benepe and Gurin. Mory Kaba, a cab driver, objected, saying he, too, used the park to escape traffic. "But what can I do?" he said.[134]

Chapter 12

Freedom to Walk

The Rise and Fall and Rise Again of Play Streets

Automobiles do not own the streets.

—Mayor John Hylan, 1925

It's not Broadway anymore.

—Donald Trump on closing of Times Square to traffic, 2009

GROVER WHALEN WAS FED UP. A Mayor Jimmy Walker appointee, the mustachioed police commissioner was determined to introduce virtue to New York. In 1929, notwithstanding his Roaring Twenties boss's love of nightlife, Whalen announced efforts to enforce Prohibition. Before Christmas—an unwise time for a campaign against libations—Whalen began a "war on speakeasies." Undeterred by the fact that there were fifteen thousand such establishments, he insisted, "I want to rid the city [of] disorderly places."[1] It didn't go well. By April, Whalen told the federal government that such actions were exhausting his officers. Washington would have to safeguard Prohibition, he concluded.[2]

Failing in stopping New Yorkers from drinking, Whalen turned to a more pedestrian problem: pedestrians. Three hundred thousand people worked in Manhattan's Garment District on the West Side, not far from Penn Station. They ate lunch between noon and 1:00 p.m., and they didn't fit onto sidewalks as they left cutting and sewing factories for pushcart food and fresh air. "With fully three-quarters of the population . . . going to lunch simultaneously—the period being specified in union regulations—the need for an outdoor forum . . . has been increasingly felt."[3] Workers stretching legs mixed with theater-going crowds, creating pedestrian jams. Whalen unsuccessfully pushed for a jaywalking law. In the meantime, officers arrested walkers for disorderly conduct. "Ella Colson, the theatre district's first woman jaywalker . . . was arrested Wednesday night as she darted across Broadway," the *New York Times* reported. She received a suspended sentence.

Enforcement wasn't effective. Walkers had numbers on their side. Police might catch one "disorderly" walker, but hundreds pushed by. Whalen attempted another solution: one-way sidewalks. For two blocks between Thirty-Sixth and Thirty-Eighth Streets, northbound pedestrians would stay on the west sidewalk; southbound walkers, on the east sidewalk. Yet this measure consumed manpower. "The ten policemen assigned to enforce the new regulation had their hands full," but success was "moderate," Whalen admitted.[4] The rule was abolished.[5]

Having failed to keep New Yorkers from walking freely, just as he had failed to keep them from drinking, Whalen arrived at a new solution: common sense. If people walked, he would give them room. "He ordered Thirty-Sixth Street, between Seventh and Eighth Avenues, closed to vehicular traffic from 12 to 1 o'clock each workday." Garment workers could "congregate in the street," the commissioner decreed. "But they must leave the sidewalks clear" for movement. At a businessmen luncheon, Whalen pronounced himself pleased. "They had to have some place to go, and we gave them one," he said.[6] The strait-laced commissioner called it a "play street for grown-ups."[7] Four years later, the "play street" remained and, even during the Depression, was "standing room only."[8]

Whalen's measure was the exception. Over the ensuing half-century, New Yorkers, children and adults, lost the right to their streets, contributing to New York's decline. Beginning in the 1960s, as New York stopped building highways, urbanists proposed reviving public spaces for people on foot or for people who wanted to sit at chairs and tables. But until the new millennium, crime and disorder deterred mayors. In the first decade of the twenty-first century, Michael Bloomberg finally took back stretches of streets from fast-moving vehicles in a place calculated to garner global attention: Times Square. New York painfully relearned what its residents had forgotten a century before: cars do not define a city.

New Rules

New Yorkers in 1929 understood Whalen's reference to "play streets." For a decade, automobile drivers, self-granted with entitlement because they could afford the contraptions, had taken over public spaces. In 1910,

72,000 people had registered a vehicle in New York City; by 1920, the figure had reached 216,000 and would double by 1926.[9] By 1930, the number of autos reached 764,000.[10] The city's population was growing, too—from 4.8 million in 1910 to 6.9 million by 1930. However, although most New Yorkers didn't have cars, vehicles multiplied faster than people, dominating the streets.

Even before Robert Moses had any public position, New York's impulse was to accommodate cars. "Motor traffic needs better roads," a *Times* headline read in 1920.[11] That year, New York got traffic lights: five "signal towers" to control cars, trucks, horse carts, and pedestrians in Midtown, then, as in the future, the most congested part of the city. Thanks to the lights, "a taxi can go from the Plaza to the Waldorf in less than seven minutes."[12] The editorial page called the lights a "toy," but made clear that they weren't toys. "Everybody has to play whether he likes it or not. Pedestrians, trucks, automobiles—they must all play the game of the lights."[13]

Pedestrians never had had to play by such a "game." Horse-cart drivers, trolley operators, pushcart vendors, cyclists, and walkers, moving slowly, had shared the road, albeit uneasily. Yet barely two decades into the century of the car, the city favored the motor vehicle minority over the majority who had to watch out for them. Engineers—and the *Times*, in praising the fast auto trip between two hotels within fifteen minutes' walking distance from each other—wanted cars flowing, ignoring that such prioritization inconvenienced greater numbers of people on foot. Walkers had to wait, in clumps at corners, for a few cars to move.

Pedestrians lost this compulsory "game." In 1910, 332 New Yorkers died in traffic, including 232 pedestrians. By 1920, 811 people had died—including 568 walkers. In 1929, the figure reached an all-time peak of 1,360, including 952 pedestrians, nearly three each day. The Depression cut this toll to 1,145 and 629, respectively, the following year. But streets remained stages for carnage.[14]

Parents had long had to worry about children being hit by trains. Now, they had to worry about a new risk. By World War I, New York City had more than a million children aged five to fifteen. Nearly 700,000 of them, in tenements or cut-up houses, had no place to play at home. A decade earlier, if they stayed away from avenues, trolley tracks, and train yards, they amused themselves on narrow streets, looking out for trotting horses and human-powered pushcarts.

Motor vehicles were not as forgiving. One two-paragraph article in 1929 noted the death of five-year-old Paul Casseni of the Bronx's 142nd Street. The boy, playing, "was instantly killed . . . when he ran into the rear of a motor truck," the *Times* reported. "The boy was crossing the street . . . when the westbound truck . . . swerved to avoid him. Confused, the boy ran into the rear wheel."[15] The paper assigned blame: the boy had run into a truck, rather than the truck having run into the boy.

Deadly Games

Parents won a guerrilla action against cars and trucks: "play streets." In 1914, Whalen's predecessor as police commissioner, Arthur Woods, determined to give space back to children. Woods, a Massachusetts native and Harvard grad who had taught Franklin Delano Roosevelt at Groton, had studied sociology. An appointee of John Purroy Mitchel, a reformist mayor, Woods launched the Police Athletic League to encourage officers to engage with children. Two decades before Robert Moses, as parks commissioner, built playgrounds, kids needed room: hence: traffic-free play streets.[16]

By 1916, play streets were a tradition—but there weren't enough. "Streets are already beginning to be filled with the many children who during the Summer season have no other playground," the *Times* wrote. "Unless more play streets and play centers are provided . . . police officers assert that the usual heavy Summer toll of . . . loss of life may be expected." Woods wanted to close one hundred streets, up from fifteen the previous summer. "The sooner we get [children] out from under the wheels of vehicles, just so soon will the street accidents begin to go down," he said. An officer concurred. "Children must have a place to play. . . . They will not walk a mile to go to a city park. Then the parks are hemmed about by so many restrictions that many children do not care to play. . . . They are going to play in the streets. Many a poor little girl, while playing 'ring around a Rosie' . . . has had her life crushed out by auto."[17] By 1920, the city had set up sixty play streets.[18]

For much of the century, play streets became synonymous with summer. In 1932, at a trough of the Depression, the city opened forty-two oases—"in neighborhoods which are overpopulated and in which no recreational space is available"—the Lower East Side, the lower West Side, northern Manhattan, and the South Bronx.[19] Thousands of children crowded each block. Moses, who became city parks commissioner in 1934, supported the never-met goal of two hundred play streets, writing that "there cannot be enough facilities of this kind."[20]

Child-welfare advocates saw play streets as diversions from dangerous pursuits. The city didn't close streets and leave children alone. PAL took in money from the city, donors, and, later, the New Deal to pay workers, many of them college students, to organize games and open fire hydrants when the temperature reached eighty degrees. In 1934, East Harlem got eleven streets, at the insistence of the city's welfare department.[21] The same summer, the Leisure Time Conference of the Lower West Side Council of Social Agencies reported that play streets had not reduced just crashes but also delinquency. In 1934, a deputy police commissioner, Miss Henrietta Additon, toured Manhattan areas where more than one thousand "underprivileged children" played paddle tennis, stickball, and shuffleboard, declaring that the fun would keep them out of children's court.[22] More than a decade later, in 1948, one thousand children spent their summer on one Harlem block, playing "hop scotch, jacks, rope jump, marbles, skellies," and participating in "novelty races."[23] The next year, college grads supervised sixty-four play streets, with "puppet shows, amateur hours, roller skating derbies, inter-street tournaments, arts and crafts and a Mardi Gras."[24] A year later, on Henry Street on the Lower East Side, one of seventy-five blocked-off streets, mothers played volleyball against their kids to "make them so tired that they won't be any trouble," as one worker said. One ten-year-old girl, minding neighborhood infants, said her mother couldn't play, as she had to work. Like many children, the preteen was on her own. A Mrs. Reitano observed, "If the children didn't have this, they'd be doing something destructive."[25]

Play streets, scarce in a city with tens of thousands of blocks, were contested. Though the city set them up on streets without much traffic, drivers coveted every inch. In 1925, a judge ruled that Mayor John Hylan had no authority to close blocks; only the Board of Aldermen, then the city's body of lawmakers, could do it. Hylan directed police to ignore the ruling. "Children are entitled to play," the mayor wrote. "Automobiles do not own the streets; and the children have some rights. . . . If a play street saves the life or limb of a single child, its existence is justified."[26] In 1928, even the Auto Club favored play streets, as long as they "avoid interference with traffic."[27] But five years later, the Uptown Chamber of Commerce protested, saying that twenty-six Manhattan play streets were "handicapping . . . traffic."[28] In 1934, Mayor Fiorello LaGuardia chatted with children on 207th Street in the Bronx; they were about to lose their street, as nearly all residents polled "wanted it restored as a thoroughfare."[29]

Children suffered further marginalization after World War II. Car registrations increased from below one million in 1940 to 1.4 million in 1950.[30] "Two streets . . . on New York City's Lower East Side, provide a microcosm of the change," wrote Simon Breines and William Dean. "As late as 1950, these streets were still prime ball-game and roller-skating areas. As the automobile gained ascendancy, . . . traffic increased, and the curbside became a parking lot."

Even when parents won a play street, the block was not free of danger. In 1949, the city's chief magistrate asked the traffic court to levy a $15 fine ($200 in 2024 dollars) on people who drove through play streets, noting that children "have the right to rely on the security the play street signs give them."[31] In 1948, a truck driver on a Lower East Side play street ran over and killed a six-year-old boy, Charles Verdon.[32] In April 1949, druggist Anthony Fischetti drove through a Brooklyn play street, killing a three-year-old boy, Jack Anconi.[33] In June 1949, a driver injured eleven-year-old Packy Ryan, also in Brooklyn, on a play street; more than 1,500 children came out in a combination-protest-block-party to support the boy, who looked out the window as he convalesced.[34] It shouldn't be too much, said the Women's City Club, for the city to "keep clear the streets which must serve as playgrounds for urban children who cannot know the joys of clean green grass or the relative safety in which the children of suburbs and country play."[35] A 1952 dragnet caught 140 drivers.[36]

Play streets endured, a refuge for more than four hundred thousand children a year by the 1950s,[37] even as the white middle class was leaving tenements for suburbs, lured not just by subsidized mortgages and highways but also by a safe place for offspring to play. Play streets were an example to the world. In 1952, Erik Groes-Peterson, Copenhagen's traffic chief, toured New York. "[He] had high praise for the practice here of closing off streets for play areas. This is a system the Danes hope to put into effect, . . . since numerous fatalities among children have occurred."[38]

Games changed with the times. In 1955, three years after the United Nations headquarters opened on the East Side, the city's sixty play streets had an international theme: "Understanding our Neighbors" through "songs, costumes, and folk dance."[39] In 1957, the city featured "Americanism," with 130 "youngsters" on one Manhattan block "whoop[ing] it up . . . in Indian headdress."[40] In June 1959, when the temperature reached a record 96.9 and the pavement "bubbled," kids splashed in hydrants, while blocks away, motorists stood by overheated cars on parkways and highways.[41]

Mean City, Kind Streets

As the century entered its second half, officials saw play streets as an outlet to relieve racial strife as southern black families escaped segregation and sought opportunity by moving north. In 1950, 9 percent of New Yorkers were black; by 1970, the figure would reach 21 percent. As Puerto Rican families moved to the mainland to seek work, New York's Hispanic population rose from barely measurable to 16 percent.

In many policies, federal, state, and local officials—as well as leaders in the real estate and construction industries—exacerbated suffering. Newcomers found themselves blocked both by barriers to jobs and by exclusion policies on the part of landlords, lenders (including the federal government), and developers. Play streets were balm, if not cure, for urban stress. As early as 1949, the *Times* noted, "cynics who snort at the idea of mixed racial groups . . . need only stand in a city play street . . . to learn that children do not seem to be born with the common prejudices." In enlightened moments, officials used streets to de-escalate conflict. In July 1961, on the Upper West Side's Eighty-Fourth Street, between Amsterdam and Columbus Avenues, "slum-bred frustration and despair . . . erupted into a brawl among 400 Negroes and Puerto Ricans." The Wagner administration made the block into a play street. Two weeks later, "400 children ran foot races, played basketball, skated and cooled themselves in a hydrant."[42] Yet the city often did the wrong thing. A year later, that Upper West Side play street was slated for urban renewal demolition. The city planned a similar street four blocks south. Officials, however, abandoned the idea, despite the pleas of a rector, who observed families "in desperate need."[43] The "main objection" was "loss of parking spaces."

With many middle-class white children now playing in suburban yards and with resentments rising in declining neighborhoods, children's noise was no longer a welcome sound. Residents of fragile blocks protested for continued access to public spaces. In April 1964, CORE, the Congress of Racial Equality, held a "sit-in" in the office of Henry Barnes, Wagner's traffic commissioner. Ten adults and forty young children, buttressed by fifteen teenage boys "picketing," demanded a play street on 123rd Street in Harlem "so that no more children would be killed."[44] The city agreed.[45]

Through street interactions, children whose families were undergoing traumas could find role models. In summer 1964, Connie Holt, a medical student at Maryland's historically black Howard University, came to Brooklyn to supervise "Negro and Puerto Rican youngsters who tugged at her arm, hugged her around the waist, and pushed her toward an open fire hydrant." Activists used play streets to address the emerging issue of environmental injustice. A decade and a half earlier, children had been content to play games fostering "Americanism." By 1970, when Mayor Lindsay inaugurated one of one hundred play streets, on Harlem's 114th Street, children "paraded" in protest, carrying signs reading "lead paint kills."[46]

A few blocks of peace could not fix iniquities that would erupt into unrest. "They hate the cops, and the cops hate them," a Brooklyn College student and play street volunteer said of children and teens.[47] As crime, unemployment, addiction, and other ills increased, play streets, ironically, seemed to many wise stewards like an irrelevant frill. "Policemen no longer play with the youngsters," the *Times* observed in 1970. Top department officials and "some influential citizens," including budget watchdogs, "felt that policemen should not be paid to play." The city diverted cops to other work.[48]

Play streets dwindled. By 1973, the city opened 48, from a high of 106 in 1967. With the broke city cutting spending, play streets, compared to teaching and sanitation, didn't seem important. Donations—from General Motors and Exxon—only partially offset budget cuts. The need hadn't diminished. "It's nice to have the streets free of cars," said twelve-year-old Beatrice Wilson of Harlem that summer.[49] Residents committed to staying fought for dwindling resources. In 1977, the Citizens Committee for New York City, a civic group created to counteract service cuts, put out a "self-help" handbook that explained how to apply for a play street.[50]

Hetty Fox, of the Bronx's Morrisania neighborhood, decided to act. Fox had moved to the South Bronx in 1940 as a three-year-old child; her parents were the first black homeowners on the Italian street.[51] Fox, after graduating from Hunter College, moved to California in the 1960s, teaching psychology and black studies. She thought leaving the Bronx was a mark of success. "The higher you go in school, the farther you get from your neighborhood," she said later.[52] As her parents considered selling their home in the decaying neighborhood, Fox knew that "communities were disappearing."

She changed her mind about what it meant to be successful, coming home in 1970. The city's policy was to shrink neighborhoods like hers through cutbacks in services, such as firefighting, even as arson raged. She said, "I knew it made sense to keep the houses" rather than allow them to burn down.[53] Undeterred by a mugging and by scavengers in near-abandoned buildings, she enlisted neighbors in a watch against crime. She petitioned the city for sidewalks and trees.

In 1977, Fox applied for a play street, closing off her block, Lyman Place. "When I heard no sounds of children on this block, I knew it was almost dead," she said years later.[54] A street peopled with well-supervised children "keep[s] the block closed to thieves and drug dealers."[55] "We could control what was going on . . . and release the energy of the children." Thanks to the Police Athletic League, Fox received a $225 weekly salary ($1,200 in 2024 dollars) and equipment for the kids. More than one hundred kids ran, shrieked, and learned.[56]

Fox's work helped stem the bleeding. "Not on our block," she told *City Limits* magazine, apropos of fires that consumed the area.[57] The number of families on the block increased from sixty-five to eighty during the 1980s, also the result of Koch-era housing reinvestment. Fox, who died in 2019, persisted into the new century, despite vanishing support; the city forced her to curtail hours during the 1990s. "Miss Fox is lucky to have a single basketball hoop, a few lonely games and a wobbly, paint-splattered table," the *Times* wrote.[58]

A generation later, Maria Forbes saw a play street as integral to saving a different Bronx neighborhood. Forbes, born in 1962 and, like Fox, a native of Manhattan, moved to the Bronx as a child. Her stepfather was a longshoreman and her father a seaman; her mother, descended from Carolina slaves, was a therapist.[59] The family owned a duplex and a three-family house in Highbridge in the southwest Bronx. Forbes and her sisters were among four black children in the Catholic School; "we used to go pick up this other boy," she says of the fourth child, to stay together. Forbes remembers childhood play streets. It was "so beautiful," she says, recalling the "skate-mobile and the game-mobile."[60]

In the 1970s, her family's tenants struggled to pay rent. "I always remember these tenants coming to ask [my mother] for one-shot deals," she says. Her mother became a renter herself, moving to a building on the Grand Concourse. But the landlord was in default and was struggling to pay Con Ed, the electricity provider, for power to common areas. Forbes's mother, Velma Thomas, wanted to keep the building occupied. Thomas went to court, winning permission to collect rent and operate the building.

In 1985, as a young adult, Forbes moved to Claremont Village to the east, eight blocks south of the Cross-Bronx Expressway. "I saw the crack epidemic destroy it," she says of her area. "They sold the fire-alarm system out of the building." She followed her mother's example. In 1990, she became head of her tenants' association, representing her neighbors to the city's housing authority, which had taken over the buildings.

The neighborhood needed more than building management and repairs. Kids needed a place to gather. Though her three sons, as children, took trips to the country with the Fresh Air Fund, a program supported by donors and rural homeowners, many children "never get to make it across

167th Street." Parents "can't afford summer camp, let alone [family] trip money," and parents were wary of sending children with strangers. A 1985 fire had destroyed a community center. Claremont Park, below the Cross-Bronx Expressway, was a long walk. Though the city, by the 1980s and 1990s, was using donations to refurbish parks, such as Manhattan's Central Park and Bryant Park, Bronx parents had to bundle children into subways to benefit from free and safe spaces with recreational programming. "I used to go to Easter egg hunts in Central Park with my sons," she said, but didn't see why she should have to travel so far.

In 1992, Forbes asked for a play street, funded through the housing authority's drug-prevention program. She had a reputation as a persistent advocate. "People call me assertive, aggressive," she says. Internally among city agencies, "they said, 'please give her the street, so she will leave us alone.'" The children who populated her play street had plenty to do. They had a "championship in track and field, flag football, baseball, basketball. . . . I became a sports mom." The children learned art and dance. "That play street did so many things for so many families," Forbes says. "We saved more little boys and girls, from going to jail, getting pregnant." Forbes, who never learned how to drive, notes that the play street "causes traffic jams. People complain." But residents were supportive. "We had so much fun."

Play streets fell out of fashion. Crime fell, graduation rates went up, and parks were reinvigorated. Playing in the street, no longer a tradition for nearly all children but rather a program for poor minority children, was a relic of the past. The nature of play changed, with children spending more time inside. Manhattan's long-serving district attorney, Robert Morgenthau, used proceeds of assets seized from drug dealers to fund play streets, but in 1993, the number was just twenty-eight.[61] In 1994, Diana Peterson of Inwood, in northern Manhattan, ran into trouble in renewing her play street: residents worried about parking. "Why can't they just use half of the street and let us park on the other half?" said one building superintendent. "Residents have told her that they will not sign the annual petitions required . . . if their cars are towed."[62] The city stopped supporting Forbes's play street in the mid-2000s. In 2017, the city had just fifteen.[63]

Hard to Walk

Even as play streets for kids dwindled in the second half of the 1960s, urban innovators were taking up Whalen's old idea: play streets for adults. From his first days in office, in 1966, Mayor John Lindsay knew that he had to improve the urban environment. Car-choked streets threatened New York's tax base.

In 1967, the mayor released a report called "The Threatened City." The report quoted an article in the Detroit *Free Press*, calling New York "a city no longer in love with itself. . . . New York is killing itself [on] congestion and paralysis." The report acknowledged that with factory employers leaving, the future would be white-collar work. People in finance, law, advertising, and "creative" industries would crowd into skyscrapers. "We hope to see several hundred thousand more office workers," the authors said. As a matter of physics, they couldn't commute in cars.

New York's worst-of-both-worlds approach had created a paradox. At great cost to neighborhoods, the city had proven that it couldn't compete with suburbs in giving people an easy car commute. People who desired such a thing would leave. Yet the city's mismanagement of streets meant that many others who didn't desire a car commute might also leave. Driving in New York was *just* tolerable enough for hundreds of thousands of people to do it daily, foisting noise, pollution, and crashes on millions who took transit or walked.

Thanks to its poisonous embrace of the car, New York was alienating people who lived in the city because they preferred not to embrace the automobile. People on trains suffered deteriorating service and people walking inhaled toxic air as they dodged drivers. "The pleasant custom of taking a walk . . . is becoming very difficult," the report noted.

One solution came from the past, repeating Whalen's Garment District experiment. "The practice of closing streets should be extended for adults as well as children," the report suggested. Advisers counseled the mayor to be more ambitious than scattered blocks. They targeted the city's core: Broadway. Two years later, the planning commission's "Plan for New York City" suggested a "wide" pedestrian thoroughfare on Forty-Eighth Street, south of Rockefeller Center, "along the axis of the new [never built] 48th Street Subway."

In 1970, another city study, "Movement in Midtown," determined that pedestrians needed room. The report, written by van Ginkel Associates, a Montreal architecture firm, observed that three-quarters of Manhattan commuters arrived by transit "despite the unbearable service." Subways and buses deposited people on streets, where they became pedestrians. Midtown "has virtually the same ratio of pedestrian space as any other part of Manhattan but the concentration of people is ten times or more," the planners noted. "Sidewalks are narrow, noisy, dirty and overcrowded."

The answer: "pedestrian streets." The report suggested "closing off a number of streets and avenues. . . . Planting of trees and vegetation will replenish oxygen . . . and will reduce noise levels. The wide walkways, the separation from fast vehicular movement and the slower pace, will stimulate relaxation." The report suggested Forty-Eighth and Forty-Ninth Streets, and Madison and Lexington Avenues. "Minibuses" and emergency vehicles could access pedestrian thoroughfares, as could, during limited hours, delivery vehicles. The report also suggested wider sidewalks on Fifth Avenue, as well as weekend closures there "for strolling, shopping and sightseeing." But the biggest target, as in the earlier report, was Broadway: "Its full width from Lincoln Center to Herald Square"—two miles—"should be designed for people on foot."

By now, New York had global examples, as Dean and Breines put it in *The Pedestrian Revolution*, of "restor[ing] the historic function and quality of city streets." In the 1950s, when Copenhagen officials had viewed New York's play streets, New York had been a pioneer. Now, it was a laggard. Copenhagen had closed its *Stroget* to cars in the mid-1960s, letting people walk the near-mile of boutiques and cafes. "Merchants who initially opposed closing the street to vehicles, report sales increases of 25 to 40 percent." Only 30 percent of traffic moved to other roads; the rest disappeared. Munich had closed its city center to vehicles and seen foot traffic increase 60 percent. Even in the United States, car-centric cities were rethinking the automobile. In Minneapolis, in 1967, city officials had transformed the Nicollet Mall, formerly scene of twelve thousand daily vehicles, into a promenade. If the city couldn't afford an expensive redesign, "any street can be closed temporarily . . . by . . . wooden police barriers," Breines and Dean wrote.

A Play Street for Adults, Again

Applying these ideas, Lindsay targeted Lower Manhattan's Nassau Street. Nassau Street, near Manhattan's southern tip, wasn't in Midtown, with modern avenues and streets, but in Lower Manhattan, with colonial-era narrow routes. The *Times*'s description of Nassau Street's challenges resembled its depiction of the Garment District's challenges five decades earlier. "Lunch crowds . . . jam the narrow road and its shops" selling luggage, cameras, and sporting goods. The crowds weren't factory workers but bankers.

In 1969—reelection year—Lindsay came up with the same solution Whalen had: a play street. In a summertime experiment, from 11:00 a.m. to 2:00 p.m., five blocks of Nassau Street became a mall. "The purpose is to end the daily conflict between office workers and executives [nine thousand an hour] who pour into the busy commercial street . . . and motorists who try to negotiate the 20-foot-wide roadway."[64] People moved off sidewalks to take over the roadbed. "This gives people a chance to walk with freedom," said one walker.[65] Stores didn't suffer.[66]

In 1970, for inaugural Earth Day, Lindsay granted New Yorkers access to one of the world's famous thoroughfares, rivaling Paris's Champs-Élysées and London's Oxford Street: Fifth Avenue. Walkers "could appreciate the beauty of the city under the cloud-studded blue skies overhead rather than the grey plumes of auto exhausts." Hundreds of thousands of pedestrians who thronged the roadbed on April 22 stood—or sat—in wonder. "It was perfectly possible for a man to sit . . . in the center of Fifth Avenue," the *Times* wrote. "The bells of St. Thomas Church tolled joyously as thousands of pedestrians streamed, [the avenue] a pedestrian mall for what seemed, to many, too brief a time." One boy flew a kite; a Girl Scout handed out flowers. "They should have this every Wednesday," said a Mrs. Barbara Youngberg, who had come from Queens with her toddler son.[67]

Lindsay announced that Fifth Avenue would close on four summer Saturdays. "The pedestrian was king," the *Times* wrote. "Thousands of men, women and children—with their dogs and bicycles . . . expressed overwhelming pleasure. No horns blew. Few gasoline fumes assailed them." Strollers cheered. "I'm for anything that will get cars out of the city," Joseph Sheering, a mechanic, told the paper. Six canopied "little trains on tires" ferried people who preferred not to walk. "Fun city," said one "train" engineer, pulling a cord to make a "merry" sound.[68] As had happened in Central Park four years earlier, pollution fell. The mayor declared, "The general concept of street closings is now firmly established."[69]

East of Fifth Avenue, Madison Avenue merchants viewed the experiment with envy. Martin Weiner, an advertising executive, and 184 merchants banded into a "Madison Avenue General Ideas Committee." This "Magic" consortium asked the mayor to shut down their thoroughfare Tuesday evenings for a "magic promenade."[70] In September, Lindsay fulfilled their wish. Nearly twenty blocks of Madison would become an evening mall every Tuesday. Stores, galleries, and museums would stay open late, restaurants putting out sidewalk tables. Shoppers and diners could hear folk singers, see "flower girls," and enjoy fashion shows and dancing. As on Fifth Avenue, "mini trains" would transport passengers who didn't want to or couldn't walk.[71] The "magic promenade" was a hit. "You're really giving the city back to the people," one man shouted as Lindsay walked with his wife and small son. Weiner "pointed happily to shops thronged with people."[72]

Promenades proved themselves hardy to colder weather. In December, Lindsay again closed Fifth Avenue to traffic each Sunday for the

Christmas-shopping season. Strollers enjoyed activities from folk dancing, "African dancing," and "singing groups" to "ice skating on thermoplastic." Lindsay wished passersby "Merry Christmas." Ken Patton, the mayor's commerce commissioner, said the closures could "change the course of history." The *Times* noted that "there seemed to be a difference in the quality of city life."[73]

For the mayor, the festive air was a reprise of summer 1966, when cyclists had taken over Central Park. Lindsay capitalized on momentum. The following February, City Hall began its project—the van Ginkel plan—"to decongest midtown Manhattan by closing portions of Broadway and Madison and Lexington Avenues to automobile traffic."[74] Downtown Brooklyn, too, would get a pedestrian mall.

Madison Avenue made sense for permanent pedestrianization. The avenue carried only three percent of Midtown's traffic, or twenty thousand car trips a day. By contrast, it saw two hundred thousand daily pedestrians.[75] In December, the city unveiled a four-million-dollar plan to narrow the four-lane avenue to two, allowing buses and deliveries. The mall would be "graced by trees, sidewalk cafes, decorative pavements, bus shelters, drinking fountains and new forms of lighting." If it worked, the city would establish malls on Lexington, Broadway, and Forty-Eighth and Forty-Ninth Streets.[76]

The project won support. "Businessmen for the Madison Mall," a coalition that included more than eighty "prominent realty men . . . , retailers, hotel men and other midtown interests," claimed that 60 percent of merchants favored the project. Major employers nearby—"Newsweek, [electronics company] Sperry Rand, IBM, Union Carbide"—favored the closures, as did the community board. ABNY's powerful Lew Rudin was cautious, desiring a "trial run."[77]

The Cars Win

A year later, "magic" Madison Avenue was dead, killed by three factions. First, on Madison Avenue, some merchants' attitudes had changed since temporary closures, now that they understood the temporary "magic" evenings were a prelude to permanent changes. Many retailers supported the transformation, but merchants were no longer speaking with one voice. Higher-end stores complained that customers didn't walk. Residents complained about noise, both from the city's official entertainment and "rowdyism."[78] In mid-June, the city halted temporary evening closures.

Second, a new group, the "Traffic Action Committee," had mobilized. Made up of the Fifth Avenue Association, the Auto Club, and restaurant and hotel associations, the group called temporary closures "a failure." Traffic hadn't disappeared, they said; it had moved to other streets, worsening congestion on Fifth and Park Avenues. Merchants were "seriously hurt."[79] The Fifth Avenue Association, whose jurisdiction extended east, said members "overwhelmingly opposed" traffic bans.[80] The taxi industry called it "poorly conceived." The powerful Real Estate Board of New York, too, came out against it. The Teamsters, the union representing 175,000 truck drivers, warned of "horrible complications" pushing up shipping costs. "Then men won't do it," said a union spokesperson, referring to night deliveries. "Why should they give up a normal life?" Kisburg charged that the only people who would enjoy the mall were the "lumpenproletariat," who "don't work," and the "elitists, who can work anytime they want."[81]

Finally, even elected officials who favored curtailing traffic were skeptical. Greitzer, the Manhattan councilwoman, said that the closure wouldn't work "unless we do something about keeping cars from entering the central business district." Eldon Clingan, Citizens for Clean Air's former chief and now a councilman, agreed that the mall would "put the air pollution problem someplace else."[82] The *Times* was unsure. "It dabbles with the automobile problem without facing the harsh truth that there can be no workable solution short of severely restricting admission of automobiles," the paper said.[83]

Lindsay blinked. "All over the world, great cities are beginning to redesign their core areas to favor the man on foot," he said in fall 1972, but he postponed the trial closure, and then delayed it again, to July 1973.[84] The postponements gave opponents a vacuum in which to mount a long-term offense. In March, a gold-plated consortium sued. The plaintiffs—trade associations, Brooks Brothers, Abercrombie & Fitch, Tiffany's, B. Altman, Saks, Lord & Taylor, and Bergdorf—won a ruling, upheld on appeal, that the mayor could not redesign the street; the Board of Estimate would have to vote.[85] In June, Lindsay brought the plan to the board. "The Mayor clearly does not see the mall as a minor matter," the *Times* said.

But two years of delay had carried a political cost. With the 1973 mayoral primary race over, Lindsay had months left in office. Abe Beame, the likely next mayor, as well as a current Board of Estimate member by virtue of his position as city comptroller, opposed the mall, as did Queens's Donald Manes and Brooklyn's Sebastian Leone, both borough presidents and board members. "The taxi industry seems to be able to produce an enormous amount of pressure," said a Lindsay spokesperson.[86] The *Times* noted, correctly, "If the mall is not approved now, it probably will be lost forever."[87]

The board was unmoved. Lindsay convinced Percy Sutton, Manhattan's borough president, to vote for the mall, as well as borough presidents of the Bronx and Staten Island. But the supporters weren't a majority. "It's all been the crude business of the political process," Lindsay said. "I have six months left in office and . . . the more futility I see."[88] Lindsay was going out the way he had come in: stymied in a progressive vision by a transportation special interest. The first time, it had been the transit union; this time, it was, in part, cab owners.

The episode was a case study in how not to achieve streetscape change. The mayor had attempted to pedestrianize a high-profile corridor without having demonstrated a sustained, successful pilot elsewhere in Midtown. Tuesday evening closures had been too short to cement opinion to such an extent that merchants would have felt foolish in going against it, and the evening closures confused constituents. Would a partly pedestrianized Madison Avenue be one big party, as the evening closures were, or would it be a place to walk?

During Lindsay's final week, to say goodbye to a demoralized New York, the mayor chose a backdrop of urban hope: car-free Fifth Avenue. Even as he had failed to achieve permanent pedestrianizations, the mayor had continued Christmastime Saturday closures. The final Sunday of 1973, walking by stores festooned with decorations, "dodging roller skaters and volleyball players . . . Lindsay loped the 23-block length of the holiday promenade," wishing New Yorkers farewell. Amid the "barbershop harmony chorus from Fordham University" and a "roving clown who sketched children" was a cyclist, Robert Jacobson, riding with his wife and daughters. "With the clean air and no cars," he said, "too bad this is the last day."[89]

Gathering in the Streets, One Day at a Time

Though the Madison Avenue pedestrian plaza had failed, Lindsay had created an expectation of nicer streets. In 1974, even as the city careened toward insolvency, the Beame administration—hardly visionary—launched a "greening" of Sixth Avenue downtown. The city spent $400,000 to spruce up "traffic triangles" where diagonal roads intersecting had created dead spaces, including at Carmine and Prince Street in the Village, adding trees as well as benches and chess tables. In the late 1970s, the Beame and Koch administrations continued a separate Lindsay-era idea. With federal funding, the city opened an eight-block pedestrian mall in downtown Brooklyn. As the promenade opened in the 1980s, it "injected new life into a dying business area."[90]

Residents took back their streets in another way: fairs. Beame didn't have money for frills. But one amenity was cheap: a festival. In 1974, the merchants of Ninth Avenue in Hell's Kitchen—a mix of Irish, Italian, and Hispanic families—proposed an event: a "mile-long movable feast." Beame attended, telling reporters, "I hope the festival will encourage people to tap the potential for entertainment and learning along our city streets." The May weekend attracted half a million people, sampling food from twenty-two countries.[91] By the 1980s, the annual festival had become the biggest celebration of New York's melting pot.

New "Greenmarkets," too, encroached on cars. In 1976, Barry Benepe launched outdoor farmers' markets to solve two problems: New York State's farmers needed markets to sell produce, so as not to lose land to development. New York's urban denizens needed fresh ingredients. The Union Square Greenmarket took over streets around the downtown park; other Greenmarkets closed streets on weekends. In the late 1980s, the Koch administration made some of this change permanent, taking space from cars to expand Union Square Park. "We're converting a chunk of mid-Manhattan from parking to park," Henry Stern, parks commissioner, said.[92]

In 1986, New York celebrated the Statue of Liberty's centennial. This local assertion of national pride didn't come via motor vehicle. For "the biggest street fair that just about anyone can remember,"[93] the city closed Lower Manhattan as well as waterfront parkways in Brooklyn to traffic for a weekend, welcoming two million people. Crowds "swallowed up" the city, watching the biggest-ever fireworks show.[94] Even Lower Manhattan residents were pleased. "It was not the nightmare everyone thought it would be," Randy Shown said.[95] Whether in summer or winter, for culinary or patriotic reasons, to save the environment or to shop, every time the city closed a street to cars, New Yorkers grasped that they needn't be confined near gutters. As play streets had dwindled, a new adult generation stood in the roadbed and liked it.

If New York Could Do It There . . .

Just before Memorial Day 2009, Alex Dzh, twenty-three, was driving a pedicab through Times Square when he noticed orange barrels with "do not enter" signs barring Broadway. "Ten minutes ago, it was open," he said. "I don't know what happened." What had happened was that Mayor Bloomberg, who had taken office seven years earlier, had gone big. The city transportation department, under Sadik-Khan, had closed New York's world-famous thoroughfare—the "bowtie," from Forty-Second to Forty-Seventh Street—overnight. In a bit of whimsy, Sadik-Khan festooned the space with lawn chairs and beach balls.

New York had grabbed back a chunk of Times Square from traffic. The move was practical, providing relief and safety to the record hundreds of thousands of walkers who traversed the area each day. But it was also symbolic. The remaking the Crossroads of the World sent a message around the world, nation, and most importantly, the city: if New York could do it here, at the center of America's media, financial, entertainment, fashion, and tourism industries, pedestrianization could work anywhere. "Closing" Times Square was the revival of the play-street philosophy: New Yorkers shouldn't have to be in cars to have a right to streets.

Pedestrianizing Times Square was not a new idea. For decades, it was an open secret among traffic officials that closing or narrowing Broadway would improve, rather than further clog, car and truck flow. Broadway posed a unique problem. Most of Manhattan is a grid: north-south avenues and east-west streets. In 1811, the city's street commissioners had decided that a perpendicular system made sense.[96] But the commissioners were too late for Broadway.

Broadway slanted through the grid, worsening jams. As Lindsay's "The Threatened City" report had noted in 1967, Broadway created "awkward intersections." At most Manhattan intersections, drivers and pedestrians face conflicting traffic from only one direction. That is, if they are going east or west, they must stop at a light to wait for traffic going north or south, at a 90-degree angle. Broadway adds a third conflict: the 45-degree angle. The longer waits make drivers and walkers impatient, tempting them to break the law, with drivers crawling into intersections despite a red light and pedestrians threading through cars on a "don't-walk" sign. Broadway gridlock was worse at major two-way roads, such as Forty-Second Street, at Times Square; Thirty-Fourth Street, at Macy's Herald Square; and Twenty-Third Street, at Madison Square Park. With cross-town traffic moving two ways, east and west, drivers and pedestrians faced four conflicts.

The triangles of space that this criss-crossing of roads created—such as the "bow tie" of Times Square, in addition to similar no-man's-zone areas of Herald Square—were, as the Lindsay-era report had noted, "dead areas." Times Square was a mass of people on special occasions, such as New Year's Eve, when people could gather in the roadbed. But the rest of the time, walkers scrambled around vehicles or were stranded on tiny islands waiting to cross. Magnifying frustration was that many visitors were tourists; they wouldn't learn from their mistakes and modify their behavior because they wouldn't be back. "The mass of Times Square and the mass of Midtown was so off," says Sadik-Khan. "It was a mess, hidden in plain sight."

For decades, city officials considered remaking Times Square, only to drop the idea. In 1974, with Beame in his fourth month in office, the city's planning commissioner, John Zuccotti, borrowed a Lindsay-era idea for an "upgrade": closing "two or three blocks" of Broadway for "pedestrian malls."[97] That fall, New Yorkers viewing a Bryant Park exhibit called "More Streets for People" perused examples of pedestrian plazas from around the world, as well as the Times Square concept. By 1975, Beame's traffic officials had approved an idea "to turn a three-block section of Broadway at the northern end of Times Square into a permanent mall," to "lead to a revival of the tarnished district." The mall "would contain benches, plantings, space for street entertainment, a tourist information center and perhaps refreshment facilities." The city was close to winning a development project, the Portman Hotel—later called the Marriott Marquis—after years of delays, and the "Broadway Plaza" could be a sightseeing spot for hotel guests. "I want to see pedestrian spaces," Beame said.[98] Two years later, Beame won a half-million-dollar federal grant to create the "experimental pedestrian mall" for one summer. The plaza, Beame said, "will be an identifiable landmark and meeting place."[99] Beame's successor, Ed Koch, who took office in 1978, took up the idea. "Cars and buses that now rush down Broadway . . . blaring horns and spewing exhaust, will be replaced by a pedestrian mall with trees, walkways, and outdoor dining."[100]

By 1982, the Times Square mall, like the Madison Avenue project a decade earlier, was dead. The usual suspects opposed it, as they had opposed Lindsay's Madison project. But the bigger impediment was fear. The city didn't create more open space in Times Square because, the question was, who would use it? Times Square had always maintained a precarious balance between wholesome activities, like Broadway shows and Howard Johnson's, and illicit ones. With the Port Authority Bus Terminal and Penn Station rail terminal, as well as a dozen subway lines, nearby, the area attracted people down on their luck, running away from something, or looking to do something they wouldn't do under the watch of family and neighbors.

For more than a decade, Times Square had been losing this equilibrium. The "Crossroads of the World" had become a crossroads of scam games, peepshows, drug sales and use, and pimping of sex-trafficked women and children. "The *Times* has had many discussions with the police about conditions in this area," publisher Arthur Sulzberger wrote to staff in 1971 after a *Times* driver was shot to death. The death was the third killing in two months in the area.[101]

A decade later, the situation was no better. Theatergoers had learned not to linger. Richard Bassini, Broadway Association chair, worried that the pedestrian mall would "fall prey to street people, drug traffickers and peddlers."[102] As theater manager Gerald Schoenfeld warned, it could "become a place for vendors or three-card monte operators."[103] Carol Bellamy, city council president, said, "the open space . . . will only serve as a stronger magnet for the illicit activities."[104]

Carl Weisbrod, then the president of New York State's Forty-Second Street Development Project and later planning commissioner, remembers the concerns. "Times Square being what it was, when conditions in Times Square were pretty awful, the theater industry was very, very opposed."[105] Koch killed the project. "Good riddance," *Times* editorialists noted.[106] But another decade of gridlock didn't make Times Square safer. In 1990, the number of murders in the two police precincts encompassing the area reached twenty-four; robberies reached 6,362.

By the mid-1990s—thanks to policing, redevelopment, and tourism—New Yorkers were feeling better about Times Square. Confidence was capped by Disney's city-subsidized refurbishment of Broadway's long-abandoned New Amsterdam Theater, reopened in 1997 for *The Lion King*. Tourists, local visitors, and office workers flocked to the bowtie.

In 1998, New Yorkers learned, via a dreadful incident, that they no longer feared street life. That July, a construction elevator at the Conde Nast skyscraper on Broadway, part of Times Square's renewal, collapsed, killing eighty-five-year-old Thereza Feliconio. The disaster disrupted routines. With the city having shut down nearby towers, "lawyers, accountants, salesmen, public relations people, and the staffs of two magazines have struggled to create offices in exile," the *Times* reported. "They have coped with missing files, vanishing mail, and overwhelmed voice-mail systems." One therapist "begged" to enter her office, saying she had to call patients.[107]

As Mayor Rudolph Giuliani reopened the area, he started with pedestrians, not cars. New Yorkers walked in the avenue and liked it. Giuliani encouraged people to return, exhorting them to see a Broadway show and to enjoy the pedestrian mall. "Some people actually are urging me to keep Times square closed to traffic forever, because they have been having such a good time," he said.[108]

The same year, Giuliani was working on a similar project, albeit on a smaller scale. North of Times Square, at Seventy-Second Street, as part of a subway renovation, the city was taking lanes of Broadway to expand a pedestrian triangle, called Verdi Park, once known as "Needle Park" for drug use.[109] Now that New York was safer, residents welcomed open space. "Before we did it, some people liked it, and some people hated it, and after we did it, nobody said anything," the former mayor remembers.[110]

A different tragedy south of Times Square illustrated another problem of growing foot traffic and uncontrolled vehicles: danger of mass casualties. Two days after Christmas 2001, workers, shoppers, residents, and visitors were strolling outside Macy's in Herald Square. With 9/11 just three months in the past, life was hardly normal. But New Yorkers and tourists were trying to act as if it were, gathering at one of the city's busiest intersections—where Thirty-Fourth Street meets the Avenue of the Americas and Broadway cuts across both—to look at holiday windows. As the last light left the sky, seventy-six-year-old Sidney Weinstein drove his van into the crowd, killing seven. The dead were a mosaic of New York, with surnames of European, Chinese, Korean, and Indian origin. There was no indication of terrorism. Rather, traffic chaos had claimed the lives. Weinstein had been illegally parked, and police had asked him to move; flustered, he hit the accelerator.

The city had known of the danger. "The intersection ranked as the third most dangerous in Manhattan," the *Times* reported, with twenty-five people killed over a four-year period. In fact, the city had been planning changes. "Recognizing the traffic problems, the city Department of Transportation has been working to reconfigure the Herald Square area by eliminating a lane of traffic on Broadway. . . . Future plans include the creation of pedestrian plazas."[111] As Iris Weinshall, then the city's traffic commissioner, remembered, even before the crash, "Herald Square was on the list, because not only did we look at pedestrian deaths and accidents, we looked at the volume of pedestrians walking, and the space they had available. . . . If you looked at Herald Square, you knew that pedestrians were walking in the street."[112]

By the mid-2000s, New York's success had stopped being a novelty and become, in its own way, a crisis. This problem was more welcome than double-digit annual murders and four-digit annual robberies. By the new century, the police precincts around Times Square had just four murders annually; the number of robberies was 403, barely one per day.[113] But Times Square was packed beyond capacity. Locals, commuters, and sightseers were squeezing the bowtie in numbers exceeding 350,000 pedestrians on busy days. In 1998, the Times Square subway station saw 41.4 million annual users; by 2008, it saw 60.9 million, all of whom became pedestrians after emerging from underground trains.

Tim Tompkins, who began his tenure as head of the Times Square Alliance of commercial interests in 2002, remembers the change. "I used to joke, the number-one complaint had gone from, 'you can't get through Times Square without getting mugged,' to, 'you can't get through Times Square.'" Walkers were creating "pedlock," squished off sidewalks and into avenues. Pedestrians suffered injury, with thirty-seven walkers hurt by cars or trucks in a six-month period. For all this inconvenience and danger, cars didn't move efficiently. The average speed was 6.7 miles per hour.

To New Yorkers growing used to functional governance, chaos felt unacceptable. In 2006, a *Times* piece exhorted readers to "stand on any corner in Times Square—if you can find an unclaimed piece of pavement. . . . There are few other places where so many objects compete . . . just to move."[114] "People would dodge taxis to stand on this little spot to take pictures," says Tompkins. A "tiny fence down the center" prohibited them from going into the road, but they did anyway.

The Times Square Alliance lobbied for space. In the mid-2000s, says Tompkins, "we did a document called 'These Streets Were Made for Walking.' . . . The cover of this glossy brochure was basically a shitload of people in the streets. We said, 'as bad as it is now, if you look at the upcoming commercial development, it's going to go . . . absolutely terrible.'" The alliance was also about to build its translucent glass "Red Steps" gathering place, a focal point of tourism, which would attract bigger crowds.

Some faction would have to give up room. It made sense that it would be the drivers: pedestrians outnumbered them ten to one.[115] Tompkins was just looking for "six more feet. . . . All these things, we showed to the city department of transportation, and said, 'we need this space.'" To expand the plaza around the new steps, "we were trying to get this lane, one lane, [and] we had to do about $70,000 of origination and destination studies." Weinshall, after deliberation, gave the go-ahead. "One night I was at the theater, I literally could not walk on the sidewalk," she remembered. "We looked at the flow of traffic. . . . The data showed us there was more than enough capacity if you narrowed the road for cars. . . . We finally said yes, cars and trucks are important . . . but we need to provide more space for pedestrians. . . . The biggest pushback was mostly from the trucking industry [which likes three lanes of traffic], because they can double-park."

When the Red Steps opened in 2008, the city took a lane of Broadway and a lane of Seventh Avenue, enlarging the triangle to double its previous size.[116] "The camel's nose was under the tent," says Tompkins.

A Dress Rehearsal for Broadway

To many observers, "pedestrianizing" Times Square a year later, in 2009, was a whim: it had happened overnight, with no planning. In fact, just as with bike lanes, it was the product of forethought. The previous year, Sadik-Khan, succeeding Weinshall, had taken away Broadway lanes from traffic far south of Times Square—at Herald Square and at Madison Square—to see what worked and what didn't. "In a surprising reshaping of the urban landscape," the *Times* said, "the city is creating a public esplanade along . . . one of its most prominent streets," cutting Broadway from four lanes to two and "setting aside the east side of the roadway for a bicycle lane and a pedestrian walkway with cafe tables, chairs, umbrellas and flower-filled planters."[117] Nearby business improvement districts would use revenue earned from fees levied on property owners as well as money from food and drink sales to maintain the plazas. Some observers were skeptical. "They'll have carbon monoxide in their tuna fish," said a fashion worker.

Yet the Broadway plazas south of Times Square proved a success. Vicki Lee, a fashion designer, said it was "dangerous"—despite cement planters to keep cars from hitting people—but sat with friends. Another couple "ate sandwiches and gazed at the passing cars." A neighborhood worker, Richie Frakes, 61, sat eating a salad. "It's the first time in my life I ever had lunch in the middle of Broadway," he told a reporter. Karis Durmer, 29, a Condé Nast worker, observed, "The minute this pops up, overnight, people are already utilizing it."[118] Over and over, when the city gave space to people standing or sitting, people took it. "We were showing what was possible, one bite at a time," says Sadik-Khan, to "lead us to the big debut on Broadway."

For the rest of 2008 and early 2009, Sadik-Khan planned the Times Square project. Sadik-Khan and deputies had met with the community board as well as the Times Square Alliance. "Janette came in," says Tompkins. "We were basically hoping" for just a little more space, beyond what the city had granted around the Red Steps. Instead, Sadik-Khan remembers saying, "Hey, I've got this even bigger idea, let's close down Broadway." Tompkins remembers thinking that the city would never do it, but then "we took a deep breath and said . . . 'let's go for it.'"

For some commercial interests in Times Square, "it was a stretch," Tompkins says. "I'm worried because I don't know if it will work," Charlotte St. Martin, the director of the Broadway League theater consortium, told the *Times*. "I certainly don't want things to be worse."[119] Many theater buffs took cabs, and St. Martin didn't want to make that choice more difficult. Retailers worried about deliveries. Investors who owned Times Squares' billboards were worried they wouldn't get maintenance access and feared that with fewer cars going by, fewer people would see their advertisements. The city modified its plan, including permission for cars to turn onto Forty-Fifth Street from Seventh Avenue to give theatergoers better access and making sure sign owners and retailers would have delivery access at off-peak times. In February, months ahead of the opening of Times Square to pedestrians, the city posted signs warning drivers. Bloomberg informed the press that "people don't come to look at cars struck in traffic." Of the risk that traffic would further clog, he observed that the city couldn't "do anything to make it worse."[120]

Tables, Chairs, and Critics

Turning Times Square's Broadway into a pedestrian plaza dominated news—and, as with bike lanes, garnered critics not known for traffic expertise. David Letterman, on his Late Night show, chuckled with Donald Trump that Times Square was a tourist "petting zoo." Trump called on Bloomberg to "reverse" the "experiment." The *Post*'s Cindy Adams, in pithy style, asked, "Could someone please kindly tell me what the frig is happening in Times Square? Why . . . are people now lying around in cheapo, crappo, junko lawn chairs?"[121] Mike Lupica, *Daily News* sportswriter, lamented the changes to "what we used to think of as Times Square before it became . . . Bloomberg Beach."[122] Lupica noted that "the red-and-blue plastic chairs and the chaise lounges are supposed to make you feel more civilized and cosmopolitan than the Champs-Élysées." But he called that a "cover story" for a conspiracy: the plaza was "Bloomberg's revenge" for having lost his congestion-pricing bid the year before, as state lawmakers had refused permission for the mayor to charge drivers to enter Manhattan. "This time he didn't have to ask Albany. . . . He went ahead and did what he wanted. . . . Pull up a chair."

That the mayor was up for reelection for his third and final term that fall didn't appear to faze him. "Sadik-Khan came to me and said, 'I want to close Broadway,' and I said, 'You want to do what?'" he said years later.[123]

Sadik-Khan hadn't brought this idea up in her job interview, two years before. "Can you imagine if I had said, let's pedestrianize Times Square?" she later wondered. The mayor did get annoyed about the plastic chairs, said another person close to him—but focused on the bigger picture.

Despite rhetoric, the plazas hadn't encountered political threats. City council Speaker Christine Quinn, whose district included much of Times Square, hadn't challenged Bloomberg's authority to redesign streets, as the now-defunct Board of Estimate had challenged Lindsay's plazas. A few outer-borough council members used Times Square's profile as a backdrop against which to vent driver-focused frustrations. "With the failure of congestion pricing, . . . other things are being done to drive car owners crazy," said Councilman James Vacca, a Democrat of the Bronx, echoing Lupica.[124] City public advocate Bill de Blasio, mindful of his affluent, car-owning Park Slope neighbors in Brooklyn, complained, "We cannot make such a fundamental change to Times Square without first giving the community a greater say."[125]

Facts on the ground outweighed words on the page. New Yorkers and tourists loved the "cheesy" chairs. "Less than a week after Times Square became an outdoor stage, it's already hard to find a seat," the *Times*'s Eleanor Randolph wrote. Locals unfolded laptops; tourists took in the scene. "There are not many places like this to stop and catch your breath," said Debbie Adam, a tourist from South Africa. "It was like this had been there for the last 40 years," said Tompkins, of how quickly people claimed the new space.[126] By late summer, the novelty chairs were gone, replaced by French-style metal tables and chairs. But the plastic had served its purpose as PR.

Data backed impressions. The change didn't worsen traffic; it sped things up. In one year, the closure improved speeds by 7 percent. By tracking GPS data from taxi trips, the city found that northbound cabdrivers along avenues through which Broadway slices went 17 percent more quickly in 2009 than in 2008. Southbound drivers *did* see a 2 percent slowdown—not surprising, since they had lost Broadway—but it was exceeded by the northbound gain. As a control measure, the city tracked speeds on the unaffected east side of town and found that they increased by about 5 percent (the Great Recession of 2008 had accelerated speeds citywide, since job losses meant that fewer cars entered).

Pedestrianization improved life for Broadway's denizens. Walker injuries fell by 40 percent in Times Square and by 53 percent in Herald Square; drivers and passengers in the two areas saw injuries fall 63 percent.[127] A Times Square Alliance survey found that two-thirds of workers liked the changes. Times Square attracted 11 percent more walkers than it had the previous year, climbing to 22,381 people per hour at peak times. New visitors weren't all tourists; they included commuters, who had switched routes because they found Times Square more pleasant. "I used to not go out at lunchtime," said one worker, because the four-block walk would take twenty minutes. After the changes, it took three.

The changes were good for the economy. The Red Steps became the nation's second-most-popular Instagram location, after Disneyworld, and billboard owners were pleased: higher "dwell time" by pedestrians who had a place to sit outweighed loss from cars and trucks. Though she didn't love the plazas, St. Martin of the Broadway League agreed. "We can't say it's cost us business," she said of theaters. Times Square's challenges remained the byproduct of success: global chains were pushing out longtime stores and restaurants, such as decades-old fixture Howard Johnson's. Less than a year later, Bloomberg announced the changes would become permanent, with the city launching a twenty-seven-million-dollar construction project to show off Broadway's roadbed with distinctive, backlit pavement markings. "The best thing that ever happened to Times Square, other than musical theater, was the pedestrian plaza," Bloomberg says. "Business boomed. And it boomed . . . because instead of cars that drove by, businesses had more foot traffic, and that meant more shoppers."[128]

In December 2013, Bloomberg, a week left in office, cut the ribbon on the first permanent Times Square plaza. Referring to what had once been an "experiment," the mayor observed, "You'd have a very tough time rolling this back," just as the city, if it tried to roll back its once-unthinkable ban on smoking in restaurants, would face a public outcry. A poll showed plazas to be one of the mayor's most popular programs, with 72 percent support.[129] "You've changed the streets of New York," Sadik-Khan, the soon-to-be ex-transportation commissioner, told the soon-to-be ex-mayor.[130]

From Times Square to the Neighborhoods

Seen from one angle, pedestrianizing Times Square was a technocratic solution to a straightforward problem: the constituency who used the space the most had the least amount of space. Seen from another angle, it did for pedestrians—and for people looking for a place to sit—what Citi Bike did for cycling. At first, the idea was crazy and then, with plastic chairs, funny, and then it seemed so normal that nobody noticed.

Rethinking who had access to the roadbed was not new: throughout the first two-thirds of the twentieth century, New York had narrowed sidewalks for cars. But for people who had grown accustomed to squeezing by strangers on crosswalks while one-occupant SUVs blocked intersections, it was a revelation. "After building a culture where you are not supposed to be in a roadbed" unless you are in a car, says Sadik-Khan, the "status quo" had become "a helluva drug."[131]

It could not have happened, she adds, without people feeling safer in Times Square. New York had proven that it didn't need gridlock to keep streets free from crime. "The taming of Times Square so that change was possible" had mattered. In 2013, Bloomberg's last year in office, the precincts around Times Square, with their tens of millions of annual visitors, saw just two murders and 299 robberies, fewer than one per day, few of them in the tourist core.

Sadik-Khan used Times Square's success to bring pedestrian plazas to other parts of New York. As Christine Berthet, who runs the Hell's Kitchen pedestrian organization CHECKPEDS, put it, "It really got the message to everybody, if you can do it at Times Square, you can do it anywhere." At Brooklyn's Grand Army Plaza, the convergence of roads into a fourteen-lane roundabout inhospitable to people crossing the street, the city clawed space back to create pedestrian "islands."[132] In the Bronx, at Fordham Plaza, along the shopping thoroughfare of Fordham Road and abutting a commuter rail and subway station as well as bus lines, the city truncated car access to create a larger, better-protected pedestrian square.

In Jackson Heights, Queens, at Roosevelt Avenue, one of the most heavily peopled thoroughfares in New York, with five subway stations and a half dozen bus lines, the city closed a block to traffic, giving residents a respite. Across the street, V. M. Gandhi, who sells gold bullion, said just after the closures that "sure, there is grumbling, [but it's] human nature [for] people to grumble." Gandhi further noted that 90 percent of his customers come by foot, either directly or via mass transit (including global visitors via airplane).

Gandhi noted that though driving and parking in the area are not easy, driving and parking in the area were not easy before the plaza. Driving to Jackson Heights is like driving to Times Square: "You've got to mentally prepare yourself." The reason some people undergo this hassle is the reason Jackson Heights thrives: density. Jackson Heights is a unique place, where a family can come from elsewhere in the region to purchase Indian groceries, clothing, jewelry, and newspapers, concentrated within blocks.

Not Perfect, Just Better

Like everything else in New York, pedestrian plazas do not work perfectly. Many New Yorkers don't like Times Square, dismissing it as tourist monoculture. But mass tourism is a forty-year global trend only briefly paused by the 2020 pandemic. Refusing to give visitors more room did not stop them from crowding Times Squares' tiny islands in the late 1990s.

So that good uses drive out bad uses such as aggressive panhandling and drug abuse, public plazas need near-constant public "programming," says Dan Biederman, whose firm has long managed two Midtown plazas (as well as Bryant Park). Public art, performances, sword-fighting and juggling lessons, and face-painting—all keep spaces populated. But programming is expensive and requires creativity, as play street organizers learned a century ago. "How complicated it is to do good programming," says Biederman, "[it's] the reason we have a large staff."[133] Foot traffic can vary within a few blocks, meaning that though pedestrians fill the core of Times Square, plaza space has often been empty just a few blocks north.

The mass of tourist numbers has attracted other phenomena. As soon as the plazas opened, scraggly "Elmos" became almost as famous as tables and chairs. Men and women dress in cartoon characters, ranging from Elmo to Minnie Mouse, and trawl for tips. Street buskers are trying to make a living, but visitors are swarmed by multiple characters for tips. CD sellers—young men appearing to give away free CDs and then surrounding and strong-arming recipients for "donations"—have proliferated. One Elmo-type character was arrested for shouting anti-Semitic slurs, another for groping, and a third for assault. Bare-chested women—"*desnudas*"—demand tips, sometimes aggressively.

"Managing the plazas has not been an easy thing," says Weisbrod, the city's former planning head. "I'm not opposed to plazas," he says, noting that as the head of the Downtown Alliance in the 1990s, he helped the city pedestrianize Stone Street, a picturesque, cobblestoned Lower Manhattan block, for dining. "But you still face the issue of what these plazas are for, who they are for, how they are managed."

In 2015, the de Blasio administration reacted to the concern. "I'd prefer to just dig the whole damn thing up and put it back the way it was," police commissioner Bill Bratton said publicly. "We're going to look at what those pros and cons would be," de Blasio said. "You could argue that those plazas have had some very positive impacts. You could also argue they come with a lot of problems." It wasn't the first time the mayor had voiced skepticism. Two years earlier, the then-candidate had confessed "mixed feelings on this issue. I'm a motorist."[134]

The backlash to the idea of ripping up the plazas was fierce. Despite costumed characters and panhandlers, most of the time, for most people, the plazas were working. Where drivers once fumed and honked, people munched on dumplings. "Sure, let's tear up Broadway—we can't govern, manage or police our public spaces," said Tompkins of the Times Square Alliance, sarcastically. "That's not a solution. It's a surrender." *Times* architecture critic Michael Kimmelman said that the controversy "brought back memories of the 1980s, when New York officials refused to install benches in some city parks" for fear they would attract vagrants.[135] De Blasio backed down—in part because of repudiation, but in part because of the sheer limitations of physical space. By the 2010s, foot traffic in Times Square exceeded 450,000 on busy days. Even *with* plazas, there wasn't room.

By then, a grimmer issue had emerged: vehicle terrorism. For decades, New York had pedestrianized a few sensitive spaces, such as Wall Street, fearful of truck-bomb attacks on buildings. Now, the threat was vehicle attacks on crowds. In July 2016, an attacker drove a truck through the beachside promenade of Nice, France, killing eighty-six people, one of multiple attacks in Europe. Less than a year later, an attacker drove into Times Square, injuring twenty people and killing Alyssa Elsman, 18, who was visiting from Michigan. One factor prevented a higher toll: steel bollards, erected as part of the pedestrian plaza. Months later, a truck terrorist murdered eight bicyclists on the Hudson River bike path, spurring police to further separate vehicles and people, plunking clunky cement blocks, dubbed "sugar cubes," across sidewalks.

As the city completed Times Square's permanent plazas in 2016, before the New Year's ball drop, Tompkins peered at record crowds. "We need every inch," he said.

Chapter 13

Killed in the Crosswalk

Turning Tragedies into Progress

This is going to be a central focus of our administration because the human cost is simply unacceptable.

—Mayor Bill de Blasio, January 15, 2014

We [turned] our grief into something more, make sure our kids did not die in vain.

—Amy Tam-Liao, bereaved parent, December 7, 2021

BELKYS RIVERA WEPT AS HER translator conveyed her words to the New York City Council in 2014. "I remember my heart breaking. . . . The last day I saw my son alive was December 25, 2011." Josbel was twenty-three, starting a job as a store manager. Belkys worried when he didn't come home. Two detectives materialized at dawn. "The police asked me to bring my other children nearby, and that's when I began to realize that something had happened." Josbel was dead—killed by a hit-and-run driver while crossing the Bronx's Mosholu Parkway. Amy Tam-Liao's story was as wrenching. She told the council about her three-year-old daughter, Allison Liao, who sang "The Wheels on the Bus Go Round and Round" as she rode the Q44 bus. Allison had died walking the previous fall, "holding Grandma's hand," after "a huge SUV" driver turned into a crosswalk in Flushing, Queens. "We are never going to see her start kindergarten."

Parents, spouses, siblings, children, and friends of traffic crash victims have banded together successfully to reduce this death toll. Unlike in the twentieth century, politicians can no longer dismiss deaths as the price of living in a mobile society. Survivor stories and activism have compelled officials to pay attention. In 1990, 701 New Yorkers died in crashes; in 2018, the figure was 206, a low not seen since the Model T conquered the city's streets nearly a century earlier. Across four mayors—David Dinkins, Rudolph Giuliani, Michael Bloomberg, and Bill de Blasio—New York's traffic deaths fell even as the nation surrendered to a rising toll of lost lives. This public-safety success, as important as cutting crime, has made New York's streets, literally, more livable.

Controlled Pedestrians, Uncontrolled Vehicles

Before World War II, New York officials were alarmed at the risk of motor vehicles to public safety. In 1926, the state's bureau of motor vehicles convened the first New York State Safety Congress. The toll hit home: as John F. Gilchrist of the tax commission told the meeting, "It is a sad and strange coincidence that the safety congress is held at the time that the people of Albany are crying out their hearts over the sad and untimely end of their mayor, whose death was the result of an accident in which a motor vehicle was involved." Leon Aronowitz, statistician, told the audience of "appalling destruction of life." The previous year, 2,210 people had been killed statewide, and "527 were children playing"; 1,092 people had died in the city, including 764 pedestrians.

Officials tried to reduce the casualty count by punishing drivers. Against 1.8 million drivers and 1.7 million vehicles, the state suspended eleven thousand licenses a year. In introducing Charles Harnett, commissioner of motor vehicles, the deputy commissioner praised his boss. Referring to driver's licenses, Dinneen said, "His is the one signature which is carried on the little piece of paper. . . . He is the man who stands . . . between the reckless driver and your children, your wives . . . with the command, 'Thou Shalt Not Kill.'"

But conventional wisdom was to make room for cars. As Jon Harriss, former New York City deputy police commissioner, told the conference, traffic safety was a "scientific business," and its principle was "adequate space of roadways." One issue, he said, was "pedestrian control." Referring to Manhattan's theater district, the area vexing Whalen, he referred to "two hundred thousand people endeavoring to get into 75 or 100 theaters and moving picture houses at the one hour . . . nothing short of a miracle could handle this vast throng." In fact, something short of a miracle had handled crowds: subways, streetcars, and walking. Nevertheless, he said, "the pedestrian . . . is equally at fault."[1]

The city punished not just bad drivers but also bad walkers. Then–police commissioner Whalen, as well as the Broadway Association, lobbied for a law against jaywalking. Traffic lights required pedestrians to obey rules—although the lights only existed because people driving cars could not regulate themselves in the way that slower vehicles and pedestrians had. As John Scheier of the Broadway Association's traffic committee put it in 1929, advocating for a law forbidding pedestrians to cross streets midblock, "New York City is way behind. . . . The rest of the country is laughing."[2] But the idea languished, and in 1936, Mayor LaGuardia dismissed pedestrian control as "goosestepping."[3]

It wasn't until 1958 that New Yorkers had to follow jaywalking rules.[4] But the rules, just as Whalen's 1920s effort to get pedestrians to walk in the same direction, consumed manpower. Police gave out two hundred thousand warnings in July, ahead of two-dollar fines.[5] Ticket blitzes resulted in only temporary decreases in deaths. Jaywalking laws reiterated the thesis that pedestrians, the city's most efficient movers, were the problem.

By then, decades of making room for motor vehicles and regulating pedestrian behavior across that deadly expanse had not worked. For more than a decade, between 1923 and 1934, New York City's deaths had remained above 1,000 annually. Though the Depression and postwar regulation cut deaths, by the late 1960s, they were rising again. Between 1968 and 1972, deaths remained above 900 per year. Deaths decreased from the mid-1970s through the mid-1980s, but never fell below 527, reached in 1983, including 304 pedestrians. Deaths rose again in the late 1980s to reach their modern 1990 peak.

Despite grim figures, New York State and City have long performed well compared to the country. Even in 1990, when the 701 fatalities represented the highest total in fifteen years, New Yorkers fared better than most Americans. That year, the city's death rate was 9.6 per 100,000, compared to a national rate of 17.9 per 100,000.

New York outperformed the nation for several reasons. The state was early to take drunk driving seriously, lowering the drunkenness threshold and strengthening penalties in 1960.[6] The country did not take the scourge seriously until the emergence of Mothers Against Drunk Driving (MADD) in the 1980s, when drunk drivers accounted for half of the country's then 51,091 annual traffic deaths. New York was the first state to get a seatbelt law, in 1984. As then-governor Mario Cuomo said, "Persons who wear seat belts are . . . less likely to be ejected." The logic is obvious, but laws were controversial. The vote was not unanimous; in the state senate, it was thirty-seven to sixteen.[7] The governor of Maine vetoed a similar bill as late as 1992, saying that it "crosse[d] the line between public interest and personal choice."[8]

New York also benefited from the perseverance of grassroots activists. In the 1980s, even with the murder level above four digits, some New Yorkers understood that reckless drivers presented as clear and present a danger as shooters. In 1982, Marion Filley was walking through Manhattan with her eighteen-month-old daughter, Jocelyn. Marion waited for the light on Fifth Avenue, then crossed. A driver ignored the signal and hit Jocelyn's stroller, dragging her thirteen blocks. "She had her scalp ripped off," Marion told *Newsday*.[9] Jocelyn recovered, but Marion and a neighbor, Paula Blasband, decided to do something about it. "We heard they had red-light cameras in Europe," she said. Determined to get New York to adopt them, they started a small organization called Stop Traffic Offenses Program, or STOP. Mayors Koch and Dinkins supported the idea.

Progress was slow. As with many issues, the city needed state lawmakers' permission to levy fines via camera. In the 1990s, New York won permission to erect a limited number of cameras, becoming a first-in-the-nation "pioneer."[10] In 1991, the Department of Transportation "experimented" with cameras at two Queens locations, including one on a multilane speedway, Queens Boulevard. In one month, the cameras caught 1,090 red-light runners. In 1993, near the end of Dinkins's term, the city deployed fifty cameras, the maximum under state law, to generate forty-five-dollar tickets.

As important as New York's assertive stance toward bad drivers was precar infrastructure. Thanks to the affordability, convenience, and ubiquity of public transportation as well as densely built housing, stores, and offices, most residents did not drive. In 1990, New York had fewer than 2.1 million household vehicle registrations against an adult population of 5.6 million. By 2015, the vehicle total had fallen below 1.9 million, despite an increase in the adult population to 6.7 million. New York also had something most American cities lacked: pedestrian mass. Pedestrians provide safety in numbers; a distracted driver in a suburb may fail to see a walker, but it is hard to miss fifty walkers.

New York's other transportation choices enable safety, as well. With for-hire taxis and car services as well as twenty-four-hour transit, a New Yorker who has had too much to drink can get home. Density works in favor of driver, cyclist, and pedestrian safety in another way. Traffic may be frustrating to drivers, cyclists, and walkers. But congestion means slow speed. Someone hit by a car going twenty miles per hour will live in 90 percent of cases; someone hit at forty miles per hour has a 30 percent chance of surviving.

Cutting Crime and Car Carnage

Near the turn of the millennium, New York built on these advantages. In reducing traffic deaths, New York benefited from a related phenomenon: falling crime. Lou Riccio, transportation commissioner in the early 1990s under Dinkins, had wanted to draw attention to pedestrian safety, proposing to put mannequins in Central Park to demonstrate how many people died each year. "I couldn't get the media," he said. "They just were not interested." That failure is because, he says, "crime was the only story that people wanted to talk about. . . . I kept trying to make the case that this is just as important."[11]

By the mid-1990s, crime had been falling for half a decade. Giuliani, who took office in 1994, took his tough-on-crime approach to traffic deaths. Rather than wait for crime to happen and respond, the police department was now mapping crimes based on location, frequency, and time of week and day and deploying officers to prevent them. Thanks in part to this "Compstat" program, murders fell. In 1997, the city applied the approach to traffic crashes, calling the program "Trafficstat."[12] The police deployed ticket writers at areas with frequent crashes, such as Herald Square in Manhattan and Queens Boulevard. "We tried to apply the same process we applied to the other problems," says Giuliani. The city supplemented enforcement with modest design changes, including wider sidewalks and medians.

Giuliani also got tough on drunk drivers. Working in the Reagan administration in the 1980s, "I went to a big conference in Seattle. It was the first time I had been exposed to MADD [Mothers Against Drunk Drivers]. . . . I sat through four or five mothers who got up and explained how their children were killed. It occurred to me that that's something that doesn't have to happen. . . . [As mayor,] I did everything I could do to reduce drunk driving."[13] In 1999, he asked his police commissioner, Howard Safir, to think creatively. He woke up to see that Safir had announced a policy on a morning TV show: the city would seize drunk drivers' cars.[14] The reasoning was that the car was instrumental to driving drunk; therefore, the vehicle was subject to forfeiture. Over two years, the city seized 4,004 vehicles.[15] "We didn't know what to do with the darned cars," the former mayor says. In the first year, drunk-driving deaths fell from thirty-two to twenty-three.[16]

Stoking Outrage

The next step was to change the story, to get New Yorkers to understand that even when drivers weren't drunk, they were responsible for crashes. Road design enabled drivers to speed and to drive distractedly, and they did. As with many challenges to groupthink, renegades changed the narrative. Starting in 1996, under the rubric of "Right of Way," transportation economist Charles Komanoff rode with a dozen cyclists at night to spots where pedestrians had been killed, illegally stenciling an orange imprint of a body along with the victim's name, date of death, and the *memento mori* "killed by automobile" onto the street.

The activists did a half-dozen stencils every month, under the "principle of, change the conversation from killer bikes to killer cars," says Komanoff. At York Avenue on the Upper East Side, Right of Way made a stencil for Jie Zhang, an AIDS researcher killed outside the hospital where she worked. Zhang's baby was born via emergency surgery. Her death upset Komanoff because her son, Samuel, "entered the world less than a week after my own first-born." At another spot, volunteers memorialized Erica Morena, a three-year-old girl killed by a driver "racing to beat the light" near the New York Public Library on Fifth Avenue.[17]

The stencils earned coverage. *Times* columnist Clyde Haberman concluded that "New Yorkers on foot [are] an embattled species." He wasn't making a breezy joke. "A New York pedestrian is statistically more likely . . . to be killed by a stranger driving a car than by . . . a gun-toting stranger," he informed readers. Stranger-on-stranger murders were rare, comprising fewer than 200 of the city's 983 homicides in 1996, whereas 235 pedestrians had died.[18]

People digesting the coverage included survivors of traffic violence. In fall 1997, six-year-old Dante Curry was enjoying a day off from school, playing on a "side street in the South Bronx." Spooked by a dog, he ran into the street as a driver, going sixty-five miles per hour, "gunn[ed] his Mustang."[19] Dante died from head injuries. A year later, his aunt, Gladys, after seeing a TV report, called Right of Way and asked for a stencil. Says Dante's mother, Evelyn Cancel, "I wanted any type of justice. . . . It's just tiring, they gave this [driver] a sixty-dollar ticket and sent him on his way." Of the stencil, she says, "It was a beautiful gesture. . . . It let me know where my son's body was" on the road. "It let me know that someone was thinking about him."[20] Yet the press still often blamed pedestrians. A 1998 *Times* editorial praising Giuliani for an anti-jaywalking campaign was typical. "More careful and alert and, dare we say it, lawful pedestrian behavior would save lives."[21]

Right of Way supplemented art with research. In 1999, the group published a booklet, "Killed by Automobile: Death in the Streets of New York City 1994–1997." For the first time, credible researchers—thanks to Komanoff's economic background—had studied who was at fault in crashes. Data gleaned from freedom-of-information requests proved that what most people thought was not true. Most pedestrians and cyclists had not been acting carelessly when they were killed. In 1997, in 58 percent of fatal crashes, the cyclist or walker had had the right of way. In another 13 percent, the driver contributed an infraction that made a crash worse; for example, a speeding driver turned a pedestrian mistake into a death sentence.[22] The *Times* picked up the story. "Drivers Are at Fault in Most Pedestrian Deaths," the headline read.[23]

The Boulevard of Death

Riccio identifies the turning point. In January 2001, the *Daily News* ran a front-page "special report." Under a half-page black-and-red headline, four people smiled out of family photos: Jennifer Brenes, Victor Marinescu, Vera Wilson, and Michael King, aged fifteen to eighty-three. The four individuals had nothing in common, save for one thing. All had died walking on Queens Boulevard, some of seventy-two people killed on the seven-mile stretch over eight years. In 1993, seventeen pedestrians had died. The *News* dubbed Queens Boulevard the "Boulevard of Death."[24] A pedestrian died every six weeks.[25] Street memorials of flowers, teddy bears, and photos—some fresh, some tattered—unnerved walkers who traversed the same footsteps as the dead.

Stories were wrenching. In 1995, Helen Freeman, walking to the store, "saw a commotion. An ambulance. A fire truck . . . and a crowd." She asked a passerby what was going on. "A woman really got it," she learned. "A guy was speeding." Freeman feared that the victim was her sister, ninety-two-year-old Ethel Gebeloff. Minutes later, she saw her sister's shoes. She overheard the driver: "She walked too slow." After a driver killed Gregory Babekov in 1998, family members told his niece, twelve-year-old Sofia Leviyev, that she couldn't cross alone; two years later, she was old enough to do so. In the fall of 2000, she was dead, at the same intersection.

Queens Boulevard showcased everything wrong with New York City's approach to traffic. Queens Boulevard is "bad design," says Riccio, an engineer. "It's so wide. You have nice stores, neighborhood stores, on each side, then you have old people living on both sides. . . . It's built like a highway," he concludes. New York had avoided building several interstate highways, particularly in Manhattan. But Queens Boulevard was a de facto interstate highway at pedestrian level.

The road's twelve to sixteen lanes traversed some of New York's densest neighborhoods—Sunnyside, Rego Park, Elmhurst, Forest Hills—at the same grade as pedestrians. Drivers sped down lanes above the thirty- to thirty-five-miles-per-hour limit, often going above fifty miles per hour. Pedestrians had to cross up to three hundred feet—the equivalent of a thirty-story building laid sideways from sidewalk to sidewalk—within half a minute. As on most New York thoroughfares, pedestrians were the majority; just 20 percent of residents in abutting neighborhoods used a car to get to work. But after LaGuardia ripped out trolley tracks, New York had redesigned Queens Boulevard for drivers.

For years, city officials had known of the dangers. But the city's response had been to blame pedestrians. "The problem with Queens Boulevard is that everyone wants to get all the way across in one shot," said a transportation department spokesman in 1993, after a drunk, speeding driver erased a married couple and their daughter during the first hours of the year. "We've been trying to teach people to be more patient, and cross half of it at a time."[26] The Department of Transportation said that giving pedestrians more time would risk "severe traffic."

After the 2001 series, the city's initial response was to stigmatize pedestrians further.[27] "Queens Boulevard drove me crazy," remembers Giuliani, then the mayor. But at the time, his idea—one that proved unworkable—was to build overpasses, further inconveniencing walkers. A Queens councilman, learning that police practice was to warn senior citizens about jaywalking, not to ticket them, said it was time for "tough love." New signs warning walkers that "a pedestrian was killed crossing here" were as disturbing as fading memorials replaced by new ones. The city would only *consider* cutting the speed limit.

The city did what it always did after attention to traffic danger: ticket walkers. In June 2001, following a ticket blitz, a line "beg[an] forming well before 8 on weekday mornings" at Queens Borough Hall. After "police began an aggressive crackdown," walkers had received more than six thousand summonses and agreed that "standing in line for several hours to pay a $10 fine in criminal court seems . . . absurd." New Yorkers ranging from "elderly ladies to sharply dressed businessmen to teens in plaid school skirts" paid.[28]

But the *News* report was a seminal event in New Yorkers' attitude toward everyday deadliness. The *News*, with a circulation of seven hundred thousand, reached nearly one out of ten New Yorkers. Now, on its front page, it treated deaths as preventable outrages, not back-page paragraphs. Residents of other neighborhoods put the "Boulevard of Death" moniker on their own death strips. In Brooklyn, residents labeled Ocean Parkway, the bucolic-looking multilane raceway where thirteen people had died in four years, "Brooklyn's boulevard of death."[29] Two sisters, Inna and Svetlana Shatman, fifteen and ten, on an evening walk with their parents in April 2001, had been fatally mown down. "You killed my family," the girls' father screamed at the driver of the crashed Porsche.

Just as "Killed by Automobile" had, follow-up *News* stories used data to demolish the idea that walkers were at fault. Pedestrians killed were not reckless. Two-thirds of them were older than fifty-five, 40 percent older than seventy. Older people are more careful; family members said that their parents, siblings, aunts, uncles never would have taken a risk. Most walkers weren't crossing outside of the crosswalk or against the light when someone ran them over. Thirty seconds to cross was insufficient; the *News* found that an able-bodied adult would need forty-three seconds to reach the median, never mind cross both sides. The same intersections were deadly over and over, with ten deaths within one three-block stretch and eight intersections with more than three deaths.

Could pedestrians be repeating the same mistakes, or did the fault lie with the city? Theodore Haiman, a retired math teacher, commented on the absurdity of punishing walkers. He wrote of having been caught in a jaywalking dragnet. After the signal flipped to "walk," he and his wife crossed "at a normal pace." Though "an avid runner," once sponsored by Nike, by the time he and his wife got to the other side, the light flashed "don't walk." A police officer, "in a most authoritarian tone," issued them tickets. "Three police officers were engaged for about 20 minutes in giving jaywalking tickets . . . while all around us traffic hazards went unheeded."[30]

Public attention forced officials to change their approach. The city built fencing to keep pedestrians in crosswalks, annoying pedestrian advocates. Critics said "we were taking away their options," recalled Weinshall. "We were redefining their options in a safer way." But finally, the city set a uniform thirty-miles-per-hour speed limit, a measure traffic engineers had long fought.[31] "We said, we're gonna try this as an experiment, and then we'll come back, and give you the information. . . . data showed that it worked." In March 2001, two months after the *News* series ran, the city said it would double the number of red-light cameras on the boulevard to four.[32]

Looking for a New Way to Enforce the Law

By the time Bloomberg took office in 2002, three mayors had cut traffic deaths from the 1990 peak of 701. Koch and Dinkins had helped through support of speed cameras. Giuliani had helped through crackdowns on antisocial behavior, particularly drunken driving. During the final three years of the Koch administration, ending in 1989, an average of 632 people died annually, including 352 pedestrians. During the final three years of the Dinkins administration, ending in 1993, an average of 585 people died annually, including 293 pedestrians—drops of 8 percent and 17 percent, respectively. By the final three years of the Giuliani term, ending in 2001, an average of 398 people died each year, including 194 people on foot, drops of 32 and 34 percent each. Since 1990, city traffic deaths had fallen by nearly half, against a nationwide drop of 5 percent. But New York could do better.

As Bloomberg succeeded Giuliani, New Yorkers who lived near Queens Boulevard made it clear that they weren't satisfied with modest progress. In July 2003, Caprice Bush and Sharon Rivers, twenty-three and thirty-four, were on their lunch break from jobs at a bank. The young women behaved as pedestrians should, standing on the Queens Boulevard median rather than running to beat the crossing signal. A driver blew a light, smashing into an SUV. The second vehicle fatally crushed Bush and Rivers.[33] One hundred and fifty residents flocked to the scene, demanding action. "I will . . . be in your faces," Bush's mother, Sharon, vowed, noting that the day would have been her daughter's twenty-fourth birthday. "I will guarantee that no one else dies."[34]

Bloomberg indicated that he would approach Queens Boulevard differently, favoring walkers. The city announced a step the city had resisted for decades, giving pedestrians an extra thirty seconds—a full minute—to cross. The city would narrow a parallel service road and reduce parking spaces to improve sightlines.[35] A businessman protested the loss of parking. Bloomberg responded: "We don't put economics higher on the list than protecting the people."[36]

For nearly a century, in its street engineering, New York *had* put economics—or the illusion of what made for a healthy economy—ahead of life. Bloomberg's remarks made a once-fringe idea less marginal. Norbert and Estelle Chwat, elderly Queens residents who headed the Forest Hills Action League, had for years advocated for a "complete rebuilding" of the boulevard, an idea long dismissed as fantasy.

The attention resulted in another important step. Frank Padavan, a state senator whose district included Queens Boulevard, worked with Weinshall to convince the state legislature to double the number of red-light cameras to one hundred. Padavan was a conservative Republican and initially skeptical of cameras; he himself had gotten tickets. "If I'm getting these, my constituents are getting them," he told Weinshall. She responded that if he was getting the tickets, he must have been violating the law.[37] He was anguished by Queens Boulevard deaths, and the data convinced him. In 2004, citing a Queens crash where a boy, hit by a truck driver who blew a red light, had suffered critical injury, Padavan noted that injuries had fallen by at least one-quarter, and as much as 60 percent, at locations with red-light cameras. "Running a red light is the most destructive of all situations involving vehicles and pedestrians . . . because drivers increase their speed. A guy going through a red light is not creeping through," Padavan added.[38]

Republican Governor George Pataki signed the red-light camera expansion in 2006. "Deaths on Queens Boulevard played a part," Pataki recalls. "I made a commitment . . . to uphold the rule of law." Cameras were "a logical extension" of that commitment. At the time, Pataki recalls, Democrats, not Republicans, were skeptical of camera enforcement, as they were concerned about civil liberties. Padavan, after seeing the crash data, even pushed for another type of automated enforcement against dangerous drivers: camera ticketing of speeders, to "put an end to some of these tragedies."[39] New York's state legislature wasn't ready for speed cameras.

Reporting on the Streets

After the turn of the millennium, a new ally emerged: *Streetsblog*. *Streetsblog* was the innovation of Aaron Naparstek, a Cleveland native and Columbia journalism grad who entered the workforce as the tech boom was taking off. "I kind of went right into the internet," he says. By the late 1990s, he lived in Brooklyn, working from home helping corporations build websites. The job was "how to make the [virtual] space pleasing" to the user.

He heard incessant honking. "It just drove me nuts," he says. "I had a totally dysfunctional user interface right outside my apartment. . . . Traffic can't move. All the users are deeply unhappy. This is a terrible interface. I kind of put my journalism hat back on." Naparstek started writing for the small *New York Press*; his first article was titled "Auto Asphyxiation."[40] A cyclist, he advocated banning cars from Brooklyn's Prospect Park, volunteering with Transportation Alternatives. Through this network, he learned that a tech entrepreneur, Mark Gorton, "wanted to expand the whole movement." Naparstek prepared a PowerPoint to pitch Gorton on the *Streetsblog* concept. A couple of slides in, Gorton was in. He "was like, 'oh, yeah, how much would it cost?'"

Streetsblog was *Voice*-style journalism: facts, opinion, and pressure. Naparstek thought of the blog in part as government watchdog: was the transportation department doing its job? He saw it as a journalism outlet, as the city's tabloid newspapers, suffering budget cuts, focused less on neighborhood issues, and the *Times* focused on national news. If a paper wouldn't send a reporter to every community-board meeting, *Streetsblog* would.

Naparstek refocused debate. *Streetsblog* became to the early twenty-first century movement what the *Voice* had been to getting buses out of Washington Square Park and killing the Lower Manhattan Expressway, but with a difference: it had a hyperlocal focus in all five boroughs. Global climate change, he notes, depended on "intense fights" around "microlevel neighborhood stuff: parking spots, bike lanes, how is the bus gonna work?" *Streetsblog* reported on progress and setbacks of bike lanes and pedestrian plazas, and it made tabloid-style attacks on politicians or appointed officials.

The site had an edge when it came to traffic deaths. Naparstek's first *Press* article had told the story of "these two little kids," fifth-graders, Juan Estrada and Victor Flores, "run over and killed, . . . walking home from school" in Brooklyn. "It just wasn't even news." Before he was born, his grandmother, in 1958, was killed by a drunk driver in New Jersey. "One of the early goals of the blog was to focus on the ongoing toll of traffic violence that . . . had just become like a background noise," he says. In its first year, 2006, *Streetsblog* launched "the weekly carnage," a roundup of crashes that had killed or injured people, featuring a photo of a mangled car, the instrument, as Giuliani had put it, of the damage. "Every Friday morning, we will tally up and present the previous week's motor vehicle mayhem," wrote reporter Aaron Donovan. "It's a grim accounting but . . . someone's got to do it."[41]

Streetsblog focused on one arm of government that wasn't treating crashes as a crisis: the NYPD. The police ticketed speeders and arrested drunken drivers. But if a driver wasn't drunk, police took the driver's word that a dead cyclist or pedestrian had acted in error. After digging,

Streetsblog found witnesses or camera footage, evidence the NYPD hadn't tracked down, that indicated otherwise. "There was an early bike crash case," Naparstek remembers. "Rasha Shamoon, she was this young graphic designer, she was run over on a Friday or Saturday evening [in Lower Manhattan], by people in town on a weekend night driving this enormous vehicle. Everything that came out seemed to be blaming the cyclist. I was like, OK, I'm gonna dig into this case, how do they even know?" Referring to reporters' reliance on "anonymous police sources," Naparstek wondered, "Who did they talk to?"

Naparstek's hunch was correct. Though police were quick to absolve the driver, *Streetsblog* found that he had previously racked up two speeding tickets, one cell phone use ticket, three seatbelt violations, and one "personal injury case." A civil jury found the driver liable. "The only known evidence that Rasha Shamoon caused the crash that took her life was the word of those in the vehicle that struck her," *Streetsblog* said. "Yet that was enough for [the] NYPD." Shamoon's sister, Saba Michaud, said that *Streetsblog*'s investigation gave comfort to her parents. Refugees from Iraq, they had expected better from America. "Her portrayal by the NYPD was that she was irresponsible. . . . For my parents this was huge," she said.[42]

Parents of children killed, frustrated with newspaper and NYPD disinterest, had *Streetsblog* for coverage of what had happened to their relatives. In a separate case, Joel Lefevre wrote a book on his family's attempt to get the police to charge the reckless truck driver who killed his brother, Mathieu, in Brooklyn, in 2011. The driver finally admitted fault. Before *Streetsblog* existed, such cases faded away. In 1989, for instance, Marty Cook told of the frustration of trying to obtain the "accident report" on the cycling death of her sister, Julia Collier, under a truck on the Upper East Side. "I was her only sister, . . . we just wanted to know what happened. They said, . . . 'We're too busy,'" Marty told *City Cyclist*.[43]

Streetsblog got the traditional press to take crashes seriously. "I would get in fights with newspaper editors," says Naparstek about the use of the word *accident*, which implied a lack of preventability. The blog's headlines made someone or some agency responsible. "Traffic Still the Top Injury-Related Killer of NYC Kids," one 2011 headline read.[44] "Bike and Pedestrian Safety Stats the *Daily News* Won't Cover," read a 2012 article chastising reporters for allowing themselves to be "fed misinformation."[45]

Streetsblog was "wildly successful, beyond our expectations," Naparstek notes. It wasn't the number of readers, but *who* perused the site. Department of Transportation staffers, elected and appointed officials, and police commanders were reading, commenting under pseudonyms, and sending tips. "You could see . . . IP addresses . . . there's a lot of nyc.gov people," says Naparstek.[46]

Expanding the Politically Possible

A year after *Streetsblog* launched, Janette Sadik-Khan succeeded Weinshall as transportation commissioner. Often lost among arguments over Sadik-Khan's bike lanes and pedestrian plazas was the fact that Sadik-Khan didn't build them just to give cyclists and pedestrians space. The infrastructure improved safety. Barrier-protected lanes made cyclists safer. But they also made pedestrians safer by reducing walkers' crossing time across multilane stretches and by improving sight lines so that walkers could see cars and drivers could see walkers. Narrowing lanes and making streetscapes more interesting forced drivers to pay attention rather than encouraging them to zone out on an open road such as Queens Boulevard. "Safety impacts were the biggest change," says Sadik-Khan. At modified intersections, fatalities fell by a third between 2005 and 2013, twice the city rate.[47]

One improvement was formalizing data. Mayors had used crude data to pinpoint dangerous sites before, but fine-grained analysis was rare. In 2010, the transportation department released a fifty-page report, "The New York City Pedestrian Safety Study & Action Plan." Just like "Killed by Automobile" a decade before, the report presented evidence that most of what New Yorkers thought about crashes wasn't true. One myth was the reckless taxi driver or truck driver. Seventy-nine percent of killer drivers were behind the steering wheels of private cars and SUVs, not commercial vehicles. Another myth was the bad woman driver; 80 percent of deadly drivers were men. Eight percent of drivers who killed walkers were drunk, below the national average of 13 percent, showing New York's success. In pedestrian deaths, driver inattention and speed were culprits. Seniors, 12 percent of the population, were 38 percent of crash victims. Children, too, particularly boys, were at risk. Deadly crashes were more likely in black and Hispanic neighborhoods.[48]

Sadik-Khan's Department of Transportation used this data to make changes beyond pedestrian plazas and bike lanes. At many intersections, pedestrians got "count-down clocks," rather than flashing "don't walk" signs, so that they would know how much time they had to cross. On some bike lanes, such as Broadway, cyclists got green lights ahead of drivers. The city retimed lights to deter speeding. On side streets, the city reduced speed limits from twenty-five to twenty miles per hour. Residents puzzled over changes, including patches of no-man's-land space, striped white, where car and truck drivers once dominated. But extra space between drivers and pedestrians reduced sharp turns.

Bloomberg achieved something else, besides design: additional automated enforcement. New York had had red-light cameras for a decade by the mid-2000s. But getting Albany to approve speed cameras was difficult, as Padavan had found. To voters, running a red light was a mortal sin, but speeding was a venial sin. In 2013, in his last few months in office, twelve years after Padavan had unsuccessfully pushed for a pilot on Queens Boulevard, Bloomberg worked to convince Albany to install twenty speed cameras.

The state senate, controlled by Republicans, balked. Two senators, Marty Golden and Simcha Felder (the latter a Democrat who usually voted with the GOP) led the opposition. The ostensible reason was horse trading: they wanted the legislature to approve an unrelated matter. Camera supporters also suspected that Golden, a former police officer, opposed the cameras because the police union opposed them (a factor that had long muted camera support on the part of both parties).

Golden was also an embodiment of what safe-streets advocates called "windshield perspective." Golden represented neighborhoods abutting crash-heavy Ocean Parkway. Yet his sympathies were with constituents who drove through the district, rather than walked it. He was famous for driving everywhere, using a government placard to park illegally. During his tenure, in 2005, he had even hit and injured a seventy-four-year-old woman, Hariklia Zafiropoulos, walking home from church in Brooklyn; she died months later.[49] As in many crashes, Golden called the crash an "accident," though he paid a $750,000 settlement.[50] He suffered no political repercussions.

Eight years later, as Bloomberg counted his last months in office, he unleashed fury at Felder and Golden. After the two refused to approve the speed-camera pilot, Bloomberg railed, "Maybe you want to give [their] phone numbers to the parents of the child when a child is killed."[51] It was hard for the senate to hold out against the pressure. In July, lawmakers passed a compromise, allowing twenty cameras in school zones during hours when school was in session. The violations wouldn't be as serious as tickets written by officers; speeders wouldn't earn a ticket unless they went more than ten miles over the speed limit, and they would face a $50 fine, rather the normal $90 to $600 fine and points on their drivers' licenses that could result in suspension.[52] But New York had its speed cameras.

As Bloomberg left office, he left a changed city in terms of risk to drivers, passengers, walkers, and cyclists. Traffic deaths, like murders, had fallen to then-record lows. In the last three years of the Bloomberg administration, an average of 276 people died annually in traffic crashes, including 159 pedestrians. The numbers were down 31 and 18 percent, respectively, from the Giuliani administration. "From speed bumps and curb extensions and bigger medians, which especially benefitted seniors, the data shows it worked—it saved a lot of lives—and that's why our successors have expanded them," Bloomberg sums up.[53]

Making Street Safety a Political Issue

In the 2013 mayoral election, for the first time in decades, New Yorkers weren't voting for a new leader in an atmosphere of crisis. In 2013, the city's problem was success: overcrowded trains, skyrocketing rents, police who policed as if crime remained high. In a record-low turnout year, Bill de Blasio, a former Brooklyn city councilman and the elected public advocate, a ceremonial position with no responsibility, targeted voters with a "tale of two cities" message of inequality, as well as with his calm demeanor—an attitude for a calm time.

The campaign stood out in another way: it was the first election in which crashes mattered. "Street Safety Gains Traction as Political Issue," the *Wall Street Journal* reported.[54] Former Congressman Anthony Weiner, now a regular Citi Bike user, was running against de Blasio that summer. He had abandoned his call to destroy bike lanes and pledged protection for pedestrians. Candidate Christine Quinn, city council speaker, pledged to halve deaths.

De Blasio had the most ambitious plan: Vision Zero. The goal: zero traffic deaths by 2023. Vision Zero, created in Sweden, was a change in philosophy. Just like a plane crash or a train derailment, a traffic crash would never be the victim's fault; rather, it was a failure of a system that *allowed* a mistake to become a disaster. When a child runs after a ball into a residential street and a driver strikes him, Vision Zero maintains, the death isn't the child's fault, but the result of road design or failure to regulate driver behavior, or both. In Stockholm, with a traffic death rate one-third of New York's, the policy had cut fatalities by 45 percent. "There is no level of death or injury that New Yorkers should accept," the aspiring mayor vowed.[55]

De Blasio's embrace of Vision Zero was an acknowledgment of the city's growing public safety. People no longer terrified of crime could focus on other issues. "The number of people being killed in crashes starting to rival

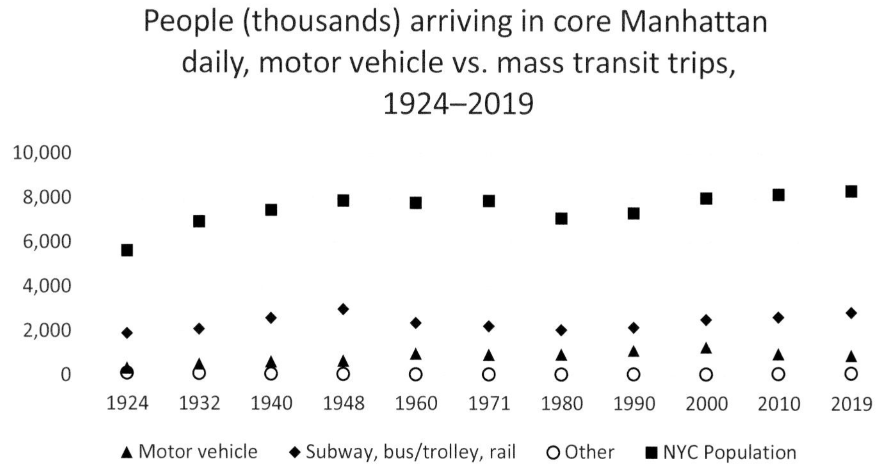

Beginning in the 1980s, as New York's population recovered from 1970s declines, the city's mass-transit system, not motor-vehicle traffic, absorbed most of this new growth. The trend was the opposite to that of the Seventies, when, as the people who remained in the city deserted mass transit, a declining population did not lead to fewer motor vehicles on the roads. Source: Author's calculations based on New York Metropolitan Transportation Council (and predecessor) annual Hub-Bound reports, 1924–2019.

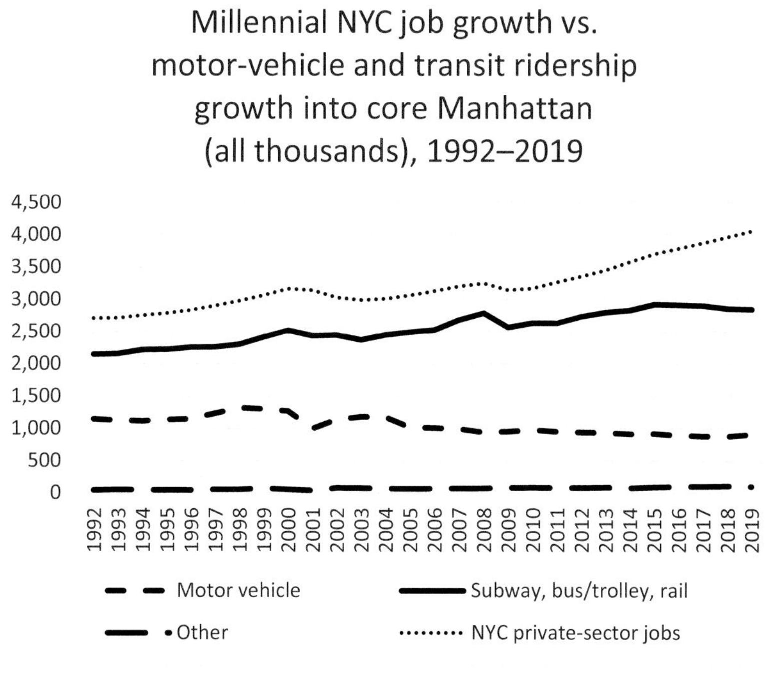

For most of the new century, until Uber and Lyft cut transit ridership in 2015, New Yorkers increasingly took mass transit, not private cars, to get to their growing employment options in Manhattan. Source: Author's calculations based on New York Metropolitan Transportation Council, Bureau of Labor Statistics data.

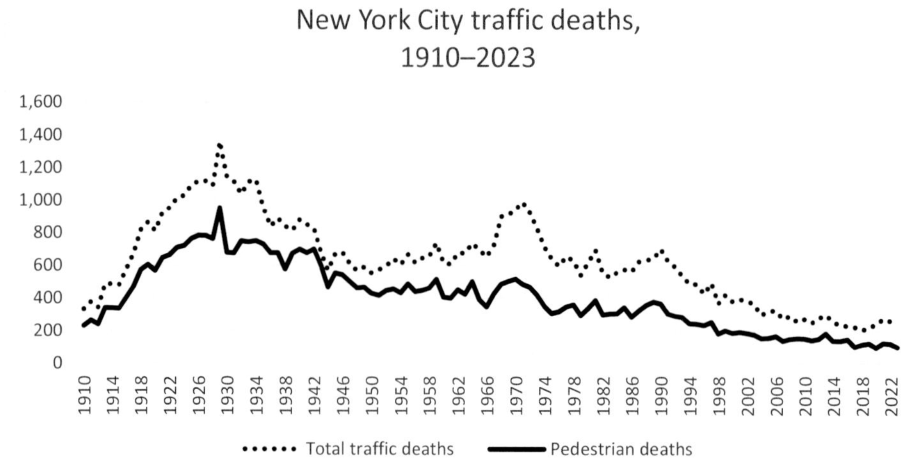

As millennial New York City grew in population and jobs, traffic deaths plummeted. Better policing, red-light and speed cameras, lower speed limits, and new pedestrian plazas and bike lanes helped keep more New Yorkers alive on the streets. Source: Author's calculations based on New York City Pedestrian Safety Study & Action Plan, New York City Department of Transportation, and the NYU Wagner Rudin Center for Transportation Policy and Management, August 2010; Vision Zero View, NYC DOT, accessed December 2023.

By the mid-teens, pedestrians and trolley passengers were losing street space to less efficient cars. Source: Afternoon crowds and traffic in Times Square, New York City, ca. January 1917. William Davis Hassler, PR 083. New-York Historical Society, nyhs_PR83_4270.

By the 1930s, motor cars dominated space that had belonged to transit riders and pedestrians. Source: A Motorman's View Down Broadway [New York City Streetcar], ca. 1932. Browning Photograph Collection, PR 009, Box 22, Folder 223. New-York Historical Society, 74042.

Cars passing under a low bridge on the Bronx River Parkway at Parkway Viaduct in Yonkers on July 13, 1925. Westchester officials, led by chief engineer Jay Downer, built the parkway years before Robert Moses dominated New York's highway planning. Source: Courtesy Westchester County Archives.

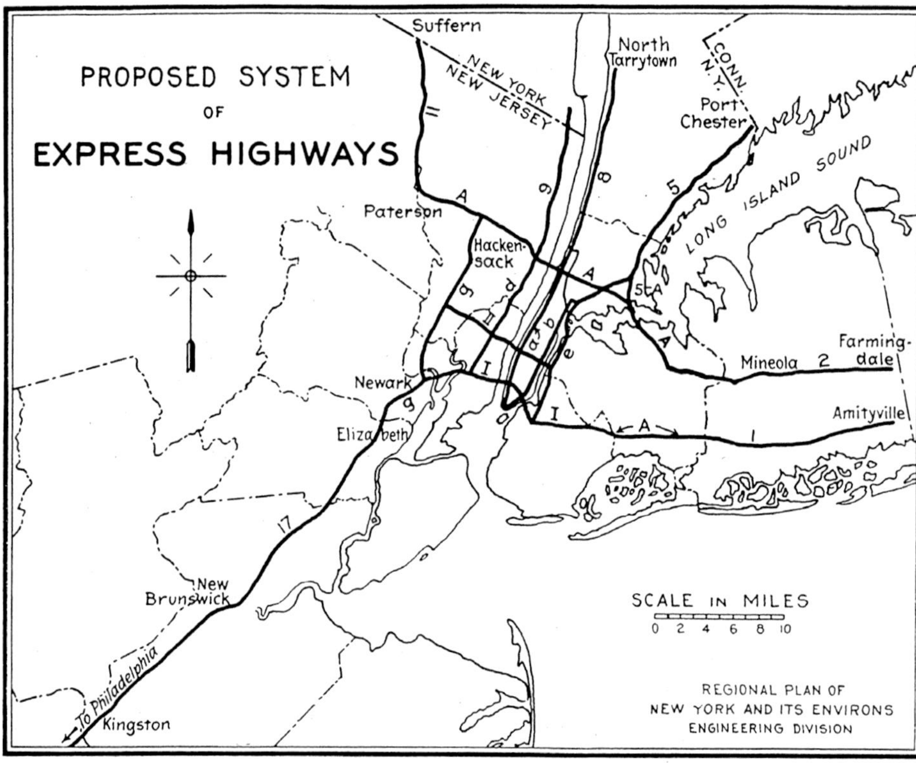

In the 1920s, without relying on Robert Moses, prominent officials proposed a system of highways for New York that included an expressway cutting across the Bronx and two expressways cutting across Manhattan. Source: Committee on Regional Plan of New York and Its Environs, "Regional Plan of New York and Its Environs, Volume One, The Graphic Regional Plan," 1929. Courtesy Regional Plan Association.

Mayor Robert F. Wagner at the controls of a steam shovel, September 22, 1958. Among the onlookers, Commissioner Robert Moses (dark suit), who needed Wagner's approval, among others', before embarking on any public works project. Source: Copyright NYC Municipal Archives. Photograph copies courtesy of the La Guardia & Wagner Archives, La Guardia Community College, CUNY.

Shirley Hayes, center, a homemaker and former actress, and fellow volunteers collect signatures—including that of actor Jerry Orbach—as part of their years-long successful effort to cancel a planned wider road through Washington Square Park and close the Greenwich Village park to car and bus traffic entirely (ca. 1958). Source: Courtesy Hayes family.

Shirley Hayes's sons (*from left*, Kerry, Dennis, Chris, and Tim), ca. 1958. She deputized them to collect petition signatures to close Washington Square Park to traffic. Source: Courtesy Hayes family.

After a celebration over the last car to drive through Washington Square Park, 1958, Hayes and fellow activists had to continue their fight for the next few years to get the buses out. Source: Tankel Collection, Courtesy Greenwich Village Society for Historic Preservation.

Firefighter Samuel Murray, at rear right, with (*from left*) Ella Ferguson, Lloyd Ramsey, and Mildred Campbell, strategizes on how to save their Queens homes from the expansion of the Clearview Expressway in March 1966. Source: *Long Island Press*, March 13, 1966. Courtesy Queens Borough Public Library, Archives, Long Island Daily Press Microfilm Collection.

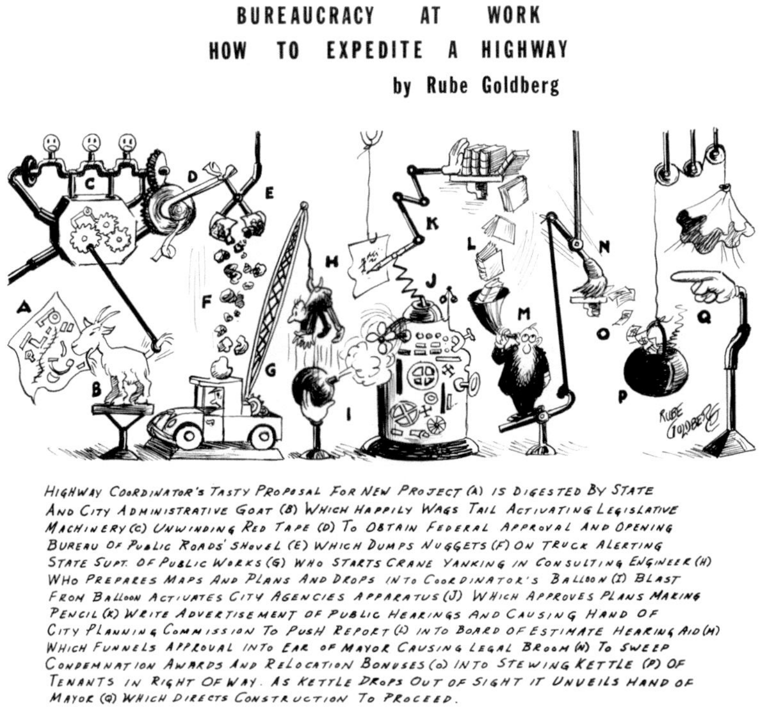

As Robert Moses came under public pressure, he asked cartoonist Rube Goldberg to create this June 1966 illustration of the bureaucratic process required to undertake his projects. Source: Courtesy MTA Bridges and Tunnels Special Archive.

With the full support of President Ronald Reagan—standing with (*from left*) then Lieutenant Governor Mario Cuomo, Mayor Ed Koch, construction worker Basil Powell, and Senator Al D'Amato—Westway seemed unstoppable on September 7, 1981. Source: Courtesy NYC Municipal Archives.

Marcy Benstock at a press conference on September 24, 1985, standing with transit advocate Gene Russianoff (*behind her on the left*), Manhattan Congressman Ted Weiss, and Beverly Dolinsky, head of the Permanent Citizens Advisory Committee to the MTA. All helped defeat the Westway highway project. Source: Copyright NYC Municipal Archives. Photograph copies courtesy of the La Guardia & Wagner Archives, La Guardia Community College, CUNY.

Mike Quill, cofounder and leader of the Transport Workers Union Local 100, tore up a judge's injunction against the transit strike in January 1966, similar to the scene in this undated photo. Source: Transport Workers Union of America Records; WAG 235; Tamiment Library/Robert F. Wagner Labor Archives, New York University.

An overwhelmed Mayor John Lindsay on the second day of the twelve-day transit strike that demonstrated the value of transit to New York City. Source: Press Conference—Transit strike: Lindsay night press conference, January 2, 1966, WNYC-TV. Courtesy New York City Municipal Archives.

In the mid-1960s, young mothers Hazel Henderson and Carolyn Konheim created the Citizens for Clean Air advocacy group to call attention to deadly air pollution. The group placed free advertisements, designed pro bono by a major ad firm, in newspapers. Source: Courtesy of the archives of Hazel Henderson.

Metropolitan Transportation Authority chairman Richard Ravitch (*second from left*) stands with Mayor Edward I. Koch (*fourth*) and city and state officials (including Congressman Bill Green, City Council President Carol Bellamy, and City Councilman Sam Horwitz) to welcome the first of 325 new Kawasaki-built subway cars, funded via Ravitch's prevailing upon the state legislature to raise dedicated taxes for the MTA. August 18, 1983. Source: Courtesy New York City Municipal Archives.

Mayor Edward I. Koch leads New Yorkers across the Williamsburg Bridge on April 2, 1980, the second day of the city's second ever transit strike. Unlike Mayor John Lindsay, Koch did not exhort New Yorkers to stay home. Source: Courtesy New York City Municipal Archives.

A K-9 police team patrols a graffiti-saturated subway car on September 12, 1981. Source: Photo by Allan Tannenbaum / sohoblues.com.

New York Mayor John Lindsay leads a summer bicycle ride through Central Park, ca. 1970, four years after having closed the park to motor vehicles on summer Sundays to make room for cyclists. Source: Photo by James R. Peipert.

After the partial collapse of the elevated West Side Highway in 1973, New Yorkers, including environmentalist Tom Stokes, used the shuttered roadway as a bike path and recreation spot, ca. 1974–78. Source: Photo by Daphne Gemmill.

Bloomberg-era transportation commissioner Janette Sadik-Khan launches New York's Citi Bike bikeshare program, with six thousand bikes available at more than three hundred stations, May 27, 2013. Citi Bike normalized biking as a commuting option. Source: Flickr via New York City Department of Transportation.

Transportation Alternatives chief Paul Steely White drives the last car through Central Park's main carriage drive, June 28, 2018. Then Mayor Bill de Blasio's action that year capped a half-century of advocacy by cyclists to build on the Lindsay-era 1966 Sunday closures and bar the carriage drives full-time to motor traffic. Source: Courtesy of the author.

Transportation Alternatives activists hold a die-in protest in Washington Square Park to protest the continuing scourge of cyclist deaths, despite half a century of progress, July 9, 2019. Source: Courtesy of the author.

By 2019, New Yorkers, whether commuting or working a delivery job, took full advantage of New York's protected bike lanes, often outnumbering cars at Midtown intersections like this one at Eighth Avenue and Forty-ninth Street, Manhattan, September 5, 2019. Source: Courtesy of the author.

In much of the twentieth century, play streets, closed to vehicles, were New York City children's respite from relentless danger from cars and trucks. Source: New York City Municipal Archives.

By the mid-2000s, Times Square was such a sea of pedestrians that, as shown in this July 5, 2009 scene, the Bloomberg administration closed much of Broadway to cars and trucks to make more room for walking, sightseeing, eating, and resting. Source: Photo by Allan Tannenbaum, sohoblues.com.

Amy Cohen, mother of 12-year-old Sammy Cohen Eckstein, who was killed in a 2013 car crash, testifies before the New York City Council in favor of a lower speed limit in February 2014. She and fellow survivors convinced Mayor Bill de Blasio to adopt a Vision Zero policy for safer streets. Source: Courtesy Families for Safe Streets.

Transit passengers waiting at the M104 bus stop, Broadway, Upper West Side, May 21, 2009. Although poorer New Yorkers rely on the bus more than wealthier residents do, riding the bus is a universal experience in New York City. Source: Photo by William Meyers.

Nilka Martell of the Loving the Bronx advocacy group points out the "heat map" of Bronx asthma rates, August 15, 2022, as part of her mission to cap a portion of the Cross-Bronx Expressway with a park. Source: Courtesy of the author.

Bronx Congressman Ritchie Torres contemplating the Cross-Bronx Expressway from above on June 20, 2022. Torres has fought for federal funding to cap part of the expressway, thus ameliorating, if not undoing, a mistake of the twentieth century. Source: Courtesy of the author.

COVID-19 pandemic dining protocol, Amsterdam Avenue, Upper West Side, October 5, 2020. New York's outdoor-dining program, begun in mid-2020 by then Mayor Bill de Blasio, was crucial to New York's gradual reopening from COVID-19 lockdowns. Source: Photo by William Meyers.

Bronx residents enjoy a fall afternoon in the Fordham Plaza pedestrian space, October 31, 2021. Photo courtesy of the author.

New Yorkers gather in the Times Square pedestrian plaza on January 18, 2022, at a vigil in memory of subway-murder victim Michelle Go, pushed in front of a moving train to her death three days earlier. Source: Photo by William Meyers.

The author on an entirely empty subway car from Midtown to downtown just after morning "rush hour," October 8, 2020. After initial COVID-19 lockdowns, New York's subways remained mostly empty for months. Source: Courtesy of the author.

As tourist crowds returned in full force for Christmas 2023, Mayor Eric Adams closed Fifth Avenue to cars for three Sundays in a row, reprising a Lindsay-era policy. Despite uncooperative weather on all three days, New Yorkers and tourists came to stroll. Source: Courtesy of the author.

the number of people killed in murders, a gigantic eye-opener for me," de Blasio remembered. "I couldn't believe that was possible."[56]

It was also the campaigner calibrating his message to events. As de Blasio sought office, a confluence of preventable tragedies—traffic deaths of children—galvanized attention. In February 2013, Amar Diarrassouba, 6, holding his older brother's hand walking to school, was hit and killed in a Harlem crosswalk by a tractor trailer driver.[57] In June, a teen driver jumped a curb on the Upper West Side, killing Ariel Russo, 4, on the sidewalk with her grandmother. In late July, Renee Thompson, 16, from the Bronx, who hoped to go to Howard University, was struck and killed by a tractor trailer driver as she walked from work to the subway on the Upper East Side.[58] Three months later, Allison Liao, 3, died in the crosswalk in Flushing holding her grandmother's hand.[59] The same week, Sammy Cohen Eckstein, 12, was killed by a van driver—not a bike rider in the controversial bike lane—on Prospect Park West.

Rich or poor, white or black, longtime New Yorkers or newcomers, private school students or public, children were in danger. It wasn't that more children were dying; it was that thanks to reforms that had showed what was possible, as well as a sharply curtailed murder rate, the carnage became unacceptable. Right of Way volunteers stenciled Allison's first name and "age three" at the crash site, with the same message as nearly a decade before: "killed by automobile." The same day in a different borough, they painted a memorial to Sammy, commemorating the lives and deaths of two children killed two days apart. "Being a parent and experiencing the fear and uncertainty of children being around super-intense traffic," de Blasio recalls, "and just seeing how unregulated and random it all was . . . the more I started thinking as a parent, what the activists were saying was making sense."

De Blasio's pledge to adopt Vision Zero didn't make or break the election. But bereaved families were paying attention during the campaign. As Amy Cohen and her husband, Gary Eckstein, grieved, they determined that other parents should not suffer. Before Sammy died, Cohen and Eckstein had been acquainted with the streets activism community. Amy, Gary, and their children were cyclists; as *Streetsblog* reported the day after Sammy's death, Eckstein had spoken in favor of the Prospect Park West bike lane two years before.[60] Before Sammy was killed, though, Cohen says, she hadn't paid attention to pedestrian safety. "I fell into the 'pedestrian must have been doing something wrong' camp. I had two bright street-savvy kids. . . . Nearly every eighth grader is walking to school by himself."[61]

After Sammy's death, Cohen determined to make the streets safer. In fall 2013, she knew that de Blasio was campaigning on Vision Zero. "My husband, he reads *Streetsblog*. He heard that the City Council was having a hearing" on cutting the speed limit from thirty to twenty miles per hour in residential zones, a goal Transportation Alternatives had pushed. Before Sammy's death, the family had visited London, where they had seen the posted lower speed limit and speed camera enforcement. Gary now told Amy, "If we had this, Sammy would still be alive."

Three weeks after Sammy's death, Amy testified before the city council. Nearly an hour in, after transportation officials had spoken in bureaucratese about progress the city had made, the council heard from Amy, Gary, and their teenaged daughter, Tamar. "On October 8 at 5:11 p.m., my twelve-year-old son, Sammy Cohen Eckstein, was struck by a van just across the street from our home," Amy said, voice wavering. Sammy had lost a ball in the intersection and waited until he had the light in his favor to retrieve it. As the light changed, "he slipped, and was hit by a van approaching the intersection at full speed." Sammy, a preteen with "strong opinions" who had just ridden one hundred miles on an organized bike tour, died hours later. Cohen clutched photos. "Our family has suffered an unspeakable loss," she said. Reducing the speed limit would "ensure that yet more lives are not needlessly cut short." Gary noted that "you would think that the large memorial to Sammy would make drivers aware," but dozens of vehicles still drove above the speed limit down Prospect Park West. Tamar read a letter she had written for her brother's funeral. Councilman James Vacca, in charge of the council's transportation committee, was in tears, as were colleagues and reporters.

A week later, Amy Tam-Liao and Hsi-Pei Liao, parents of three-year-old Allison, wrote a *Daily News* op-ed. Allison's killer had "violated our daughter's right of way as she was walking in the crosswalk, with the light." The parents would work to "never let this happen again." They urged the incoming administration to focus on cutting pedestrian deaths rather than surrender to the "massive distraction [of the] bike debate. . . . Bikes rarely . . . kill people," they said, but fights over bike lanes obscured "the single biggest traffic problem we face: the threat of cars and trucks." Of de Blasio, they said, "We are . . . watching."

As de Blasio prepared to take office, deaths continued. That December, Noshat Nahian, eight, an immigrant who had embraced New York in his months in the city, was killed in the crosswalk walking to school near Northern Boulevard in Queens by a truck driver with a suspended license.[62] In January, the second week of de Blasio's administration, Cooper

Stock, 9, died holding his father's hand in an Upper West Side crosswalk, hit by a taxi driver who failed to yield.[63] A new special interest—bereaved survivors—vowed to hold the new mayor to what he pledged.

Holding Politicians Accountable

Over decades, New York had built pro-cycling lobbies, pro-environmental lobbies, and anti-car lobbies. But the city had not built a street-safety lobby. The bereaved would change that. "I can't be the only crazy mom who has so much pain, and it has to go somewhere," Cohen said to herself. "When we learned more about how often this happens," says Tam-Liao, "we . . . felt like there had to be some change."

Cohen talked with Caroline Samponaro, deputy director of Transportation Alternatives. Samponaro had written her Columbia University thesis on bicycle activism. She had long spoken with survivors of crashes and participated in memorials, such as the city's white "ghost bikes," placed by activists at crash sites. What was missing was an organized body. "[After the] high-profile deaths involving small children," she says, "the parents that I ended up meeting . . . wanted to meet each other."

Another survivor, Mary Beth Kelly, was interested in organizing. Kelly had begun cycling as a student at Boston University, where she met her husband, Carl Henry Nacht. Moving to New York in the 1970s, remembers Kelly, cycling "felt less safe than either Boston or Philadelphia . . . [but] we did it anyway." Kelly had joined Transportation Alternatives but wasn't active until 2006, when her husband, a doctor, was killed on the Hudson River bike path by a NYPD tow truck driver. "When Henry was killed," she says, "I even put it in the funeral printout, if people wanted to make donation, it was Transportation Alternatives, Fresh Air Fund, Doctors Without Borders." After her husband's death, "Paul [Steely White] asked me to form a newly formed advisory council for TA." She grew accustomed to public speaking.

Another mother, Lizi Rahman, was drawn by de Blasio's promise. Rahman had lost her son in 2008 in a cycling crash. Asif, 22, had been killed by a truck driver while avoiding a double-parked vehicle—on Queens Boulevard. Lizi had often expressed worry to Asif as the young man prepared to ride his bike to work. "Don't worry, ma," he would say. "There are bike lanes everywhere." But when Lizi went to the site, "I was surprised to see there was no bike lane. I said, how come? This street has six or seven lanes each way. There is no room for a bike lane? . . . Other lives would be saved."[64]

For years before de Blasio's election, she had petitioned politicians, but she was "frustrated." Despite Bloomberg's progress elsewhere, he "stayed mum" on Queens Boulevard. A council member she declines to name sent her a private message. "Re: the bike line on QB," the council person wrote, "I'm sorry this is a continuing source of frustration for you. . . . I don't believe there is any possibility whatsoever that a protected bike lane on QB will ever happen. It seems to me that your choices are to have it be a continuing source of frustration for you or just let it go. . . . Cycling in NYC is, and always will be, I fear, a very dangerous endeavor." Walking by Asif's memorial, marked by a "ghost bike" painted white by activists, she hoped that the new mayor would reconsider. But in making political progress, "I didn't really know how to do that," she remembers.

In January 2014, two dozen survivors crowded Cohen's borrowed workplace conference room. "It was so raw," Samponaro remembers. Dana Lerner, Stock's mother, came weeks after her son was killed. Cooper's uncle, Barron Lerner, had written a book about drunk driving, and the death showed how traffic violence could hit anyone.

Families for Safe Streets was born. The group's debut was at a press conference de Blasio held in February. Earlier that month, he had met with families privately, and he acknowledged their presence before the press. Visibly moved, he said they "have been extraordinary." Praising their "courage and strength," he noted, "They could have chosen to turn away. Instead, they have devoted themselves to protecting others, so no other family has to experience what they experience."[65] De Blasio later recalled, "We had all gotten used to car culture, seeing people die. . . . The whole thing felt just wasteful."

The new transportation commissioner, Polly Trottenberg, released a Vision Zero blueprint. The book promised several efforts: tackling dangerous, wide roads such as Queens Boulevard, which made up 15 percent of road space but comprised 60 percent of deaths, lowering speed limits, and enforcing speeding laws. In de Blasio's plan to add speed cameras, cut the speed limit, and redesign mayor roads, one element was missing. The city would no longer go after jaywalkers. Standing next to de Blasio, new police commissioner Bill Bratton confirmed the change. "Over a five-year period," he said, "in 70 percent of pedestrian fatalities . . . the speed of the vehicle and inappropriate turning was a significant . . . factor." Bloomberg had unofficially stopped making pedestrians scapegoats for their deaths. Now, it was policy. "Bratton and I . . . didn't even have to have a real discussion," says de Blasio. "It was obvious." It was obvious only because a generation of activists had made it so.

Families for Safe Streets flexed power. The same month, the city council held another hearing. Families for Safe Streets members were a formidable speakers' row. "We demand an end to traffic violence," said Cohen, reading a group statement.[66] Council members sent a home-rule message to Albany asking legislators to cut the speed limit on local roads to twenty-five miles per hour. (The city council could cut the speed limit on smaller residential streets without state permission, but not on broader roads.) Families for Safe Streets was "essential," says Trottenberg. "They were an incredibly powerful political force, people who, as they always say, are an advocacy group that doesn't want any new members."[67]

The mayor needed Albany's permission to achieve another Vision Zero goal: expanding the speed camera program from twenty cameras to 140. There was no indication that Albany would act; the previous year, it had approved twenty speed cameras only after pressure exerted by Bloomberg. "People told us it would take ten years," remembers Cohen. Red-light cameras had taken a decade. The group said, "We don't have ten years. . . . People were going to die."

Families for Safe Streets members, in bright-yellow shirts and carrying photos of loved ones, lobbied Albany. The group met with Sheldon Silver, then the powerful speaker of the state assembly. Though Silver had approved the speed camera pilot the year before, he had often showed skepticism of camera-based programs. "We had a dozen people who shared their stories," said Cohen. "I remember him crying. He shared that he lost his mother in a crash." (His mother, with whom he had been close, had been killed by a reckless driver in Florida years earlier, and, a former aide says, he drove carefully after her death.) "He really became a strong supporter."

In the senate, which had fought speed cameras months before, opposition melted away. Christine Berthet—head of the CHECKPEDS pedestrian safety group in Hell's Kitchen, which had for years lobbied for pedestrians—marvels at the sea change. "Politically, these elected officials, if they are face to face to somebody who has been suffering . . . cannot deny those people," she says. The lower speed limit and more speed cameras in school zones passed on the first try.

De Blasio got to work on another part of Vision Zero: a protected bike lane on Queens Boulevard. The Department of Transportation proposed to cut into parking and travel lanes on the boulevard's service roads to make room for cyclists; it would also add pedestrian islands and stop signs at intersections to prevent high-speed lane changes and merges.[68] Rahman, keeping the promise she had made to herself after Asif died, was a tireless advocate. De Blasio understood how important Queens Boulevard was, Rahman says, because she kept telling him. In January 2014, when he came to a memorial on Northern Boulevard for eight-year-old Noshat Nahian, Rahman remembers, "His office called me. He showed me a lot of respect." In 2015, de Blasio, Rahman standing beside him, observed that "my children are just a little younger than Lizi's son was."[69]

As the project launched, Rahman says, "We went through a lot of hassles, convincing people, different community boards. We collected petitions, stood . . . in the cold." Queens residents' reception of the bike lane depended on where they lived along the corridor. "The first phase was easier," says Rahman. In Sunnyside, "people are mostly immigrants. They needed to ride a bike." During the second phase, de Blasio ran into trouble. In 2016, the area community board, comprised of middle-class residents, many of whom owned cars, rejected the bike lane. "This is not a park," said chairman Lou Walker. "This is a very heavily traveled vehicular roadway."[70]

Rahman was distraught. Holding down a teaching job, finishing her master's degree, and tending to her terminally ill husband, she left the meeting early. "I got a call that night. 'Lizi, they voted no to the bike lane.' I was really miserable. . . . [But] in the morning, I started getting messages, calls. Mayor de Blasio overrode the decision," she learned. Phase three, though, passing through affluent Forest Hills, was more difficult. In 2018, de Blasio responded to pressure over parking spaces by splitting phase three into two separate phases, creating a phase four and delaying the project nearly three years.[71] That year, the Forest Hills community board voted against the fourth phase. The concern was losing two hundred parking spots. "Is this going to allow a retail environment to continue to exist?" wondered one board member.[72]

Again, de Blasio overrode the board. Says Trottenberg, "[De Blasio] viewed Queens Boulevard as an incredibly iconic and important street, both because it had been a place of so many fatalities [and because] it's the kind of roadway that, if you can move the needle, you can do it all over the city." De Blasio appreciated "the incredible symbolism, that was the street where there were years with double-digit lives lost." Concurs the mayor, "I respected community boards, but I also understood their statutory place"—advisory only. "They were being Nimby . . . [but if] we were going to show that Vision Zero was the way, it had to be proven in some place like that. We were not going to buckle."

He also had data from the first two phases. As Laura Shepard, Queens organizer for Transportation Alternatives, says, statistics from "Woodside and Elmhurst," two neighborhoods along the first two corridors, "showed a significant decline in pedestrian injuries. There had been no fatalities. That was a very persuasive point." Pedestrian injuries had fallen 55 percent.[73] People were using the bike lane. Ridership had more than doubled, says Shepard, a lifetime Queens resident who had grown up riding with her father. "It was really challenging," as a child, teen, and young adult, she says, "because the streets were so dangerous." But with part of the bike lane complete, "more and more people [were] going longer distances, people of all ages and abilities."

Families for Safe Streets even succeeded in changing language. In 2016, the Associated Press told its journalists that they should refer to traffic wrecks as "crashes," not "accidents," in incidents in which "negligence is claimed or proven." An accident implies that no one could have prevented it.[74] "Getting the AP style guide to change its terminology"—a decade after New York City had stopped using the term *accident*—was "a big . . . cultural change," says Samponaro.

Claiming a Political Scalp

By 2018, Families for Safe Streets's power appeared to have waned. By then, de Blasio was no longer a new mayor; he was a second-term incumbent. Crime stayed down, and the economy hummed along. But the mayor, after his 2017 reelection, seemed out of touch, more interested in running for president. The city was consumed by Donald Trump's presidency.

Traffic deaths and Vision Zero had receded from the news, ironically because of the success of speed cameras combined with the lower speed limit, as well as the continuation of street redesigns. No pedestrian or cyclist died on Queens Boulevard between 2013 and 2017. "The Boulevard of Death is no more," the *Times* said.[75] In speed camera zones, crashes with injuries had decreased 14 percent.[76] On Ocean Parkway, crash injuries had fallen 23 percent.[77]

The politicians who had fought speed cameras four years earlier saw their chance. In the state senate, Golden and Felder held the renewal of the speed camera program hostage to unrelated projects. Golden still claimed not to be against speed cameras in theory, but Felder was less shy: he was also pushing a bill to re-raise the speed limit on Ocean Parkway. The goal was to "ensure that the high volumes of traffic on those roads move," he said.[78]

Albany maneuvering didn't go unnoticed. *Streetsblog* ran article after article attacking Golden. Now, reporters uncovered a new reason that windshield-oriented politicians and the police union had opposed speed cameras. "Golden's Cadillac Has Been Caught Speeding in School Zones Three Times in 2018," the blog reported that June. Since 2014, he or his driver had netted fourteen violations, putting him in a tiny percentage of scofflaws; most drivers received a single ticket.[79] (He had also been caught driving in a bike lane.) *Streetsblog* tied the personal to the policy: "Marty Golden does not care if speeding drivers kill more New York City children."

Golden didn't let small-scale press trouble him. The average south Brooklyn resident didn't read *Streetsblog*. His district was conservative; he had served for sixteen years with little opposition; and his two potential Democratic opponents, vying in a primary to challenge him in November, were a thirty-two-year-old unknown political staffer and a twenty-nine-year-old journalist. As the summer wore on, Albany declined to take up the measure.

Families for Safe Streets mobilized. The group protested in front of Golden's Brooklyn office. "Marty Golden a No Show. . . . While Demonstrators Hold 24-Hour Vigil," blared *Streetsblog*. Family members clocked miles as they walked around his block; four survivors of traffic violence were arrested for blocking the road. The two Democrats vying to replace Golden, writer Ross Barkan and Brooklyn borough president staff lawyer Andrew Gounardes, were regular participants.

The protests broke through mainstream press. The *Post* covered the arrests and reminded readers of Golden's reckless driving.[80] *Times* columnist Jim Dwyer cracked that "the senator has rare expertise on speed cameras."[81] In November, Golden lost. Gounardes, who had won the primary, won, fifty-one to forty-nine. The margin of loss was 1,271 votes. "Street Safety Impediment Marty Golden Admits He's a Loser," *Streetsblog* informed readers. Golden didn't just lose his seat; he lost Republican control of the senate for the first time in two generations.

It's impossible to know how much the speed camera issue swung the vote. Trump's presidency had galvanized voters into voting Democratic; in an anti-incumbency mood, this was also the year that Alexandria Ocasio-Cortez deposed a sitting Democrat. Barkan, who observed the general election after losing the primary, said, "It definitely became an issue, though, because Golden was so willing to flout the law." Referring to Golden's then-thirteen-year-old fatal car crash, finally, "it becomes a liability for him." Regarding fears about speeding, he adds, "These are complaints that . . . cross party lines. . . . Younger parents were concerned, middle-aged persons and seniors." As for Families for Safe Streets, says Barkan, "They definitely mattered."

In 2019, the Democratic-controlled legislature convened. Gounardes, Golden's successor, introduced a bill to allow New York City to quintuple speed cameras to cover 750 school zones. The city could also keep the cameras on all day and evening, from 6:00 a.m. to 10:00 p.m. The bill passed. Gounardes called it "depoliticizing . . . pedestrian safety."[82]

Mission Incomplete

By 2019, de Blasio was far from accomplishing Vision Zero. Traffic deaths were nowhere near zero and remained higher than in European cities. That year, London, with the same population as New York, lost 125 people to traffic violence, including 68 pedestrians and 5 cyclists.[83] In New York, 220 people died, including 124 pedestrians and 28 cyclists. As the mayor responded slowly to cyclist deaths in Brooklyn during his second term, Transportation Alternatives held a "die-in" protest for victims in Washington Square Park in summer 2019. The city was also slipping in design standards. The design of bike lanes "has become a little less safe," says Berthet. The Queens Boulevard bike lane was an example; for much of the stretch, the only protection was plastic.

Activists achieved little progress in one important area: getting police and prosecutors to treat crashes as crimes. The de Blasio administration had gotten the city council to pass a law making failing to yield, and in the process injuring or killing a pedestrian, a misdemeanor rather than just a traffic violation. But the penalty was light. Killer drivers still walked free. In the wake of the national anti-policing movement that began in the mid-2010s, much of the safe streets community stopped asking for criminal law enforcement.

And yet, the city had made streets safer. The 220 traffic deaths in 2019, though higher than the record low of 206 the previous year, was less than one-third of the 701 souls snatched in 1990. The 124 pedestrians killed in 2019 were two-thirds below the 366 killed in 1990. During the three years ending in 2019, traffic deaths were 22 percent below the final three years of the Bloomberg administration. Pedestrian deaths had fallen 29 percent. "Vision Zero was our proudest accomplishment," says Trottenberg. "You're dealing with life and death. Families for Safe Streets made it feel like . . . more people . . . got home to dinner."

Over the three decades until 2019, New York also made its drivers, cyclists, and pedestrians even safer relative to the rest of the country. In 2019, across the country, 11 out of every 100,000 people died in crashes, whether in motor vehicles or on bicycles and on foot. In New York City, the rate was 2.6 per 100,000.[84] In contrast to New York's progress, America saw decades of progress disappear after 2009, when pedestrian deaths hit a low of 4,109. In 2019, 6,590 walkers died nationwide, higher than the 1990 figure. Larger and faster SUVs driven by distracted drivers on suburban roads—many without sidewalks—killed a growing number of people on foot.[85]

New York City's relative street safety in a country with the highest street fatality rate in the Western world—four times the United Kingdom's rate, three times Germany's and Japan's, and twice France's—was cold comfort for the survivors of the 10,894 people killed in New York City traffic crashes between 1990 and 2019. Still, Vision Zero worked. It just hadn't gone far enough.

Months before he left office in 2021, de Blasio inaugurated the final section of the Queens Boulevard bike lane. "New York City is proud to . . . give new life to the notorious 'Boulevard of Death,'" said the mayor. Rahman, alongside him, said, "Today's announcement is a testament to years of relentless organizing by Families for Safe Streets members who have turned anguish into action." Later, she said, "He kept his promise." Part of taking back New York's streets was keeping more people alive on them.

Chapter 14

Yellow, Green, Black

The Struggle to Limit Ride Services

You are not earning a living wage and . . . the hours which you are compelled to work create a danger.

—Mayor Fiorello LaGuardia, 1934

No more suicides!

—Cabdrivers' call outside City Hall, 2019

THE YELLOW CAB IS AN EMBLEM OF New York—and the reason is its simplicity: put your arm in the air and hail a ride. Behind this simplicity is the complexity required to make the simple succeed. New York's taxi medallion system, created in the Depression and evolved over the decades through innovative competition within regulatory limits, was an exercise in political economy.

Taxis are a critical part of urban transportation. Though New York is a transit city, most people occasionally need a car. Enabling them to ride efficiently, safely, and affordably cuts traffic, as it discourages people from purchasing cars. Yet New York couldn't rely on an unregulated cab market. The city had to balance customers' demand for rides with the fact that street space was scarce. The city had to balance cabdrivers' desire to cruise for passengers in Manhattan, where most customers were by virtue of density and wealth, with outer borough residents' need for taxis. It had to balance customer and driver safety with the spontaneity of getting into a car with a stranger. It had to balance investors' need to earn a return on assets—vehicles and medallions—with drivers' need to earn a living.

The medallion system wasn't ideal. But every day, the system worked. By the twenty-first century, hundreds of thousands of New Yorkers—commuters and visitors, lone women and unaccompanied children—safely got into a car with a stranger each day.[1] Tens of thousands of drivers earned a living. In 2011, this New York world was "disrupted" by the "move-fast-and-break-things" tech industry at the height of powers. Uber forced New York to relearn what it had learned nearly a century before: whether you're a cabdriver or customer, an unlimited number of cars on finite city streets is bad for you—and for the city.

Too Many Cabs

When Mayor LaGuardia took office in 1934, New York City's unemployment rate was near one-third.[2] Men in frayed hats lined up for bread. Conditions were so dire that LaGuardia, a Republican and "Fusion" multiparty candidate, refrained from an inauguration party, instead noting in a speech, "New York City was restored to the people this morning at one minute after midnight." After years of Walker corruption—the former mayor had resigned in 1932 and two short-term officeholders had governed since—LaGuardia pledged to "clean house and clean it thoroughly," disavowing "dishonesty or cowardice."[3]

One month later, LaGuardia faced his test of how thoroughly he would stand up against special interests. At 4 a.m. on February 2, thirty thousand taxi drivers called a strike. The previous October, to raise money for unemployment relief, New York City had imposed a nickel-a-ride levy on taxicab fares. The powerful United Taxicab Board of Trade, a coalition of cab owners, sued, and the state's supreme court declared the tax invalid. Now, the question was: what to do with the half-million dollars that cab companies had collected and put in reserve pending court resolution? LaGuardia suggested that cab owners should give the proceeds to their drivers. Big companies owned half the city's taxis, or "fleets," employing the drivers behind the wheel. People who owned and drove their own cabs for a living controlled the remaining half.

Big companies, the largest of which was Parmelee, controlled by the Checker cab manufacturer, balked—so drivers struck. Though the cabdrivers' immediate rage was their employers' hoarding of all those nickels—"get the nickels" was the cry—the bigger issue was the Depression.[4] With many New Yorkers out of work or earning less, customer numbers were down. Driver income had fallen from $21 to $8.50 a day, as Graham Russell Gao Hodges writes in *Taxi!: A Social History of the New York City Cabdriver*. The half of drivers who didn't own their cabs had to pay 60 percent to their employer. "Drivers have long insisted that they could not make a living," the *New York Times* reported.[5]

Across the economy, employers were responding to lack of demand by reducing supply and producing fewer goods and services. Yet the number of cabdrivers was up. The industry had seen "a stampede of those of fallen fortunes,"[6] with "Wall Street brokers," "architects," "bookkeepers and lawyers," and "thousands [of] mechanics" driving cabs. Eighty thousand drivers, up from seventy thousand in 1929, fought for customers. Fleet companies had removed cabs from the streets, retiring older vehicles; the number of taxis had fallen from 24,291 in 1929 to 20,000.[7] But too many drivers still plied the streets. "Six thousand too many, said Parmelee counsel Harold Riegelman."[8]

The city had no way to reduce driver ranks. Fleet owners had no incentive to idle operable cabs and lose market share. For drivers, earning 40 percent of a few fares was better than earning nothing. Many newcomers drove infrequently, on weekends or during rain, when business was better. These "occasionals"—derided as "button-hole makers" by full-time drivers, because they had previously worked in the Garment District[9]—competing on the best shifts threatened livelihoods of men for whom cabdriving was a profession.

Oversupply didn't harm only cabdrivers. Cabdrivers "cruised" 70 percent of the time before finding a passenger, adding to congestion. Five hundred empty taxis went by Thirty-Fourth Street and Fifth Avenue every hour. "The casual visitor to New York may be . . . not a little scared at the way his taxi driver whirls him through congested traffic. But his confusion is not comparable to that in which the entire taxicab industry of this city finds itself," the *Herald Tribune* wrote.[10]

The Board That Failed to Limit the Number of Cabs

Earlier in the Depression, then-mayor Walker had confronted this crisis. In 1930, in what seemed an uncharacteristic instance of good governance, Walker named an independent body, headed by well-respected former War Labor Board chairman Frank Walsh. In 1931, the commission proposed its solution: a "Board of Taxicab Control." Walsh concluded that the board should reduce the number of cabs from twenty-one thousand to fifteen thousand "by gradually stiffening the requirements for financial and other responsibility."[11] In granting licenses, the board would consider "traffic congestion and parking space and safe use of the streets" as well as crash insurance.[12] The board also would regulate the fare, working conditions, and location of hack stands where cabs could wait for fares rather than cruising—even "dictating color schemes of vehicles."[13] Though a limit on cabs would be vulnerable to "political tampering," it would be better than "the present chaotic condition," the *Herald Tribune* concluded.[14]

Walker faced opposition. Large companies—Yellow, controlled by General Motors, in addition to Parmelee—welcomed the cap as well as standards for cars and driver uniforms. If everyone had to shrink, no company would lose market share. But small companies and independent owners feared "taxi trusts": that is, Parmelee and Yellow would take advantage of the cap to consolidate the industry, squeezing owner-operators out and creating a "monopoly" that would "drive the private hackman from the streets."[15] The industry had two warring publications, the *Taxi Sun* and the *Taxi Weekly*, whose publishers were for and against the regulations, respectively. "We have been bombarded with complaints about the measure, which affects thousands of taxicab owners and drivers, as well as their friends and relatives," said one alderman. "Almost all of them are voters."[16]

Walker got Tammany Hall, which controlled the aldermen, into line. In 1931, after a hearing enlivened by a mysterious "threat of exposure of 'scandal' in connection with the taxi-cab regulation bill,"[17] aldermen passed the measure, fifty-two to six, to "eliminate 4,500 taxis."[18] The mayor signed it into law in January 1932.[19] The taxi control board tackled its tasks. The board considered drivers' comportment, creating a requirement for coats and hats (but without dictating "the color, cut or cloth") and prohibiting smoking. It considered morality, forbidding drivers from "steering" customers to speakeasies. It regulated fares. It considered safety, limiting hours to twelve per day and warning that it might not renew the license of anyone "who has been convicted of driving a cab in which a person has been killed, or who in one year has had four accidents resulting in personal injury."

One thing the board *didn't* consider was what it had been created for: reducing the number of cabs. By May, the taxicab board was defanged. That month, a taxicab broker, J. A. Sisto, had information for the Seabury commission, the state body looking into Walker's misdeeds. "Mayor James J. Walker in November 1929 accepted a $26,535.51 payment" from Sisto, who had worked as an agent for Checker, the *Herald Tribune* reported. Sisto told the committee that he had given Walker one thousand shares of the Cosden Oil pool out of "admiration."[20] Checker's Parmelee, the press reminded readers, "had most at stake in the mayor's taxicab regulation."

The revelation would help push Walker to resign, but it had another effect. The taxicab board became too self-conscious to impose caps. In June, one member, Best & Co. department store chairman Phillip LeBoutillier, said, "I was a member of Mayor Walker's commission . . . and I never heard that it was the aim to limit the number of taxicabs."[21] After Walker resigned, the *Herald Tribune* observed, "The memory of the Sisto bonds appears to have hung heavy above the board's deliberations . . . another consequence of the former Mayor's peculiar ways of doing business. The idea of regulating the industry in the public interest was a sound one. But when it became known that Mr. Walker had been so careless as to accept valuable securities from a promoter of one of the large taxicab companies, it also became impossible for any honorable board appointed by him to do anything which might seem to benefit the large companies."[22]

Walker's successor abolished the board. The surplus of cabs trawled streets. "Taxi drivers are not . . . beggars. They are not asking alms," drivers' representative Jacob Panken said as the drivers went on their 1934 strike.[23]

A Bill That Capped the Number of Cabs

LaGuardia was a natural supporter of cabdrivers. The mayor had won because his promises of a New Deal for New York and his cross-party ties with President Roosevelt had appealed to the working man. "I cannot take sides," he told the strikers, "but as Mayor, I am interested in the welfare of the people. . . . I know that you are not earning a living wage and that the hours which you are compelled to work create a danger."[24] He warned fleets against hiring strike breakers and told his police commissioner to treat picketers lightly.

But the mayor miscalculated. First, he underestimated some strikers' wrath. Second, he overestimated the ability of drivers to discipline themselves. Cabbies weren't traditional union men but loose groups. Strikers had no factory gates to picket, so they protested in streets, where potential for confrontation was greater; they had no leadership that could steer them from mob action or keep rabble-rousers from joining marches. Finally, the mayor misjudged both sides' inability to act to mutual advantage. It was in neither side's welfare to idle fleets. He predicted the sides would settle.

He was wrong. That February, violence shocked New Yorkers. Wealthier New Yorkers didn't seem to realize there was a Depression. On February

3, after midnight, Broadway theatergoers who had attended a performance of *Ziegfeld Follies*, *Whatever Possessed Her*, *Wednesday's Child*, *The Joyous Season*, or *Oliver* climbed into nonstriking taxis. One thousand strikers and sympathizers were waiting, angry that some cabdrivers were not respecting the walkout.

These "scabs," in pro-labor parlance, were keeping the strike from an intended effect: to inconvenience elite residents. "[Striking] drivers . . . rioted through the Broadway theatrical district . . . , ordering men and women passengers out of cabs, smashing doors, windows and headlights . . . , and wielding ice picks, blackjacks and brass knuckles."[25] Independent operators chalked "OWNER/DRIVER" on cabs to deter vandals, but strikers didn't spare their property. "Outside the Public Library . . . thirty to forty hoodlums pounced upon two taxis, ripped the doors off, twisted the hoods and pummeled the chauffeurs." Agitators were not only angry at strikebreakers but also at passengers. Men with "high hats became the target. . . . Crushed and battered silk hats were strewn on the sidewalks." In Times Square, "a woman was dragged from a taxicab and knocked unconscious." A month later, strikers ravaged Midtown, "leaving a trail of damaged cabs, harried police and a few cracked heads."[26] Strikers "hop[ped] from roof to roof of stalled cars and chastised cabbies."[27] Two men hailed a cab and directed the driver to an isolated location, where they burned his taxi.

LaGuardia bore anger from the business and political world for having lost control. Parmelee took out a newspaper ad blaming LaGuardia. "Mayor LaGuardia . . . cannot allow the streets to be left free for rioters," the *Times* said.[28] "[LaGuardia] is stultifying his administration and making his Police Commissioner an object of contempt and derision," the *Herald Tribune* concluded.[29] In Palm Sunday sermons, clergymen blamed booze—such violence hadn't happened during Prohibition, which had ended the previous year, one pastor observed—or anarchists and Communists. "I can understand how men . . . with children just on the edge of hunger are easily led into mischief. But . . . cobblestones are not arguments," said Dr. George Drew Egbert to the First Congregational Church of Queens.[30] The mayor finally stopped the "taxi riots." Police arrested 160 people.[31]

Machine politicians who controlled the Board of Aldermen, already resentful of the reformist mayor, launched an inquiry. An assistant district attorney showed riot footage to a special jury, calling the episodes "the most disgraceful thing seen in this city in a long time." The police commissioner, former rival John O'Ryan, was clear on assigning blame. "The mayor told me that he felt very strongly in principle as to the right of assemblage," the commissioner told the panel. "I didn't share this view [to let strikers march], but I commended his liberal policy and principle, and we followed his views."[32] The jury ruled LaGuardia responsible. "I can't control the actions of seven million people," the mayor said.[33] The strike fizzled as strikers lost confidence in disorganized leadership. "Many strikers . . . made no secret of their resentment against the interference of Communists," the *Times* noted.[34] The drivers received 50 percent of nickels collected.[35]

The mayor wouldn't let cab companies declare victory, however. "The companies have had their way [for] a long time," the mayor said.[36] He promised to help strikers earn a living wage. To accomplish this goal, ironically, he had to exploit attention created by the strike to do what Parmelee had suggested years earlier and what Walker had failed to do: limit the number of cabs. The concerns were the same. "I don't see any sense in destroying the independent," said Samuel Nidetch, a "hackman" since 1906. "There's no right for a corporation to manufacture a cab, sell it to an independent and then operate a fleet of 100 against him," he said. Aldermen compromised: divide licenses between fleet and independent owners and maintain the ratio as cab numbers fell.[37]

In 1937, again corralled by Tammany, aldermen voted on the bill, sponsored by Manhattan's Lewis Haas.[38] Under the "Haas Law," cab "medallions" would be capped at 17,858. As owners declined to renew licenses, the total would permanently shrink to 11,787. Without a medallion, a cabdriver could not pick up a customer.[39]

The Haas Act: An Imperfect Solution

The Haas Act proved imperfect. In 1937, aldermen had no traffic analyses to divine the number of necessary taxis not only in that year but decades into the future. Just a decade later, after World War II, the price of a taxi medallion had soared. One city councilman (whose new governing body had replaced the aldermen) unsuccessfully proposed to release one thousand medallions to cut off the "black market" harming returning soldiers. "Veterans . . . are compelled to buy old and worthless cabs, paying several thousand dollars apiece, only because of the value of the medallion," the Manhattan Republican, Stanley Isaacs, said.[40] By the 1950s, a license that was nearly worthless in 1937 was worth five thousand dollars on the secondary market, a measure of how the city's population had grown, and grown wealthier. By the 1960s, the medallion had reached twenty-eight thousand dollars. Independent cab owners who had bought medallions cheaply could use the asset to add to their retirement savings. But the rising value made it harder for newcomers to earn a living.

This scarcity was also customers' complaint: not enough cabs. One problem was scarcity outside Manhattan. Yellow cab drivers—the city decreed the color in the 1960s—preferred to remain in Manhattan or at the airports. This preference was partly a function of density. In Manhattan, farepayers from the business, tourist, and entertainment worlds were plentiful. Lucrative short trips were common. Drivers also preferred not to stray far from Manhattan because, if they couldn't get a fare on the trip home from an outer-borough destination, they would lose money "deadheading" back to where customers were. Cabdrivers would sometimes gruffly—and illegally—eject a passenger who hopped in the backseat wanting to go to Brooklyn, the Bronx, or Queens.

As New York grew racially diverse, a growing group of potential customers had cause to complain: black New Yorkers. Cabdrivers illegally passed by black people hailing a cab. In 1986, city councilman Hilton B. Clark, from Harlem, noted, "Yellow cabs do not pick up black people."[41] Over the decades, prominent black people ranging from actor Danny Glover to weatherman Al Roker have said that taxi drivers ignored them.

Yet over decades, businesses emerged to serve the city's complex needs for car service across incomes and geographies while helping the city maintain its goal: not to return to the pre-Haas era, with cars flooding Manhattan streets. The first business was "gypsy cabs." In the 1970s, to meet the need outside of Manhattan, unlicensed entrepreneurs began plying the streets. Some drivers even painted their cars yellow. Many "gypsy" drivers were black and Puerto Rican, serving a market that yellow cabbies avoided. But many cars were unsafe, without seat belts or well-functioning brakes.

The *Times* illustrated tensions between the need for outer-borough service and the need for safety: "Passengers, finding it increasingly difficult to get taxis, run the risk of falling prey to gypsy drivers . . . , charging whatever the traffic will bear and uncovered by insurance. Often these drivers have criminal records. . . . An airline stewardess was murdered by a gypsy driver not long ago. Against these hazards is the reality that in . . . the slums, gypsies provide the only taxi service."[42]

In 1971, the Lindsay administration determined that it would be futile to eradicate "gypsy cabs." Instead, to legalize newcomers, the Lindsay administration created the Taxi and Limousine Commission. The city invited drivers to register and meet safety requirements. Thereafter, drivers in this "livery-cab industry," as it became known, could provide service via a prearranged phone call to a radio in the cab, but they couldn't pick up customers who hailed them on the streets.

In the 1980s, Manhattanites noticed a new problem: a lack of empty yellow cabs in Manhattan, a byproduct of the city's resurgence. "It's always been hard to find a taxi at rush hour," the *Times* lamented. "But the recent boom in Manhattan, combined with decay of the subways, has made it hard to find a taxi at any time."[43] Four years later, the editorial board noted that the lack of cab availability "depresses the quality of life. . . . A monopoly industry has seized power."[44]

The taxi monopoly was real, whether fighting Lindsay's 1971 Madison Avenue Mall or a plan floated by 1980s Mayor Ed Koch for "green stripe" cabs that could pick up street hails in outer boroughs. The industry stymied efforts to increase the yellow fleet. Koch attempted to sell 1,800 new medallions, but the industry stopped him. In 1985, Koch admitted that "we haven't been able to increase the number of taxis," "because the opposition says you'll reduce the value."[45] A year later, the *Times* editorialized that he "has been brushed aside by a Council that marches only to the tune played by the taxi cartel."[46]

Corruption remained a monopoly byproduct. In the decades since Walker, the city never solved the bad dealing endemic to regulated industry. In the 1970s and 1980s, machine Democrat Stanley Friedman, head of the Bronx Democratic Party, did double duty representing taxi fleet owners, which were no longer big companies such as Parmelee and Yellow, but groups of smaller investors. Friedman "exerted broad influence on taxi matters and exercised virtual veto power over legislation."[47] In 1986, when Koch brought in a new taxi commissioner, Gilbert Gorman, who had never lived in New York, the *Times* saw unfamiliarity as an advantage: "He'll start without political debts" in an industry "overwhelmed by incompetence and corruption."[48] A year later, Gorman had given up.[49]

Yet monopoly was not impervious to outside innovation. Another entrepreneurial business emerged: "black car" service for Wall Street. As early as the mid-1960s, a few yellow cab owners outfitted their cabs with radios, so that they could pick up fares via telephone call rather than rely on street hails. By the 1980s, "at rush hour, as many as one-third of the city's taxis [were] on radio call."[50] This phenomenon annoyed Manhattanites, who would put their hand in the air for a cab only to see the light notifying would-be customers that it was "on radio call." Regulators ordered radios removed. Entrepreneurs survived by moving the business model away from yellow cabs into "black cars." Just like livery-cab drivers, black-car drivers, if they didn't pick up customers via street hail, did not have to buy medallions.[51] Bankers and lawyers working late would call to arrange service, paying a premium for a nicer car and certainty of pickup.

These markets complemented each other, even if coexistence was uneasy. Speaking of the possibility of radio-controlled black cars taking over the yellow business in Manhattan, Columbia University economist Edward Rogoff said, "If any such service began seriously to compete with yellow cabs . . . there'd be blood."[52] Nevertheless, consumers had a choice, depending on price as well as comfort and reliability. A Manhattan architect looking for an after-work ride to a restaurant might put up his hand, hailing a yellow cab. A Wall Street lawyer working until 10:00 p.m. would have her office call a "black car" half an hour in advance and exit her lobby to find the sedan to take her to the Upper East Side. An elderly woman looking for a ride to church would call a livery cab service, climbing into the beat-up model. A Brooklyn family with a morning flight would "dial the sixes" (666–6666) to arrange a ride.

Regulating these businesses allowed the city to control traffic, at least modestly, by maintaining the cap on yellow-cab service. Despite complaints of scarcity, the city had a reason for regulating medallions, the same reason it had had half a century earlier. In 1984, Sam Schwartz, then-head of the city's traffic-operations bureau, said that too many taxis would mean "all you'd accomplish is to provide seating in midtown Manhattan," as cabs sat in congestion.[53] People could wait *for* a cab, or they could wait *in* a cab.

Angry and Frightened Cabbies

Regulations were not a protection from the city's overall governance failures as the booming Sixties deflated into the busted 1970s. In 1972, the *Times* reported that conditions for cabbies were the worst since the Great Depression. Even the medallion, a "prized possession," was declining in value. Cabs were "battered and dirty." Gas prices and inflation cut earnings. Drivers were also at risk. As city crime soared, so did robbery murders of cabdrivers. "The hazards of cab driving . . . are reflected in the frightening toll of deaths," the *Times* said in 1970, as the number of murders climbed to eight that year and the number of robberies doubled to more than two thousand.[54]

The group most in danger was livery cab drivers, because of "the refusal of most regular [yellow cab] drivers to go into ghetto areas for fear of robbery or even death," the *Times* noted.[55] In 1981, two cabbies were killed in two days, bringing the year's total to ten livery drivers and seven medallion cabbies. Albert H. Kapel, slain in the Bronx, was a sixty-nine-year-old former button supplier in the garment industry who drove because he "loved to be with people."

The city had no solution. "Drivers are angry and frightened," said an industry spokesperson.[56] In 1993, forty-two taxi drivers were killed, thirty-five of them livery drivers. One of the year's last victims was Tarek Abdel Hamid, an Egyptian immigrant. Hamid died in Harlem as bullets came "smashing through the windshield."[57] A year later, the city required bulletproof partitions in yellow cabs.[58] In 2003, after two decades of falling violence, New York marked a milestone in public safety. That year, no cabdriver died—not even a livery driver in a dangerous neighborhood. "In the last 30 years, there has never been a 12-month period in which no livery driver was killed," said a driver representative.[59]

Earning a Fair Wage

The system accomplished another Haas-era goal beyond regulating Manhattan traffic. Cabdrivers earned a decent wage. In 1970, the average fleet driver made $150 weekly; by comparison, a transit worker earned $175.[60] Abe Mittleman, a Brooklyn native, says, "It was the perfect job for someone who didn't want [a regular job]"—that is, someone like Mittleman, who "hated school" and hated his pre-Army post as a bank teller. "I used to watch the clock all day, pray for 3:00 . . . so we could close," he remembers.[61]

When the military released him in 1970 (he avoided the Vietnam War through luck), Mittleman took a friend's suggestion to drive a cab. "Time would go by, it would be twelve hours . . . , where the heck did time go? . . . I loved meeting people." Mittleman worked two long days weekly, moving upstate and returning to the city Thursdays and Sundays. There were drawbacks: "I could not find a legal toilet."

Mittleman did what cabdrivers had done since the Great Depression: purchase his medallion to ensure independence and an asset for retirement. In 1976, after six years of taking his "49.51 percent" of the proceeds as a driver, he and his brother put together a five-thousand-dollar down payment and bought a "mini fleet" of two medallions for fifty-six thousand dollars. On days that he didn't work, another driver—a Vietnamese refugee—paid to drive his cab. When he inherited both medallions after his brother's death, Mittleman turned the management of the cabs over to a third party, a common arrangement. He retired in 2012.

Sam Schwartz, who would eventually become the city's traffic commissioner, began driving a cab around the same time as Mittleman, in the late

1960s. "The money was really good," he says, and the screening process benefited a person with little experience. "I lived in Bensonhurst, I walked over to Tone Taxi . . . to apply for a job. There was no [instruction] class or anything. You answered ten questions, which you were pretty much given in advance. You had to pass a physical. They listened to your heartbeat—once. You had to have one heartbeat." (The city did not launch its "taxi school" until 1984, in response to complaints about lack of language and direction skills.)[62] Schwartz made "thirty to thirty-five dollars a shift, a little more at night."[63]

For a college student and, later, graduate, the money was better than any comparable job; the legal minimum wage in 1971, when Schwartz stopped driving because he got a job with the city's transportation department, was $1.45. Schwartz remembers his first fare, who jumped into the cab and demanded to go to Manhattan; the fare was $3.35, and Schwartz didn't have 65 cents change. "He thought I was ripping him off." Schwartz liked the work, although he was surprised at how many men wanted to find prostitutes and "how many New Yorkers had serious alcohol problems," vomiting in the cab.

Unlike many cabbies, he enjoyed driving in Brooklyn. He recalls that many drivers racially discriminated. He remembers "an elderly black woman who wanted to go to Brooklyn Hospital." Nearby police approached one driver: "The first cabdriver refused. The second cabdriver refused." When Schwartz accepted the fare, she tipped him generously, typical of black customers, who were glad to see a yellow cab. Schwartz gained insight into cabdrivers' habits, which alienated pedestrians. "What I learned is part of wild taxi behavior . . . people didn't know their right from their left," he says. A customer would get in and say, "Go right." But when Schwartz started to turn right, the customer would say, "No, I said right."

Most cabbies drove full-time. They were part of the New York background. At the time, cabdrivers were "guys in their fifties and sixties, largely Jewish, not born here." It was "the profile of my parents," says Schwartz. Cabdrivers "were [amateur] psychologists, psychiatrists," Schwartz says. "The drivers would have opinions, . . . it was a free psychology visit."

Nearly four decades later, in 2011, Pat Johnson, a Columbia University history graduate, was searching for a way to pay off student loans after the 2008 recession. He saw a bumper sticker on a cab: "Drivers wanted." Working four evenings a week—5:00 p.m. to 5:00 a.m.—he earned one thousand dollars after paying his lease fee and for gas. "Medallion owners at my garage could buy their house, put their kids through school," he says. Like Mittleman and Schwartz, he liked the work. "You could put a revolving door on the side of the vehicle, that's what it felt like," with twenty-five fares a shift. "I got to meet all kinds of crazy people from all fifty states, probably six continents." He liked the fact that he could leave his work at work. "So many people I take around the city, their job goes with them."

By then, a fraction of drivers (9 percent) had been born in America. Earlier generations of immigrants had given way to cabdrivers from the Dominican Republic, Bangladesh, Pakistan, India, China, Uzbekistan, and Haiti. Nearly all were still men.[64] Like Mittleman, the new generation saved to buy medallions, albeit for prices in the six rather than five figures. "I started driving for the better life," says Steven Wong. He bought his medallion in 2006, for $400,000, to "invest for the future." Prudip Kundu started driving in 2004 to "fund a good education for my child." He bought his medallion in 2007, for $450,000. Everyone said, "It's better . . . to own."

As the second decade of the new millennium started, a New Yorker procuring a ride—from home to airport, from office to hospital, from supermarket to home—had a wealth of options. Between 1996 and 2014, in response to growing demand and to encourage wheelchair-accessible taxis, the city finally sold more medallions, bringing the total to 13,587. In 2013, New York got yet another service to increase street-hail availability in the boroughs: "green cabs." The owner of a green-painted cab, in exchange for paying a $1,500 fee, could pick up street hails outside of core Manhattan.[65] But the city was clear that it had no intention of eliminating the cap on yellow medallions. The problem New York had addressed in the twentieth century persisted into the twenty-first: streets could only handle so many cars.

By 2010, cabs and for-hire cars not only provided service to residents and visitors; they also provided a living for more than one hundred thousand drivers; 49,128 medallion drivers owned or drove 13,587 yellow cabs, many of them in shifts for fleets. An additional 53,755 "black car" or livery drivers drove one of 37,782 for-hire vehicles, either their own car—bought for the business, not a personal car—or a car for a fleet.[66]

Most important, the system assured public safety. "Even in taxi-saturated Manhattan," one city report on pedestrian crashes notes, "only 16 percent of pedestrian [injury or death] crashes involved a taxi or livery car. . . . Professional drivers [earning a living] are highly incentivized to avoid crashes."[67] Background checks deterred bad actors; sexual assault or other wrongdoing was low. Meanwhile, the price of a yellow-cab medallion reached a milestone: one million dollars, a fivefold increase from 2001.[68]

Moving Fast and Breaking Things

In February 2016, Travis Kalanick strode to the stage of a Vancouver hall. Costumed in a gray vicuña sweater pulled snugly over a pristine-white cotton T-shirt, tailored dark jeans, red Nike sneakers, and glossed black hair, the thirty-nine-year-old Uber cofounder paced before a rapt audience. "I want to talk about the future of human-driven transportation," he said, "about how we can cut congestion, pollution and parking by getting more people into fewer cars."[69]

Kalanick pointed out the absurdities of car-based urban life. "We have skyscrapers built for cars," he said, as a backdrop of the multistory garage at the base of Chicago's Marina City "corn cob" buildings flashed behind him. Uber would end these absurdities: "technology that's in our pockets"—the smartphone—enabled people "to push a button and get a ride."

The "hitch" was "regulation." The hubris of government officials attempting to regulate Uber was obvious from history, Kalanick implied. A century before, in 1914, Kalanick told his audience, "A car salesman from LA . . . had an idea. . . . He was cruising around downtown Los Angeles, my hometown, and he saw trolleys with long lines of people. . . . He said, 'Why don't I just put a sign on my car that takes people wherever they want to go for a jitney'—that was slang for a nickel." But "the trolley guys"—"the existing transportation monopoly"—were not happy about this "juggernaut." They prodded the city to regulate jitneys "out of existence." The result was "unfortunate, because when you can't share a car, you have to own one."

Thanks to this shortsightedness, cities became a car-choked mess. "How would our cities be different" if Los Angeles and other cities hadn't killed the jitney? he wondered. "Would we have parks in the place of parking lots?" Transit was fine, but "transit hasn't yet figured out how to get to everybody's doorstep." Even in "a city like New York City," with "one of the most sophisticated mass transit systems in the world, there are still 2.5 million cars that go over those bridges every day." Uber—"to match you up with one of your neighbors on your way to work" in a carpool—was the answer. But, Kalanick warned, "It goes back to the lesson of the jitney. . . . Technology has given us another opportunity." Only government could ruin this once-a-century chance.

What Kalanick said didn't add up. Kalanick didn't explain why it was necessary to bring urban residents with no disabilities to their "doorsteps." Even as Kalanick spoke, many cities—including New York—still had jitney service, whether "dollar vans" plying Queens avenues or shared taxicab rides from Washington, D.C.'s Union Station. Never mind that most New York residents already didn't own a car. Never mind that most Uber rides weren't carpools; the company's main business was akin to a taxi or car service, the difference being that customers hailed the service via app, not by raising their hand on the street or phoning a dispatcher.

Kalanick's host, former journalist Chris Anderson, wasn't interested in sober questions. He was content to inform the guru that "you're being forced to be . . . a kind of global visionary." Nor was Kalanick's host interested in parsing the Uber chief's history lesson. Perhaps it wasn't wise for Kalanick to use trolleys as an example of irrelevant technology. At their peak, New York trolleys carried one billion passengers a year,[70] compared to the 678 million people who took the buses that replaced them.[71]

New York had never perfectly regulated cab service. But the city regulated for-hire vehicles to do what Uber would purportedly do: control pollution, congestion, and parking.

A Taste of Luxury for Everybody

Half a decade before Kalanick delivered his 2016 speech, Uber had debuted in New York as a black-car service. "Once you sign up for Uber's free app and enter your credit card," the *Times* informed readers, "you can call a car by opening the app and telling it your location. . . . You do feel important when a black Cadillac Escalade pulls up. . . . There is also a feeling of camaraderie with the drivers."

Uber was expensive. "The gee-whiz factor comes with a price," the *Times* reported, calling Uber "clever but costly. . . . A ride that would have cost about twenty dollars in a yellow cab costs thirty-six dollars with Uber. The premium seems steep," even compared to a black car.[72] The company was pitching New Yorkers who wanted "a taste of luxury." Targeting a niche market, Uber became big but not dominant. For a while, growth in car rides spurred by Uber wasn't alarming. In 2010, taxis and other for-hire vehicles made 168.9 million trips citywide. By 2014, the figure was 181 million.

But faced with competition, Uber metastasized. In 2014, Uber's competitor, Lyft, entered New York.[73] Uber slashed prices by 20 percent on something called UberX, not a premium service but a "hodgepodge fleet of unglamorous sedans, minivans, and other vehicles," as the *Times* described it. Uber would now be "less expensive than the typical yellow taxi ride." The city wasn't worried: taxi commissioner Meera Joshi said that "the consumer can choose." Neither was the taxi industry worried.

Evgeny Freidman, owner of hundreds of taxi medallions, cracked that with UberX, "you have a guy showing up in an old Chevy with flames on the side of his car, without a shirt."[74] These readings were naïve. There was no "hodgepodge fleet." Uber required UberX drivers to buy a late-model vehicle, which low interest rates after the 2008 recession enabled them to do. Drivers didn't show up without shirts. They wanted to earn a five-star customer rating.

If Uber and Lyft had been competing fairly, Joshi would have been correct: the consumer would have chosen, just as consumers who wanted premium service could call a black car and consumers looking for a lower-priced service could call a livery cab. But Uber wasn't competing fairly. Unlike yellow cab owners or livery cab drivers, or jitney owners a century earlier, it could operate at a loss, indefinitely. By the time Kalanick gave his speech, Uber was losing four hundred million dollars annually. The next year, as its global rides exploded from 1.8 billion to 3.7 billion, Uber lost four billion dollars.[75]

To gain riders, the company subsidized every trip. It could do so because Silicon Valley's funders were confident that once Uber built market share through low pricing, it could build what tech financiers called a transportation "network monopoly," much like Facebook had built a social network monopoly. Theoretically, anyone could create a competitor. But once enough customers and drivers joined the existing platform, few would join a competitor, because drivers and customers would be sparser. Uber grew exponentially to justify its forty-billion-dollar stock-market valuation, a tenfold increase in three years.[76]

Uber's losses weren't between it and its shareholders because its product wasn't private. The product wasn't the car but urban streets. The company, pricing rides below cost, was inducing demand. Because of the price war, Uber offered a service that could compete not just with cabs but with transit. By summer 2015, through its carpooling service, UberPool, Uber promised New Yorkers a "ride in Manhattan for $10 or less. . . . Whether you're matched with another rider or not."[77] Below-cost Uber rides were luring people from crowded subways into Suburbans and Camrys; convenience tempted the person who would have taken a bus down Fifth Avenue.

Artificial demand for cars meant more cars on scarce streets. Between 2010, the year before Uber launched in New York, and 2015, the number of for-hire vehicle licenses in the city rose from 53,852 to 89,686.[78] The growth didn't come from yellow cabs, whose numbers the city had long capped; it came from Uber and new competitors. At first, Uber trips had risen as yellow cab trips had fallen; now, though cab trips were still falling, overall trips were growing, fast. In 2015, cabs and for-hire vehicles made 228.7 million trips, more than a quarter over the previous year's levels, the highest growth in history. Uber wasn't keeping people out of their vehicles, as Kalanick argued; household cars and SUVs registered in the city rose slightly.[79]

Uber caused rather than cut congestion, particularly in Manhattan. Uber did serve the city's other four boroughs. But like cabs, Uber was mostly in Manhattan, because density and money were there. More than half of new for-hire vehicle rides—that is, mostly Uber rides—touched core Manhattan, Bruce Schaller, former deputy traffic commissioner turned independent traffic expert, would later write.[80] By 2015, vehicles in core Manhattan were traveling at just 7.4 miles per hour, down from 9.1 half a decade earlier, a 26 percent drop.

It dawned on experts: Uber was not just another black car service. It was taking over the market, including demand for yellow cabs—and, absent regulation, it would do so in months. Uber drivers couldn't pick up people who hailed them on the street, as they didn't have medallions. But technology transformed a phone screen touch into the equivalent of a street hail: a car would show up not in half an hour, as with the older black car market, but within minutes.

This ease was a problem. Uber was different from the yellow taxi in another way that had devastating impacts for traffic speeds. People had long complained that they couldn't get a cab in Manhattan, but this friction served a purpose. Since cabs were occupied most of the time, they didn't have to "deadhead" within Manhattan—going back and forth without passengers. To serve customers quickly, Uber had an idle car waiting for everyone who wanted to summon one car. That way, nobody would have to wait or take a train, just as generations of would-be cab passengers had done.

This deadheading—drivers circling a Midtown block in hopes of an e-hail—was adding traffic. Uber wasn't making up for inefficiencies by getting more people into fewer cars, as Kalanick said. More than three-fourths of Uber trips weren't shared rides. People taking advantage of Uber's cheapest rides, the five-dollar carpools, hadn't previously been riding in cars but had been "carpooling" on buses and subways. "Nobody's going to get out of a car to get into a shared car," says Schaller. "You can get people" in their own cars "to share" only "if you give them a real travel-time advantage," such as a special lane for carpooling.[81]

Uber's model had implications for drivers across the industry. For eighty years, the city had regulated yellow-cab fares to assure drivers a decent wage. In 2013, a driver's gross revenue per hour ranged from $26 to $44.[82] By 2015, it was down to between $22 and $35. The economy and city were doing well. Only one factor had changed. "[As] I saw more and more of the T-plated vehicles [Uber cars affixed with TLC as the first three letters of the license plate] income just dropped. Over four days, I couldn't pull in $1,000. Maybe, $600, $650, $700," says Johnson, the yellow cab driver.

New York's leaders weren't sure what to do. Uber provided employment. Nearly 150,000 people were by then driving a for-hire car, nearly 50 percent higher than half a decade earlier.[83] People liked the service. It wasn't surprising that New Yorkers would prefer a cheap, clean car ride to a train or bus ride.

One constituency was pleased, after decades of frustration: people of color, who had long had trouble hailing a taxi. In 2014, Antonio Reynoso, Brooklyn city councilman, told the taxi commissioner that he found it "almost impossible" to find a yellow cab. "My race is still an issue," he said, but also his destination: cabbies didn't want to go to Brooklyn. "It takes me forever to try to get a yellow cab, even when I'm wearing a suit and tie." With Uber, like other "young men of color, if I click my app, the closest vehicle comes."[84]

Absent an easy fix, the city determined to do something responsible: slow the problem, to devise a solution. City council member Stephen Levin—who represented Brooklyn Heights, Williamsburg, and other areas of traffic-clogged north Brooklyn—determined it was necessary to curtail Uber's two-thousand-car-a-month growth. "In late 2014," he says, "we had a hearing. . . . I remember looking at the data and seeing the rapid increases and thinking really that that was not really a sustainable thing."

Levin introduced a bill requiring e-hail companies such as Uber—those with five hundred or more vehicles—to cap growth to 1 percent a month. Uber couldn't keep taking over streets, as the city took time to devise regulations for a new age. "We need to limit the growth so that the findings [from a study] can be accurate and not obsolete when they come out in a year," Levin said in mid-2015.[85] The de Blasio administration agreed. "The onslaught of vehicles is so tremendous that it seems actually irresponsible not to legislate," taxi commissioner Joshi said.[86]

The mayor was clear that he would grant Uber no favors. In July, de Blasio opined on a favorite topic: capitalism. "Uber is a multi-billion-dollar corporation," he said. "The people depend on us to make sure the public's interest comes ahead of corporate interest. . . . [Despite] millions and millions of dollars and lots of lobbyists. . . . I don't care how much money they have—there will be rules."[87]

An Aggressive Monopolist Upstart

Uber came down with fire and fury. The start-up had been readying itself for battle, hiring premier public affairs officials, from former Obama adviser David Plouffe to a former top aide to then Governor Andrew M. Cuomo.[88] Now, it organized drivers for a City Hall rally, outfitted in Uber T-shirts and caps. "De Blasio: Don't Destroy Brooklyn Jobs," one professionally printed sign read. "Levin: Stand up for Brooklyn Jobs."[89]

Uber got that clearinghouse for elite wisdom on its side: the *Times*. "The main reason traffic is slowing down is that the city's economy is improving," its editorialists intoned. The paper did not explain how adding tens of thousands of unregulated cars improved matters.[90] Business and news pages had already been indulging tech mythmaking. Writers called Uber "ride-sharing," even though most rides were not shared. Opinion writers conflated tech with progress. One 2014 article was typical. "In its long-established markets, using Uber every day is already arguably cheaper than owning a private car," wrote columnist Farhad Manjoo. "Now that Uber, Lyft, and other rivals are embroiled in a vicious match for dominance across the globe, ride-sharing prices over all are sure to plummet. The competition is likely to result in more areas of the country in which ridesharing becomes both cheaper and more convenient than owning a car, a shift that could profoundly alter how people navigate American cities."[91] There was no evidence that Uber was reducing car ownership or trips.

Pro-tech bias was so strong that writers did not hide sloppy rationalization. "Even if Uber's vehicles added 5 percent more traffic and if this caused meaningful congestion," economics writers wrote in 2015, "a few more drivers from Brooklyn might have switched to the subway."[92] Counting on entrenched car riders to switch to the subway to make room for entrenched subway riders who had switched to cars was hardly viable.

Few people wanted to question on-demand tech solutions to intractable problems. The clunky taxi and for-hire car industry, albeit safe and efficient, was hardly a model of tech utopianism. "Tech was new. Cabs were not new," says Michael Woloz, a yellow cab lobbyist. The city's regulation of taxis as well as fleets' management of shifts was perplexing to customers who just wanted a car, no questions asked. Why did cabdrivers change shifts at 5:00 p.m., bringing them "off duty," as the light said, when commuters wanted a taxi? Why, in the 1990s, did the city require cabs to install annoying backseat televisions as well as recordings featuring celebrities entreating riders to buckle seatbelts? Why did it take so long for cabs to accept credit card payments? From regulators' perspectives, taxi service was a utility, efficient and safe but hardly glamorous or instantaneously convenient, but from consumers' perspectives, thanks to Uber, it was an outdated product.

Uber won pop culture. As Citi Bike was attracting cool people for the right reasons—or coinciding with the right reasons—Uber was attracting them for the wrong reasons. Ashton Kutcher, the millennial *That Seventies Show* actor and Uber investor, defended the company. "The residents of New York need access to affordable and reliable transportation," this non–New Yorker without transportation expertise, seemingly unaware of the subway, tweeted.[93] Another celebrity, Neil Patrick Harris—"Doogie Howser" to youngish adults—encapsulated this reasoning. "25K new residents use Uber NYC each week," he tweeted. "How is a fixed number of cars supposed to serve this demand?" Like a luxury Manhattan developer offering an expert opinion on Times Square's pedestrian plaza, the actor was out of his depth. The question was how streets could handle demand.

De Blasio's Uber

Uber's most potent campaign had nothing to do with jobs or tech. Rather, it was directed at one person: the mayor. De Blasio was vulnerable because the mayor's political support was not deep. Just a year and a half earlier, de Blasio had won his mayoralty in a race with record-low turnout; only 20 percent of voters had participated in the primary election.

De Blasio had one weakness that Uber could exploit: perception of corruption, notwithstanding the fact that Uber was spending far more money on lobbying, ads, and former government officials than the taxi industry. The mayor faced investigations into whether he had provided favors to developers who had donated to his campaign, and the taxi industry was another supporter. In 2013, the yellow cab industry had donated more than half a million dollars to his campaign.[94] One Uber ad said that de Blasio was "pushing the agenda of his big taxi donors."

It didn't hurt Uber's case that bad dealing persisted in the industry. Two fleet medallion owners, Evgeny Freidman and Symon Garber, had recently admitted to overcharging drivers for leases.[95] Freidman, in tabloid lore the "taxi king" in control of 925 yellow cabs, was hardly a sympathetic small businessman. "Every day that I wake up, you know, I'm like, this is great," Freidman told the *Times*. "You know, I live on Park Avenue, got a bunch of, like, Ferraris. . . . I have a house in the south of France. I can have breakfast, like, at Cipriani." Much of his wealth had come from borrowing to bid up the price of medallions, from cash earned by overcharging drivers for use of the cab and from skimping on taxes.[96] In 2013, Freidman pleaded guilty to failing to turn over to the state fee payments collected from passengers.[97]

Uber's hardest pressure point on the mayor, though, had nothing to do with corruption but harnessed the on-demand instinct that tech enabled. The tech customer isn't just always right but expects instant gratification. To encourage customers to protest proposed regulations, Uber created what one former top aide to de Blasio calls a "customer-outrage tool." In one Uber ad, a woman strode toward her Uber to see it vanish into thin air. When customers tapped the app to order a car, they saw a "de Blasio's Uber" screen: a screen with no cars available or with twenty-five-minute waits. The feature was to "demonstrate what life for NYC riders would be like if de Blasio's plan to limit Uber is passed," Uber told a tech publication.[98] "Every time New Yorkers logged on to order a car, they were reminded of the mayor's threat ("NO CARS—SEE WHY") and were sent directly to a petition," the *Times* reported. The city received seventeen thousand emails.[99]

De Blasio's anti-corporate messaging wouldn't help him against such an onslaught. To customers, Uber wasn't a "multinational corporation," as the mayor had intoned. It was their app, on their phone. Few people would consider broader congestion issues in their votes in the mayor's reelection, two years away, but people *would* remember that de Blasio had snatched away their cheap, convenient car.

The strongest vein of Uber's customer-is-always-right argument was the one with merit. Benjamin Jealous, former NAACP president and an Uber investor, told radio host Brian Lehrer, "I moved to New York City when I was 17 years old, lived there until I was 28. . . . I can recall days waiting half an hour on the Upper West Side, only to be thrown out of the cab at 125th St." The cab industry has "consistently discriminated against us."[100]

Positioning Uber as a better alternative to cabs for people of color threatened a mayoral strength, the top aide says. De Blasio was a white man married to a black woman, with two biracial children; his 2013 campaign had centered on this biography. De Blasio could not ignore black New Yorkers saying that Uber would pick them up when a cabdriver wouldn't. Uber neutralized what might have been another potent force of people of color: immigrant yellow cab drivers and owners. "Another savvy move by Uber [was] to paint the [yellow cabs] as purely owned by the Gene Freidmans of the world," says Levin. "People didn't really know that half of the [medallion owners] were owner-drivers, small owners."

Finally, Uber had an age-old trick: it was too good to be true—but seemed true. The fiction that lured New Yorkers was the below-cost price. Elderly women in outer boroughs ditched livery cab services or the bus, taking Uber to church.[101] For decades, New Yorkers of all races had had trouble hailing taxis in Manhattan or had had to wait for livery cars in the boroughs. Yet this cost and inconvenience had been useful, from a policy perspective: if it were cheap and easy to summon a car, dense New York would collapse under traffic.

Uber's effort worked. City council support for a cap "started to melt away," says Levin. The governor gave his opinion. "Uber is one of these great inventions, start-ups, of this new economy," Andrew Cuomo said. "And it's taking off like fire through dry grass"—not the most apt metaphor. "And it's offering a great service for people, and it's giving people jobs."[102]

The mayor changed his mind. The city would not slow Uber's growth; instead, it would be business as usual, pending a study.[103] To conduct the study, City Hall chose McKinsey, the consulting firm known to be compliant with customers' desired outcomes; around the same time, it was counseling Purdue Pharma on opioid sales.[104] In 2016, the Friday before a holiday weekend, when few people were paying attention, City Hall released the results, two months late. As the *Times* put it, the study was "very short—and very expensive," two million dollars for twelve pages of old information.[105]

The verdict was unsurprising. "Vehicles of all types play a role in congestion. . . . The study does not recommend a cap on for-hire vehicles."[106] In 2016, the number of registered for-hire cars reached 101,308, nearly twice the 2010 level. The number of drivers reached 155,620. Taxi and for-hire car trips reached 279 million, two-thirds higher than six years earlier.

Death and Taxis

In February 2018, Doug Shifter, 61, parked his luxury vehicle near City Hall and shot himself in the head. Shifter, who had called himself a "professional driver" and "executive" chauffeur, had explained his reasoning on Facebook. Though he hadn't worked for Uber, Uber had cut the prices he could charge. "I have been financially ruined," he wrote. "I cannot survive . . . working 120 hours! Due to the huge numbers of cars available with desperate drivers trying to feed their families, they squeeze rates to below operating costs." Referring to the Haas law, he added, "That old law was working. . . . Now the politicians have flooded the streets with unlimited cars."[107]

Suicide followed suicide. Six weeks earlier, livery driver Danilo Castilo had jumped out of his Manhattan window, lamenting the situation on the back of a ticket he had received.[108] A month after Shifter died, Nicanor Ochisor, a Romanian immigrant, hanged himself in his Queens garage, Ochisor had owned his taxi medallion for thirty years. But the asset, falling in value, would never fund his retirement. He and his wife, who also drove the cab, were having trouble picking up fares. "I was going downtown, uptown, and nothing," said his widow, Helen.[109] After a fourth death, cabdrivers displayed mock coffins outside City Hall.[110] In May, Yu Mein "Kenny" Chow, an immigrant from Burma, parked his taxicab not far from Gracie Mansion and jumped into the East River. Chow had seen no way out of debt he had amassed to buy a taxi medallion.[111] By summer, six were dead.

Cabdrivers and other for-hire drivers questioning Uber's dominance had previously been dismissed as against competition; now, they were sympathetic figures. "The economic devastation and desperation, where people were killing themselves, that's what changed the public discourse," says Levin. Uber's drivers, too, began protesting the company. This time, Uber drivers' signs were handwritten, not sleekly printed, and drivers were wearing their own clothes, not Uber T-shirts.[112]

Uber drivers were fighting the same thing yellow cab drivers were fighting: more drivers meant lower pay. Uber drivers were not "gig workers," the term tech boosters used. Rather, "half of the drivers support children and provide the bulk of their family's income," the New School's James Parrott and Michael Reich found. Drivers realized that being one of an unlimited number of providers vying to be the first one to a customer pickup didn't benefit them. As driver Pedro Acosta told the paper, "They dropped the price so much. We have to work so many hours."[113] One driver, Jacky Lin, said that without Uber adding thousands more drivers every month, there would be "a better chance of drivers getting better trips."[114] Parrott and Reich found that after Uber's commission as well as car loan, insurance, maintenance, and fuel costs, Uber drivers made fourteen dollars an hour, below the city's minimum wage, which the city was increasing to fifteen dollars.[115]

Drivers were the opposite of gig workers, too, in that they put much at stake in their livelihoods. Cabdrivers working for yellow fleets never had had to take the risk of purchasing cars. Unlike those drivers, and unlike bartenders or bike messengers doing "gig" work to support an acting career, Uber drivers had taken on risk in borrowing money to buy fast-depreciating vehicles. "Uber enticed drivers, promising they would make $5,000 during the first month," the *Times* noted.

Drivers noticed more congestion. "When you have the city crawling with traffic, everybody's losing," taxi driver Carl Dauphin told the *Times*. Congestion concentrated in Midtown. "In the afternoon peak from 4 p.m. to 6 p.m.," he wrote in 2017, "there are over 10,000 taxi/TNC vehicles in the [central business district], more than double the number in 2013." One-third were empty, "clogging the streets without any mobility benefit."[116]

Something else had changed since 2015. "Our city's subway system is completely broken," said an Uber spokesman.[117] It was an overstatement: the subway was moving millions each day. Yet the charge was rooted in truth: as the Metropolitan Transportation Authority had lost focus on maintenance work after the 2008 recession, the subway's on-time performance had fallen to 59 percent some months, the lowest since the 1980s. Yet the decline of the subways didn't help Uber's case. New Yorkers liked Uber, but they knew that it could not replace subways.

In summer 2018, six months after Shifter's death and three years after it had declined to slow Uber's growth, the city council acted. Members voted, 39 to 6, to restrain Uber and its competitors. This time, in contrast to the proposal three years earlier, the limit was a hard one: a cap on Uber cars rather than slower growth. The mayor signed the bill.

In contrast to 2015, the mayor was on comfortable ground. Capping Uber was now pro-worker, not anti-job, and the mayor could balance interests of minority taxi customers against interests of minority for-hire drivers. "More than 100,000 workers and their families will see an immediate benefit," the mayor said. De Blasio acknowledged the congestion crisis. "This action will stop the influx of cars . . . grinding our streets to a halt."[118]

Luxury for Manhattan

As LaGuardia had had to finish what Walker had started in capping cabs in the 1930s, it had taken New York City two tries to cap Uber. Back then, Parmelee had pressured the city to cap cars, and critics had feared it would use this cap to create a monopoly. Parmelee had had its own interests at heart when it advocated for a cap on cabs and lavished Walker with rewards. But its proposal was in the best interest of the city.

Eighty years on, Uber's pressure had been only in Uber's interest, not in the city's interest. Just as five-dollar Uber rides weren't good for taxis, they weren't good for streets. This time, it was taxi-industry pressure to constrain the number of cars that aligned with public interest. The taxi industry's time horizon was long because medallion owners who drove their own cabs had an interest in long-term value. Uber's time horizon—with the company under pressure to consolidate its own monopoly to raise prices and turn a profit—was short term.

The 2018 cap came too late for Shifter. It also came too late for Fausto Luna, an Uber driver who jumped in front of a subway train that September, just after de Blasio signed the new law. Luna's death marked the seventh suicide in a year. Joshi, the taxi commissioner, came to Luna's memorial, but needed her spokesman to act as "bodyguard."[119] In December, Roy Kim became the year's eighth self-harm death. Kim, a Korean immigrant, had purchased his medallion for $600,000. "[He] had complained to friends this year that he could not find fares," the *Times* reported.[120] By now, 200,000 drivers were competing with one other, nearly twice as high as in 2010.[121]

The 2018 cap also came too late to control traffic; 135,993 for-hire cars were plying the streets, triple the number of cars in the pre-Uber era. The number of daily trips for for-hire vehicles, including cabs, had topped one million, up from 766,000 in 2016; it had nearly doubled in less than a decade. None of the top e-hail locations were in an outer borough. "The most popular locations . . . tend to be in Manhattan," the taxi regulator said, with more than half of pickups. Uber and new competitors did their best business on the Upper West Side and in the East Village and Tribeca—New York's wealthiest neighborhoods.[122]

Even the small percentage of Uber carpools didn't make the streets efficient. Schaller estimated that for every "mile of personal driving removed," Uber and its competitors added 2.6 miles.[123] Manhattan speeds had fallen to 7 miles per hour, 22 percent below the 2010 level. In Midtown, speeds had fallen to 4.9 miles per hour, not faster than a horse carriage. Subway ridership, which had reached a record nearly 1.8 billion trips in 2015, had fallen for the third year.[124] In 2018, despite or because of record trips, Uber lost $1.8 billion. The next May, Uber, still unprofitable, went public on the stock market at a valuation of $75 billion, a different level of removal from free-market reality than a million-dollar taxi medallion.[125]

Too Good to Be True

The Uber cap slowed the flood of cars. (New regulations also raised driver pay.) But what would happen to drivers who had bought cab medallions at inflated prices? The value of yellow medallions had risen too high before

Uber, and lenders had lured buyers into loans they couldn't afford. Yet the city itself had told buyers that medallions were "better than the stock market."[126] "They were conned," one specialist told the *Times*.[127] The city's failure to control the number of cars on the streets had turned what might have been a price correction into a decimation.

Bhairavi Desai, of the Taxi Workers' Alliance, noted that small medallion owners were trapped.[128] The average owner owed $600,000 and was paying close to $3,000 monthly. With the number of passengers down, "whenever the meter is going, it goes straight to the loan." Their original lenders, largely credit unions, had gone into receivership because of this bad debt. Hedge funds and other investors had purchased the loans from the original lenders at cheap prices, a common practice. But they hadn't reduced the debt that driver-owners owed. "You start with one credit union, it goes to the next bank, it goes to the next, and each time it is marked down. But the owner driver is still paying on a $700,000, $800,000 debt," she said, asking the city to help.

"No more suicides" was the rallying cry at a July 2019 City Hall protest. Medallion owner after medallion owner told his story. The city failed to act. In 2021, a year into a pandemic that further decimated income, a dozen taxi driver-owners launched a hunger strike. "We've got one chance to make this right," said Desai.[129] That November, City Hall bowed to human and economic reality. The city offered grants to people who owned five or fewer medallions to help them refinance debt. To entice lenders to cut the amount of money that medallion holders owed to $170,000, the city offered loan guarantees. The refinancing lowered monthly payments to a maximum $1,122.[130] The biggest hedge fund purchaser of distressed medallion loans, after months of driver protests outside its headquarters, agreed to debt reductions. By then, Kalanick was out at Uber, among his governance failures having tolerated sexual harassment. Gene Freidman, the former "taxi king," was dead, at fifty, of a heart attack.[131]

Self-Driving to Urban Gridlock

Another innovation tantalizes tech gurus: self-driving cars. Google's Waymo has logged millions of miles in autonomous-driving tests since 2009. In the mid-2010s, Uber was testing its own self-driving cars in Pittsburgh and Arizona. Tesla founder Elon Musk sells his company's electric cars with "Autopilot," implying that they can drive themselves. "Elon Musk is Travis [Kalanick] all over again," says Schaller. "Big, sexy assertions."

As tech enthusiasts embraced the idea that "shared" Ubers could solve urban traffic, they are lulled by the idea that self-driving cars can not just solve congestion, but help government avoid investments in transit. In an *Atlantic* article called, "The New York Subway Is Beyond Repair," tech writer Peter Wagner said, "Forget trains. It's time for something radically different." Wagner called for the city to "rip out the tracks and fill the tunnels with fleets of autonomous vehicles."[132] Another case for autonomous vehicles (AVs) is that they would reduce deaths, as robot drivers would be safer. Musk has accused AV skeptics of "killing people."

Technology behind autonomous vehicles is not proven. An autonomous vehicle relies on sensors to "see" what's around it. Massive processing power enables the car to "decide" instantly what to do with millions of data inputs—how it should respond to what's going on around it. For now, the real world of urban streets requires computing that is beyond the capacity of driverless cars.

Crashes demonstrate AV fallibility. In 2016, a Tesla on Autopilot—in which it can maintain its lane, change lanes, speed up or slow down, and brake—steered into a truck crossing a Florida highway, killing the Tesla driver. In 2018, a Tesla Model X in Autopilot mode veered into a barrier on a Mountain View, California, highway, also killing the driver, an Apple engineer. Through August 2023, Tesla Autopilot was associated with fourteen deaths in the United States. With no public data on how many hours drivers engage Autopilot, it was impossible to discern whether Autopilot was safer than human-driven cars. Likewise, in 2018, an Uber prototype SUV in autonomous mode, with a human driver in the front seat, hit a pedestrian, Elaine Herzberg, in Tempe, Arizona, killing her (and leading Uber to abandon its driverless-car program).

Intermediate levels of technology between human-driven cars and self-driven cars may be most dangerous. The need for a human to take over a car within milliseconds after he has sat disengaged from the road for a long period is one peril of intermediate AV technology. In all fatal Tesla crashes and the fatal Uber crash, the human operator was supposed to be paying attention. But the driver stopped doing so—because technology encouraged complacency.

Even as technology advances, another risk is that cities reshape themselves around technology, not the other way around. New York made this mistake once in narrowing sidewalks and building highways. Easier paths for autonomous vehicles could similarly degrade cities. If an autonomous car can't "see" a cyclist crossing an intersection in a bike lane, or if it gets "confused" by pedestrians, the sensible course would be for city officials to ban that car from operating on its roads. But a tempting solution would be to restrict access for pedestrians and cyclists. An interstate highway is safe for pedestrians—because no pedestrians are allowed. Cities could "end up with pedestrians and cyclists effectively not being able to use urban areas," warns Oliver Carsten, professor at Britain's University of Leeds. Cities may have to resist pressure to set traffic lights to favor caravans of fast-moving driverless cars rather than pedestrians and cyclists.

Tellingly, few AV experts seem interested in how pedestrians react to driverless cars. Wendy Ju, assistant professor in Cornell Tech's information science program on Manhattan's Roosevelt Island, is one exception. As Ju explains, "The way that cars and pedestrians interact . . . is not completely cooperative." New Yorkers are "good at this game," she says. In New York, pedestrians expect cars to defer to them. New Yorkers walk in crosswalks expecting drivers to stop. If New Yorkers waited for a driver to signal his stop, though, as pedestrians do in much of the country, the driver wouldn't stop. Conversely, a conservative safety model, where a car stops at any hint of pedestrian encroachment rather than "understanding" that the pedestrian has correctly judged the spacing, could create more gridlock—and another temptation to reduce pedestrian freedom. Ju notes, "When we're designing the interactions, we have to do a lot more to model people's behavior." Behavior differs from city to city, but carmakers design for a national market.

Autonomous vehicles can't compensate for poor road and vehicle design. In Uber's fatal crash, road design and speed limits, as well as the heavy vehicle, an SUV, were factors. The road, like many in suburbs, was a high-speed multilane thoroughfare with a narrow sidewalk, few pedestrian crossings, and no bike lanes. Reducing crashes involves fixing road conditions, installing bike lanes and sidewalks, and cutting speed limits.

Driverless cars may be safer, eventually—but for whom? SUVs protect occupants but contributed to an 83 percent increase in pedestrian deaths nationwide between 2009 and 2022. A Mercedes-Benz executive noted in 2016 that, when an autonomous car has a "choice" between saving its driver or a pedestrian, it may be best for it to choose its own driver. "If you know you can save at least one person, . . . save the one in the car." The comment sparked backlash, but drivers and passengers cocoon themselves in large vehicles at the expense of people outside.

Another promise is that autonomous vehicles will reduce traffic. Urban dwellers could hail a free, autonomous minibus and share rides on commuting corridors rather than hail individual taxis. It's possible that with an AV available, two people who otherwise would have commuted in separate cars would team up to ride in the same autonomous car. Yet "just as with safety, what cities do with the new technology will matter," says Ju.

It's likely, based on history, that people would prefer to ride in their own AVs. If cheap driverless cars proliferate, they could overwhelm cities. "If ride-sharing does not become the norm," says Schwartz, "more cars . . . means more pollution, more congestion, and an excellent chance the road will privilege drivers." Drivers would be in even larger vehicles "because . . . people, once freed from the restriction of having to operate the vehicle, may want . . . to stretch out, relax, read, text, work, watch movies, and even nap."[133] It's also likely that with cars at the ready, busy fathers would summon two separate vehicles to pick up two separate children at two separate schools and drive them to two separate appointments for ballet lessons and a dentist appointment. Then, too, just as people want to hail taxis at rush hour, people would want to hail AVs at rush hour. Where would AV fleets store vehicles to meet peak-hour demand—in "a skyscraper built for cars," to borrow Kalanick's phrase?

In this AV future, pedestrians and cyclists would wait longer at intersections, as the city would have reengineered streets to favor self-driving vehicles. There would be fewer cyclists and pedestrians, anyway, as they would have succumbed to the temptation of the ever-available, ever-cheaper autonomous car. A dwindling number of people would use an unreliable subway. "Transit systems are best funded when they are used by both the well-to-do and the not-doing-so-well," adds Schwartz. "A system viewed as 'for the poor' will be poorly maintained." Mentally ill and eccentric people would make up a growing percentage of pedestrians, discouraging other people from walking.

All this risk for a problem that doesn't need solving. Cities accomplished the supposed AV goal more than a century ago. Technology exists to keep people safe, to encourage them to share vehicles, and to cut congestion. It is called the subway. "Even if driverless cars are 90 percent safer [than driving]," says Schwartz, "transit remains 95 percent safer [than driving]. So, if we take people out of transit . . . and put them into robo-cars, . . . they will be less safe." Transit solves the capacity problem that autonomous cars are supposed to solve. Autonomous cars "can't replicate transit capacity," says Schwartz. A single highway lane carries two thousand vehicles an hour; a lane for close-following autonomous vehicles could move 3,600, or, with two people in each vehicle, 7,200. A subway train can move 2,000 people every two minutes, 60,000 people per hour.

As Kalanick put it in 2014, "The reason Uber could be expensive" without investors subsidizing below-cost rides "is because you're not just paying for the car—you're paying for the other dude in the car. When there's no other dude in the car, . . . taking an Uber anywhere becomes cheaper than owning a vehicle."[134] Ubiquitous cars on demand—summoned by a smartphone or by a raised hand on a street, driven by a taxi driver, a "gig worker," or by no one—are not the future of a healthy New York.

Chapter 15

Thou Shalt Not Park Here

The Politics of Public Parking

> The business man who objects to the congestion that his customers encounter . . . will resent most vigorously any attempt to curtail the privilege of stopping in the public street.
>
> —Police Commissioner Grover Whalen, 1930

> Children first learn about free parking when they play Monopoly. The chance of landing on free parking is low, about the same as the chance of going to jail.
>
> —Donald Shoup, *The High Cost of Free Parking,* 2005

PARKING HAS BEEN AN URBAN PEST—for people doing it and people surrounded by it—since the car created a problem that the horse and buggy had not posed: storage. Throughout the nineteenth century, few urban dwellers owned horse-drawn carriages, and nobody who did so abandoned his horse for hours while he shopped or worked.[1] People who could not afford to shelter large animals—most people—took public transportation, including horse-drawn omnibuses.

By the 1920s, a small number of people had a dilemma: what to do with their cars? In 1900, three hundred New Yorkers had registered vehicles.[2] By 1910, the figure had reached 72,000, and by 1920, 216,000, on the way to 764,000 by 1930.[3] These people began engaging in strange behavior: leaving their property on the street. Patrons would drive to Manhattan's theater, shopping, and business districts and strand their vehicles as they went indoors to watch, shop, or work.

Public storage of bulky belongings in New York's marquee commercial districts—Midtown and Lower Manhattan—became untenable. In contrast to much of New York City's approach to the car, the city created an elegant system, even if accidentally: let free markets control this disorder.

No Parking

Officials were unsure about what to do about the nuisance of parking in commercial districts. The city had no transportation department; traffic had previously governed itself. The police, in charge of disorder, were, by default, responsible for devising a solution. In 1924, the police department determined that "a large part of the traffic congestion is due to parked cars."[4] Cars were not only blocking other cars; they were blocking emergency vehicles.

The fix was obvious: ban street storage. Police decreed that "parking automobiles for long periods in the business districts will be prohibited . . . parking will be permitted for twenty minutes" on Fifth Avenue, Broadway, and other "main arteries."[5] (Enforcement was racially uneven; in 1927, Chief Magistrate William McAdoo—observing that "seven Negroes were the only defendants . . . who received jail terms [for illegal parking,] although there were numerous white men charged"—reminded witnesses that "we have no color line," and reduced the sentences to five-dollar fines.)[6]

People who had grown accustomed to parking were not happy; nor were storekeepers and theater managers. For centuries, people had found their way around without having a machine as an appendage; now, they could no longer figure out how to do so. Merchants told city officials that customers were suffering. The Broadway Association wanted an extension of the twenty-minute limit.[7] As the holidays approached, Mayor John Hylan relented. He increased the parking limit below Fifty-Ninth Street to one hour.

Magistrate McAdoo warned of the precedent. McAdoo's tenure, begun in 1910, had predated the proliferation of the automobile. He saw parked cars as adding to road peril. "A man or woman may be a reckless driver when . . . parking for the smallest space of time . . . ties up all traffic and endangers life and limb," McAdoo said. He also feared that once New York allowed people to park, the city would have a difficult time revoking this gift. McAdoo foresaw "protest going up from those who consider what they call 'my rights' interposing as against communal rights."[8]

The advice went unheeded. Because car drivers, of all street users, were least able to govern themselves and coordinate with one another to avoid crashes and congestion, they would get the most room and attention. In Times Square's theater district, a "semi-military system" could achieve the impossible, law enforcement officials promised: "permit . . . parking near theatres" and "end congestion" at the same time. Despite fifteen thousand cars descending each night, all of whose occupants arrived and left at the same time, police promised that "three classes of motorists—those who come by taxi, those who drive their own and those who have chauffeurs . . . can . . . be well on their way home within five minutes." From now on, area streets would be one-way, rather than two-way, eliminating the danger of cars moving "in opposite directions head-on" because drivers were desperate to claim a parking space. Police would direct theatregoers where to park. "Cars destined for a certain theatre are . . . assembled in a block . . . in the same street in which the place of entertainment is situated," police explained. "If the street be even-numbered, and therefore eastbound, the cars assemble in that street west of Eighth Avenue."[9]

The rules didn't work. By 1929, Grover Whalen, by then police commissioner, applied his zeal—the same energy he applied to his project to force pedestrians to walk in the same direction—to revisiting Times Square's parking crisis. For a two-week experiment, Whalen would "marshal an army"—four hundred officers—to enforce "foolproof" rules:[10] in addition to prohibiting turning as well as commercial traffic during theater hours, he forbade parking during playgoers' arrival and departure times, encouraging people who arrived by car to take taxis, not their own vehicles.[11] "No parking of any sort," reinforced the *New York Times*, from 7:30 to 9:30 p.m., as diners and theatergoers arrived, and between 10:30 and 11:30 p.m., as they left.[12] "Wrecking crews will . . . cart off parked locked automobiles to the nearest police station."[13]

The test merited daily front-page chronicling.[14] Before "he stepped into his waiting limousine," the commissioner declared the project a success.[15] Subways were busier than usual: the rules "caused many to resort to the underground [subway] routes."[16] It was an early example of successful urban management: make it more difficult to drive, and people will choose a more efficient way.

After two weeks, Whalen had defeated what the *Times* called "the parking evil." The rules became permanent. To remove parked cars on an indefinite rather than emergency basis, Whalen invoked an 1897 law prohibiting people from depositing "movable property" in streets. The law held that owners of such "encumbrances" would have to pay a ten-dollar fee to the street-cleaning commissioner to retrieve their property. "In this way," Whalen said, "[the city could] impose a fine that is heavier than that usually imposed in court."[17] Entertainment venues were not pleased. The Broadway Association believed "the restrictions are robbing Broadway of its gaiety." Whalen dismissed them, saying that their numbers "would not stand up."[18]

Whalen went further as broader Manhattan's parking crisis persisted. "If a conflagration were to sweep away property in the heart of Manhattan valued at $500,000,000, it would correctly be regarded as a major disaster," *Times* reporters wrote, yet congestion was costing that much in lost time annually.[19] Occupants of moving vehicles were forced to wait behind parked cars, with "half the automobiles . . . standing still."

By March, "parkers having exhausted Police Commissioner Whalen's patience," Whalen said that the city would apply the Times Square towing procedure to cars overstaying past time limits anywhere in the city, hailing the system of confiscaton for its "greater inconvenience" to scofflaws.[20] By 1930, the city was "whisking away" 1,119 cars monthly. The *Times* was uncertain about this extremity. "The commissioner . . . may be able to devise a method to sheathe his iron hand in something more like a velvet glove," the paper suggested.[21]

Whalen wanted to go beyond time limits; he was so pleased with his Times Square system that he proposed to extend it beyond the theater district. In February, he wrote to Walker, observing, "One of the greatest helps to traffic congestion . . . would be the elimination of parking." He suggested that the city encourage developers to build "hotel garages" so that people could pay to park vehicles off of the street.[22] Existing garage owners supported the move, noting that the city shouldn't provide free competition on behalf of "motor squatters"— the estimated quarter of Manhattan parkers who violated the one-hour street-parking limit where the city still allowed parking.[23]

By June, Whalen was gone, as "the publicity which [he] was acquiring for himself and his consistent domination of the front page had become irksome and annoying to Mr. Walker." The theater and restaurant industries intensified their "clamor," hoping to find a sympathetic listener in Whalen's successor, Edward Mulrooney. Mulrooney lifted the parking ban.[24] All the new commissioner accomplished, however, was a demonstration of why Whalen had implemented the rules. By fall, Mulrooney reinsitated the prohibition, with a difference: offenders would not have their cars towed but would get a ticket.

As the Depression deepened, impresarios and merchants pressed for relief. "Restrictions are keeping people away," said theater owner Walter Reade in 1933. "If they wish to eat at a certain restaurant or go to a show they are forced almost to leave their automobiles in Long Island City [the area of Queens closest to Manhattan] or Weehawken [in New Jersey]."[25] Like future opponents of traffic curbs, the pro-parking lobby painted limitations not as a matter of physics, but as one person's obsession, deriding the rules even after Whalen had left as "Whalen's personal ordinance." Drivers didn't understand that discouragement of driving was the purpose of the rules, not an unintended drawback. Car owners lamented that "regulations governing . . . the vicinty of theatres were too stringent," rendering "their machines . . . almost useless . . . so much that it might be better . . . not to buy an automobile." Motorists declared that "these regulations forced them either to add to the expense and inconvenience by leaving their cars in garages . . . or by not using their automobiles."[26]

Complaints showed that the policy was working, and the police stood firm. In 1935, under Mayor Fiorello LaGuardia, police turned a "a deaf ear" to protests that "regulations now virtually prohibit the use of a private automobile." Officials made a terse statement: "Streets do not belong to any particular individual. They were not intended for parking."[27] In New York's business and entertainment destinations, block by block, successive mayors expanded the Manhattan ban on long-term free parking. In 1938, the city "entirely prohibited" parking of "space-taking machines" on ten east-west streets, creating "express streets" for moving traffic, a policy that would continue, notwithstanding sporadic enforcement, over decades.[28] Trip times fell by 60 percent, from twenty minutes, "when cars lined every inch of the curb," to eight minutes.[29] Deputy police inspector James Sheehy asked, "Why should some dowager in a fur coat spend three or four hours shopping in a store with her car parked outside?" In three years, police increased annual violations from 167,000 to 400,000; the fine doubled, from one to two dollars.[30]

Six years after World War II, New York installed parking meters in commercial districts. The American Automobile Association complained of "another financial burden on motorists," a dime an hour.[31] But after testing meters in shopping areas of Harlem, the Lower East Side, and the Bronx's Fordham Road, T. T. Wiley, commissioner of the city's year-old traffic department, hailed the devices. In ninety days, the 1,500 meters "reduced double parking and eased traffic congestion" and produced a yearly surplus of $2.3 million.[32]

Less than a decade later, New York created a corps of enforcers to make sure that parkers fed the by-then 50,000 meters: "meter maids." In 1959, Mayor Wagner hired one hundred women to write tickets,[33] supervised by an officer who was "to be a man."[34] The women had to meet a weight requirement: of the six thousand who applied, a reporter observed that "some appeared too stout."[35] Like many jobs assigned to women, the role of "meter maid," though comparatively well-paid, was low status, as implied by the word "maid." Meter maids were heckled, harassed, punched, bitten.

Encouraging Parking

After World War II, Manhattan parking rules encountered stronger resistance. Department-store owners, fearful of losing customers to free suburban parking, proferred an infrastructure solution: government-built garages. The American Retail Federation released a study titled "Keep Customers Coming: Practical Suggestions for Obtaining Off-Street Parking."[36] With the automobile "at the top of the list of postwar wants . . . customers will go where the going—and parking—is easiest," the study said. "Unless the pressure of traffic is counterattacked with adequate city arteries and parking facilities, downtown business districts will suffer."

The prescription for traffic—highways—required a complement: parking. The study suggested "bypass highways" to downtowns, including to "adequate terminal parking." The study listed examples: Oakland, California, had built parking fields to "anchor business downtown." Across the Bay, San Francisco, in 1942, "by burrowing four stories underground," had built a 1,700-car garage, a "daring step." The United States Chamber of Commerce, at a conference on urban problems in Washington, D.C., in 1950, praised New York for clearing slums but said parking must be the next priority. Fred W. Moe of the Ramp Buildings Corporation on 230 Park Avenue told conferencegoers that garages could serve a "dual purpose" as nuclear bomb shelters.

Industry wanted government to step in because companies were not building garages. Manhattan property owners did not tear down buildings on block after block to erect multistory garages or convert land to parking lots. Exceptions and near exceptions existed. In 1951, a seven-hundred-space, above-ground garage opened northeast of Times Square on the site of the demolished Hippodrome, a red-brick theater.[37] A decade later, the NBC network sold the historic Hudson Theater on Forty-Fourth Street—where Ethel Barrymore had trod the boards—so that a developer could raze it for a garage. Ralph Bellamy, Actors Equity head, termed it "an act of violence."[38] A tenant above the theater stalled the plan, which fell through.[39] Although developers built garages below new office buildings, they were not enough to accommodate cheaply tens of thousands of would-be daytime parkers.

The city explored government funding. In 1946, Mayor O'Dwyer determined that the "first positive step toward solving the growing parking problem" would be "non-profit parking lots at six mid-Manhattan locations," totaling six thousand spaces. A year later, the planning commission approved sixteen garages, including fourteen Manhattan facilities.

Opposition came from an odd source: Robert Moses. The city wanted Moses to build the garages, but he was skeptical. Moses didn't oppose paid parking, as his twenty-five-cent lots at Rockaway Beach and Coney Island attested.[40] He supported parking meters. Moreover, parking was linked to the expressways Moses wanted to build, including across Midtown and Lower Manhattan. The *Times* included a rendering of an eight-story Midtown parking garage, "which would be linked to the highway located on the Avenue of the Americas between Thirtieth and Thirty-first Streets"—Moses's proposed mid-Manhattan expressway.[41]

But Moses knew that Manhattan garages were a different concept from outer-borough garages and lots. He doubted the city would charge fees high enough for garages to pay for themselves. If not, garages would drain finances, unlike his Triborough Bridge and Tunnel Authority. Moses's correspondence with Lawrence Paul Wolf, manager of Skyway Service Stations, which ran a four-hundred-car Midtown lot, influenced his thinking. In 1946, Wolf complained to Moses, the police department wanted to turn two vacant sites near his lot into government-subsidized parking. Wolf noted that his lot was never full; it operated at 75 percent of capacity.[42] "We have never turned away a customer. . . . If the mayor permits the commissioner to open this parking lot" and charge a lower fee, "it will syphon [*sic*] off our yard enough business to make our parking stations unprofitable, the net result being a loss to the city" of parking spaces. Concluded Lawrence, "A publicly financed and operated parking station . . . is a distinct hazard to both our community and to us in the car parking business." Moses replied that it "emphasizes precisely what I told the Board [of Estimate]."[43]

In a letter to Mayor O'Dwyer, Moses dismissed the idea of the city running Midtown parking lots before it could build garages for a different reason: they would cause traffic, not reduce it.[44] "Any City department head who assumes the burden of operating small surface parking lots . . . is a likely candidate for a lunatic asylum," he said. "Such parking fields would not make the slightest impression on . . . Midtown congestion. They might, indeed, increase it. They would fill up quickly."

This argument may seem inconsistent with Moses's highway reasoning: wouldn't people driving into Manhattan via expressways need to park? But from a regional perspective, Moses thought of Manhattan as a place to drive through, not park in, and he also thought that people could park underneath his expressways. In 1946, he said, the alternative to parking garages would be "expressways and parkways with service roads and incidental parking facilities."[45] A selling point of the Lower Manhattan Expressway would be that "some 1,400 cars will be accommodated . . . underneath," a brochure promised.

For the most part, though, Moses thought that people parking in commercial Manhattan, rather than making deliveries and drop-offs, should use transit. As one Triborough deputy, George Spargo, wrote to a Baltimore counterpart in 1946, "I doubt if there is a single proposal" for garages "that will not need to be subsidized. . . . This screwball notion . . . that you can spend millions of dollars building garages, and then charge a dime for parking [is] fantastic. . . . Mass transportation is provided into the center of the City . . . and, so far as possible, this method of transportation should be used" rather than "subsidizing that individual . . . to permit him to drive his car."[46] A year later, Moses told O'Dwyer that people "who can afford to use their automobiles . . . into Manhattan" should pay fully for parking.[47]

Moses's love of parks and understanding of construction, too, led him to oppose officials' most fantastical idea: garages under parks. In the late 1940s, O'Dwyer wanted to build a parking garage beneath Bryant Park, Midtown's only green space,[48] and suggested allowing people to park in train tunnels."[49] Such garages would "do lasting damage to the parks and would create new congestion," Moses warned. As for cost, Moses noted that though it was possible to fund under-park garages, it was also possible to build a "tunnel to China if no one cared about costs [or] destruction."

Finally, Moses understood economics because he was experiencing them in the rising cost of land for highways. In 1946, Moses reiterated that "public ownership of garages . . . is . . . financially impractical" because "they would have to be built on land of such high value."[50] Moses knew that Manhattan real estate owners did not view garages as the most profitable use of property, because high land values were threatening his Manhattan expressways. Manhattan property had a use superior to driving or parking, as the market made clear.

By December 1946, Triborough informed the Board of Estimate that it couldn't take responsibility for sixteen proposed garages. Rather,

Triborough would build two garages that might pay their way, with city subsidy of land: the Battery Parking Garage, opened in 1950, charging 50 cents for the first hour and 25 cents for each additional hour, up to a maximum of $1.25 a day, for 1,050 cars.[51] Triborough would also take on the 2,000-slot Coliseum Garage, part of the (now-demolished) Coliseum convention center at Columbus Circle, opened in 1956. The independent Port Authority bus terminal, too, opened in 1950, made room for 450 cars.[52]

The Coliseum vindicated Moses's concerns that garages would aggravate traffic. "The Columbus Circle area . . . became a traffic nightmare," the *Times* reported that December, as "motorists inching toward the Coliseum underground parking entrance" on Fifty-Eighth Street slowed travel. They had been coming to see the National Automobile Show.[53] The Coliseum also confirmed financial concerns. Triborough had to modify the lease with an oil company "because the lessee was ready to cancel the lease which had not proven profitable."

Despite Moses's reluctance, the city accelerated plans. Wiley, the traffic commissioner, had come to New York in 1949 from Detroit. One of his selling points was that he had devised "a system of parking garages" in the Motor City.[54] In 1950, the state legislature approved a New York City Parking Authority.[55] The city determined to spend one hundred million dollars to build parking for forty thousand cars. The parking authority, new mayor Vincent Impellitteri said, would be the "cornerstone of the program for the relief of traffic congestion." Though half of the spaces would be near transit stations outside of Manhattan to "intercept" cars before they entered the business districts, half "would be built in business centers."[56]

Moses realized that the city would proceed with or without him. If his refusal to participate wasn't going to end the program, he wanted to play a role. Moses, even as he dismissed proponents of public parking garages as demonstrating a "political and hysterical character," said he would fund the city's parking authority, separate from Triborough, via bonds.[57] He was a good sport once he realized he had lost. In 1953, opening the East Side Airlines Terminal for buses to the airport, Moses said, "If we can get the City Parking Authority on its feet . . . we can also lick the problem of parking."[58]

Despite Moses's financial sophistication, he couldn't conjure investor confidence. In 1953, Moses approached businesses, including department stores, asking them to sign leases guaranteeing payments to planned garages in case customer fees fell short.[59] The Commerce and Industry Association rejected this idea. The group noted that "shoppers in the large retail stores use rapid transit and bus facilities, and that garages couldn't be built close enough to stores to overcome the reluctance of customers to 'walk more than 1,000 feet from a parking garage to shop.'" Businesses wanted garages but didn't want to pay.

Investors understood that garages carried not just market risk, but political risk. Without higher prices for metered street spaces and stricter enforcement of illegal parking, drivers would continue to circle for a meter space or take their chances of a ticket. Investors also remained alarmed at the city's lack of understanding of market forces. In 1953, when private Manhattan parking garages raised their prices by one-third, to an hourly rate of one dollar, "capitalizing on the laws of supply and demand," Wiley, the traffic commissioner, said the higher rates were "disastrous from a traffic-policy perspective."[60] By 1954, Moses had another idea: pledge money from the city's forty thousand parking meters to build the garages.[61] But the city didn't want to give up this revenue.

By 1960, Mayor Wagner was still pursuing garages "to bring shoppers back from the suburbs." The mayor had halved the plan for Manhattan spaces to ten thousand. Still, fifteen garages, each within one thousand feet of a department store, would cost $52.5 million. The RPA called the proposal "bold."[62] Moses agreed, again, to finance the program.[63] This time, opposition came from another quarter: the Transport Workers Union. Mike Quill "denounced" garages that would siphon subway customers.[64]

Drivers continued to push for garages underneath recreational space. In 1961, the Auto Club begged the Board of Estimate to dig up Bryant Park. The group "contended the garage was essential to alleviate congestion."[65] As late as 1965, Wagner, in his last year in office, planned a garage under Madison Square Park, a small park near Twenty-Third Street. The traffic commissioner, Henry Barnes, who, like his predecessor, had experience in car-centric Michigan (Flint), said that three hundred cars parked illegally around the park every day and that the eight-hundred-space garage would "alleviate that problem."[66]

Yet political sentiment had joined financial sentiment against digging for parking under parks. Robert Meister, then a law-school student, remembers protesting the garage. Meister lived near the park, in a "rent controlled apartment three flights up on 25th Street," he recalls. "My parents couldn't believe I was going to live in a slum." He remembered a snowstorm during which the city banned cars. "The air smelled differently," he said. He took interest in the city's plan. "The concept was dig everything up, put in new trees" afterward, he remembers. "I was already thinking like a lawyer. You can only use parkland for park purposes."

Meister was a member of the East Midtown Reform Democratic Club, which, in 1959, had helped him find his apartment. Within the club he began strategizing with Ray Rubinow, who had fought the wide road through Washington Square Park. William F. R. Ballard, of the city's planning commission, protested that a garage under a park would make "every park a potential parking garage." As the Wagner administration came to an end, the planning commission opposed the project, with Ballard saying, "Manhattan's business district core is the most heavily used, most densely occupied, most intensively involved urban center in the world. Under no stretch of the imagination can we assign this greatness to easy auto access or good parking." Parks commissioner Newbold Morris, too, opposed the garage.[67]

As he opposed highways, John Lindsay, who took office in 1966, opposed Manhattan garages, particularly a garage under green space. "I happen to be against garages under parks," Lindsay said.[68] By fall, New York had abandoned the mass-scale garage idea, just as it was abandoning highways. "Expansion of off-street parking capacity" was no longer policy, wrote Joseph Mc C. Leiper, director of city planning for transportation.[69] "[It] will generate more automobile travel. . . . Existing highways and river crossings entering the Central Business District are already used to capacity at peak hours. More parking facilities in Manhattan would generate pressures to expand this highway capacity." Building highways had once been an argument for building garages; now, killing highways was an argument for killing garages.[70] As for merchants, "department stores must face the fact that their future is dependent upon customers who are workers, visitors, and residents in Manhattan, rather than futilely try to become 'drive in' competitors of . . . suburban shopping centers."

Ironically, Moses, clinging to power, remained a lone voice for garages. He wrote in *Newsday*, "Ramp garages are essential in the central city core."[71] In a 1966 statement supporting Moses, New York's Auto Club cited the proposition that "parking spaces would only attract more cars" as one of the "specious arguments" made by the anti-car lobby, along with the argument that "the auto is creating congestion" and "highways only would attract more traffic."[72]

Outside Manhattan, prominent citizens still supported garages. In 1966, in Queens, "businessmen whose establishments stand to be demolished in favor of the proposed Bridge Plaza municipal off-street parking garage agree that the move is 'the best thing that could happen.'" The 1,100-space garage at Jackson Avenue would be "the greatest thing that ever happened to Long Island City," says Michael Sheehan, part owner of Doherty's Restaurant.[73]

Yet mass-scale garages in Manhattan were dead, with few completed. By the mid-1960s, the traffic department operated forty-three parking facilities citywide with 12,265 spaces. The city also had 56,000 parking meters. But most garages and metered spaces were outside of core Manhattan, which had just 6,303 meters. The Auto Club's vice president, Charles Murphy, lamented in 1967 that Wiley's 1955 plan had "gathered dust," with only 30 percent of promised spaces built.[74] The city had halted this program, he noted, despite the "overwhelming success of the only such [city-run] garage in Manhattan. Located at Eighth Avenue and 52nd Street, this garage . . . has—since . . . 1960—taken 3.5 million cars off crowded city streets."

New York, by accident, had arrived at a good-enough result. Legal parking in core Manhattan remained available. When Lindsay foreclosed further construction, 115,000 off-street parking spaces existed in Manhattan below Fifty-Ninth Street.[75] Most were in small-scale underground lots in private buildings, not in mass-scale garages. Nobody was ever turned away for lack of a space. But parking was scarce and expensive. The market had worked. Would-be garage builders, absent government subsidy, hadn't built free-standing facilities, both because they had more lucrative uses for property and because they had been wary of city competion, real—the garages Triborough and the city did build—and potential: any time, New York could have built the garages it threatened, ruining their business.

Discouraging Parking

Manhattan parking would get even scarcer and pricier. Mayors have policies—but they also have pet peeves. Mayor Lindsay saw illegal Midtown parking as a traffic challenge—and he also hated it. "We were going to a black-tie event," said one former aide. "He would get out of the limousine, telling some double-parked guy to move. It was crazy." Once, he became "furious" at "triple-parked" cars blocking his limo.[76] Irony aside, during eight years in office, Lindsay would transform this dislike into policy—improving enforcement and taking away more of the legal parking spaces that remained.

Even before he took office, Lindsay showed a zeal for parking rules—using himself as an example. In 1965, after the election, police found a car illegally parked by Midtown's Roosevelt Hotel, Lindsay's transition headquarters. The windshield featured a note, informing meter maids that it was the "official car" of the mayor-elect. A motorcycle enforcer slapped a fifteen-dollar ticket on the vehicle.[77] Lindsay seized upon the publicity, writing the officer to tell him that the ticket was "deserved" and that "rigid enforcement of illegal parking is urgently needed."[78] The *Times* agreed. "The most dramatic initial action Mayor Lindsay could take . . . would be to strengthen and enforce the traffic laws," the paper editorialized. "For most problems, . . . there is no magic wand," but he could cure congestion "miraculously . . . by a single command": "Enforce the law."

The paper counseled "ruthless" enforcement against double parking. "It should not be beyond the wit of man" to devise a more efficient system of writing traffic tickets.[79] The *Times* was not wrong. Each day, 200,000 passenger cars—as opposed to taxis or trucks—entered Manhattan business districts, joining 50,000 cars owned by Manhattan residents. Nearly 40 percent of parked vehicles were illegally parked. An RPA study estimated that one-third of afternoon drivers were looking for parking.[80]

Lindsay engaged in enforcement theater: crackdowns. Weeks into his term, in a media event delayed by the transit strike, Lindsay chose Broadway for his assault. Lindsay did something that his predecessor hadn't done in nearly a decade: mass towing. With seventy-five thousand people parked illegally every day on Manhattan streets,[81] the situation was so bad that even the Auto Club endorsed the program.[82] "We want to make a clear demonstration that this will not be permitted," vowed Lindsay.[83] By fall, the city was towing one thousand Midtown cars a week, "ranging from a silver-gray Rolls Royce to an engineless jalopy."[84]

Towing worked better than ticketing. It raised the financial penalty, from fifteen to forty dollars. More important to affluent drivers, the tow often damaged their vehicles and was a tax on their time.[85] One driver called it a "Gestapo" tactic. The penalty for running into a store was no longer the chance of getting a ticket; it was the loss of a day trekking to the tow pound.[86] "There's nothing like a towaway operation to get . . . compliance," said traffic commissioner Henry Barnes.[87] As in the 1930s, drivers complained that crackdowns were forcing them to leave cars at home, but inconvenience was the point, not an unfortunate byproduct.

The mayor targeted drivers who had been immune to enforcement: elected officials, diplomats, and doctors. "The new broom did not become fully effective until it began to touch . . . favored groups," the *Times* said.[88] "What good does it do to tow away 10 or 20 cars," Lindsay said, "when you have one or two special exceptions?"[89] Victims grumbled. "We were supposed to be guests of the city," one diplomat told the *Times*. "We have to go to two, three sometimes four parties in one night."[90] Lindsay revoked three aides' cars for two weeks for illegal parking.[91] His enthusiasm risked a charge of hypocrisy. Reporters found his own double-parked car, a "shiny Lincoln," despite his "no exceptions" decree. The mayor moved his car—but wasn't cowed by the jeers.

Where the mayor made a longer-term difference was in forcing people to pay tickets, ensuring that ticketing would be a deterrent. The $15 ticket ($150 in 2024 dollars) should have been adequate—except that drivers risked what Frazer Dougherty, a forty-five-year-old industrial designer with homes in Manhattan and on Long Island and with outstanding parking tickets with total fines due of $2,100 ($21,000 in 2024 dollars)—called a "game which some people play excellently."[92] As Dougherty noted, drivers knew that they ran a good chance of not being ticketed. They knew, too, that they did not have to pay. Ticket compliance had fallen from 92 percent in 1952 to 47 percent.[93] This result was partly a function of how many tickets the city was writing: "meter maids" wrote nearly four million tickets each year, too many to process.

Lindsay introduced efficiency. The city moved tickets from criminal court to a civil "parking violations bureau." The bureau was "the city's answer to the thousands of motorists who habitually ignored parking tickets and to those who felt they were not guilty, but who had to wait hours before a Criminal Court judge."[94] ("I'm not guilty," said college junior Rena Smilowitz over her $25 ticket for parking near a hydrant. "I can't say I'm responsible for something when I'm not there.") Hours of waiting fell to fifteen minutes; police no longer had to wait with drivers. The bureau saved the equivalent of 156 police officers per year.[95] Automating tabulation of fines—thanks to a "new IBM computer," costing $350,000—helped in this "war on scofflaws."[96] Dougherty admitted defeat. He put his overdue tickets and a check in a box and mailed them to the city.

With enforcement, Lindsay could beef up the rules, knowing that drivers could no longer ignore them. As he began his second term in 1970, he made it clear that he would make parking in core Manhattan scarcer than it already was—and would be enthusiastic about it. Theodore Karagheuzoff, Lindsay's traffic commissioner following Barnes's death in 1968, predicted that "daytime parking of passenger cars at all one thousand metered spots in mid-Manhattan will be banned by next Thanksgiving." The city took away business-hour parking on First and Second Avenues in favor of a bus lane. The project and the elimination of 635 metered spaces, roughly 10 percent of Manhattan's metered total, was "the forerunner of the elimination of every legal parking space for passenger cars between First and Ninth Avenues from Thirty-Fourth to Seventy-Second

Streets, the commissioner indicated." Karagheuzoff told reporters whose idea the ban was: Lindsay's.[97] Weeks into the experiment, Karagheuzoff pronounced it a success, noting that vehicles entering downtown in the morning had fallen to 2,200 an hour, 15 percent below normal; travel time across Wall Street was down by one-third.[98]

As Lindsay prepared to leave office in 1973, he enacted reform that was "the most sweeping of its kind."[99] The goal was to "drive private autos out of the central business district."[100] Civilians would replace police officers directing traffic. The city empowered meter maids—and now "meter men"—to issue tickets for more violation types.[101] As June temperatures broke records—ninety-five degrees—and the city suffered brownouts, the mayor, walking the streets, told meter maids to "show no mercy."[102] To drivers, he said, "Stay out of Manhattan. Don't bring your car."[103]

The Auto Club was no longer a supporter of the tow program, questioning a more aggressive version, which directed tow-truck drivers to deposit cars on less cluttered streets when they had run out of room at the pound. This "push and clear" policy would "put the city in the ridiculous . . . position of playing hide and-seek with a citizen's personal possession worth thousands of dollars," the Club complained. Unasked was why people were leaving "personal possessions" illegally unattended.[104] By then, the city was towing two thousand cars weekly in Midtown, "all that we can handle."[105]

Lindsay's mark was enduring—through a provision that few people noticed. In 1973, to comply with the Clean Air Act, Lindsay and Governor Rockefeller submitted their plan to the federal Environmental Protection Agency. This "transportation control plan" committed the city to banning most rush-hour parking in commercial Manhattan, binding future mayors to Lindsay's anti-parking mania. No successor could undo his rules on a whim; Lindsay's hatred of parked cars became enshrined in the city's promise, under federal law, to scrub the air.

Looting, Fires, and Parking

On July 13, 1977, the lights went out. Marauders smashed windows and shot guns into the air.[106] The stock exchange closed, and merchants armed themselves.[107] Patrolman Paul Migdalen called the looting "brutal" compared to the "fun and games" of the blackout twelve years earlier. Governor Hugh Carey ordered troopers to keep order. Mayor Abe Beame was spooked by the "night of terror." When the lights came back on, New Yorkers remained uneasy. The "Son of Sam" killer terrifying New York City with his pistol killed his sixth and final victim.[108] Police caught the killer, David Berkowitz, by putting a name to a suspicious person . . . via a Brooklyn parking ticket.[109]

For Beame, the blackout and the "Son of Sam" terror punctuated a summer otherwise defined by a parking crisis, one that he had exacerbated. Upon taking office in 1974, the former-accountant mayor, overwhelmed by fiscal turmoil and urban disarray, had determined that he had no interest in implementing the Lindsay-era mandate to eliminate rush-hour parking in commercial Manhattan. Ideologically, Beame was more sympathetic than Lindsay to parkers. His approach represented a return to the Wagner approach—build off-street facilities—rather than the Lindsay stance: discourage people from driving. In 1974, even as the city careened toward a default on its bonds a year later, the administration proposed to knock down the Tweed Courthouse, across from City Hall, to build a garage for municipal workers.

The press reception illustrated why Beame was not deluded to figure that the public would be on his side. The courthouse, built in 1872, was an irreplaceable Italianate showpiece; the seat of Tammany Hall for decades, it was an emblem of New York's history. In a *Times* story on the teardown, though, the building was "soot-smudged"; the article neglected to say that the soot came from cars. A garage would prevent city workers' cars from "disfiguring" City Hall's plaza, the article said; the reporter didn't find a source to wonder if the answer wasn't fewer government workers driving to Manhattan.[110]

The city had considered banning workers from parking in the plaza—or rather, since such parking was illegal, enforcing the ban. But "that idea apparently has been rejected. It is a status symbol . . . to have a City Hall parking sticker. One well-to-do, long-term [sticker] holder, threatened with ouster from the plaza, broke into tears" because paying to park would harm "his reputation as a man with connections." It was more practical to tear down a landmark of Tammany corruption than to fight corruption: illegal government parking.[111] The same year, Morningside Heights residents in Upper Manhattan gathered three thousand signatures to kill a plan to build a library, desiring to preserve a garage, and "putting its parking convenience . . . above the scholarly life so characteristic of the neighborhood" (it would be more than twenty-five years before the city built the library).[112]

Beame's intrasigence in implementing the Clean Air Act plan, including banning rush-hour Manhattan parking, spurred the Natural Resources Defense Fund to sue in federal court. Beame had tried to run out the clock, appealing ruling after ruling. But by 1977, the court was holding him to the city's agreement with the EPA. In the meanwhile, a quarter of the city's by-then sixty-five thousand parking meters were broken, but the city said that people could park for free in front of them.[113]

Banning rush-hour parking in commercial Manhattan was controversial, and Beame determined to make it even more controversial. Beame's strategy was simple: take the narrow federal decree and expand it so that it seemed worse. Two years earlier, Beame's administration, in an early and now-abandoned move to cooperate with the plan, had identified 206 parking meters in core Manhattan to "hood" during business hours, thus making the spaces illegal.[114] By spring 1977, though, Beame was insisting that the federal court order would mean the loss of all 12,700 curbside spaces in core Manhattan, including in residential areas, all the time. In June, even as the city started to hood the 206 meters (again) to avoid contempt of court, Beame protested that he was doing so "angrily" and predicted a "ghost town."[115] Beame aimed his message at business, predicting that this loss of parking would "wreak economic destruction."

The prediction spooked the *Times*, a previous supporter of the transportation-control plan. The mayor had once called Beame's stance "pollution paralysis."[116] Less than two years earlier, the paper's editorialists had said that the "influx of motor vehicles . . . already chokes the commerce of the city as well as the lungs."[117] Yet the paper had since determined that the federal government "has no business demanding environmental action that fails to look at its economic and planning consequences." Editorialists pronounced the paper "horrified by this pattern of government conduct"—not just by the mayor, but by the federal government. "If the federal government wishes to stimulate local action on . . . pollution, let it provide incentives."[118] The editorial board called the plan a "parking farce" and considered it "fanciful" to assume that "if parking were made more difficult and costly, that would reduce the volume of traffic." The *Times* added that "environmentalists have no business promising better air and traffic from measures that are . . . untested."[119]

The business community, too, blamed the federal government for enforcing the plan rather than blaming Beame for recalcitrance and incompetence. "Our patrons come by car," said Broadway's Richard Barr, president of the League of New York Theaters and Producers. "It's a strange way to kill off pollution . . . to kill off the theater."[120] "I'm angry," said the powerful chief of the Association for a Better New York, real estate developer Lew Rudin. "This . . . plan is a disgrace."

The NRDC attorneys Ross Sandler and David Schoenbrod pushed back against the air of crisis Beame was creating. In response to the *Times* editorial, the men wrote a letter that the *Times* printed, unusually, on its editorial page.[121] "Your criticism . . . is based upon confusion," they argued. "The order seeks to restrict only that on-street parking which blocks traffic. Most such parking is illegal parking. . . . The court's order applies no restriction to parking in residential areas [of Manhattan,] but does limit the time of use of the relatively few legal on-street spaces in commercial areas. In most cases, this limitation applies only during rush hours," they added. That is: nighttime theatergoers, to the limited extent they could find legal street parking before the order, thanks to restrictions going back to the 1920s, would be able to find limited legal street parking after the order. Schoenbrod called the city's focus on a fake parking ban "a cruel hoax."[122]

Days before the blackout distracted everyone, the NRDC lawyers found support from another corner: *Times* columnist John Oakes. Oakes derided Beame's "smoggy view." The mayor had "distort[ed] the meaning of the parking-limitation program" to scare New Yorkers rather than accept change. "A mixture of petulance, panic and politics . . . tells much about what is wrong with his administration."[123]

By August, the city reached an "understanding" with the federal government and the NRDC. "The parking ban that the city began implementing under duress . . . will be scrapped. The hoods will be removed from 206 parking meters in midtown, and parking will be permitted there after 6 P.M. Parking at 871 downtown meters will be banned only between 8 and 9 A.M."[124] Instead of the ban, the city would crack down on illegal parking.

Lost in Beame's supposed victory was the fact that the NRDC had gotten what it had asked for: a ban on rush-hour and some daytime parking. The transportation control plan "did fairly directly lead to a significant reduction in parking," says Michael Gerrard, environmental lawyer, Columbia professor, and former NRDC staffer. Of Midtown spaces, particularly during rush hour, "they're gone. . . . You can't park, or it's very expensive." By the 1980s, the city enacted a further reform, in compliance with the Clean Air Act. To discourage private off-street parking spaces, it largely prohibited new garages in Manhattan.[125]

Months after the NRDC compromise, Beame was gone, succeeded by Koch. Midtown drivers received no succor from the mayor who had taken the bus to his inauguration.[126] By 1978, the city was giving out 9.3 million parking summonses annually.[127] In 1979, Koch "smiled" as officials affixed an immobilizing boot to a "gleaming" Porsche that owed $570. "An excellent example of how New York works," the mayor told reporters.[128] In 1982, in unveiling bus lanes, Koch showcased his "favorite" sign: "Don't Even THINK of Parking Here."[129]

The Permanent Parking Scandal

In January 1986, Donald Manes, the Queens borough president, was "found dazed, with his left wrist and ankle slashed, in his car on the Grand Central Parkway."[130] Manes claimed that he was "kidnapped by two assailants who had hidden in . . . his car," a story that fell apart.[131] Two months later, Manes was dead, having stabbed himself in the heart in his kitchen.[132] Though Manes suffered mental illness, he was also caught up in corruption—a scandal that would mar Koch's third term and make famous a prosecutor named Rudolph Giuliani.

Machine Democrats from Queens, Brooklyn, and the Bronx had long controlled patronage in the city's parking violations bureau, no longer the efficient agency Lindsay had envisioned. Manes and fellow party bosses had used the bureau to enrich themselves. They had demanded kickbacks from companies that collected parking tickets on behalf of the city. They had also steered a twenty-two-million-dollar contract for a handheld computer for meter maids to a company, it turned out, that was part-owned by Bronx Democratic leader and Koch supporter Stanley Friedman. The company had no viable product. The scandal yielded six federal convictions as well as costing the jobs of the transportation commissioner, Anthony Ameruso, and staffers.[133]

For New Yorkers, this "parking violations bureau" scandal was the biggest corruption case connected to parking. Yet the real scandal remains. Unlike in the Lindsay era, it is not diplomats who leave cars illegally unattended without risking tickets. Rather, it is government workers, parking private vehicles and throwing fake "placards" in windshields to avoid a ticket. The issue isn't just money but congestion and pollution. One study found that "government workers, many of whom have free parking, are twice as likely to drive to work" in core Manhattan—27 percent versus 14 percent for private-sector workers.[134]

Elected officials, staffers, and uniformed workers have long seen illegal parking in Manhattan as a perk. One measure of how city workers consider parking a mark of rank, not just a financial benefit, is "ticket-fixing" scandals that have regularly emerged. In 1973, a parking violations bureau official in Brooklyn pled guilty to fixing one thousand tickets for "politically active" people.[135] As proceedings revealed, "judges, assemblymen, commissioners, marshals and their deputies had made nighttime trips to an apartment in Brooklyn to get their parking tickets fixed."[136] Ticket-fixing made little sense economically. Well-paid men, many of them officeholders with valuable reputations, had spent scarce time importuning flunkies to save them a few dollars. They risked exposure and arrest. Ticket-fixing was a status symbol, as was the ability to skirt a ticket in the first place. Tickets were for little people.

Since then, New York has solved the ticket-fixing problem the wrong way. First, the city issues too many parking placards to government workers. By 2008, when then-mayor Michael R. Bloomberg vowed "to take the passes away from city workers who view what should be a rare perk as an entitlement," as the *Times* put it, the number of legal placards had reached 142,000, seven times the level of the Lindsay years.[137] Bloomberg revoked some passes, but his successor, Bill de Blasio, re-awarded placards to tens of thousands of teachers. Second, the city unofficially refrains from issuing tickets to vehicles marked by fake placards. "Placard corruption," in the phrase of one anonymous activist who uses social media to publicize pictures of illegally parked cars, harms New York's ability to strengthen traffic laws: rules are meaningless if a good portion of the driving population can ignore them.

Back to No Parking

In Midtown and Lower Manhattan, little has changed since Whalen's 1920s-era rules. Private garages are expensive—upwards of $400 to $500 for a monthly space. Street parking remains mostly illegal, and where it's not, metered pricing works. It costs $5.50 an hour to park in Midtown's limited street spaces, $7 for commercial vehicles. Prices accelerate to discourage long-term parking, reaching $13 for the third and final hour. Prices fall short of garage prices, but parking is not an incidental cost.[138] It's not the "performance-based parking" expert Donald Shoup suggests, under which parking would be expensive enough to discourage demand and ensure that a space on every block remained free—but it comes close. Moreover, enforcement (except for vehicles with government placards) is consistent. Ticket prices, reaching $115, are not lower than garage prices.[139] The biggest parking problem in Midtown is not private cars. Rather, the problem is trucks stopping, double-parked, to deliver parcels. Construction staging clogs streets, taking up lanes of traffic for years as crews use their indefinitely parked equipment to demolish, build, or renovate skyscrapers.

Manhattan's lack of cheap parking is a success. Even as New York suffered population and job loss in the 1970s, Manhattan never endured degradation to such an extent that developers thought the best use of entire blocks of real estate was to store cars. New York avoided the fate of many American cities. Detroit, New Haven, New Orleans, and St. Louis downtowns lost chunks of their central cities, including offices and theaters, to acres of parking. The ultimate reason for New York's escape from the parking scourge was transit. In the mid-twentieth century, subways and commuter rail lines, even in their distressed state, poured millions of people into Manhattan daily. New York did not destroy its business and entertainment centers to lure commuters by car.

Core Manhattan has fewer parking spaces today than in the middle of the twentieth century. Between 1978 and 2010, garage and lot spaces shrunk from 128,000 to 102,000.[140] In the second decade of the new millennium, office and apartment projects further consumed parking. Residents and workers lived and worked where empty cars once sat.

Chapter 16

Our Right to Park

The High Cost of Residential Parking

> No citizen has the legal or moral right to use the public thoroughfare for parking his car.
>
> —New Yorker Saul Sigelschiffer, 1959

> If car owners can't leave their cars parked on the street overnight, where should the cars be parked?
>
> —New Yorker Norman Romanick, 1960

AS THE SUN SET ON SEPTEMBER 11, 2001, Manhattan, New York, America, and the world were in disbelief. The World Trade Center was gone. The vice president was in a bunker; the president had spent the day aboard Air Force One, evading potential attack. TV experts were explaining who Osama bin Laden was. Members of Congress from opposite parties were vowing to work together. New York reporters were interviewing people searching for family members.

After 9:00 p.m., networks and cable channels focused on the mayor, Rudolph Giuliani. The ashen mayor updated the world on the "horrific site" in Manhattan. "We'll do everything we can do support the efforts of the people who are trying to recover people from the—from the debris and the horror," he said. He praised volunteers. He warned against price gouging. He said schools would stay closed. Before he left the podium, Giuliani added one thing: "Alternate-side street parking is suspended."[1]

That Giuliani had devoted a moment on the most traumatic day in American history to parking regulation wasn't a sign of shock. Giuliani knew that New Yorkers would go to bed sleepless but also that many residents would wonder: Would I have to go outside and move my car, parked at the curb, the next morning, for street cleaning? Even though more than half of New York households do not have cars, large percentages who do own automobiles park their vehicles on the street. The logistics of parking, including having to move their cars from one side of the street to the "alternate" side to make way for street sweepers, pervade their lives, from what time to wake up to whether to visit a relative.

In the early days of the auto era, even as officials determined that parking in core Manhattan and other commercial districts could not be infinite and free, successive mayors and police officials groped witlessly toward expanding parking at the *other* end of car owners' journeys: homes. In residential districts, city officials, rather than discouraging this irritant, normalized the dysfunctional.

New York's parking hordes view parking on the street for free as an inalienable right. Parking politics also permeates life for New Yorkers who don't own automobiles. A right to park in residential neighborhoods has hindered New York's ability to reduce congestion and design safer streets. Even as New York has sliced slivers of road away from drivers, the city provides billions of dollars in real estate annually to car owners for public storage of this private asset, hampering goals of improving urban life by creating more space for biking, walking, sitting, dining, and trees.

No Overnight Parking

In the early twentieth century, if New York's burgeoning automotive class couldn't park their private property for a few hours in front of a store, they certainly couldn't park their cars for days in front of their homes. Describing a 1925 photo of the Upper West Side's Ninety-Sixth Street, writer Christopher Gray noted "much wider" sidewalks and fewer vehicles parked. "In the 1925 view there are only two vehicles parked on a street that now serves as a permanent garage for 120. . . . New Yorkers still considered the streets as built for transportation, not car storage."[2] Though residential roads were less congested than Manhattan thoroughfares, streets were narrow. With cars lining each curb, drivers would have only one lane. Any driver stopping to drop off a passenger or package would create traffic.

New Yorkers agreed with the ban on overnight parking, which had existed since the appearance of the car. In 1931, when police were, "during hard times," easing enforcement of "all-night anti-parking laws," Thomas Farmer Jr., chairman of the New York Board of Trade, objected. Business owners who had invested in private garages could not understand why the city would provide free competing space. "If . . . cars can stand in the streets all night," Farmer said, "garages should be free of taxes."[3]

In 1934, Mayor LaGuardia's police commissioner, John O'Ryan, announced "a new drive on illegal parking." Police "would remove to storage yards all automobiles parked in streets over night" where they "would be redeemable only after payments of fines." O'Ryan reminded New Yorkers further that cars "constitute obstructions . . . [and] are an expensive nuisance."[4]

Judges weren't lenient. In 1936, Dominco Dolonino, twenty-eight, of 413 W. Thirty-First Street, parked in front of his home overnight. "Two dollars' fine," Magistrate Anthony F. Burke told him. "Why don't you get a garage?" he inquired. "Do you think the public streets are garages?" "Well, your honor," Dolonino responded, "I only bought the thing for $5 . . . and it isn't worth the garage rent." The magistrate turned the economics of owning a cheap car against the offender. "Well, in that case, the fine will be $5," he said. "You have purchased a cheap automobile, but by the time you get through with it you'll find it a very expensive proposition."[5]

As resistence to anti-parking laws grew, New Yorkers grew annoyed with their neighbors' rudeness, and worse. The self-asserted right to parking—one not even legal—provoked passions. In 1937, fifty-year-old Archie Woods, a "retired builder," the *New York Times* reported, "died in front of his home at 3222 Bronx Boulevard . . . following an altercation and an exchange of blows with Joseph Vimmatore, 26, . . . over the latter's habit of parking his car in front of the Woods home."[6] In 1938, the *Times* noted, "The drive . . . against overnight parking serves as a useful reminder of a growing evil."[7]

Yet after World War II, police had trouble keeping up with car ownership. By 1940, the number of vehicles registered in New York City reached nearly one million; by 1950, it would soar to 1.4 million.[8] Veterans who weren't leaving for the suburbs with infant baby boomers still wanted to enjoy a car-based lifestyle. In 1947—the same year that Levittown opened on Long Island, luring white city dwellers to single-family homes—city police brass issued a memo telling officers not to be overzealous in issuing tickets to overnight parkers.

This "confidential" memo made news, with reporters interpreting it as a lifting of the ban. "Motorists hereafter may park their cars overnight . . . without fear," read one story. "The lifting of the ban . . . was in answer to mounting protests from individuals, the Automobile Club of New York and civic groups." After the directive became public, the commissioner, Arther Wallander, disavowed it. "I am opposed to overnight parking," Wallender said. "Parking of cars on the public thoroughfares constitutes one of the great problems."[9] The controversy was on the front page. New York's leaders had seemingly given drivers something, only to take it away—a result worse, from a political standpoint, than never having given in. "Motorists, who had looked hopefully for relief," were stunned," the *Times* said. The Auto Club president, Wlliam J. Gottlieb, charged police with adding "confusion to chaos."[10]

The biggest argument for on-street parking was lack of garage space. Most apartment buildings did not have garages; fire concerns had spurred the state legislature to declare most of them unlawful. "The city has not yet accommodated itself to a motor age," the *Times* said in 1938. Solutions included "inexpensive community garaging, which might be fostered by the city itself. Another is apartments which include housing for cars. . . . The city of the future must be built for cars as well as people."[11] When the legislature approved "fireproof garages" in 1939, the Merchants Association endorsed the plan "as a means of relieving the overnight parking problem."[12]

In 1950, to maintain its street-parking ban, the city turned this option for developers to build parking into a mandate. A zoning amendment required developers building apartment houses with more than forty units "in the most congested areas" to build parking spaces for one out of every five units and, in less congested areas, make space for off-street car parking for every home.[13] "Many families . . . are sure to own automobiles," the *Times* said. "Why complicate further the city's traffic future by not planning for the housing of these cars?"[14]

The *Times*'s argument was bolstered by the fact that in Stuyvesant Town and Peter Cooper Village, two 1940s Lower Manhattan housing developments, proximity to the subway and a lack of garage space didn't deter residents from purchasing vehicles. Within a decade, 11,250 families in the two developments had acquired 5,500 cars, with spaces for 2,400. City officials cut parking rates on nearby public land, from twenty to ten dollars. Residents weren't satisfied. People parked illegally, storing vehicles "for years at no-parking signs" with "comparative immunity."[15]

Even as developers built garages, they were expensive, compared to free. "Those who are so fortunate as to have garage space pay rental rates that are beginning to approach the housing rental," wrote Upper West Side resident Alexander Rubin in 1947. He called the practice of ticketing or towing vehicles "grossly unjust."[16] Gottlieb, of the Auto Club, called garage owners "unscrupulous" and accused them of "having a Roman holiday at motorists' expense."[17] Two years later, Henry Volk, a resident of a "quiet residential street" in Queens, argued, "As every one knows, cars are tightly parked on both sides of every residential and non-restricted street. . . . Every one knows that by parking his car overnight in front of his residence he breaks the law. . . . Every day of the year I break the city's parking law."[18]

Garage owners countered that space was plentiful; residents didn't want to pay for it. "While automobiles are parked bumper-to-bumper on most of the curb spaces from Eighty-Sixth Street north to the city line . . . space for 10,350 cars for day parking and 4,688 cars for night storage remains idle," a Chamber of Commerce report noted in 1949. Half of garages charged less than $25 a month ($325 in 2024 dollars).[19] "Motorists have had a lot of undeserved sympathy," the chamber concluded.

New York's government made a concession. Even without legal parking overnight, streets had become so crowded that the Sanitation Department was having a hard time keeping them clean. "There were curbs," one sanitation official said, "that we hadn't been able to see, much less sweep, for months."[20] Officials launched a novel practice, effective August 1, 1950: alternate-side-of-the-street parking. On the front page, the *Times* explained the rules. "Restrictions to prevent parked vehicles from hampering street cleaning will be tested on the Lower East Side," the paper told readers. "Rules will prohibit parking on the north side of numbered streets and the west side of avenues on Mondays, Wednesdays and Fridays, and on the south side of numbered streets and east side of avenues on Tuesdays, Thursdays and Saturdays." From 7:00 a.m. to 3:00 p.m., "the Sanitation Department will be able to make a clean sweep of one side of a street, . . . returning the next day to clean the other side."[21] "Alternate-side parking" expanded citywide, with the exception of Staten Island, whose residents lived in homes with driveways.

This rule resulted in cleaner streets—but normalized parking all night. By requiring people to move vehicles only every other day, the city was acknowledging reality: cars were parked indefinitely. Politically, alternate-side parking, as it became a New York institution, gave car owners a self-identity. "Alternate parking rules keep motorists grimly on the move," the *Times* said.[22] As car owners descended from apartments and homes three times a week (later reduced to two), at the same time, to move their cars, they were no longer affluent oddities deserving of no favors.

Rather, they became a persecuted class with a common interest. "Are you a traffic neurotic?" A *Herald Tribune* humor piece asked in 1953.[23] "Let's take the case of a man we'll call Harry Lee. He's married, two kids, good job, comes out of his house one morning and goes to get into a car. There's a ticket on the windshield. . . . His blood pressure shoots up. There's only one garage in his neighborhood, and it has a two-year waiting list. What do they expect him to do, swallow the car at night?" The idea of parking for days was no longer absurd; rather, the idea that one *couldn't*, as long as one put up with the "alternate side" dance, was absurd.

In 1954, Mayor Wagner capitulated to frustration. He commissioned experts to rewrite traffic laws. The biggest feature was "abolition of the one-hour and three-hour limits on parking in non-restricted areas [that is, most residential areas] and substitution of a seventy-two-hour limit." Now, people could park around the clock. "This is tantamount to legalizing free overnight parking in most residential areas for more than 600,000 motorists." From now on, "the city did not intend to strike at motorists who use their automobiles only on week-ends." The *Herald Tribune* approved, observing that "to legalize twenty-four-hour parking . . . is . . . accepting the facts of life. . . . As long as there are not enough built-in garages . . . it is only common sense."[24]

Wagner's decision wasn't unanimously applauded. William Bird, of the Twenty-Third Street Association, said it would "induce persons now keeping cars in garages to use the streets."[25] Though hundreds of thousands of New Yorkers parked on the street for free, most, still carless, did not. For them, parking remained a nuisance. In 1955, R. Bernstein wrote to the *Times* from Flatbush, Brooklyn, that nights had once been "peaceful." But since the free-parking decree, "there has been an influx of cars that has seriously interfered with the advantage of a private home. . . . The only beneficiaries . . . have been the automobile dealers, who have been able . . . to sell more cars to apartment-house dwellers."[26]

In legalizing all-night parking, Wagner had given away this benefit for free. Several groups, and the *Times*, had suggested a $60-a-year charge ($700 in 2024 dollars). But "that nuisance tax was rejected as . . . damaging politically."[27] The time to impose the fee would have been when the city first allowed all-night parking. Once people grew accustomed to free storage, they did not want to pay. Over ensuing decades, whenever the city encountered budget problems, good-government groups and minority-party politicians suggested the fee. But the idea always died a "quiet death." By the latter half of the twentieth century, more than eight hundred thousand people—voters—were parkers.[28] When the *Times* reminded readers in 1961 that "streets were never meant for unrestricted twenty-four-hour free parking," it lamented that the city had once again "balked" at levying an overnight tax because of "motorists' wrath."[29] In 1961, a zoning update required developers to build even more parking spaces, for at least 40 percent of apartments in denser parts of the city.[30] "The proposed zoning accepts the existence of the automobile," the planning commission said.[31]

Yet there never was enough off-street parking to induce people off the free curb. Officials were regularly reminded of how difficult it would be to revoke free parking. In the late 1960s and early 1970s, Lindsay attacked Midtown parking abuse, but he had no hope of enforcing parking laws outside of core Manhattan. As Capt. Thomas Guthrie of the police's traffic-enforcement division said in 1973, the strategy was to "capture the midtown area" and move outward, but the enemy in this territorial war was never vanquished.[32] Meter-maid ranks numbered in the hundreds; police were overwhelmed with crime.

Even with free parking, abuses were emblematic of disorder. In 1971, FDNY commander William C. Rinsdale died at a fire in the Bronx's Tremont neighborhood, a fire that had raged because of double-parked cars blocking hydrants. Fire commissioner Robert Lowery condemned "parking violations that impede fire-fighting and jeopardize lives" and noted that a civilian had died under similar circumstances.[33] A year later, a retired surgeon died in a Bronx fire when firefighters couldn't get through, again blocked by illegally parked cars. Lowery termed the death "homicide."[34]

In 1971, Lindsay installed two hundred parking meters in Greenwich Village. The reasoning was that the area wasn't entirely residential; round-the-clock parkers were taking spaces that shoppers needed. Elected officials demanded the meters' removal. One politician who showed up at a rally to oppose meters: Ed Koch, by then a congressman. Koch was untroubled by inconsistency between his opposition to new roads and his support for clogging existing road space up with parked cars.[35] The *Times* reported, "In the East Village, residents spray paint on parking meters so meter maids cannot tell how long the car has been there."[36]

Until the mid-1990s, when broken-windows policing helped bring order to the streets, car owners were themselves victims. "Gwen Krause has a problem," was one 1993 tale. "She has a car in New York City. One rainy night, vandals smashed a window, and the passenger compartment turned into a little lake. Another day, another headache: a double-parked BMW boxed her into a parking space. She had to interrupt a drug deal."[37] The era was plagued by radio thefts; "NO RADIO" signs in windshields encapsulated disorder. "The best thing to do is carry your stereo off with you as conspicuously as possible," a writer counseled in 1990, so that thieves would know it wasn't in the car.[38]

An Entrenched Entitlement, with a Personal Cost

In the modern era, New York's parking stasis is exacerbated by the fact that few car owners use them for common tasks: driving to work, to the supermarket, to the doctor. In Manhattan, before the COVID-19 pandemic, just 6 percent of workers drove to their jobs. Even on Staten Island, whose car ownership mirrors the nation's, just 56 percent of people drove to work alone.

Even for the wealthy, using a car to commute and run errands has long been expensive and inconvenient. In 1984, Donald Tober, president of Sugar Foods Corporation, rented two Manhattan garage spaces—one near his Upper East Side home, for $450 monthly ($1,380 in 2024 dollars) and one near Wall Street, at a price he "declined to disclose"—commuting in his BMW between the two. Tober, though, said that for noontime lunch, he would "take a taxi."[39]

Cars, then, particularly in residential Manhattan and Brooklyn, sit at the curb, unused except, ironically, for the reason Moses-era New York built parkways: so middle-class and affluent city dwellers could leave the city for recreation. In May 2008, a fifty-one-year-old graphic designer named Sarah returned with her husband to their Prospect Park West home in leafy Park Slope, Brooklyn, from a Hamptons weekend. For twenty-five minutes, the couple circled their neighborhood until they found a spot for their high-end Infiniti. "I was lucky," said her sixty-four-year-old husband, David.

But the couple didn't enjoy their luck. The city had suspended area alternate-side parking rules to replace metal signs with updated rules meant to reduce drivers' burden, as the city was cutting sweeping time from three hours each cleaning day to ninety minutes. Sarah and David were glad they wouldn't have to move their car for a few hours each week. They realized, however, that the suspension of the rules meant that other people wouldn't have to move their cars either. "Everyone is making these dire predictions that people from other neighborhoods are going to park here," Sarah said. "We're a little concerned. . . . One neighbor said he was thinking of getting a car [because of greater ease of parking]. In summer, parking is usually great because everyone is gone [to summer homes]. So if there aren't spots, we'll know if people from outside are parking."

When street sweeping resumed after two months, an Alfa Romeo began collecting tickets for not complying with the rules. Its owner, eighty-five-year-old Vincent Banescu, "shy but friendly," had died. Although Banescu rarely drove his car, he had "moved it from one side of the street to the other on alternate-side parking days," a neighbor said. "The man is dead," someone wrote on one of his parking-ticket envelopes.

People who park on the street for free are not irrational. For them, the benefit outweighs the cost. Errol, a resident of Crown Heights, Brooklyn, who has parked on the street for thirty-seven years, needs a car to take him across the city for work on short notice. "Until the black cars arrived [in the 1980s]," he notes in 2022, "you weren't going to get a cab back to Brooklyn." For work trips, taking the train from the Bronx to Coney Island is out of the question because it takes too long. After hours, when "I feel like it's dangerous, I don't have to take the subway."

An even bigger reason for residents to hold on to their cars is "freedom and mobility." When Errol attended grad school outside of the city, he could stop to see his parents in the suburbs. Like many car owners, the need for a personal vehicle increased with his family size. "I get married, I have a lovely wife who is pregnant, one time too many, nobody [on the subway] would get up and give her a seat." Renovating a brownstone, he notes, "I'm not hauling stuff on a frickin' bus." He drives his child to school because "bus service to Red Hook [a different part of Brooklyn] may as well be nonexistent."

Owning a car hasn't been easy. In the 1980s, the problem was vandalism. "I got one of those radios that would pull out," Errol says, because replacing a broken window was expensive. By 2019, he had a new problem: when he first moved to Crown Heights, many properties were empty, and it was easy to find a spot. "It is becoming increasingly difficult . . . as the Park Slope-ization of Crown Heights continues. I can try to console myself with the thought that this is what you were hoping for, people would come." As for paying for a garage, at $250 to $300 a month, it's "just expensive."

Greg, of the Upper West Side, agrees that benefits of car ownership, including free parking, outweigh costs. Greg and his wife bought a car because they had a baby. His wife uses the car to drive to her parents' house in the suburbs once a week; the two will pick up groceries. Taking the subway with a baby, Greg says, "is hard; it's stressful." Greg also grew annoyed with subway delays. "I really don't like the subway," says Greg. "I was finding the subways exhausting and annoying right before the pandemic because of all the delays. I usually just take it to work. I had stopped using the subways for leisure activities," taking an Uber or renting a Zipcar instead.

But surge pricing, for both services, put him off. The price to rent or hire a car "surges . . . when everyone . . . needs a car," he says, such as on holiday weekends. Greg and his wife park on the street rather than in a garage. "My wife felt pretty confident in her ability to find parking," he says. "It's not hard. [There are] only a few weeks of the year when parking is terrible." When going out of town for the weekend, "we would just have to be back by 2 p.m. on Sunday, or parking is hard to find." He'll still take Uber, though, when the price is reasonable, because "I'm not going to waste my parking spot."

Parking or Safe Biking?

If something is free, why not take it? But, as economists say, free is not free. As early—or late—as the 1970s, urbanists objected to parked cars. They "disfigure block after block," lamented *The Pedestrian Revolution* in 1974. "Streets are despoiled for the convenience of a small number." Residential parking creates traffic: one city study showed that between 28 and 45 percent of drivers were cruising for parking.[40]

Aesthetics and inconvenience, though, are not the biggest problems. Parking impacts safety and transit. People sit on buses behind double-parked cars because of politicians' fear of removing parking. Pedestrians and cyclists have suffered injury and died because of an unwillingness to cede space. When New Yorkers oppose bike lanes, it's often because they are fearful of losing parking spots. In 2018, when the community board in Forest Hills, Queens, opposed the Queens Boulevard bike lane, they did so because it would cost 202 parking spaces.[41] Lizi Rahman, whose son, Asif, had died riding his bicycle on Queens Boulevard in 2008—trying to avoid a double-parked vehicle—notes that the city delayed the project for two years, over people "losing the parking spots."

On the Upper West Side, too, residents have chosen parking over bike lanes. "I would come home in tears" from community board meetings, says Mary Beth Kelly, the Upper West Side resident whose husband, Carl Henry Nacht, was killed in 2006 on the Hudson River bike path. "There was such animosity. It took four years to get a protected bike lane on Columbus Avenue. . . . It took so goddamm long." Referring to the UCLA professor who has long advocated for market pricing of parking spaces, Kelly says, "Donald Shoup was on to the whole thing. It was almost like [a right to parking] was in the Bill of Rights, even though here on the Upper West Side, less than half the people own cars."

Fear of parking-space loss impedes transit by harming support for bus lanes. In 2018, the city "significantly scaled" back a proposed bus lane through Brooklyn. Some residents had feared the loss of 134 parking spots and preferred to inconvenience 28,000 daily bus riders.[42] In 2019, when area resident Arthur Schwartz sued to prevent the Fourteenth Street busway near Manhattan's Union Square, he charged that the city had "already installed their bike lanes . . . and eliminated 1,075 parking spaces."[43]

Street advocates have tried a fun approach. In 2007, activists launched annual "Parking Days." One fall day, Transportation Alternatives and other groups paid the meter charge for eighteen parking spaces and set up grass, lawn chairs, picnic tables, and umbrellas, asking passersby to join them sunning in these "parks." "People stopped, stared," Peter Goldwasser, then policy director for Upper West Side councilwoman Gale Brewer, who had commandeered one space, told the *Times*. "It's a visually incongruous thing that gets people thinking."[44]

The Pushback to Pricing Parking

For residential parking, in contrast to commercial district parking, New York has never used one valuable tool to change behavior: pricing. The free market, via the scarcity of garage space and the high price for such space, sends a message to New Yorkers in dense neighborhoods: it makes little sense to have a car in a city in which relatives, neighbors, friends, jobs, schools, and entertainment are accessible by public transportation or by walking or cycling. The reason New York is so accessible by train, bus, or foot is density. That density makes car ownership burdensome and costly.

But the city has thwarted this signal with free parking. "You're never going to get efficient use of the street giving it away for free," says Howard Yaruss, a native Brooklynite and longtime Manhattan resident who is co-chairman of the transportation committee of the Upper West Side's community board.[45] The goal is not to eliminate parking, as New York is never going to eliminate cars.

The goal, rather, is to reveal the true cost of parking. If the city were to charge for residential spaces, the price would reveal to New Yorkers whether they need a car. As Greg, the Upper West Side parker, notes, "[Pricing would] weed out the people who don't need the cars. Half my neighborhood only takes it to the weekend house." The person who inherited a cheap car might decide that the cost is not worth the benefit. "The best way to do it is to use price," Shoup says. By charging New Yorkers, the city might learn that "the value . . . may be higher" for another use, Shoup adds.[46] An Upper West Side resident might pay two hundred dollars a month for a corner space; the restaurant on the same corner might pay one thousand dollars, because its owner generates more economic activity by serving dozens of people rather than just one.

Neighborhood residents, too, whether they own cars or not, could benefit from pricing street parking. As Shoup has suggested, the city could devote money from parking fees in a neighborhood to street-scale amenities, such as transit passes for everyone on the block. The city could even distribute the cash to all nearby households. A superior use of a parking space might not even be private or priced. Planting trees and grass where cars once sat could mitigate flooding from storms; replacing parking with a bus lane would speed transit trips.

In 2019, Yaruss took a step toward exploring charges for residential parking. He proposed a resolution to fellow transportation committee members on the Upper West Side board: "Allowing the vast majority of street space . . . to be used for free parking needs to be revisited," the resolution read. "City-owned land is a precious resource, . . . and . . . should be used in a manner that helps those in need and/or creates the greatest good for the greatest number of people. Free parking for private cars strongly encourages private car use. . . . It also exacerbates economic inequality by directing limited city resources to private car owners." The committee asked the city to consider paid parking permits or meters "capable of surge pricing."[47]

Yaruss explains his reasoning. He notes the "opportunity cost" in lost opportunities for bus and bike lanes. "Every parking spot is a fight," he says. For example, an area apartment building asked the community board to approve the removal of one spot in favor of a loading zone so that "disabled people can get in and out of a taxi—it was voted down." (Parking beneficiaries often argue that disabled people suffer from parking space loss, but better street management would make room for people with disability license plates to park.)

Yaruss's resolution provoked a firestorm. A retired doctor told the *Times* that the idea was "insanity. . . . There are fewer parking spaces now than . . . ever," he added, citing "bicycle lanes" that were "punishing drivers." Another Upper West Side resident, who said he "mostly uses the car on weekends," saw an "anti-car agenda." "There are people who were living in this neighborhood when it was crack-infested and who . . . are now being forced out because they can't afford . . . a $500-a-month garage."[48]

Comments in the *West Side Rag* community paper were similar. "Do they want us to double park?" asked one resident.[49]

The committee toned down the resolution, asking the city for a study. Yaruss wasn't surprised. "I was surprised at the vehemence," he adds. Even the proposal for a study—never completed—was controversial. "People were saying, 'we prefer ignorance.'"

Part 4

UNFINISHED BUSINESS

Chapter 17

Fast Forward

Plans to Fix New York's Bus System

> The city doesn't work if the buses don't work.
>
> —Danny Pearlstein, Riders Alliance policy director

> Bus lanes on 149th St. have been a great addition . . . yet more needs to be done to alleviate congestion, especially cars.
>
> —Karen S., Melrose, the Bronx, 2021

COMPARED TO THE SUBWAY BACKBONE, buses are New York's atrophied muscles. Before COVID-19 hit the city in 2020, bus ridership had been falling for years, from 908 million passengers in 2008 to 678 million in 2019.[1] As traffic worsened, riders with options had deserted the lumbering vehicles for Ubers and bicycles. Elected officials were more interested in posing at a ribbon-cutting ceremony for the Second Avenue Subway that cost billions of dollars than in finding new ways for buses to serve their communities. Fewer than two-thirds of New Yorkers live within walking distance of a subway station; to those who don't—as well as to elderly and disabled residents, pregnant women, and parents of children in strollers, who find it difficult to navigate stairs—buses are the only affordable form of transportation.

New York's bus network serves lower-income people who commute from one part of a sprawling outer borough to another rather than to a Manhattan office. According to a pre-COVID MTA survey, 36 percent of bus riders had household incomes of under $50,000, compared to

28 percent of subway riders; 35 percent of people who commuted both by bus and subway had incomes under $50,000; 26 and 27 percent of bus-only and bus-and-subway commuters were black, higher than the 19 percent share of the population and compared to 20 percent of subway-only commuters; 6 percent of bus riders were over sixty-five years old, 50 percent higher than on subways.[2]

Statistics also pointed up New York's complexity. Although bus riders were more likely to be poor, they weren't universally poor; 16 percent of bus commuters had incomes exceeding $150,000. For many people, the bus was the only choice, yet some New Yorkers took the bus by choice, including down Fifth Avenue from Upper East Side apartments to Midtown offices. The bus can serve riders better than it has—and attract more customers. But buses need more room on New York's streets, room that the city is reluctant to take away from cars.

The Trolleys' Sad Successors

Buses that replaced trolleys starting in the 1930s never had their golden age. One drawback, compared to the trolleys, was speed: in 1947, the Broadway streetcar had run at 6.5 to 7 miles per hour; the buses ran at 6 miles per hour.[3] Another drawback was cost. Despite Mayor Hylan's promise as he dismantled streetcars, neither private companies nor the city could profit from a five-cent bus fare. In 1947, the city bought out bankrupt bus lines.[4] The lines remained "chronic and heavy money losers."[5] In 1948, the city, in charge of all subways and substantial portions of bus routes, capitulated to reality, increasing the subway fare from a nickel to ten cents and the bus fare to seven cents. In 1953, the fare for both increased to fifteen cents (although fare hikes for remaining private bus lines remained irregular).

Sudden fare hikes were harder on riders than gradual fare increases would have been. The 1953 fare hike alienated transit passengers, but buses performed worse. Subways lost 9 percent of passengers, but buses lost 18 percent, with ridership on city-owned lines falling from 547 million to 449 million.[6] City officials disavowed the idea that the higher fare had chased passengers away, with the top transit official saying that people staying home to watch television were to blame.[7]

Passengers suffered poorer service. As early as 1948, one bus rider noted that a twenty-five-minute wait in the rain afforded "time to wonder why they called the changeover from trolleys to buses 'progress.'" Buses were crowded and dirty.[8] Private-line buses "were so overcrowded that people waiting at bus stops could not get on."[9] Cold weather strikes against the dwindling number of private lines, as the Transport Workers Union insisted that workers for private companies earn what their counterparts earned on city-owned buses, caused customers to choose an alternative, often the car, further slowing buses.[10]

The creation in 1953 of the New York City Transit Authority to manage previously private sector bus lines didn't result in better service or cost control. The idea, as with the authority's management of the subways, was that an organization with an independent board, removed from politics, could rein in costs and raise fares. But costs continued to rise.[11] Worsening the deficits was the fact that the government first took over bus routes that lost the most money, as private operators held onto profitable lines.

As it took over buses, the city didn't inherit the shiny vehicles that had replaced trolleys. Buses were old. In 1955, three hundred of the city's two thousand buses "would have to be junked."[12] Faced with the need to buy replacements and to placate the union, the city adopted a policy that would become a template: as passengers fled and lower ridership could "not justify all the service now provided," service fell further, alienating more riders.[13] Figures for ridership are not reliable because of the persistence of private lines, but news accounts hint that by the mid-1950s, ridership had fallen to 750 million, a drop of 25 percent from billion-rides-a-year trolley peaks.[14]

By 1955, the union and the remaining private bus lines commissioned Theodore Kheel, labor arbitrator and transit expert, to study the crisis. "The sharp drop in riding," Kheel concluded, "is tied directly and inseparably to the city's Number One Problem: Traffic."[15] Kheel warned the city to "solve these related twin evils of traffic congestion and transit declines."[16] The city remained passive, and less than a decade later, most private lines were gone. In 1962, after a management misjudgment—the company laid off senior workers, precipitating a strike—Fifth Avenue Coach's buses fell into city hands. The transit authority was now responsible for nearly all money-bleeding buses.[17] Between 1963 and 1973, ridership on the now city-owned Manhattan and Bronx lines fell another 20 percent.[18]

Outside Manhattan, buses faced new competition: illegal "dollar vans." Dollar vans were the result of abysmal bus service. Harris Schechtman, an MTA bus planner, remembers that even with lower ridership in the 1970s, "five or six buses would go by before you could even get a bus that would stop for you, because the buses were so packed. You take this situation and add an entrepreneurial mind, I can buy a crummy fifteen-passenger van for peanuts, all I have to do is swoop in [down major corridors] and fill it up for a dollar a passenger." Most dollar-van operators were immigrants, and word spread within ethnic groups that vans were dependable. New York eventually reluctantly embraced dollar van operators. The city licensed operators for driver and vehicle safety, forbidding drivers from picking up passengers at bus stops. "Many of them created parallel routes a block away," Schechtman says, and customers "were so loyal" that they followed.[19]

Experimenting with Express Bus Lanes

During the latter half of the twentieth century, bus ridership did increase in one field. As New Jersey suburbs increased in population, commuters returned to work in Manhattan. But New Jersey did not have adequate rail. New Jersey depended on buses to bring commuters into the Port Authority Bus Terminal, completed in 1950. By 1963, 120,000 people were coming into the Manhattan terminus each day.[20]

The Port Authority pioneered another innovation: bus lanes. In 1970, the authority inaugurated an exclusive bus lane, XBL, that allowed buses to cut through highway traffic through the Lincoln Tunnel to Manhattan. The XBL featured a "contraflow" lane, meaning that during rush hours, buses could use a lane that normally went in the opposite direction. Once through the tunnel in New York, buses used ramps, part of the original terminal, to bring them into the midtown drop-off point, avoiding traffic.[21]

The Port Authority's experiment proved that when people did not have to sit in traffic, they were willing to take buses. By 2015, more than 225,000 people were entering Manhattan from New Jersey, Staten Island, and other points north and west of Manhattan each weekday by bus. New Jersey's bus commuters comprised 40 percent of people coming into Manhattan each day from that state, dwarfing the number coming in by car (the rest came in by rail). Indeed, within a little over three decades—since 1981, when the city's economy and population began growing—the number of people commuting from New Jersey had risen by two-thirds, from 342,000 people to 568,000, but the number of vehicles coming from New Jersey into Manhattan had risen by just 3,000, or 3 percent, from 88,000 to 91,000.[22] Buses made up more than half of people coming over the Hudson River into Manhattan, but they did so in less than 7 percent of vehicles.[23] New York City could not have absorbed these commuters via automobile.

New York City pioneered an innovation around the same time the Port Authority did: express buses. In 1968, Lindsay, in another effort to cut traffic, launched a premium service to take workers from the Bronx, eastern

Queens, and Staten Island into Manhattan without having to make stops. Express buses were part of Lindsay's initiative to improve quality of life for middle-class people who might leave the city. For a higher fare—one dollar, compared to the twenty-cent subway and bus fare—riders could enjoy a faster direct ride to and from an outer-borough neighborhood, and, later, ride on a smoother bus with comfortable seats. "It's a great way to commute," said Herb Solomon, an accountant who lived in Fresh Meadows, a leafy Queens neighborhood, and commuted to Herald Square. "When I was taking the subway, I arrived home a nervous wreck." By 1970, ten thousand people were taking express buses daily; 17 percent of the customers had previously taken a car.[24] In 1971, Lindsay took the express bus into Manhattan from Fresh Meadows—after first arriving there by "limousine"—to celebrate the ten millionth rider.[25] During that year's Christmas crush, the city followed the Port Authority's and New Jersey's lead, reversing a traffic lane on the Long Island Expressway and creating a bus-only lane on Fifty-Seventh Street, to cut ten minutes from six thousand Queens residents' commute. One paper praised it as an "earlier supper." Express buses were a refuge from subway crime: "People sleep without fear," wrote a Bronx resident in 1981.[26]

Express buses had shortcomings. Because many riders had previously taken the subway, they created traffic. They became expensive to run, the MTA's most heavily subsidized service. Still, in the 1970s, express buses were the bright spot in a deteriorating transit system. As Brian Ketcham wrote in his air-quality implementation report in 1973, a recent 2 percent increase in bus ridership, "mostly from Queens," was "due entirely to the advent of the new express bus." By 2013, more than forty-eight thousand people were taking a New York City express bus into Manhattan each day.[27] By then, subways were so packed that relieving trains of passengers was a benefit.

New Yorkers' Resistance to Bus Lanes

Express buses succeeded because they had a powerful constituency—semi-suburban commuters, many in swing districts. But regular bus riders continued to suffer. The biggest problem was making room for buses on car-crowded streets. In the 1970s, seeking an improvement to air quality and trying to stanch depopulation, New York City officials gave some room to buses, but progress was as halting as the bus.

Lindsay cracked down on illegally parked and idling cars in 1970, not just to improve air quality, but to allow buses to move. In January, the mayor said the city would install bus lanes on First and Second Avenues, east of Midtown.[28] Bus speeds increased by 20 percent.[29] Two years later, traffic control agents could write tickets to vehicles in bus lanes. Ketcham's 1973 blueprint for complying with the Clean Air Act suggested eight bus-only lines in Midtown and along outer-borough thoroughfares, including Queens Boulevard and Ocean Parkway. Outside of Manhattan, though, even modest steps encountered opposition.

A decade later, the Koch administration, as part of its program for "profound change" after the 1980 transit strike, proposed bus lanes.[30] In 1981, over the objections of the Fifth Avenue Association, the city reserved two Madison Avenue lanes for buses during rush hours. Twenty-four thousand people traveled by bus in the corridor during the afternoon, while only eleven thousand traveled by car. As Sam Schwartz, then-assistant transportation commissioner, noted, "It is not only that the buses will move more swiftly, but they will move with more reliability," with fewer buses bunching together.[31] The lanes were a success, with speeds up 68 percent. By 1982, the city expanded bus lanes to other Manhattan avenues, including Sixth and Fifth, this time with the Fifth Avenue Association's approval. Signs in "red zones" warned, "Don't even THINK about parking here," on penalty of a $100 fine.[32] Other signs told drivers, "It's this bus or 50 cars."[33]

Not everyone was happy. When the city restricted crosstown traffic to buses on Forty-Ninth and Fiftieth Streets, thoroughfares through Rockefeller Center, hotels, store owners, and customers complained. Mrs. Edwin L. Hilson, a Waldorf-Astoria hotel resident, fretted, "My chauffeur won't be able to get the car."[34] One complainer was Katharine Hepburn, who wrote Schwartz a clipped letter. Writing as "the owner of property," she wrote, "it is impossible to confine deliveries . . . to the morning hours." The plan "deprives us of access to our homes . . . and . . . reduces the commercial value."[35] As bus lanes expanded, enforcement waned, especially as government employees parked in the lanes.[36]

Rebuilt Buses, Rebuilt Interest

In the 1980s, bus riders benefited from the MTA's new tax money. One impetus was a crisis. In 1980, the MTA began running a new, comfortable bus: the Grumman Flexible, built by a Long Island–based defense contractor diversifying business lines as the Cold War waned. The buses were lemons. "We were under tremendous political pressure to ignore the problems," says Schechtman, "because this was a New York corporation. Grumman would meet with the elected [officials], and say, there's nothing wrong with our buses, it's the poor quality of the streets." Officials visited other cities using Grumman buses and found the same problems. In 1984, a bus caught fire in Midtown. The MTA pulled all 871 out of service.[37] "It was a disaster," says Schechtman, because the buses accounted for a quarter of the fleet. The MTA procured temporary buses from other cities. "The only buses that these places offered us, was their worst buses. . . . A ragtag fleet was operating . . . under the livery of other cities." The crisis concentrated attention on the importance of buses. "The crisis was so bad that it . . . did kind of trigger things," says Schechtman. By then, bus depots "were over 95 years old, and none were less than 25. The [oldest] were built as horse-car barns. They didn't function well. You see these movies with the abandoned mental hospital, that's what these depots were like."[38] The MTA rebuilt depots.

Riders benefited from better operating practices. "The bus operation wasn't particularly well run," remembers Ted Orosz, a bus-planning manager for the MTA for three decades, who had grown interested in buses as a child riding a Queens Boulevard route to school, wondering why buses bunched up. "They weren't clean. There certainly wasn't any concept of customer service. In the Eighties, [though,] there started to be a lot more . . . professionalism." Just as subway managers stopped sending trains out unless they were graffiti-free, bus managers stopped sending buses out if they weren't in good condition. "A bus didn't leave the garage unless someone said yes, it is fit to go out, there are no rats in the back in sexual congress."[39]

Beyond infrastructure, the MTA took "baby steps," as Schechtman puts it, toward customer service. It did things as simple as listing bus routes in papers in geographical order, rather than alphabetical order, to help customers navigate multi-bus journeys. It renamed bus routes so that they matched streets. "The M106 was 42nd Street," Orosz recalls, a legacy of private routes' numbering. "We said, why don't we make it the M42? . . . Not really a Nobel Laureate concept." Schechtman convinced the MTA's board to approve a limited program called Add-a-Ride, allowing customers to transfer between buses without paying another fare. "The board was reluctant to approve it because [board members] worried about losing money." Instead, the pilot gained customers and "demonstrated . . . free transfers could work."

Unlike subways, buses didn't gain riders as the city reversed 1970s population losses. By 1996, as subway ridership increased, bus patronage was at a record low of 436 million, less than half of the number of passengers trolleys had moved.[40] The consolation was that for many riders, thanks in part to Schechtman's earlier work, the bus became free. After 1997, passengers transferring to a bus from the subway, and vice versa, could swipe magnetic MetroCards and pay one fare.

Mayor Bloomberg: A Champion of Buses

In July 2001, Michael Bloomberg, the long-shot Republican candidate, presented a "vision for traffic." It featured an odd idea: to "establish a 'subway on the surface' on the East Side of Manhattan."[41] The mayor said that on First and Second Avenues, site of Lindsay's first bus lanes, and far from any subway, "high-speed, limited-stop" buses could run along an "enforced, semi-dedicated right of way"—like trolley tracks. As to how to keep cars out of the lanes, the would-be mayor suggested cameras. "Cameras could even be mounted on the buses themselves, as is done in London." In his pledge to take "at least one form of mass transit" each day, Bloomberg added, at Sam Schwartz's private suggestion, "It could be a bus." Unlike bike lanes and pedestrian plazas, Bloomberg focused on bus service from his first days in office.

Gene Russianoff of the Straphangers Campaign, with his knack for gimmicks to gain attention, was in the vanguard of press coverage. In 2002, Bloomberg's first year, Straphangers and Transportation Alternatives launched the "Pokey" awards, with "winners"— buses running from just 4.3 to 5.6 miles per hour—receiving a virtual golden snail. Advocates were coming together to support faster buses. Joan Byron, then-director of policy for New York's Pratt Center for Community Development, a planning organization affiliated with the Pratt Institute design college, was one of the first to realize the possibilities. Byron, a Brooklyn resident, was originally from upstate New York. An architect by training, Byron had dropped out of Pratt, having run out of money, but remained there to work. Until the 2000s, her job involved working with community groups to build and maintain "deeply affordable housing." Starting in the Koch administration, Pratt worked with community groups purchasing land or buildings from the city, which had taken over properties abandoned by their owners. By the new century, "that pipeline of abandoned buildings had dried up."[42]

It was a good-news, bad-news problem: without abandoned housing to rebuild and with a booming population, "people who work service jobs, manual jobs, [were] pushed further and further away [from workplaces]," Byron says. As lower-income New Yorkers were priced out of neighborhoods such as Harlem and Bedford-Stuyvesant, workplaces also "became even more dispersed." Women were working as home-health aides, and men were working on construction sites. With funding from Brooklyn and Manhattan congressman Jerrold Nadler, "the first map we ever did was . . . people who had to commute more than an hour and made less than the median income." The pattern jumped out so clearly that Pratt researchers called it the "rash map" of red dots: "Folks who were not close to subway lines," with "no prospect of subway lines. . . . That left buses."

By "chance," Byron met Enrique Peñalosa, mayor of Bogota, Columbia, who was building "bus rapid transit" lines. In a city with no subway, buses functioned like trains, with dedicated lanes, multiple entrance and exit points, and fast fare payment, with customers paying at kiosks before boarding. Byron thought advocating for better buses in New York fit "our mission, [which] was to work at the intersection of the physical planning . . . and longstanding issues of social and economic justice."

At the same time, a traditional advocacy group, the Tri-State Transportation Campaign, was growing interested in buses. Veronica Vanterpool joined Tri-State in 2007. She had grown up in the Bronx and understood the necessity and frustration of the bus. "I lived in Castle Hill. I needed to take three city buses to Spellman," a Catholic school. "I would rely on the buses, not the subways, just because" as a child, "I didn't have much reason to get to Manhattan." She absorbed that "getting from the East Bronx to the West Bronx was always a hassle."[43]

Bloomberg was interested in buses for the same reason he became interested in bikeshare: the world was doing it. Peñalosa's bus rapid transit project in Bogota "was getting global attention," remembers Jon Orcutt, the Tri-State Transportation Campaign director who later worked at City Hall. London, too, as part of its program to charge cars to enter the central city, had put three hundred more buses in new bus lanes in 2003, and ridership had risen 37 percent.[44] Bloomberg, Orcutt says, was "susceptible to the argument that other [cities] were doing it better."[45] Advocates had another factor on their side: ridership was up. In 1998, following the beginning of free transfers between buses and subways, 626.6 million New Yorkers rode the bus, up from the low of 436 million in 1996.[46] Nudged by transfers, people were growing so fed up with overcrowded subways that they chose the bus.

The city faced a problem, though: it controlled streets, but the state-run Metropolitan Transportation Authority controlled buses. Deputy mayor Dan Doctoroff, readying the city for environmentally sustainable growth, asked the department of transportation to talk to the MTA, which, in 2004, identified five potential routes in five boroughs. As Janette Sadik-Khan took control of the transportation department in 2007, the city and the

MTA prepared a demonstration. "It would not have happened without her," says Orosz. "You labor away in government, and you prepare a lot of plans and a lot of them aren't going anywhere. But once in a while the stars will line up, and when the stars line up for you, for goodness sake, don't mess it up."[47]

The new service—"select bus service"—wasn't quite bus-rapid transit. Buses wouldn't have dedicated rights-of-way entirely protected from cars by barriers. But riders would pay before boarding, inserting their MetroCard into a curbside machine. They could use multiple doors to enter the longer-than usual "accordion" bus with a distinctive design—a "psychedelic, polka-dot bus," the *New York Times* called it—saving minutes queuing. Buses would have their own lane (although enforcement was, as ever, iffy). Signal communication enabled the bus to keep a light green for longer. Bus operators would no longer stick to a set schedule, but rather would go from one end of the route to the other and then turn around, cutting delays created when a bus was ahead of schedule and idled at a stop.

The test: Fordham Road, one of the mid-Bronx's busiest thoroughfares. Fordham Road was a natural pilot. Crossing the Bronx east and west, "it served so many purposes," says Vanterpool. "It served so many destinations, connected with so many subway lines" for people who didn't have subway access near their homes, "hospitals, the high school, shopping districts." To the east, it connected to Co-op City, a high-rise neighborhood with no subway. The avenue crossed where population was dense and "where car ownership is low." Nearly two-thirds of households in the corridor had no car, with 71 percent commuting via transit, cycling, or walking.[48]

Advocates spent months explaining the concept to Fordham Road residents and businesses. "I remember going to a lot of community board meetings," says Vanterpool, "building relationships. . . . Over and over, look[ing] at transit data, . . . we really broke down who was using transit. . . . We were able to . . . say, look, in this community, a very high percentage of residents are using the bus."[49] At meetings, says Orosz, people would say, "you were nice enough to come and talk to us, no one ever comes and talks to us." Businesses were concerned about parking. But once the city made it clear that they could unload goods during certain hours—the first use in New York of a "delivery window" for a bus lane—they were mollified. Another factor: once business leaders understood that elected officials unanimously supported the plan, they knew there wasn't much point in objecting. "It is not every day that bus riders in the Bronx find themselves on the cutting edge," the *Times* said in June 2008, when the service launched. By fall, travel time had fallen by 20 percent. The number of riders had increased by 7 percent, to forty-six thousand each day. Ninety-eight percent of riders were happy.[50]

Bloomberg used the success to gain support for selected-bus lines elsewhere. By 2013, when he left office, New York City had six select bus routes in four boroughs.[51] These routes comprised a small number of the MTA's 244 bus routes. But by 2010, bus ridership had reached 817 million and remained stable.[52] The de Blasio administration, which took office in January 2014, continued the program.

As the city broadened de Blasio's select bus service (SBS), officials ran into the tired objection: loss of space for cars. In Brooklyn, lawmakers who objected to speed cameras objected to removal of parking spaces and driving lanes. The city's response was, often, to dilute plans. On Kings Highway in south Brooklyn, just as on Fordham Road, most shoppers, close to three-quarters, arrived by foot or transit.[53] Yet in 2018, the city pulled back from providing a dedicated lane along an entire 6.5-mile route, leaving a patch littered with parked cars. "It has resulted in shorter bus trips," with a 21 percent times savings, "but those trips could have been even shorter," *Streetsblog* wrote.[54]

De Blasio's marquee project was, in the fall of 2019, to give buses priority across busy Union Square in downtown Manhattan, via Fourteenth Street. During the day and evening, the city would forbid all other vehicles save for trucks and cars making short stops for deliveries or drop-offs. The impetus for the busway arose from a crisis: "It started in emergency context," said de Blasio, because the MTA was planning to shut down a subway line from Brooklyn across Manhattan, the L line, for reconstruction.

When the governor, Andrew Cuomo, decreed that the subway would stay open during construction, the city went ahead with the busway, anyway. "It grew on me," de Blasio says of the proposal. "I was worried about, how would it affect people who lived on the street, senior citizens getting to their front door? I was certainly worried about congestion. . . . [But,] the more we looked at the traffic, [the small number of drivers affected] was making buses much more appealing." The busway on a major Manhattan thoroughfare also sent bold message of, "What's it going to take to have a mass transit city, a true mass transit city?"[55]

What it took was withstanding criticism. Replacing car storage with a bus lane, says Polly Trottenberg, "[was] the toughest battle I ever had. . . . [It was] rather extraordinary, just the battles, the difficulty, the level of anger. . . . It was just a pretty searing experience."[56] The city had to beat back a lawsuit filed by Village residents. They sued, ironically, on environmental grounds, charging that the city hadn't studied traffic and noise.[57] The real issue was parking. Arthur Schwartz, the lawyer who filed the suit, told *Streetsblog* that "parking is an issue." He argued that parkers didn't cause traffic, because "people who park on 12th Street [just south of 14th] never use their cars," not bothering to wonder why people should store property for free.[58]

The project, says Trottenberg, "in the end . . . was such a great success." Bus speeds surged by 22 to 47 percent for the line's twenty-eight thousand daily riders, whose numbers, too, surged by 30 percent as they shaved ten minutes off trips.[59] When de Blasio left office in 2021, twenty SBS routes were running in all five boroughs.[60] By 2019, SBS routes comprised seven of the MTA's top-ten ridership routes and 74.5 million riders a year, more than 10 percent of bus ridership.[61]

Yet SBS highlighted shortcomings of the rest of New York's bus system. Most buses remained stuck in traffic. Local bus speeds remained below eight miles per hour. Select buses fared better, but they, too, stagnated.[62] As e-hailing car services, Uber and Lyft, flooded streets with tens of thousands of cars and as construction and delivery vehicles clogged streets, the bus was too slow for people with choices. By 2019, bus ridership had declined to 698 million, 15 percent below the 2010 level.[63] Even Fordham Road's flagship route had lost riders, as the city had failed to keep lanes clear. As one rider said, Bronx buses "suffer from horrible traffic. . . . I've had to cough up money for Ubers."[64]

Buses remained frustrating to people with disabilities. Sasha Blair-Goldensohn, a disability rights advocate who has used a wheelchair since 2009, would prefer to get around in the same way that most New Yorkers do: by subway. For long-distance trips, he says, "[the bus is] not how you get around New York. . . . Buses are not how you get to Flushing from the West Side, they're not how you get to a Mets game." But the subways' dearth of elevators prevents such mobility. A hassle of the bus, he notes, is finding his way: it is "infuriating," he notes, that there "will always be a police car parked in the bus stop. . . . UPS trucks, taxicabs, it's just sort of seen as a place where [people in vehicles] can park." Getting on the bus, too, is difficult, compared to London: in London, a ramp "telescopes" out, making for a milder incline, but in New York, the ramp comes "flapping down." Once on board, he must rely on the driver to strap his chair into a designated area; in London, passengers propel themselves up the ramp, and other customers move out of the way. "By having that open area," he says, "you're included. Other people can . . . hang out with you."[65]

Riders Alliance: The New Advocates for Buses

To woo riders, advocates realized that New York would have to speed service on all bus routes. TransitCenter, a new transportation advocacy group, brought to the decade-old cause money and a fresh approach. Unlike most transportation activist groups such as Transportation Alternatives, TransitCenter wasn't built from the bottom up; it became a well-funded nonprofit by accident. TransitCenter's predecessor was a nonprofit company that processed tax-exempt transit fare cards for employers who offered the benefit to workers. When a for-profit company bought the business, the capital gain realized in the sale came under the purview of state charity regulators. As TransitCenter's predecessor had earned the money under tax exemption, the proceeds, by law, would go to the mission outlined under the nonprofit charter to advocate for transit. In 2013, David Bragdon, whose career had led him from Nike to heading the regional government in Portland, Oregon, to running Mayor Bloomberg's sustainability office, became one of two employees. Bragdon knew that New York already had a transit advocacy world. But there was "a real gap," he realized, "in advocacy on buses."

TransitCenter teamed up with another new group, Riders Alliance, then less than half a decade old, but with a mailing list of thousands of volunteers. "Their strength was the community connections," says Bragdon. Danny Pearlstein, policy director of Riders Alliance, is a native Brooklynite. A "transit enthusiast growing up," he came of age riding the subways during their 1990s "heyday." After working in local politics, he joined Riders Alliance in 2017. Money from the Rockefeller Foundation and TransitCenter helped Riders Alliance "scale up the lessons of SBS."[66]

The result, in 2016, was a proposal called Turnaround: Fixing New York's Buses, published with Tri-State and the Straphangers Campaign. "Buses in New York are slow, unreliable, and increasingly unpopular," the report noted. Fixes weren't complicated: all-door boarding and fare collection (through a tap-and-go card, then under development) for faster boarding, more dedicated bus lines and better enforcement, timing more traffic signals to give buses the green light, and tweaking routes to direct people to higher ridership lines, where the MTA could provide frequent service.[67]

After the report, says Bragdon, "the challenge . . . was to get the attention of elected officials. . . . Usually when the political class talks about transit, they think . . . subways." Riders Alliance members created "a show of strength," including protests at City Hall, in Albany, and outside MTA headquarters. "We are an Alinsky-like organization," says Pearlstein—organizing people and following a set of tactical prescriptions to achieve a goal. As Pearlstein observes, the mayor must "decide how many chips to use" in setting aside space for buses. Protesters could make sure that though the mayor heard from drivers upset about bus lanes, de Blasio would also hear from riders. Like the Straphangers Campaign before it, Riders Alliance compiled testimonials from riders too busy for advocacy. "Our messaging has largely been, is it fair that buses are so bad? . . . The people on the bus, people you want to help the most, low-income people of color, are the people having their time squandered," says Pearlstein. Riders Alliance also offered a technocratic argument. It's not just that people can't go to work or to school without faster buses. Fire trucks and ambulances need bus lanes to avoid car traffic.

In 2017, bus riders got serendipity: Andy Byford. In 2017, a crisis in the New York City subway system shadowed Governor Andrew Cuomo's reelection race the next year. Cuomo appointed Byford, one of the world's preeminent transit leaders thanks to his experience running transit systems on three continents, to come manage the New York City subways and buses. Byford, a veteran of London's transit system, with double-decker buses moving through traffic via strictly enforced lanes, knew how important buses were. "It was a huge turning point when Andy Byford came . . . because Andy valued the bus in a way that other folks who came up through the subways here didn't," says Pearlstein. "We had a meeting with him in the executive suites in the MTA building," Bragdon remembers. "We went in preparing to present a list of demands. Before we could do that, he asked if he could show a PowerPoint. . . . His plan incorporated everything we were about to ask for."[68]

In 2018, Byford unveiled his Fast Forward plan. "Our plan envisioned the wholesale reimagination of the bus network," says Byford. The city made progress—slowly. In 2019, the state legislature approved cameras aboard buses to ticket cars in bus lanes—in part because of the Democratic takeover of the senate the year before, after Republicans had refused the speed camera renewal. But by 2020, Andy Byford was gone, having charged that Cuomo's micromanagement prevented him from doing his job. "The abrupt end to my tenure and the disastrous onset of Covid [weeks later] stalled what we set out to do," he says.[69]

In the meanwhile, bus riders suffer. "I am a home attendant . . . in Southwest Queens," wrote one rider, Vinnie S. "The bus is consistently late and unreliable and I often have to wait 20 minutes. . . . Being late for work is upsetting and impacts my professional life." Wrote another, Celine P., "I work as an occupational therapist at the Jamaica Hospital and live in Jamaica, Queens. . . . There are so many cars parked in front of the bus stops that drivers don't recognize you standing there and miss you. . . . Even in the bus lanes there are cars there. My commute is mentally draining."[70]

Chapter 18

Ban, Charge, or Suffer

The Forever Politics of Congestion Pricing

> I propose . . . what's called congestion pricing.
>
> —Governor Andrew M. Cuomo, January 15, 2019

> Circumstances have changed, and we must respond to the facts on the ground—not from the rhetoric from five years ago. . . . I have directed the MTA to indefinitely pause the program.
>
> —Governor Kathy Hochul, June 5, 2024

IN 1971, SAM SCHWARTZ, Brooklyn native and former cabdriver, was a junior engineer at the New York City traffic department. Two years earlier, after graduating from Brooklyn College, Schwartz wanted to become a physicist but—discouraged by his brother, who said he wouldn't take well to academia—decided to learn a skill with which he could help his hometown. As he lost friends to suburbs, he saw that even as the population fell, cars made city life miserable for everyone, including drivers. At the University of Pennsylvania, he earned a master's in transportation engineering.

Schwartz was happy to have a job in traffic science. In the earliest part of the twentieth century, engineers had fought road expansion, preferring to move people efficiently, via mass transit, on scarce streets. Even before World War II, though, they had lost that battle to "motordom."[1] For half a century, traffic engineers had responded to more cars by making more room. It was all about "increasing capacity," Schwartz remembers.

By the time Schwartz got his city job, the old idea of regulating traffic rather than building more roads for more cars became new again.

Schwartz saw streets as a scarce resource to be managed for everyone, not as an entitlement for drivers. Over five decades, in pursuit of this principle, he would persist in the quest to get city government to charge drivers to use congested roads. More than two decades into a new century, New York's failure to competently implement such "congestion pricing" shows that despite progress, New York has yet to grasp that it cannot succeed as a driving city.

A Maniacal Scheme

At the city traffic division in 1971, Schwartz's first project was to take the extreme step of banning drivers from a big part of Manhattan. "One of my very first assignments . . . was 'the Red Zone,'" he later wrote. The plan "would have banned passenger cars, excepting taxis, from a huge chunk of Midtown," from 11:00 a.m. to 4:00 p.m.[2]

The Red Zone was a rational response to crisis: a jam-up of cars in the city's skyscraper blocks. The number of people coming into Manhattan each day was at a then-modern low, down to 3.2 million from 3.7 million in 1948. But traffic was worse, as people were deserting transit for cars. The number of people making a car trip into core Manhattan each day was up by 12 percent in less than a decade. But the number of car *trips* was up 22 percent, as the number of people in each car declined. Each day, nearly 576,000 passenger cars and taxis were entering Manhattan's business districts.[3] The average speed through cross streets was 6.9 to 7.5 miles per hour during the proposed ban hours. To design the Red Zone, between Fifty-Seventh and Thirty-Seventh Streets, Broadway and Third Avenue, Schwartz counted vehicles: 40.7 percent were private cars, 44.5 percent were taxis, and only 14.7 percent were trucks and buses.

Cars were expendable: they were less necessary than trucks and less efficient than taxis. As Lindsay was trying to comply with the Clean Air Act, the ban would also improve the environment. Finally, the Red Zone would favor the majority. Despite the surge in car use and the falling number of New York City residents and jobs, 2.3 million people arrived in Manhattan daily via mass transit. The percentage was lower than a decade before—71.1 percent compared to 74.3 percent—but was still most people. The Lindsay administration approved the plan, and the traffic department erected signs. "RED ZONE, NO CARS," read one, with a car in a circle, covered by a black slash.

The signs became artifacts, rescued by Schwartz for posterity. "Two weeks before the start," Schwartz recalls, "the mayor, bowing to pressure from the hotel and other business groups, abandoned the plan." Pro-car sentiment appeared in a letter to the *Times*. One Charles L. Goldenberg called the plan, drawn up by "mental midget" advisers, "the final blow for every thinking citizen who doesn't rely on welfare." Goldenberg predicted longer welfare lines as people who depended on cars—"automobile salesmen, garage attendants, retail auto supply stores, chauffeurs, limousine services"—joined the dole. Foreseeing that the plan would plunge the city into "no other choice but bankruptcy," Goldenberg observed that "Mr. Lindsay seems absolutely bent on destroying this city" with his "maniacal scheme."[4]

Nearly a decade after Lindsay's attempt, a different mayor tried a different ban. In July 1980, Ed Koch was buoyed at how well carpooling had worked during the transit strike months earlier. Still, too many people arrived by car. Thanks to unreliable subways and buses, the share of people arriving in Manhattan via transit had fallen to 69.1 percent.[5] Tens of thousands of workers streaming from subways threaded around cars blocking crosswalks.

The word *gridlock* had entered New Yorkers' vocabulary. *New York Times* "On Language" columnist William Safire popularized it after the strike. "'Gridlock' is to highway engineers what 'meltdown' is to nuclear engineers. . . . Everything stops," Safire wrote. "Gridlock is a fine neologism for the automobile's Armageddon."[6]

Then-mayor Koch proposed a permanent ban on people driving over the Brooklyn Bridge and three parallel spans into Manhattan with no passengers aboard, the measure he had implemented during the strike. Together, bus lanes, bike lanes, and carpooling would be "the most profound changes in decades in the way goods and people move," the *Times* wrote.[7] "There will be lots of yelling and screaming," Koch warned.[8]

Koch failed to understand that people viewed emergencies differently from day-to-day life. In the strike, drivers had been willing to sacrifice by sharing a ride with a stranger. But they balked at doing so regularly. The Automobile Club, garage owners, and the National Council of Salesmen's Organizations sued, the latter noting that "salesmen . . . can't use carpools."[9] "Why should the people of Brooklyn and Queens . . . be penalized?" asked Brooklyn borough president Howard Golden. By October, the ban was stalled, and then dead. A state appeals court ruled that the mayor didn't have the authority to make such a decree absent an emergency.[10]

Two decades later, another emergency—9/11—revived the impulse to restrict traffic. Two weeks after the 2001 attacks, traffic tie-ups were worse than ever. Closed Lower Manhattan roads and security checks on bridges backed up cars. Nearly two-thirds of vehicles contained a single person. As Koch had, Mayor Giuliani temporarily banned single-occupancy cars over bridges during rush hours, and traffic fell 15 percent.[11] In 2002, his successor, Michael Bloomberg, proposed to make the ban permanent and was reminded of the Koch precedent. "If the mayor wants to make the ban a part of regular city traffic regulations,"[12] the *Times* warned, "he would need the approval of the State Legislature." The idea withered.[13]

Mayor Lindsay's Failed Try

Thwarted from restricting traffic, mayors have attempted a different tactic: charging drivers to enter the island of Manhattan. Some crossings, including the Port Authority's Holland and Lincoln Tunnels from the west and the Triborough Bridge and Tunnel Authority's Queens-Midtown and Brooklyn-Battery Tunnels from the south and east, have long levied tolls. Separate public authorities, not city government, built them, relying on toll revenue to repay bondholders and to fund maintenance.

Even the now-free Brooklyn Bridge and its parallel East River spans once charged tolls to fund their construction—ten cents for automobiles.[14] (Originally, in 1883, the pre-car Brooklyn Bridge charged ten cents for "one horse and vehicle," five cents for "neat cattle," and two cents for "sheep and hogs, each.")[15] But in 1911, Mayor William Gaynor said that the "the tolls are oppressive" and abolished levies.[16]

Half a century later, Lindsay advisors thought reviving tolls on all crossings was a good idea. The concept made sense not just to raise money, but from a fairness perspective. Beginning in 1968, the year-old Metropolitan Transportation Authority controlled both Moses's old domain, the Triborough authority, and the mass transit system. Drivers going across the Triborough Bridge, through two tunnels into Manhattan, and over other Moses-built crossings began to pay tolls not only to pay for bridge and tunnel upkeep but also to support subway and bus service.

The state and city thought this subsidy was reasonable because subway riders kept cars off roads, helping people who chose to drive. The chaos caused by the 1966 transit strike demonstrated that not everyone could drive in. But now that Triborough drivers were subsidizing transit, why should Brooklyn, Manhattan, Williamsburg, and Queensboro Bridge drivers be exempt from paying such a subsidy?

In 1969, Lindsay asked Theodore Kheel, labor negotiator and transportation expert, to head a "save the fare" commission, finding revenues to avoid a subway price hike. Kheel "suggested assessing a toll on various bridges."[17] Although the point of Kheel's proposal was to raise money, he hinted at using price to control traffic. "Should there be a variable toll system, heavier during rush hours?" asked a former city administrator.[18]

Without using the term, he was talking about congestion pricing. Because Manhattan lacks street space for everyone who wants to use it, this economic theory goes, the city should charge for that space during busy hours. The idea would not be to punish drivers but, just as with charges for parking, to get them to change behavior. Facing a toll at peak hours, some drivers would switch to a less crowded time, and some would find another form of transportation. New York's drivers had already shown they would respond to price: free bridges were more congested than the tolled Queens-Midtown and Brooklyn-Battery tunnels. The concept found its academic champion in Columbia professor William Vickrey, who had won the Nobel prize in economics.[19] (Vickrey's original target for congestion pricing was rush-hour subways.)

The city could use the price not just to discourage traffic, but to account for damage that drivers created, fulfilling another economic theory: pricing "externalities." That is, if behavior caused crashes or pollution, the person or company engaged in that behavior should pay for that impact. Tom Wicker, *Times* columnist, noted that the auto caused such a burden on Manhattan that "it makes profound good sense . . . to raise substantially if not prohibitively the cost of reaching that island."[20] Kheel estimated the subsidy to the motorist at "$5 a ride" ($44 in 2024 dollars), meaning drivers paying $1 round-trip would get a good deal.[21]

Drivers did not appreciate these theories. The Auto Club branded the idea "shallow and destructive." Accusing Kheel of "demagoguery," the club's chief, Gilbert Phillips, said that "responsible segments of our community [must] call upon Mr. Kheel to halt his vendetta against the automobile." Moses, speaking before the American Right of Way Association, called Kheel's plan "absurd."[22] (Moses's comments had more subtlety than he got credit for: he said that the subway fare was "doomed," regardless of new tolls to support it, and that the state and city would need to levy broader taxes to support transit, which proved true.) Kheel didn't help his cause by saying that tolls should be charged on expressways and parkways, as well.[23]

The potent opposition was political. It came from quarters where more people drove over free bridges into Manhattan: Brooklyn and Queens. Of the eighty-nine thousand new vehicle trips into Manhattan each day by 1971, relative to a decade earlier, most new trips—seventy-seven thousand—came from adjacent boroughs. Queens borough president Mario

Cariello said tolls would be "an unconscionable attack on the long-suffering tax-paying wage earners of Queens who have been denied adequate mass transit."[24] Two years later, comptroller Abe Beame, eyeing his mayoral run, called on Lindsay to halt a study on bridge tolls. Beame, a Brooklyn resident, had risen through the borough's Democratic ranks, and he needed Queens and Brooklyn votes to rise further. "The people . . . paid for these bridges a long time ago," Beame wrote. Channeling Gaynor, he added that "East River bridges are . . . extensions of city streets."[25] He miscast a benefit of congestion pricing as a drawback: "This toll system . . . would make it impossible to drive into or out of Manhattan without paying a toll."[26]

Mayor Koch's Failed Try

In 1973, bridge tolls became the law of the land, without many people noticing. That year, in signing off with the federal government to comply with the Clean Air Act, Lindsay and Rockefeller committed to impose tolls on the Brooklyn and other East River bridges. Based on a $1 toll (levied in one direction), the state and city could earn $105 million a year for transit.[27]

Research conducted for the city's clean-air compliance plan that year explained another reason that absent consistent tolling, traffic would grow more distorted. As transit deficits grew, the MTA regularly increased bridge and tunnel tolls. Yet the higher the MTA set the toll on Triborough facilities, such as the Brooklyn-Battery Tunnel, the more people drove out of their way to avoid that toll. In 1972, Brian Ketcham noted that the MTA had doubled tolls and saw a 9 percent decrease in traffic. But free bridges experienced an *increase* in traffic of 13.2 percent. "There has been a large diversion from tolled facilities to free facilities," Ketcham wrote. Driving to avoid a toll added traffic, pollution, and danger for people who lived or worked near a bridge approach.

When he took office in 1974, Mayor Beame did everything he could to avoid carrying out Lindsay's commitment to the EPA. In 1977, Beame finally annoyed the federal judge overseeing the suit to such an extent that the jurist, Kevin Duffy, ordered the city to charge tolls by 1978. As the deadline loomed, Donald Manes, Queens borough president, called tolls "foolish and counterproductive."[28] Beame found an entity more powerful than a federal judge or a borough president: Congress. Brooklyn congresswoman Elizabeth Holtzman and New York senator Daniel Patrick Moynihan led lawmakers in amending the Clean Air Act to remove the bridge toll remedy.

Though the EPA, after the 1977 congressional amendment, couldn't require tolls, New York could impose them voluntarily. By 1987, the city was more breathable than it had been in the 1970s, thanks to vehicle emissions technology required by federal law. But New York remained out of compliance with the Clean Air Act. With the city reviving, traffic was unbearable. The number of daily visitors into Manhattan had risen to nearly 3.4 million, up 13 percent since 1980. But so had traffic: the number of people arriving by car was up 22 percent, nearly 1.2 million, or about one-third of travelers.[29]

Traffic was worse, too, in part because, the year before, Congress had further distorted driving patterns. In 1986, at the request of Staten Island congressman Guy Molinari, Congress had passed a law forbidding the MTA from collecting tolls in both directions on the Verrazzano-Narrows Bridge between Staten Island and Brooklyn (and, indirectly, through Brooklyn to Queens and Manhattan). Now, the MTA could collect tolls only on the Brooklyn side. The ostensible reason was to avoid traffic backing up at Staten Island tollbooths.[30]

The one-way edict created a loophole for savvy drivers. The Port Authority, which controlled the Holland Tunnel between Manhattan and New Jersey, already charged a one-way-only toll in the other direction—from New Jersey to Manhattan—to avoid Manhattan backups. Motorists gamed this new system. By driving in a circle—from New Jersey to Staten Island over the Verrazzano to Brooklyn or Queens and then from Queens over a free East River bridge through Manhattan back to New Jersey via the Holland or Lincoln Tunnel—drivers could avoid tolls. Truck drivers, in particular, had an incentive to take this detour, as the toll was much higher for trucks. Not surprisingly, trucks clogged Brooklyn, Queens, and Manhattan streets to access free bridges.

In 1987, Koch had an idea: a $10 fee to drive into Manhattan. "There are a number of good reasons to consider imposing tolls on the four free East River bridges," Gurin had written in a memo to him years earlier, especially if "adjusted by time or day."[31] Tolls would eliminate thirty thousand bridge trips daily, or 5 percent. Tolls would raise money: at $1.25, $114 million a year. Some proceeds could go to bridge repairs, neglected since the 1975 fiscal crisis (in 1988, Koch would shutter the Williamsburg Bridge for emergency work); the rest would go to transit.

By then, the city had evidence that every small change would have a big impact. "During the 1979 fuel crisis," Gurin wrote, some drivers had switched to transit. "Weekday traffic volumes were reduced by 15 percent," resulting in an increase of Midtown speeds of nearly half, from 6 to

8.5 miles per hour. As a successful example, Gurin mentioned Singapore's "restricted zones," launched in 1975. He even noted that in the United Kingdom, "[the Greater London Council] is considering an Area Control Scheme under which a cordon would be drawn around the central business district." (Prime Minister Margaret Thatcher abolished the Council, thinking its liberals were too independent of national government, and London waited nearly two decades for congestion pricing.)

Speaking in 1987 before a hearing of the House's subcommittee on the environment, held at the World Trade Center, Koch said that the $10 fee he proposed "will have to be done in less than two years."[32] Now, the public learned the formal term. Transportation commissioner Ross Sandler, exhorting New Yorkers to "think of space in midtown as an economic commodity," called the idea "congestion pricing."[33]

Capital and labor hit back. A "coalition for improved transportation and air quality" claimed to represent four thousand businesses and a half-million workers.[34] On the list of New York's great and good, it was hard to find who *wasn't* represented. Shubert theater chairman Gerald Schoenfeld and Lew Rudin of the Association for a Better New York, two influential citizens, signed, accompanied by trade groups and unions representing theaters, restaurants, hotels, motels, supermarkets, and retailers. They convened at Midtown's Grand Hyatt to call congestion pricing "ill-conceived." The group warned that congestion pricing "discriminates in favor of the affluent and will wreak severe personal hardship on hundreds of thousands of New Yorkers who must use their automobiles."[35] Koch never mentioned the fee again.

Mayor Bloomberg's Failed Tries

On Earth Day 2007, Mayor Michael R. Bloomberg, in his second term, took the stage at the American Museum of Natural History to unveil his plan for environmentally compatible growth, called PlaNYC. "As our city continues to grow," the mayor said, "the costs of congestion to our health, to our economy and to our environment are only going to get worse. . . . How do we want to pay—with an increased asthma rate, with more greenhouse gases, with more wasted time, lost business, and higher prices? Or do we charge a modest fee to encourage more people to take mass transit?" The mayor proposed an eight-dollar fee for drivers into Manhattan below Eighty-Sixth Street, from 6:00 a.m. to 6:00 p.m., levied via camera.[36]

Bloomberg's 2007 effort wasn't the first time the mayor had floated congestion pricing. The concept appealed to the mayor, a former Wall

Street entrepreneur, who had made his fortune selling data about financial instruments—that is, prices. Anything could be priced according to supply and demand, so why not roads? In 2002, his first year in office, to address deficits caused by 9/11, he had proposed congestion pricing. But opponents—again, Queens and Brooklyn politicians—quashed it.

However, 2007 was a good time to re-try. The mayor didn't have to worry about reelection, as city law limited him to two terms (he later convinced the city council to suspend the provision and won a third term). New York was no longer reeling from 9/11. Growth was the challenge: in 2007, more than 3.7 million people entered Manhattan's business districts each day, surpassing the 1948 peak.[37]

Car and truck entrances into Manhattan were down over a decade, evidence that people would switch to transit when transit was a better option than leaving the city or avoiding Manhattan, as 1970s- and 1980s-era opponents of congestion pricing had feared. Subways were in better shape than they had been in the 1970s and early 1980s; they needed money to keep up with growing demand. Climate change had become a political issue. Technologically, drivers had become accustomed to paying tolls electronically, and the city would not need to build booths, causing vehicles to idle.

New York even had an example in a competitor. In 2003, London implemented a five-pound ($8) fee to enter the densest parts of the city during business hours, using some of the money for buses. By 2006, this scheme had reduced daytime vehicle entries by 16 percent and car entries by 36 percent; congestion had fallen 8 percent.[38] London saw a 20 percent decline in carbon dioxide emissions and a 12 percent cut in particulates.[39] Stockholm, too, had introduced congestion pricing in 2006.

New York drivers going to or from New Jersey even experienced congestion pricing at home. In 2001, the Port Authority had implemented variable pricing on Hudson River crossings, framing different prices for different times not as peak-hour surcharges but as off-peak "discounts."[40] Rush-hour traffic fell.[41] Finally, the federal government, under President George W. Bush, offered five hundred million dollars to cities to pilot this free-market idea.

By the twenty-first century, the business community didn't oppose congestion pricing as it had in 1987. Executives who had once pushed for Manhattan expressways and opposed Lindsay's Red Zone and Koch's ten-dollar fee were gone; in their place were executives who understood, including through travels to cities outside of the United States, that New York would never solve traffic by creating more room for cars. Even before Bloomberg revived his proposal, the Partnership for New York City, representing employers ranging from Wall Street firms to corporate headquarters, commissioned a study finding that congestion cost New Yorkers thirteen billion dollars a year. Most of the problem remained cars: "Trucks are responsible for only 8 percent of the daily travel within the Manhattan [business district]," the report noted, "with about 44,000 trucks representing just 5.4 percent of the 810,000 vehicles."[42] By June 2007, 130 business, community, and advocacy groups, from the Brooklyn Chamber of Commerce to a coalition of doctors, had signed up; Transportation Alternatives rallied cycling advocates.

Bloomberg needed to convince two more constituencies: the governor and the legislature. In June, the governor, Democrat Eliot Spitzer, in his first year in office, signaled approval.[43] Yet the state legislature did not. The problem wasn't Republicans. State senate leader Joe Bruno called congestion pricing a "bold, creative measure."[44] Rather, Democrats, who controlled the assembly, proved uncooperative. Lawmakers, particularly those from Brooklyn and Queens, were "cool."[45] The governor would not convince them. Spitzer was unpopular with legislators, having promised to "steamroll" over them on other issues.[46]

Bloomberg tried to reverse this skepticism. He visited churches in Brooklyn, Queens, and Harlem, talking about the fourfold asthma rate in poorer neighborhoods compared to wealthier ones, in part because of trucks moving to and from free bridges connecting Manhattan to the boroughs. Air quality in Manhattan was cleaner, thanks to technology; New York City attained compliance with EPA standards for particulate and carbon monoxide in the late 1990s (though not for ozone).[47] But trucks traversed the South Bronx and industrial areas of Brooklyn and Queens, spewing particulate; vehicles also posed a danger to pedestrians.

In day-to-day news, though, Bloomberg was on the defense. Business travelers and economic theorists were familiar with London's example, but to most people, congestion pricing was a strange concept. Every week, they learned a bad thing about it. In mid-June, it emerged that to keep people from parking above the congestion district and then taking transit into commercial Manhattan, upper Manhattan residents might have to pay for parking permits.[48] Weeks later, it emerged that Manhattanites would have to pay the fee to leave and reenter the zone.[49] Neither of these measures were bad ideas, but they were surprises.

Supporters of congestion pricing found dark motives in assembly obstinacy. "The money trail clearly leads back to the parking lobby," said Paul Steely White of Transportation Alternatives, noting that opponents had taken donations from parking lot interests.[50] Parking lot owners played a role.[51] Yet the reality was that democracy is neither economics nor urban planning. Lawmakers were representing constituents. A survey pointed out the problem: most Manhattanites, 62 percent, supported congestion pricing, but most outer-borough residents—ranging from 61 to 69 percent—opposed it.[52]

Unsurprisingly, people who drove to Manhattan regularly thought the idea was "insanity."[53] "The day that New York adopts congestion pricing . . . is the day I move to Long Island," wrote David Spiel of Queens. "I have lived in Queens most of my life and have always considered it the best of both worlds. I can drive to Manhattan in 20 minutes, yet I have a yard for my children."[54] Spiel was a good proxy for people who opposed congestion pricing: someone who had chosen to live in an area of the city without transit, because it afforded his family more space than an apartment, but who did not want to pay the full cost of that decision. Even outer-borough residents who didn't drive, however, opposed the program. It was a classic political problem: only a few people strongly favored congestion pricing, but people who opposed it were passionate, as the city would be revoking a right.

Some elected officials had less-than-pure motives for opposition. As Kathy Wylde of the Partnership for New York remembers, Vito Lopez, Brooklyn assemblyman and the borough's Democratic boss, "came barreling in and screamed at us. [He] screamed at me, you're going to cost me $8 a day. Same with Shelly [Silver, assembly leader], who drove himself around town. This was about the personal impact on assembly members." Wylde notes that because "legislators . . . have parking placards, none of them have to pay [for parking], congestion pricing . . . is sticker shock."[55]

Yet supporters ignored meritorious concerns. In the Bronx and Harlem, people were skeptical that the program would alleviate traffic in their neighborhoods rather than just benefit Manhattan. Warehouses, wholesale food markets, and industrial facilities in the South Bronx, all of which required truck trips, wouldn't disappear. "I'm sort of torn," said Assemblyman Ruben Diaz Jr., Bronx Democrat. "I really want to address the environmental issues. . . . [But I also worry] that folks from other places are going to park their cars in my community" to avoid the charge.[56]

As predecessors had decades earlier, Queens and Brooklyn lawmakers worried that residents of outlying parts of those boroughs would view congestion pricing as a tax. Mark Weprin, a state assemblyman from eastern Queens, remembers that when Bloomberg officials "came around" to pitch him, "in theory, I thought it was a good idea." But he worried about his constituents. "There's no subway," Weprin says. "No LIRR stops. The bus routes are crappy." Bloomberg officials had tried to address this issue by informing him that of his constituents, only a small percentage drove into Manhattan every day—which was true. Yet "compared to other districts, it was very high. . . . It just felt unfair."[57] Furthermore, even for suburbs and parts of outer boroughs theoretically well-served by rail and subways, transit on paper is not transit in reality. A borough resident who wants to remain in Manhattan after work to see a play, dine out, or to bring her family in on the weekend faces a long wait for a train home in off hours.

Rather than engaging in endless debate, Bloomberg officials focused on a deadline. If the state didn't act, New York would lose federal funds. "Time is short," said the *Times*.[58] Bloomberg, when confronted with a report warning that congestion pricing would harm poorer people, warned that lawmakers' stance was "absolutely ridiculous" and that the "window of opportunity is rapidly closing."[59]

The rush tactic backfired. Sheldon Silver, the speaker of the state assembly, said the federal deadline wasn't the "be all and end all."[60] When the legislature adjourned without acting, Bloomberg maintained, "New York City is today poorer because of Albany's inaction. . . . Some people have guts, and some don't."[61] This acrimony soured New Yorkers further, with 57 percent of people against the idea, up from 52 percent earlier.[62] Even Manhattan was split.[63]

Bloomberg got one more chance. A year later, in spring 2008, Spitzer again proposed congestion pricing, moving the border from Eighty-Sixth to Sixtieth Street.[64] The city council offered support, with thirty local lawmakers calling on Albany to approve the plan, and twenty opposed. In addition to the *Times*, the *Daily News* and *Newsday* supported the idea.[65]

Once again, congestion pricing was up to the assembly. Yet lawmakers' opinions hadn't changed, and Bloomberg hadn't changed. Those twenty "no" votes in the city council were a sign that support remained weak. Leroy Comrie, Queens councilman, had voted against the plan, saying not only that "the residents of Queens will be unfairly taxed," but that "the lack of outreach was evident."[66]

The Bloomberg administration demonstrated impatience. "You are either for this historic change in New York or you're against it, and if you're against it, you're going to have a lot of explaining to do," said Janette Sadik-Khan.[67] With no public groundswell, lawmakers didn't feel pressure to explain anything. Elected officials didn't like being called corrupt, dumb, and shortsighted any more than they had when Lindsay had made the same charges in asking the state to unify the transit system forty years before.[68]

Bloomberg ran into bad luck. By March, Spitzer was out as governor, resigning after a sex-trafficking scandal. The new governor, David Paterson, supported congestion pricing. A second time, congestion pricing supporters focused on the person who seemingly held the remaining power. "It's up to you, Mr. Silver," the *Times* said.[69] Silver was unmoved. "The congestion pricing bill did not have anywhere near a majority of the Democratic conference, and will not be on the floor of the Assembly," he said.[70] Bloomberg lashed out. "It takes a special type of cowardice for elected officials to refuse to stand up and vote their conscience." About Silver, the *Times* said, "Rarely does one man have a chance to do so much harm to so many."[71]

Like Robert Moses, Silver was a villain in an oversimplified narrative. Silver had not brought congestion pricing to a vote because he didn't have the votes. "They said, 'Shelly [Silver] killed it,'" recalled Weprin. In reality, "more than half the city Assembly" caucus—lawmakers who represented New York City districts—"was against it." The animosity exacerbated a preexisting handicap: the state legislature's historical reluctance to give New York City new powers—as demonstrated, forty years earlier, by then Governor Rockefeller's rejection of Mayor Lindsay's plan to use Triborough surpluses for transit in favor of the governor's own such state-controlled proposal.

Bloomberg also suffered poor timing. Though congestion pricing offered money for transit, subways were working fine; few commuters sensed an emergency. A year later, after the global financial crisis plunged the transit system into deficit, the legislature had to raise $1.5 billion in new funding annually for the MTA. But congestion pricing was so toxic that lawmakers created a levy on employer payrolls rather than charge drivers.

A New, Bottom-up Approach

Bloomberg's failure distressed Sam Schwartz, who by then had joined the private sector as a transportation and planning consultant. "I really thought Bloomberg would be successful," Schwartz remembers. "When that collapsed, I had a very Brooklyn conversation with myself, 'If you really believe in this, put your money where your mouth is.'"[72] Schwartz spent the next decade correcting mistakes proponents of congestion pricing had made.

He didn't do it alone. Charles Komanoff, the transport economist and former head of Transportation Alternatives, had crunched the numbers behind the scenes during Bloomberg's congestion pricing effort. In

2007, Theodore Kheel, the labor negotiator and transit supporter, hired Komanoff to create an alternative plan to generate money for free transit. Komanoff created the Balanced Transportation Analyzer, an intricate spreadsheet model that could estimate any combination of congestion fees. The idea of free transit went nowhere, but in 2009, when Komanoff heard that environmentalist Alex Matthiessen was about to leave Riverkeeper—the Hudson River conservation group, which he had run for ten years—he invited him to breakfast to chat.[73]

Matthiessen had studied economics at Harvard Kennedy School and concluded that "internalizing externalities"—forcing polluters to pay for their pollution—was critical to solving many environmental problems. At Riverkeeper, he had helped shift the burden of pollution from the public to polluters via lawsuits, including forcing ExxonMobil to clean up Brooklyn's Newtown Creek and forcing General Electric to remove PCBs it had dumped into the Hudson. Congestion pricing would achieve such an end through policy, not after-the-fact remediation.

Komanoff introduced Matthiessen to Kheel, who hired Matthiessen to determine whether a new campaign was viable. After interviewing proponents and opponents of the Bloomberg plan, Matthiessen concluded that "congestion pricing could be done." He knew, from the Bloomberg failure, that it was a mistake to rush. "I gave this a five-year timeline," he remembers; "2015 was my goal [because] that would be the next time the MTA needed to go to Albany to fund its next five-year capital program." Matthiessen's strategy was to build a coalition of "odd bedfellows" and propose benefits beyond Manhattan. He began recruiting organizations—many of them skeptical veterans from the Bloomberg effort—and raising money, three million dollars over five years, including from the Rockefeller Foundation.[74]

Komanoff knew Schwartz and knew that he had been working on his own version of congestion pricing. He introduced Schwartz and Matthiessen. Schwartz had put together a plan but didn't have the capacity to run the campaign required to get it passed. Matthiessen had the campaign experience, but his coalition's plan wasn't bold enough. Division of labor among "the three amigos," as Schwartz dubbed them, became clear: Schwartz was the policy architect, Komanoff was the data guy, and Matthiessen was the campaigner who understood what it took, in time, money, and coalition-building, to achieve results. Rather than unveiling a proposal to see it die, Schwartz, Komanoff, and Matthiessen found out *why* so many New Yorkers were against congestion pricing—and worked to change their minds, one by one.

Schwartz became the campaign's public face. Where other advocates had been worn out by naysayers, Schwartz was patient. Weprin, then in the city council, was won over. "Sam Schwartz came to me. . . . He said, how do we sweeten the pot?" The idea Schwartz cobbled together was to put money from congestion pricing aside for projects for people living in transit-scarce neighborhoods. First, new bus routes and more frequent service in Queens. Second, lower Long Island Railroad fares for city-only trips (the railroad runs through Queens and parts of Brooklyn). Third, lower tolls on MTA bridges that were nowhere near Midtown or Lower Manhattan, as such areas had fewer mass-transit options. "It had a lot of benefits for Queens," says Weprin. "We're going to get things in return for paying extra." (Schwartz even had an idea to build a new pedestrian and cyclist bridge from Queens to Manhattan.) After praising Schwartz's plan, Weprin heard from constituents who "hate the idea that they had to pay for something that was free." But he felt it was fair.

Matthiessen wanted to rebrand "congestion pricing." As the three advocates wondered, "Who's going to get behind an idea called 'congestion pricing'—two words that no one, separately or together, wants to hear?" The coalition came up with a new name—mainly to get reporters to adopt a positive term: MoveNY Fair Plan. The name shifted focus from costs and toward benefits.

Next, the group focused on fairness. "Toll equity" would ensure that all drivers would pay their fair share, but that drivers living in less congested and less transit-friendly parts of the city would pay less, thanks to their cheaper bridge tolls. Finally, MoveNY would "reduce grinding traffic jams." In real life, few people complained about "congestion"; they complained about traffic. This was no longer a dry economics lecture; it was a *hey, why didn't I think of that?* moment.

At breakfast after breakfast, before group after hostile group, Schwartz sold the plan. Each time a person asked him a question, he acted as if he were considering this objection for the first time. He never dismissed concerns with condescension. The MoveNY team even got the American Automobile Association to acknowledge that the plan "merits serious consideration."[75] "All previous attempts came from the top," says Schwartz—that is, an elected official imposing a theory without figuring out what people thought. "They were grateful, even . . . ardent opponents, that we reached out." Over decades, Schwartz had built himself up as an honest broker. Everyone knew "Gridlock Sam" through his *Daily News* traffic column and appearances on local news. Schwartz was also working on this project pro bono—beholden to no one. "No client paid for it," wrote Bill Keller, who had just retired as the *Times* executive editor in 2012.[76]

Matthiessen built support. Beyond transit and business groups, the New York City Environmental Justice Alliance and the Community Service Society (CSS) joined. CSS's support was particularly important. A trusted anti-poverty group that was advocating for half-price subway fares for poorer residents, CSS produced a study finding that congestion pricing would not hurt the poor. "Only two percent of the working poor would potentially pay," the study concluded.[77] "That really helped us make the case, particularly with legislators in the non-Manhattan boroughs representing some of the largest black and brown communities," Matthiessen says. He spent years convincing constituencies, such as labor unions, who, in concept, were on board, but remained quiet, as they were fearful of angering Governor Andrew Cuomo, who had taken office in 2011, by pressuring him.

In 2015, after year upon year of tinkering to make as many people as possible happy, MoveNY unveiled its plan. Drivers would pay a nearly $6.00 toll to enter Manhattan. Tolls on remote outer-borough bridges that didn't touch Manhattan would fall to $3.00.[78] The program would raise $1.5 billion a year for transportation, including $500 million for road and bridge upkeep. Every borough got investments. Queens would get "ferries . . . , [a] new Triboro RX [rail] line connecting Brooklyn, the Bronx, and Queens, . . . new select bus routes, . . . [and] bike and pedestrian lanes."[79] Even the *New York Post*, a skeptic of charging drivers, was cautiously supportive. "MOVE NY has been fine-tuning its proposal since 2012 in hopes of avoiding the mistakes that doomed a similar proposal by then-Mayor Mike Bloomberg," its editorial board wrote. "MOVE NY's plan . . . merits serious consideration."[80]

Albany's reaction was hardly encouraging. Carl Heastie, who had replaced Silver as speaker of the assembly after the former resigned on corruption charges, said that "the speaker has not supported tolls."[81] (Silver died in federal prison in 2022.) Cuomo was quiet. One problem was the lack of crisis. "You can't manufacture a crisis," says Matthiessen.

Enter Governor Cuomo

MoveNY ran into good luck—or bad luck. New York's transportation system crumpled. Tens of thousands of Uber and Lyft cars stalled Midtown traffic to below five miles per hour. Below ground, by mid-2017, subway service reached a modern nadir. For years, the MTA had skimped on maintenance, cutting maintenance staff 10 percent after the 2008 financial crisis; Cuomo's insistence that the new, long-delayed Second Avenue Subway open on time, on New Year's Eve 2016, further drew MTA attention away from day-to-day upkeep.[82] As ridership neared record levels, the system's inability to cope was obvious. Subway journeys completed on time sank to a then-modern low, 78.8 percent.

The year 2017 featured transit's "summer of hell." The *Times* tallied "human costs, financial and otherwise, of a single subway disruption," when such disruptions occurred every week. "One woman never made it to housing court and now faces eviction. Another missed a doctor appointment made months earlier. A graphic designer lost $100 in wages. A computer technician paid more than $50 for an Uber car to make a meeting. A lawyer was late for a sentencing. . . . A psychoanalyst never made it to her session with a patient. Neither did her patient."[83] Mishaps, including a Harlem derailment that injured thirty-nine people, further angered the public. Ridership fell.

Other governors may have wriggled out of responsibility by claiming that the MTA, though managed by state appointees, was an independent organization. But Cuomo couldn't do that. The politically astute governor had made several misjudgments. First, he himself had coined the phrase "summer of hell." That spring, Cuomo had used the phrase to gird New Yorkers for planned work by the federal railroad, Amtrak, that would make traveling to Manhattan's Penn Station difficult. Since he didn't control Amtrak and wouldn't take the blame if Amtrak failed to finish the work on time, the governor didn't shy from the memorable phraseology. But as performance across the transit system that he *did* control became a crisis, the governor's opponents used the phrase against him.

Second, Cuomo had invited the public to hold him responsible for the MTA. In cutting the ribbon to open the Second Avenue Subway on the last day of 2016, he had rhetorically asked, "You know who runs the MTA? It's me." Now, he took the blame for the rest of the system.

Transit advocates focused on Cuomo. Says Riders Alliance founder John Raskin, "As the subways were falling apart, we . . . made a very deliberate decision to make sure Governor Cuomo had to own the problems. . . . Our goal was not to let the governor off the hook publicly."[84] Pressure on legislators would not have been as effective. As Matthiessen observes, lawmakers are "a huge, large diffuse mass. No one [was] going to feel individual pressure" besides the governor.

Third, the Riders Alliance magnified its Cuomo strategy in a way it couldn't have in a previous era. In the worse subway service crisis of the early 1980s, New Yorkers had not had an instant rage outlet. Russianoff and Straphangers volunteers had to go subway car to subway car, taking riders' comments. Now, riders on a delayed train could vent online, via Twitter. "Our members specifically came up with [a] #CuomosMTA hashtag, . . . holding the governor accountable," recalls Raskin.

Finally, 2018 was an election year. Rival politicians seized on this hashtag campaign. Cuomo faced a progressive challenger for the Democratic nomination for reelection: actress Cynthia Nixon. Nixon ran against #CuomosMTA and trended on Twitter.[85] "Tax the rich. Fix the subway," was a Nixon slogan.[86]

Cuomo had to out-progress this progressive. He announced a "subway action plan"—and, to pay for it, embraced the policy transit advocates had been pushing for years. "Congestion pricing is an idea whose time has come," Cuomo said in August. "Sometimes," he said, "society needs a wake-up call." The governor appointed a commission, Fix NYC, to advise him on details. The fifteen members were the usual business and real estate suspects, but one name stood out: Sam Schwartz.[87]

In 2018, Cuomo advanced the idea in his state of the state address, his highest-profile speech of the year, calling for "additional charges" in an "exclusive zone in Manhattan."[88] The move came just in time. After the summer of hell had turned into the winter of hell, riders stymied by delays caused by broken rails, frozen signals, and ice-covered tracks conducted their online insurgency more furiously.[89] "This is the state of #CuomosMTA," one Queens rider tweeted after an eighty-five-minute commute. "The subway is always the last resort," another tweeted. "In 25 min, I have moved 2 stops," tweeted a third. "Only the governor can lead us out of this crisis," summed up Riders Alliance.[90]

Cuomo's commission released its plan. Drivers would pay $12 to enter core Manhattan from 6:00 a.m. to 8:00 p.m. on weekdays ($25, for trucks). The money would raise $1 billion for the MTA annually, mostly for subways. The legislature remained skeptical. "The proof will be in the expensive pudding," said Queens Assemblywoman Nily Rozic. "It's not that residents can't turn to public transit to offset the costs of proposed tolls because service isn't reliable; it's because service doesn't exist."[91] The driving public remained more opposed than skeptical. A New Jersey driver found the concept "appalling"; a hot-dog vendor said he "could not pull [his cart] by hand."[92] The governor calibrated his response. Despite his commission's recommendation, he did not push hard for full congestion pricing that year. But in that April's annual budget, he extracted one half-measure that he could present as a victory without alienating regular drivers: a $2.50 to $2.75 fee on taxi, Uber, and Lyft pickups in core Manhattan.

Over his 2018 election campaign, Cuomo turned the never-ending "summer of hell" into an asset. Rather than suffer from attention to the subway, he seized momentum. Cuomo had an asset that Bloomberg hadn't enjoyed: his own image. The public had trusted Bloomberg, but never stopped seeing him as a Manhattan elite, one who could hardly relate to a Queens driver. Cuomo, conversely, amplified his outer-borough persona. "As a born-and-raised Queens boy, I have outer-borough blood in my veins," he said. "It is my priority that we keep costs down for hard-working New Yorkers and encourage use of mass transit." Cuomo, like Schwartz, framed the concept as fairness: "Everybody pays the same toll when you go into the zone," he said. "It stops what we call bridge shopping. I'm a Queens boy. You can take the 59th Street Bridge and not pay a toll or you can go through the Queens Midtown tunnel and pay a toll. I'm cheap, so I go to the 59th Street Bridge, but literally you are directing traffic [to] where there is a toll-free bridge."[93]

To head off Nixon without turning off drivers, Cuomo spent the election year focusing on the MTA's needs, not how to pay for them. He even gave frustrated New Yorkers a fresh face. In late 2017, he interviewed Andy Byford, a Briton who hailed from the Plymouth coast. Byford had run transit systems in Australia and Canada after having worked his up from trainee to help manage the London Underground, having been self-diverted from his original career choice of the Royal Navy by his intense "interest in the logistics and complexity of transit." In his interview with the governor, Byford recalls, "I was asked . . . if I could deliver improvements within a year, to which I emphatically replied, yes. The governor seemed satisfied." It was "an absolute dream to run New York City Transit."[94]

Starting work in early 2018, with his British accent, practiced humility—he liked to tell breakfast audiences of business and real estate notables that he was the "spotty kid from Plymouth"—and ubiquitous presence on trains, name tag around his neck, Byford became a "rock star," as one MTA official put it. Byford gained trust from riders and adoration from advocates. That spring, he unveiled his Fast Forward plan to modernize subway and buses. The plan would upgrade subway signals, allowing for faster service, renovate stations, and accelerate repair and replacement. It would cost forty billion dollars over five to ten years—so required congestion pricing.[95]

Cuomo's Congestion Pricing, on Paper

By 2019, Cuomo was no longer the second-term governor in a subway malaise. He had handily beat both Nixon and his Republican opponent the previous fall. He would expend some rebuilt political capital getting congestion pricing passed. "This was all the governor," says Pat Foye, then the MTA chairman. "He was at the height of his powers." Cuomo was no longer even mildly reticent about congestion pricing in his state of the state address. "This would say, basically, everyone pays a toll," the governor said.

As part of the state budget, Cuomo proposed to the legislature a bill that wasn't quite the MoveNY plan and wasn't quite the plan his commission had suggested. Instead, it would authorize the MTA, through its Triborough affiliate, to toll vehicles entering core Manhattan, raising at least one billion dollars annually. The bill was short on details: it said nothing about what the toll would be, what times of day the MTA would levy it, or which drivers and vehicles, if anyone, would be exempt.

In pushing congestion pricing through the legislature, Cuomo benefited from the failures of a decade before. Cuomo had a concrete spending plan: Fast Forward. "Our plan, and the positive press and excitement that it generated, indisputably helped secure the case for action in Albany," says Byford. The governor enjoyed backup from well-practiced congestion-pricing advocates as parallel "fix our transit" and "fix the subways" coalitions emerged to replace MoveNY and meet the political moment. It was no accident that advocates named the coalitions (comprised of the same groups that had supported the MoveNY plan) after Cuomo's "Fix NYC" commission. As Matthiessen pointed out, "It was our intention to tee up a politically viable plan, get Cuomo to embrace it and then give him all the credit." The first group ("Fix Our Transit"), Matthiessen recalls, was comprised of "polite civil-society groups," such as the Regional Plan Association, "that had to play nice," pushing benefits of congestion pricing. The second group ("Fix the Subway") was made up of "the more in-your-face, grassroots groups, the tougher groups that thrived . . . in their criticism of the governor."

The Regional Plan Association, nearly a century removed from proposing Manhattan highways, dispatched its board of developers and executives to Albany. "We'd been through it a couple of times before," says Kate Slevin, who spearheaded the RPA campaign. "We knew what the opposition points were, we had very clear answers to them, addressing the equity concerns, explaining how the outer boroughs were going to benefit." The Tri-State Transportation Campaign marshaled data to answer opposition points. A Tri-State study found that despite cries from eastern Queens and south Brooklyn, "not one district has more than single-digit percentages of commuters driving into the zones."[96]

But transportation experts and advocates weren't the most influential voices. With Cuomo now behind congestion pricing, construction and transit unions got behind the plan, as it meant jobs—and staying in Cuomo's favor. The thirty-five-thousand-strong, vote-rich Transport Workers Union, whose president, John Samuelsen, was a Cuomo ally, leafleted subways and paid for newspaper ads, including some that scolded then-mayor Bill de Blasio for his failure to advocate for congestion pricing.

Unanimity wasn't total. De Blasio remained lukewarm, preferring a millionaire's tax. The *Post* remained skeptical, saying congestion pricing had "become the gov's cure-all for fixing mass transit's substantial woes."[97] The paper asked, "How high will the tolls be? How many drivers will have to pay them? No details." Three lawmakers from Brooklyn and Queens, including Assemblyman David Weprin (Mark's brother), held rallies against the proposal. But transit advocates deployed the weapon that had worked with bike lanes and pedestrian plazas: counterprotest. A rally against congestion pricing lost potency when counter-ralliers outnumbered ralliers.[98]

The governor wielded another element of his personality, his reputation for retribution. In one speech, the governor blamed a potential 30-percent subway-fare hike on lawmakers who wouldn't pass congestion pricing. "Either the rider pays in fares and tolls or it's congestion pricing," the governor said.[99] Carl Heastie, the assembly speaker, said, "We're at the point where the Assembly members understand the need to fund the M.T.A."[100] The MTA needed money, and "all the other options were worse," says Wylde, of the Partnership for New York City, of lawmakers' thinking. Assemblywoman Amy Paulin, in charge of the body's transportation committee, says that "a combination of advocacy that we hadn't seen in the earlier [attempts] . . . [combined] with the work of the speaker [Heastie] . . . [in] allaying concerns for different individual legislators."[101] Some lawmakers wanted accessibility for riders with disabilities; others wanted attention to suburban rail. Heastie "assured them that . . . these priorities would be addressed." To woo suburban legislators, 20 percent of funding would go to suburban transit. To woo Manhattan lawmakers, Manhattanites earning less than sixty thousand dollars would be exempt.

Cuomo benefited from the passage of time in another way: a new generation of legislators had taken power. The way in which their predecessors had departed helped congestion pricing. By 2019, Silver was on his way to federal prison for an unrelated corruption conviction. The idea that Silver had stopped congestion pricing, and that this had had something to do with venality, had stuck.

Cuomo dismisses any impact advocates had. Advocates meant "zero to me," he says, "because they're not in the real world. Nobody cares." What *did* matter, in his and his top aide's telling, was how closely the summer of hell followed the opening of the Second Avenue Subway just months before; as Cuomo had taken credit for that project's completion on time, he could not disavow responsibility for the rest of the system. "The summer of hell was hell, and the only reason [coupled with the fact that] we had just come off the high-profile Second Avenue Subway, that congestion pricing happened," says Melissa DeRosa, the governor's secretary. "I remember lying on my office floor," she adds, after the report of yet another subway incident came in. "When the subways don't work, New York City doesn't work. . . . We had no choice."[102]

Cuomo says of the legislature, "I was too strong for them to stop. How did I get politically strong? I worked at it very hard." In his telling, he informed Heastie, "I'm gonna do congestion pricing, or I'm gonna go to the people of this state and say you're stopping congestion pricing." Reframed, even people who didn't understand congestion pricing or didn't support it would frown upon legislative obstruction on something as critical about fixing the MTA. The average voter might not understand the specifics of congestion pricing and even oppose it, but "they know, [if] Andrew Cuomo is saying Carl Heastie is trying to stop this, it is Discovery Channel, it is the stronger animal eats the weaker animal." It also helped that, as Cuomo puts it, legislators "don't exist" outside their own districts. "[Lawmakers] said to themselves that people will blame Cuomo" for congestion pricing when the state started levying the toll.[103]

The governor's positioning of the congestion pricing proposal as a provision of the all-important state budget, rather than a standalone bill, was clever politicking, appealing to lawmakers' competing priorities. In that year's budget were bills important to lawmakers who didn't care about congestion pricing, such as bail reform, to reduce the number of pretrial inmates incarcerated. Putting congestion pricing in the budget also gave lawmakers cover when it came to defending their vote to drivers. They could claim, later, that they hadn't voted for congestion pricing, but had voted for some other item in the budget. "It is easier to vote for it in an omnibus package," says John Liu, a Queens senator.[104] Finally, Cuomo ensured that the congestion-pricing bill prohibited the MTA from launching congestion pricing until at least 2021, giving the public time to forget which lawmakers had voted for it.

In March 2019, congestion pricing became law. The initiative "reforms and funds the MTA with an estimated $15 billion to be raised through Central Business District tolling" over ten years, the governor said.[105] One constituency had never been convinced: the public. Voters opposed congestion pricing, 54 to 41 percent.[106] Even Manhattanites opposed it, 51 to 48 percent. Despite MoveNY's best efforts, people still called it by that phrase. But it was the end—and beginning—of an era.

Blindsided and Misled?

But it wasn't. By March 2020, Manhattan's central business district was devoid of traffic—not because of congestion pricing but because of the pandemic. By 2022, traffic was back, yet congestion pricing was still a paper tool. The MTA, in charge of the program, didn't launch it in 2021, as scheduled. One ostensible reason was Trump administration hold-ups; the federal government had to approve an environmental review. But even as President Joe Biden took office, the federal government didn't sign off, and the MTA remained sluggish in determining tolls, time-of-day pricing, and exemptions. Later that year, Cuomo was gone, having resigned after a sexual harassment scandal.

In 2022, New Yorkers learned unwelcome details about congestion pricing. That summer, the MTA finally released details, required under the federal environmental process. First, price: up to twenty-three dollars for cars, higher than Cuomo's commission or Schwartz had proposed. Second, universality: congestion pricing would apply twenty-four hours a day, with a minimum fee of five dollars, different from London, which charges drivers only during business hours, and not what advocates had proposed. Third, the MTA refused to say whether it would exempt government employees driving their cars to work, even though the environmental impact documents implied that such an exemption would undo much of the congestion reduction benefit.

Worst was the traffic impact. Traffic volumes in Manhattan's core would fall by 7 to 9 percent, a salutary result. Traffic citywide, though, would fall only by a maximum of 1.5 percent. The results would not fall evenly. Staten Island and the Bronx, as well as northern New Jersey, would see increases in traffic. Worst of all: in six of seven tolling scenarios the MTA laid out, the number of trucks on the Cross-Bronx Expressway would increase, by 170 to as many as 704 new trucks each day.

New Yorkers had not been wrong to be skeptical. Congestion pricing *would* mostly benefit Manhattan, as opponents had charged. And it would not do so neutrally: the Bronx and Staten Island would suffer. Further, despite long-ago promises of the MoveNY plan, with the MTA facing multiyear deficits far exceeding the amount of money congestion pricing would yield, it was unlikely that Staten Island or the Bronx would receive better transit service.

History was repeating itself. Trucks needed somewhere to go, and if trucks couldn't go across Manhattan for free, they would go *around* Manhattan. For decades, transportation advocates had wielded the Cross-Bronx Expressway as everything wrong with New York traffic—and everything they wanted to fix. But the Bronx would continue to be Manhattan's sacrifice zone. Congressman Ritchie Torres, who represents the South Bronx and supports congestion pricing in theory, said that he felt "ambushed" as well as "blindsided and misled." He added, to "divert diesel truck traffic from Manhattan to the Bronx . . . is not fair, that is not right, and that is not what the people of the Bronx were promised."[107]

The MTA and congestion-pricing advocates couldn't afford this fresh criticism. To counter it, the MTA agreed to spend money lessening this potential impact on the Bronx, including $15 million to replace up to 1,000 idling diesel trailers at the Hunts Point produce market and $20 million to establish an asthma "case management center" in the borough. The MTA would also help pay for electric-truck charging stations, install air filtration systems in schools near highways that would see more traffic, and "install roadside vegetation to improve near-road air quality."[108]

Both New York and the federal government eventually determined that even higher projected truck traffic across truck-burdened Bronx neighborhoods was an acceptable price to pay for less traffic in Manhattan. In May 2023, the Biden administration approved the MTA's environmental review, judging extra trucks in the Bronx to be insignificant. Statistically, the federal government wasn't wrong: the Bronx was already so oversaturated with heavy trucks that a few hundred more didn't matter.

The final federal approval allowed for the MTA to present a firm plan to the public. By early 2024, the MTA had finally approved a firm toll schedule: $15.00 for cars entering Manhattan between 5:00 a.m. and 9:00 p.m. and $3.75 during the overnight hours, new surcharges for taxis and for-hire vehicles, no exemption for workers commuting to government jobs, and a much higher daytime rate—up to $36—for trucks. As MTA chairman Janno Lieber, who had taken the post in 2022, said in March 2024, "New York has more traffic than any place in the United States, and now we're doing something about it." Despite several ongoing lawsuits by the state of New Jersey, Staten Island elected officials, and the teachers' union, the MTA soon set a date: June 30, 2024. New Yorkers walking or driving around Manhattan could see the long gray-steel arms of toll-collection cameras, costing half a billion dollars to erect, projecting out above and over every avenue, delineating the Sixtieth Street congestion-zone line.

Yet even as the MTA set a firm date, it remained unclear how substantially congestion pricing would improve mass transit. Yes, congestion pricing would raise money for the MTA, including funding for the second phase of the Second Avenue Subway—but its estimated $1 to $1.5 billion a year would not be enough to build New York the transit it needs, in part because of New York's high transit-construction costs, compared to other global cities. Even when Cuomo signed congestion pricing into law in 2019, before COVID ravaged the MTA's finances, the MTA's plan was to borrow up to thirty years' worth of congestion-pricing revenues to raise $15 billion immediately—enough for just two years' worth of improvements in physical assets. Its champions, eager to build support, glossed over this fact.

On June 5, 2024, Governor Kathy Hochul stunned New Yorkers. Just three and a half weeks before those new cameras extending across Sixtieth Street were to start snapping photos of license plates and receiving signals from E-ZPass readers, and months after reaffirming her support, the governor announced what she termed an "indefinite pause."[109] The reasons she cited were financial pressures on New York's inflation-weary middle class and the city's slow recovery from COVID-19. "I have come to the difficult decision that implementing the planned congestion-pricing system risks too many unintended consequences for New Yorkers," she said. "It was . . . enacted in a pre-pandemic period, where workers were in the office five days a week, crime was at record lows, and tourism was at record highs." The MTA immediately announced that it, in turn, would indefinitely delay construction on the next few stations of the Second Avenue Subway, as well as some upgrades to subway signals.

The transit advocates and safe-streets advocates who had labored for years—some, decades—were understandably outraged and marshalled hundreds of protesters to march through Times Square and to picket outside the governor's office as well as her events. On social media, activists began holding her responsible for everything from ordinary subway delays to pedestrian deaths, calling her a "traitor" and a "sellout." Progressive politicians castigated the governor for her turnabout.

But the outrage failed to gain political potency. Hochul paid no immediate political price: an April poll had shown that 64 percent of city voters opposed congestion pricing, and a poll following the governor's announcement showed support for her "pause."[109] The carefully crafted coalition that, in 2019, had supported then-Governor Cuomo as he had inserted congestion pricing into the state budget had fractured; the Transport Workers Union, for example, had withdrawn its support. Lawmakers had never had to go on record as supporting congestion pricing, instead voting for it five years earlier as part of that budget; few lawmakers criticized Hochul's pause. The coalition was no longer sufficiently broad, and it had never been deep: a few ardent congestion-pricing supporters would not be a factor in a future statewide election in which voters' post-COVID concerns remained crime, quality of life, and affordability. Advocates threatened lawsuits, but no obvious legal framework for such a suit existed: Cuomo had crafted the congestion-pricing law carefully, ensuring that the program could not start before a particular date, but forcing no firm deadline by which it had to begin. The MTA faced no immediate fiscal crisis or service cuts, thanks to the governor's 2023 move to increase a different tax, a tax on downstate payrolls, for the transit system, and most voters were not concerned about a delay to an abstract project such as the Second Avenue Subway, already far in the future.

Moreover, the governor was not wrong to point out that 2024 New York City was a different place from 2019 New York City. "The idea behind congestion pricing is that it will encourage many current drivers to shift to public transit," she said in announcing her pause. "But there is a third possibility that ow poses a greater threat than it did at the program's inception. Drivers can now choose to stay home altogether, telling employers they need to work fully remote again," or at least on more days of the week. "Or they might just change their patterns and skip the visits to the city." In 2019, New York had enacted congestion pricing from a position of strength; in 2024, it was pausing congestion pricing from a position of weakness.

Chapter 19

Two Miles

Bronx Mothers versus the Ghost of Moses

What motivates me is asthma.

—Bronx Congressman Ritchie Torres, June 20, 2022

The first time he was hospitalized, he must have been two or three weeks old.

—Nilka Martell, Bronx activist, speaking of her son, August 15, 2022

NILKA MARTELL, BORN IN 1975, has lived her entire life in the southeast Bronx, within two blocks of the Cross-Bronx Expressway. As a child, when her father was at work, her mother took her to Virginia Playground, above the open-cut highway. "When you're young, you don't really understand that you're breathing these fumes," she says. Martell never developed asthma, but her son, born in 1998, suffered from the ailment, caused by pollution. "When I was pregnant," Martell says, "I lived in an apartment that was on the Cross-Bronx." She would come home from work and ask herself, "Why is this window so grimy? I just washed it." Her weeks-old baby was hospitalized, and doctors diagnosed him with asthma. "The first year of his life, he was probably hospitalized . . . five times." Martell, a paralegal, was focused on survival. "I was a single mom, I was working, it was . . . about keeping a roof over our heads," she says. It wasn't until her son attended school that Martell grasped the pervasion of Bronx asthma. When she handed her son's medication to the school nurse, she was shocked. "[The nurse] had a Rubbermaid tote. She just opened it up and it was like dozens and dozens of ziplocked bags with Albuterol pumps, and I was like, holey, moley."[1]

Now, Martell has an audacious vision: for New York to cover a portion of the Cross-Bronx Expressway that has marked her family's lives. Stitching up the gash with parks and playgrounds would be the culmination of decades of activism to undo harm done by generations of politicians and planners. "Capping" the Cross-Bronx would build on recent successes as well as reverse recent setbacks—both illustrating how arduous the project is politically and why it is necessary.

From Dirty River to Ribbon Parks

On January 20, 2023, the *Post* featured a sensational headline: "Dolphins spotted in Bronx River." The sea mammals got "a proper Bronx welcome" from a neighbor. "Somebody please explain to me why the f-ck is there dolphins," he observed, training his camera on their distinctive fins. "Shit had me shocked."[2] The dolphins were the river's latest photo-friendly animals; in 2007, biologists had spotted a beaver and named it José, after José Serrano, the Bronx congressman who had supported the water's revitalization. Once a repository for abandoned cars, the river was so clean that fish could survive and attract predators.

The dolphin-friendly river was the result of a half-century-long effort. In the 1960s, Ruth Anderberg, a resident of the Fordham neighborhood, noticed that the river was "buried in trash."[3] A decade later, she attended a speech given by Bronx borough police commander Tony Bouza, who spoke of a contrast. A native of Spain, he had grown up in "abject poverty" in Brooklyn, on Prospect Park West. He was now fortunate enough to live in Scarsdale, a Westchester suburb. "My wife and I often walked the Bronx River in Westchester . . . on Sundays, and I was always struck by the bucolic beauty," he recalled. Westchester had cleaned that stretch of the river decades before in creating the pre-Moses Bronx River Parkway. But as the river wound its way down the Bronx, "it looked like a sewer to me. It had refrigerators, automobiles, tires. . . . And I thought, this has to change, because it was an insult to the people of the Bronx, that the dominant society would be so neglectful."[4]

The two launched a cleanup, called the Bronx River Restoration Project. "[Anderberg] got [Bouza] to give her a desk and a phone in the police office," recalls Diana Hartel, who interviewed her. The two convinced the National Guard and local tow truck owners to haul debris—"six wrecked cars, two rusted horse trailers, 50 to 60 refrigerators . . . and the remains of an upright piano"[5]—out of the river; kids scythed weeds. "I saw environmental issues as being central to my duties as the Bronx borough commander," said Bouza." As for Anderberg, "her devotion to her faith was a driver. She really did not only want to help the river, but to help those kids."

To less committed individuals, the task would have been frustrating. Illegal dumpers, many of them garbage haulers whose bases were in the nearby industrial Bronx, returned. Bouza didn't find the work discouraging. "I expect humans to be humans," he recalled, but he figured that "once you restore it to a certain point, then you have people with an interest in the restoration. . . . People begin to respect it."

Even polluted, the Bronx River was one of a few scarce recreational opportunities available to a city kid. Freddy Ferrer, born in 1950, grew up a short walk away, in the Hunt's Point neighborhood. His mother, a bookkeeper, worked at the Hunts Point market, the acres of land near the borough's southeast tip that serve as the food-distribution center for much of the mid-Atlantic United States. "My own personal interest in the river is that I used to swim in it," he recalls. "I should be glowing in the dark."[6]

Two decades later, to a new generation, the lure of the river remained. "This was personal," says Ruben Diaz Jr., born in 1973, "as this was my neighborhood, and it's still my neighborhood." As a kid, Diaz and his friends, sporting their oldest sneakers, used to walk to the river, detouring to "avoid the beefs we had with the guys in the Bronx River [housing] projects." They would arrive at "the Tarzan swing," a rope-tire swing beneath the 174th Street bridge, and jump in. The boys would take off their clothes and "stand up on cars that were dumped in the river."[7]

Ferrer and Diaz grew up to be elected officials—Ferrer as Bronx borough president from the late 1980s to 2001 and Diaz in the state assembly from the late 1990s until 2009, when he, too, became borough president. They used their power to improve the environmental state of their borough—not a goal that earlier generations of black and Hispanic politicians, concerned about immediate issues such as unemployment and housing, had pursued. In 1993, Ferrer helped create a plan that recommended "establishing a Bronx Greenway via linear parks and bikeways"—an idea that seemed fanciful.[8] "When I was a young Assembly member," says Diaz, "if you [were] a young black Latino official," the conventional advice was that "you want to get on all the social service committees." But his chief of staff "convinced me that . . . I should sit on the environmental conservation committee." As Serrano worked in Congress to bring federal dollars to revive the river, Ferrer and Diaz worked to bring state and local dollars.

At the turn of the century, they found an odd ally: Republican governor George Pataki. Pataki was a natural environmentalist. "I grew up on the shores of the Hudson," north of New York, he recalls. "As a kid, we were told, don't put your foot in it, it's polluted. . . . I worked in a factory in the summers. Whenever you had waste or pollution, you'd just turn a valve and change the color of the river." Upon election in 1994, Pataki says, "one of the most important things to me [was] recapturing the waterfronts [across the state]. The Bronx River was obviously one that desperately needed it."[9]

Pataki was mindful of politics; a Republican governor in a Democratic state, he courted Democratic support. In 2005, Diaz recalls, when Pataki was pushing to get voters to approve a bond act to authorize the state to borrow money for infrastructure, "I was helpful in adding a Latino voice . . . [and] we were able to secure some of the [funds] for the Bronx." Pataki provided millions to clean up the river more thoroughly than neighborhood volunteers could. Once again, the National Guard pulled cars out of the water. The Guard "loved doing it," says the former governor, "because they were doing something creative rather than training." As the work finished in the early 2000s, "I remember kayaking with Jose Serrano. He was just stunned."

What would keep the Bronx River clean was activity. By then—thanks to lower crime, public investment in housing, and immigration—the Bronx had reversed population losses. Residents needed a refuge from asphalt. That meant creating parks along the river—Ferrer's long-desired greenway. Ferrer is no fan of former mayor Rudy Giuliani nor of his parks department commissioner, Henry Stern. But, he says, "to give the devil his due," Stern supported the project, declaring 1999 to be "the year of the Bronx River." A year later, the city inaugurated the first park path along the river, the Soundview Park Greenway; Stern promised a corridor of such paths, as the state and city were building along Manhattan's waterfront.

In 2001, advocacy groups formed a nonprofit, the Bronx River Alliance, to raise money, coordinate volunteers, and advocate for more government investment. The next year, a new mayor, Michael Bloomberg, took office, and supported waterfront parks. In 2008, the city transformed an illegal dump into Hunts Point Riverside Park. To give children a safe place to cool off—multiple children had drowned in the river—the city placed the "floating pool lady," a supervised pool on a barge, where the Bronx and the East Rivers met; the following year, the city conjured another park, Concrete Plant Park, from a long-shuttered concrete plant. In 2013,

Bloomberg's last year, the city opened the first part of the thirteen-acre Starlight Park, once the site of an early twentieth-century amusement park. What was once a neglected waterfront was becoming a ribbon of parks, playgrounds, and ballfields.

Facing a Wall of Traffic

There was one problem: hundreds of thousands of parents, grandparents, and children who lived within walking distance had no convenient, safe way to get to their new open spaces. Grandparents wheeling carriages and teenagers looking to play ball had to navigate wide intersections menaced by fast-moving trucks and traipse upstairs to a highway overpass just to reach their theoretically walkable parks. People coming from other directions had to scramble across highway ramps. For years, groups had fought for "these beautiful parks," says Danny Peralta, head of The Point Community Development Corporation. "[But] it was not safe to get to them." Walking to a park, "you're going to come up against industry," including trucks going to and from Hunts Point warehouses. Even getting bus service was a struggle. The Point CDC and fellow groups fought every year to get a bus to the "floating lady" pool, only to repeat the process the following summer, until, finally, "it became a permanent fixture."[10]

The most egregious barrier was a twentieth-century highway: the Sheridan Expressway. The Sheridan—named after a Bronx engineer, Arthur Sheridan, who died in a 1952 Bronx car crash with an oil truck—was one of the Moses era's last highway projects. In the 1940s, the state and city conceived the Sheridan to connect the southern Bronx's other planned highways, the Bruckner and the Cross-Bronx. The Sheridan was to cut north from the Cross-Bronx past the Bronx Zoo and beyond. But anti-highway groups halted the completion of the Sheridan. In 1963, all Moses was able to open of the Sheridan was a one-mile stretch between the Cross-Bronx and the Bruckner: a "highway to nowhere," as critics derided it. The state "de-mapped" unbuilt portions, along with the Lower Manhattan Expressway, in 1971.

Yet thousands of trucks each day rumbled through the Bronx via the stub. To the west, people lived in single- to three-family homes and small apartment buildings; to the east, beginning in the new century, beckoned the new Starlight and Concrete Plant parks. In between was the six-lane interstate, at the same level as surrounding streets, but cut off from pedestrians and cyclists by concrete walls. Rather than cross from one side of the road to the other, the two hundred thousand New Yorkers who lived within a mile had to walk out of their way on a desolate service road to a single overpass littered with trash. "Here we are, cleaning up the Bronx River," says Diaz. "We have fish in the river. I even put in a ladder for heron. We have two beavers in the river, Joe the beaver, Justin Beaver. Now . . . what do we do with the Sheridan?"

An umbrella group called the Southern Bronx River Watershed Alliance, created in 1999, had considered this problem even before the parks' creation. Wanda Salaman is executive director of Mothers on the Move, one of the groups that joined the alliance. (The other local groups included Youth Ministries for Peace and Justice and Nos Quedamos ["We Stay"]; the coalition received technical assistance from the Tri-State Transportation Campaign and the Pratt Center.) Salaman came to New York from Puerto Rico in 1975, at eight, and remembers "the burning, the destruction, . . . [and] then learn[ing] what community organizing was."[11]

A preventable tragedy spurred Mothers on the Move and fellow organizations. In 1998, a six-year-old girl named Crystal Vargas was cycling in a patch of the Hunts Point green space. "A truck jumped the sidewalk and killed her," says Salaman. As with the death of three-year-old Anna Pellone in Washington Square Park fifty-six years earlier, New York's press, to the extent that it noticed the death, blamed the victim. "[The girl] was riding her bike around . . . a small grassy area . . . when she veered off the sidewalk . . . and hit the rear of a passing truck," the *Times* reported, quoting a police determination that the death was "truly an accident."[12]

Vargas's neighbors would have none of this. "That [death] got the members in Mothers on the Move upset," recalls Salaman. "[They] started to look at the truck route . . . [and] did this whole study," finding that more than fifteen thousand trucks were traversing Hunts Point every day. Over the more than half century since the market had opened and grown, "the city had not changed the route" for trucks. The group convinced the city to add traffic-calming measures. "Before, they didn't have islands," says Salaman. "Trucks cannot just go anywhere. That is something that our members were proud of . . . that took us into [considering] the Sheridan."

The alliance's next target was harder than anything Jane Jacobs and fellow twentieth-century anti-highway advocates had accomplished: not preventing a highway but unbuilding one. "We kept having all these meetings," she remembers. "We did our own study ourselves." The alliance decided to "go for the highest thing . . . [and] tell elected officials [we] want to decommission [the Sheridan] and close it down," creating a green space in its place.

The groups became savvy in local politics. "Some stuff was city, some stuff was state," Salaman adds. In 1999, they gained the attention of local officials. That year, Adolfo Carrión, Jr., an urban planner before he won office as a Bronx city councilman in 1997, asked the state transportation department to consider converting the expressway into parkland, observing that "there are so many highways through residential areas" that "these communities have been taken for granted."[13]

The state and city balked. (The state controlled the Sheridan but wouldn't act without city cooperation.) As the state said in 2001, getting rid of the expressway would force thirty-seven thousand vehicles each day, including two thousand trucks, onto nearby roads. Yet, as Majora Carter, then leading the Point CDC, pointed out, such vehicles were *already* using local roads; competing roads were saturated, contributing to the Bronx's traffic plague.[14]

Faced with a demand that they were reluctant to meet, state and city government chose an old tactic: stall. In 2012, after a study conducted with Obama-era federal funds, then-mayor Bloomberg came to the same conclusion, calling the displacement of highway traffic to streets a "fatal flaw."[15] A year later, with weeks left in office, Bloomberg released a compromise: turn the interstate into a boulevard. Barriers would come down, and three new crosswalks, protected by traffic signals, would connect western neighborhoods to the river. The Sheridan would continue to move cars and trucks, but it would resemble Manhattan's new West Side Highway, crossable to the river on foot at grade level.[16] A year later, the city council endorsed the idea.

Erasing an Interstate, with a Catch

Yet transforming the Sheridan would need the support of the governor: Andrew Cuomo. Cuomo was an exception to political antipathy toward big infrastructure projects. Pursuing what he called "the most ambitious transportation development plan in modern history," he often invoked Robert Moses as an example of what New York could do. "We lost our daring. . . . We don't think big anymore," he told business leaders in 2016.[17] From the replacement of the Tappan Zee Bridge across the Hudson River to building a third track for the Long Island Rail Road; from rebuilding LaGuardia Airport to completing the Moynihan Station train hall across from Penn Station, Cuomo upgraded New York.

Bronx officials wanted him to take on one more project: the Sheridan. Marcos Crespo succeeded Diaz as assembly member in 2009. He saw Diaz as a mentor; as an intern in 2003, he had admired Diaz as "the hip-hop assemblyman and a young guy. . . . I was impressed with someone who could wear his TIMs and listen to hip-hop, then put on a suit and debate environmental justice." For years, as a legislative staffer, Crespo followed the progress of Sheridan activists. After his own election, he found, as Diaz had, that "as a person of color, they tend to steer you to social services. . . . I said, there are three committees I have to have, environmental conservation, transportation, and energy." Of groups working to decommission the Sheridan, he says, "I felt pressure. We had to find a way to deliver this."[18]

Crespo redirected pressure to Cuomo. "When Andrew got elected," he says, "he would hold these breakfasts. I would get up every year and raise my Bruckner Sheridan project," a megaproject that included the conversion of the Sheridan into a boulevard. For decades—dating to 1997 but discussed informally before that—the state had mulled ways to ease traffic to the Hunt's Point market. A reason the southeast Bronx was an attractive location for wholesale meat, fish, produce, and prepared-food vendors was the convergence of interstates that could move perishable goods quickly in all directions: the Bruckner Expressway, the Cross-Bronx Expressway, and the Major Deegan Expressway and their connections to New Jersey, New England, and Long Island. But no interstate brought trucks directly into the market, meaning that truck drivers had to exit highways and traverse Bronx streets. The state had long considered building highway connections directly from the Sheridan and Bruckner to the market, and widening the latter, to reduce the temptation for trucks to choose local streets, but officials had never acted. The project was expensive, area residents were skeptical, and it would involve years of construction in a traffic-choked corridor. "Build a new road?" Cuomo asks rhetorically. "Are you kidding me? Did you read Robert [Caro on] Moses?"[19]

Crespo notes that the governor was always "championing his investments in Buffalo. . . . We would tell him, look, I know you're focused on Buffalo, if you take a second to look what's happening in the Bronx, everything you're trying to do in Buffalo, you're accomplishing in the Bronx . . . [with] major investments in the Hunt's Point [food] market." Finally, the governor said, "'Ruben, Marcos, let's talk, what is this project?' We said, 'well, it's an important project.'" Trucks on the streets were "hurting our community, creating asthma." The governor told the two men, "I'm committed."[20]

Cuomo took on the Hunts Point Interstate Access project and combined it with converting the Sheridan into a boulevard. That latter part was a concession exacted by Diaz and Crespo. Diaz notes that when the governor decided to do the project, "they were telling me, look, we're willing to do this, willing to invest real money . . . [but] they wanted to move quickly. As the borough president, I cannot leave a billion-plus dollars on the table." Diaz remembers the March 2017 conversation he and Crespo had with the governor, down to the date and time, because the governor's plan omitted crosswalks at the same level as the Sheridan, instead proposing a new overpass. "Marcos was fighting with the governor," he says, "saying, 'there's no way, we're just gonna accept one overpass.'"[21] As Crespo recalls, "They said, 'we can address this by putting in some elevated crosswalks.' I said, 'absolutely not. I have an entire network of these along that Bruckner that your agencies won't maintain, and I have residents risking their safety running across.'"[22] With Diaz acting as "good cop," the governor compromised, approving the at-grade crosswalks.

Cuomo says he was motivated by the prospect of removing trucks from local streets. "When I was nineteen years old," he recalls, "I sat in a meeting with my father, with people in the South Bronx talking about their asthma. . . . I sat there saying, this is the most outrageous disgusting situation, where because these people are poor, [the government] is letting their kids get sick rather than just build new roads. You didn't have to cure cancer here, it was just, stop the trucks from coming down my block." Of the Bruckner-Sheridan plan, he says, "people had been talking about it for fifteen years . . . [but] nobody really cared, because it was the Bronx. . . . The poverty and power of a district has a lot to do with it."

Cleverly, from a political perspective, the governor positioned the aspect of the two-part project that local people wanted—the Sheridan teardown—ahead of the aspect that activists were less enthusiastic about: new highway infrastructure. In 2016, the governor approved nearly $100 million to begin tearing down the Sheridan. The move garnered a nod in *Streetsblog*, not normally a Cuomo fan. A year later, Cuomo unveiled the second part of the $1.8 billion project: the new interstate connections.[23]

A Calm Boulevard, but at a Cost

As details of the new interstate connections became clear, though, activists felt hoodwinked. They had agreed to the interstate access portion of the project, they maintained, because officials had told them that new interstate ramps would avoid residential areas; ramps would bring trucks right to industrial areas. Now, though, the state insisted that it could not put the ramps where residents desired, away from homes and parks.

As state transportation officials put it in the project's environmental review, to build one ramp where residents desired would require agreements with both Amtrak and CSX, the freight railroad. But both Amtrak and CSX had "expressed opposition," with the latter saying the ramp would "significantly reduce [railyard] efficiency." The state, it reminded the public, was "prohibited by prior court decisions from using eminent domain to acquire property rights from the railroad," so, effectively, there was nothing it could do.[24] The state's final proposal "would put an elevated highway segment over Concrete Plant Park, with truck traffic running between the residential heart of Hunts Point and the waterfront, including Hunts Point Riverside Park," *Streetsblog* reported.[25]

Diaz and Crespo tried to convince community groups that this plan was the best they could achieve. Diaz candidly explains how his own views had changed over the years, from considering converting the Sheridan altogether into a park to accepting the final compromise. "As an assemblymember [representing a portion of the Bronx]," he says, "I thought we should really consider [eliminating the Sheridan]. . . . [But, as borough president,] my views of the world are much amplified. I see that Hunt's Point is an economic engine for the Bronx. We feed the whole northeastern market. . . . What we get is the boulevard [as well as bike lanes,] which is a compromise. You get [an interstate] flyover from the Sheridan [Boulevard] . . . to get the trucks through."[26] Crespo, too, acknowledges that "the ramp . . . was one of the major problems," with "the same groups excited about this . . . turn[ing] their back." Crespo argued to constituents that "this needed to move forward. . . . It wasn't plan A. But it was a good B+."[27]

Advocates split. In 2018, Maria Torres, then president of the Point CDC, pronounced the plan "disgraceful," adding, "This city built this beautiful park and finally gave residents access to a cleaner Bronx River. Now the Department of Transportation plans to create a barrier by sending more trucks to this area. Children and families would have to cross a major truck route and breathe in all that pollution just to enjoy open space on the waterfront."[28] As Dariella Rodriguez, who advocated for the South Bronx at Youth Ministries for Peace and Justice before moving to the Point CDC as community development director, puts it, "It's really, really frustrating. . . . We have this community-led solution, all this support and participation, put together a coalition and alliance, and say, this is what we need to do, all that work, but instead of the government saying, hey, this is what we're seeing, they're like . . . we're going to do it our way. . . . There's this big, bad Robert Moses that we're all acknowledging, but our government now is doing the same thing. The only difference is that Robert Moses was not an elected representative, and we have elected officials now making solutions for neighborhoods that they are not in. . . . There's a highway on top of you, there's highway all around you, it smells, it's disgusting."[29]

Tawkiyah Jordan was also frustrated, from the perspective of having worked for the city on its plan, only to be thwarted by the state. Born in the Bronx, she moved as a child to Queens. As her mother ran a Bronx child-care center, she estimates that she spent about 80 percent of her childhood there. In 2005, she began working at Youth Ministries for Peace and Justice, advocating for Starlight and Concrete Plant Park; later, she worked for the city planning department, presenting Sheridan possibilities to residents. Were it not for Carrión, Crespo, and Diaz, she says, "[as well as] the way these community organizations navigated . . . "[the Bronx] would not have seen the Sheridan [become a boulevard.] . . . When you watched a Diaz Jr. move from that community to becoming the borough president," she says, "it's a big deal. He's still carrying the history and the connections to the neighborhood. . . . Not that it means he's going to do whatever the community asked, because that's not what happened, but grassroots intentions liv[ed] in him." Nevertheless, Jordan pronounces herself "horrified" by the state's locations for the highway ramps. "It's like a bait and switch, [an] age-old story, it kind of pisses me off. . . . It's so annoying, so frustrating and disheartening," she says. Building the ramp "more in the industrial section would have preserved the investment and hard work."[30]

In 2019, the state inaugurated the new Sheridan Boulevard. "The Sheridan Expressway is opened up, giving back beautiful greenspace to the Bronx River," Cuomo said. Some longtime anti-highway activists are conciliatory. "We spent seventeen years on this project," says Salaman of Mothers on the Move. "[Yet] crosswalks are a compromise. . . . People can at least cross the street and go to the other side without going up those steps on 174th Street that are filled with garbage and needles." Similarly, says Elena Conte, an advocate and organizer who worked on the Sheridan project at the Pratt Center, "I have very mixed emotions about the final plan. There was a real missed opportunity." And yet, though "twenty years for three crosswalks" may not sound like much, "walking across the Sheridan on those crosswalks can bring me to tears, knowing how hard the community fought." To get to Starlight Park, she says, "I don't have to go up, down and around, I can just cross. The wall is down. The access is . . . tangible."[31]

The Sheridan improvement notwithstanding, New York had, once again, in a new century, chosen the old century's solution to traffic: build highway capacity. Mychal Johnson is a Chicago native who has lived in the Bronx for more than two decades; he fights the Bronx's asphalt curse through South Bronx Unite. The larger issue than the location of highway ramps or the number of crosswalks is that the South Bronx is the center of "heavy intense industrial use": not just the Hunts Point market, but power plants, waste-processing sites, oil-tank storage, truck depots. The concentration of trucks, industry, and roads makes the South Bronx "a heat sink," he notes, as he and a visitor walk around on a day approaching ninety degrees. A community garden offers modest relief, but it sits in the Bruckner's shadow and is often shuttered. Pedestrians must holler to one another on streets as trucks rumble overhead, exhaust visibly magnifies the heat, and heavy loads echo overhead from one bumpy interstate segment to another. During the pandemic, he says, "when things shut down, it was so much quieter."[32]

Yes, it is better for Bronx pedestrians and cyclists that trucks use an interstate rather than local streets, and it makes sense to connect the interstate more directly to Hunts Point, if not directly into the market. But since before the building of the Cross-Bronx, New York has proven that when it builds more capacity, it will get more trucks and cars. Absent enforcement of truck routes, truck drivers frustrated with traffic on the new interstate connections will detour to streets, anyway, saturating the South Bronx with more traffic. Every time the city has a choice of whether to burden the South Bronx with more trucks, it always chooses the burden. Not much more than a decade ago, Johnson notes, the city subsidized the relocation of FreshDirect, a high-end grocery-delivery service, from Queens to the Bronx. Yet FreshDirect added one thousand truck trips each day. Manhattan residents accept their FreshDirect deliveries without thinking of the people who live near the trucks. "It should never be OK to do that again," says Johnson. South Bronx residents must "show community power," he says, so officials "understand that there is a possibility of losing your seat or your job if you don't represent the desires of your community members."

No Moses to Blame Anymore

On November 15, 2021, President Joe Biden signed into law the Infrastructure Investment and Jobs Act. Thanks to $1.2 trillion in investments, the president promised, "your life is going to change for the better." The same month, Bronx Congressman Ritchie Torres and New York senator Chuck Schumer stood near a small sliver of green, Virginia Park, a chain-link fence behind them. A sheer drop below, cars and trucks sped down the trench of the Cross-Bronx. "The Cross Bronx Expressway, built by Robert Moses, is both literally and metaphorically a structure of racism," Torres said. "It has left [in] its wake decades of . . . environmental degradation." Meeting with Biden's transportation secretary, Pete Buttigieg, months earlier, he recounted, "I said, 'Mr. Secretary, . . . you have the opportunity to be the transportation secretary who dismantles a legacy of Robert Moses.' Cap the Cross-Bronx Expressway, to liberate the South Bronx from its greatest environmental and public-health burden." Schumer noted that the infrastructure law included $7.5 billion for cities around the nation to stitch highway-riven communities together.

Standing with Torres and Schumer was Nilka Martell, whose organization, Loving the Bronx, had been advocating to cap part of the Cross-Bronx for nearly half a decade. Martell wasn't an activist until 2010, when she lost her job. The next spring, waiting to hear from potential employers, she looked for ways to channel energy. The Bloomberg-era MillionTrees NYC project had planted trees on her block, so she and her children "started taking care of the trees. . . . We were impressed by how many kids want to do volunteer work." From fellow volunteers, she learned about the Bronx River Alliance, on whose board she now sits, as well as Youth Ministries for Peace and Justice.

Through her son's involvement with Youth Ministries, "I started learning about . . . the high asthma rates, the lack of waterfront access, the fact that we have all these highways." She had also "started picking up books," particularly Kevin Walsh's *Forgotten New York*, which "led me down a rabbit hole of wanting to know more about this borough I called home." She had already suffered the Cross-Bronx's impact. As a child in the late 1970s and early 1980s, she remembers having friends who lived on the other side of the expressway, and "it really created a divide. . . . We weren't allowed to go visit them. . . . It really just destroyed communities." Now, she learned that "Moses had no problem just bulldozing these buildings down for . . . car traffic."

Martell got a grant to improve her own block and expanded her scope, considering ways to improve nearby Virginia Park. At a meeting of the South Bronx River Watershed Alliance, she saw a presentation for the Sheridan. Part of the presentation was "different things going on in different cities. One of them was this concept of deck parks, portions of highways that were capped." Because the Sheridan was not a below-grade highway, "we knew that [concept] didn't really [apply to] the Sheridan"; and because the Bruckner, by contrast, was elevated well above grade, "it wasn't something that could be done on the Bruckner. . . . [But] when we went back to Virginia Park [above the Cross-Bronx]," she notes, "we were like, holy shit . . . can that be implemented on the Cross-Bronx? . . . We were like, oh, wow, we didn't even know this could be possible."[33]

Through Loving the Bronx—so grassroots that "we don't have a budget," Martell says—she took that knowledge and applied it practically. "We're pretty sick and tired of top-down decisions," she says. "People coming in and telling us what's best for us. We're experts, too. We live here, we are the ones who are impacted by the air pollution, by the noise pollution." Since 2016, she and fellow advocates have been talking to "anyone who would listen, neighbors, elected officials, businesses, business improvement districts." At first, she said, "people would laugh, and say, that's a cute idea. . . . [But] we were like, listen, this is being done in other cities, we're not pulling an idea out of a hat."

At first, Martell and fellow advocates pushed just to cap the small sliver of the Cross-Bronx between Virginia Park and Virginia Playground, to make one green space. But in 2018, Loving the Bronx approached Assemblywoman Karines Reyes, a freshly elected official, for her support. Says Martell, "We thought, we have a shot . . . because Reyes is a registered nurse." Reyes encouraged the group to be ambitious. "Why are we only advocating for this one portion?" she said. "If there's a little bit over two miles [of the 6.5-mile highway that are open-cut trench, and thus appropriate for capping,] let's advocate for the whole thing." Above the Cross-Bronx, Martell says, instead of dead, dirty air, "could be playgrounds and open space," and perhaps housing and small-business kiosks. "No one is gonna come give us new land. If we can cap these portions, we have two miles of new land." Loving the Bronx worked with students from a nearby high school to consider different ideas. "This is going to be ten, fifteen years," says Martell, meaning students will be tomorrow's adult advocates.

Martell expanded her circle to add formal expertise. She read a 2018 analysis led by Dr. Peter Muennig, health policy professor at Columbia University's Mailman School. The study, published in the *American Journal of Public Health*, found that capping a 2.4-mile portion of the expressway would pay for itself in benefits to the more than two hundred thousand people who lived within a half-mile: health benefits, ranging for more opportunities for exercise to lower noise pollution, would add nearly two months of life expectancy. Together with increased property values, if properly distributed, the investment would yield $1,629 per resident. Such gains "more than made up for the project's steep price tag," then estimated at $757 million, the authors concluded. Muennig became interested in the Cross-Bronx during his medical residency in the Bronx; at the time, he read *The Power Broker*, and the story of the highway's creation and neighborhood destruction "was always in the forefront of [his] mind."

Muennig worked at the Fordham Family Health Center, treating patients with diseases resulting from poor community design, including asthma and obesity. He went back to school to get a policy degree to "look at nonmedical policy interventions that can prevent disease." From that perspective, the Cross-Bronx "seemed like a really logical area." He is heartened that advocates have found his study useful: "My job is to provide good science. Their job is to turn the science into actionable policy."[34]

In 2020, Martell notes, "[the pandemic] provided a platform to look at these issues. Our environment was shitty to begin with," exacerbating pandemic suffering. In 2021, Torres, former city councilman, took office as congressman for the South Bronx—the country's poorest district. Loving the Bronx contacted him. On Earth Day 2021, Torres, Reyes, and Martell unveiled their vision. Months later, they stood with Schumer. Thanks to the federal infrastructure law, the city won a two-million-dollar grant to study the possibility, to be released in 2024.

For Torres, too, the Cross-Bronx is personal. "What motivates me is asthma," he says. Torres can cite statistics—the Bronx has nearly the highest asthma death rate in the nation, at almost four times the national average—but he has also lived it. Torres, born in 1988, grew up in the Throgs Neck public-housing development, near where the Cross-Bronx dumps traffic onto the bridge of the same name. As a child, Torres was hospitalized repeatedly for asthma. "You are breathing through no fault of your own," he says, gesturing just above the Cross-Bronx to the air that, on a 90-degree-plus day, he and his visitor could see as well as feel. Referring to the pandemic, "When we were sheltering in place," he says, "the rate of asthma fell" along with traffic.[35]

Referring to highway scars, he says, they are "not an accident. . . . Communities of color paid a heavy price" for infrastructure that benefits not the local area but the broader region. Referring to the hashtag promoted by the Black Lives Matter movement, "I can't breathe," he adds, "We can't breathe in the Bronx." Like Martell, Torres notes that capping a highway is not a new idea. "There's precedent," he says, referring to Boston's Big Dig, as well as projects in Seattle and Dallas. Unlike Boston, "capping is far less extreme than digging"; the hole, in effect, is the existing open-cut highway. Maintaining an open-cut highway, he notes, is a "choice"—to inflect bad air on people who cannot use money to escape. "There would be no greater manifestation of racial equity" than green space instead of a sheer drop to asphalt.

Capping the Cross-Bronx Expressway faces obstacles. The project doesn't have official support from the governor or mayor—something that, as Cuomo's years in office prove, is vital to any large project. Notwithstanding the Mailman School estimate, the price tag is likely billions of dollars. In New York, the Cross-Bronx competes with multiple projects, including rebuilding a deteriorated portion of the Brooklyn-Queens Expressway that goes through Brooklyn Heights, a wealthy neighborhood. In the mid-twentieth century, community pressure forced New York to cover that BQE stretch with a cap of a kind Cross-Bronx neighbors want: the Brooklyn promenade. In the United States, the Cross-Bronx proposal is competing for dollars against projects in swing states. Cuomo is sanguine. "You would need a political force that doesn't exist," he says, "a visionary force that doesn't exist." Torres says that "[his] greatest point of pessimism is America's seeming inability to build." Muennig observes that "how slowly things get done in New York" has a public health impact. "While this deliberative process is happening, all this bureaucratic red tape going on . . . people are dying." He calls it "the human cost of bureaucracy."[36]

"Long-term," says Martell, "if we want to change the trajectory of the Bronx, we have to make this a healthier borough. The only way to do that is correct the wrong that Moses did. The federal government funded the creation of the Cross Bronx. Why wouldn't they want to invest in correcting it?" Moses has been out of power for more than half a century and dead for nearly that long. Who is in charge—Moses's apparition or us? "We may be low-income families, we may be people of color," says Martell. "But that doesn't mean that we don't deserve clean air. We don't realize how powerful we are."

Chapter 20

Deliveristas and Dining Sheds

Locked-Down New York Unlocks Its Streets

> Citi Bike . . . quelled all of my transportation worries during the height of the pandemic!
>
> —Elizabeth G., hospital pharmacist in a Tweet, February 23, 2022

> It's a parking war. . . . I've slept in my car to wait for a spot.
>
> —Sandy Blackwell, Bronx resident, March 26, 2022

ON MARCH 2, 2020, Mayor Bill de Blasio and Governor Andrew Cuomo had inevitable news. The nation had already closed its border to China and was about to close the border to Europe; Manhattan's streets had been less peopled for weeks. The city confirmed its first COVID-19 case. The mayor tried to comfort city dwellers. "We have the ability to keep this contained," he said. "If, God forbid, it spread, spread, spread, . . . we have 1,200 [hospital] beds ready." Two weeks later, seven New Yorkers were dead. "We're going to repeat ourselves a lot," de Blasio said. "Stay home as much as you can. That guidance might get a lot sharper."[1] Four days later, COVID deaths reached forty-three. The mayor issued a decree: "Effective Sunday, March 22nd, at 8:00 p.m., all non-essential businesses in New York City will be closed."[2] On one day, April 7, 816 New Yorkers died of COVID—nearly one out of every 10,500 city souls, gone within twenty-four hours.

By then, the unthinkable was routine. Door by door, shopkeepers and restaurant managers had posted handwritten signs as they locked up. As weeks passed, the hastily scrawled sheets, many promising a reopening "next week" or "in a few days," were out of date, relics of optimism along with bright-green St. Patrick's Day shamrocks and pink-and-white Easter bunnies stranded in storefronts. Broadway was dark. New York lost nine hundred thousand—22 percent—of its private-sector jobs in days. Though white-collar workers kept their jobs, offices were empty—lone, masked guards pacing marble lobbies. Bankers and lawyers worked from kitchens and bedrooms. Hundreds of thousands of wealthier residents fled the city.

That spring, the sound of New York was stillness. The streets' few walkers stood in the middle of avenues, their selfies memorializing the phenomenon. Residents sequestered in apartments marveled at quiet, punctuated by ambulances. Birds were louder. Dogs on walks made a racket with metal tags clanging.

As spring turned to summer and beyond, COVID-19 revealed the best and worst of New York, moment to moment. As nurses and bus drivers risked their lives, murders soared. As New Yorkers made friends with neighbors, fatal overdoses broke records.[3] As peaceful crowds took over streets to protest the Minneapolis police murder of George Floyd, looters took advantage of a law enforcement vacuum to smash shop windows. One could walk by a refrigerated morgue truck but enjoy the sun on one's face.

COVID-19 upheavals further revealed the city's transportation strengths—and weaknesses. New Yorkers depended on decade-old bike lanes and pedestrian streetscapes as never before—but also sought refuge, from disease and crime, in anti-urban cars. The year 2020 harbored hints at two possible futures for a post-COVID city: a decisive victory for cyclists, pedestrians, and outdoor activities over the car as the city recovered or a return to the automobile and a diminishment of New York.

The Good Year

By 2019, New York hadn't won the battle to control the car, but it was in the best position it had been in for three-quarters of a century. Traffic deaths, at 220 overall and 124 pedestrians, were below one-third of 1990 levels. As then-mayor de Blasio said in his state of the city speech, "We're getting safer in ways we couldn't even have imagined decades ago. Last year, . . . we had the fewest traffic fatalities since 1910." He reminded the audience that "in 1910, . . . New York City had half as many people, and there were more horses . . . than cars." By 2019, half a million people were cycling each day, twice as many as a decade earlier.[4] Every day, hundreds of thousands of tourists crowded Times Square, and New Yorkers enjoyed pedestrian spaces from Jackson Heights in Queens to Fordham Plaza in the Bronx. The city and state were regulating Uber. In less than two years' time, if all had gone as planned, Manhattan would have had congestion pricing.

So many tourists and workers crowded Rockefeller Center and Times Square that Christmas that de Blasio gave walkers more room. "When the world descends on Rockefeller Center for a month," the mayor said just before Thanksgiving, "additional tools are clearly necessary." The mayor closed streets around the famed tree until New Year's and gave pedestrians an additional lane on Fifth Avenue. The "historic pedestrianization," as the mayor called it, allowed locals and tourists to spread out, laughing as they took pictures rather than being squeezed by strangers. As New Year's week ticked down to 2020, it was as common to overhear Chinese and Italian on Midtown streets as it was to overhear English.

New York's streets weren't perfect. That year, the city suffered twenty-eight cyclist deaths, up from ten the previous year. Bike and bus lanes remained clogged with illegally parked cars. More than half a century since urbanists had killed the Lower Manhattan Expressway, too many New Yorkers breathed in fumes and dodged traffic created by highways. Clunky "sugar cube" barriers to protect pedestrians from vehicle attacks cluttered bike paths and sidewalks. Notwithstanding these deficiencies, able-bodied people could walk or bike the streets more comfortably and safely than at any other time in auto history.

New York's uneasy transportation peace reflected and enabled the city's robust health. By 2019, the city had a record population, between 8.5 and 8.8 million, a quarter above its late-1970s low. The city had a record number of private sector jobs, nearly 4.2 million. The roaring economy and teeming streets were the cause and effect of public safety. With annual murders at 319, nearly 90 percent below 1990 figures, New Yorkers and visitors were less likely to be victims of violent crimes than they had been in generations. (In 2017 and 2018, annual murders had fallen below 300, levels not seen since the 1950s.)[5] Traffic deaths and murders had peaked in 1990, and for three decades since, they had fallen.

Hints of trouble were emerging. The number of people entering core Manhattan daily had stagnated since 2015, near 3.9 million, and the population had perhaps peaked. But data were mixed and not necessarily bad. Some white-collar jobs were moving to Brooklyn and Queens. If a few people were leaving the city altogether, they were leaving because the city had gotten too crowded and expensive—a challenge, but a different one from four decades earlier. In 2019, when the delivery giant Amazon, facing public opposition to its city and state tax breaks, canceled plans to build a headquarters in Queens, New Yorkers' reaction was to shrug: we had enough jobs and people. If any American city could withstand a crisis in 2020, it was New York.

A Ghost Town Needs Its Buses

Regan Weal couldn't stay home during COVID's worst days. By 2020, Weal, raised on Manhattan's Lower East Side, had operated a bus for the Metropolitan Transportation Authority (MTA) for fourteen years. She had followed both her mother and grandfather into transit. "I love driving," she says. "I get to know my regulars."

In the weeks leading up to March 2020, Weal paid attention to the pandemic spreading in China and Italy. But, she said, "I honestly thought about it like you think about anything, it's not going to happen here." Her concerns grew as she saw, "It's starting to come closer." On her route down and up Manhattan's Fifth and Sixth Avenues, "my regular [customers] started to disappear," people with discretionary schedules locking themselves down before the city did. Weal's route passes through Times Square. By mid-March, "it was a complete ghost town. I have never seen New York looking like this." It was "eerie," she remembered, "to see Times Square without even a parked car."[6]

Weal's mother worried about her going to work—as did she. "It was a struggle," she recalled. "The world is on fire; you have to go to work." Weal had to go to work because some of her customers had to go to work. Ridership reflected who had to keep commuting, despite danger to themselves and their families. Before COVID, in 2019, MTA buses saw 2.2 million weekday trips, compared to the subways' nearly 5.5 million.[7] The grim first week of April 2020, New Yorkers rode the subway for just 423,294 trips each weekday—not even 7 percent of normal, the smallest number in history. Ridership on the region's two commuter railroads for suburbanites was nearly nonexistent. Each day that week, though, buses logged 423,720 trips, 19 percent of pre-COVID numbers. For the first time, bus ridership exceeded subway ridership.

People taking the bus as COVID spread could not work at home. Hospitals needed nurses' aides; supermarkets needed stockers. The city's lowest-paid workers, now "essential workers," lived far from easy subway commutes. Bus riders stayed quiet, but "people who did talk, talked about how scary the situation was," Weal says. Bus operators were fearful of

COVID, especially as many passengers worked in hospitals. At the request of the union, the MTA required riders to enter through the back door, far from the farebox, making the $2.75 ride temporarily free.

Louis Ortiz, a Bronx native and a bus operator for nine years, remembers driving through Manhattan, as "everyone was locking everything down." It was so empty, "I didn't even know if I was going to have a job. [My family told me,] stay home. My wife was certain of me catching it." Ortiz caught COVID-19 that March. He was hospitalized for seven days, "hooked up to oxygen" when being in the hospital seemed "a death sentence," and out of work seventeen days.

Ortiz returned April 17. "It was kind of surreal," he says. "I'm driving down the West Side Highway, you could bowl a ball down there." Manhattan wasn't entirely empty, though. "If I had fifteen people" on the bus, he says, "that was a full bus. . . . Hospital workers . . . would thank me for getting them to work. . . . We are as essential as essential workers can be."[8]

The people on the bus notched a bitter victory. With few cars on the road—bridge and tunnel traffic fell to a quarter of normal—and with fare-free boarding eliminating payment delays, bus speeds shot above nine miles an hour, the highest in decades. With "no cars and no people," Weal idled at stops to keep to her schedule, which had built-in time for traffic. "Not one parked car" obstructed her route, Weal remembered. "The weirdest thing."[9]

Weal and Ortiz were among the first New Yorkers to observe social and public-safety dislocations that COVID-19 began to magnify. Mentally ill homeless people taking the bus with no destination made for an "uncomfortable situation," Weal remembers. Even before COVID, as bus drivers who interact with the public, "we had a high assault rate." Ortiz, Weal's colleague, remembers that asking people to wear masks, as the MTA required starting in April, caused tension. A customer might board the bus with no mask only to react badly to being asked to wear one. The customer would put the mask on, but then another unmasked customer would board. "There's pressure because that [first] person is watching," Ortiz says. If Ortiz avoided confronting a maskless passenger, another passenger "will start yelling at them, yelling at you."

Bikes as Lifelines

Essential workers used bike lanes as never before. What had been a handy, healthful way to get around became a lifeline. The city had reshaped its streetscape over the previous decade to take a relatively few miles of pavement away from cars and create safer passage for cyclists. This transformed map helped New Yorkers who couldn't stay home to get to work.

New Yorkers following orders to stay home depended on delivery riders to bring them groceries. These workers depended on bikes. Outside the Whole Foods Market near Midtown's Bryant Park, shuttered to customers and transformed into a warehouse, cargo cyclists loaded bright-yellow grocery tubs and cycled up the Sixth Avenue bike lane to Manhattan homes. Hospital workers shunned subways in favor of open-air rides. In April, the city's top Citi Bike docking station was near three Upper East Side hospitals; before COVID, the station was only thirty-one on the list. "On a normal, pre-coronavirus week, the busiest stations were near transit hubs such as Grand Central. . . . Now, all the action is at hospitals," *Streetsblog* reported.[10]

The city responded, building temporary bike lanes along major corridors and connections to bridges. "We did nine miles of bike lanes in a week and a half, which, for us, is pretty astonishing," said Polly Trottenberg, de Blasio-era transportation commissioner.[11] The city worked with Citi Bike to add stations near hospitals. "Will there be a Citi Bike dock at NYP Columbia Hospital???" one worker tweeted in early April.[12] Nobody would dare say that a nurse's aide commuting via Citi Bike was "begriming" a neighborhood. During the summer and fall, New Yorkers fortunate enough to have been able to stay home during lockdown began to navigate their city again. They, too, rode bicycles.

New Yorkers' reliance on bicycles showed up in numbers. Bridges and bike lanes showed a 33 percent increase from May to December, from 5.4 million cycling trips in 2019 to more than 7.2 million. On Prospect Park West, the bike lane some locals had fought barely a decade previously, ridership exceeded 800,000, compared to 600,000 in 2019.[13] In 2020, 40,000 people used a bicycle to enter core Manhattan each day, up from 33,000 the year before. Travel by bicycle into Manhattan rose, even though white-collar workers stayed home most of that year; overall travel into Manhattan below Sixtieth Street—by any means—fell by more than half. In 2021, New York City saw 550,000 cycling trips daily, an increase over the 530,000 rides in 2019, even though most office workers continued to stay home and the city was missing hundreds of thousands of jobs. Subway ridership, by contrast, rarely exceeded half of normal in 2021.

With supply-chain woes creating a shortage of bikes for purchase and with novice cyclists having no idea how to maintain a bike, Citi Bike became a workhorse for a traumatized city. In 2020, notwithstanding lockdowns, an average 54,459 people used Citi Bikes each day, only 5 percent below the 2019 level. On nice days, Citi Bike broke the 100,000-ride-a-day figure. The trend held in 2021.[14] By the end of the second COVID year, Citi Bike was the only form of organized transportation to surpass pre-COVID levels.[15] In the cold-weather month of December 2022, with subway ridership at two-thirds of pre-COVID normal, 51,204 riders used Citi Bike each day, compared to 31,458 each day in December 2019.

Yet though COVID-19 revealed strengths of the city's bike network, it also revealed weaknesses. Progress on protected bike lanes remained slow, resulting in unnecessary deaths. Though cycling was safer than ever before, relative to the number of riders, it was still less safe than taking the subway, walking, or riding in a car. It didn't have to be that way: London, Paris, and other global cities boasted better safety. Six cyclists died in London in 2020 and ten in 2021, one-third of the number of people killed over those two years in New York (45), despite similar populations.

New York's food-delivery cyclists, mostly immigrants, faced disproportionate risk. Like bike messengers in the 1980s, they faced pressure to deliver food quickly from restaurants that were miles away—so much pressure that, unlike messengers, they had to spend up to $2,000 to purchase a motorized "e-bike," legalized by the city and state in early 2020. This expensive equipment made workers vulnerable to violence, which soared in 2020. In March 2021, an assailant shot and killed Francisco Villalva Vitinio, 29, in Harlem, stealing his e-bike.[16] In September, an assailant knifed a Grubhub worker to death in a Lower East Side park, also for his e-bike.[17]

The bigger risk was crashes. In 2021, at least fourteen *deliveristas* died in traffic.[18] One victim was Babacar Dia, 44, a Haitian immigrant, killed in Brooklyn in September by a speeding motorist who fled. "For somebody to just hit him and keep going like that is just inhumane—as if he was an animal," his widow, Hanifah Dia, said.[19] Because delivery workers were "independent contractors" for tech companies such as Uber, not hourly-wage employees, they didn't receive compensation for injury. Their families did not receive compensation after a death. The "apps" also disavowed responsibility for humane working conditions, including providing bathrooms.

The industry's refusal to take responsibility in another area proved deadly: storage, maintenance, and charging of e-bikes. Poorly built and maintained e-bike batteries are flammable, and fires spread quickly. But delivery workers stored, charged, and maintained work equipment at home, in overcrowded apartments. Between 2021 and late 2023, twenty-seven New Yorkers died in e-bike fires sparked by faulty batteries. Until 2020, this cause of fire death was nonexistent.

Delivery workers' frustrations spurred them to organize, as messengers had protested three and a half decades previously. A new advocacy group, El Diario de los Deliveryboys en la Gran Manzana, or the Diary of the Delivery Boys in the Big Apple, attracted 2,900 members. Leader Sergio Solano, a New Yorker for sixteen years, has delivered food since 2007. He's been robbed "two times, almost three. . . . No place [is] safe," he said in 2021.[20] That summer, *Streetsblog* reported, "about 85 delivery workers . . . marched . . . to the 40th [police] Precinct house . . . in Mott Haven, [the Bronx,] and later rode to the 25th Precinct station house on East 119th Street in Harlem to express their frustration with the slew of attacks."[21]

The city's failure to grapple with e-bike safety had repercussions beyond delivery workers. When the city legalized e-bikes in 2020, it did so without building wider bike lanes. Spacious lanes would enable faster e-bike riders to ride separately from pedal-bike riders, including children. The city also failed to enforce laws against riding above the twenty miles per hour speed limit and riding the wrong way in parks and on sidewalks. These deficiencies caused friction. A family with children on Central Park's bike paths had to watch for an e-bike delivery worker traveling faster than twenty miles per hour. The ubiquity of e-bike riders in narrow lanes also deterred women from taking up cycling. Until 2018, the number of women cycling to work climbed for more than a decade, to 30 percent of the total. After, it fell, in percentage and in real numbers.[22]

Higher speeds created a danger for non-working e-cyclists, as well. In 2023, thirty cyclists died, "the deadliest year for cyclists in New York City since 1999," the *Times* reported. Twenty-three of the dead cyclists were e-cyclists, most of them not working for a delivery company but either commuting or riding recreationally. Nearly one-third of the e-bike riders who died in crashes died in single-vehicle crashes—that is, they were not hit by a car or truck. In other words, e-cyclists were dying in motorcycle-style crashes into poles or medians, driven by high motorized speed and recklessness. Citi Bike was contributing to the higher death toll; whereas once the bike-share program encouraged people to take up slow-speed urban pedal cycling for the first time, now, its new e-bike fleet encouraged people who had neither ridden a bike in city traffic nor ridden a motorcycle to drive a motorized two-wheel vehicle in urban traffic. The results were tragic: four Citi Bike e-bike riders died in 2023.[23]

The proliferation of e-bikes presented a new danger to pedestrians as well. Between 2021 and 2023, ten pedestrians died after being hit by e-bikes or other motorized two-wheeled vehicles. Through 2020, it had taken thirteen years for ten pedestrians to die under the wheels of bicyclists, e-cyclists, or mopeds, fewer than one per year. In September 2023, after a decade of operations, Citi Bike claimed its first pedestrian: the operator of a Citi Bike e-bike ran a red light in Lower Manhattan and killed sixty-nine-year-old Priscilla Loke.[24] E-bike legalization also coincided with the proliferation of two-wheeled motorized devices, such as dirt bikes and gas-powered mopeds, that remained illegal. The city's unwillingness to keep such illegal two-wheeled vehicles off streets and to enforce speed-limit and route laws for e-bikes created conditions for a renewed "bikelash."

The new dominance of e-bikes on New York's streets posed a challenge beyond the physical; it posed a philosophical and intellectual challenge. For decades, New York cycling advocates argued that anyone, or almost anyone, could ride a pedal bike; the major impediment was the lack of safe places to cycle on city streets. Yet beginning in 2020, pedal cyclists found themselves crowded out of their protected bike lanes by fast-moving e-bikes. The ubiquity of e-bikes represented the triumph of a car-culture argument: that is, that the average person needed a motorized, fast-moving vehicle to get around a dense city.

Outdoor Space Is the Only Space

In 2020, New Yorkers who wanted to socialize, exercise, or get a change of scenery from their apartments had to do so outdoors. Before the pandemic, pedestrian plazas had been an amenity; during the pandemic, they became a necessity. From Times Square to Jackson Heights to Fordham Plaza, a car-free space was one of the city's only pleasures.

In April, the Times Square pedestrian plaza was surreal. It was possible to stand in the bowtie and not see a soul. The daily pedestrian count fell from an average of 375,224 walkers to just 33,320, a 91 percent drop.[25] Famed billboards featured not advertisements, but messages of support to locked-down New Yorkers. The Red Steps were gated to discourage congregating. Yet 33,320 people is not nothing—and the people who were there were different from the people who had preceded them weeks before: locals, not tourists. The Naked Cowboy never left; half-masked, he chatted in his underwear with New Yorkers. By summertime, Times Square's break dancers were back, watched by entertainment-starved locals who had never given the young men's dance routines any mind before.

Outdoor space had proved such a necessity that New York made more of it: hundreds of blocks of car-free streetscapes. In April, as the weather warmed, Mayor de Blasio launched Open Streets. "This summer is going to look different from any other in our city's history, and we're ready to give New Yorkers more ways to leave home while staying safe," the mayor said.

The mayor did on a grand scale what Janette Sadik-Khan had done the previous decade in Times Square: throw up barriers and decree a street closed to traffic. De Blasio gives the city council credit for this idea. "I was worried, could it be done safely? Are people still going to drive on them?" the former mayor remembers.[26]

Some Open Streets became dead spaces—but "some of them were fantastic," the former mayor remembered. On the Upper West Side's Columbus Avenue, residents walked with children and dogs, greeting neighbors from a distance and giving their kids space to run. In Jackson Heights, a dense area of mid-rise apartment buildings and two- and three-family homes without much parkland, the city made thirty-six long blocks of Thirty-Fourth Avenue into a promenade. Teens rode bicycles unaccompanied, while children skipped as parents walked behind them. The Thirty-Fourth Avenue program proved so popular that locals petitioned the city to make it permanent. "Everybody basically has a park right outside their door" now, said one resident, Jim Burke. "One of the densest parts of Queens has become a small town."[27] (Although not without complaining: as one resident lamented, "If I would have wanted to move to a park, I would have saved my money to go to Central Park.")[28]

Pedestrian streetscapes remained a respite as COVID wore on. In the mid-Bronx, on a sunny, chilly Halloween afternoon, children dressed as Spiderman and ghosts filed Fordham Plaza, needing prodding from parents to hold out baskets for trick-or-treating. A singer belted out a number and announced a cupcake-eating contest. Teens dressed as cats and witches chatted as they walked. Entrepreneurs displayed merchandise, from homemade vegan coquito to crystal rock jewelry, under the Fordham Flea Market's white tents. Families purchased lobster rolls or chicken *pinchos*, taking food to French café-style tables and chairs. "This place is a beautiful place," said Kenya Mighty, a performer whose NEST Music Conservatory works with neighborhood children. After being "shut up for a year, we can be alive." Before New York had expanded Fordham Plaza a half-decade previously, remembered Mighty, who lives nearby, "God, it was desolate. . . . This was really just a circle for the buses"—much like Manhattan's Washington Square Park six decades earlier.[29]

New Year's Day 2021 was the strangest such occasion Times Square had ever hosted. The evening before, the festivities had gone on, for TV—but the shimmering ball had dropped without guests below. The next morning, a few hundred New Yorkers ventured out to see the ball at the bottom of its pole. They took pictures of the "2021" emblem, a sign that the city would move on from the pandemic, if only through time's passage. Confetti gathered under hot-dog carts. Strangers smiled at one another as adults took videos of their children running and shouting. Grover Whalen would have recognized the scene: for the first time ever, Times Square was a play street just for New Yorkers.

Dining in the Street

New York's biggest pandemic initiative to take back streets from cars wasn't for walking, cycling, or sitting. It was for dining. For most of 2020, the state and city prohibited indoor dining and even forbade groups from meeting at residences. To save restaurants that had been closed for months and to buoy individuals who longed to eat a meal with a pal, New York moved restaurants outdoors. Under de Blasio's new "Open Restaurants" initiative, which launched in June, owners put tables and chairs on the sidewalk and in the street, taking over parking spots.

Open Restaurants took over the city. More than twelve thousand restaurants took over 8,550 parking spaces, out of three million spaces citywide.[30] It "was one of the scariest things I ever did, and definitely the most popular," says Trottenberg. Open Restaurants was "urgent," says de Blasio. "I talked to a lot of people in the industry. They were just scared to death. It looked like just massive business failures. We believed that hundreds of thousands of jobs were at stake," permanently.

De Blasio had seen outdoor dining on a 2018 family trip to Montreal and thought New York could do the same. "I was hesitant about some of the negatives," the former mayor said, including the possibility of cars crashing into diners, "but I said, let's just do this. Let's just go for it. I was worried about the jobs." In creating a permit process, "what was really important [was] to keep it incredibly simple. . . . They were dealing with so much stress, they needed this process to be extremely stripped down. The [Department of Transportation] brought me this application form, I said, I want you to get me something that you can do in a few clicks." Visiting Melba's restaurant in Harlem, he remembered, he learned from owner Melba Wilson, "It took less than five minutes. That was a triumph of anti-bureaucratic thinking."[31]

"What we did not assume," the mayor said, "was that it would have a huge psychological impact." All summer and afterward, from Queens' Long Island City to Greenwich Village, Harlem's Central Park North to the Bronx's Arthur Avenue, New Yorkers desperate for conviviality ate and drank where empty cars had sat inert. In many cases, they were seeing friends for the first time in months. Manhattan's Ninth Avenue became a cocktail party; in the morning, locals doing grocery shopping threaded through al fresco brunch. New Yorkers walking or cycling enjoyed the sound of conversation and clanking glass. Some restauranteurs built elaborate plywood sheds, festooned with fairy lights and plastic flowers, and commissioned murals.

Open Restaurants brought human-scale activity to neighborhoods oppressed by the relentless infrastructure of cars and trucks. Nestled between the Bruckner Expressway and the Bronx River in Hunts Point is the Boogie Down Grind Café, owned by Majora Carter, a small-scale business owner and activist. As she reopened Boogie Down, Carter built two dining sheds, one "fabulously" decorated. In an area defined by cars and trucks, whether bumping overhead on the Bruckner or jammed at intersections honking and spewing exhaust, Carter's tables were an opportunity for residents to claim a portion of their streets. "Open-restaurant seating" where drivers had parked "literally doubled the capacity of our 30-seat café," Carter notes.[32]

Even locals who didn't eat or drink at Boogie Down embraced the idea. As Carter set up the open-dining structure in a parking space, she remembered, "There was this one guy who decided he was the decider of how the space should be used [and he wanted parking]. What was really interesting was the response of most of the people who were around, whether or not they were patrons. [People said,] 'No, he's wrong.' I thought that was a really interesting thing, coming from a community [where] even people without cars would talk about how bad parking is. . . . People said, 'no, streets are not just for cars.'" Carter says, though, that what is "super annoying" is that drivers who lost spots parked in crosswalks, making it difficult for neighbors to navigate.[33]

For New Yorkers suffering the trauma of COVID, as well as double-digit unemployment and urban unrest, Open Restaurants and Open Streets were the first glimmer of joy in months. With two-thirds of New Yorkers supporting outdoor dining, the mayor planned to make it permanent.[34] The streets repurposing "is a rather dramatic step," said William Dean, who had cowritten *Pedestrian Revolution* five decades before. "We are going through a cataclysmic event in the city. . . . When the thing is over, you sometimes see changes that are made for the good stay around."[35]

As COVID-19 fears lessened, Open Streets and Open Restaurants garnered opposition. On some Open Streets, as in Play Streets days, drivers got out of cars and moved barriers out of the way or drove over them.

Conflict arose between drivers and restaurants, too, because despite restaurants in parking spaces, most street space still belonged to cars. To protect diners from cars and trucks rushing by, the city required restaurants to set up ugly crash barriers. Within the barriers, dining sheds—some complete with windows and heating—oriented diners away from the street and sidewalk, not toward them, as in cities such as Paris and Milan. Even as drivers enjoyed multiple lanes of Ninth Avenue, dining structures crammed on the side of the roadway made it difficult for people with disabilities to navigate streets. Waiters crossing a bike lane to reach diners had to watch for cyclists and vice versa. New Yorkers in restaurant-packed neighborhoods such as the Lower East Side revived their perennial issue of noise, something the city has long failed to enforce; with bars outdoors, noise was louder. New Yorkers complained that in cold weather, dining sheds were unused.

Some complaints were from drivers who wanted what they considered their space back. They had grown accustomed to parking unused vehicles on public streets for free, and they didn't want people eating there. In Greenwich Village, one man held a sign: "MIND IF I PARK ON TABLE #4?"[36]

Pedestrian Plazas' First Crime Test

Decades earlier, when officials had proposed a Times Square pedestrian refuge, New Yorkers had feared that taking space from cars would encourage loitering, disorder, and crime. New York inaugurated its Times Square pedestrian plaza in 2009, when crime was reaching record lows. In late 2019, though, crime began to rise, and in 2020, it rose quickly, creating a test of how the new Times Square would handle disorder and violence.

As in the 1970s and 1980s, no single factor caused New York's rise in violent crime. COVID's spread came as New York was grappling with the state legislature's reforms to the criminal justice code, made over the previous three years, to keep people charged with nonviolent and even some violent crimes out of jail pending trial and to impose new burdens of evidence discovery on prosecutors; the jail population fell precipitously.[37] COVID hobbled social and homeless outreach services, and New York's police department was understaffed in early 2020 because of sickness and quarantine; later that spring, resources were stretched responding to protests, both peaceful and violent, against George Floyd's murder. Courts were closed. People with severe mental health problems or records of violent crime, or both, were left to their own devices; arrests, already falling steadily for years, plummeted by one-third in 2020.[38] Teenagers with no school had nothing to do. Streets were unpeopled with passersby whose presence, in Jane Jacobs's "eyes on the street" theory, prevented disorder.

New York became less safe than it had been in years. Between 2019 and 2020, the city's murder level rose by 47 percent, to 468, the fastest increase in history. In 2021, at 488, the number of murders was 53 percent above pre-pandemic levels, outpacing the 37 percent increase nationwide. In 2022, the number of murders, at 433, remained 36 percent above 2019 levels. The number of felonies in 2022, 126,537, was 31 percent higher than the 2019 level, the highest level since 2006.

In Times Square, history reverberated across decades. As in the 1970s and 1980s, the bowtie was the epicenter of disorder. As they always had, people suffering from mental illness or drug addiction traveled to Times Square from around the city and the country because they were out of options. But crowds and police enforcement that had constrained behavior were gone. The situation was even more fragile, because in the pandemic, to avoid sheltering people in communal shelters and spreading COVID further, the city's social services agency housed thousands of homeless men—many afflicted with mental illness and addiction—in Manhattan hotels, with nothing to do during the day; drug dealers congregated to prey on addicts.

Times Square became the sharp edge of a new reality of danger. Between 2019 and 2022, in the two police precincts that encompass Times Square, felonies increased 41 percent; murders rose from two in 2019 to seven in 2020 to eight in 2021 to nine in 2022.[39] A May 2021 shooting injured three regional tourists who had ventured back to New York, including a child. The following month, another shooting injured an off-duty Marine. That October, Maria Ambrocio, a fifty-eight-year-old emergency room nurse visiting from New Jersey to lunch with a friend, was knocked to the ground by a suspect who had just robbed someone; the suspect had been freed without bail after a sexual assault. Ambrocio died of head injuries.

Yet core Manhattan's surge in stranger-on-stranger crime wasn't concentrated in Times Square's pedestrian plazas. The area's most troubled spot was nearby Eighth Avenue, a heavily traveled car and truck route. Between fall 2020 and spring 2023, Eighth Avenue was the site of three murders, ranging from a homeless man stabbed to death to a fatal shooting by drug dealers. Drug users and dealers preferred to conduct their activity on sidewalks or under buildings' scaffolding, far from the daylight of even mostly empty plazas. Though pedestrian spaces weren't immune to the city's new chaos, neither were car-heavy thoroughfares.

Manhattan's most troublesome spots of car-free disorder weren't pedestrian plazas but traditional parks. Starting in 2020, Washington Square Park became an attractive nuisance: a magnet for drug sales and use, brawling and boxing matches, gambling, and all-night partying. In 2022, in Washington Square Park, two men were stabbed in two separate incidents over marijuana sales. Few people, though, would suggest paving parks.

Soaring crime demonstrated not that public spaces are ungovernable, but that New York must police public spaces, because public spaces are critical to a successful city. In 2021 and 2022, neighbors around Washington Square Park petitioned the city to resume enforcing rules. Times Square Alliance officials similarly petitioned the city to enforce laws against drug dealing. As Tim Tompkins, who left the Times Square Alliance in 2021, says, "All these things come back to the effective management of public space. This very delicate mix of order and disorder, spontaneity, and order," is "incredibly tightly related to these issues of safety." By 2022, tourists were back in Times Square. To deter antisocial activity, the alliance, like play street supervisors decades before, offered programming from high school choruses to art installations. That July, the number of visitors to the bowtie topped 350,000, 87 percent of normal.

Mayor de Blasio, who had once considered ripping up the Times Square plaza, made more room for visitors on foot. In 2021, de Blasio permanently widened car-free streets to the north and south of Times Square itself. "These improvements will make Broadway more vibrant," the mayor said. Junior's Cheesecake set out bright orange tables and chairs for returning tourists. South of Times Square, along Broadway, New Yorkers in the Flatiron District and near Union Square sat licking ice cream, sipping coffee, scrolling phones.

De Blasio acknowledges his turnabout. "My own path started in a pretty traditional place," he says. "A lot of progressives are culturally traditionalist. It's not [that] I was like, 'oh my God, aren't cars great?' But I did like the life of the city, the flow of traffic, . . . the honking of horns." His work cutting traffic deaths before the pandemic, though, influenced his thinking. "It made me feel more and more that we could lean into pedestrian plazas."[40]

A Bad New Dependence

One of the paradoxes of COVID-19 New York was that as New Yorkers took refuge in car-free streets, they also took refuge in cars. As the city reopened, traffic returned. By summer, bridge and tunnel traffic had reached three-quarters of normal, and by mid-2021, it reached pre-COVID-19 numbers. By 2022, bridge and tunnel traffic surpassed 2019 levels. Cars returned even as Manhattan's offices remained half empty.

As in the 1970s—but to a severer degree—fewer people coming into core Manhattan created more traffic. In fall 2020, the number of people coming to core Manhattan each day fell by nearly two million, compared to the pre-COVID year. On an average fall day in 2020, fewer than 1.7 million people entered core Manhattan, less than 44 percent of the nearly 3.9 million people who had entered the previous year. But many people who returned chose the car.[41] In 2020, 727,000 people arrived via motor vehicle, 80 percent of the 2019 level of 910,000. By contrast, just 738,000 people arrived by subway, barely one-third of the more than 2.2 subway arrivals in 2019. In late 2019, people arriving by subway had comprised 58 percent of Manhattan commuters and visitors and motor-vehicle occupants 24 percent; in 2020, by contrast, the percentage of people arriving by subway was 44 percent, barely exceeding the 43 percent arriving by motor vehicle. It was the first time the numbers were close to parity. (The balance commuted via commuter rail, bus, ferry, bicycle, or foot.)

This phenomenon intensified in 2021, as Broadway theaters, Madison Square Garden sporting events, and other venues reopened. Traditional rush hours remained quiet, but weekend streets backed up, as people who once would have taken transit to entertainment drove to Manhattan instead. By November 2022, tolled trips through the two MTA tunnels leading into Manhattan were 3.6 percent above 2019 levels; on weekends, trips were 6.3 percent higher than in 2019. "They're driving in more," observed Ortiz, the MTA bus driver. As they drove, they resumed parking in bus lanes.

Shifting Congestion from Manhattan

The city's biggest post-COVID traffic problem wasn't in Manhattan but in the outer boroughs. For the first time ever, people didn't *have* to go to Manhattan to perform well-paying jobs. In 1966 and in 1980, during the city's two twentieth-century transit strikes, white-collar New Yorkers had done everything in their power, from roller-skating to chartering boats, to come to Manhattan every day, lest they prove themselves irrelevant. During COVID, they worked from home, far longer than the government asked them to, and reoriented routines.

New York's mass-scale commuting cessation made the transit system less convenient for hundreds of thousands of people. With time saved not commuting, people embarked on other trips—and those trips weren't convenient by transit. New York built its transit system starting in the nineteenth century to get people to Manhattan jobs—first in factories and warehouses, later in offices—from outer-borough and suburban homes. Much of the transit system was designed, in routes and scheduling, to bring people into Manhattan in the morning and bring them home in the afternoon.

Peter Madonia, a Bronx native whose family owns a bakery in the storied Arthur Avenue Italian district, explains the modern problem that arises from the fact that planners did not think of how to get someone from Brooklyn to the Bronx or from New Jersey to Queens. "To get from borough to borough, every single human [via train] has to go through Midtown Manhattan," Madonia observes. "If you came from Brooklyn and moved to the Bronx, how are you going to get [back to Brooklyn] to visit your family?" The city's highways, by contrast, were built to go around Manhattan, not through it, and are convenient for borough-to-borough trips. Yes, it is possible to take a train, or multiple trains, from New Jersey to the Bronx, or from the Bronx to Queens, or from Westchester to Brooklyn. But it is faster and easier to drive, even with traffic. Driving is even more convenient on weekends and during evening hours, when trains are infrequent and slow.

Of the Bronx's Arthur Avenue, Madonia observes, many former residents long ago moved to the suburbs, following the pattern of twentieth-century migration. But they and their children and grandchildren return to shop at Italian stores and eat at Italian restaurants, just as Indian Americans who migrated to the suburbs from Queens' Jackson Heights return. For a family to take commuter rail to Arthur Avenue involves a drive to a station, round-trip tickets costing more than fifty dollars, and a half-hour walk or bus ride. A family eating a meal in the evening risks missing an infrequent train home. "There is some role for cars," Madonia says, and the issue is "how to manage it."[42]

For people freed from commuting by COVID, if they didn't want to confine themselves to grocery stores and restaurants within walking distance, and if they didn't want every leisure trip to be into Manhattan, it made sense to use a car. In mid-2020, New Yorkers purchased cars at a record pace. "In Manhattan, Brooklyn, Queens, and the Bronx, the number of [new] vehicles registered between August and October jumped 37 percent compared with the same period the previous year," the *Times* reported.

As New York woke up from its COVID coma, more cars and more time freed from a transit commute meant more traffic. "A pandemic that has transformed countless work routines and shopping habits is now upending long-established traffic patterns, shifting the congestion that has paralyzed Manhattan for years to the city's other boroughs," the *New York Times* reported in 2021. On major arteries, including the Cross-Bronx, speeds were slower than before COVID.

New car owners meant that even as New York demonstrated how convivial it was to dine in the street, a larger parking constituency wanted to reclaim that street. As he waited for his normal Brooklyn spot after street sweeping, one car owner, Anthony Fauci (no, not that Anthony Fauci) observed in 2021 that "the gentlemen's agreement allowing drivers to reclaim their [parking] spots once cleaning is finished has been nullified. Now drivers swoop." Another Brooklyn parker, Noreen O'Donnell, lamented competition. "It's like the Hunger Games for parking," the Boerum Hill resident said. "It's not harder now—it's relentless."[43] In Kingsbridge Heights, a Bronx neighborhood, Sandy Blackwell told the *Daily News*, "It's a parking war. Everybody got a car. I've slept in my car to wait for a spot."[44]

Scarce Ubers

Even as some New Yorkers bought cars, the pandemic pointed up what the mania over Uber a half-decade eariler had obscured: for-hire car service could never be a substitute for transit. In March 2020, the pandemic pushed yellow taxi and Uber drivers off the streets. March 9 was Pat Johnson's last day. "I took home $40," he says. "People were fearful. The city was obviously dead." By April, trip levels were 84 percent below pre-COVID levels. Only one-quarter of drivers remained on the road.[45]

By 2021, passengers were back—but drivers were not. Uber prices skyrocketed to attract drivers via higher fares. As drivers returned, new city rules mandated higher pay, and the companies, under investor pressure to turn a profit, could no longer heavily subsidize rides. In November, *The Points Guy*, a travel website, noted that prices to one of New York's three airports exceeded $150. A taxi, by contrast, cost $72, including tip. "Taxis are just more convenient—that is, if you can find one," author Caroline Tanner informed readers.[46]

Johnson, the cabdriver, returned to work. With less competition from Uber, he could make a living. "People have told me they're glad to see the yellows, because Uber is charging more." The system was working again, at least for a while, as it was supposed to. People who wanted to take a premium service in a transit-rich city could pay the Uber price. People who could not afford a premium could wait to hail a cab. Said another customer, "It's so fun to hail a cab like the olden days."[47]

People who couldn't regularly afford any car or cab service—which is many people—needed transit. "I ride the bus every day [to work] from . . . Ozone Park [Queens] to the hospital in Jamaica Hills," Fermina H. of Queens told Riders Alliance. "My biggest challenge is how unreliable the Q24 is. . . . The other day I waited for forty minutes for the bus. . . . Sometimes, the unreliability results in a taxi ride, which is too big of a cost."[48]

A Resurgent Street Menace

New Yorkers were in greater peril starting in 2020 not just from random knifing, shoving, and shooting attacks, but from drivers, as one type of antisocial behavior bled into another. Murders and traffic deaths had fallen in tandem from 1990 until 2019. Now, they rose together.

For the first COVID months, New York's streets brought more strangeness than danger to pedestrians. Pedestrian crashes fell as New Yorkers heeded the call to stay home. By mid-May 2020, the city had gone fifty-eight days without a pedestrian killing—the longest ever. That full year, thanks to the spring pause, the number of pedestrian fatalities was 96, 23 percent lower than the 124 walkers killed in 2019.

As pedestrians returned to streets in modest numbers, by summertime, the lull was over. In June, ten pedestrians died, compared to nine the previous year; in July, eight pedestrians died, compared to six the previous July. Manhattan pedestrians encountered another alienation, in addition to the revived danger: a blank wood-scape where well-tended windows once beckoned. Storefront after storefront, from boutiques to chain drugstores, were boarded up with fragrant plywood to deter opportunistic looters and organized thieves who had begun menacing New York.

As traffic careened toward normal, so did deaths: 126 walkers died in 2021. Fatality numbers would have been comparable to 2019 figures, but the number of pedestrians remained fewer, so the rate was higher. Pedestrians had lost the safety-in-numbers phenomenon, wherein drivers had no choice but to move carefully because of the mass of people on foot.

Ironically, given their resistance to traffic-calming measures, motor-vehicle and motorcycle drivers were mostly killing themselves, their passengers, and fellow drivers in greater numbers. A small percentage of drivers, particularly teens and young men, in the absence of school or work, spent the pandemic drag-racing and joyriding. Police did little to deter them, in line with the city's lighter approach to disorder: summonses for moving violations fell from nearly one million in 2019 to 510,000 in 2020 and recovered only to 607,000 by 2022.[49]

Drivers are "behaving outrageously," said Sam Schwartz, former traffic commissioner, after a young, speeding, late-night BMW driver fatally drove himself and two passengers off the Henry Hudson Parkway onto train tracks below. In 2020, 122 motorists or passengers died, 79 percent higher than the 68 who died in 2019. The situation improved somewhat in 2021 and 2022 with 113 and 99 deaths, respectively. Motorists pushed the city's overall 2020 traffic toll, despite lower pedestrian and cyclist deaths, to 242, up 10 percent from the 220 killed in 2019. In 2021 and 2022, the figures were 275 and 263, respectively. As with murders and felonies, the 264 deaths in 2023, along with the previous two years' fatalities, represented nearly a decade's lost progress.

In September 2021, New York recorded one of its youngest-ever traffic victims. Three-month-old Apolline Mong Guillemin, in her stroller in Brooklyn, died under the wheels of a car driven the wrong way by an unlicensed driver who had racked up dozens of speed- and red-light camera tickets.[50] The city agreed to two thousand petitioners' request to close the block and create a refuge called "Apolline's Garden"—despite objections from neighbors who didn't want to lose parking spots.[51]

That November, Families for Safe Streets held its annual "world day of remembrance" for traffic victims. On the steps of Brooklyn Borough Hall, as the sun set on a wan, chilly afternoon, family member after family member stood in lemon-yellow T-shirts with photos of loved ones, reciting names to mark the year's toll. Eighteen hundred flowerpots were arrayed on the steps, each sprouting a stick with a lemon-yellow placard of the name of someone who had died on New York's streets since the launch of Vision Zero eight years earlier.[52] "There are no names yet for December," said traffic-violence widow Mary Beth Kelly. "The saddest thing is, we know there will be."

Chapter 21

Sick Transit

Whither the Subways—and New York?

People may permanently alter their commutation behavior.
—MTA warning to bondholders, March 18, 2020

The best way we can honor him is change things.
—Delilah Goble at Garrett Goble memorial, March 26, 2023

WHEN PAT FOYE, chairman of the Metropolitan Transportation Authority (MTA) from 2019 to 2021, recalls the moment he realized that COVID-19 would be a crisis of unfathomable depths, he doesn't talk about near-vanished ridership, multi-billion-dollar deficits, or his own COVID case in March 2020. Instead, he remembers the news he received March 27: "Garrett Goble." Around 3:00 that morning, an arsonist—a homeless man with a recent history of violent crime—had set fire to the inside of a subway moving through Harlem. The fire, with few riders to stamp it out, destroyed the car and damaged the 110th Street station. The arsonist injured seventeen people. He killed Garrett Goble, the thirty-six-year-old train operator who put himself in danger to bring passengers to safety. The Brooklyn man had a "beautiful family," says Foye—wife, Delilah, sons Noah, then ten, and Hunter, an infant, and mother, Vicki. Delilah and Garrett had been together for fourteen years. Garrett had taken a job with the MTA because, Delilah says, "he wanted to provide for us."[1] Delilah believes the death was preventable. "When I say my husband died, automatically, it's like, 'oh, COVID,'" Delilah said later. "And I'm like, 'no, it's not how he lost his life, it's because some idiot tried to set a train on fire.'"[2]

Goble's murder by fire in the first dark weeks of COVID was a harbinger. In the nearly 116 years since October 27, 1904, when Mayor George McClellan Jr. had taken the ceremonial silver controls of New York's first subway and guided riders from City Hall to 103rd Street, the transit system had endured crashes, fires, strikes, floods, crime, and terror attacks. But neither transit nor the city had confronted anything like COVID: a crisis that crippled both the means of transit—crowding people together to get them from point A to point B—and the goal of transit, to congregate people in cities. Beginning in March 2020, COVID-19 repelled riders. After the acute public-health risk abated, passengers stayed away. Office workers grew accustomed to working from home, and New Yorkers grew accustomed to walking or taking bikes or cars. As the city attempted to lure commuters back, violent crime also rematerialized, after decades of dormancy. New York wouldn't recover from COVID-19 and its aftermath unless it revived public confidence in public transit.

A Subway Hero's Departure

February 21, 2020, was Andy Byford's last day as subway and bus chief. After two years, Byford had resigned, frustrated by what he called Governor Cuomo's "intolerable" micromanagement.[3] Byford had accomplished something unusual, becoming a transit president with public name recognition. On that final day, he hopped aboard a crowded F train to say goodbye. "You did the best job," one passenger told him.[4]

One group of riders was particularly distressed to see Byford go: disability rights activists. In 2017, a new group called the Elevator Action Group had begun a campaign, Elevators Are for Everyone, for access to mass transit. Disability rights organizations had sued the MTA, charging that the MTA's substantial station renovations amounted to building new stations, which, under federal law, must be accessible to all. Byford was the first transit chief who seemed moved by their concerns; in 2018, he had appointed the transit system's first-ever "accessibility" officer.

Yet to most people, Byford's departure seemed more like inside-baseball politicking than another crisis. Nearly 83 percent of trains were on time, up from the low of 58 percent in 2018.[5] For 2019, ridership, after three years of decline, was up slightly, close to 5.5 million trips each weekday.[6] Throughout the subway maintenance turmoil of the past few years, riders had continued to benefit from a longer-term success: thanks to public safety gains over decades, men, women, and even older children alone could take the subway—day or night, whether in the South Bronx or Times Square—without fear. With an average of one to two murders in the subways annually, people never thought about violence.

That day, the *Times* featured a story on the business page: "Why the stock market isn't too worried about coronavirus." If investors had been on the subway, they might have thought differently. As early as January, before New York confirmed a COVID case, riders encountered a novelty: passengers sporting masks and latex gloves. "I don't touch the poles," one rider told the *New York Post*. "I don't want to get it. I am really scared." Other passengers, the reporter noted, "shot side-eyes at anyone who dared to cough."[7]

Riders noticed something else: each day, the train was less full. By March 9, even without government warnings to stay home, ridership fell below five million; more than 10 percent of passengers weren't there. With masks in short supply, more of the ever-smaller band of riders were wearing something—a scarf, a T-shirt—around their nose and mouth, though nobody had told them to do so. Another alien experience was the absence of human noise. Chattering tourists and college students were gone, as were gossiping bankers shuttling between Wall Street and Midtown. People rode alone, fearful and mute.

Like passengers, transit workers wanted to wear masks. The MTA forbade this practice, saying masks were not part of the uniform. The MTA's reasoning was that masks would scare passengers. The MTA was trying to avoid frightening its riders at the same time it was discouraging them from crowding trains, a contradiction summed up in a March 9 *Post* headline: "Coronavirus in NY: MTA Chief Calls Subways Safe—But Also Says Avoid Them." The MTA's further reasoning was that the agency, with no public health expertise, was following federal Centers for Disease Control guidance, which discouraged public mask use, in part to preserve mask supply for hospitals.

Increasingly, though, MTA managers doubted federal advice. Officials noticed that "the CDC was making that decision based on mask availability, not on what made the most sense," recalls Sarah Feinberg, the Obama-era federal transportation official who succeeded Byford as acting transit president as the pandemic hit.[8] By the second week of March, the MTA reversed course. As the Transport Workers Union sent a bulletin to members telling them that if they ignored the MTA's directive, the union would back them, and in response to the reality of COVID's spread, the authority allowed workers to mask up. By April, ahead of the national government, it required both customers and workers to wear face coverings, handing them out at stations. Many people wore two masks or a scarf over a mask. "A reflection of how horrible things were in New York for so long [was the fact that] we had 92, 96, 97, 98 percent of people wearing masks," says Feinberg. "It's hard to get 90-something percent of New Yorkers to do anything," and compliance was "a sign not necessarily of deep respect for the MTA" but a sign that passengers were terrified.

Ridership was nearly nonexistent. Having fallen from three-quarters of normal on March 12 to below one-quarter of normal within a week, it was in the single digits by April. To comfort people who had to ride, the MTA began a cleaning program, taking every train out of service at the end of each run. Trains were cleaner than ever, smelling like freshly washed kitchens. Trains hurtled lightly from stop to stop, not weighed down by thousands of pounds of passengers. In core Manhattan, entire stations, from Columbus Circle to Times Square, were empty at rush hour. When delays arose because train crews were out with COVID, commuters with long trips from the Bronx and Queens to Manhattan hospitals or supermarkets didn't complain; they were grateful that the train was coming sometime.

Even masked, with near-empty trains, transit workers were dying. The union's website became an obituaries page. Bus Operator Maqueda Lewis, 51. Conductor Nevie Lacayo, 41. Train Operator Alain Walker, 44. Bus Operator Walter "Wats" Watson, 55. Conductor Elecier Williams, 41. Power maintainer Rodney Sparrow, 50. During the first eighteen months of COVID-19, 172 transit workers perished.

Trump and the MTA

Empty trains created a fiscal crisis. On March 12, the MTA informed the people and institutions, including major banks, that had invested money in its forty-four billion dollars' worth of bonds that it was experiencing a "material event"—something so out of the ordinary that it might affect the authority's ability to repay debt. Less than a week later, as New York's governor and mayor suggested that people stay home, suggestions that became orders, the MTA updated its distress call. "People may permanently alter their commutation behavior," the MTA warned. The MTA was losing twelve million dollars a day in fares. "The impacts . . . are clearly severe." The MTA drew down one billion dollars in credit it held with banks—the equivalent of borrowing cash on your credit card. As investors know, corporations and public authorities may *have* letters of credit—but they are not supposed to *use* them.

The MTA's announcements rattled investors. Municipal-bond holders do not like to take risks; they purchase the bonds because they are a sure thing. "MTA Chief Wants Federal Aid to Make Bond Payments," *Bloomberg* reported in late March. The MTA insisted that it had "sufficient liquidity and resources to fund its debt service," an assurance that healthy entities do not make. On March 24, Standard & Poor's downgraded the MTA's debt, the first of several moves by bond-rating agencies. "Debt service coverage, liquidity, and debt metrics will worsen," analysts said, noting "prospects for permanent negative dislocation of transit and traffic volume."[9] In April, Moody's, a rival bond-analysis firm, said in its own downgrade that one factor in the MTA's favor was "strong political and financial support from New York State, New York City, and the U.S. Government."[10]

The MTA was too big to fail. As COVID terror spread from New York to the nation, the spring of 2020 was a terrifying time for people who watched investment markets. Between early February and March 23, the stock market lost a quarter of its value. With restaurants and stores across the country closing by late March, people who kept their jobs curtailed spending. Corporations stopped advertising because there was nothing to sell; television stations filled space with advisories telling people to wash their hands. (Carmakers were an exception to the advertising void.) As the economy shut down, 19.4 million Americans lost their private sector jobs by the end of April—15.2 percent of workers, the most abrupt recession ever. Investors feared that jobless people or people earning less would have trouble paying debts, precipitating a new financial crisis.

The MTA's fiscal woes exacerbated Wall Street panic. If the biggest municipal debt issuer in the country—comprising 1 percent of the four-trillion-dollar market—was issuing warning after warning to investors, new investors wouldn't risk fresh money. That spring, the MTA couldn't borrow at any interest rate it could afford. Interest rates for cities and states across the country soared.[11]

In late March, Congress acted to quell panic. On March 27, President Donald J. Trump approved the $2.2 trillion CARES Act, funneling a record amount of money into the economy. The CARES Act delivered hundreds of billions of dollars to Americans and a further hundreds of billions to businesses. It did *not* include broad relief for state and local governments.

The one exception: transit. Of $25 billion for transit nationwide, the MTA would get $3.9 billion, against the authority's then $17.1 billion annual budget. The CARES Act also contained a provision allowing the

Federal Reserve to lend directly to distressed municipalities, a step not even taken during the 2008 financial crisis. By the end of the year, only two borrowers, repelled by high interest rates in private markets as their risk rose, had to borrow from the Fed. The MTA, drawing $2.9 billion, was one (Illinois was the other).

One reason that a Republican president and Republican-controlled Senate approved this historic aid was the scope of the crisis; across the country, from Texas to Ohio, transit systems, mostly bus systems, were running empty. But the MTA also had two friends in powerful places. The first was Brooklyn's Chuck Schumer, New York's senior senator, then the Senate's minority leader. "New York's subways, trains, and buses are our very lifeblood," Schumer told *Politico* in March.[12]

The second reason was Andrew Cuomo. In mid-2020, the governor commanded national audiences via televised COVID updates. Cuomo's strategy for the MTA was to focus on a different New Yorker with power in Washington: Trump. His tactic was to give Trump what he wanted: positive attention. "With Trump, politicians say, 'I hate Trump,'" remembers Cuomo. "I don't have that luxury, 'well, I hate Trump.' Who cares if you hate Trump? . . . I said to Trump, I need help." Cuomo offered Trump what he knew the latter man needed as he ran for reelection during the COVID crisis: praise. "I said, 'Donald,' which I called him, 'I know you; you know me. Watch the briefing.'" Aid to New York would mean praise from the most popular governor in America: "I will be the first to say you did the right thing. . . . I have a bigger audience than you do."[13] When Trump delivered for the MTA, so did Cuomo for Trump. "He delivered for New York," Cuomo told Howard Stern on his satellite show. "He's expediting a $3.9 billion payment to MTA," Cuomo told reporters in mid-May. "I'm grateful . . . and I thank him." Trump was so pleased about one such paean that he played the clip for reporters.

It wasn't enough. As spring progressed to summer, New York's commercial real estate owners and business executives understood that though the immediate goal was to keep people home, soon the long-term goal would be to coax them back. Were the MTA to slash service after its CARES Act aid ran out, it would have no hope of reattracting riders. White-collar workers who had spent months at home were hardly going to return to trains that ran less frequently and reliably. Billions of dollars in office buildings would be a write-off.

In late April, business, real estate, and labor leaders came together under the umbrella of the Regional Plan Association to call for more. They sent an open letter to Congress, signed by everyone from top Manhattan office-tower landlord Scott Rechler of RXR to Julie Samuels of the city's TechNYC tech-economy lobby; from Kathy Wylde of the Partnership for New York City business group to Tony Utano of the Transport Workers Union. "New York will not return to work and other aspects of our lives primarily in automobiles," the signatories beseeched Washington. "We not only need the MTA to continue to function through the worst of the crisis, but also to be poised to rebound. . . . Helping New York get back to work will be an important component of getting America back to work."

The lobbying worked. Via two additional rescue packages, the nation's transit systems would win a total of $69.5 billion, including $14.5 billion for the MTA, enough money to keep it running until 2024. In December 2020, weeks after having lost reelection, Trump approved the second round of MTA help, $4 billion, part of $900 billion in COVID aid. The president who signed this aid into law was a former Manhattan real estate developer who, four decades earlier, had told a fawning Tom Brokaw of NBC, "I see the inner cities as being sort of the wave of the future . . . with the problem of fuel and the gasoline shortages."[14] In 2021, with Schumer as Senate majority leader, Trump's successor, President Joe Biden, signed the $1.9 trillion American Rescue Plan Act, which included another $6.5 billion in MTA funding. The MTA's budget crisis was fixed—for a few years.

Fear Stalking the Trains

In March 2020, the few passengers on trains felt something they hadn't felt for decades: fear. The fewer New Yorkers on the train—disproportionately New Yorkers of color, commuting long distances to essential jobs—contended with a greater risk of being a crime victim. As the MTA's fiscal crisis receded, a new violence crisis raged.

Subways became more dangerous than they had been in nearly three decades. In 2020, seven people, including Goble, lost their lives to subway homicide, more victims than over the entire previous half-decade. In 2019, the year before COVID, subway passengers had suffered 917 violent felonies; by 2020, the figure was 928. Yet with so many New Yorkers working at home—ridership never exceeded one-third of normal after March of that first COVID year—the per-ride violent-felony rate had tripled, from 0.54 per million rides to 1.45. By late 2020, only 42 percent of riders said they felt safe from crime, a decrease from 67 percent during the pre-COVID year.[15] In 2021, the situation hadn't improved. Transit passengers suffered seven murders and 999 violent felonies, though ridership rarely exceeded half of pre-COVID normal.

Why did subway crime soar during COVID? In fact, crime had begun to rise in the final weeks of 2019 as judges began to implement the looser criminal justice laws affecting both bail and evidence-discovery terms that would take effect in the new year. In January and February 2020, subway passengers suffered a 60 percent increase in violent felonies, compared to the previous year, as transit arrests fell by one-fourth and fare-beating arrests fell by nearly two-thirds. Robberies nearly doubled, to 151. A week before New York locked down, twenty-five-year-old Rudolph "Rudy" Dunning, a fashion designer, bled out on the floor of a station in the Soundview area of the Bronx, fatally stabbed by a stranger for whom he had kindly—if illegally—opened the fare gate. This deterioration in safety reversed nearly three decades of declining transit crime.

The mid-March cessation of passenger activity magnified the pullback in policing and the increase in crime at a time when mentally vulnerable people were suffering the most protracted social dislocations experienced in living memory. During 2020, transit arrests fell by nearly two-thirds; civil summonses fell by nearly 60 percent. Crowds that deterred at least some crimes were gone. But people engaged in violent behavior hadn't fled the transit system. Many of them—afflicted by mental illness or addiction—had nowhere to go. Robbers not suffering mental illness were also emboldened. One measure of disorder was the number of people who entered subways without paying: in mid-2020, fare evaders comprised 13.6 percent of subway entrants, compared to 3.8 percent two years previously. At best, subway fare evaders cost the MTA hundreds of millions of dollars in lost revenue annually; at worst, they disproportionately committed more serious crimes underground, preying on other passengers.[16]

In May 2020, disorder helped compel the MTA to do something it had never done: shutter subways overnight, from 1:00 to 5:00 a.m., both to empty trains and stations for cleaning and to protect daytime passengers from entrenched vagrancy. Thousands of people were living on trains and in stations, many of them alarming passengers with their erratic behavior and drug use. Closing the trains once a day forced everyone to exit. As subways shut down, police watched as civilian homeless-outreach workers moved homeless adults into hotel rooms.

The closure was inconvenient to essential workers; those commuting to early-morning or late-night shifts had to take the bus or participate in a car hail program the MTA provided. As one airport worker, William L., a resident of the Bronx's Melrose neighborhood, told Riders Alliance of his two-hour commute, "With the subway closed, it was even harder, as I had to start . . . at 4:00 a.m." That month, Mamadou Diallo, 32, a food-delivery worker, waiting for the bus in Harlem at 2:30 a.m., was robbed, shot, and killed. "Family says he'd be alive if NYC subways were running overnight," read one headline.[17] Trains didn't reopen to overnight riders for more than a year.

Of course, most of the time, the trains remained open—and transit officials grew alarmed at increased danger for passengers and workers. Goble's March 2020 death was "absolutely horrifying," says Feinberg. The killing was "a horrible example of the things that could go wrong when you allowed that level [of disorder]. . . . [It could] have been a mass casualty incident."[18] But horrifying incidents kept coming. In February 2021, Claudie Roberts, a homeless woman, and Dwayne Dixon, a homeless man, were separately stabbed to death. The alleged assailant was a homeless man whose family said he suffered from mental illness. He recently had been released on several pending charges under the state's justice reforms with no follow-up care.

In mid-2021, MTA officials called on city government to step up policing. After five armed robberies at three subway stops within twelve minutes, Feinberg called on de Blasio to act. "The responsibility for these vicious attacks . . . falls on City Hall," she said. "The mayor is risking New York's recovery."[19] The mayor, though, balked at consistent action. After the stabbing deaths of Roberts and Dixon, he added five hundred police to the subways, but the measure was temporary. Rather than confront the crisis, he minimized the problem, accusing Feinberg, a Cuomo appointee, of playing politics.

The mayor had several reasons for inaction. First, ideologically, he shied from aggressive policing; he had won two elections on promises to pull back. Second, he was in his final year; his lame-duck status gave him little incentive to act decisively on any issue. Finally, the mayor didn't face pressure from a once-potent force on safety: transit advocates. Three decades earlier, even before Brian Watkins's murder, the Straphangers' Campaign's Gene Russianoff had called for more subway officers and tougher enforcement. But a new generation of transit advocates opposed assertive policing. For much of 2020 and 2021, New York's transit-advocacy community even minimized the fact that violence was up. "Total felonies are down on the subway," *Streetsblog* said in May 2021, summing up transit advocacy conventional wisdom.[20] The statement ignored that felonies were down only because nonviolent felonies—larcenies—were down; by any measure, violence was up.

Even advocates who acknowledged that violence was up bristled when the MTA called attention to this fact. "By constantly calling into question the subway's safety, they risk scaring riders away," Riders Alliance's Danny

Pearlstein said. "And that in itself makes the subway less safe."[21] When advocates acknowledged the problem, they called for social services, not policing. Nobody disputed the need for effective mental health and drug treatment; the immediate problem for the city was: How to protect riders from mentally ill individuals repeatedly failed by a disorganized state and city public health system or from a group of teenagers, desocialized from having missed more than a year of school, looking to commit a robbery? How to stop a drug addict resistant to help from injecting herself in view of riders?

The mainstream press was slow to grasp the issue. The *Times* insisted that "data was mixed." Against a backdrop of disorder, horrors kept coming. In July 2021, Than Than Htwe, 58, an immigrant seamstress from Myanmar, died after being pushed down the stairs at a Canal Street station, even though her adult son had accompanied her on her way to the doctor to keep her safe. In November, Akeem Loney, 32, a former star soccer player who had become homeless, was fatally stabbed on a train near Penn Station. Nearly three years later, prosecutors presented evidence that his assailant had entered a Brooklyn subway station without paying his fare.

The Murder That Shocked New York

On Saturday, January 15, 2022, Michelle Alyssa Go, 40, took advantage of a three-day weekend to venture from her Upper West Side apartment into the core of the city. New York was nowhere near back to normal: subway ridership hadn't reached 50 percent of pre-COVID levels on any day the previous week. But Go, like most New Yorkers, was resuming daily life. Around 9:30 a.m., Go was standing on a Times Square subway platform. Nearby, a man was behaving erratically; one woman moved away. Screams rang out, and Go was dead—pushed under the onrushing train by Martial Simon, 61, a stranger. Go was the fifteenth murder victim since March 2020; her killing wasn't even the first of 2022. On New Year's morning, Roland Hueston, 36, defended a stranger under attack by teens who had entered the Fordham Road subway without paying their fares; the teens forced Hueston to the tracks, where a train hit him.

Go's killing, though, was different. Thirty years earlier, Watkins's death had risked the city's tourism industry; now, a new death, that of a young woman at a high-profile station in the middle of the day, risked the city's COVID recovery. Like Watkins, Go was a compelling victim. A California native, she had "spent a third of her life in New York City, . . . [the] city she came to love," her father wrote. Go, an avid traveler and volunteer helping homeless women and children, had graduated from NYU business school and worked her way through New York's financial industry to attain a management job at Deloitte, the global consultancy. With more than half of office workers still working from home, Go's murder further deterred them from returning to routines that involved riding trains.

Go was also of Asian descent; hate crimes against Asians were rising, and the Asian American community was outraged at the lack of enforcement. "It resonated a lot with the younger [Asian American Pacific Islander] community in five boroughs, and then nationally," says Jan Lee, a civic leader in Chinatown. "She looked like everyone's sister, daughter, cousin. . . . Michelle was young, she was a professional, she was basically a target that was so 'real' . . . that we woke up to the fact that . . . it can be me next."[22] Thousands of people, many of them Asian Americans, attended a Times Square vigil for Go not just to mourn, but to demand change. Rage was compounded by the fact that Go's death was preventable. Go's killer had a violent history, a history of untreated mental illness, and an outstanding warrant for arrest for violating parole at the time of the murder. After Go's killing, it was impossible for transit advocates and the *Times* to deny that violence had risen.

Finally, Go's death galvanized outrage because New Yorkers sensed the possibility of change. Three decades earlier, Watkins's murder had occurred just as New York had elected a new mayor, David Dinkins. New Yorkers weary of nearly two years of COVID also had just elected another new mayor, Eric Adams, in November 2021. During election season, New Yorkers' main issue, for the first time in nearly decades, was crime. New Yorkers who hadn't felt fearful in decades grappled with smashed windows, stray bullets, and violent robberies.

Carnage on trains reflected and magnified disorder above ground. Adams, a sharply dressed former NYPD captain, spoke to New Yorkers' insistence that they would not go back to the bad old days. "I . . . call for more police officers on our subway system and serious mental health resources, so that New Yorkers can feel safe enough to ride our subways again," he vowed in his campaign.[23] Eight months later, during his first week in office and a week before Go's murder, Adams stood in the subway with the new governor, Kathy Hochul, promising more outreach to the mentally ill and drug addicted as well as more policing.

Yet after Go's killing, change came slowly. Adams lacked focus. He had announced his plan without having devoted new resources toward carrying it out. Over decades of calm, the transit-police ranks had fallen from

4,100 officers to 2,730.[24] His idea was not to add to police officers underground and direct them to do additional enforcement, as had happened three decades earlier. Rather, officers on street patrol would park their cars and enter subway stations for momentary "visual" inspections. That May, a Goldman Sachs employee, Daniel Enriquez, 48, was shot and killed by a stranger on the Q train as he rode from Brooklyn to Manhattan to brunch, the second white-collar worker to be randomly executed in five months.

As 2022 progressed, crime kept people from returning to subways; ridership remained at around 60 percent. The share of people who said they felt safe on the trains was 33 percent, half the pre-COVID rate. An MTA survey of 175,000 subway riders found that four out of five riders' concerns encompassed safety: "personal security" on trains, "personal security" in stations, "people behaving erratically" on trains, and "people behaving erratically" in stations.[25]

More people were riding, but gradually higher passenger numbers didn't deter violence, nor did a slow return to pre-COVID job numbers. Instead, higher ridership meant more victims. Starting in September 2022, even as ridership climbed toward two-thirds of pre-COVID figures, four people lost their lives in four separate subway murders in one month. One victim was Brooklyn steamfitter Tommy Bailey, 43, randomly stabbed on his way home from work, allegedly by a suspect who had committed a similar, nonfatal random subway stabbing the year before—only to be released under the state's justice reforms. Charles Moore, 38, a Citi Field maintenance worker, was killed in a similar attack in the Bronx; Jayjon Burnett, 15, was killed in a dispute on a Queens train; Heriberto Quintana, 48, a construction worker, was thrown under a Queens train by a stranger.

Only then did the governor and mayor act decisively. That season, Hochul was running in her first election as governor (previously lieutenant governor, she had succeeded Cuomo after his 2021 resignation). Yet in a Democratic state and during an election year that was supposedly a sure win for Democrats because of the Supreme Court's overturning of *Roe versus Wade* that spring, she was in a tight race with a Trumpian tough-on crime Republican, Long Island Congressman Lee Zeldin. A major issue was subway crime.

Two weeks before the election, Hochul and Adams launched an aggressive initiative: "Cops, Cameras, and Care." The "care" part referred to the continuation of mental health outreach. But the "cops" part was a departure from Adams's earlier announcement. Henceforth, the state would pay for 1,200 police shifts each day in the subways, more than doubling coverage. "Riders will see more officers . . . and so will those thinking of breaking the law," the mayor said. "We will do whatever it takes to make our subways safer," vowed the governor.[26] In a state where no Republican had won statewide office for two decades, Hochul won—by just three points. The deadly violence eased, but not before subway violence took eleven lives in 2022, a number not seen since the early 1990s.

The policing surge worked—to an extent. Arrests and summonses returned to pre-COVID levels. As in the past, interrupting petty crimes deterred larger ones. In nine days of March 2023, police recovered four illegal guns from four people caught evading the fare. Violent felonies dipped below one per million rides, 50 percent below persistent COVID peaks—but twice as high as before COVID-19. Arrests were less effective than in a previous era; as the Manhattan Institute's Hannah Meyers has found, the percentage of transit arrests that resulted in a dismissal or a prosecutor's refusal to prosecute steadily rose from 15.6 percent percent in 2017 to 65.5 percent in 2023, as the justice system became less forceful. With no serious penalty for low-level crimes despite more police enforcement, fare evasion remained rampant, reaching 14 percent in mid-2023.[27]

The city's newfound failure to keep repeat offenders behind bars once arrested and to effectively contain and treat the seriously mentally ill resulted, in May 2023, in yet another preventable tragedy. On May 1st, Jordan Neely, 30 and homeless, boarded a Manhattan F train and began threatening other passengers; one witness said that he repeatedly screamed, "I would kill a motherfucker. . . . I'll go to jail." Another passenger, Daniel Penny, a college student and former Marine, put Neely in a chokehold, killing him (Penny faces a manslaughter charge). New York's criminal-justice system and mental-health system had missed chance after chance to place Neely in a hospital or in jail; he had been arrested 42 times, including for fracturing an elderly woman's nose in a random subway attack less than two years previously, and he was also on the city's list of the top fifty people most in need of intensive mental-health treatment. Yet he had been left to roam the subways screaming.[28]

Without a functional criminal-justice or mental-health treatment system, a grim cycle took hold: after each high-profile crime, the city would surge the number of police in the subways, relying on overtime shifts. As the memory of the most recent crime faded in an ever-shorter news cycle, the extra police presence faded away, too. In the first six weeks of 2024, four people lost their lives to subway violence, all random victims. The first victim was 45-year-old Richard Henderson, a grandfather, shot to death in January after intervening on a Brooklyn train in a dispute over a passenger's loud music, a classic example of disorder becoming deadly.[29]

The fourth victim was Jason Volz, 54, pushed under a Bronx subway train in March by an alleged assailant with a long history of mental illness, who had been out on bail after his arrest for another unprovoked assault just months previously.[30]

Between March 2020 and early March 2024, thirty-five New Yorkers had lost their lives to subway homicide, more than the previous sixteen years' toll, when consequences for lower-level lawbreaking were greater, incapacitating violent individuals before they could take a life. As Lieber observed in March 2024, "I grew up in New York riding the trains at a time when crime and subway breakdowns were much more frequent. My kids grew up in a different subway era. They were able to come and go at all hours of the night feeling safe. We're not going back. We're not going back!"[31]

That month, Governor Kathy Hochul called in the National Guard to patrol subway stations, searching would-be passengers' bags for weapons. New York's subway system had felt like a low-grade conflict zone for four years, with even a seemingly calm commute requiring constant vigilance, and now, it looked like one.

Adjusting to a New Era

More than three years after COVID-19 cloaked New York in a miasma of anxiety, the city's vexing recovery problem persisted: how to get people back on subways, buses, and commuter rail in numbers close to 2019 levels. As of spring 2024, long after car traffic returned to normal, transit ridership remained at just 71 percent of pre-COVID levels, barely a percentage point above the previous year. With fewer than four million people on the subways each day, compared to 5.5 million four years previously, New York had lost decades of progress. "I don't know if we're going to get there anytime soon," MTA chairman Janno Lieber said in December 2023. "We have room to bring people back."[32] Once again, the challenge is to serve not only people who have no other options but also to convince people who have choices to choose transit for comfort, speed, reliability, safety, and price.

For the first time ever, office workers can decide whether and how often to commute to Manhattan. White-collar workers can work at home at least some of the time, indefinitely; by fall 2023, New York's office occupancy hovered below two-thirds of pre-COVID figures, with the five-day-a-week commuting schedule seemingly receding into history.[33] Major financial firms have found that their highly paid employees can work productively elsewhere, from Miami to Nashville. New York is thus experiencing a compressed version of dislocations it experienced three-quarters of a century earlier, when the city's previous economic base, manufacturing, discovered that it did not have to locate factories in New York City. Largely because Manhattan's missing office workers—some still working at home much of the time, some having relocated altogether—Manhattan's business districts were still missing one-third of their foot traffic, relative to 2019, one of the worst results in the country.[34]

These changing patterns have jarring implications for the future of America's densest city. Fewer commuters mean lower demand for restaurant and retail workers, so New York has not led the nationwide jobs recovery. The divergence marked a historical turn: for the first time since the 1970s and 1980s, New York is faring worse than the nation. New York can't predict the future; it is a fool's errand to guess whether tech workers in 2030 will prefer to work in an office three days a week or no days a week. It is a fool's errand to predict, if office workers don't return four to five days a week, how New York can replace that lost activity with something else.

New York can control one factor in whether the city remains attractive to workers with a choice, though: the MTA must offer transit service that is an amenity, not a utility. Beyond the commute, New Yorkers' habits have changed—and transit doesn't easily change. Even before COVID-19, changing work and living patterns demanded that New York build convenient, cheap transit from one outer borough to another or within one part of a single borough to another, accommodating people whose lives don't center around Manhattan. "Whether our transportation system is flexible enough to respond to the post-COVID changing demand from the riders, . . . where they want to go and when," will shape the future, says Kathy Wylde of the Partnership for New York City.[35] One idea is an "Interborough Express" train, a passenger service to run between Brooklyn and Queens, without touching Manhattan. New York could dedicate more lanes on outer-borough parkways and avenues to buses, enabling riders to glide through traffic. State and regional counterparts can provide cheaper, more frequent commuter rail service.

A transit system that serves a constituency beyond Manhattan commuters must change in another respect: it cannot require people to climb up and down stairs. A subway system built for able-bodied, working-aged people to reach Manhattan jobs is not universal; it excludes people with bad knees, people with baby carriages, people with suitcases. "It's in the MTA's interest to make travel more convenient and accessible for everyone," says Jessica Murray, a disability-rights activist. The state, city, and MTA must jettison "the idea that people with disabilities somehow don't deserve the same access. . . . It goes back to their mentality of, this is only a small percentage of the population. Actually, it helps all these people."[36] In 2022, advocates settled their lawsuit with the MTA, with the agreement requiring the MTA to make all subway stations step-free—but the MTA won't complete the project until 2055.

For New York to adapt transit to a post-COVID world, state and city officials must absorb a difficult fact: even before COVID slashed fare revenue, the MTA faced deficits. The authority's budget gaps were not caused by a lack of tax or fare revenue; both had exceeded inflation since the early 1980s. Rather, costs had grown faster than inflation, far exceeding developed-world averages.[37] As federal COVID aid ran out, the MTA won a new tax from Albany, worth $1.1 billion annually, in April 2023—but to make the most of its new revenue, it must cut the cost of delivering service in line with global norms.

New York's enduring post-COVID obstacle is also its enduring advantage: heavy rail transit, the only way to move millions of people daily in a dense city. The pandemic and New York's lurching recovery reveal a tale of two transportation futures. In one, New Yorkers, commuters, and visitors ride subways and buses in safety and confidence. Even if white-collar workers don't commute to Manhattan five days a week, they come in two or three days a week. More people live in the city's office districts, in older buildings converted into apartments. Because most of their fellow residents, visitors, and commuters rely on transit, not cars, New Yorkers walk and bicycle safely on streets, zip smoothly along bus lanes, and eat at outdoor cafes. People traveling from one outer borough to another or from one suburb to an outer borough can do so via faster, cheaper, and more frequent rail and bus lines. Driving isn't banned, but the city restricts it in dense areas, recognizing that people who choose the least efficient mode of transportation in the densest city in the United States mustn't expect other people to sacrifice safety, comfort, and health for their convenience. The state and city charge drivers for moving and parking vehicles on dense streets at congested hours, where alternatives to driving exist.

In an alternate future, New York fails to rebuild confidence in its mass-transit system, and the Manhattan business district fails to recover. As riders stay away, the MTA cuts service, repelling more passengers. Subways and buses become the domain of people with few options, and the state and city can no longer muster political will to further subsidize fare revenues with tax revenues. Without well-designed congestion pricing, drivers crowd Manhattan roads, even as the population falls. Nobody wants to walk, cycle, or dine outdoors amid gridlock, noise, and danger. This lack of activity justifies handing streets back to cars; traffic is worse than ever, the reasoning goes, and drivers need extra space. People who had wanted to live or work in a big city because they wanted to walk and bike the streets are repelled by motor vehicles making urban life less livable. New York loses the wealth generated by Manhattan's density, harming its ability to fund social services and public education. Poorer New Yorkers must buy second- or third-hand cars to get to work to school or sacrifice hours of scarce leisure time waiting for trains and buses that don't come.

The future of mass transit and of the streets will determine the future of New York City. As the *Times* wrote in 1904 of the city's first subway, "It was astonishing . . . how easily the passengers fell into the habit of regarding the subway as a regular thing. While the crowds above were still eagerly watching the entrances to see men emerge, were still enthralled by the strangeness of it all, the men on the trains were quietly getting out at their regular stations and going home, having finished what will be to them the daily routine of the rest of their lives. It is hard to surprise New York permanently."[38]

ACKNOWLEDGMENTS

ON MARCH 12, 2020, I sat in the New York Public Library's manuscripts room, unmasked, rushing more quickly than usual through Robert Moses's papers, attuned to stray coughs and looking up to my laptop to click every once in a while (okay, more than every once in a while) on COVID-19 news. By late afternoon, it was clear that the library, like most cultural institutions, would be shutting its doors to stop the spread. "See you in a couple weeks," I said to the archivist as I handed back my box. The air of disaster—familiar from 9/11—was upon us. The library wouldn't reopen for research for more than a year. On my way home, I stopped at the Bryant Park Whole Foods; a good idea, I thought, to stock up. Everyone else had had the same idea, and the shelves were bare. I grabbed what was left and waited, still unmasked, in a line that stretched out the door. The Whole Foods itself would be temporarily closed and boarded up by the end of the spring. Because I both live and work in Midtown Manhattan, for almost all of 2020, all of 2021, and even much of 2022, I had Midtown to myself. I didn't know you could research, write, and revise a book mostly at the kitchen table, but, apparently, you can.

I am most grateful to Mary Hedge, the archivist at the Metropolitan Transportation Authority's MTA Bridges and Tunnels Special Archive. By August 2020, I was out of documents and books to read at home and out of things to read on the NYPL's internet. Who else had Robert Moses documents? The MTA, which had long ago absorbed Moses's Triborough Bridge and Tunnel Authority. I knew that it was a long shot, but I couldn't stand sitting in my apartment anymore; it couldn't hurt to ask. I thought maybe the answer would be "perhaps in a few months," but at least I would have something to look forward to do.

Mary's immediate answer to when I asked if I could come over and start to look through the MTA's Moses documents? Yes, I could come next week. I'll never forget that late summer, fall, and early winter, biking down the West Side Highway to the MTA, or taking the E train, often all by myself on the platform and then all by myself in the train car, and then walking the streets of Lower Manhattan, nearly entirely alone. After I got my temperature checked at the MTA building entrance each day, Mary and I sat, well more than six feet away from each other, fully masked, two days a week for months, on an almost entirely empty Triborough floor, enjoying our Pret lunches outdoors for our break. Without the ability to do that research, this book would be a year late(r), and it would be a different book. As I walked Lower Manhattan in the lowering autumn dusk, largely alone, and then took the E train back home, also alone, I wondered: what is going to happen to us—to those of us marooned in an empty Manhattan for three seasons now, to Manhattan's business hubs, to the trains, to the city?

I will be forever grateful to people—some friends and some at the time strangers—who opened their homes or offices to me in the middle of a pandemic: the late Mary Frances Dunham and her daughter, Kate Dunham; Marcy Benstock; Sam Schwartz; Gene Russianoff and his wife, Pauline Toole; Charles Komanoff. I am also grateful to the people who helped me build a municipal library at home, mailing me or handing me old government documents and news clippings from their home offices and garages; by April of 2020, I had a pile of paper close to three feet tall to go through: David Gurin, the late Steven Polan (I know some of you want to remain anonymous). I am also grateful to early full readers, Wendy Feuer, David Gurin (again), and Carl Weisbrod; and early partial readers, Charles Komanoff, Ted Orosz, Sam Schwartz, Lou Venech, John Samuelsen, and Andrew Sidamon-Eristoff.

I thank the archivists at the New-York Historical Society, particularly former librarian Erin Weinman, and at the New York Public Library, particularly Tal Nadan, Cara Dellatte, and John Cordovez. I'll never forget walking through an almost entirely empty NYPL starting in the late spring of 2021: the Rose Reading room, empty. The people who had been waiting more than a year to resume their research were so glad just to have a library again that they didn't mind wearing masks for hours each day. I also thank Nellie Hankins at the MTA Bridges and Tunnels Special Archive for inventorying the TBTA files in the mid-2010s, as well as, as Nellie puts it, "the unsung generations of TBTA secretaries who ran the file room for forty years." Thank you, too, to Tim Minton and John McCarthy at the MTA.

I thank my colleagues at the Manhattan Institute and *City Journal*, Reihan Salam, Bernadette Serton, Brandon Fuller, John Ketcham, Hannah Meyers, Brian Anderson, Paul Beston, Teddy Kupfer, and Jamie Meggas, as well as Michele Jacob and Nora Kenney for putting up with my transit obsessions and indulging my interest in bikes and pedestrian plazas. I thank my old boss Myron Magnet for teaching me how to write things that are longer than seven hundred words. I thank agent Janet Rosen, and the publisher, Fred Nachbaur at Fordham University Press, for believing in this book and for not making me make it too short. I thank editor Michael Koch for his gentle insight and for being kind and patient as he deleted all the words that didn't belong and guided the rearrangement of the rest of them. I thank Kem Crimmins at Fordham for shepherding this from Microsoft Word to print, Will Cerbone for the crash correspondence course in photo editing, Kate O'Brien-Nicholson and Jeremy Wang-Iverson for their marketing and PR expertise respectively, and Aldene Fredenburg for her careful attention to commas (and to math).

I thank my friends Seth Barron, Stephen Eide, E. J. McMahon, Ann Weisbrod, Paul Berk, Alex Armlovich, and Peter Cohen for their moral support. I thank my mom, Mary Gelinas, my dad, John Gelinas, and his partner, Linda Turner, my sister and brother-in-law, Melissa and Tim Prudente, my brother, Sean, and my nephews, Odin and Deacon Prudente, for their love. I thank my husband, Matthew Civello, for not minding when I clatter away at the computer when I am supposed to be doing the dishes (after he has done the cooking).

NOTES

1. New York's Original Sin: Scrapping Street Transit

1. "State Erases Laws on Trolleys; Last One Quit Streets In 1957," *New York Times*, July 24, 1960, https://timesmachine.nytimes.com/timesmachine/1960/07/24/99764131.pdf.

2. "Trolleys Challenged by Growth of the Bus," *New York Times*, January 4, 1925, https://timesmachine.nytimes.com/timesmachine/1925/01/04/101630583.pdf.

3. Meyer Berger, "Fifth Avenue Bus Line, Oldest in the Nation, Becomes Local Institution Again by Sale," *New York Times*, May 28, 1954, https://timesmachine.nytimes.com/timesmachine/1954/05/28/83757729.pdf.

4. "5th Av. Line Upheld on Bus Franchises," *New York Times*, May 24, 1933, https://timesmachine.nytimes.com/timesmachine/1933/05/24/105136848.pdf.

5. Berger, "Fifth Avenue Bus Line."

6. "London's Motor 'Buses," *New York Times*, November 4, 1906, https://timesmachine.nytimes.com/timesmachine/1906/11/04/101849771.pdf.

7. "Favors Restricting Motor Bus Service," *New York Times*, November 16, 1913, https://timesmachine.nytimes.com/timesmachine/1913/11/16/100661385.pdf.

8. "Hylan Adds Pinchot to Presidency List; Foresees a Revolt," *New York Times*, December 10, 1922, https://timesmachine.nytimes.com/timesmachine/1922/12/10/109339923.pdf.

9. John Francis Hylan, *Mayor Hylan of New York: An Autobiography* (New York: Rotary Press, 1922), https://upload.wikimedia.org/wikipedia/commons/c/ce/Autobiography_of_John_Francis_Hylan%2C_mayor_of_New_York_%28IA_autobiographyofjoohylao%29.pdf.

10. New York City Municipal Archives, "Guide to the Records of Mayor John F. Hylan, 1918–1925," accessed April 10, 2022, https://www1.nyc.gov/assets/records/pdf/OM-JFH_REC0013_Finding%20Aid-MASTER.pdf.

11. "Take Over Subways, Keep a 5-Cent Fare, Is Hylan's Platform," *New York Times*, October 6, 1921, https://timesmachine.nytimes.com/timesmachine/1921/10/06/98749901.pdf.

12. "Bars Buses on Lines Reopened by B.R.T.," *New York Times*, September 8, 1920, https://timesmachine.nytimes.com/timesmachine/1920/09/08/96899885.pdf.

13. "City Had to Supply New Bus Service," *New York Times*, September 23, 1919, https://timesmachine.nytimes.com/timesmachine/1919/09/23/96341863.pdf.

14. John Hylan, "Mayor Reviews His Stewardship, Backs 5-Cent Fare," *New York Times*, January 9, 1921, https://timesmachine.nytimes.com/timesmachine/1921/01/09/103530461.pdf.

15. John Walker Harrington, "Back to the Village in New York's Jitney Bus," *New York Times*, November 30, 1919, https://timesmachine.nytimes.com/timesmachine/1919/11/30/118182963.pdf.

16. "Says Queens Wants Cars," *New York Times*, August 19, 1920, https://timesmachine.nytimes.com/timesmachine/1920/08/19/96894085.pdf.

17. "Loft Seeks Routes for Electric Buses," *New York Times*, October 8, 1924, https://timesmachine.nytimes.com/timesmachine/1924/10/08/119044786.pdf.

18. "Excoriates Hylan as a Lawbreaker," *New York Times*, July 30, 1922, https://timesmachine.nytimes.com/timesmachine/1922/07/30/99046108.pdf.

19. "Creel Sees Hylan City's Best Mayor," *New York Times*, October 30, 1921, https://timesmachine.nytimes.com/timesmachine/1921/10/30/98762511.pdf.

20. "Hylan Boom Seen in Plea for Buses," *New York Times*," July 31, 1922, https://timesmachine.nytimes.com/timesmachine/1922/07/31/99047528.pdf.

21. "Mayor Hylan Opens Trackless Trolley," *New York Times*, October 9, 1921, https://timesmachine.nytimes.com/timesmachine/1921/10/09/107027729.pdf.

22. "Transit Plan Drops 26 Brooklyn Lines, 146 Miles of Track," *New York Times*, March 2, 1922, https://timesmachine.nytimes.com/timesmachine/1922/03/02/98992162.pdf.

23. "Hylan Bus Pilgrims Leave for Albany," *New York Times*, March 13, 1923, https://timesmachine.nytimes.com/timesmachine/1923/03/13/105853732.pdf.

24. "Transit Line Buses, If Free, Suit Hylan," *New York Times*, September 6, 1924, https://timesmachine.nytimes.com/timesmachine/1924/09/06/104262272.pdf.

25. "Hylan Turned Down Plan to Run Buses," *New York Times*, November 17, 1922, https://timesmachine.nytimes.com/timesmachine/1922/11/17/99102403.pdf.

26. "Whalen in a Rage Hurls Epithets at Transit Council," *New York Times*, November 2, 1922, https://timesmachine.nytimes.com/timesmachine/1922/11/02/99093410.pdf.

27. "5-Cent Fare Failure, Says Bus Company," *New York Times*, November 21, 1925, https://timesmachine.nytimes.com/timesmachine/1925/11/21/104195280.pdf.

28. "New York Is Seen as a City of Buses," *New York Times*, August 24, 1924, https://timesmachine.nytimes.com/timesmachine/1924/08/24/98805361.pdf.

29. "Brooklyn Opposes City-Wide Buses," *New York Times*, July 11, 1926, https://timesmachine.nytimes.com/timesmachine/1926/07/11/99996756.pdf.

30. "Mayor's 'Low Voice' Issue in Bus Suit," *New York Times*, August 9, 1927, https://timesmachine.nytimes.com/timesmachine/1927/08/09/94914617.pdf.

31. "Walker Is Beaten in Bus Showdown; Stays Here to Fight," *New York Times*, January 21, 1927, https://timesmachine.nytimes.com/timesmachine/1927/01/21/118638572.pdf.

32. "Secret Bus Parley Held," *New York Times*, December 30, 1926, https://timesmachine.nytimes.com/timesmachine/1926/12/30/98411249.pdf.

33. "Equitable Routes Approved by Board," *New York Times*, February 16, 1929, https://timesmachine.nytimes.com/timesmachine/1929/02/16/95733217.pdf.

34. "Suit on Franchise Won by Equitable," *New York Times*, March 9, 1929, https://timesmachine.nytimes.com/timesmachine/1929/03/09/91761561.pdf.

35. "'Slush Fund' Charged in Equitable Deal," *New York Times*, January 29, 1929, https://timesmachine.nytimes.com/timesmachine/1929/01/29/95720780.pdf.

36. "Equitable Doomed to Lose Bus Grant; B.M.T. Award Likely," *New York Times*, January 30, 1929, https://timesmachine.nytimes.com/timesmachine/1929/01/30/95876115.pdf.

37. "Equitable Balked at Airing Finances," *New York Times*, March 6, 1929, https://timesmachine.nytimes.com/timesmachine/1929/03/06/121608819.pdf.

38. "City Bus System Stirs Wide Protest," *New York Times*, April 21, 1932, https://timesmachine.nytimes.com/timesmachine/1932/04/21/100721116.pdf.

39. George H. Copeland, "Seeking a City Bus System: The Tangle of Efforts to Date," *New York Times*, May 15, 1932, https://timesmachine.nytimes.com/timesmachine/1932/05/15/100739684.pdf.

40. "Walker to Shelve Berry Bus Report," *New York Times*, October 14, 1931, https://timesmachine.nytimes.com/timesmachine/1931/10/14/94242938.pdf.

41. "Walker's Administration Turbulent, but Mayor Maintained Wide Popularity," *New York Times*, September 2, 1932, https://www.nytimes.com/1932/09/02/archives/walkers-administration-turbulent-but-mayor-maintained-wide.html.

42. "Walker's Administration Turbulent, but Mayor Maintained Wide Popularity," *New York Times*, September 2, 1932, https://www.nytimes.com/1932/09/02/archives/walkers-administration-turbulent-but-mayor-maintained-wide.html.

43. "General Motors Seeking Control of 5th Ave. Bus and Green Lines," *New York Herald Tribune*, April 4, 1930.

44. "5th Av. Coach Group Seeks Bus Monopoly," *New York Times*, August 14, 1932, https://timesmachine.nytimes.com/timesmachine/1932/08/14/100788625.pdf.

45. "Witness Says Lynch Got Financial Aid before Bus Award," *New York Times*, November 25, 1931, https://timesmachine.nytimes.com/timesmachine/1931/11/25/98347184.pdf.

46. "Says Car Tracks Must Go," *New York Times*, March 9, 1922, https://timesmachine.nytimes.com/timesmachine/1922/03/09/98997687.pdf.

47. "Trolleys 'Archaic,' Walker Asserts," *New York Times*, September 25, 1929, https://timesmachine.nytimes.com/timesmachine/1929/09/25/91948254.pdf.

48. "Buses to Oust Manhattan Bridge Trolleys," *New York Times*, January 9, 1929, https://timesmachine.nytimes.com/timesmachine/1929/01/09/95705638.pdf.

49. "Vehicles Killed 423 in This City in 1911," *New York Times*, January 3, 1912, https://timesmachine.nytimes.com/timesmachine/1912/01/03/100506313.pdf.

50. "1931 Transit Fares Decline 91,200,000," *New York Times*, April 11, 1932, https://timesmachine.nytimes.com/timesmachine/1932/04/11/100824636.pdf.

51. "426 Homicides Reported in City Last Year; 1,521 Died in Street Accidents," *New York Times*, September 7, 1930, https://timesmachine.nytimes.com/timesmachine/1930/09/07/118380359.pdf.

52. George P. Le Brun, "Surface Cars and Buses," letter, *New York Times*, September 7, 1933, https://timesmachine.nytimes.com/timesmachine/1933/09/07/99925488.pdf.

53. "Straus Advocates Mayor Hylan Plan," *New York Times*, December 27, 1921, https://timesmachine.nytimes.com/timesmachine/1921/12/27/98778899.pdf.

54. "2d Av. Trolley Line Now Offered to City," *New York Times*, June 23, 1926, https://timesmachine.nytimes.com/timesmachine/1926/06/23/98383187.pdf.

55. "Association Votes for Broadway Buses," *New York Times*, January 19, 1920, https://timesmachine.nytimes.com/timesmachine/1920/01/19/106360183.pdf.

56. "Prefer a Bus Line to Trolley Cars," *New York Times*, December 16, 1923, https://timesmachine.nytimes.com/timesmachine/1923/12/16/104975168.pdf.

57. "New York Is Seen as a City of Buses," *New York Times*, August 24, 1924, https://timesmachine.nytimes.com/timesmachine/1924/08/24/98805361.pdf.

58. "Bus Plan Proposes Abolishing Trolley Cars in Manhattan," *New York Times*, February 25, 1926, https://timesmachine.nytimes.com/timesmachine/1926/02/25/100052835.pdf.

59. Editorial board, "Sober Thoughts on Buses," *New York Times*, June 24, 1926, "https://timesmachine.nytimes.com/timesmachine/1926/06/24/98383870.pdf.

60. Editorial board, "Buses and Electric Cars," *New York Times*, February 26, 1926, https://timesmachine.nytimes.com/timesmachine/1926/02/26/119062268.pdf?pdf.

61. "Calls City Bus Plan Economic Waste," *New York Times*, March 9, 1925, https://timesmachine.nytimes.com/timesmachine/1925/03/09/98818144.pdf.

62. "Expert Analyzes Street Congestion," *New York Times*, August 10, 1924, https://timesmachine.nytimes.com/timesmachine/1924/08/10/98804081.pdf.

63. "Buses Fail to Stem Gain in Street Cars," *New York Times*, June 13, 1926, https://timesmachine.nytimes.com/timesmachine/1926/06/13/98480482.pdf.

64. "Buses, Street Cars Share 42d St., with One Electric Line Supplanted," *New York Times*, November 18, 1946, https://timesmachine.nytimes.com/timesmachine/1946/11/18/93180922.pdf.

65. "Staten Islanders Are Tired of Buses," *New York Times*, February 6, 1920, https://timesmachine.nytimes.com/timesmachine/1920/02/06/118258453.pdf.

66. "Staten Islanders Complain of Buses," *New York Times*, February 21, 1920, https://timesmachine.nytimes.com/timesmachine/1920/02/21/96874266.pdf.

67. E. C. Morris, "Bus vs. Street Car," letter, *New York Times*, June 8, 1922, https://timesmachine.nytimes.com/timesmachine/1922/06/08/99028361.pdf.

68. H. W. Buck, "Noise Factor in Trolley-Bus Debate," letter, *New York Times*, July 2, 1926, https://timesmachine.nytimes.com/timesmachine/1926/07/02/98487025.pdf.

69. "Trolley Mileage Still Near Peak," *New York Times*, January 23, 1927, https://timesmachine.nytimes.com/timesmachine/1927/01/23/97136508.pdf.

70. New York City Department of Transportation, "New York City Mobility Report," October 2016, https://www1.nyc.gov/html/dot/downloads/pdf/mobility-report-2016-screen-optimized.pdf.

71. Editorial board, "Another Year of Old Buses," *New York Times*, October 13, 1932, https://timesmachine.nytimes.com/timesmachine/1932/10/13/100863154.pdf.

72. "New York City's Buses," letter, *New York Times*, October 20, 1932, https://timesmachine.nytimes.com/timesmachine/1932/10/20/100867477.pdf.

73. "New Transit Plan Scraps 10 Car Lines," *New York Times*, December 21, 1921, https://timesmachine.nytimes.com/timesmachine/1921/12/21/107037902.pdf.

74. Emanuel Strum, "Bronx Trolley Service," letter, *New York Times*, February 7, 1934, https://timesmachine.nytimes.com/timesmachine/1934/02/07/95032375.pdf.

75. "Would Rid Streets of Unused Tracks," *New York Times*, September 4, 1924, https://timesmachine.nytimes.com/timesmachine/1924/09/04/101608040.pdf.

76. "New Transit Plan Scraps 10 Car Lines."

77. Herbert Kaufman, "Trolley Cars Preferred," letter, *New York Times*, August 26, 1939, https://timesmachine.nytimes.com/timesmachine/1939/08/26/93950764.pdf.

78. "Transit Traffic Fell 7.8% in Year," *New York Times*, November 6, 1933, https://timesmachine.nytimes.com/timesmachine/1933/11/06/105815148.pdf.

79. "Passengers Gain on Transit Lines," *New York Times*, October 31, 1934, https://timesmachine.nytimes.com/timesmachine/1934/10/31/94576384.pdf.

80. "Trolleys to Vanish on 9 Lines in City," *New York Times*, September 6, 1934, https://timesmachine.nytimes.com/timesmachine/1934/09/06/93765363.pdf.

81. "Trail's End for Old Trolleys," *New York Times*, January 19, 1936, https://timesmachine.nytimes.com/timesmachine/1936/01/19/85208733.pdf.

82. "Madison Av. Buses Begin Service Feb. 1," *New York Times*, January 21, 1935, https://timesmachine.nytimes.com/timesmachine/1935/01/21/93443881.pdf.

83. "Swift Buses Oust Madison Trolleys," *New York Times*, February 1, 1935, https://timesmachine.nytimes.com/timesmachine/1935/02/01/101513879.pdf.

84. "Buses Crowd Out Historic Car Line," *New York Times*, January 27, 1935, https://timesmachine.nytimes.com/timesmachine/1935/01/27/93446040.pdf.

85. "Trolleys Doomed, Mayor Reveals," *New York Times*, January 30, 1935, https://timesmachine.nytimes.com/timesmachine/1935/01/30/93448092.pdf.

86. "City Starts Removal of Madison Av. Tracks; Cost of ERB Project Put at $6,500 a Block," *New York Times,* June 11, 1935, https://timesmachine.nytimes.com/timesmachine/1935/06/11/95078280.pdf.

87. "Queens Boulevard to Get a Bus Line," *New York Times*, October 6, 1935, https://timesmachine.nytimes.com/timesmachine/1935/10/06/93777901.pdf.

88. "Last Trolley Cars Clang on Eighth Av.," *New York Times*, November 13, 1935, https://timesmachine.nytimes.com/timesmachine/1935/11/13/93501252.pdf.

89. "Broadway Bus Line to Run Next Week," *New York Times*, February 4, 1936, https://timesmachine.nytimes.com/timesmachine/1936/02/04/93517924.pdf.

90. "Broadway Buses to Run Wednesday," *New York Times*, February 9, 1936, https://timesmachine.nytimes.com/timesmachine/1936/02/09/85241948.pdf.

91. Robert L, Banks, "New Buses Disliked," letter, *New York Times*, February 9, 1935, https://timesmachine.nytimes.com/timesmachine/1935/02/09/93770453.pdf.

92. J. W., "Criticizing the Buses," letter, *New York Times*, April 8, 1936, https://timesmachine.nytimes.com/timesmachine/1936/04/08/85293598.pdf.

93. Ellen Garrigues, "Trolley Removal Protested," letter, *New York Times*, August 24, 1939, https://timesmachine.nytimes.com/timesmachine/1939/08/24/93950157.pdf.

94. "3,000 Sign Plea for Street Cars," *New York Times*, November 18, 1939, https://timesmachine.nytimes.com/timesmachine/1939/11/18/113370534.pdf.

95. Herman Rinke, "Trolley Cars Win Approval," *New York Times*, March 10, 1941, https://timesmachine.nytimes.com/timesmachine/1941/03/10/85460337.pdf.

96. Everett A. White, "Trolley Cars Preferred," letter, *New York Times*, March 18, 1941, https://timesmachine.nytimes.com/timesmachine/1941/03/18/85466282.pdf.

97. "Trolley Diehards Boo Bus Drivers," *New York Times*, October 14, 1940, https://timesmachine.nytimes.com/timesmachine/1940/10/14/94005744.pdf.

98. "Trolleys May Stay on One Brooklyn Line," *New York Times*, March 10, 1942, https://timesmachine.nytimes.com/timesmachine/1942/03/10/85025322.pdf.

99. "U.S. Orders Halts 2 New Bus Lines," *New York Times*, March 14, 1942, https://timesmachine.nytimes.com/timesmachine/1942/03/14/85523041.pdf.

100. "Warns of Return to Trolley Riding," *New York Times*, June 14, 1943, https://timesmachine.nytimes.com/timesmachine/1943/06/14/85106670.pdf.

101. "Bus Service Slash Is in Effect Here," *New York Times*, May 30, 1943, https://timesmachine.nytimes.com/timesmachine/1943/05/30/223828402.pdf.

102. "Mayor Promises More Bus Service for Next Sunday," *New York Times*, May 31, 1943, https://timesmachine.nytimes.com/timesmachine/1943/05/31/85105248.pdf.

103. "Knell of 59th St. Trolleys Sounds as Buses Take Up Rounds Tomorrow," *New York Times*, November 9, 1946, https://timesmachine.nytimes.com/timesmachine/1946/11/09/93174785.pdf.

104. "42d St. Trolleys End Runs Today," *New York Times*, November 17, 1946, https://timesmachine.nytimes.com/timesmachine/1946/11/17/93178984.pdf.

105. "Last Broadway Trolley Ends Run with Ceremony," *New York Times*, December 15, 1946, https://timesmachine.nytimes.com/timesmachine/1946/12/15/305856902.pdf.

106. "Buses on 3d Ave. Sunday," *New York Times*, May 16, 1947, https://timesmachine.nytimes.com/timesmachine/1947/05/16/88782334.pdf.

107. "76 Buses Replace 3d Ave. Trolleys," *New York Times*, May 19, 1947, https://timesmachine.nytimes.com/timesmachine/1947/05/19/87526408.pdf.

108. "The Last of the Streetcars to Run in Manhattan," *New York Times*, June 29, 1947, https://timesmachine.nytimes.com/timesmachine/1947/06/29/104321496.pdf.

109. "Manhattan to Lose Last Trolley Sunday," *New York Times*, June 25, 1947, https://timesmachine.nytimes.com/timesmachine/1947/06/25/87772520.pdf.

110. "Bronx Trolleys Retire," *New York* Times, August 23, 1948, https://timesmachine.nytimes.com/timesmachine/1948/08/23/96597334.pdf.

111. "City Speeds Buying of 130 New Buses," *New York Times*, November 4, 1947, https://timesmachine.nytimes.com/timesmachine/1947/11/04/104363782.pdf.

112. "Brooklyn Bridge Back in Full Use," *New York Times*, May 4, 1954, https://timesmachine.nytimes.com/timesmachine/1954/05/04/84119972.pdf.

113. Sam Schwartz papers.

114. "Bronx Gets Buses; Brooklyn Is Left," *New York Times*, August 22, 1948, https://timesmachine.nytimes.com/timesmachine/1948/08/22/86906687.pdf.

115. "Brooklyn to Keep 11 Trolley Lines," *New York Times*, June 3, 1949, https://timesmachine.nytimes.com/timesmachine/1949/06/03/84269347.pdf.

116. "Era to Rattle Out Aboard a Trolley," *New York Times*, March 4, 1951, https://timesmachine.nytimes.com/timesmachine/1951/03/04/356878592.pdf.

117. "City Trolley Cars Near End of Line," *New York Times*, April 20, 1956, https://timesmachine.nytimes.com/timesmachine/1956/04/20/121637908.pdf.

118. Ralph Katz, "Last Stop Looms for City's First Trolley Line," *New York Times*, March 3, 1957, https://timesmachine.nytimes.com/timesmachine/1957/03/20/85007871.pdf.

119. "Sunday Will Clang End of Trolley Era in City," *New York Times*, April 4, 1957, https://timesmachine.nytimes.com/timesmachine/1957/04/04/90789525.pdf.

120. Editorial board, "The Last Trolley Car," *New York Times*, April 5, 1957, https://timesmachine.nytimes.com/timesmachine/1957/04/05/90790277.pdf.

2. The 1929 Regional Plan: Paving New York's Car Future

1. Robert A. Caro, *The Power Broker: Robert Moses and the Fall of New York* (New York: Vintage Books, 1974), 5, 16, 21.

2. Maurice Carroll, "Moses' 11 Titles Now Down to One," *New York Times*, July 13, 1966, https://timesmachine.nytimes.com/timesmachine/1966/07/13/93853301.pdf.

3. "Joint Legislative Committee on Metropolitan and Regional Area Studies," January 7, 1966, TBTA records, box 107-4. During his testimony, Moses said, "My grandfather was in business down here in Lower Manhattan. He was on a committee to take the tracks off what they called 'Death Avenue.' . . . There used to be a man on horseback, . . . a man on a horse, with a red flag, who went in front of these trains, the freight trains that ran at grade and cut off the city proper from the waterfront [to warn pedestrians and carriage drivers]."

4. "Children Parade against Death Ave.," *New York Times*, October 25, 1908, https://timesmachine.nytimes.com/timesmachine/1908/10/25/105013865.pdf; Christopher Gray, "When a Monster Plied the West Side," *New York Times*, December 25, 2011, https://www.nytimes.com/2011/12/25/realestate/the-railroad-tracks-that-turned-a-street-into-death-avenue.html.

5. Joshua B. Freeman, *In Transit: The Transport Workers Union in New York City, 1933–1966* (Philadelphia: Temple University Press, 2001), 13.

6. State of New York Bureau of Motor Vehicles, "First New York State Safety Congress," March 1926, Moses papers, box 3.

7. William P. Vogel Jr., "Atlantic Ave. Grade Crossings Reach Beginning of the End," *New York Herald Tribune*, July 9, 1939.

8. New York Department of State, "Votes Cast for and against Proposed Constitutional Conventions and Also Proposed Constitutional Amendments," Manual for the Use of the Legislature of the State of New York, https://history.nycourts.gov/wp-content/uploads/2019/01/Publications_Votes-Cast-Conventions-Amendments-compressed.pdf.

9. Warren Moscow, "Smith Turns Tide for Crossing Bill in Plea at Albany: Backs Moses," *New York Times*, July 6, 1938, https://www.nytimes.com/1938/07/06/archives/smith-turns-tide-for-crossing-bill-in-plea-at-airany-backs-moses.html.

10. Editorial board, "Amendment No. 3: The Grade Crossing Plan," *New York Times*, October 28, 1938, https://timesmachine.nytimes.com/timesmachine/1938/10/28/98204038.pdf.

11. "Boroughs Mark Finish of Grade Crossing Work: Brooklyn and Queens," *New York Herald Tribune*, October 17, 1943.

12. "Memorandum from Triborough Bridge and Tunnel Authority," May 23, 1966, via TBTA records, box 107-3.

13. Committee on Regional Plan of New York and Its Environs, "Regional Plan of New York and Its Environs," vol. 1, "The Graphic Regional Plan," 1929, https://s3.us-east-1.amazonaws.com/rpa-org/pdfs/RPA-Plan1-v1-Regional-Plan-of-New-York-and-Its-Environs.pdf.

14. "Bronx River Park Has Rural Beauty," *New York Times*, June 6, 1920, https://timesmachine.nytimes.com/timesmachine/1920/06/06/96350676.pdf.

15. "Reports Progress of Bronx Parkway," *New York Times*, July 19, 1914, https://timesmachine.nytimes.com/timesmachine/1914/07/19/100098615.pdf.

16. "New Parkway Nearly Done," *New York Times*, March 7, 1920, https://timesmachine.nytimes.com/timesmachine/1920/03/07/118267625.pdf.

17. "Motor Routes Attractive in Westchester," *New York Herald Tribune*, April 24, 1924.

18. "Building New Motor Route to New England Resorts," *New York Times*, February 1, 1925, https://timesmachine.nytimes.com/timesmachine/1925/02/01/104165406.pdf.

19. "Big Crowd to Hear the Regional Plan," *New York Times*, May 26, 1929, https://timesmachine.nytimes.com/timesmachine/1929/05/26/91794494.pdf.

20. "Vast 'City-State' Girdled in Rail and Highway Loops Set Up in Regional Plan," *New York Times*, May 28, 1929, https://timesmachine.nytimes.com/timesmachine/1929/05/28/95957868.pdf.

21. "Paul Windels, Lawyer, 82, Dies," *New York Times*, December 16, 1967, https://timesmachine.nytimes.com/timesmachine/1967/12/16/90908963.pdf.

22. Robert Moses papers, box 3.

23. Caro, *Power Broker*, 6.

24. Caro, 8.

25. Transcript, "Hearing of State Finance and Assembly Ways and Means Committees," February 11, 1925, Moses papers, box 3.

26. Downer letter to Moses, October 29, 1928, Moses papers, box 5.

27. "Progress Made on Long Island's Parks and Parkways," *New York Times*, April 29, 1928, https://timesmachine.nytimes.com/timesmachine/1928/04/29/118338534.pdf.

28. Moses papers, boxes 5 and 7.

29. TBA records, box 121-1.

30. Caro, *Power Broker*, 546–47.

31. Stephen G. Thompson, "Idea of Buses on L. I. Parkways Draws More Fire Than Approval," *New York Herald Tribune*, January 29, 1950.

32. "No Buses on Parkways," *New York Times*, June 2, 1960, https://timesmachine.nytimes.com/timesmachine/1960/06/02/119104563.pdf.

33. Caro, *Power Broker*, 12.

34. "F. K. Bowers Dead; Revenue Collector," *New York Times*, October 16, 1930, https://timesmachine.nytimes.com/timesmachine/1930/10/16/102172421.pdf.

35. "Proposed Triborough Bridge across the Harlem and East Rivers," *New York Times*, January 14, 1917, https://timesmachine.nytimes.com/timesmachine/1917/01/14/102309271.pdf.

36. "M'Laughlin Named to Bridge Board," *New York Times*, January 17, 1934, https://timesmachine.nytimes.com/timesmachine/1934/01/17/94483910.pdf.

37. "Protest Queens Evictions: 600 Families Ordered to Move from Site of Approaches," *New York Times*, January 17, 1934, https://timesmachine.nytimes.com/timesmachine/1934/01/17/94483951.pdf.

38. "1,227 Families Face Higher Rents as the City Forces Them to Move," *New York Times*, November 29, 1936, https://timesmachine.nytimes.com/timesmachine/1936/11/29/93323921.pdf.

39. John E. Morris, *Subway: The Curiosities, Secrets and Unofficial History of the New York City Transit System* (New York: Black Dog and Leventhal Publishers, 2020), 17–19; Jill Jonnes, *Conquering Gotham: The Construction of Penn Station and Its Tunnels* (New York: Viking, 2007), 128–129.

40. Moses statement, January 3, 1935, Moses papers, box 74.

41. "New Span Climax Of 23-Year Effort: Unique among World Bridges," *New York Times*, July 12, 1936.

42. "Roads Gain in This Area," *New York Times*, May 23, 1937, https://timesmachine.nytimes.com/timesmachine/1937/05/23/94379627.pdf.

43. R. L. Duffus, "Manhattan Reclaims Her Rim of Water," *New York Times*, June 6, 1937, https://timesmachine.nytimes.com/timesmachine/1937/06/06/101011298.pdf.

44. Caro, *Power Broker*, 542.

45. "4,000,000th Car on Span," *New York Times*, August 28, 1937, https://timesmachine.nytimes.com/timesmachine/1937/08/28/94415815.pdf.

46. "Moses Says City Leads World in Aid for Traffic," *New York Herald Tribune*, April 17, 1943.

47. Peet Creighton, "Motorists' Millennium: Tunnels, Underground Parking," *New York Herald Tribune*, January 28, 1945.

48. Robert Moses, "The Traffic Menace, in Both Peace and War: Civilian Defense," *New York Times*, April 29, 1951.

49. O'Brien Boldt, "Area Lacks Web Roads," *New York Times*, February 1, 1942, https://timesmachine.nytimes.com/timesmachine/1942/02/01/85514586.pdf.

50. Editorial board, "Our New Expressways," *New York Times*, March 13, 1950, https://timesmachine.nytimes.com/timesmachine/1950/03/13/87132350.pdf.

51. "540 Bronx Families to Get New Homes," *New York Times*, April 12, 1946, https://timesmachine.nytimes.com/timesmachine/1946/04/12/84631948.pdf.

52. "Apartments to Be Moved," *New York Times*, May 14, 1947, https://timesmachine.nytimes.com/timesmachine/1947/05/14/87754927.pdf.

53. Charles G. Bennett, "Bronx Expressway Dispute Has Estimate Board Fuming," *New York Times*, April 24, 1953, https://timesmachine.nytimes.com/timesmachine/1953/04/24/83720113.pdf.

54. "Moses Threatens to Halt Bronx Job," *New York Times*, March 12, 1953, https://timesmachine.nytimes.com/timesmachine/1953/03/12/83809525.pdf.

55. "Bronx Residents Lose Road Fight," *New York Times*, December 3, 1954, https://timesmachine.nytimes.com/timesmachine/1954/12/03/96511864.pdf.

56. Caro, *Power Broker*, 859.

57. Charles G. Bennett, "Bronx Expressway Route Approved to 'Demagogue,' 'Blackmail' Cries," *New York Times*, May 15, 1953, https://timesmachine.nytimes.com/timesmachine/1953/05/15/96621653.pdf.

58. Moses papers, box 75.

59. Letter from Mueller to Moses, July 8, 1954, Moses papers, box 75.

60. Letter from Moses to Buckley, April 5, 1956, Moses papers, box 76.

61. "Moses Sees Close of Big-Bridge Era," *New York Times*, June 24, 1957, https://timesmachine.nytimes.com/timesmachine/1957/06/24/102278117.pdf.

62. Triborough Bridge and Tunnel Authority press statement, October 22, 1957, Moses papers, box 76.

63. "Throgs Neck Bridge," Triborough Bridge and Tunnel Authority brochure, October 22, 1957, Moses papers, box 76.

64. William R. Conklin, "Battery Bridge Plans Put Through in a Rush," *New York Times*, April 2, 1939.

65. Charles G. Bennett, "Triborough Drops Midtown Crossing," *New York Times*, June 20, 1950, https://timesmachine.nytimes.com/timesmachine/1950/06/20/113161695.pdf.

66. Bernard Stengren, "Wagner Lectures Aides on Bus Ads: He Bids Moses Comply with Policy," *New York Times*, June 13, 1959.

67. "Moses Agrees to Head '64 Fair," *New York Times*, April 14, 1960, https://timesmachine.nytimes.com/timesmachine/1960/04/14/99945803.pdf.

68. "Throgs Neck Bridge," Triborough Bridge and Tunnel Authority brochure, October 22, 1957, via Moses papers, box 76.

69. Spargo memo to Moses, March 14, 1956, Moses papers, box 76.

3. Kids versus Cars: A Housewife's Fight to Save Washington Square Park

1. "Girl, 3, Killed by Bus near Washington Arch: Pinned under Rear Wheel as She Runs into Vehicle," *New York Herald Tribune*, June 8, 1942.

2. "Remembering Edith Lyons," Greenwich Village Society for Historic Preservation, February 18, 2015, https://www.villagepreservation.org/2015/02/18/remembering-edith-lyons/.

3. Charles G. Bennett, "One-Way Roads Set for Washington Square," *New York Times*, February 2, 1952, https://timesmachine.nytimes.com/timesmachine/1952/02/17/84239643.pdf.

4. John LoCicero, interview with the author, July 9, 2021.

5. Helen Lawrenson, "The Four Faces of Greenwich Village," *New York Herald Tribune*, August 23, 1959.

6. "Greenwich Village Statistical Trends and Observations," New York University, Hayes papers, October 1969.

7. Shirley Hayes, "An Oral History Interview Conducted for the GVSHP Preservation Archives," interview by Josh Berman (Greenwich Village Society for Historic Preservation, 2000), https://media.villagepreservation.org/wp-content/uploads/2020/05/15034903/hayes_transcript.pdf; Edith Lyons, "An Oral History Interview Conducted for the GVSHP Preservation Archives," interview by Vicki Weiner (Greenwich Village Society for Historic Preservation, 1997 and 1998), https://media.villagepreservation.org/wp-content/uploads/2020/05/15034857/lyons_transcript.pdf.

8. Shirley Hayes papers.

9. *Villager*, April 3, 1952, Hayes papers.

10. "Traffic Ban Is Aim in Washington Sq.," *New York Times*, June 4, 1962, https://timesmachine.nytimes.com/timesmachine/1952/06/04/93373632.pdf.

11. "Moses' Plan on Washington Square Decried: 'Stop That Man' Is Tenor of 300 Villagers' Meeting on Rehabilitation Scheme," *New York Herald Tribune*, January 24, 1940.

12. Hayes papers.

13. Hayes papers.

14. 1963 Hub Bound Travel, New York Metropolitan Transportation Council report, https://www.nymtc.org/Utility-Menu/Archive/Data-and-Modeling-Archive/Hub-Bound-Travel-Archive.

15. Council minutes, Hayes papers.

16. "Traffic Ban Is Aim in Washington Sq."

17. Joseph C. Ingraham, "City Plan Gains in Washington Sq.," *New York Times*, April 15, 1955, https://timesmachine.nytimes.com/timesmachine/1955/04/15/91359693.pdf.

18. "Traffic Plan for Square Hit Hard," *Villager*, March 10, 1955, Hayes papers.

19. *Villager*, April 28, 1955, Hayes papers.

20. "The Battle over Washington Square," *Village Voice*, December 7, 1955.

21. "Call Mass Meeting on Fate of Square," *Village Voice*, November 2, 1955.

22. "The 'Voice' Number 1," *Village Voice*, October 26, 1955.

23. Lyons, "An Oral History."

24. Hayes papers.

25. *New York World Telegram and Sun*, May 30, 1956, Hayes papers.

26. Moses papers, box 76.

27. Moses papers, box 76.

28. Moses papers, box 76.

29. "Statement of Robert Moses Regarding Washington Square," *Village Voice*, January 1, 1958.

30. Hayes papers.

31. New School press release, April 1958, Hayes papers.

32. New School press release, April 1958, Hayes papers.

33. Hayes papers.

34. Carol Greitzer, interview with the author, November 6, 2019.

35. Hayes papers.

36. Warren Moscow, *The Last of the Big-Time Bosses: The Life and Times of Carmine De Sapio and the Rise and Fall of Tammany Hall* (New York: Stein and Day, 1971), 114.

37. Moscow, *Last of the Big-Time Bosses*, 163.

38. Hayes papers.

39. "De Sapio Wins Local Fight, but Village Democrats Give VID a Strong Vote," *Village Voice*, September 18, 1957.

40. *Villager*, December 19, 1957, Hayes papers.

41. Peter Kihss, "Throng Debates Road in Village," *New York Times*, May 15, 1958, https://www.nytimes.com/1958/05/15/archives/throng-debates-road-in-village-mrs-roosevelt-supports-a-majority-of.html.

42. Hayes papers.

43. Robert A. Poteete, "De Sapio in Plea to Bar Washington Square Road," *New York Herald Tribune*, September 19, 1958; Charles G. Bennett, "Village Protesters Led by De Sapio," *New York Times*, September 19, 1958.

44. "Mr. De Sapio's Decision," *Village Voice*, October 22, 1958.

45. "Victory and Anniversary," *Village Voice*, October 29, 1958.

46. Jane Jacobs, "An Oral History Interview Conducted for the GVSHP Preservation Archives," interview by Leticia Kent, Greenwich Village Society for Historic Preservation, 1997.

47. Hayes papers.

48. "Revolt against De Sapio Goes on TV Next Week," *Village Voice*, September 2, 1959.

49. "City Shifts to Hayes Plan—Cars, Buses, Everything Out!," *Village Voice*, August 26, 1959.

50. Hayes papers.

51. "De Sapio Almost Defeated as VID Landslide Sweeps Square Area," *Village Voice*, September 23, 1959.

52. "Citizens of Village Unite Momentarily to Hail Bus Victory," *New York Times*, September 3, 1963.

53. Hayes, "An Oral History."

54. Community Planning District minutes, May 1962, Hayes papers.

55. Courtesy Hayes family.

56. Hayes papers, box 5.

4. Changing Times (and Minds): Defeating the Lower Manhattan Expressway

1. O'Brien Boldt, "Area Lacks Web Roads," *New York Times*, February 1, 1942, https://timesmachine.nytimes.com/timesmachine/1942/02/01/85514586.pdf.

2. Robert Moses, "Statement before the New York State Temporary Highway Finance Planning Commission," January 5, 1956, Moses papers, box 76.

3. Charles G. Bennett, "Canal St. Expressway Gets Planning Body's Approval," *New York Times*, February 4, 1960, https://timesmachine.nytimes.com/timesmachine/1960/02/04/119452621.pdf.

4. Editorial board, "Waiting until 1962?," *New York Times*, June 6, 1960, https://timesmachine.nytimes.com/timesmachine/1960/06/06/105440490.pdf.

5. Bennett, "Canal St. Expressway Gets Planning Body's Approval."

6. Paul Crowell, "Downtown Road Linking Two Rivers Is Voted by City," *New York Times*, September 16, 1960, https://timesmachine.nytimes.com/timesmachine/1960/09/16/99870314.pdf.

7. "Lower Manhattan Elevated Expressway," Triborough Bridge: A Tunnel Authority Brochure, TBTA records, box 115-3.

8. Joseph C. Ingraham, "Moses Asks City to Double Relocation Bonus," *New York Times*, February 17, 1960, https://timesmachine.nytimes.com/timesmachine/1960/02/17/105178967.pdf.

9. Crowell, "Downtown Road Linking Two Rivers Is Voted by City."

10. John F. Murphy, "2,000 Families to Be Uprooted," *New York Times*, February 27, 1961, https://timesmachine.nytimes.com/timesmachine/1961/02/27/118024740.pdf.

11. Jane Jacobs, *The Death and Life of Great American Cities* (New York: Vintage Books, 1961), 4.

12. Roberta Brandes Gratz, *The Battle for Gotham: New York in the Shadow of Robert Moses and Jane Jacobs* (New York: Nation Books, 2010), 100.

13. Mary Perot Nichols, "Battle Waxes Hot (and Short) over 9th St. Expressway, *Village Voice*, November 22, 1962.

14. Stephanie Gervis, "Political Powerhouse Kills Broome St. Expressway," *Village Voice*, December 13, 1962.

15. Grace Glueck, "Artists Assail Downtown Expressway," *New York Times*, June 20, 1969, https://timesmachine.nytimes.com/timesmachine/1969/06/20/78352290.pdf.

16. "Lindsay Attacks Broome St. Plan; Mayor Delays," *Village Voice*, August 23, 1962.

17. David Gurin, "Last Exit to Lower Manhattan," *Village Voice*, January 28, 1965.

18. "Home Owners Protest X-way Route," *Long Island Press*, March 13, 1966, TBTA records, box 107-3.

19. Samuel Murray, interview with the author, May 7, 2021.

20. "Legislator Raps X-way Extension," *Long Island Press*, March 12, 1966, TBTA records, box 107-3.

21. Lewis Mumford, "The Roaring Traffic's Boom—IV," *New Yorker*, June 11, 1955.

22. Robert Moses papers, box 75.

23. Joseph C. Ingraham, "Autos Rule and Frustrate Life in the Urban Region," *New York Times*, January 28, 1957.

24. Tri-State Transportation Commission, "Hub-Bound Travel 1963," August 1966.

25. Joseph C. Ingraham, "L.I. Expressway: A Dilemma," *New York Times*, August 4, 1963.

26. Editorial board, "Highway Merry-Go-Round," *New York Times*, June 15, 1963, https://www.nytimes.com/1963/06/15/archives/highway-merrygoround.html.

27. Joseph C. Ingraham, "L.I. Expressway to Be Snarled for Years: Improvements Begun," *New York Times*, August 21, 1967.

28. Walter Thabit, "Troubles in the Way of the Open City," *New York Times*, November 15, 1964.

29. TBTA records, box 107-3.

30. TBTA records, box 106-2.

31. TBTA records, box 106-2.

32. Editorial board, "Twenty-one Years to Act," *New York Times*, April 10, 1962, https://timesmachine.nytimes.com/timesmachine/1962/04/10/89856716.pdf.

33. John V. Lindsay, "A Modern Transportation System for New York City," November 1965, TBTA records, box 107-4.

34. Robert Alden, "Business Leaders Press Tax Battle in City Hall Talk," *New York Times*, April 8, 1966, https://timesmachine.nytimes.com/timesmachine/1966/04/08/79992562.pdf.

35. TBTA records, box 107-3.

36. Editorial board, "Twenty-one Years to Act."

37. Editorial board, "Mr. Moses and the Expressway," *New York Times*, November 20, 1965, https://timesmachine.nytimes.com/timesmachine/1965/11/20/95003491.pdf.

38. Editorial board, "Lower Manhattan Expressway," *New York Times*, March 11, 1966, https://timesmachine.nytimes.com/timesmachine/1966/03/11/82429599.pdf.

39. TBTA records, box 107-3.

40. TBTA records, box 107-3.

41. Maurice Carroll, "Moses' 11 Titles Now Down to One," *New York Times*, July 13, 1966, https://timesmachine.nytimes.com/timesmachine/1966/07/13/93853301.pdf.

42. Peter Kihss, "Downtown Tunnel Studied Instead of an Expressway," *New York Times*, January 17, 1967.

43. Moses papers, box 76.

44. "Jane Jacobs Is Arrested at Expressway Hearing," *New York Times*, April 11, 1968, https://www.nytimes.com/1968/04/11/archives/jane-jacobs-is-arrested-at-expressway-hearing.html.

45. Maurice Carroll, "Mayor Drops Plans for Expressways across 2 Boroughs," *New York Times*, July 17, 1969, https://timesmachine.nytimes.com/timesmachine/1969/07/17/81554329.pdf.

46. Joseph C. Ingraham, "Airport Buses to Use Grand Central Road," *New York Times*, September 5, 1969, https://timesmachine.nytimes.com/timesmachine/1969/09/05/81546291.pdf.

47. Allegra Hobbs, "Chapel of San Lorenzo Ruiz in Little Italy Selling to Developer for $7.35M," *dnainfo*, July 11, 2017, https://www.dnainfo.com/new-york/20170711/little-italy/san-lorenzo-ruiz-chapel-sold.

48. 378 Broome Street, https://www.378broome.nyc/building-residences, accessed April 23, 2024.

49. Donald Janson, "Expressway Construction Lags as Officials Heed Urban Outcry," *New York Times*, February 15, 1970, https://www.nytimes.com/1970/02/15/archives/expressway-construction-lags-as-officials-heed-urban-outcry.html.

5. No Way on Westway: A Watery Grave for Manhattan's Last Highway

1. Alfred E. Clark, "Boy on West Side Highway Dies in Fall through Hole," *New York Times*, August 17, 1974, https://www.nytimes.com/1974/08/17/archives/boy-on-west-side-highway-dies-in-fall-through-hole.html.

2. "Truck and Car Fall as West Side Highway Collapses," *New York Times*, December 16, 1973, https://www.nytimes.com/1973/12/16/archives/truck-and-car-fall-as-west-side-highway-collapses.html.

3. Robert Lindsey, "It Once Set the Pace Instead of Slowing It," *New York Times*, June 23, 1974, https://www.nytimes.com/1974/06/23/archives/west-side-highway-43-years-all-downhill-closing-down-sections.html.

4. William E. Farrell, "About New York," *New York Times*, January 21, 1981, https://www.nytimes.com/1981/01/21/nyregion/about-new-york.html.

5. "Boy's Fatal Fall on W. Side Highway Is a Puzzle," *New York Daily News*, August 17, 1974.

6. State-city memorandum, Benstock papers.

7. Murray Schumach, "Project Brings New Cooperation by State, City and Community," *New York Times*, August 20, 1973, https://www.nytimes.com/1973/08/20/archives/project-brings-new-cooperation-by-state-city-and-community-memo.html.

8. Sam Roberts, "Battle of the Westway: Bitter 10-Year Saga of a Vision on Hold," *New York Times*, June 4, 1984, https://www.nytimes.com/1984/06/04/nyregion/battle-of-the-westway-bitter-10-year-saga-of-a-vision-on-hold.html.

9. Editorial board, "Westway," *New York Times*, March 5, 1975, https://www.nytimes.com/1975/03/05/archives/westway.html.

10. John P. Keith, "A Westway Trade-In Won't Heal Public Transit," letter, *New York Times*, April 18, 1980, https://timesmachine.nytimes.com/timesmachine/1980/04/18/111230553.pdf.

11. U.S. Department of Transportation, Federal Highway Administration, and New York State Department of Transportation, "West Side Highway Project, Final Environmental Impact Statement," public comments, Benstock papers.

12. David Gurin, interview with the author, June 26, 2018.

13. David Gurin, "New Highway in Town: What, More Cars?," *Village Voice*, November 30, 1972.

14. Carson papers, box 12.

15. Linda Greenhouse, "Highway Project Spurs Some Doubt," *New York Times*, September 27, 1973, https://www.nytimes.com/1973/09/27/archives/highway-project-stirs-some-doubt-west-side-consultants-see-little.html.

16. Steven R. Weisman, "City's West Side Highway Plan Criticized by Community Boards," *New York Times*, November 28, 1974, https://timesmachine.nytimes.com/timesmachine/1974/11/28/80261667.pdf.

17. Bunny Gabel, interview with the author, February 28, 2019.

18. Edward C. Burks, "West Side Rail Line Urged Instead of a New Highway," *New York Times*, August 27, 1973, https://www.nytimes.com/1973/08/27/archives/west-side-rail-line-urged-instead-of-a-new-highway-kheel-says-us.html.

19. Frank Lynn, "Competing Political Pressures Underlie the Carey-Koch Dispute," *New York Times*, December 25, 1977, https://www.nytimes.com/1977/12/25/archives/competing-political-pressures-underlie-the-careykoch-dispute.html.

20. Citizens for Clean Air, "Westway Is Worth Being Scared About," April 1977 newsletter.

21. Benstock resume, Benstock papers.

22. Clean Air Campaign correspondence, Benstock papers.

23. Marcy Benstock, interview with the author, October 1, 2018, and follow-ups.

24. City of New York Office of the Mayor, "Brooklyn-Queens Expressway Expert Panel Report," January 30, 2020, https://archive.c2smart.engineering.nyu.edu/wp-content/uploads/2020/02/BQE_Expert_Panel_Report_FINAL.pdf.

25. U.S. Department of Transportation, Federal Highway Administration, and New York State Department of Transportation, "West Side Highway Project, Final Environmental Impact Statement," Benstock papers.

26. *Action for Rational Transit, et al., Plaintiffs, v. West Side Highway Project, By Its Executive Director, Lowell K. Bridwell, et al., Defendants*, March 1982 court decision document.

27. Kathleen Johnston, "Brian Ketcham: Political Engineering," *New Engineer*, January 1974.

28. Brian Ketcham, interview with the author, April 8, 2019, and unpublished autobiography, Ketcham papers.

29. Brian T. Ketcham, "Beyond Autocracy: The Role of the Consumer and Public Interest Organizations in Regulating the Auto," talk at Harvard University, October 1978, Ketcham papers.

30. Maurice Carroll, "Buckley Accuses Moynihan of 'Shading' His Positions; Moynihan Depicts Buckley as Casting Harmful Votes," *New York Times*, October 11, 1976, https://www.nytimes.com/1976/10/11/archives/buckley-accuses-moynihan-of-shading-his-positions-moynihan-depicts.html.

31. Edward C. Burks, "Moynihan Aims for Top Panel: Senate Finance," *New York Times*, January 23, 1977, https://www.nytimes.com/1977/01/23/archives/moynihan-aims-for-top-panel-senate-finance.html.

32. "EPA Putting New Curve in Westway," *New York Daily News*, August 28, 1980.

33. Sydney H. Schanberg," Corruption Ignored," *New York Times*, June 9, 1984, https://www.nytimes.com/1984/06/09/opinion/new-york-corruption-ignored.html.

34. John LoCicero, interview with the author, July 9, 2021.

35. "Durst Uses Times Page-One Ads to Promote Housing and Oppose Westway," *Real Estate Weekly*, April 9, 1984.

36. Al Butzel, interview with the author, October 9, 2018.

37. Peter Kihss, "U.S. 'No' to State Air Plan Is 'Devastating,' Carey Says," *New York Times*, June 26, 1980, https://timesmachine.nytimes.com/timesmachine/1980/06/26/111250481.pdf.

38. Charles Warren, interview with the author, July 20, 2021.

39. Editorial board, "Wrong Way on Westway," *New York Times*, December 15, 1978, https://www.nytimes.com/1978/12/15/archives/wrong-way-on-westway.html.

40. "Three U.S. Agencies Said to Drop Their Objections to Westway Plan," *New York Times*, March 11, 1981, https://www.nytimes.com/1981/03/11/nyregion/three-us-agencies-said-to-drop-their-objections-to-westway-plan.html.

41. Edward A. Gargan, "Building Westway, Now That It's Real," *New York Times*, August 2, 1981, https://www.nytimes.com/1981/08/02/weekinreview/building-westway-now-that-it-s-real.html.

42. Sydney H. Schanberg, "Westway Deceit (1), *New York Times*, June 26, 1982, https://www.nytimes.com/1982/06/26/opinion/new-york-westway-deceit-1.html.

43. Arnold H. Lubasch, "U.S. Judge Blocks Westway Landfill as Threat to Fish," *New York Times*, April 1, 1982, https://www.nytimes.com/1982/04/01/nyregion/us-judge-blocks-westway-landfill-as-threat-to-fish.html.

44. Editorial board, "Westway, Blocked by a Fin," *New York Times*, April 3, 1982, https://www.nytimes.com/1982/04/03/opinion/westway-blocked-by-a-fin.html.

45. Maureen Dowd, "The Westway's Man in the Middle," *New York Times*, June 27, 1984, https://www.nytimes.com/1984/06/27/nyregion/man-in-the-news-the-westway-s-man-in-the-middle.html.

46. Fletcher Griffis, interview with the author, May 13, 2019.

47. Griffis interview.

48. "Westway Decision Delayed by Army," *New York Times*, October 16, 1984, https://www.nytimes.com/1984/10/16/nyregion/the-city-westway-decision-delayed-by-army.html.

49. "Excerpts from Statement Recommending Westway Permit," *New York Times*, January 25, 1985, https://www.nytimes.com/1985/01/25/nyregion/excerpts-from-statement-recommending-westway-permit.html.

50. Sam Roberts, "Westway Landfill Wins the Support of Army Engineer," *New York Times*, January 25, 1985, https://www.nytimes.com/1985/01/25/nyregion/westway-landfill-wins-the-support-of-army-engineer.html.

51. Randy Mastro, interview with the author, August 19, 2020.

52. Mitch Bernard, interview with the author, July 26, 2021.

53. No. 81 Civ. 3000. United States District Court, S.D. New York. Aug. 7, 1985.

54. John P. Keith, "A Westway Trade-In Won't Heal Public Transit" (letter), *New York Times*, April 18, 1980, https://timesmachine.nytimes.com/timesmachine/1980/04/18/111230553.pdf.

55. Jack Newfield, *The Education of Jack Newfield* (New York: St. Martin's Press).

56. Albin Krebs and Robert Mcg. Thomas Jr., "Westway Is among Golden Fleece Winners," *New York Times*, November 11, 1981, https://www.nytimes.com/1981/11/11/nyregion/notes-on-people-westway-is-among-golden-fleece-winners.html.

57. Steven Polan, interview with the author, July 30, 2021; Richard Ravitch, interview with the author, July 1, 2020.

58. Maurice Carroll, "Reagan Aid Requested on Westway," *New York Times*, December 23, 1984, https://www.nytimes.com/1984/12/23/nyregion/reagan-aid-requested-on-westway.html.

59. Marcy Benstock, "For a Westway Trade-In," *New York Times*, November 8, 1980, https://timesmachine.nytimes.com/timesmachine/1980/11/08/112171122.pdf.

60. John B. Oakes, "Westway's Liabilities," *New York Times*, February 13, 1978, https://www.nytimes.com/1978/02/13/archives/westways-liabilities.html.

61. John Oakes, "Westwaygate," *New York Times*, March 21, 1983, https://www.nytimes.com/1983/03/21/opinion/westwaygate.html.

62. John B. Oakes, "Wasteway, Governor? No Way!," *New York Times*, June 6, 1983, https://www.nytimes.com/1983/06/06/opinion/wasteway-governor-no-way.html.

63. Sydney H. Schanberg, "Time to Put Westway Away," *New York Times*, June 6, 1981, https://www.nytimes.com/1981/06/06/opinion/new-york-time-to-put-westway-away.html.

64. Sydney H. Schanberg, "The Risks of Westway," *New York Times*, July 21, 1981, https://www.nytimes.com/1981/07/21/opinion/new-york-the-risks-of-westway.html.

65. Schanberg, "Westway Deceit (1)."

66. Michael Orestes, "House Votes by Big Margin to Bar Funds for Westway," *New York Times*, September 12, 1985, https://www.nytimes.com/1985/09/12/nyregion/house-votes-by-big-margin-to-bar-funds-for-westway.html.

67. Michael Oreskes, "To New Yorkers, Border War with Jersey Has Claimed a Victim: Westway," *New York Times*, September 25, 1985, https://www.nytimes.com/1985/09/25/nyregion/to-new-yorkers-border-war-with-jersey-has-claimed-a-victim-westway.html.

68. Congressional Record, United States Congress, September 11, 1985, https://www.congress.gov/bound-congressional-record/1985/09/11/house-section.

69. Michael Oreskes, "Moynihan Sees No Way to Win a Westway Vote," *New York Times*, September 19, 1985, https://www.nytimes.com/1985/09/19/nyregion/moynihan-sees-no-way-to-win-a-westway-vote.html; Editorial, "Westway at the Brink," *New York Times*, September 13, 1985, https://www.nytimes.com/1985/09/13/opinion/westway-at-the-brink.html.

70. Trade-In Plan, "Half May Go for Transit," *New York Times*, September 24, 1985, https://www.nytimes.com/1985/09/24/nyregion/trade-in-plan-half-may-go-for-transit.html.

71. Cuomo and Koch letter to Dole (copy), Benstock papers.

72. Michael Oreskes, "Westway Funds Trade-In Wins Federal Approval," *New York Times*, October 1, 1985, https://www.nytimes.com/1985/10/01/nyregion/westway-funds-trade-in-wins-federal-approval.html.

73. Richard F. Weingroff, "A Moment in Time: President Ronald Reagan Launches Construction of Westway," Highway History, Federal Highway Administration, accessed April 17, 2022, https://www.fhwa.dot.gov/highwayhistory/moment/westway.cfm.

74. Letter from Cuomo to Benstock, Benstock papers.

75. "Schanberg Resigns After N.Y. Times Cancels His Column," September 26, 1985, https://www.latimes.com/archives/la-xpm-1985-09-26-mn-1376-story.html.

76. Griffis interview.

77. Nicole Gelinas, "Lessons of Boston's Big Dig," *City Journal*, Autumn 2007, https://www.city-journal.org/htmol/lessons-boston%E2%80%99s-big-dig-13049.html.

6. Struck City: The Shutdown That Stressed the Value of Transit

1. Clayton Knowles, "2,500 Cheer Mayor," *New York Times*, January 2, 1966, https://timesmachine.nytimes.com/timesmachine/1966/01/02/355972222.pdf.

2. 1963 Hub Bound Travel, New York Metropolitan Transportation Council Report, https://www.nymtc.org/Utility-Menu/Archive/Data-and-Modeling-Archive/Hub-Bound-Travel-Archive.

3. Andrew J. Sparberg, *From a Nickel to a Token: The Journey from Board of Transportation to MTA* (New York: Fordham University Press, 2015), 143.

4. "New Year's Eve Transit Gala," *New York Herald Tribune*, December 22, 1965.

5. Editorial board, "The Quill Candidate," *New York Times*, October 30, 1953, https://timesmachine.nytimes.com/timesmachine/1953/1/30/84428313.pdf.

6. "Closed Shop Here," *New York Times*, May 28, 1937, https://timesmachine.nytimes.com/timesmachine/1937/05/28/118972406.pdf.

7. "Tough-Talking Mike Quill Was Gentle Off Stage," *New York Times*, January 29, 1966, https://timesmachine.nytimes.com/timesmachine/1966/01/29/79295140.pdf.

8. Damon Stetson, "Talks Continued; Wagner Works with Labor Panel," *New York Times*, January 1, 1964, https://www.nytimes.com/1964/01/01/archives/talks-continued-wagner-works-with-labor-panelpolice-on-standby.html.

9. Editorial board, "A Costly Transit Deal," *New York Times*, January 2, 1964, https://www.nytimes.com/1964/01/02/archives/a-costly-transit-deal.html.

10. Thomas P. Ronan, "Lindsay Says He Will Run against Wagner to Halt 'Decline and Fall' of City," *New York Times*, May 15, 1965, https://timesmachine.nytimes.com/timesmachine/1965/05/14/101546474.pdf.

11. John V. Lindsay, "A Modern Transportation System for New York City," Lindsay campaign, October 1965.

12. "Lindsay Rules Out a Subway Strike," *New York Daily News*, November 17, 1965.

13. "Quill Threatens Dec. 15 Walkout on Transit Lines," *New York Times*, December 3, 1965.

14. "Where's Money? Mike Says City's 'Lousy' with It," *New York Journal-American*, December 13, 1965, TBTA records, box 107-3.

15. Editorial board, *New York Journal-American*, November 11, 1965, TBTA records, box 107-3.

16. "New TWU Plea Made to Lindsay," *New York Times*, December 1, 1965.

17. Damon Stetson, "Quill Asks Pact Put at 250 Million by Transit Body," *New York Times*, November 5, 1965.

18. Emanuel Perlmutter, "Quill Calls Halt to Transit Talks," *New York Times*, December 2, 1965, https://www.nytimes.com/1965/12/02/archives/quill-calls-halt-to-transit-talks-denounces-lindsays-stand-in-city.html.

19. Emanuel Perlmutter, "Lindsay Demands Fair Settlement in Transit Talks," *New York Times*, December 28, 1965, https://timesmachine.nytimes.com/timesmachine/1965/12/28/98465929.pdf.

20. Damon Stetson, "Quill, On TV, Tears Up Court Order in Act of Defiance," *New York Times*, December 31, 1965, https://timesmachine.nytimes.com/timesmachine/1965/12/31/95922486.pdf.

21. Homer Bigart, "New Talks Today," *New York Times*, January 2, 1966, https://timesmachine.nytimes.com/timesmachine/1966/01/02/355972302.pdf.

22. Damon Stetson, "Quill Quits Talks," *New York Times*, January 1, 1966, https://timesmachine.nytimes.com/timesmachine/1966/01/01/79262839.pdf.

23. Tri-State Regional Planning Commission, "Hub Bound Travel Trips Crossing the Manhattan Central Business District Cordon in 1971," February 1973.

24. Robert E. Dallos, "Mayor-Elect Asks Curb on Autos in Case of Strike," *New York Times*, December 31, 1965, https://timesmachine.nytimes.com/timesmachine/1965/12/31/95922490.pdf.

25. Peter Kihss, "Doors at 2 Rail Stations Locked for Time in Crush," *New York Times*, January 4, 1966, https://timesmachine.nytimes.com/timesmachine/1966/01/04/79267542.pdf.

26. Douglas E. Kneeland, "People with a Will Find a Way to Work," *New York Times*, January 4, 1966, https://timesmachine.nytimes.com/timesmachine/1966/01/04/79267544.pdf.

27. Homer Bigart, "$100-Million Loss Each Day Is Seen," *New York Times*, January 5, 1966, https://timesmachine.nytimes.com/timesmachine/1966/01/05/79268395.pdf.

28. "Worst Traffic Jam Yet," *New York Post*, January 5, 1966.

29. "Excerpts from Two Lindsay Press Conferences on the Transit Strike," *New York Times*, January 4, 1966, https://timesmachine.nytimes.com/timesmachine/1966/01/04/79267697.pdf.

30. Peter Kihss, "Auto-Train Crisis Is More Serious," *New York Times*, January 5, 1966, https://timesmachine.nytimes.com/timesmachine/1966/01/05/79268396.pdf.

31. Douglas E. Kneeland, "People Return to City, But Holiday Mood Is Over," *New York Times*, January 5, 1966, https://timesmachine.nytimes.com/timesmachine/1966/01/05/79268741.pdf.

32. Douglas E. Kneeland, "Mayor's Schedule Ignored by Many, Including City Hall," *New York Times*, January 7, 1966, https://timesmachine.nytimes.com/timesmachine/1966/01/07/79269731.pdf.

33. Homer Bigart, "Rockefeller Requests Aid and Johnson Acts Quickly," *New York Times*, January 8, 1966, https://timesmachine.nytimes.com/timesmachine/1966/01/08/79270410.pdf.

34. Bigart, "Rockefeller Requests Aid."

35. Homer Bigart, "Retailers' Losses Put at 35-Million," *New York Times*, January 4, 1966, https://timesmachine.nytimes.com/timesmachine/1966/01/04/79267541.pdf.

36. Ralph Blumenthal, "Mayor Tours City Control Post and Urges Caller to Stay Home," *New York Times*, January 3, 1966, https://timesmachine.nytimes.com/timesmachine/1966/01/03/79266633.pdf.

37. Homer Bigart, "President Asked to Enter Strike," *New York Times*, January 6, 1966, https://timesmachine.nytimes.com/timesmachine/1966/01/06/105231877.pdf.

38. "Transit Tie-up Hit Low-Pay Groups Hard," *New York Post*, September 19, 1967.

39. Bigart, "President Asked to Enter Strike."

40. "Business Groups Warn on Impact," *New York Times*, January 13, 1966, https://timesmachine.nytimes.com/timesmachine/1966/01/13/79278768.pdf.

41. Terence Smith, "Mayor Chats with Victims of Strike," *New York Times*, January 9, 1966, https://timesmachine.nytimes.com/timesmachine/1966/01/09/355996102.pdf.

42. Richard Witkin, "Turning Point: Late Sunday Night," *New York Times*, January 14, 1966, https://timesmachine.nytimes.com/timesmachine/1966/01/14/79279914.pdf.

43. Peter Kihss, "Cost of Strike Settlement," *New York Times*, January 14, 1966, https://timesmachine.nytimes.com/timesmachine/1966/01/14/79279917.pdf.

44. Transport Workers Union of America Records; WAG 235; Tamiment Library/Robert F. Wagner Labor Archives, New York University.

45. John Samuelsen, interview with the author, April 24, 2024.

46. "Widow of Quill Upheld by Court," *New York Times*, November 7, 1970, https://timesmachine.nytimes.com/timesmachine/1970/11/07/83675180.pdf.

47. Editorial board, *New York Post*, January 4, 1966, TBTA records, box 107-4.

48. Terence Smith, "Kennedy Is Critical of Lindsay's Timing on Strike," *New York Times*, January 13, 1966, https://timesmachine.nytimes.com/timesmachine/1966/01/13/79278769.pdf.

49. Jay Kriegel, interview with the author, June 20, 2019.

50. Robert Alden, "Picking Up Pieces Is Chief Aim Now," *New York Times*, January 14, 1966, https://timesmachine.nytimes.com/timesmachine/1966/01/14/79279912.pdf.

51. Editorial, *New York World-Telegram*, January 18, 1966.

52. "New York City's Economy: A Perspective on Its Problems," *Federal Reserve Board of New York Quarterly Review* (Summer 1977), https://www.newyorkfed.org/medialibrary/media/research/quarterly_review/1977v2/v2n2article8.pdf.

53. New York City Office of the Mayor, "Mayor Bloomberg and Police Commissioner Kelly Announce 2013 Saw the Fewest Murders and Fewest Shootings in Recorded City History at NYPD Graduation Ceremony," December 27, 2013, https://www1.nyc.gov/office-of-the-mayor/news/436-13/mayor-bloomberg-police-commissioner-kelly-2013-saw-fewest-murders-fewest/#/0.

54. A. M. Rosenthal, "The Fatigued City," *New York Times*, January 13, 1966, https://timesmachine.nytimes.com/timesmachine/1966/01/13/79278789.pdf.

55. "Joint Legislative Committee on Metropolitan and Regional Area Studies," transcript, January 7, 1966, TBTA records, box 107-4.

56. *New York Daily News*, January 7, 1966.

57. Martin Gansberg, "Expressway Plan Definitely 'Out,' Price Discloses," *New York Times*, March 7, 1966, https://timesmachine.nytimes.com/timesmachine/1966/03/07/79968362.pdf.

58. Editorial board, "Unified New York Transit," *New York Times*, January 20, 1966, https://timesmachine.nytimes.com/timesmachine/1966/01/20/79283533.pdf.

59. Press release, mayor's office, City of New York, February 13, 1966.

7. Skull Practice at Triborough: Confronting Decades of Mass-Transit Deficits

1. "City Transit Loss 1.7c on Each Rider," *New York Times*, March 11, 1946, https://timesmachine.nytimes.com/timesmachine/1946/03/11/88342574.pdf.

2. David McConnell, "Subway Snarl Is Tightening on O'Dwyer: Issue of City Hall Rule," *New York Herald Tribune*, May 12, 1946; Editorial board, "The Transit Authority," *New York Herald Tribune*, March 5, 1952.

3. "Rise in City Budget Put at $105,029,625," *New York Times*, April 2, 1948, https://timesmachine.nytimes.com/timesmachine/1948/04/02/93724691.pdf.

4. David McConnell, "O'Dwyer Stands By 5-Cent Fare as Debt Soars: Names Committee," *New York Herald Tribune*, January 9, 1947.

5. Leo Egan, "15-Cent Fare Seen If City Runs Lines, 12½ By Authority," *New York Times*, March 6, 1952.

6. Andrew J. Sparberg, *From a Nickel to a Token: The Journey from Board of Transportation to MTA* (New York: Fordham University Press, 2015).

7. Tony Schwartz, "The Subway: City's Lifeline for 75 Years," *New York Times*, April 4, 1980, https://timesmachine.nytimes.com/timesmachine/1980/04/04/111147192.pdf.

8. Richard Phalon, "'65 Transit Pay Exceeded Fares," *New York Times*, January 6, 1966, https://timesmachine.nytimes.com/timesmachine/1966/01/09/355996152.pdf.

9. Peter Kihss, "Cost of Strike Settlement: $60-Million Seen Likely, but Estimates Change with Operating Experience," *New York Times*, January 14, 1966.

10. David McConnell, "Moses Asserts 5c Fare Curbs City Projects: Cuts Billion from Works," *New York Herald Tribune*, April 15, 1946.

11. Robert Moses, "Solving Traffic Woes to Take Years: Moses," *New York Daily News*, October 17, 1953, Moses papers, box 75.

12. "Joint Legislative Committee on Metropolitan and Regional Area Studies," transcript, January 7, 1966, TBTA records, box 107-4.

13. "Moses Wants 2% Sales Tax Back to Get 145 Millions for Subways," *New York Herald Tribune*, December 21, 1945.

14. "Moses Bars Train on Narrows Span," *New York Times*, April 9, 1956, https://timesmachine.nytimes.com/timesmachine/1956/04/09/84931432.pdf.

15. Editorial board, "Tracks on Narrows Bridge," *New York Times*, April 19, 1956.

16. Joseph C. Ingraham, "Moses Outlines 10-Year Plan for Relief of Traffic in the City," *New York Times*, March 31, 1966, https://timesmachine.nytimes.com/timesmachine/1966/03/31/284442432.pdf.

17. Richard Phalon, "Gilhooley Sees $51 Million Need in 1966 Alone to Save 15c Fare," *New York Times*, January 16, 1966, https://timesmachine.nytimes.com/timesmachine/1966/01/16/121592073.pdf.

18. David Wise, "Moses' Authority Rule Challenged in Report," *New York Herald Tribune*, January 18, 1957.

19. Jay Kriegel, interview with the author, June 20, 2019.

20. "TA Plan—Back to Moses," *New York Journal-American*, January 26, 1966, TBTA records, box 107-3.

21. Editorial board, "New York Program: Transit," *New York Times*, December 21, 1965, https://timesmachine.nytimes.com/timesmachine/1965/12/21/95011699.pdf.

22. Editorial board, *New York Herald Tribune*, January 22, 1966, TBTA records, box 107-3.

23. TBTA records, box 136-2.

24. Joseph C. Ingraham, "Rail Subsidy Idea Scored by Moses," *New York Times*, January 23, 1960.

25. Samuel Kaplan, "Moses Calls Transit Unity 'Hogwash,'" *New York Times*, January 8, 1966.

26. Transcript, "Joint Legislative Committee on Metropolitan and Regional Area Studies," January 7, 1966, TBTA records, box 107-4.

27. TBTA records, unboxed.

28. TBTA records, unboxed.

29. TBTA records, box 107-4.

30. Memo from Moses, March 5, 1966; Memo to Moses, February 16, 1966, TBTA records, box 107-3.

31. Poletti written testimony, March 10–11, 1966, TBTA records, box 107-4.

32. TBTA records, box 107-3.

33. Memo from Moses, February 21, 1966, TBTA records, box 107-4.

34. Letter, March 15, 1966, TBTA records, box 106-2.

35. "Program for Arterial Recreation Areas," TBTA brochure, July 21, 1966, TBTA records, box 106-2.

36. "Bossism Charged as Council Picks Majority Leader," *New York Times*, March 25, 1964, https://www.nytimes.com/1964/03/25/archives/bossism-charged-as-council-picks-majority-leader-wagner-and.html.

37. TBTA records, box 107-4.

38. Andrew Sidamon-Eristoff, "Political leadership at the Metropolitan Transportation Authority" (senior thesis, Princeton University, April 16, 1985).

39. *Long Island Press*, June 4, 1966, TBTA records, box 107-3.

40. "Rocky'd Give JVL Transit Czardom," *Long Island Star Journal*, February 6, 1966.

41. "Rocky Gets Low Mark for Transit Strike Reaction," *Staten Island Advance*, March 10, 1966, TBTA records, box 107-3.

42. Sidney H. Schanberg, "Governor Signs 2d Transit Bill," *New York Times*, May 3, 1967.

43. TBTA records, box 110-4.

44. Homer Bigart, "Moses Backs Plan on Transit Unity," *New York Times*, March 11, 1967.

45. Moses statement, March 17, 1967, TBTA records, box 109-1.

46. Moses papers, box 76.

47. Richard P Hunt, "Moses Quits 5 State Posts," *New York Times*, December 1, 1962, https://timesmachine.nytimes.com/timesmachine/1962/12/01/89890845.pdf.

48. Robert A. Caro, *The Power Broker: Robert Moses and the Fall of New York* (New York: Vintage Books, 1974), 1074–1076.

49. *New York Motorist*, February 1955, TBTA records, box 136-2.

50. Moses papers, box 75.

51. "Transit Role for Moses," *New York World Journal-Telegram*, January 16, 1967.

52. Robert Moses, "Why NY Needs the Transportation Bond Issue," *Newsday*, October 28, 1967.

53. TBTA records, box 110-4.

54. TBTA records, box 109-1.

55. TBTA records, box 109-1.

56. TBTA records, box 110-4.

57. TBTA records, box 110-4.

58. TBTA records, box 109-1.

59. TBTA records, box 109-1.

60. TBTA records, box 110-4.

61. TBTA records, box 110-4.

62. Richard L. Madden, "Moses Condemns Fund Plan Again," *New York Times*, June 14, 1967.

63. Sydney H. Schanberg, "Triborough Accord on Transit Nearer," *New York Times*, February 7, 1968.

64. TBTA records, box 115-3.

65. TBTA records, box 110-4.

66. Metropolitan Transportation Authority, annual report, 1968.

67. Sydney H. Schanberg, "Transit Power Shift: Ronan Is Expected to Have Vastly More Authority Than Moses Had in Heyday," *New York Times*, March 24, 1967.

68. Fred C. Shapiro, "The Wholly Ronan Empire: 'The Terrible Thing Is That It's Working,'" *New York Times*, May 17, 1970.

69. Sparberg, *From a Nickel to a Token*, 161.

70. 1969 annual report, Metropolitan Transportation Authority, TBTA papers.

71. Richard Witkin, "Triborough Agency Has Surplus of $26-Million," *New York Times*, April 3, 1968.

72. Richard Witkin, "Stalled City Subway Expansion: Fourfold Cost Rise," *New York Times*, November 12, 1974.

73. Milton Leebaw and Harriet Heyman, "The Region in Summary," *New York Times*, October 20, 1974, https://www.nytimes.com/1974/10/20/archives/the-region-fares-up-it-figures-endorsing-the-arts-us-strings-on.html.

74. Andrew Cuomo, interview with the author, April 3, 2023.

75. Bill de Blasio, interview with the author, May 24, 2023.

76. Tri-State Regional Planning Commission, "Hub Bound Travel: 1980, Interim Technical Report," January 1982.

77. Tri-State Regional Planning Commission, "Hub Bound Travel Trips Crossing the Manhattan Central Business District Cordon in 1971," February 1973; Tri-State Regional Planning Commission, "Hub Bound Travel: 1980, Interim Technical Report," January 1982.

78. "New York City's Economy: A Perspective on Its Problems," *Federal Reserve Board of New York Quarterly Review*, Summer 1977, https://www.newyorkfed.org/medialibrary/media/research/quarterly_review/1977v2/v2n2article8.pdf.

79. *Long Island Press*, September 20, 1967, TBTA records, box 115-3.

80. Editorial Board, *New York Daily News*, July 21, 1967, TBTA records, box 115-3.

81. TBTA records, box 115-3.

8. Nixon's Nudge: The Federal Laws That Forced a New Direction

1. Terence Smith, "Contrasts Mark Thanksgiving Day," *New York Times*, November 25, 1966, https://timesmachine.nytimes.com/timesmachine/1966/11/25/82968739.pdf.

2. Stuart H. Loory, "Conspiracy of Nature's Forces Is Blamed for Smog," *New York Times*, November 26, 1966, https://timesmachine.nytimes.com/timesmachine/1966/11/26/83566843.pdf.

3. "10% Here Suffered Effects of Smog, Private Study Finds," *New York Times*, December 10, 1966, https://timesmachine.nytimes.com/timesmachine/1966/12/10/82974341.pdf.

4. "Smog Emergency Called for City," *New York Times*, November 26, 1966, https://timesmachine.nytimes.com/timesmachine/1966/11/26/83566779.pdf.

5. David Bird, "November Smog Killed 168 Here," *New York Times*, October 27, 1967, https://timesmachine.nytimes.com/timesmachine/1967/10/27/82162296.pdf.

6. Editorial board, "We're the Tops in Air Poison," *New York Times*, August 5, 1967, https://timesmachine.nytimes.com/timesmachine/1967/08/05/90388102.pdf.

7. Eliza Griswold, "How *Silent Spring* Ignited the Environmental Movement," *New York Times*, September 23, 2012, https://www.nytimes.com/2012/09/23/magazine/how-silent-spring-ignited-the-environmental-movement.html.

8. Hazel Henderson, interview with the author, June 16, 2021.

9. Henderson interview.

10. Henderson papers.

11. Charles G. Bennett, "3 Candidates Give Pollution Plans," *New York Times*, July 30, 1965, https://www.nytimes.com/1965/07/30/archives/3-candidates-give-pollution-plans-lindsay-ryan-and-screvane-take.html.

12. Robert Mcg. Thomas Jr., "Carl Ally, Hard-Hitting Adman, Is Dead at 74," *New York Times*, February 17, 1999, https://www.nytimes.com/1999/02/17/business/carl-ally-hard-hitting-adman-is-dead-at-74.html.

13. "Text of President Johnson's Message to Congress on Pollution and Resources," *New York Times*, January 31, 1967, https://timesmachine.nytimes.com/timesmachine/1967/01/31/83573670.pdf.

14. "Acrid, Dirty Air Here Expected to Move On with Wind Today," *New York Times*, August 18, 1967, https://timesmachine.nytimes.com/timesmachine/1967/08/18/90393566.pdf.

15. David Schoenbrod, interview with the author, June 26, 2018.

16. "Text of Nixon Statement," *New York Times*, January 2, 1970, https://www.nytimes.com/1970/01/02/archives/text-of-nixon-statement.html.

17. Richard Nixon, "Remarks on Signing the Clean Air Amendments of 1970," December 31, 1970, https://www.presidency.ucsb.edu/documents/remarks-signing-the-clean-air-amendments-1970.

18. Christopher D. Ahlers, "Origins of the Clean Air Act: A New Interpretation," March 12, 2015, https://law.lclark.edu/live/files/19115-45-1ahlers.

19. "Clean Air Act (CAA) and Federal Facilities," United States Environmental Protection Agency, accessed April 19, 2022, https://www.epa.gov/enforcement/clean-air-act-caa-and-federal-facilities.

20. New York City Office of the Mayor, "Mayor Bloomberg and Police Commissioner Kelly Announce 2013 Saw the Fewest Murders and Fewest Shootings in Recorded City History at NYPD Graduation Ceremony," December 27, 2013, https://www1.nyc.gov/office-of-the-mayor/news/436-13/mayor-bloomberg-police-commissioner-kelly-2013-saw-fewest-murders-fewest/#/0.

21. "Lindsay Also Cuts Back Top Speed Here," *New York Times*, November 11, 1973, https://www.nytimes.com/1973/11/11/archives/lindsay-also-cuts-back-top-speed-here-governor-reduces-speed-limit.html.

22. David Bird, "Governor Offers a Clean Air Plan," *New York Times*, April 18, 1973, https://www.nytimes.com/1973/04/18/archives/governor-offers-a-cleanair-plan-waives-privatecar-device-as-not.html.

23. Brian Ketcham, interview with the author, April 8, 2019.

24. New York City Metropolitan Area Air Quality Implementation Plan, Transportation Controls, New York State Department of Environmental Conservation, April 1973.

25. Editorial board, "Tragedy for the City," *New York Times*, January 3, 1970, https://www.nytimes.com/1970/01/03/archives/tragedy-for-the-city.html.

26. Schoenbrod interview.

27. Edward C. Burks, "Suit Threatened on Subway Noise," *New York Times*, January 22, 1974, https://www.nytimes.com/1974/01/22/archives/suit-threatened-on-subway-noise-transit-police-and-abrams-give.html.

28. "Suit on Subway Din Dismissed by Judge," *New York Times*, June 29, 1974, https://www.nytimes.com/1974/06/29/archives/suit-on-subway-din-dismissed-by-judge.html.

29. Edward Hudson, "U.S. Asks Tighter Curbs on Cabs Here," *New York Times*, August 31, 1975, https://www.nytimes.com/1975/08/31/archives/us-asks-tighter-curbs-on-cabs-here.html.

30. "City Seeks to Block U S. Plan for Tolls on Bridges," *New York Times*, September 12, 1975, https://www.nytimes.com/1975/09/12/archives/city-seeks-to-block-us-plan-for-tolls-on-bridges.html.

31. Edward C. Burks, "U.S. Formally Orders Tolls on Bridges to Manhattan," *New York Times*, September 30, 1975, https://www.nytimes.com/1975/09/30/archives/us-formally-orders-tolls-on-bridges-to-manhattan-city-to-fight.html.

32. Editorial board, "The Case for Tolls," *New York Times*, October 7, 1975, https://www.nytimes.com/1975/10/07/archives/the-case-for-tolls.html.

33. Editorial board, "E.P.A. Gets Tough," *New York Times*, February 24, 1976, https://www.nytimes.com/1976/02/24/archives/epa-gets-tough.html.

34. Arnold H. Lubasch, "Court Orders New York to Effect Clean-Air Plan," *New York Times*, April 27, 1976, https://www.nytimes.com/1976/04/27/archives/court-orders-new-york-to-effect-cleanair-plan.html.

35. Arnold H. Lubasch, "Judge Demands a Parking Plan within 10 Days," *New York Times*, July 6, 1977.

36. "New York Ready for Parking Ban," *New York Times*, June 24, 1977, https://www.nytimes.com/1977/06/24/archives/new-york-ready-for-parking-ban.html.

37. Editorial board, "The Parking Farce," *New York Times*, June 18, 1977, https://www.nytimes.com/1977/06/18/archives/the-parking-farce.html.

38. Nathaniel Sheppard Jr., "New Yorkers in Congress Will Fight River Tolls," *New York Times*, February 28, 1977, https://www.nytimes.com/1977/02/28/archives/new-yorkers-in-congress-will-fight-river-tolls.html.

39. Elizabeth Holtzman, interview with the author, January 13, 2022.

40. Warren Weaver Jr., "New York Fails in Bid to Block Parking Ban," *New York Times*, October 18, 1977, https://www.nytimes.com/1977/10/18/archives/new-york-fails-in-bid-to-block-parking-ban-high-court-declines-to.html.

41. Lee Dembart, "Backing of Parking Plan Explained," *New York Times*, August 20, 1977, https://www.nytimes.com/1977/08/20/archives/backing-of-parking-plan-explained.html.

42. Lee Dembart, "New York Wins Clean-Air Accord, Easing Limit on Midtown Parking," *New York Times*, August 19, 1977, https://www.nytimes.com/1977/08/19/archives/new-york-wins-cleanair-accord-easing-limit-on-midtown-parking-new.html.

43. Editorial board, "Small Steps against Smog," *New York Times*, August 27, 1977, https://www.nytimes.com/1977/08/27/archives/small-steps-against-smog.html.

44. Ross Sandler, interview with the author, November 19, 2021.

45. Judith Cummings, "Rocky Roadbed for Subways," *New York Times*, July 12, 1981, https://www.nytimes.com/1981/07/12/weekinreview/rocky-roadbed-for-subways.html.

46. Michael Stern, "Rep. Koch Finds 27 Major Companies in Midtown Area Are Weighing a Move from City," *New York Times*, November 3, 1971, https://www.nytimes.com/1971/11/03/archives/rep-koch-finds-27-major-companies-in-midtown-area-are-weighing-a.html.

47. Maurice Carroll, "Consultants Give Ideas for Changes to a Budget-Tight City," *New York Times*, December 26, 1978, https://www.nytimes.com/1978/12/26/archives/consultants-give-ideas-for-changes-to-a-budgettight-city-times.html.

48. Maurice Carroll, "Planners Urge Spending More on Fixing Subways," *New York Times*, December 29, 1978, https://www.nytimes.com/1978/12/29/archives/planners-urge-spending-more-on-fixing-subways-report-called-impetus.html.

49. Ross Sandler and David Schoenbrod, "Subways: Cash & Carey," *New York Times*, July 3, 1979, https://www.nytimes.com/1979/07/30/archives/subways-cash-carey-for-a-55cent-farenow.html.

9. The Lion of the MTA: The Push to Rebuild New York's Transit

1. Richard Ravitch, *So Much to Do: A Full Life of Business, Politics, and Confronting Fiscal Crises* (New York: PublicAffairs, 2014), 140.

2. Richard Pérez-Peña, "Hugh Carey, Who Led Fiscal Rescue of New York City, Is Dead at 92," *New York Times*, August 8, 2011, https://www.nytimes.com/2011/08/08/nyregion/hugh-carey-who-led-fiscal-rescue-of-new-york-city-dead-at-92.html.

3. Richard Ravitch, oral history by Wendy Feuer, June 7, 2021, MTA Capital Program Oral History Project, 7.

4. Steven Polan, interview with the author, July 30, 2021.

5. Andrew Sidamon-Eristoff, "Political Leadership at the Metropolitan Transportation Authority" (senior thesis, Princeton University, April 16, 1985).

6. Ravitch, Oral History Project, 9.

7. E. J. Dionne Jr., "Carey Names Ravitch to Head M.T.A.," *New York Times*, October 18, 1979, https://www.nytimes.com/1979/10/18/archives/carey-names-ravitch-to-head-mta-heads-construction-company.html.

8. Ravitch, interview with the author, July 1, 2020.

9. "What They Said of the 50c Fare," *New York Times*, June 28, 1980, https://timesmachine.nytimes.com/timesmachine/1980/06/28/113948333.pdf.

10. Dionne, "Carey Names Ravitch to Head M.T.A."

11. Ravitch, interview with the author.

12. David A. Andelman, "M.TA. May Face Deficit Next Year of $200 Million," *New York Times*, November 21, 1979, https://www.nytimes.com/1979/11/21/archives/mta-may-face-deficit-next-year-of-200-million-four-solutions.html.

13. Editorial board, "Getting the Transit Debate Moving," *New York Times*, November 23, 1979, https://www.nytimes.com/1979/11/23/archives/getting-the-transit-debate-moving.html.

14. Robert Hanley, "Odd-Even Sales of Gasoline Due Tomorrow in New York," *New York Times*, June 19, 1979, https://www.nytimes.com/1979/06/19/archives/oddeven-sales-of-gasoline-due-tomorrow-in-new-york-similar-plan.html.

15. Richard J. Meislin, "Carey Will Propose Statewide Plan for Surcharge on Car Registration," *New York Times*, February 15, 1980, https://timesmachine.nytimes.com/timesmachine/1980/02/15/111762687.pdf.

16. Joyce Purnick, "Carey Asking Fuel Taxes," *New York Times*, February 21, 1980, https://timesmachine.nytimes.com/timesmachine/1980/02/21/111764789.pdf.

17. "Paying the Cost of Transit: Fares or Taxes?," *New York Times*, February 2, 1980, https://timesmachine.nytimes.com/timesmachine/1980/02/02/112062413.pdf.

18. Richard J. Meislin, "Legislature and the Fare," *New York Times*, March 13, 1980, https://timesmachine.nytimes.com/timesmachine/1980/03/13/111140654.pdf.

19. Ari L. Goldman, "Albany Senate Leaders Reluctant to Act on Fiscal Plan for M.T.A.," *New York Times*, March 6, 1980, https://timesmachine.nytimes.com/timesmachine/1980/03/06/111226028.pdf.

20. Ari L. Goldman, "Carey Urges Action on Full Transportation Package," *New York Times*, March 10, 1980, https://timesmachine.nytimes.com/timesmachine/1980/03/10/111138885.pdf.

21. Joyce Purnick, "Transit Politicking Complicates Maneuvers over Aid Package," *New York Times*, March 16, 1980, https://timesmachine.nytimes.com/timesmachine/1980/03/16/111770963.pdf.

22. David A. Andelman, "Half-Fare Setup on City Transit Sharply Curbed," *New York Times*, March 15, 1980, https://timesmachine.nytimes.com/timesmachine/1980/03/15/111141151.pdf.

23. David A. Andelman, "Transit Authorities in New York Region Foresee Fare Rises," *New York Times*, February 22, 1980, https://timesmachine.nytimes.com/timesmachine/1980/02/22/111222499.pdf.

24. Ari L. Goldman, "Ravitch Predicts 75c Transit Fare If Legislature Doesn't Act by July," *New York Times*, April 21, 1980, https://timesmachine.nytimes.com/timesmachine/1980/04/21/111231241.pdf.

25. David A. Andelman, "M.T.A. Proposes Rise of Up to 25 Cents in New York Fares," *New York Times*, April 30, 1980, https://timesmachine.nytimes.com/timesmachine/1980/04/30/113941040.pdf.

26. "Ravitch, in Albany, Warns of Fare Rise," *New York Times*, May 8, 1980, https://timesmachine.nytimes.com/timesmachine/1980/05/08/111240855.pdf.

27. Ari L. Goldman, "Tolls Are Raised for Two Tunnels and Six Bridges," *New York Times*, May 17, 1980, https://timesmachine.nytimes.com/timesmachine/1980/05/17/111242146.pdf.

28. Ari L. Goldman, "City Turnstiles Being Modified to Accept New Tokens," *New York Times*, June 3, 1980, https://timesmachine.nytimes.com/timesmachine/1980/06/03/111245089.pdf.

29. Richard J. Meislin, "Republicans Reject Carey's M.T.A. Plan," *New York Times*, June 5, 1980, https://timesmachine.nytimes.com/timesmachine/1980/06/05/111245631.pdf.

30. Richard J. Meislin, "Plan to Aid M.T.A. Passes Legislature; 60-Cent Fare Likely," *New York Times*, June 15, 1980, https://timesmachine.nytimes.com/timesmachine/1980/06/15/111785743.pdf.

31. "Koch Endorses Fare-Rise Plan to Fight Crime," *New York Times*, October 4, 1980, https://timesmachine.nytimes.com/timesmachine/1980/10/04/111296948.pdf.

32. Judith Cummings, "Decline in Riders Forebodes a Rise in Subway Fares," *New York Times*, January 16, 1981, https://www.nytimes.com/1981/01/16/nyregion/decline-in-riders-forebodes-a-rise-in-subway-fares.html.

33. Judith Cummings, "Subway Riders Frazzled by Delays and Crowding," *New York Times*, January 27, 1981, https://www.nytimes.com/1981/01/27/nyregion/subway-riders-frazzled-by-delays-and-crowding.html.

34. Editorial board, "Mr. Ravitch Clears the Track," *New York Times*, December 5, 1980, https://timesmachine.nytimes.com/timesmachine/1980/12/05/111321547.pdf.

35. Judith Cummings, "Ravitch Listens, and Waits, on Tour of Subways; Says He's No Stranger to Subway," *New York Times*, November 7, 1980, https://www.nytimes.com/1980/11/07/archives/ravitch-listens-and-waits-on-tour-of-subways-says-hes-no-stranger.html.

36. David Plavin, interview by Wendy Feuer, July 1, 2021, MTA Capital Program Oral History Project, 8.

37. "Ravitch Hopes He'll Find the Silver Lining in Albany," *New York Times*, February 1, 1981, https://www.nytimes.com/1981/02/01/weekinreview/ravitch-hopes-he-ll-find-the-silver-lining-in-albany.html.

38. "Capital Revitalization for the 1980s and Beyond," accompanying press statement by Richard Ravitch, Metropolitan Transportation Authority, November 25, 1980.

39. Judith Cummings, "Transit Decline Poses a Threat to Jobs in City," *New York Times*, April 5, 1981, https://www.nytimes.com/1981/04/05/nyregion/transit-decline-poses-a-threat-to-jobs-in-city.html.

40. Judith Cummings, "Ravitch Warns of a $1 Fare without Rise in Transit Aid," *New York Times*, May 14, 1981, https://www.nytimes.com/1981/05/14/nyregion/ravitch-warns-of-a-1-fare-without-rise-in-transit-aid.html.

41. Judith Cummings, "Transit Authority Agrees to Proposal for Executive Help," *New York Times*, April 27, 1981, https://www.nytimes.com/1981/04/27/nyregion/transit-authority-agrees-to-proposal-for-executive-help.html.

42. Shawn G. Kennedy, "Five Members of Carey Transit Panel Visit Subway and Bus Operations," *New York Times*, June 6, 1981, https://www.nytimes.com/1981/06/06/nyregion/5-members-of-carey-transit-panel-visit-subway-and-bus-operations.html.

43. Ravitch, Oral History Project, 11.

44. Judith Cummings, "Transit Agency Chief Seeks Cut in Bus Air Conditioning," *New York Times*, May 1, 1981, https://www.nytimes.com/1981/05/01/nyregion/transit-agency-chief-seeks-cut-in-bus-air-conditioning.html.

45. Edward A. Gargan, "Koch Seeks Statewide Tax for MTA," *New York Times*, March 5, 1981, https://www.nytimes.com/1981/03/05/nyregion/koch-seeks-statewide-tax-for-mta.html.

46. Gene Russianoff, interview with the author, March 15, 2022.

47. Ronald Sullivan, "Ravitch and Wagner Assailed at Transit Speakout," *New York Times*, March 8, 1981, https://www.nytimes.com/1981/03/08/nyregion/ravitch-and-wagner-assailed-at-transit-speakout.html.

48. Robin Herman, "Legislative Chiefs Seek Votes for Aid to Transit," *New York Times*, July 9, 1981, https://www.nytimes.com/1981/07/09/nyregion/legislative-chiefs-seek-votes-for-aid-to-transit.html.

49. Richard J. Meislin, "Carey Panel Urges 2 Tax Rises to Help MTA with Deficits," *New York Times*, June 5, 1981, https://www.nytimes.com/1981/06/05/nyregion/carey-panel-urges-2-tax-rises-to-help-mta-with-deficits.html.

50. Richard J. Meislin, "Governor Proposes 3-Part Tax Program to Close MTA Gap," *New York Times*, June 27, 1981, https://www.nytimes.com/1981/06/27/nyregion/governor-proposes-3-part-tax-program-to-close-mta-gap.html.

51. Richard Levine and Carlyle C. Douglas, "In the Short Run Saving Transit Is Left to the Riders," *New York Times*, June 28, 1981, https://www.nytimes.com/1981/06/28/weekinreview/the-region-in-summary-in-the-short-run-saving-transit-is-left-to-the-riders.html.

52. "Transit Plan Is Assailed at a Moynihan Session," *New York Times*, April 5, 1981, https://www.nytimes.com/1981/04/05/nyregion/transit-plan-is-assailed-at-a-moynihan-session.html.

53. Judith Cummings, "Ravitch Says Fare Will Go Up to 75c by This Weekend," *New York Times*, July 1, 1981, https://www.nytimes.com/1981/07/01/nyregion/ravitch-says-fare-will-go-up-to-75-by-this-weekend.html.

54. Judith Cummings, "City's Fare Rises to 75c And Rails Increase by 25%," *New York Times*, July 3, 1981, https://www.nytimes.com/1981/07/03/nyregion/city-s-fare-rises-to-75-and-rails-increase-by-25.html.

55. Herman, "Legislative Chiefs Seek Votes for Aid to Transit."

56. "Quotation of the Day," *New York Times*, July 10, 1981, https://www.nytimes.com/1981/07/10/nyregion/quotation-of-the-day-188815.html.

57. "Excerpts from Address by Ravitch on Transit System's Progress and Plans," *New York Times*, November 29, 1981, www.nytimes.com/1981/11/26/nyregion/excerpts-from-address-by-ravitch-on-transit-system-s-progress-and-plans.html.

58. Richard Ravitch, "Transitory Federalism," *New York Times*, October 21, 1981, https://www.nytimes.com/1981/10/21/opinion/transitory-federalism.html.

59. Ari L. Goldman, "Koch Asks New Agency on Funds for Westway," *New York Times*, July 21, 1981, https://www.nytimes.com/1981/07/21/nyregion/koch-asks-new-agency-on-funds-for-westway.html.

60. City's Subways Still Declining, a Survey Finds," *New York Times*, October 15, 1981, https://www.nytimes.com/1981/10/15/nyregion/city-s-subways-still-declining-a-survey-finds.html.

61. Ari L. Goldman, "Straphangers Rate Quality of Their Rides," *New York Times*, May 6, 1983, https://www.nytimes.com/1983/05/06/nyregion/straphangers-rate-quality-of-their-rides.html.

62. Michael Oreskes, "Bond Rating Service Gives MTA Issue a Favorable Grade," *New York Times*, July 10, 1982, https://www.nytimes.com/1982/07/10/nyregion/bond-rating-service-gives-mta-issue-a-favorable-grade.html.

63. Mortimer Downey, interview by Wendy Feuer, July 5, 2021, MTA Capital Program Oral History Project, 11.

64. Lena Williams, "Legislators Told of a Transit Gap up to $400 Million," *New York Times*, May 6, 1982, https://www.nytimes.com/1982/05/06/nyregion/legislators-told-of-a-transit-gap-up-to-400-million.html.

65. Damon Stetson, "Better Controls in Transit Pact Seen by Ravitch," *New York Times*, May 1, 1982, https://www.nytimes.com/1982/05/01/nyregion/better-controls-in-transit-pact-seen-by-ravitch.html.

66. Josh Barnabel, "Albany Sesson to Begin with Fare Issue Cloudy," *New York Times*, December 13, 1982, https://www.nytimes.com/1982/12/13/nyregion/albany-session-to-begin-with-fare-issue-cloudy.html.

67. Ari L. Goldman, "Cuomo Has Plans on Transit Fare That He Hopes Can End Deadlock," *New York Times*, December 20, 1982, https://www.nytimes.com/1982/12/20/nyregion/cuomo-has-plans-on-transit-fare-that-he-hopes-can-end-deadlock.html.

68. Josh Barnabel, "Utilities Plan to Pass Along Transit Aid Tax Surcharge," *New York Times*, December 14, 1982, https://www.nytimes.com/1982/12/24/nyregion/utilities-plan-to-pass-along-transit-aid-tax-surcharge.html.

69. "Quotation of the Day," December 23, 1982, *New York Times*, https://www.nytimes.com/1982/12/23/nyregion/quotation-of-the-day-119391.html.

70. Ravitch, interview with the author.

71. Ari L. Goldman, "MTA Plan to Save Money: Sell Buses, Rent Them Back," *New York Times*, September 12, 1981, https://www.nytimes.com/1981/09/12/nyregion/mta-plan-to-save-money-sell-buses-rent-them-back.html.

72. Mortimer Downey, interview with the author, June 18, 2021.

73. Steven M. Polan, interview by Wendy Feuer, June 1, 2021, MTA Capital Program Oral History Project, 12.

74. Tom Goldstein, "D'Amato: At Home in the Senate," *New York Times*, February 13, 1983, https://www.nytimes.com/1983/02/13/magazine/d-amato-at-home-in-the-senate.html.

75. Editorial board, "Mr. Cuomo's Pointless Transit Repair," *New York Times*, June 9, 1983, https://www.nytimes.com/1983/06/09/opinion/mr-cuomo-s-pointless-transit-repair.html.

76. Ravitch, Oral History Project, 17.

77. Ari L. Goldman, "Ravitch Leaving MTA to Return to Private Sector," *New York Times*, August 30, 1983, https://www.nytimes.com/1983/08/30/nyregion/ravitch-leaving-mta-to-return-to-private-sector.html.

78. "Stanley Fink, 61, Dies; A Legend at State Capitol," *Times Union*, March 6, 1997.

79. "Warren M. Anderson," *Times Union*, June 5, 2007.

80. Jerry Kremer, interview with the author, June 7, 2021.

81. Sidamon-Eristoff, "Political Leadership at the Metropolitan Transportation Authority."

82. "Carey Rebuts Criticism of Clean-Air Plan by E.P.A.," *New York Times*, September 3, 1980.

83. David Schoenbrod, interview with the author, June 26, 2018.

84. Bruce Lambert, "Here and There, City Repairs and Renovations Start to Show," *New York Times*, September 7, 1986, https://www.nytimes.com/1986/09/07/weekinreview/here-and-there-city-repairs-and-renovations-start-to-show.html.

85. "New York's Economy in 1980," *Federal Reserve Board of New York Quarterly Review*, Spring 1981, https://www.newyorkfed.org/medialibrary/media/research/quarterly_review/1981v6/v6n1article1.pdf.

86. M. A. Farber, "Transit System Is Facing a Troubled Future," *New York Times*, August 1, 1984, https://www.nytimes.com/1984/08/01/nyregion/transit-system-is-facing-a-troubled-future.html.

87. Nicole Gelinas, "New York's Economic Future Rides on Its Subways," Manhattan Institute, July 10, 2018, https://media4.manhattan-institute.org/sites/default/files/IB-NG-0718.pdf.

88. "The Next New York: Renewing and Reforming the Empire State," Empire Center, December 2022.

89. Andrew Cuomo, interview with the author, April 3, 2023.

90. Ravitch, interview with the author.

10. From Fear Train to Packed Train: Securing New York's Subways

1. Jesus Rangel, "Statistically, At Least, It Is Rather Safe Down There," *New York Times*, February 10, 1985, https://www.nytimes.com/1985/02/10/weekinreview/statistically-at-least-it-is-rather-safe-down-there.html.

2. "Step Taken to Curb Subway Robberies," *New York Times*, July 25, 1936, https://timesmachine.nytimes.com/timesmachine/1936/07/25/88682725.pdf.

3. "Menaced by Crowds as Subway 'Masher,'" *New York Times*, August 29, 1937, https://timesmachine.nytimes.com/timesmachine/1937/08/29/512907742.pdf.

4. "City Acts to Curb Subway Crime; Would Add 300 to the 354 Police," *New York Times*, December 10, 1949, https://timesmachine.nytimes.com/timesmachine/1949/12/10/96486822.pdf.

5. Ray Kelly, interview with the author, May 5, 2016.

6. "Crime in Subways Shows Drop in '59," *New York Times*, January 27, 1960, https://timesmachine.nytimes.com/timesmachine/1960/01/27/99338834.pdf.

7. Editorial board, "Crime in the Subways," *New York Times*, July 8, 1964, www.nytimes.com/1964/07/08/archives/crime-in-the-subways.html.

8. "Youth Invasions Upset IRT Riders," *New York Times*, November 2, 1964, https://timesmachine.nytimes.com/timesmachine/1964/11/02/118686393.pdf; "Gangs Beat and Rob 2 Riders on Upper Manhattan Subways," *New York Times*, July 18, 1964, https://www.nytimes.com/1964/07/18/archives/gangs-beat-and-rob-2-riders-on-upper-manhattan-subways.html.

9. New York City Office of the Mayor, "Mayor Bloomberg and Police Commissioner Kelly Announce 2013 Saw the Fewest Murders and Fewest Shootings in Recorded City History at NYPD Graduation Ceremony," December 27, 2013, https://www1.nyc.gov/office-of-the-mayor/news/436-13/mayor-bloomberg-police-commissioner-kelly-2013-saw-fewest-murders-fewest/#/0.

10. Charles Mohr, "Apathy Is Puzzle in Queens Killing," *New York Times*, March 28, 1964, https://www.nytimes.com/1964/03/28/archives/apathy-is-puzzle-in-queen-skilling-behavioral-specialists-hard-put.html.

11. Editorial board, "Crime in the Subways."

12. "Subway Ride from Coney Island Can Be Long, Lonely, Fearful," *New York Times*, June 8, 1964, https://www.nytimes.com/1964/06/08/archives/subway-ride-from-coney-island-can-be-long-lonely-fearful.html; Charles G. Bennett, "20% Rise Sought in Subway Police," *New York Times*, March 25, 1964, https://timesmachine.nytimes.com/timesmachine/1964/03/25/97174534.pdf.

13. Emanuel Perlmutter, "Police Appeal to 10 Witnesses in Search for Subway Killers," *New York Times*, March 14, 1965, https://timesmachine.nytimes.com/timesmachine/1965/03/14/96699069.pdf.

14. Emanuel Perlmutter, "Drifter, 17, Named as Killer of Youth on Subway Train," *New York Times*, March 17, 1965, https://timesmachine.nytimes.com/timesmachine/1965/03/17/97187201.pdf.

15. "Subway Killer, 18, Gets Life Sentence," *New York Times*, February 11, 1966, https://timesmachine.nytimes.com/timesmachine/1966/02/11/79295394.pdf.

16. "12-Year-Old Girl Stabs Woman in a Senseless Subway Murder," *New York Times*, May 23, 1965, https://timesmachine.nytimes.com/timesmachine/1965/05/23/101548631.pdf.

17. "City Is Advised to Guard Subways," *New York Times*, June 2, 1964, https://www.nytimes.com/1964/06/02/archives/city-is-advised-to-guard-subway-2way-train-radios-and-more.html; Philip H. Dougherty, "Quill Seeks 2,000 to Guard Subway," *New York Times*, April 1, 1965, https://timesmachine.nytimes.com/timesmachine/1965/04/01/106987763.pdf.

18. Clayton Knowles, "Wagner Offers a Night Patrol on All Subways," *New York Times*, April 6, 1965, https://timesmachine.nytimes.com/timesmachine/1965/04/06/101536383.pdf.

19. "Brooklyn Residents Get Delay in Closing 2 Subway Entrances," *New York Times*, April 29, 1965, https://timesmachine.nytimes.com/timesmachine/1965/04/29/106991267.pdf.

20. "Mayor Describes 'Stunning' Decline in Subway Crime," *New York Times*, September 11, 1965, https://timesmachine.nytimes.com/timesmachine/1965/09/11/94976801.pdf.

21. Robert E. Dallos, "Nights Are Quiet on Subway Front," *New York Times*, July 16, 1966, https://timesmachine.nytimes.com/timesmachine/1966/07/16/82488754.pdf.

22. James Q. Wilson, "Do the Police Prevent Crime?," *New York Times*, October 6, 1974, https://www.nytimes.com/1974/10/06/archives/do-the-police-prevent-crime-scenes-from-the-330-to-1130-pm-patrol.html.

23. Subway Crime 29% Over 1968 Despite 15.4% Nighttime Drop," *New York Times*, October 30, 1969, https://timesmachine.nytimes.com/timesmachine/1969/10/30/81869720.pdf.

24. "1,800 More Police Sought for Subway," *New York Times*, September 24, 1970, https://www.nytimes.com/1970/09/24/archives/1800-more-police-sought-for-subway-to-cut-crime-rise.html.

25. "1,500 More Police Proposed to Patrol Daytime Subways," *New York Times*, February 13, 1968, https://www.nytimes.com/1968/02/13/archives/1500-more-police-proposed-to-patrol-daytime-subways.html.

26. Thomas F. Brady, "Gunman and Policeman Die in Times Sq. Area Battle," *New York Times*, March 1, 1970, https://www.nytimes.com/1970/03/01/archives/gunman-and-policeman-die-in-times-sq-area-battle-2-shot-to-death-in.html.

27. "Fire Bomb Thrown on Subway Train; 3 Persons Burned," *New York Times*, May 5, 1971, https://www.nytimes.com/1971/05/02/archives/fire-bomb-thrown-on-subway-train-3-persons-burned.html.

28. Robert D. McFadden, "IND Rider Slain in Holdup; Wife's Cries Go Unheeded," *New York Times*, July 29, 1974, https://www.nytimes.com/1974/07/29/archives/ind-rider-slain-in-holdup-wifes-cries-go-unheeded-ind-rider-is.html.

29. Deirdre Carmody, "Beame Demands Safer Subways," *New York Times*, July 30, 1974, https://www.nytimes.com/1974/07/30/archives/beame-demands-safer-subways-with-codd-and-transit-aides-following.html.

30. Barbara Campbell, "Transit Patrolmen Step Up Effort to Curb Young Gangs," *New York Times*, November 21, 1970, https://www.nytimes.com/1970/11/21/archives/transit-patrolmen-step-up-effort-to-curb-young-gangs-police-act-to.html.

31. "Unidentified Man Found Slain in Empty Car of an IRT Train," *New York Times*, March 28, 1978, https://www.nytimes.com/1978/03/28/archives/unidentified-man-found-slain-in-empty-car-of-an-irt-train.html.

32. Charles Kaiser, "Boy, 15, Who Killed 2 and Tried to Kill a Third Is Given 5 Years," *New York Times*, June 29, 1978, https://www.nytimes.com/1978/06/29/archives/boy-15-who-killed-2-and-tried-to-kill-a-third-is-given-5-years.html.

33. Richard J. Meislin, "Carey, in Shift, Backs Trial in Adult Court for Some Juveniles," *New York Times*, June 30, 1978, https://www.nytimes.com/1978/06/30/archives/new-jersey-pages-carey-in-shift-backs-trial-in-adult-court-for-some.html.

34. Irving Spiegel, "Transit Police Seek Full Force," *New York Times*, January 3, 1976, https://www.nytimes.com/1976/01/03/archives/transit-police-seek-full-force-ask-for-restoration-of-jobs-in-wake.html.

35. Robert Hanley, "Shotgun Bandits Rob 20 on Subway," *New York Times*, December 29, 1975, https://www.nytimes.com/1975/12/29/archives/shotgun-bandits-rob-20-on-subway-300-taken-from-those-aboard-2-men.html.

36. Peter Kihss, "Koch Says Police Reinforcements Curb Subway Crime," *New York Times*, March 23, 1979, https://www.nytimes.com/1979/03/23/archives/koch-says-police-reinforcements-curb-subway-crime-decreases-in-off.html.

37. Robert D. McFadden, "Rider Is Shot Dead on IND in Village after Argument as 35 Witness Crime," *New York Times*, June 5, 1976, https://www.nytimes.com/1976/06/05/archives/rider-is-shot-dead-on-ind-in-village-after-argument-as-35-witness.html.

38. Matthew L. Wald, "Woman Slain in IRT at Lincoln Center," *New York Times*, August 8, 1977, https://www.nytimes.com/1977/08/08/archives/woman-slain-in-irt-at-lincoln-center-woman-is-slain-in-irt-at.html; Joseph B. Treaster, "Parents' Long Wait Ends as Police Identify Palsy Victim Slain on IRT," *New York Times*, September 18, 1977, https://www.nytimes.com/1977/09/18/archives/parents-long-wait-ends-as-police-identify-palsy-victim-slain-on-irt.html.

39. "Crime on Subways Up 17% Last Year," *New York Times*, January 30, 1981, https://www.nytimes.com/1981/01/30/nyregion/the-city-crime-on-subways-up-17-last-year.html.

40. Morris Kaplan, "At 6, He Was a Purse-Snatcher . . . and at 18, a Convicted Killer," *New York Times*, November 17, 1971, https://www.nytimes.com/1971/11/17/archives/at-6-he-was-a-pursesnatcher-and-at-18-a-convicted-killer.html; Robert Hanley, "Woman Felled by Purse-Snatcher Is Crushed to Death by IRT Train," *New York Times*, October 9, 1976, https://www.nytimes.com/1976/10/09/archives/woman-felled-by-pursesnatcher-is-crushed-to-death-by-irt-train.html.

41. "Man Held in Death under an IND Train," *New York Times*, February 2, 1974, https://www.nytimes.com/1974/02/02/archives/man-held-in-death-under-an-ind-trainin.html; Wolfgang Saxon, "Stranger Pushes Woman to Death under a Train," *New York Times*, February 2, 1975, https://www.nytimes.com/1975/02/02/archives/stranger-pushes-woman-to-death-under-a-train.html.

42. Laurie Johnston, "Girl Pushed in Front of IND Train," *New York Times*, June 8, 1979, https://www.nytimes.com/1979/06/08/archives/girl-pushed-in-front-of-ind-train-hand-severed-girl-pushed-in-front.html.

43. "Ex-Mental Patient Arrested in Subway-Hurling Killing," *New York Times*, March 1, 1979, https://www.nytimes.com/1979/03/01/archives/exmental-patient-arrested-in-subwayhurling-killing.html.

44. "$1,000 Reward Offered in Slaying of IND Clerk," *New York Times*, June 1, 1973, https://www.nytimes.com/1973/06/01/archives/1000-reward-offered-in-slaying-of-ind-clerk.html.

45. For some stakeout coverage, see, for example, "Two Subway Holdup Suspects Are Shot by Hidden Policemen," *New York Times*, April 26, 1971, https://www.nytimes.com/1971/04/26/archives/two-subway-holdup-suspects-are-shot-by-hidden-policemen.html; "2 Slain in Toll-Booth Holdup in a Bronx Subway Station," *New York Times*, October 31, 1971, https://www.nytimes.com/1971/10/31/archives/2-slain-in-tollbooth-holdup-in-a-bronx-subway-station.html; "3 Suspects Seized in Subway Holdups," *New York Times*, December 29, 1971, https://www.nytimes.com/1971/12/29/archives/3-suspects-seized-in

-subway-holdups.html; "2 Shot by Transit Police after Attempted Robbery," *New York Times*, August 19, 1972, https://www.nytimes.com/1972/08/19/archives/2-shot-by-transit-police-after-attempted-robbery.html; "Transit Policeman Shoots and Wounds Holdup Suspect," *New York Times*, January 15, 1973, https://www.nytimes.com/1973/01/15/archives/transit-policeman-shoots-and-wounds-holdup-suspect.html; "Policeman Wounds Bandit as IND Holdup Is Foiled," *New York Times*, March 5, 1973, https://www.nytimes.com/1973/03/05/archives/policeman-wounds-bandit-as-ind-holdup-is-foiled.html; "2 Boys Shot in 2 IRT Incidents, One, 14, in an Alleged Holdup," *New York Times*, April 20, 1973, https://www.nytimes.com/1973/04/20/archives/2-boys-shot-in-2-irt-incidents-one-14-in-an-alleged-holdup.html; "Boy, 13, Shot as IND Stakeout Thwarts Holdup Attempt by 3," *New York Times*, August 19, 1973, https://www.nytimes.com/1973/08/19/archives/boy-13-shot-as-ind-stakeout-thwarts-holdup-attempt-by-3-air-pistol.html; "Suspect Killed in IND Station Holdup," *New York Times*, August 2, 1974, https://www.nytimes.com/1974/08/02/archives/suspect-killed-in-ind-station-holdup.html; "Police Slay Youth in Subway Holdup," *New York Times*, November 17, 1974, https://www.nytimes.com/1974/11/17/archives/police-slay-youth-in-subway-holdup.html.

46. Wilson, "Do the Police Prevent Crime?"

47. "BMT Clerk Gagged and Fatally Burned in a Change Booth," *New York Times*, February 15, 1977, https://www.nytimes.com/1977/02/15/archives/bmt-clerk-gagged-and-fatally-burned-in-a-change-booth.html.

48. Judith Cummings, "3 Seized in Flame Attack on 2 Clerks in IND Booth," *New York Times*, January 18, 1979, https://www.nytimes.com/1979/01/18/archives/3-seized-in-flame-attack-on-2-clerks-in-ind-booth-held-without-bail.html.

49. Judith Cummings, "One of Victims in IND Attack Dead of Burns," *New York Times*, January 20, 1979, https://www.nytimes.com/1979/01/20/archives/one-of-victims-in-ind-attack-dead-of-burns-how-the-attack-took.html.

50. "Off-Duty Patrolman Slain in IRT Station Gun Battle," *New York Times*, June 29, 1972, https://www.nytimes.com/1972/06/29/archives/offduty-patrolman-slain-in-irt-station-gun-battle.html.

51. "Ex-Policeman Fatally Stabbed in Times Sq Subway Station," *New York Times*, January 15, 1973, https://www.nytimes.com/1973/01/15/archives/expoliceman-fatally-stabbed-in-times-sq-subway-station.html.

52. "Transit Officer Buried as Neighbors Rage at Slaying," *New York Times*, February 29, 1980, https://timesmachine.nytimes.com/timesmachine/1980/02/29/112055575.pdf.

53. Carey Winfrey, "Newest Aid for Subway Riders: Quick-Reference Crime Primer," *New York Times*, July 13, 1980, https://timesmachine.nytimes.com/timesmachine/1980/07/13/112159232.pdf.

54. Ross Sandler and David Schoenbrod, "Reducing Crime in the New York City Subway System: Nine Recommendations," Project on Urban Transportation, National Resources Defense Council, December 1979, Straphangers Campaign papers, NYPL, box 1.

55. Robert D. McFadden, "Police Force Goes from 500 to 900 as 'War' on Subway Crime Begins," *New York Times*, March 20, 1979, https://www.nytimes.com/1979/03/20/archives/police-force-goes-from-500-to-900-as-war-on-subway-crime-begins.html.

56. Tom Goldstein, "Suit on a Fear of Subways Wins Woman Jobless Pay," *New York Times*, June 5, 1975, https://www.nytimes.com/1975/06/05/archives/suit-on-a-fear-of-subways-wins-woman-jobless-pay.html.

57. David Burnbaum, "Most Call Crime City's Worst Ill," *New York Times*, January 16, 1974, https://www.nytimes.com/1974/01/16/archives/most-call-crime-citys-worst-ill-2-of-3-term-crime-worst-city.html.

58. Eric Pace, "Passenger with a Licensed Gun Shoots 2 Assailants in Subway," *New York Times*, October 15, 1971, https://www.nytimes.com/1971/10/15/archives/passenger-with-a-licensed-gun-shoots-2-assailants-in-subway.html.

59. Robert Mcg. Thomas Jr., "Harasser Shot by IRT Passenger," *New York Times*, November 1, 1979, https://www.nytimes.com/1979/11/01/archives/harasser-shot-by-irt-passenger.html.

60. Walter H. Waggoner, "Man in Civilian Patrol Injured in an Attempt to Stop IRT Mugging," *New York Times*, February 20, 1979, https://www.nytimes.com/1979/02/20/archives/man-in-civilian-patrol-injured-in-an-attempt-to-stop-irt-mugging.html.

61. Glenn Fowler, "'Angels' Refuse Auxiliary Status," *New York Times*, October 17, 1980, https://timesmachine.nytimes.com/timesmachine/1980/10/17/112890487.pdf.

62. Curtis Sliwa, interview with the author, May 15, 2023.

63. Molly Ivins, "Police Will Train Subway 'Angels' under City Plan," *New York Times*, January 15, 1981, https://www.nytimes.com/1981/01/15/nyregion/police-will-train-subway-angels-under-city-plan.html.

64. "Subway Ridership Lowest Since '18," *New York Times*, April 6, 1975, https://timesmachine.nytimes.com/timesmachine/1975/04/06/83169540.pdf.

65. Frank J. Prial, "Bus and Subway Vandals Cost City 2.6 Million in '70," *New York Times*, March 30, 1971, https://www.nytimes.com/1971/03/30/archives/bus-and-subway-vandals-cost-city-26million-in-70.html.

66. Editorial board, "How to Remember Michael Stewart," *New York Times*, November 26, 1985, https://www.nytimes.com/1985/11/26/opinion/how-to-remember-michael-stewart.html.

67. Sandler and Schoenbrod, "Reducing Crime in the New York City Subway System."

68. Shawn G. Kennedy, "First Violators to Clean Subway Cars Get to Work," *New York Times*, May 16, 1982, https://www.nytimes.com/1982/05/16/nyregion/first-violators-to-clean-subway-cars-get-to-work.html.

69. "Suzy and Red vs. the Graffiti Painters," *New York Times*, September 16, 1981, https://www.nytimes.com/1981/09/16/opinion/suzy-and-red-vs-the-graffiti-painters.html.

70. Edward C. Burks, "Subways Lose Riders but Are on Time More," *New York Times*, October 8, 1973, https://www.nytimes.com/1973/10/08/archives/subways-lose-riders-butare-on-timemore-1000-trains-eliminated.html.

71. Ross Sandler and Steven M. Jurow, "More Sub Than Way," *New York Times*, December 11, 1982, https://www.nytimes.com/1982/12/11/opinion/more-sub-than-way.html.

72. Editorial board, "Danger, Above Ground and Below," *New York Times*, April 27, 1979, https://www.nytimes.com/1979/04/27/archives/the-editorial-notebook-danger-above-ground-and-below.html.

73. Judith Cummings, "Koch Subway-Crime Program Passes Its First Test," *New York Times*, March 21, 1979, https://www.nytimes.com/1979/03/21/archives/koch-subwaycrime-program-passes-its-first-test-koch-pleased-with.html.

74. Josh Barnabel, "6 Slain in City in First 8 Hours of the New Year," *New York Times*, January 2, 1980, https://timesmachine.nytimes.com/timesmachine/1980/01/02/113930042.pdf.

75. "New York Will Spend More Money to Fight Rise in Subway Crime," *New York Times*, October 22, 1980, https://timesmachine.nytimes.com/timesmachine/1980/10/22/111301978.pdf; Robert D. McFadden, "Transit Police Act on Koch's Directive," *New York Times*, March 18, 1979, https://www.nytimes.com/1979/03/18/archives/transit-police-act-on-kochs-directive-personnel-and-schedules.html.

76. Judith Cummings, "Dog Patrols Put Teeth into Subways Crime Fight," *New York Times*, December 16, 1980, https://timesmachine.nytimes.com/timesmachine/1980/12/16/111835420.pdf.

77. Joseph B. Treaster, "Felonies in Subway Fall for First Time in 4 Years," *New York Times*, February 3, 1984, https://www.nytimes.com/1984/02/03/nyregion/felonies-in-subway-fall-for-first-time-in-4-years.html.

78. David A. Andelman, "Police May Shut Some Entrances to City Subways," *New York Times*, October 6, 1980, https://timesmachine.nytimes.com/timesmachine/1980/10/06/111297161.pdf.

79. Ari L. Goldman, "Felonies in Subways Leveled Off in 1982, Transit Police Reported," *New York Times*, January 4, 1983, https://www.nytimes.com/1983/01/04/nyregion/felonies-in-subways-leveled-off-in-1982-transit-police-reported.html.

80. Richard Levine, "The Numbers Say Subways Are Safer Than They Seem," *New York Times*, June 28, 1987, https://www.nytimes.com/1987/06/28/weekinreview/the-numbers-say-subways-are-safer-than-they-seem.html.

81. Deirdre Carmody, "High School Senior Dies after Clubbing by Gang," *New York Times*, March 27, 1982, https://www.nytimes.com/1982/03/27/nyregion/high-school-senior-dies-after-clubbing-by-gang.html.

82. Don Terry, "Subway Token Clerk Dies after Booth Was Set Afire," *New York Times*, June 5, 1988, https://www.nytimes.com/1988/06/05/nyregion/subway-token-clerk-dies-after-booth-was-set-afire.html.

83. Judith Cummings, "Many Riders Are Giving Up on Subways," *New York Times*, November 13, 1980, https://timesmachine.nytimes.com/timesmachine/1980/11/13/111308380.pdf.

84. Selwyn Robb, "4 Youths Shot by Goetz Faced Criminal Counts," *New York Times*, January 10, 1985, https://www.nytimes.com/1985/01/10/nyregion/4-youths-shot-by-goetz-faced-criminal-counts.html.

85. Marcia Chambers, "Goetz Rejects Offers on Bail from a Stranger and Family," *New York Times*, January 5, 1985, https://www.nytimes.com/1985/01/05/nyregion/goetz-rejects-offers-on-bail-from-a-stranger-and-family.html.

86. Editorial board, "Why Surrender on the Subway?," *New York Times*, January 4, 1985, https://www.nytimes.com/1985/01/04/opinion/why-surrender-subway-bernhard-goetz-hero-for-allegedly-shooting-four-teen-agers.html.

87. David N. Dinkins, "Fears That Are Tearing New York Apart," *New York Times*, June 20, 1987, https://www.nytimes.com/1987/06/20/opinion/fears-that-are-tearing-new-york-apart.html.

88. Peter Kerr, "Token Clerk Shoots a Robbery Suspect," *New York Times*, January 7, 1986, https://www.nytimes.com/1986/01/07/nyregion/token-clerk-shoots-a-robbery-suspect-gun-is-called-illegal.html.

89. Ronald Sullivan, "Self-Defense Claim in Subway Death," *New York Times*, January 24, 1990, https://www.nytimes.com/1990/01/24/nyregion/self-defense-claim-in-subway-death.html.

90. James C. McKinley Jr., "Youth Held in Attack on Subway Killer," *New York Times*,

April 15, 1990, https://www.nytimes.com/1990/04/15/nyregion/youth-held-in-attack-on-subway-killer.html.

91. James C. McKinley Jr., "Man Is Killed on a Subway Train While Trying to Thwart a Robbery," *New York Times*, May 19, 1990, https://www.nytimes.com/1990/05/19/nyregion/man-is-killed-on-a-subway-train-while-trying-to-thwart-a-robbery.html.

92. Sam Roberts, "Robert Kiley, Mass Transit Chief in Boston, London and New York, Dies at 80," *New York Times*, August 10, 2016, https://www.nytimes.com/2016/08/10/nyregion/robert-kiley-mass-transit-dead.html.

93. James Lemoyne, "Man in the News: New President of the City Transit Authority, David Lawrence Gunn," *New York Times*, January 12, 1984, https://www.nytimes.com/1984/01/12/nyregion/man-in-the-news-new-president-of-the-city-transit-authority-david-lawrence-gunn.html.

94. David Gunn, interview with the author, May 2016.

95. Edward A. Gargan, "2 Troubled Years on Subways Seen by MTA Nominee," *New York Times*, October 10, 1983, https://www.nytimes.com/1983/10/10/nyregion/2-troubled-years-on-subways-seen-by-mta-nominee.html.

96. Richard Levine, "Transit Authority Proclaims a Success: 50% of Cars Clean," *New York Times*, October 6, 1986, https://www.nytimes.com/1986/10/06/nyregion/transit-authority-proclaims-a-success-50-of-cars-clean.html.

97. James Brooke, "Subways Are Cleaner, Transit Authority Says," *New York Times*, June 14, 1986, https://www.nytimes.com/1986/06/14/nyregion/subways-are-cleaner-transit-authority-says.html.

98. George L. Kelling and James Q. Wilson, "Broken Windows: The Police and Neighborhood Safety," *Atlantic*, March 1982, https://www.theatlantic.com/magazine/archive/1982/03/broken-windows/304465/.

99. Calvin Sims, "With Subway Crime Up, Transit Police Get a New Chief," *New York Times*, April 12, 1990, https://www.nytimes.com/1990/04/12/nyregion/with-subway-crime-up-transit-police-get-a-new-chief.html.

100. Calvin Sims, "No End to Rising Subway Crime; It May Get Worse, Chief Asserts," *New York Times*, September 6, 1990, https://www.nytimes.com/1990/09/06/nyregion/no-end-to-rising-subway-crime-it-may-get-worse-chief-asserts.html.

101. The People of the State of New York against Johnny Hincapie, Indictment No. 10641/90, trial transcript, 184-7, 286-7.

102. William Glaberson, "Chilled by Violence, New Yorkers Are Questioning Life in Their City," *New York Times*, September 16, 1990, https://www.nytimes.com/1990/09/16/nyregion/chilled-by-violence-new-yorkers-are-questioning-life-in-their-city.html.

103. James C. McKinley Jr., "Stray Bullet Claims Another New York Child," *New York Times*, July 27, 1990, https://www.nytimes.com/1990/07/27/nyregion/stray-bullet-claims-another-new-york-child.html.

104. Celestine Bohlen, "Dinkins Offers Plans to Reduce Crime," *New York Times*, July 16, 1989, https://www.nytimes.com/1989/07/16/nyregion/dinkins-offers-plans-to-reduce-crime.html.

105. Todd S. Purdham, "Dinkins Proposes Increases in Taxes in His First Budget," *New York Times*, May 25, 1990, https://www.nytimes.com/1990/05/25/nyregion/dinkins-proposes-increases-in-taxes-in-his-first-budget.html.

106. Don Terry, "Council Gains Budget Pact with Dinkins," *New York Times*, June 30, 1990, https://www.nytimes.com/1990/06/30/nyregion/council-gains-budget-pact-with-dinkins.html.

107. Normal Steisel, interview with the author, August 26, 2021.

108. "Mr. Dinkins Clears the Air," *New York Times*, August 26, 1990, https://www.nytimes.com/1990/08/26/opinion/topics-of-the-times-mr-dinkins-clears-the-air.html.

109. Timothy Egan, "Family in Fatal Mugging Loved New York," *New York Times*, September 6, 1990, https://www.nytimes.com/1990/09/06/nyregion/family-in-fatal-mugging-loved-new-york.html.

110. Bill Bratton, interview with the author, March 23, 2022.

111. Watkins family, "From the Watkins Family," *New York Times*, September 12, 1990, https://www.nytimes.com/1990/09/12/opinion/from-the-watkins-family.html.

112. Karen de Witt, "Watkins Family Endorses a Plan to Hire More Police," *New York Times*, September 18, 1990, https://www.nytimes.com/1990/09/18/nyregion/watkins-family-endorses-a-plan-to-hire-more-police.html.

113. "Dinkins Says He'll Show Anger at Violent Crimes," *New York Times*, September 6, 1990, https://www.nytimes.com/1990/09/06/nyregion/dinkins-says-he-ll-show-anger-at-violent-crimes.html.

114. Straphangers, box 31.

115. Editorial board, "Deferred Maintenance—And Murder," *New York Times*, September 6, 1990, https://www.nytimes.com/1990/09/06/opinion/deferred-maintenance-and-murder.html.

116. Editorial board, "A Subway Tragedy's Aftermath: Mr. Vallone Stands Up to Crime," *New York Times*, September 8, 1990, https://www.nytimes.com/1990/09/08/opinion/a-subway-tragedy-s-aftermath-mr-vallone-stands-up-to-crime.html.

117. David N. Dinkins, "New York City Will Prevail," *New York Times*, September 13, 1990, https://www.nytimes.com/1990/09/13/opinion/new-york-city-will-prevail.html.

118. Elizabeth Kolbert, "Cuomo, Upstaging Dinkins, Says City Police Will Add 'Thousands,'" *New York Times*, September 12, 1990, https://www.nytimes.com/1990/09/12/nyregion/cuomo-upstaging-dinkins-says-city-police-will-add-thousands.html.

119. Ralph Blumenthal, "Dinkins Proposes Record Expansion of Police Forces," *New York Times*, October 3, 1990, https://www.nytimes.com/1990/10/03/nyregion/dinkins-on-crime-dinkins-proposes-record-expansion-of-police-forces.html.

120. Kevin Sack, "Dinkins Crime Plan Wins the Backing of Top Lawmakers," *New York Times*, February 8, 1991, https://www.nytimes.com/1991/02/08/nyregion/dinkins-crime-plan-wins-the-backing-of-top-lawmakers.html.

121. Bratton interview.

122. Calvin Sims, "Transit Police to Eject Subway Panhandlers," *New York Times*, May 31, 1990, https://www.nytimes.com/1990/05/31/nyregion/transit-police-to-eject-subway-panhandlers.html.

123. Calvin Sims, "The Emerging Subway-Fare Thief: Frustrated, Irritated or in a Hurry," *New York Times*, June 25, 1990, https://www.nytimes.com/1990/06/25/nyregion/the-emerging-subway-fare-thief-frustrated-irritated-or-in-a-hurry.html.

124. Calvin Sims, "Fare Beaters in Subway Pay in the End, in Sweat," *New York Times*, February 18, 1991, https://www.nytimes.com/1991/02/18/nyregion/fare-beaters-in-subway-pay-in-the-end-in-sweat.html.

125. Alan Finder, "Chief of Transit Officers Resigns after 21 Months," *New York Times*, January 17, 1992, https://www.nytimes.com/1992/01/17/nyregion/chief-of-transit-officers-resigns-after-21-months.html.

126. George James, "Subway Crime Drops Sharply at Year's End," *New York Times*,

February 15, 1991, https://www.nytimes.com/1991/02/15/nyregion/subway-crime-drops-sharply-at-year-s-end.html.

127. "Subway Crime Is Down in First Drop in 2 Years," *New York Times*, December 15, 1990, https://www.nytimes.com/1990/12/15/nyregion/subway-crime-is-down-in-first-drop-in-2-years.html.

128. Alan Finder, "Fare Beating Is Up and So Is Ire of Paying Riders," *New York Times*, January 13, 1992, https://www.nytimes.com/1992/01/13/nyregion/fare-beating-is-up-and-so-is-ire-of-paying-riders.html.

129. Finder, "Chief of Transit Officers Resigns."

130. Jacques Steinberg, "Subway Crime Fell in 1991, Officials Say," *New York Times*, February 21, 1992, https://www.nytimes.com/1992/02/21/nyregion/subway-crime-fell-in-1991-officials-say.html.

131. Alan Finder, "Subway Felonies Decline in First 3 Months of Year," *New York Times*, May 15, 1992, https://www.nytimes.com/1992/05/15/nyregion/subway-felonies-decline-in-first-3-months-of-year.html.

132. Alan Finder, "Open Season on Fare Beaters," *New York Times*, May 17, 1992, https://www.nytimes.com/1992/05/17/nyregion/open-season-on-fare-beaters.html.

133. Craig Wolff, "Subway Crime Declining, New Transit Figures Show," *New York Times*, November 12, 1993, https://www.nytimes.com/1993/11/12/nyregion/subway-crime-declining-new-transit-figures-show.html.

134. "Crime in Subway Declines," *New York Times*, January 20, 1995, https://www.nytimes.com/1995/01/20/nyregion/crime-in-subway-declines.html.

135. Andy Newman, "Fare Beating in the Subways Falls Off under a Tougher Arrest Policy," *New York Times*, November 18, 1997, https://www.nytimes.com/1997/11/18/nyregion/fare-beating-in-the-subways-falls-off-under-a-tougher-arrest-policy.html.

136. David Kocieniewski, "Subway Crime Bringing Calls to Add Police," *New York Times*, November 22, 1997, https://www.nytimes.com/1997/11/22/nyregion/subway-crime-bringing-calls-to-add-police.html.

137. Metropolitan Transportation Authority, "Transit and Bus Committee Meeting," January 2020, https://new.mta.info/document/13821.

138. Homer Bigart, "Wagner Bolsters Police on Subway to Deter Attacks," *New York Times*, June 3, 1964, https://timesmachine.nytimes.com/timesmachine/1964/06/03/106975448.pdf.

139. William Bratton, "Bridging the Cop-Community Divide: NYPD Commissioner Bill Bratton's Plans to Build Bridges after a Season of Extreme Tension," *New York Daily News*, May 10, 2015, https://www.nydailynews.com/opinion/william-bratton-bridging-cop-community-divide-article-1.2215958.

140. Alan Finder, "Subway Crime Declines in First Drop Since 1987," *New York Times*, November 15, 1991, https://www.nytimes.com/1991/11/15/nyregion/subway-crime-declines-in-first-drop-since-1987.html.

141. Edwin McDowell, "New York Tourism Industry Says '91 Was 'a Pretty Miserable Year,'" *New York Times*, February 9, 1992, https://www.nytimes.com/1992/02/09/nyregion/new-york-tourism-industry-says-91-was-a-pretty-miserable-year.html.

142. New York Metropolitan Transportation Council, "Hub Bound Travel Data 2019," https://www.nymtc.org/Portals/0/Pdf/Hub%20Bound/2019%20Hub%20Bound/DM_TDS_Hub_Bound_Travel_2019.pdf.

11. Splitting Lanes: From Bike Nuts to Bike Share

1. Alan Finder, "New York to Ban Bicycles on 3 Major Avenues," *New York Times*, July 23, 1987, https://www.nytimes.com/1987/07/23/nyregion/new-york-to-ban-bicycles-on-3-major-avenues.html.

2. David Gurin, interview with the author, June 26, 2018.

3. "Bicycle Habitat—The History," Bicycle Habitat, accessed April 14, 2022, https://www.bicyclehabitat.com/articles/bicycle-habitat-the-history-pg540.htm.

4. "Street Widening Is Urged for City," *New York Times*, August 26, 1963, https://timesmachine.nytimes.com/timesmachine/1963/08/26/89956326.pdf.

5. Lloyd E. Millegan, "Annual Bike Race Closes Roadways in the Morning," *New York Times*, May 2, 1966, https://timesmachine.nytimes.com/timesmachine/1966/05/02/83531158.pdf.

6. Richard J. H. Johnston, "Barnes against Closing Park Drives," *New York Times*, April 6, 1966, https://timesmachine.nytimes.com/timesmachine/1966/04/06/79991973.pdf.

7. Barry Benepe, interview with the author, October 24, 2018.

8. Paul L. Montgomery, "Autos Have a Rough Day in Central Park," *New York Times*, May 2, 1966, https://timesmachine.nytimes.com/timesmachine/1966/05/02/83531156.pdf.

9. Robert E. Dallos, "Mayor Pedals into Central Park and Supports Proposed Car Ban," *New York Times*, June 6, 1966, https://timesmachine.nytimes.com/timesmachine/1966/06/06/80007721.pdf.

10. Jay Kriegel, interview with the author, June 18, 2019.

11. "Bike Riding Days Added to 2 Parks," *New York Times*, September 3, 1966, https://timesmachine.nytimes.com/timesmachine/1966/09/03/82508651.pdf.

12. "New Car Ban Set for Central Park," *New York Times*, April 17, 1967, https://timesmachine.nytimes.com/timesmachine/1967/04/17/90335283.pdf; Val Adams, "A Park Bike Night Set for Tuesday," *New York Times*, May 19, 1967, https://timesmachine.nytimes.com/timesmachine/1967/05/19/90342892.pdf; "Central Park Bans on Cars to Be Extended to Winter," *New York Times*, August 3, 1967, https://www.nytimes.com/1967/08/03/archives/central-park-bans-on-cars-to-be-extended-to-winter.html.

13. Jay Kriegel, *John V. Lindsay: 50th Anniversary Commemoration* (McLean, Va.: International Publishers, 2015), 3.

14. "Autumn Brings Bicycle Traffic Jams on Central Park Paths," *New York Times*, October 12, 1968, https://timesmachine.nytimes.com/timesmachine/1968/10/12/76935616.pdf.

15. Ted Mastroianni, interview with the author, September 23, 2021.

16. Gerald Scorse, "Thanks, Mayor Lindsay," letter, *New York Times*, January 26, 2000, https://www.nytimes.com/2000/01/26/opinion/l-thanks-mayor-lindsay-517020.html.

17. Barry Fishman, interview with the author, October 6, 2021.

18. "Pedaling to Be Pushed by Mayor Wednesday," *New York Times*, September 14, 1970, https://www.nytimes.com/1970/09/14/archives/pedaling-to-be-pushed-by-mayor-wednesday.html.

19. Editorial board, "Bike for a Better City," *New York Times*, September 15, 1970, https://www.nytimes.com/1970/09/15/archives/bike-for-a-better-city.html.

20. "Brooklyn Bridge Opens Special Bicycle Ramps," *New York Times*, April 1, 1971, https://www.nytimes.com/1971/04/01/archives/brooklyn-bridge-opens-special-bicycle-ramps.html.

21. "Bicyclists Denied a Push by Mayor," *New York Times*, September 26, 1971, https://www.nytimes.com/1971/09/26/archives/bicyclists-denied-a-push-by-mayor-lindsay-cools-on-support-for.html.

22. "Bicyclists Denied a Push by Mayor."

23. David Gurin, "Provo: Blasting Back at the Brave New World, Report from the Netherlands," *Village Voice*, August 25, 1966.

24. David Gurin, "The Everyday Never Seemed So Obscene," *Village Voice*, April 30, 1970, https://news.google.com/newspapers?nid=KEtq3P1Vf80C&dat=19700430&printsec=frontpage&hl=en.

25. Paul L. Montgomery, "400 Bicyclists Pedal Demands," *New York Times*, April 8, 1973, https://www.nytimes.com/1973/04/08/archives/400-bicyclists-wheel-down-fifth-avenue-in-drive-for-bike-lanes.html.

26. Martin Tolchin, "Fuel Crisis Seen as Boon to Cities," *New York Times*, November 18, 1973, https://www.nytimes.com/1973/11/18/archives/fuel-crisis-seen-as-boon-to-cities-transit-called-a-key-officials.html.

27. Charles Komanoff, "The Bicycle Uprising: Remembering the Midtown Bike Ban 25 Years Later," *Streetsblog*, August-September 2012, http://www.komanoff.net/bicycle/Bicycle_Uprising.pdf.

28. "Metropolitan Briefs," *New York Times*, July 14, 1978, https://www.nytimes.com/1978/07/14/archives/metropolitan-briefs-bike-lane-test-starts-marshals-win-reprieve.html.

29. City of New York, "New York City's Bicycle Program," March 1983, via Schwartz papers.

30. David A. Andelman, "Koch Unveils Traffic Control Plan for Use If Transit Employees Strike," *New York Times*, March 25, 1980, https://timesmachine.nytimes.com/timesmachine/1980/03/25/112146477.pdf.

31. "The 1980 Transit Strike, Transportation Impacts and Evaluation," New York City Department of Transportation, April 1980, Sam Schwartz personal archive.

32. "Add Your Strength to TA's New People Power," *City Cyclist*, Transportation Alternatives, August/September 1986, http://www.komanoff.net/citycyclist/Aug-Sep-1986.pdf.

33. Clyde Haberman, "Koch Opens Two Bike Lanes Already Used to Cyclists," *New York Times*, October 16, 1980, https://timesmachine.nytimes.com/timesmachine/1980/10/16/111807092.pdf.

34. Glenn Flower, "A Hit-Run Bike Case Spurs City Safe-Cycling Campaign," *New York Times*, July 14, 1980, https://timesmachine.nytimes.com/timesmachine/1980/07/14/112162139.pdf.

35. Glenn Fowler, "Third Person Struck by Bicycle Dies," *New York Times*, July 17, 1980, https://timesmachine.nytimes.com/timesmachine/1980/07/17/111251884.pdf.

36. Flower, "A Hit-Run Bike Case."

37. "Bike Lanes' Removal Ordered by Mayor," *New York Times*, November 14, 1980, https://timesmachine.nytimes.com/timesmachine/1980/11/14/111816805.pdf.

38. Clyde Haberman, "Koch Says He's Prepared to Get Rid of Bicycle Lanes," *New York Times*, June 30, 1981, https://www.nytimes.com/1981/06/30/nyregion/koch-says-he-s-prepared-to-get-rid-of-bicycle-lanes.html.

39. Sam Schwartz, "Rolling Thunder," *New York Times*, November 5, 2006, https://www.nytimes.com/2006/11/05/opinion/05CI-Schwartz.html.

40. Josh Barbanel, "New Bike Lanes: Perils of Progress; Accidents Common Near Music Hall New Lanes for Bicyclists in City: Safety and the Perils of Progress," *New York Times*, September 24, 1980, https://www.nytimes.com/1980/09/24/archives/new-bike-lanes-perils-of-progress-accidents-common-near-music-hall.html.

41. Peter Samton, "Bikes without Lanes," *New York* Times, November 27, 1980, https://timesmachine.nytimes.com/timesmachine/1980/11/27/114018315.pdf.

42. William R. Greer, "Bicycle Riders Vie for Space on Streets," *New York Times*, August 15, 1983, https://www.nytimes.com/1983/08/15/nyregion/bicycle-riders-vie-for-space-on-streets.html.

43. New York City Department of Transportation, "The New York City Pedestrian Safety Study & Action Plan: Technical Supplement," August 2010, https://www1.nyc.gov/html/dot/downloads/pdf/nyc_ped_safety_study_action_plan_technical_supplement.pdf.

44. Joe Hendry, "In Memory of Steve 'The Greek' Athineos," December 15, 2019, https://www.youtube.com/watch?v=XgL-2s6ZCD8&ab_channel=JoeHendry.

45. Boone, interview.

46. Editorial board, "Lax Pursuit of Reckless Bikers," *New York Times*, June 50, 1986, https://www.nytimes.com/1986/06/05/opinion/the-worm-and-the-apple-lax-pursuit-of-reckless-bikers.html.

47. Seth L. Amgott, "For the Bicycle Messenger, No Roadbed of Roses," letter, *New York Times*, November 10, 1985, https://www.nytimes.com/1985/11/10/opinion/l-for-the-bicycle-messenger-no-roadbed-of-roses-143166.html.

48. Robert McGlynn, "Possible Solutions," *City Cyclist*, Transportation Alternatives, October/November 1986, http://www.komanoff.net/citycyclist/Oct-Nov-1986.pdf.

49. Elizabeth Neuffer, "City's Cyclists Leave Outrage in Their Paths," *New York Times*, May 16, 1987, https://www.nytimes.com/1987/05/16/nyregion/city-s-cyclists-leave-outrage-in-their-paths.html.

50. Jane Gross, "Despite Crackdown by City, Cyclists Stay In High Gear," *New York Times*, October 26, 1985, https://www.nytimes.com/1985/10/26/nyregion/despite-crackdown-by-city-bicyclists-stay-in-high-gear.html.

51. Editorial board, "Easy, Riders: This Bike Rule Helps Everyone," *Crains New York Business*, August 3, 1987.

52. Charles McCorkell, correspondence with the author, November 14, 2021.

53. "Bicycle Blueprint: A Plan to Bring Bicycling into the Mainstream in New York City," Transportation Alternatives, April 1993, courtesy Mary Frances Dunham personal archive.

54. "Koch Delays Ban as Support Crumbles," *City Cyclist*, Transportation Alternatives, March/April 1988, http://www.komanoff.net/citycyclist/Mar-Apr-1988.pdf.

55. Todd S. Purdham, "Koch Drops Plan to Ban Bikes," *New York Times*, April 13, 1988, https://www.nytimes.com/1988/04/13/nyregion/koch-drops-plan-to-ban-bikes.html.

56. Charles Komanoff, "Report from the President," *City Cyclist*, Transportation Alternatives, January/February 1989, http://www.komanoff.net/citycyclist/Jan-Feb-1989.pdf.

57. Jon Orcutt, interview with the author, October 4, 2021.

58. Jeff Parker, "Three Who Died," *City Cyclist*, Transportation Alternatives, May/June 1989, http://www.komanoff.net/citycyclist/May-Jun-1989.pdf.

59. "Wall Street Bank Paves the Way," *City Cyclist*, Transportation Alternatives, March/April 1991, http://www.komanoff.net/citycyclist/Mar-Apr-1991.pdf.

60. Jon Orcutt and Charles Komanoff, "1991: Wheels of Change," *City Cyclist*, Transportation Alternatives, January/February 1991, http://www.komanoff.net/citycyclist/Jan-Feb-1991.pdf.

61. Tom Fox, "David Dinkins Was a Founding Father of Hudson River Park," *Village Sun*, November 30, 2020, https://thevillagesun.com/david-dinkins-was-a-founding-father-of-hudson-river-park.

62. David W. Dunlap, "Officials Approve Plans to Rebuild West Side Artery," *New York Times*, August 2, 1994, https://www.nytimes.com/1994/08/02/nyregion/officials-approve-plans-to-rebuild-west-side-artery.html.

63. Rudolph W. Giuliani, interview with the author, November 5, 2021.

64. Vera Haller, "Gray-Flannel Suit with Helmet: Bike Path Is a Hit with Commuters," *New York Times*, July 8, 2001, https://www.nytimes.com/2001/07/08/nyregion/neighborhood-report-west-side-gray-flannel-suit-with-helmet-bike-path-hit-with.html.

65. Kit R. Roane, "Fatal Bicycle Accidents Reach 10-Year High," *New York Times*, February 27, 1998, https://www.nytimes.com/1998/02/27/nyregion/fatal-bicycle-accidents-reach-10-year-high.html.

66. Andy Newman, "Cyclist Fatalities Increased 75% in 1999, Puzzling Police," *New York Times*, January 8, 2000, https://www.nytimes.com/2000/01/08/nyregion/cyclist-fatalities-increased-75-in-1999-puzzling-police.html.

67. Charles Komanoff and Michael J. Smith, "The Only Good Cyclist: NYC Bicycle Fatalities—Who's Responsible," *Right of Way*, May 2000.

68. Lydia Polgreen, "The Bike Helmet as Riot Gear?," *New York Times*, November 4, 2004, https://www.nytimes.com/2004/11/04/nyregion/the-bike-helmet-as-riot-gear.html.

69. "Remarks by Mayor Michael R. Bloomberg as Prepared for Delivery at the 2004 Republican National Convention on Monday, Aug. 30, 2004," Fox News, August 20, 2004, https://www.foxnews.com/story/transcript-bloombergs-speech.

70. Jennifer 8. Lee and Matthew Sweeney, "Monthly Mass Bicycle Ride Leads to 49 Arrests in Manhattan," *New York Times*, August 27, 2005, https://www.nytimes.com/2005/08/27/nyregion/monthly-mass-bicycle-ride-leads-to-49-arrests-in-manhattan.html.

71. Diane Cardwell, "Mayor Bloomberg Doubts Paris-Style Bike Program Will Work in New York," *New York Times*, September 30, 2007, https://www.nytimes.com/2007/09/30/world/americas/30iht-paris01.7685347.html.

72. New York City Office of the Mayor, "Mayor Bloomberg and Police Commissioner Kelly Announce 2013 Saw the Fewest Murders and Fewest Shootings in Recorded City History at NYPD Graduation Ceremony," December 27, 2013, https://www1.nyc.gov/office-of-the-mayor/news/436-13/mayor-bloomberg-police-commissioner-kelly-2013-saw-fewest-murders-fewest/#/0.

73. New York City Department of Health, "Summary of Vital Statistics 2017," July 2019, https://www1.nyc.gov/assets/doh/downloads/pdf/vs/2017sum.pdf.

74. Thomas J. Lueck, "Bloomberg Draws a Blueprint for a Greener City," *New York Times*, April 23, 2007, https://www.nytimes.com/2007/04/23/nyregion/23mayor.html.

75. New York City Office of the Mayor, "PlaNYC: A Greener Greater New York," April 2007, http://www.nyc.gov/html/planyc/downloads/pdf/publications/full_report_2007.pdf.

76. New York City Department of Transportation et. al., "Bicyclist Fatalities and Serious Injuries in New York City 1996–2005," https://www.nyc.gov/html/dot/downloads/pdf/bicyclefatalities.pdf.

77. Michael Flegenheimer, "Turning the City's Wheels in a New Direction," *New York Times*, December 30, 2013, https://www.nytimes.com/2013/12/30/nyregion/turning-the-citys-wheels-in-a-new-direction.html.

78. Dan Doctoroff, interview with the author, March 16, 2022.

79. Sewell Chan, "New Limits on Central Park Car Traffic," *New York Times*, July 31, 2007, https://cityroom.blogs.nytimes.com/2007/07/31/new-restrictions-on-central-park-car-traffic/.

80. Janette Sadik-Khan, "Bike Lanes in New York," letter, *New York Times*, January 23, 2008, https://www.nytimes.com/2008/01/23/opinion/lweb23bikes.html.

81. "Answers from the Transportation Commissioner," Part 2, *New York Times*, June 26, 2007, https://cityroom.blogs.nytimes.com/2007/06/26/answers-from-the-transportation-commissioner-part-2/.

82. New York City Department of Transportation, "Protected Bicycle Lanes in NYC," September 2014, https://www1.nyc.gov/html/dot/downloads/pdf/2014-11-bicycle-path-data-analysis.pdf.

83. J. David Goodman, "For Bike Advocates, Delayed Gratification," *New York Times*, August 12, 2012, https://www.nytimes.com/2012/08/12/nyregion/for-new-york-bike-advocates-delayed-gratification.html.

84. Paul Steely White, interview with the author, October 7, 2021.

85. Michael M. Grynbaum, "City Will Crack Down on Scofflaw Cyclists," *New York Times*, October 22, 2010, https://www.nytimes.com/2010/10/22/nyregion/22bike.html.

86. Sewell Chan, "Will Car-Free 'Summer Streets' Work?," *New York Times*, August 8, 2008, https://cityroom.blogs.nytimes.com/2008/08/08/will-summer-streets-work-2/.

87. Javier C. Hernández, "No Traffic on a Saturday? Well, No Cars, Anyway," *New York Times*, August 10, 2008, https://www.nytimes.com/2008/08/10/nyregion/10closed.html.

88. Aaron Naparstek, "A Ride Down NYC's 'Street of the Future,'" *Streetsblog*, October 4, 2007, https://nyc.streetsblog.org/2007/10/04/streetfilms-nycs-first-legit-on-street-cycle-track/.

89. J. David Goodman, "Expansion of Bike Lanes in City Brings Backlash," *New York Times*, November 23, 2010, https://www.nytimes.com/2010/11/23/nyregion/23bicycle.html.

90. Steve Cuozzo, "Idiotic DOT Takes a Walk on the Wild Side," *New York Post*, November 13, 2008, https://nypost.com/2008/11/13/idiotic-dot-takes-a-walk-on-the-wild-side/.

91. Steve Cuozzo, "Killing Times Square," *New York Post*, August 24, 2009, https://nypost.com/2009/08/24/killing-times-square/.

92. Steve Cuozzo, "Bike Lanes, Bike Lies," *New York Post*, April 18, 2011, https://nypost.com/2011/04/18/bike-lanes-bike-lies/.

93. Michael M. Grynbaum, "Shops Want Back Parking Lost to Columbus Ave. Bike Lane," *New York Times*, February 7, 2011, https://cityroom.blogs.nytimes.com/2011/02/07/shops-want-back-parking-lost-to-columbus-ave-bike-lane/.

94. Michael M. Grynbaum, "For City's Transportation Chief, Kudos and Criticism," *New York Times*, March 6, 2011, https://www.nytimes.com/2011/03/06/nyregion/06sadik-khan.html.

95. New York City Department of Transportation, "Prospect Park West Bicycle Path and Traffic Calming," Presentation to Community Board 6, April 16, 2009, https://www1.nyc.gov/html/dot/downloads/pdf/prospectpark_west.pdf.

96. J. David Goodman, "Dueling Protests over a Brooklyn Bike Lane," *New York Times*, October 21, 2010, https://cityroom.blogs.nytimes.com/2010/10/21/dueling-protests-over-a-brooklyn-bike-lane/.

97. Andrea Bernstein, "Power, Politics, and the Prospect Park Bike Lane," WNYC, October 20, 2011, https://www.wnyc.org/story/283578-power-politics-and-the-prospect-park-bike-lane/.

98. Letters, "Unruly Streets: Cyclists and the City," *New York Times*, December 23, 2010, https://www.nytimes.com/2010/12/23/opinion/l23bike.html.

99. Michael M. Grynbaum, "Lawsuit Seeks to Erase Bike Lane in New York City," *New York Times*, March 8, 2011, https://www.nytimes.com/2011/03/08/nyregion/08bike.html.

100. Michael M. Grynbaum, "Judge Rejects Groups' Effort to Remove Bike Lane," *New York Times*, August 17, 2011, https://www.nytimes.com/2011/08/17/nyregion/effort-to-remove-prospect-park-west-bike-lane-is-rejected.html; Selina Cheah, "Prospect Park West Bike Lane Antagonists Finally Drop Lawsuit," *Curbed New York*, September 28, 2016, https://ny.curbed.com/2016/9/28/13098378/prospect-park-west-bike-lane-lawsuit-dropped.

101. Iris Weinshall, interview with the author, April 28, 2023.

102. Robin Finn, "A New Commissioner Enters the Fray against Gridlock," *New York Times*, June 22, 2007, https://www.nytimes.com/2007/06/22/nyregion/22lives.html.

103. Grynbaum, "For City's Transportation Chief, Kudos and Criticism."

104. Steve Cuozzo, "The Bike-Lane Cancer," *New York Post*, December 13, 2012, https://nypost.com/2012/12/13/the-bike-lane-cancer/.

105. Nicole Gelinas, "Listening to Bike Lane Bashers," June 10, 2013, https://issuu.com/cityandstate/docs/city_and_state_jun_10_2013/41.

106. "Answers from the Transportation Commissioner," Part 5, *New York Times*, June 29, 2007, https://cityroom.blogs.nytimes.com/2007/06/29/answers-from-the-transportation-commissioner-part-5/.

107. Michael M. Grynbaum, "City Hall to Give Council Role in Bike-Share Program," *New York Times*, September 10, 2011, https://www.nytimes.com/2011/09/10/nyregion/city-council-gets-role-in-bike-share-program.html.

108. Matt Flegenheimer, "Flooding Apparently Damaged Equipment for Bike-Share Program," *New York Times*, November 15, 2012, https://www.nytimes.com/2012/11/15/nyregion/bike-share-equipment-apparently-damaged-by-flooding.html.

109. Matt Flegenheimer, "For Bloomberg and Bike-Sharing Program, the Big Moment Arrives," *New York Times*, May 27, 2013, https://www.nytimes.com/2013/05/27/nyregion/on-eve-of-bike-sharing-debut-watching-for-a-fiasco-or-a-success.html.

110. Matt Flegenheimer, "Out for a First Spin: City's Bike Share Program Begins," *New York Times*, May 28, 2013, https://www.nytimes.com/2013/05/28/nyregion/bike-share-program-opens-in-new-york-city-after-long-delay.html.

111. Matt Flegenheimer, "Bike-Share Effort Draws Riders and Hits Snags," *New York Times*, June 12, 2013, https://www.nytimes.com/2013/06/12/nyregion/two-weeks-in-riders-and-errors-for-bike-share-effort.html.

112. Citi Bike, "Citi Bike June 2013 Monthly Report," https://s3.amazonaws.com/citibike-regunits/pdf/2013_06_June_Citi_Bike_Monthly_Report.pdf.

113. Citi Bike, "Citi Bike August 2013, Monthly Report," https://s3.amazonaws.com/citibike-regunits/pdf/2013_08_August_Citi_Bike_Monthly_Report.pdf.

114. Alex Goldmark, "Truckloads of Bikes Not Enough to Meet Citi Bike Demand at Penn Station," WNYC, July 23, 2013, https://www.wnyc.org/story/308448-citi-bike-penn-station-so-popular-even-truckloads-bikes-arent-enough/.

115. Bill Cunningham, "Spoke Spinners," *New York Times*, May 31, 2013, https://www.nytimes.com/video/fashion/100000002256686/bill-cunningham-spoke-spinners-.html.

116. Gabrielle Noone, "Leo DiCaprio Takes His Life into His Hands," *The Cut*, May 11, 2016, https://www.thecut.com/2016/05/leonardo-dicaprio-citi-bike.html.

117. "Paul McCartney, Barry Gibb and Madonna Guest Star on Saturday Night Live," ABC News Radio, December 22, 2013, http://abcnewsradioonline.com/music-news/2013/12/22/paul-mccartney-barry-gibb-madonna-guest-star-on-saturday-nig.html.

118. Anemona Hartocollis, "Looking Smart on the Pedals," *New York Times*, July 11, 2013, https://www.nytimes.com/2013/07/11/fashion/looking-smart-on-the-pedals.html?searchResultPosition=98.

119. Matt Flegenheimer, "In Sickness and in Health, Long after the Bike Is Due Back," *New York Times*, October 12, 2013, https://www.nytimes.com/2013/10/12/nyregion/in-sickness-and-in-health-long-after-the-bike-is-due-back.html.

120. New York City Department of Transportation, "NYC Pedestrian Fatalities Bicycle-Pedestrian and Motor Vehicle-Pedestrian Crashes," https://www1.nyc.gov/html/dot/downloads/pdf/nycdot-pedestrian-fatalities-by-bike-motor-vehicle.pdf.

121. Dorothy Rabinowitz, "Death by Bicycle," *Wall Street Journal*, May 31, 2013, https://www.wsj.com/video/opinion-death-by-bicycle/C6D8BBCE-B405-4D3C-A381-4CA50BDD8D4D.html.

122. Matt Flegenheimer, "City to Close 2 Drives in Central Park Through Labor Day," *New York Times*, July 4, 2013, https://www.nytimes.com/2013/07/04/nyregion/city-to-close-2-drives-in-central-park-through-labor-day.html.

123. Citi Bike, "Citi Bike September 2017 Monthly Report," https://d21xlh2maitm24.cloudfront.net/nyc/September-2017-Citi-Bike-Monthly-Report.pdf.

124. Doctoroff, interview.

125. Janette Sadik-Khan, interview with the author, October 6, 2021.

126. Michael R. Bloomberg, correspondence with the author, April 27, 2023.

127. New York City Department of Transportation, "Cycling in the City," September 2021, https://www1.nyc.gov/html/dot/downloads/pdf/cycling-in-the-city-2021.pdf.

128. New York City Department of Transportation, "New York City Cycling Risk: Changes in Cyclist Safety Relative to Bicycle Use in New York City 2000–2018," https://www1.nyc.gov/html/dot/downloads/pdf/nyc-cycling-risk.pdf.

129. Michael Barbaro and Megan Thee-Brenan, "Poll Shows New Yorkers Are Deeply Conflicted over Bloomberg's Legacy," *New York Times*, August 18, 2013, https://www.nytimes.com/2013/08/18/nyregion/what-new-yorkers-think-of-mayor-bloomberg.html.

130. Citi Bike, "Citi Bike September 2019 Monthly Report," https://d21xlh2maitm24.cloudfront.net/nyc/September-2019-Citi-Bike-Monthly-Report-marketing.pdf.

131. New York City Department of Transportation, "Bicyclists: Ridership Statistics and Reports," accessed April 13, 2022, https://www1.nyc.gov/html/dot/html/bicyclists/bikestats.shtml.

132. New York City Department of Transportation, "Vision Zero View," accessed April 13, 2022, https://vzv.nyc/.

133. Bill de Blasio, interview with the author, April 28, 2023.

134. Jeffrey C. Mays, "Central Park's Scenic Drives Will Soon Be Car-Free," *New York Times*, April 20, 2018, https://www.nytimes.com/2018/04/20/nyregion/central-park-car-ban.html.

12. Freedom to Walk: The Rise and Fall and Rise Again of Play Streets

1. "Whalen Begins Shakeup, Ousting Two Inspectors; Will War on Speakeasies," *New York Times*, December 20, 1928, https://timesmachine.nytimes.com/timesmachine/1928/12/20/95683023.pdf.

2. "Whalen Turns Back the Speakeasy Task to Federal Dry Chief," *New York Times*, August 29, 1929, https://timesmachine.nytimes.com/timesmachine/1929/08/29/94176464.pdf.

3. "The Needle City Has Play Space," *New York Times*, February 10, 1929, https://timesmachine.nytimes.com/timesmachine/1929/02/10/95878893.pdf.

4. "Ban on 'Jaywalking' by City Law Planned to Ease Traffic Jam," *New York Times*, January 27, 1929, https://timesmachine.nytimes.com/timesmachine/1929/01/27/113327859.pdf.

5. "Garment Workers Get a 'Play Street,'" *New York Times*, January 30, 1929, https://timesmachine.nytimes.com/timesmachine/1929/01/30/95876358.pdf.

6. "Whalen Would Bar 5th Av. Left Turns," *New York Times*, January 31, 1929, https://timesmachine.nytimes.com/timesmachine/1929/01/31/91750823.pdf.

7. "Garment Workers Get a 'Play Street,'" *New York Times*, January 30, 1929, https://timesmachine.nytimes.com/timesmachine/1929/01/30/95876358.pdf.

8. "Survey of Midtown Manhattan Made by 42d Street Association," *New York Times*, January 8, 1933, https://timesmachine.nytimes.com/timesmachine/1933/01/08/282529582.pdf.

9. Committee on Regional Plan of New York and Its Environs, *Regional Plan of New York and Its Environs*, vol. one, *The Graphic Regional Plan*, 1929, https://s3.us-east-1.amazonaws.com/rpa-org/pdfs/RPA-Plan1-v1-Regional-Plan-of-New-York-and-Its-Environs.pdf.

10. New York City Department of Transportation, "New York City Mobility Report," October 2016, https://www1.nyc.gov/html/dot/downloads/pdf/mobility-report-2016-screen-optimized.pdf.

11. "Heavy Motor Traffic Needs Better Roads," *New York Times*, January 25, 1920, https://www.nytimes.com/1920/01/25/archives/heavy-motor-traffic-needs-better-roads.html.

12. "Traffic Ills Remedied," *New York Times*, March 25, 1920, https://timesmachine.nytimes.com/timesmachine/1920/03/25/102738772.pdf.

13. Editorial board, "The Traffic Lights," *New York Times*, March 15, 1920, https://timesmachine.nytimes.com/timesmachine/1920/03/15/97739015.pdf.

14. New York City Department of Transportation, "The New York City Pedestrian Safety Study & Action Plan: Technical Supplement," August 2010, https://www1.nyc.gov/html/dot/downloads/pdf/nyc_ped_safety_study_action_plan_technical_supplement.pdf.

15. "Auto Truck Kills Boy, 5, in the Bronx," *New York Times*, May 31, 1929, https://timesmachine.nytimes.com/timesmachine/1929/05/31/95960329.pdf.

16. Police Athletic League, "1914–1929: Creation of Playstreets," December 31, 2015, https://www.palnyc.org/history.

17. "To Turn Open Lots into Playgrounds," *New York Times*, June 11, 1916, https://timesmachine.nytimes.com/timesmachine/1916/06/11/101573669.pdf.

18. "Play Streets Set Apart," *New York Times*, July 22, 1920, https://timesmachine.nytimes.com/timesmachine/1920/07/22/103200756.pdf.

19. "42 Play Streets Open Today for Children in Crowded Areas," *New York Times*, July 6, 1932, https://timesmachine.nytimes.com/timesmachine/1932/07/06/100775662.pdf.

20. "$100,000 Is Sought for Playgrounds," *New York Times*, July 1, 1934, https://timesmachine.nytimes.com/timesmachine/1934/07/01/95048842.pdf.

21. "Open 11 Play Streets," *New York Times*, June 25, 1934, https://timesmachine.nytimes.com/timesmachine/1934/06/25/118512751.pdf.

22. "Play Streets Cut Accident Volume," *New York Times*, June 30, 1934, https://timesmachine.nytimes.com/timesmachine/1934/06/30/98426245.pdf.

23. "Play Street Meet Held on East Side," *New York Times*, July 16, 1948, https://timesmachine.nytimes.com/timesmachine/1948/07/16/84540150.pdf.

24. "P.A.L. Play Street Seminar on Lower West Side," *New York Times*, June 30, 1950, https://timesmachine.nytimes.com/timesmachine/1950/06/30/91106963.pdf.

25. "Family Day on the Lower East Side," *New York Times*, August 17, 1951, https://timesmachine.nytimes.com/timesmachine/1951/08/17/84683545.pdf.

26. "Hylan Defies Court Ruling on Play Streets," *New York Times*, April 10, 1925, https://timesmachine.nytimes.com/timesmachine/1925/04/10/98821409.pdf.

27. "Favors 'Play Streets,'" *New York Times*, December 21, 1928, https://timesmachine.nytimes.com/timesmachine/1928/12/21/95686628.pdf.

28. "Assails Play Streets," *New York Times*, April 15, 1933, https://timesmachine.nytimes.com/timesmachine/1933/04/15/99224062.pdf.

29. "Mayor Tours Bronx to Study Its Needs," *New York Times*, May 12, 1934, https://timesmachine.nytimes.com/timesmachine/1934/05/12/94525876.pdf.

30. New York City Department of Transportation, "New York City Mobility Report," October 2016, https://www1.nyc.gov/html/dot/downloads/pdf/mobility-report-2016-screen-optimized.pdf.

31. "Bromberger Asks Heavy Fines to Protect Children in Play Streets from Injury," *New York Times*, June 28, 1949, https://timesmachine.nytimes.com/timesmachine/1949/06/28/84216785.pdf.

32. "Fined $50 In Boy's Death," *New York Times*, April 3, 1948, https://timesmachine.nytimes.com/timesmachine/1948/04/03/86896714.pdf.

33. "Killed on Play Street," *New York Times*, April 26, 1949, https://timesmachine.nytimes.com/timesmachine/1949/04/26/84210224.pdf.

34. "Injured Boy's Party Packs 1,500 In Block," *New York Times*, August 28, 1949, https://timesmachine.nytimes.com/timesmachine/1949/08/28/110059754.pdf.

35. "Dirty Play Streets Attacked by Club," *New York Times*, October 15, 1949, https://timesmachine.nytimes.com/timesmachine/1949/10/15/96475226.pdf.

36. "Play Streets Get Safety Deputies," *New York Times*, July 11, 1952, https://timesmachine.nytimes.com/timesmachine/1952/07/11/84332899.pdf.

37. "400,000 Use Play Streets," *New York Times*, November 21, 1955, https://timesmachine.nytimes.com/timesmachine/1955/09/21/79393336.pdf.

38. "Dane Scans Ideas on Traffic Safety," *New York Times*, November 1, 1952, https://timesmachine.nytimes.com/timesmachine/1952/11/01/83832044.pdf.

39. "60 Areas for Play Will Open Tuesday," *New York Times*, July 3, 1955, https://timesmachine.nytimes.com/timesmachine/1955/07/03/91361429.pdf.

40. "Play Streets Get Touch of Fantasy," *New York Times*, August 23, 1957, https://timesmachine.nytimes.com/timesmachine/1957/08/23/84754602.pdf.

41. "96.1 Sears City for Two-Year High," *New York Times*, June 30, 1959, https://timesmachine.nytimes.com/timesmachine/1959/06/30/80588952.pdf.

42. John Sibley, "84th St. Trouble Block Becomes Play Street," *New York Times*, July 18, 1961, https://timesmachine.nytimes.com/timesmachine/1961/07/18/101471198.pdf.

43. "Police Play Street Balked by Petitions," *New York Times*, July 13, 1962, https://timesmachine.nytimes.com/timesmachine/1962/07/13/81791533.pdf.

44. "CORE Leads a Sit-In at Barnes's Office," *New York Times*, April 1, 1964, https://timesmachine.nytimes.com/timesmachine/1964/04/01/118655592.pdf.

45. "City Block Shut for Play Following CORE Protest," *New York Times*, April 8, 1964, https://www.nytimes.com/1964/04/08/archives/city-block-shut-for-play-following-core-protest.html.

46. "Mayor Hails P.A.L for Play Program at Harlem Opening," *New York Times*, July 7, 1970, https://www.nytimes.com/1970/07/07/archives/mayor-hails-pal-for-play-program-at-harlem-opening.html.

47. "44 Play Streets Opened by P.A.L., 100,000 Children to Join in Recreation Program," *New York Times*, July 7, 1964, https://www.nytimes.com/1964/07/07/archives/44-play-streets-opened-by-p-a-l-100000-children-to-join-in.html.

48. "Image and Role of Men in Blue Are Fading from the Police Athletic League Here," *New York Times*, July 3, 1973, https://www.nytimes.com/1970/09/13/archives/image-and-role-of-men-in-blue-are-fading-from-the-police-athletic.html.

49. "Summer Play Streets Open with Games and Parade," *New York Times*, July 3, 1973, https://timesmachine.nytimes.com/timesmachine/1973/07/03/99151081.pdf.

50. "Citizens Group Handbook Urges New Yorkers to Help Themselves," *New York Times*, December 11, 1977, https://www.nytimes.com/1977/12/11/archives/citizens-group-handbook-urges-new-yorkers-to-help-themselves-block.html.

51. Hetty Fox, Interview with the Bronx African American History Project, BAAHP Digital Archive at Fordham University, October 1, 2015, https://research.library.fordham.edu/cgi/viewcontent.cgi?article=1203&context=baahp_oralhist.

52. David Gonzalez, "Play Street Becomes a Sanctuary," *New York Times*, August 2, 2009, https://www.nytimes.com/2009/08/02/nyregion/02ritual.html.

53. Jarrett Murphy," Film Offers Instruction on Self-Defense against Urban Displacement," *City Limits*, February 13, 2020, https://citylimits.org/2020/02/13/film-offers-instruction-on-self-defense-against-urban-displacement/.

54. Kiley Armstrong, "Woman Leaves Plush Life to Save Crumbling Bronx Block," *Associated Press*, August 4, 1987, https://apnews.com/article/9d14706f28b736dca04823800a0709b2c.

55. "Bronx Woman's Goal: Revive a Block," *New York Times*, July 24, 1988, https://www.nytimes.com/1988/07/24/nyregion/bronx-woman-s-goal-revive-a-block.html.

56. Steven Goodstein, "Bronx Activist Hetty Fox Still Helping after 45 Years," *Bronx Times*, April 12, 2015, https://www.bxtimes.com/bronx-activist-hetty-fox-still-helping-after-45-years/.

57. Jarrett Murphy, "Film Offers Instruction on Self-Defense against Urban Displacement," *City Limits*, February 13, 2020, https://citylimits.org/2020/02/13/film-offers-instruction-on-self-defense-against-urban-displacement/.

58. David Gonzalez, "Play Street Becomes a Sanctuary," *New York Times*, August 2, 2009, https://www.nytimes.com/2009/08/02/nyregion/02ritual.html.

59. "Maria Forbes," Neighborhood Women, accessed April 12, 2022, http://neighborhoodwomen.org/maria-forbes/.

60. Maria Forbes, interview with the author, October 26, 2021.

61. Richard D. Lyons, "Seized Drug Cash Pays for Children's Play Sites," *New York Times*, July 18, 1993, https://www.nytimes.com/1993/07/18/nyregion/seized-drug-cash-pays-for-children-s-play-sites.html.

62. Randy Kennedy, "Balancing Act: When Play and Parking Clash," *New York Times*, July 31, 1994, https://www.nytimes.com/1994/07/31/nyregion/neighborhood-report-washington-heights-balancing-act-when-play-and-parking-clash.html.

63. Jim Dwyer, "Heard on the Stoops: A Nostalgia for Playstreets," *New York Times*, July 11, 2017, https://www.nytimes.com/2017/07/11/nyregion/about12.html.

64. Joseph P. Fried, "Midday Vehicle Ban Due in Five Downtown Blocks," *New York Times*, May 12, 1969, https://timesmachine.nytimes.com/timesmachine/1969/05/12/78345163.pdf.

65. "Nassau St. Mall Called Success; Extension Is Urged," *New York Times*, June 2, 1971, https://timesmachine.nytimes.com/timesmachine/1971/06/02/79704069.pdf.

66. "City Is Seeking More Streets for Pedestrian Malls," *New York Times*, August 23, 1969, https://timesmachine.nytimes.com/timesmachine/1969/08/23/78392446.pdf.

67. McCandlish Phillips, "The Day the City Caught Its Breath," *New York Times*, April 23, 1970, https://www.nytimes.com/1970/04/23/archives/the-day-the-city-caught-its-breath.html.

68. Murray Schumach, "Crowds Stroll in Fifth Avenue," *New York Times*, July 12, 1970, https://www.nytimes.com/1970/07/12/archives/crowds-stroll-in-fifth-avenue-traffic-barred-for-day-pollution.html.

69. Edward Ranzal, "Mayor Will Extend Shopping Mall Plan to 8 More Streets," *New York Times*, August 6, 1970, https://www.nytimes.com/1970/08/06/archives/mayor-will-extend-shopping-mall-plan-to-8-more-streets-mayor-to.html.

70. Edward Ranzal, "Mall Is Proposed for Madison Ave.," *New York Times*, July 21, 1970, https://www.nytimes.com/1970/07/21/archives/mall-is-proposed-for-madison-ave-group-wants-section-shut-to-cars.html.

71. "Madison Ave. Becomes a Mall Once a Week," *New York Times*, September 22, 1970, https://www.nytimes.com/1970/09/22/archives/madison-ave-becomes-a-mall-once-a-week.html.

72. Lawrence Van Gelder, "A Mile of Madison Ave. Becomes a Mall for the Night," *New York Times*, September 23, 1970, https://www.nytimes.com/1970/09/23/archives/a-mile-of-madison-ave-becomes-a-mall-for-the-night-a-mile-of.html.

73. Paul L Montgomery, "Fifth Ave. Is Car-Free and Carefree," *New York Times*, December 14, 1970, https://timesmachine.nytimes.com/timesmachine/1970/12/14/78232378.pdf.

74. Martin Tolchin, "City Studying Proposal to Close Parts of Broadway and 2 Avenues as Malls," *New York Times*, January 29, 1971, https://www.nytimes.com/1971/01/29/archives/city-studying-proposal-to-close-parts-of-broadway-and-2-avenues-as.html.

75. Simon Breines and William J. Dean, *The Pedestrian Revolution: Streets without Cars* (New York: Random House, 1974).

76. Frank J. Prial, "Network of Malls Urged by City for Midtown Area," *New York Times*, December 8, 1971, https://www.nytimes.com/1971/12/08/archives/network-of-malls-urged-by-city-for-midtown-area.html.

77. Glenn Flower, "Showdown Looms on Madison Mall," *New York Times*, February 10, 1972, https://www.nytimes.com/1972/02/10/archives/showdown-looms-on-madison-mall-businessmen-debating-plan-as-city.html.

78. Fred Ferretti, "Madison Ave. Closings Stir Dissent," *New York Times*, May 13, 1971, https://www.nytimes.com/1971/05/13/archives/madison-ave-closings-stir-dissent-madison-ave-closings-upset-some.html.

79. Frank J. Prial, "Traffic-Ban Test Called Failure," *New York Times*, June 4, 1971, https://www.nytimes.com/1971/06/04/archives/trafficban-test-called-failure-businessmen-cite-4-studies-of.html.

80. "Madison Traffic Ban Opposed by Merchants," *New York Times*, April 27, 1971, https://www.nytimes.com/1971/04/27/archives/madison-traffic-ban-opposed-by-merchants.html.

81. Paul L. Montgomery, "Teamsters Oppose Suggested Closing of 3 Main Streets," *New York Times*, February 2, 1971, https://www.nytimes.com/1971/02/02/archives/teamsters-oppose-suggested-closing-of-3-main-streets.html.

82. David Bird, "New Mall Plan Draws Criticism," *New York Times*, November 9, 1971, https://www.nytimes.com/1971/11/09/archives/new-mall-plan-draws-criticism-draft-for-madison-ave-calls-for.html.

83. Editorial board, "The Madison Ave. Mall," *New York Times*, February 26, 1973, https://www.nytimes.com/1973/02/26/archives/the-madison-ave-mall.html.

84. Peter Kihss, "Madison Ave. Mall Test Due to Begin Next March," *New York Times*, September 17, 1972, https://www.nytimes.com/1972/09/17/archives/madison-ave-mall-test-due-to-begin-next-march-madison-ave-mall-test.html.

85. C. Gerald Fraser, "Judge Rules against Madison Ave. Mall," *New York Times*, March 6, 1973, https://www.nytimes.com/1973/03/06/archives/judge-rules-against-madison-ave-mall-judge-rules-out-mell-on-mdison.html.

86. Frank Lynn, "Lindsay and Beame Clash over Madison Ave. Mall," *New York Times*, July 11, 1973, https://www.nytimes.com/1973/07/11/archives/lindsay-and-beame-clash-over-madison-ave-mall-lindsay-and-beame.html.

87. Editorial board, "For the Madison Mall," *New York Times*, July 11, 1973, https://www.nytimes.com/1973/07/11/archives/for-the-madison-mall.html.

88. Frank Lynn, "Madison Ave. Mall Is Defeated, 12–10, by Estimate Unit," *New York Times*, July 12, 1973, https://www.nytimes.com/1973/07/12/archives/madison-ave-mall-is-defeated-1210-by-estimate-unit-beame.html.

89. Laurie Johnston, "Lindsay Marks Last Sunday in Office amid Thousands Strolling on the Mall," *New York Times*, December 31, 1973, https://www.nytimes.com/1973/12/31/archives/lindsay-marks-last-sunday-in-office-amid-thousands-strolling-on-the.html.

90. Frank J. Prial, "Mall Stands Alone in Brooklyn 'Renaissance,'" *New York Times*, April 9, 1982, https://www.nytimes.com/1982/04/09/nyregion/mall-stands-alone-in-brooklyn-renaissance.html.

91. Glenn Fowler, "Event Next Weekend Offers Foods and Entertainment," *New York Times*, May 6, 1974, https://www.nytimes.com/1974/05/06/archives/twoday-feast-on-9th-ave-set-event-nextweekend-offers-foods-and.html.

92. Susan Heller Anderson, "Plan Aims to Double Union Sq," *New York Times*, July 16, 1987, https://www.nytimes.com/1987/07/16/nyregion/plan-aims-to-double-union-sq.html.

93. Deirdre Carmody, "Liberty Event to Bring Big Fair to City Streets," *New York Times*, May 12, 1986, https://www.nytimes.com/1986/05/12/nyregion/liberty-event-to-bring-big-fair-to-city-streets.html.

94. Robert D. McFadden, "A Very Special Day; Millions Watch Festive Harbor Salute to Liberty," *New York Times*, July 5, 1986, https://www.nytimes.com/1986/07/05/nyregion/very-special-day-millions-watch-festive-harbor-salute-liberty-fireworks-fill-sky.html.

95. Robert D. McFadden, "On Day of Record Heat, Liberty Weekend Ends," *New York Times*, July 7, 1986, https://www.nytimes.com/1986/07/07/nyregion/on-day-of-record-heat-liberty-weekend-ends.html.

96. "The Great Grid: The Master Plan of Manhattan, 1811—Now," Museum of the City of New York, Accessed April 12, 2022, https://thegreatestgrid.mcny.org/greatest-grid/the-1811-plan.

97. Joseph P. Fried, "City Weighs New Tourist Center and Malls for Times Sq. Area," *New York Times*, April 21, 1974, https://www.nytimes.com/1974/04/21/archives/city-weighs-new-tourist-center-and-malls-for-times-sq-area-business.html.

98. Glenn Fowler, "Decision Awaited on a Permanent Times Sq. Mall," *New York Times*, January 21, 1975, https://www.nytimes.com/1975/01/21/archives/decision-awaited-on-a-permanent-times-sq-mall.html.

99. Charles Kaiser, "Pedestrian Mall on Times Square Will Be Tested with U.S. Funds," *New York Times*, January 28, 1977, https://www.nytimes.com/1977/01/28/archives/pedestrian-mall-on-times-square-will-be-tested-with-us-funds.html.

100. Leslie Oelsner, "'New' Times Square Waiting in the Wings," *New York Times*, November 14, 1978, https://www.nytimes.com/1978/11/14/archives/new-times-square-waiting-in-the-wings-projects-include-mall-and-big.html.

101. "Jersey Youth Slain near Times Square," *New York Times*, December 27, 1971, https://www.nytimes.com/1971/12/27/archives/jersey-youth-slain-near-times-square.html.

102. Carter B. Horsley, "Broadway Poised for New Growth; Mall Questioned," *New York Times*, May 10, 1981, https://www.nytimes.com/1981/05/10/realestate/broadway-poised-for-new-growth-mall-questioned.html.

103. Paul Goldberger, "Portman Hotel's Plan Seems to Assure Mall on Broadway," *New York Times*, January 17, 1982, https://www.nytimes.com/1982/01/17/nyregion/portman-hotel-s-plan-seems-to-assure-mall-on-broadway.html.

104. Paul Goldberger, "Project Mall in Times Square Area Losing Support," *New York Times*, May 5, 1982, https://www.nytimes.com/1982/05/05/nyregion/projected-mall-in-times-sq-area-losing-support.html.

105. Carl Weisbrod, interview with the author, October 27, 2021.

106. Editorial board, "Times Square after the Mall," *New York Times*, May 17, 1982, https://www.nytimes.com/1982/05/17/opinion/times-square-after-the-mall.html.

107. Dan Barry, "After Collapse, Midtown Stress Hits New Highs," *New York Times*, July 23, 1998, https://www.nytimes.com/1998/07/23/nyregion/construction-collapse-times-square-overview-after-collapse-midtown-stress-hits.html.

108. Lois Weiss, "Deadly Accident Shuts Times Square; 43rd Street Building Scaffolding and Elevator Tower Collapses in Manhattan," *New York City Real Estate Weekly*, July 29, 1998.

109. Anthony Ramirez, "New Station, Less Pavement at West 72nd St.," *New York* Times, April 5, 1998, https://www.nytimes.com/1998/04/05/nyregion/neighborhood-report-upper-west-side-new-station-less-pavement-at-west-72d-st.html.

110. Giuliani, interview with the author, November 5, 2021.

111. David M. Herszenhorn, "6 Killed in Herald Square by Out-of-Control Van," *New York Times*, December 28, 2001, https://www.nytimes.com/2001/12/28/nyregion/6-killed-in-herald-square-by-out-of-control-van.html.

112. Iris Weinshall, interview with the author, April 28, 2023.

113. New York Police Department, "Seven Major Felony Offenses," Accessed April 12, 2022, https://www1.nyc.gov/assets/nypd/downloads/pdf/analysis_and_planning/historical-crime-data/seven-major-felony-offenses-by-precinct-2000-2020.pdf.

114. Carolyn Curiel, "Hey! Hey! I'm Walking Here!—How New York (and Other Big Cities) Should Solve the Traffic Problem," *New York Times*, September 13, 2006, https://www.nytimes.com/2006/09/13/opinion/tpTRAFFIC.html.

115. New York City Department of Transportation, "Green Light for Midtown Evaluation Report," January 2010, https://www.nyc.gov/html/dot/downloads/pdf/broadway_report_final2010_web.pdf.

116. David W. Dunlap, "Atop the New TKTS Booth, Ruby-Red Stairs with a View of the Great White Way," *New York Times*, October 17, 2008, https://www.nytimes.com/2008/10/17/nyregion/17tkts.html.

117. William Neuman, "Closing on Broadway: Two Lanes of Traffic," *New York Times*, July 11, 2008, https://www.nytimes.com/2008/07/11/nyregion/11broadway.html.

118. William Neuman, "In New York, Broadway as Great Walk Way," *New York Times*, February 27, 2009, https://www.nytimes.com/2009/02/27/nyregion/27broadway.html.

119. Neuman, "In New York."

120. Neuman, "In New York."

121. Cindy Adams, "It's Broadway—Not Rockaway!," *New York Post*, August 23, 2009, https://pagesix.com/2009/08/23/its-broadway-not-rockaway/.

122. Mike Lupica, "Mayor Bloomberg Does in Times Square What He Could Not with Congestion Pricing," *New York Daily News*, June 8, 2009, https://www.nydailynews.com/news/mayor-bloomberg-times-square-not-congestion-pricing-article-1.375811.

123. Erin Durkin, "Bloomberg Predicts Times Square Pedestrian Plaza Will Stay under de Blasio," *New York Daily News*, December 23, 2013, https://www.nydailynews.com/new-york/bloomberg-crows-times-square-pedestrian-plaza-article-1.1557047.

124. "City Councilman: Baghdad's Roads Better Than Many in NYC," CBS News New York, May 4, 2011, https://newyork.cbslocal.com/2011/05/04/city-councilman-baghdads-roads-better-than-nycs/.

125. John Del Signore, "Broadway Pedestrian Plaza: Conflicting Data Won't Stop Mayor," *Gothamist*, February 12, 2010, https://gothamist.com/news/broadway-pedestrian-plaza-conflicting-data-wont-stop-mayor.

126. Eleanor Randolph, "The Best Seats in Times Square," *New York Times*, June 8, 2009, https://www.nytimes.com/2009/06/08/opinion/08mon4.html.

127. New York City Department of Transportation, "Green Light for Midtown Evaluation Report," January 2010, https://www.nyc.gov/html/dot/downloads/pdf/broadway_report_final2010_web.pdf.

128. Michael R. Bloomberg, correspondence with the author, April 27, 2023.

129. Michael Barbaro and Megan Thee-Brenan, "Poll Shows New Yorkers Are Deeply Conflicted over Bloomberg's Legacy," *New York Times*, August 18, 2013, https://www.nytimes.com/2013/08/18/nyregion/what-new-yorkers-think-of-mayor-bloomberg.html.

130. Durkin, "Bloomberg Predicts Times Square Pedestrian Plaza Will Stay."

131. Janette Sadik-Khan, interview with the author, October 6, 2021.

132. New York City Department of Transportation, "NYC DOT Commissioner Sadik-Khan Announces Historic Safety Redesign at Grand Army Plaza, Enhancing Access to Prospect Park," November 9, 2011, https://www1.nyc.gov/html/dot/html/pr2011/pr11_93.shtml.

133. Dan Biederman, interview with the author, September 1, 2022.

134. Lauren Evans, "Will De Blasio Kill the Times Square Pedestrian Plaza?," *Gothamist*, October 24, 2013, https://gothamist.com/news/will-de-blasio-kill-the-times-square-pedestrian-plaza.

135. Michael Kimmelman, "Challenging Mayor de Blasio over Times Square Plazas," *New York Times*, August 22, 2015, https://www.nytimes.com/2015/08/22/arts/design/challenging-mayor-de-blasio-over-times-square-plazas.html.

13. Killed in the Crosswalk: Turning Tragedies into Progress

1. "First New York State Safety Congress, State of New York Bureau of Motor Vehicles, March 1926," transcript, Moses, NYPL, box 3.

2. "Jay-Walking Law Urged for Whole City," *New York Times*, April 11, 1929, https://timesmachine.nytimes.com/timesmachine/1929/04/11/95908038.pdf.

3. "Mayor Signs New Traffic Code, But Rejects Ban on Jaywalking," *New York Times*, December 23, 1936, https://www.nytimes.com/1936/12/23/archives/mayor-signs-new-traffic-code-but-rejects-ban-on-jaywalking-finds.html.

4. Bernard Stengren, "Anti-Jaywalk Rules Will Start June 23," *New York Times*, June 15, 1958, https://timesmachine.nytimes.com/timesmachine/1958/06/15/91391542.pdf.

5. "Jaywalking Warnings to 210,726 Cut Toll," *New York Times*, July 28, 1958, https://timesmachine.nytimes.com/timesmachine/1958/07/28/82707112.pdf.

6. Bernard Stengren, "State's New Motor Laws," *New York Times*, September 25, 1960, https://timesmachine.nytimes.com/timesmachine/1960/09/25/99874970.pdf.

7. Michael Oreskes, "Leaders in Albany Agree to Require Use of Seat Belts," *New York Times*, June 20, 1984, https://www.nytimes.com/1984/06/20/nyregion/leaders-in-albany-agree-to-require-use-of-seat-belts.html.

8. Tamar Lewin, "Seat-Belt Laws Grow, But by Fits and Starts," *New York Times*, August 15, 1993, https://www.nytimes.com/1993/08/15/us/seat-belt-laws-grow-but-by-fits-and-starts.html.

9. "Up Against Killer Cars; Lights, Camera, Citation!," *Newsday*, May 11, 1992.

10. New York City Department of Transportation, "City to Add 50 New Cameras to Red Light Camera Program," September 14, 2006, https://www1.nyc.gov/html/dot/html/pr2006/pr06_51.shtml.

11. Lou Riccio, interview with the author, November 21, 2021.

12. Clemente Lisi, "City Slashes Crashes," *New York Post*, December 23, 2003, https://nypost.com/2003/12/23/city-slashes-crashes-traffic-fatalities-hit-a-six-year-low/.

13. Rudy Giuliani, interview with the author, November 5, 2021.

14. Paul Zielbauer, "Police to Seize Cars of People Accused of Drunken Driving," *New York Times*, February 21, 1999, https://www.nytimes.com/1999/02/21/nyregion/police-to-seize-cars-of-people-accused-of-drunken-driving.html.

15. New York City Office of the Mayor, "Mayor Giuliani and Police Commissioner Kerik Announce Increased DWI Enforcement during Fourth of July Holiday and throughout Summer," July 2, 2001, http://www.nyc.gov/html/om/html/2001b/pr236-01.html.

16. C. J. Chivers, "Recklessness behind Wheel Will Mean No Wheels," *New York Times*, January 14, 2000, https://www.nytimes.com/2000/01/14/nyregion/recklessness-behind-wheel-will-mean-no-wheels.html.

17. Charles Komanoff, "The History of a Movement," Part I, "Hazmat Suits and Street Memorials," *Streetsblog*, December 6, 2021, https://nyc.streetsblog.org/2021/12/06/the-history-of-a-movement-part-i-hazmat-suits-and-street-memorials/.

18. Clyde Haberman, "Why Streets Aren't Safe: The Drivers," *New York Times*, April 25, 1997, https://www.nytimes.com/1997/04/25/nyregion/why-streets-aren-t-safe-the-drivers.html.

19. Charles Komanoff, "The History of a Movement," Part III, "The Death of Dante Curry," *Streetsblog*, December 10, 2021, https://nyc.streetsblog.org/2021/12/10/the-history-of-a-movement-part-iii-the-death-of-dante-curry/.

20. Evelyn Cancel, interview with the author, December 21, 2021.

21. Editorial board, "Car-Dodging with the Mayor," *New York Times*, January 14, 1998, https://www.nytimes.com/1998/01/14/opinion/car-dodging-with-the-mayor.html.

22. Charles Komanoff, "The History of a Movement," Part IV, "'Killed by Automobile,'" *Streetsblog*, December 13, 2021, https://nyc.streetsblog.org/2021/12/13/the-history-of-a-movement-part-iv-killed-by-automobile/.

23. Andy Newman, "Drivers Are at Fault in Most Pedestrian Deaths, Study Reports," *New York Times*, https://www.nytimes.com/1999/03/19/nyregion/drivers-are-at-fault-in-most-pedestrian-deaths-study-reports.html.

24. "Police to Step Up Patrons on 'Boulevard of Death,'" *Newsday*, December 9, 2000.

25. Roberto Santiago, Maki Becker, Warren Woodberry Jr., and Pete Donohue, "Boulevard of Death Takes Terrible Toll," *New York Daily News*, January 11, 2001, https://www.nydailynews.com/archives/news/boulevard-death-takes-terrible-toll-killed-queens-article-1.898166.

26. Seth Faison, "Pedestrians at Risk on Queens Boulevard," *New York Times*, January 3, 1993, https://www.nytimes.com/1993/01/03/nyregion/pedestrians-at-risk-on-queens-boulevard.html.

27. "Queens Blvd. Crackdown: City Vows to Speed Up Changes to Make Roadway Safer," *New York Daily News*, January 12, 2001.

28. Corey Kilgannon, "Kew Gardens Journal; Crossing at Peril of Life and Limb (and a $10 Fine)," *New York Times*, June 10, 2001, https://www.nytimes.com/2001/06/10/nyregion/kew-gardens-journal-crossing-at-peril-of-life-and-limb-and-a-10-fine.html.

29. "Road Beautiful but Deadly: Ocean Pkwy. Carnage Rivals Queens Blvd.'s," *New York Daily News*, April 25, 2001.

30. "Shattered Illusions on Queens Boulevard," *Newsday*, March 16, 2001.

31. Jim O'Grady, "Despite 'Maniacs,' A Better Report Card for a Troubled Road," *New York Times*, February 24, 2002, https://www.nytimes.com/2002/02/24/nyregion/neighborhood-report-update-despite-maniacs-better-report-card-for-troubled-road.html.

32. "More Red-Light Cameras Set for Blvd," *New York Daily News*, March 8, 2001.

33. Colin Gustafson, "Street Renamed to Honor 2 'Blvd. of Death' Victims," *Queens Chronicle*, July 12, 2007, https://www.qchron.com/editions/central/street-renamed-to-honor-2-blvd-of-death-victims/article_3487c4d1-8640-5da3-9b69-47a5d0e44817.html.

34. "Vigil for Life on Queens Blvd.; Residents Seek Improvements to 'Deadly' Thoroughfare," *Newsday*, August 1, 2003.

35. David Seifman, "Qns. Blvd. Pedestrians Will Get a 'Death' Reprieve," *New York Post*, February 12, 2004, https://nypost.com/2004/02/12/qns-blvd-pedestrians-will-get-a-death-reprieve/.

36. David Seifman, "'Boulevard of Death' Upgrade," *New York Post*, April 6, 2004, https://nypost.com/2004/04/06/boulevard-of-death-upgrade/.

37. Iris Weinshall, interview with the author, April 28, 2023.

38. Lorena Mongelli, "Red-Light Cam Call," *New York Post*, July 12, 2004, https://nypost.com/2004/07/12/red-light-cam-call/.

39. Betty M. Cooney, "New Senate Bill Takes Aim at Queens Blvd. Radar Pilot," *Queens Chronicle*, March 22, 2001, https://www.qchron.com/editions/central/new-senate-bill-takes-aim-at-queens-blvd-radar-pilot/article_5b7bc903-b5ef-5db2-8438-e5e9e939bd89.html.

40. Aaron Naparstek, "Auto Asphyxiation," *New York Press*, November 11, 2014, https://www.nypress.com/news/auto-asphyxiation-BANP1020040309303099998.

41. Aaron Donovan, "The Weekly Carnage," *Streetsblog*, July 28, 2006, https://nyc.streetsblog.org/2006/07/28/the-weekly-carnage/.

42. Brad Aaron, "Driver Cleared by NYPD Found Negligent in Death of Cyclist Rasha Shamoon," *Streetsblog*, February 14, 2012, https://nyc.streetsblog.org/2012/02/14/driver-cleared-by-nypd-found-negligent-in-death-of-cyclist-rasha-shamoon/.

43. Jeff Parker, "Three Who Died," *City Cyclist*, Transportation Alternatives, May/June 1989, http://www.komanoff.net/citycyclist/May-Jun-1989.pdf.

44. Noah Kazis, "Traffic Still the Top Injury-Related Killer of NYC Kids," *Streetsblog*, September 13, 2011, https://nyc.streetsblog.org/2011/09/13/traffic-still-the-top-injury-related-killer-of-nyc-kids/.

45. Ben Fried, "The Bike and Pedestrian Safety Stats the Daily News Won't Cover," *Streetsblog*, August 9, 2012, https://nyc.streetsblog.org/2012/08/09/the-bike-and-pedestrian-safety-stats-the-daily-news-wont-cover/.

46. Aaron Naparstek, interview with the author, November 16, 2021.

47. Nicole Gelinas, "New York's Next Public Safety Revolution," *City Journal*, Spring 2014, https://www.manhattan-institute.org/html/poverty-and-progress-nyc-xi-vision-zero-10306.html.

48. New York City Department of Transportation, "The New York City Pedestrian Safety Study & Action Plan," August 2010, https://www1.nyc.gov/html/dot/downloads/pdf/nyc_ped_safety_study_action_plan.pdf.

49. Brad Aaron, "Marty Golden Fatally Wounded a Senior with His SUV in 2005," *Streetsblog*, December 13, 2017, https://nyc.streetsblog.org/2017/12/13/marty-golden-fatally-wounded-a-senior-with-his-suv-in-2005/.

50. James Fanelli, "Cop-Impersonating State Sen. Marty Golden Knocked 74-Year-Old Pedestrian into Coma with 2005 Wreck, Paid Out $750G Settlement," *New York Daily News*, December 15, 2017, https://www.nydailynews.com/new-york/cop-impersonating-pol-2005-suv-wreck-left-elderly-woman-coma-article-1.3699120.

51. Michael Powell, "When Fury Can Be a Force for Good Ends," *New York Times*, April 2, 2013, https://www.nytimes.com/2013/04/02/nyregion/bloombergs-ire-on-defeat-of-red-light-cameras-is-justified.html.

52. Thomas Kaplan, "New York City Gets Legislature's Nod to Install Speed Cameras," *New York Times*, June 23, 2013, https://www.nytimes.com/2013/06/23/nyregion/city-gets-legislatures-nod-to-install-speed-cameras.html.

53. Michael Bloomberg, interview with the author (via email), April 27, 2023.

54. Ted Mann, "Street Safety Gains Traction as Political Issue," *Wall Street Journal*, August 6, 2013, https://www.wsj.com/articles/SB10001424127887323968704578652383311616100.

55. Bill de Blasio, "De Blasio Calls for Visionary Street Safety Goal: No Fatalities or Serious Injuries on New York City Streets."

56. Bill de Blasio, interview with the author, April 28, 2023.

57. J. David Goodman and Randy Leonard, "Truck Kills Boy, 6, as He Walks to School," *New York Times*, March 1, 2013, https://www.nytimes.com/2013/03/01/nyregion/6-year-old-fatally-hit-by-truck-in-east-harlem.html.

58. Gillian Kleiman, "Teen Staffer Killed by Tractor-Trailer While Walking Home from Dylan's Candy Bar," August 1, 2013, https://nypost.com/2013/08/01/teen-staffer-killed-by-tractor-trailer-while-walking-home-from-dylans-candy-bar/.

59. Dana Varinsky, "3-Year-Old Fatally Struck by SUV in Queens," *dnainfo*, October 7, 2013, https://www.dnainfo.com/new-york/20131007/flushing/3-year-old-fatally-struck-by-suv-queens/.

60. Stephen Miller, "Samuel Cohen Eckstein, 12, Killed by Van Driver on Prospect Park West," *Streetsblog*, October 9, 2013, https://nyc.streetsblog.org/2013/10/09/samuel-cohen-eckstein-12-killed-by-van-driver-on-prospect-park-west/.

61. Amy Cohen, interview with the author, November 16, 2021.

62. Michael Schwirtz and Rebecca White, "Tractor-Trailer Kills 8-Year-Old Boy Walking to School in Queens," *New York Times*, December 21, 2013, https://www.nytimes.com/2013/12/21/nyregion/boy-8-fatally-struck-by-tractor-trailer-in-queens.html.

63. Michael Schwirtz, "9-Year-Old Killed by Taxi Was 'Spirited' and 'Wise,'" *New York Times*, January 12, 2014, https://www.nytimes.com/2014/01/12/nyregion/9-year-old-killed-by-taxi-was-spirited-and-wise.html.

64. Lizi Rahman, interview with the author, December 2, 2021.

65. New York City Office of the Mayor, "Transcript: Mayor de Blasio Releases 'Vision Zero' Action Plan, Launching Citywide Effort to Prevent Traffic Fatalities," February 18, 2014, https://www1.nyc.gov/office-of-the-mayor/news/056-14/transcript-mayor-de-blasio-releases-vision-zero-action-plan-launching-citywide-effort-to#/0.

66. Families for Safe Streets, "Families to City Council: Accelerate Plan to Stop Traffic Deaths," *Gothamist*, February 23, 2014, https://gothamist.com/news/families-to-city-council-accelerate-plan-to-stop-traffic-deaths.

67. Polly Trottenberg, interview with the author, February 15, 2022.

68. New York City Department of Transportation, "Queens Boulevard Proposed Corridor Safety Improvements," Presentation to Community Board 2 Transportation Committee, March 31, 2015, https://www1.nyc.gov/html/dot/downloads/pdf/2015-03-queens-blvd-safety-improvements.pdf.

69. New York City Office of the Mayor, "Transcript: Mayor de Blasio Announces Department of Transportation Commencing Work on $100 Million Vision Zero Overhaul of Queens Boulevard," July 23, 2015, https://www1.nyc.gov/office-of-the-mayor/news/510-15/transcript-mayor-de-blasio-department-transportation-commencing-work-100-million.

70. Katie Honan, "Bike Lanes Left Out of Community Board's Approval of Queens Boulevard Fixes," *dnainfo*, May 11, 2016, https://www.dnainfo.com/new-york/20160511/elmhurst/bike-lanes-left-out-of-community-boards-approval-of-queens-boulevard-fixes/.

71. Katie Honan, "Queens Boulevard Will Get Bike Lanes That Community Board Rejected: Mayor," *dnainfo*, May 11, 2016, https://www.dnainfo.com/new-york/20160511/elmhurst/queens-boulevard-will-get-bike-lanes-that-community-board-rejected-mayor/.

72. "Community Board 6 Votes 'No' to Queens Boulevard Redesign," *Forest Hills Post*, June 14, 2018, https://foresthillspost.com/community-board-6-votes-no-to-queens-boulevard-redesign.

73. New York City Department of Transportation, "Queens Boulevard Yellowstone Boulevard to Union Turnpike Proposed Corridor Safety Improvements," Presentation to Community Board 6 Transportation Committee, May 23, 2018, https://www1.nyc.gov/html/dot/downloads/pdf/queens-blvd-yellowstone-union-may2018.pdf.

74. Angie Schmitt, "Associated Press Cautions Journalists That Crashes Aren't Always 'Accidents,'" *Streetsblog*, April 4, 2016, https://usa.streetsblog.org/2016/04/04/associated-press-cautions-journalists-that-crashes-arent-always-accidents/.

75. Winnie Hu, "No Longer New York City's 'Boulevard of Death,'" *New York Times*, December 3, 2017, https://www.nytimes.com/2017/12/03/nyregion/queens-boulevard-of-death.html.

76. New York City Department of Transportation, "Automated Speed Enforcement Program Report 2014–2017," June 2018, https://www.nyc.gov/html/dot/downloads/pdf/speed-camera-report-june2018.pdf.

77. Jim Dwyer, "Vision Zero Has Made Ocean Parkway Safer, but Some See Red," *New York Times*, March 28, 2017, https://www.nytimes.com/2017/03/28/nyregion/vision-zero-ocean-parkway-traffic-safety.html.

78. Dwyer, "Vision Zero."

79. Brad Aaron, "Marty Golden's Cadillac Has Been Caught Speeding in School Zones Three Times in 2018 Alone," *Streetsblog*, June 25, 2018, https://nyc.streetsblog.org/2018/06/25/marty-goldens-cadillac-has-been-caught-speeding-in-school-zones-three-times-in-2018-alone/.

80. Paul Martinka, Amanda Woods, and Gina Daidone, "Speed Camera Advocates Arrested While Protesting Outside Senator's Office," June 29, 2018, https://nypost.com/2018/06/29/speed-camera-advocates-arrested-while-protesting-outside-senators-office/.

81. Jim Dwyer, "Senator Does a U-Turn on Speed Cameras in School Zones," *New York Times*, July 12, 2018, https://www.nytimes.com/2018/07/12/nyregion/speed-cameras-martin-golden.html.

82. Vivian Wang, "Speed Cameras Will Surround Every New York City Public School," *New York Times*, March 19, 2019, https://www.nytimes.com/2019/03/19/nyregion/speed-cameras-schools-nyc.html.

83. Transport for London, "Casualties in Greater London during 2019," September 2020, https://content.tfl.gov.uk/casualties-in-greater-london-2019.pdf.

84. Insurance Institute for Highway Safety, "Fatality Facts 2019 State by State," March 2021, https://www.iihs.org/topics/fatality-statistics/detail/state-by-state.

85. Governors Highway Safety Association, "Pedestrian Traffic Fatalities by State," February 2020, https://www.ghsa.org/sites/default/files/2020-02/GHSA-Pedestrian-Spotlight-FINAL-rev2.pdf.

14. Yellow, Green, Black: The Struggle to Limit Ride Services

1. New York City Department of Transportation, "New York City Mobility Report," August 2019, https://www1.nyc.gov/html/dot/downloads/pdf/mobility-report-print-2019.pdf.

2. Pauline Toole, "Unemployment in the Great Depression," New York City Department of Records and Information Services, October 9, 2020, https://www.archives.nyc/blog/2020/10/9/90vdpgn8lc5zxcildoooltvzmfwx22.

3. Stephen Farrell, "Inaugurations, through the Decades," *New York Times*, December 30, 2013, https://archive.nytimes.com/www.nytimes.com/interactive/2013/12/30/nyregion/nyc-mayor-inaugurations.html.

4. "Cab Drivers Strike, Backed by Mayor, to Get 5c Tax Fund," *New York Herald Tribune*, February 3, 1934.

5. "Taxi War a Result of Lower Profits," *New York Times*, February 11, 1934, https://timesmachine.nytimes.com/timesmachine/1934/02/11/93749514.pdf.

6. "City Taxi Board Seeks to Solve Cab Problem: Faces Task of Regulating," *New York Herald Tribune*, June 5, 1932.

7. "Lewis B. Sebring Jr., "Taxicab Operators War among Themselves over Rates and Regulations," *New York Herald Tribune*, February 16, 1930.

8. "Taxi War a Result of Lower Profits," *New York Times*, February 11, 1934, https://timesmachine.nytimes.com/timesmachine/1934/02/11/93749514.pdf.

9. Sebring, "Taxicab Operators War among Themselves."

10. Sebring, "Taxicab Operators War among Themselves."

11. "Mayor Placates 200 Protesting Cab Control Bill," *New York Herald Tribune*, May 7, 1931.

12. "Walker's Bill Makes Utility of Taxi Industry," *New York Herald Tribune*, January 17, 1931.

13. "Taxicab Control Bill Scheduled to Pass Today," *New York Herald Tribune*, December 22, 1931.

14. Editorial board, "The Taxicab Bill," *New York Herald Tribune*, March 1, 1931.

15. John T. Whitaker, "Taxi Monopoly War Predicted on Walker Plan," *New York Herald Tribune*, January 19, 1931.

16. "Threaten Aldermen on New Taxicab Bill," *New York Times*, June 10, 1931, https://timesmachine.nytimes.com/timesmachine/1931/06/10/96917247.pdf.

17. "Aldermen Told to Vacate Jobs as Budget Saving," *New York Herald Tribune*, November 24, 1931.

18. "Aldermen Pass Taxicab Control Bill by 52 to 6," *New York Herald Tribune*, December 23, 1931.

19. "Mayor Signs Bill for Control of Taxicab Industry by City," *New York Herald Tribune*, January 30, 1932.

20. "Taxicab Broker Admits $26,535 Gift to Walker," *New York Herald Tribune*, May 13, 1932.

21. "Cab Monopoly Fight Revived before Board," *New York Herald Tribune*, June 2, 1932.

22. Editorial board, "A Charter for Taxicabs," *New York Herald Tribune*, November 15, 1932.

23. "Tipplers Poor Tippers, Taxi Inquiry Hears," *New York Herald Tribune*, February 14, 1934.

24. "Cab Drivers Strike, Backed by Mayor, to Get 5c Tax Fund," *New York Herald Tribune*, February 3, 1934.

25. Joseph Driscoll, "Taxi Passengers Beaten in Riots on Broadway as Strikers Wreck Cabs," *New York Herald Tribune*, February 4, 1934.

26. "Taxi Strikers Crack Pates in Midtown Tour: Damaged Cabs," *New York Herald Tribune*, March 21, 1934.

27. "Strikers Hurl Police Aside, Rip Up Taxis: 5,000 Paralyze Times Sq.," *New York Herald Tribune*, March 22, 1934.

28. Editorial board, "Public Disorder," *New York Times*, March 23, 1934, https://timesmachine.nytimes.com/timesmachine/1934/03/23/93756754.pdf.

29. Editorial board, "Plebiscite by Riot," *New York Herald Tribune*, March 27, 1934.

30. "Taxi Disorders Condemned by City Ministers," *New York Herald Tribune*, March 26, 1934.

31. "Cab Strikers Curbed after Riots; Scores Injured; Mob Halts Mayor," *New York Herald Tribune*, March 23, 1934.

32. "O'Ryan Lays Cab Riots at Mayor's Door: Wanted to Use Police," *New York Herald Tribune*, April 10, 1934.

33. "Cab Riots Laid to Mayor and Police by Jury," *New York Herald Tribune*, April 12, 1934.

34. "Taxi Men Oust Reds and Seek to Settle," *New York Times*, March 30, 1934, https://timesmachine.nytimes.com/timesmachine/1934/03/30/95038718.pdf.

35. "Taxi Strike Ends as Peace Is Signed," *New York Times*, February 9, 1934, https://timesmachine.nytimes.com/timesmachine/1934/02/09/94491491.pdf.

36. "Mayor Calls Parley Today in Cab Strike," *New York Herald Tribune*, March 24, 1934.

37. "Would Divide Taxi Trade," *New York Times*, May 21, 1935, https://timesmachine.nytimes.com/timesmachine/1935/05/21/95076862.pdf.

38. "Aldermen Adopt Limits on Taxicabs," *New York Times*, March 2, 1937, https://timesmachine.nytimes.com/timesmachine/1937/03/02/96731983.pdf.

39. "Taxi Limit Law Signed," *New York Times*, March 10, 1937, https://timesmachine.nytimes.com/timesmachine/1937/03/10/118961185.pdf.

40. "Isaacs Sponsors Cab Bill," *New York Times*, June 11, 1946, https://timesmachine.nytimes.com/timesmachine/1946/06/11/100998799.pdf.

41. Robert O. Boorstin, "Panel Votes to Broaden Power of Taxi Agency," *New York Times*, November 20, 1986, https://www.nytimes.com/1986/11/20/nyregion/panel-votes-to-broaden-power-of-taxi-agency.html.

42. Editorial board, "Metered Madness," *New York Times*, September 9, 1970, https://www.nytimes.com/1970/09/09/archives/metered-madness.html.

43. Editorial board, "To Get More Taxis, Get More Taxis," *New York Times*, December 20, 1981, https://www.nytimes.com/1981/12/20/opinion/to-get-more-taxis-get-more-taxis.html.

44. Editorial board, "Cabs and City Hall 'Off Duty,'" *New York Times*, August 7, 1984, https://www.nytimes.com/1984/08/07/opinion/cabs-and-city-hall-off-duty.html.

45. Jesus Rangel, "Koch Offers a Plan to Double Number of Taxi Medallions," *New York Times*, January 16, 1985, https://www.nytimes.com/1985/01/16/nyregion/koch-offers-a-plan-to-double-number-of-taxi-medallions.html.

46. Editorial board, "Higher Fares? If There Are More Cabs," *New York Times*, October 13, 1986, https://www.nytimes.com/1986/10/13/opinion/higher-fares-if-there-are-more-cabs.html.

47. James Barron, "22% Rise in New York Cab Fares Recommended by Taxi Panel Staff," *New York Times*, March 24, 1987, www.nytimes.com/1987/03/24/nyregion/22-rise-in-new-york-cab-fares-recommended-by-taxi-panel-staff.html.

48. Editorial board, "Mr. Outside Tackles the Taxis," *New York Times*, June 1, 1986, https://www.nytimes.com/1986/06/01/opinion/mr-outside-tackles-the-taxis.html.

49. Kirk Johnson, "Scholar's Time as Taxi Chief: Politics Made It a Hard Ride," *New York Times*, June 2, 1988, https://www.nytimes.com/1988/06/02/nyregion/scholar-s-time-as-taxi-chief-politics-made-it-a-hard-ride.html.

50. Editorial board, "To Get More Taxis, Get More Taxis," *New York Times*, December 20, 1981, https://www.nytimes.com/1981/12/20/opinion/to-get-more-taxis-get-more-taxis.html.

51. "500 Radio Cabs Are Converted to Street-Hail Duty," *New York Times*, November 7, 1982, https://www.nytimes.com/1982/11/07/nyregion/500-radio-cabs-are-converted-to-street-hail-duty.html.

52. David A. Andelman, "Taxi Medallion Worth $68,000, but What's a Ride Worth?," *New York Times*, March 2, 1980, https://timesmachine.nytimes.com/timesmachine/1980/03/02/111767298.pdf.

53. Suzanne Daley, "New York Making Changes to Improve Its Taxi Service," *New York Times*, May 26, 1984, https://www.nytimes.com/1984/05/26/nyregion/new-york-making-changes-to-improve-its-taxi-service.html.

54. Editorial board, "Trouble on the Taxis," *New York Times*, November 14, 1970, https://www.nytimes.com/1970/11/14/archives/trouble-on-the-taxis.html; Emanuel Perlmutter, "Man, 21, Charged with City's First Murder of a Taxi Driver in Nearly Two Years," *New York Times*, July 16, 1970, https://www.nytimes.com/1972/07/16/archives/man-21-charged-with-citys-first-murder-of-a-taxi-driver-in-nearly.html.

55. A. H. Raskin, "Taxis: The One Sure Thing Is That Fares Will Go Up," *New York Times*, November 22, 1970, https://www.nytimes.com/1970/11/22/archives/taxis-the-one-sure-thing-is-that-fares-will-go-up.html.

56. Glenn Flower, "Cabdriver Is Killed in Bronx," *New York Times*, October 19, 1981, https://www.nytimes.com/1981/10/19/nyregion/cabdriver-is-killed-in-bronx-2d-holdup-in-48-hours.html.

57. Michel Marriott, "Harlem Shots Kill a Cabby; Rider Is Hurt," *New York Times*, December 23, 1993, https://www.nytimes.com/1993/12/23/nyregion/harlem-shots-kill-a-cabby-rider-is-hurt.html.

58. Norimitsu Onishi, "Taxi Panel Requires Bullet-Resistant Partitions," *New York Times*, January 21, 1994, https://www.nytimes.com/1994/01/21/nyregion/taxi-panel-requires-bullet-resistant-partitions.html.

59. Michael Luo, "Police Measures Avert Livery-Cab Killings," *New York Times*, February 7, 2004, https://www.nytimes.com/2004/02/07/nyregion/police-measures-avert-livery-cab-killings.html.

60. Emanuel Perlmutter, "Mayor Will Seek Rise in Cab Fares to Avert Strike," *New York Times*, November 16, 1970, https://www.nytimes.com/1970/11/16/archives/mayor-will-seek-rise-in-cab-fares-to-avert-strike-does-not-specify.html.

61. Abe Mittleman, interview with the author, December 21, 2021.

62. Craig Wolff," Aspiring Cabbies Take Course before Taking Wheel," *New York Times*, April 8, 1984, https://www.nytimes.com/1984/04/08/nyregion/aspiring-cabbies-take-course-before-taking-wheel.html.

63. Sam Schwartz, interview with the author, February 27, 2021.

64. New York City Taxi and Limousine Commission, "New York City Taxi and Limousine Commission 2020 Annual Report," https://www1.nyc.gov/assets/tlc/downloads/pdf/001-annual-report-2020.pdf.

65. Ginia Bellafante, "Green Cabs Appear as Bloomberg Prepares to Depart," *New York Times*, September 22, 2013, https://www.nytimes.com/2013/09/22/nyregion/green-cabs-appear-as-bloomberg-prepares-to-depart.html.

66. New York City Taxi and Limousine Commission, "New York City Taxi and Limousine Commission 2011 Annual Report," https://www1.nyc.gov/assets/tlc/downloads/pdf/annual_report_2011.pdf.

67. New York City Department of Transportation, "The New York City Pedestrian Safety Study & Action Plan," August 2010, https://www1.nyc.gov/html/dot/downloads/pdf/nyc_ped_safety_study_action_plan.pdf.

68. New York City Council, "Report of the Taxi Medallion Task Force," January 2020, https://council.nyc.gov/data/wp-content/uploads/sites/73/2020/01/Taxi-Medallion-Task-Force-Report-Final.pdf.

69. "Uber's Plan to Get More People into Fewer Cars," TED, February 2016, https://www.ted.com/talks/travis_kalanick_uber_s_plan_to_get_more_people_into_fewer_cars/transcript.

70. "Last Trolleys Rolled in the City in 1957," *New York Times*, July 9, 1975, https://www.nytimes.com/1975/07/09/archives/last-trolleys-rolled-in-the-city-in-1957.html.

71. Metropolitan Transportation Authority, "Subway and Bus Ridership for 2019," https://new.mta.info/agency/new-york-city-transit/subway-bus-ridership-2019.

72. Joshua Brustein, "The Smartphone Way to Beckon a Car," *New York Times*, May 15, 2011, https://www.nytimes.com/2011/05/15/nyregion/uber-and-weeels-offer-car-services-by-phone-app.html.

73. Mike Isaac, "Lyft Expands Its Car Hailing Service to New York," *New York Times*, July 8, 2014, https://bits.blogs.nytimes.com/2014/07/08/lyft-expands-its-car-hailing-service-to-new-york-city/.

74. Matt Flegenheimer, "A Taxi Alternative, UberX, Offers Lower Fares," *New York Times*, July 8, 2014, https://www.nytimes.com/2014/07/08/nyregion/a-taxi-alternative-uberx-offers-lower-fares.html.

75. Uber Technologies, Inc., "Form S-1 Registration Statement," April 11, 2019, https://www.sec.gov/Archives/edgar/data/1543151/000119312519103850/d647752ds1.htm.

76. Dana Olsen, "Uber by the Numbers: A Timeline of the Company's Funding and Valuation History," PitchBook, November 29, 2017, https://pitchbook.com/news/articles/uber-by-the-numbers-a-timeline-of-the-companys-funding-and-valuation-history.

77. Uber, "Ride in Manhattan for $10 or less," July 10, 2015, https://www.uber.com/blog/new-york-city/ride-in-manhattan-for-10-or-less/.

78. New York City Taxi and Limousine Commission, "New York City Taxi and Limousine Commission 2015 Annual Report," https://www1.nyc.gov/assets/tlc/downloads/pdf/001-annual-report-2015.pdf.

79. New York City Department of Transportation, "New York City Mobility Report," August 2019, https://www1.nyc.gov/html/dot/downloads/pdf/mobility-report-print-2019.pdf.

80. Schaller Consulting, "UNSUSTAINABLE? The Growth of App-Based Ride Services and Traffic, Travel and the Future of New York City," February 27, 2017, http://www.schallerconsult.com/rideservices/unsustainable.pdf.

81. Schaller Consulting, "UNSUSTAINABLE?"

82. New York City Taxi and Limousine Commission, "2014 Fact Book," https://www1.nyc.gov/assets/tlc/downloads/pdf/2014_tlc_factbook.pdf.

83. New York City Taxi and Limousine Commission, "2016 Fact Book," https://www1.nyc.gov/assets/tlc/downloads/pdf/2016_tlc_factbook.pdf.

84. Patrick McGeehan, "New York City Council Explores the Woes of Hailing a Taxi," *New York Times*, December 4, 2014, https://www.nytimes.com/2014/12/04/nyregion/new-york-city-council-explores-the-woes-of-hailing-a-taxi.html.

85. Reem Nasr, "A Cap on the Number of Uber Cars in NYC?," CNBC, June 26, 2015, https://www.cnbc.com/2015/06/26/a-cap-on-the-number-of-uber-cars-in-nyc.html.

86. Colleen Wright, "Uber Says Proposed Freeze on Licenses in New York City Would Limit Competition," *New York Times*, July 1, 2015, https://www.nytimes.com/2015/07/01/nyregion/uber-says-proposed-freeze-on-licenses-would-limit-competition.html.

87. New York City Office of the Mayor, "Transcript: Mayor de Blasio Announces Department of Transportation Commencing Work on $100 Million Vision Zero Overhaul of Queens Boulevard," July 23, 2015, https://www1.nyc.gov/office-of-the-mayor/news/510-15/transcript-mayor-de-blasio-department-transportation-commencing-work-100-million.

88. Mike Isaac, "Uber Picks David Plouffe to Wage Regulatory Fight," *New York Times*, August 20, 2014, https://www.nytimes.com/2014/08/20/technology/uber-picks-a-political-insider-to-wage-its-regulatory-battles.html.

89. Fitz Tepper, "Uber Stages Protest at NYC City Hall," *TechCrunch*, June 30, 2015, https://techcrunch.com/2015/06/30/uber-stages-protest-at-nyc-city-hall-against-bill-throttling-new-driver-signups/.

90. Editorial board, "Limiting Uber Won't End Congestion," *New York Times*, July 18, 2015, https://www.nytimes.com/2015/07/18/opinion/limiting-uber-wont-end-congestion.html.

91. Farhad Manjoo, "With Uber, Less Reason to Own a Car," *New York Times*, June 12, 2014, https://www.nytimes.com/2014/06/12/technology/personaltech/with-ubers-cars-maybe-we-dont-need-our-own.html.

92. Jeremy B. Merrill and Alastair Coote, "Blame Uber for Congestion in Manhattan? Not So Fast," *New York Times*, July 28, 2015, https://www.nytimes.com/2015/07/28/upshot/blame-uber-for-congestion-in-manhattan-not-so-fast.html.

93. Adam Edelman, Alfred Ng, and Leonard Greene, "Kate Upton, Neil Patrick Harris, Ashton Kutcher Lead Twitter War on Mayor de Blasio over Controversial Bill That Would Cap Uber's Growth," *New York Daily News*, July 23, 2015, https://www.nydailynews.com/news/politics/kate-upton-leads-celebrity-charge-de-blasio-uber-article-1.2300747.

94. "Taxi Industry Gave De Blasio over $550,000 for Campaign," *New York Post*, May 17, 2014, https://nypost.com/2014/05/17/taxi-industry-gave-de-blasio-over-550000-for-campaign/.

95. William K. Rashbaum, Danny Hakim, Brian M. Rosenthal, Emily Flitter, and Jesse Drucker, "How Michael Cohen, Trump's Fixer, Built a Shadowy Business Empire," *New York Times*, May 5, 2018, https://www.nytimes.com/2018/05/05/business/michael-cohen-lawyer-trump.html.

96. Sam Roberts, "Gene Freidman, 'Taxi King' Who Upended His Industry, Dies at 50," *New York Times*, October 25, 2021, https://www.nytimes.com/2021/10/25/nyregion/gene-freidman-dead.html.

97. Pete Donohue, "Taxi Mogul to Pay $1.2 Million over Allegations He Was Ripping Off Cab Drivers," *New York Daily News*, December 19, 2013, https://www.nydailynews.com/new-york/taxi-mogul-pay-1-2m-alleged-rip-off-article-1.1552626; Brian M. Rosenthal and William K. Rashbaum, "Michael Cohen's Ex-Partner Gets Probation after Turning on Him," *New York Times*, October 30, 2019, https://www.nytimes.com/2019/10/30/nyregion/gene-freidman-taxi-medallion-michael-cohen.html.

98. Fitz Tepper, "Uber Launches de Blasio's Uber Feature in NYC with 25-Minute Wait Times," *TechCrunch*, July 16, 2015, https://techcrunch.com/2015/07/16/uber-launches-de-blasios-uber-feature-in-nyc-with-25-minute-wait-times/.

99. Edward T. Walker, "The Uber-ization of Activism," *New York Times*, August 7, 2015, https://www.nytimes.com/2015/08/07/opinion/the-uber-ization-of-activism.html?searchResultPosition=8.

100. The Brian Lehrer Show, "Is Ride-Sharing 'Color-Blind'?," WQXR, July 22, 2015, https://www.wqxr.org/story/ride-sharing-color-blind/.

101. Winnie Hu, "Uber, Surging Outside Manhattan, Tops Taxis in New York City," *New York Times*, October 12, 2017, https://www.nytimes.com/2017/10/12/nyregion/uber-taxis-new-york-city.html.

102. Will Bredderman, "Ripping de Blasio Uber Bill, Cuomo Calls E-Hail Apps 'Great Inventions,'" *Observer*, July 22, 2015, https://observer.com/2015/07/ripping-de-blasio-uber-bill-cuomo-calls-e-hail-apps-great-inventions/.

103. Matt Flegenheimer, "De Blasio Administration Dropping Plan for Uber Cap, for Now," *New York Times*, July 23, 2015, https://www.nytimes.com/2015/07/23/nyregion/de-blasio-administration-dropping-plan-for-uber-cap-for-now.html.

104. Tom Peters, "McKinsey's Work on Opioid Sales Represents a New Low," *Financial Times*, February 15, 2021, https://www.ft.com/content/82e98478-f099-44ac-b014-3f9b15fe6bc6.

105. Emma G. Fitzsimmons, "Uber Not to Blame for Rise in Manhattan Traffic Congestion, Report Says," *New York Times*, January 16, 2016, https://www.nytimes.com/2016/01/16/nyregion/uber-not-to-blame-for-rise-in-manhattan-traffic-congestion-report-says.html.

106. New York City Office of the Mayor, "For-Hire Vehicle Transportation Study," January 2016, https://www1.nyc.gov/assets/operations/downloads/pdf/For-Hire-Vehicle-Transportation-Study.pdf.

107. Doug Shifter, "To Those It May Concern," Facebook, February 5, 2018, https://www.facebook.com/people/Doug-Schifter/100009072541151.

108. Dan Rivoli, Edgar Sandoval, and Leonard Greene, "Distraught Livery Driver Killed Himself Weeks before Second City Hall Suicide," *New York Daily News*, February 6, 2018, https://www.nydailynews.com/new-york/distraught-driver-killed-weeks-city-hall-suicide-article-1.3803684.

109. Emma G. Fitzsimmons, "A Taxi Driver Took His Own Life. His Family Blames Uber's Influence," *New York Times*, May 1, 2018, https://www.nytimes.com/2018/05/01/nyregion/a-taxi-driver-took-his-own-life-his-family-blames-ubers-influence.html.

110. Danielle Furfaro and Max Jaeger, "Cabbies Lay Down Caskets in Protest of City's Taxi Rules," *New York Post*, March 28, 2018, https://nypost.com/2018/03/28/cabbies-lay-down-caskets-in-protest-of-citys-taxi-rules/.

111. Nikita Stewart and Luis Ferré-Sadurní, "Another Taxi Driver in Debt Takes His Life. That's 5 in 5 Months," *New York Times*, May 27, 2018, https://www.nytimes.com/2018/05/27/nyregion/taxi-driver-suicide-nyc.html.

112. Emma G. Fitzsimmons, "Uber Hit with Cap as New York City Takes Lead in Crackdown," *New York Times*, August 8, 2018, https://www.nytimes.com/2018/08/08/nyregion/uber-vote-city-council-cap.html.

113. Emma G. Fitzsimmons, "Taxi Drivers in New York Are Struggling. So Are Uber Drivers," *New York Times*, June 17, 2018, https://www.nytimes.com/2018/06/17/nyregion/uber-taxi-drivers-struggle.html.

114. Emma G. Fitzsimmons and Aaron Robertson, "Taxi and Uber Drivers Are United in Backing a Cap on Ride-Hail Vehicles," *New York Times*, August 6, 2018, https://www.nytimes.com/2018/08/06/nyregion/taxi-and-uber-drivers-are-united-in-backing-a-cap-on-ride-hail-vehicles.html.

115. James A. Parrott and Michael Reich, "An Earnings Standard for New York City's App-Based Drivers: July 2018 Economic Analysis and Policy Assessment," Report for the New York City Taxi and Limousine Commission, https://static1.squarespace.com/static/53ee4f0be4b015b9c3690d84/t/5b3a3aaa0e2e72ca74079142/1530542764109/Parrott-Reich+NYC+App+Drivers+TLC+Jul+2018jul1.pdf.

116. Schaller Consulting, "Empty Seats, Full Streets: Fixing Manhattan's Traffic Problem," December 21, 2017, http://www.schallerconsult.com/rideservices/emptyseats.htm.

117. Jeffrey C. Mays, "3 Years Ago, Uber Beat Back a Cap on Vehicles. What's Changed? A Lot," *New York Times*, August 9, 2018, https://www.nytimes.com/2018/08/09/nyregion/uber-cap-nyc-decision-strategy.html.

118. Fitzsimmons, "Uber Hit with Cap."

119. Tyler Pager and Emily Palmer, "Uber Driver's Death Marks Seventh For-Hire Driver Suicide Within a Year," *New York Times*, October 7, 2018, https://www.nytimes.com/2018/10/07/nyregion/uber-driver-suicide-for-hire-taxis-new-york.html.

120. Emma G. Fitzsimmons, "Why Are Taxi Drivers in New York Killing Themselves?," *New York Times*, December 2, 2018, https://www.nytimes.com/2018/12/02/nyregion/taxi-drivers-suicide-nyc.html.

121. New York City Taxi and Limousine Commission, "2018 Annual Report," https://www.nyc.gov/assets/tlc/downloads/pdf/annual_report_2018.pdf.

122. New York City Taxi and Limousine Commission, "2018 Fact Book," https://www1.nyc.gov/assets/tlc/downloads/pdf/2018_tlc_factbook.pdf.

123. Bruce Schaller, "Can Sharing a Ride Make for Less Traffic? Evidence from Uber and Lyft and Implications for Cities," *Transport Policy*, March 2021, http://www.schallerconsult.com/rideservices/sharingride.htm.

124. New York City Department of Transportation, "New York City Mobility Report," August 2019, https://www1.nyc.gov/html/dot/downloads/pdf/mobility-report-print-2019.pdf.

125. Stephen Edelstein, "Uber Lost $1.8 Billion in 2018 Despite Record Ride-Hailing, Food-Delivery Gains," *Drive*, February 16, 2019, https://www.thedrive.com/news/26514/uber-lost-1-8-billion-in-2018-despite-record-ride-hailing-food-delivery-gains.

126. Winnie Hu, "New York Attorney General Accuses N.Y.C. of Fraud over Taxi Crisis," *New York Times*, February 20, 2020, https://www.nytimes.com/2020/02/20/nyregion/nyc-taxi-medallion-lawsuit.html.

127. Brian M. Rosenthal, "'They Were Conned': How Reckless Loans Devastated a Generation of Taxi Drivers," *New York Times*, May 19, 2019, https://www.nytimes.com/2019/05/19/nyregion/nyc-taxis-medallions-suicides.html.

128. Nicole Gelinas, "New York City Taxi Drivers Need Debt Relief, But Not from Taxpayers," *City & State New York*, July 15, 2019, https://www.cityandstateny.com/opinion/2019/07/new-york-city-taxi-drivers-need-debt-relief-but-not-from-taxpayers/177162/.

129. Brian M. Rosenthal, "N.Y. Cabbies Stage Hunger Strike for More Aid: 'We're Not Backing Down,'" *New York Times*, November 1, 2021, https://www.nytimes.com/2021/11/01/nyregion/ny-taxi-drivers-hunger-strike.html.

130. New York City Office of the Mayor, "Taxi Medallion Relief Program Achieves Debt Relief for 144 Owners," October 23, 2021, https://www1.nyc.gov/office-of-the-mayor/news/706-21/taxi-medallion-relief-program-achieves-debt-relief-144-owners; Brian M. Rosenthal, "N.Y.C. Cabbies Win Millions More in Aid After Hunger Strike," *New York Times*, November 3, 2021, https://www.nytimes.com/2021/11/03/nyregion/nyc-taxi-drivers-hunger-strike.html.

131. Sam Roberts, "Gene Freidman, 'Taxi King' Who Upended His Industry, Dies at 50," *New York Times*, October 25, 2021, https://www.nytimes.com/2021/10/25/nyregion/gene-freidman-dead.html.

132. Peter Wayner, "The New York City Subway Is Beyond Repair," *Atlantic*, June 9, 2018, https://www.theatlantic.com/technology/archive/2018/06/the-new-york-city-subway-is-beyond-repair/562472/.

133. Schwartz, Samuel I., *No One at the Wheel: Driverless Cars and the Road of the Future* (New York: PublicAffairs, 2018), 185.

134. Casey Newton, "Uber Will Eventually Replace All Its Drivers with Self-Driving Cars," *Verge*, May 28, 2014, https://www.theverge.com/2014/5/28/5758734/uber-will-eventually-replace-all-its-drivers-with-self-driving-cars.

15. Thou Shalt Not Park Here: The Politics of Public Parking

1. Henry Grabar, *Paved Paradise: How Parking Explains the World* (New York: Penguin, 2023), xv.

2. New York City Planning Commission, "Selected Measures for Partial Traffic Relief in New York City," September 30, 1946, TBTA records, box 121-1.

3. New York City Department of Transportation, "New York City Mobility Report," October 2016, https://www1.nyc.gov/html/dot/downloads/pdf/mobility-report-2016-screen-optimized.pdf.

4. "20-Minute Parking Rule to Aid Traffic," *New York Times*, June 5, 1924, https://timesmachine.nytimes.com/timesmachine/1924/06/05/104039604.html.

5. "Broadway Closed to Cruising Cabs," *New York Times*, June 6, 1924, https://timesmachine.nytimes.com/timesmachine/1924/06/06/104040432.html.

6. "Jails 7 for Parking, Goodman Is Rebuked by M'Adoo," *New York Times*, November 11, 1927, https://timesmachine.nytimes.com/timesmachine/1927/11/11/94918251.html.

7. "Business Men Ask 'Park' Rule Changes," *New York Times*, November 20, 1924, https://timesmachine.nytimes.com/timesmachine/1924/11/20/101621600.html.

8. "Auto Parking Rule Changed to One Hour," *New York Times*, December 9, 1924, https://timesmachine.nytimes.com/timesmachine/1924/12/09/101624828.html.

9. "New Traffic Plan in Theatre Zone," *New York Times*, November 23, 1924, https://timesmachine.nytimes.com/timesmachine/1924/11/23/104162350.html.

10. "400 Police Drilled for Traffic Test," *New York Times*, January 20, 1929, https://timesmachine.nytimes.com/timesmachine/1929/01/20/91745268.html.

11. "Traffic Plan Faces First Test Tonight," *New York Times*, January 21, 1929, https://timesmachine.nytimes.com/timesmachine/1929/01/21/95711977.html.

12. "Police Map Tactics for Theatre Traffic," *New York Times*, January 17, 1929, https://timesmachine.nytimes.com/timesmachine/1929/01/17/95872749.html.

13. "Whalen to Ask Law Fining 'Jaywalkers,'" *New York Times*, January 16, 1929, https://timesmachine.nytimes.com/timesmachine/1929/01/16/95871717.html.

14. "Traffic Plan Faces First Test Tonight."

15. "Theatre Traffic Speeded 50% in Plan's First Test," *New York Times*, January 22, 1929, https://timesmachine.nytimes.com/timesmachine/1929/01/22/95874032.html.

16. "Taxi Travel Drops in Theatre Zone," *New York Times*, January 22, 1929, https://timesmachine.nytimes.com/timesmachine/1929/01/22/95874050.html.

17. "Traffic Plan Stays, Whalen Declares," *New York Times*, January 26, 1929, https://timesmachine.nytimes.com/timesmachine/1929/01/26/95875373.html.

18. "Curb Will Continue on Theatre Traffic," *New York Times*, February 5, 1929, https://timesmachine.nytimes.com/timesmachine/1929/02/05/95729131.html.

19. R. L. Duffus, "Trying to Unlock the Wheels of Traffic," *New York Times*, January 20, 1929, https://timesmachine.nytimes.com/timesmachine/1929/01/20/91746681.html.

20. "Police to Seize All Autos Parked Illegally without Wasting Time Issuing Summonses," *New York Times*, March 31, 1929, https://timesmachine.nytimes.com/timesmachine/1929/03/31/95897673.html.

21. Editorial board, "Opposing the Tow-Off," *New York Times*, February 14, 1930, https://timesmachine.nytimes.com/timesmachine/1930/02/14/96048313.pdf.

22. "Whalen Advocates Ban on All Parking below 61st Street," *New York Times*, February 3, 1930, https://timesmachine.nytimes.com/timesmachine/1930/02/03/95747282.html.

23. "Civic Traffic Board Urges 'Auto Hotels,'" *New York Times*, May 15, 1929, https://timesmachine.nytimes.com/timesmachine/1929/05/15/issue.html.

24. "Theatre Parking Ban Lifted for Summer; Mulrooney Weighs New Rules for Trucking," *New York Times*, July 9, 1930, https://www.nytimes.com/1930/07/09/archives/theatre-parking-ban-lifted-for-summer-mulrooney-weighs-new-rules.html.

25. "Broadway Fights to End Parking Ban," *New York Times*, February 4, 1933, https://timesmachine.nytimes.com/timesmachine/1933/02/04/99291017.html.

26. "Police Deaf to Motorists' Plea for Less Stringent Parking Rules," *New York Times*, October 24, 1935, https://timesmachine.nytimes.com/timesmachine/1935/10/24/101515014.pdf.

27. "Police Deaf to Motorists' Plea."

28. "Cities Try Out Traffic Cures," *New York Times*, January 2, 1938, https://timesmachine.nytimes.com/timesmachine/1938/01/02/99530649.html.

29. "84 Get Summonses in No-Parking Area," *New York Times*, January 11, 1938, https://timesmachine.nytimes.com/timesmachine/1938/01/11/96775430.html.

30. "New Rules Listed on Traffic Fines," *New York Times*, September 28, 1940, https://timesmachine.nytimes.com/timesmachine/1940/09/28/94002086.html.

31. E. L. Yordan, "City Parker Studied," *New York Times*, November 29, 1936, https://timesmachine.nytimes.com/timesmachine/1936/11/29/93326173.html.

32. Joseph C. Ingraham, "15,000 New Parking Meters Urged," *New York Times*, May 15, 1953, https://timesmachine.nytimes.com/timesmachine/1953/05/12/issue.html.

33. "More Powers Voted to the Meter Maids," *New York Times*, January 27, 1965, https://timesmachine.nytimes.com/timesmachine/1965/01/27/95523480.pdf.

34. "'Meter-Maid' Bill Passed by Council," *New York Times*, August 14, 1959, https://timesmachine.nytimes.com/timesmachine/1959/08/14/80543196.html.

35. "6,000 Hopefuls Seek 100 Meter Maid Jobs," *New York Times*, October 8, 1959, https://timesmachine.nytimes.com/timesmachine/1959/10/08/88827767.html.

36. American Retail Federation, "Keep Customers Coming: Practical Suggestions for Obtaining Off-Street Parking," via TBTA records, box 121-1.

37. "700-Car Garage Opens," *New York Times*, December 9, 1952, https://timesmachine.nytimes.com/timesmachine/1952/12/09/93594900.html.

38. Milton Esterow, "Hudson Theatre Sold by N.B.C.; Garage Will Be Erected on Site," *New York Times*, September 14, 1961, https://timesmachine.nytimes.com/timesmachine/1961/09/14/118925963.pdf.

39. Sam Zolotow, "Producer Stalls Theater's Razing," *New York Times*, October 18, 1961, https://timesmachine.nytimes.com/timesmachine/1961/10/18/97253530.html.

40. "New Parking Lots Planned by Moses," *New York Times*, August 18, 1949.

41. "Digest of City Planning Group Report on Relieving Traffic Here," *New York Times*, November 14, 1946, https://timesmachine.nytimes.com/timesmachine/1946/11/14/93177726.html.

42. Letter from Lawrence Paul Wolf to Robert Moses, August 13, 1946, via TBTA records, box 121-1.

43. Letter from Wolf to Moses, TBTA records, box 121-1.

44. Letter from Robert Moses to mayor, August 14, 1946, via TBTA records, box 121-1.

45. David McConnell, "O'Dwyer Hunts Solution to City Traffic Jams," *New York Herald Tribune*, July 14, 1946.

46. George Spargo, letter to Baltimore's Downtown Committee on parking, September 23, 1946, via TBTA records, box 121-1.

47. "Moses Warns City Garages Must Pay Way," *New York Herald Tribune*, July 21, 1947.

48. Murray Snyder, "Mayor to Urge City to Set Up 6 Parking Lots," *New York Herald Tribune*, August 13, 1946.

49. "City Will Survey Parking Facilities in Subway System," *New York Times*, July 29, 1946.

50. McConnell, "O'Dwyer Hunts Solution to City Traffic Jams."

51. "Battery Garage Opens Tomorrow," *New York Times*, June 30, 1950, https://timesmachine.nytimes.com/timesmachine/1950/06/30/91106971.html.

52. "450 Cars to Be Parked on Roof of Bus Terminal," *New York Times*, December 14, 1950.

53. "Autos Inside Coliseum Cause a Jam Outside," *New York Times*, December 10, 1956, https://timesmachine.nytimes.com/timesmachine/1956/12/10/105220916.html.

54. "Mayor Names Detroit Expert to Traffic Post: Wiley to Head Engineering," *New York Herald Tribune*, February 2, 1949.

55. "Compromise Terms on Parking Passed," *New York Times*, March 23, 1950, https://timesmachine.nytimes.com/timesmachine/1950/03/23/113146449.html.

56. "Traffic Aid Plans Put to City Board," *New York Times*, February 5, 1954.

57. "City Will Seek Right to Build Public Garages: Facilities for 40,000," *New York Herald Tribune*, January 10, 1952.

58. Robert Moses, Remarks at the Opening of the East Side Airlines Terminal, November 30, 1953, via TBTA records, box 136-2.

59. Leo Widlicka, "Group Bars Moses Plan for Garages," *New York Herald Tribune*, October 14, 1953.

60. Joseph C. Ingraham, "Parking Lots Here to Increase Rates," *New York Times*, September 30, 1953, https://timesmachine.nytimes.com/timesmachine/1953/09/30/84064242.pdf.

61. "Traffic Aid Plans Put to City Board."

62. Don Ross, "Plan Association Supports Wiley Parking Program," *New York Herald Tribune*, April 4, 1960.

63. Joseph C. Ingraham, "Mid-City Garages for 10,000 Autos Urged by Wiley," *New York Times*, January 18, 1960.

64. Stanley Levey, "Quill Denounces City Garage Plan," *New York Times*, January 20, 1960.

65. Joseph C. Ingraham, "Mayor Is Backed on 42d St. Garage," *New York Times*, December 4, 1961, https://timesmachine.nytimes.com/timesmachine/1961/12/04/119430014.html.

66. Thomas P. Ronan, "Barnes Dropping Plans for Garage," *New York Times*, December 24, 1965, https://timesmachine.nytimes.com/timesmachine/1965/12/24/96726523.pdf.

67. Editorial board, "Wrong Way on Every Count," *New York Times*, August 28, 1965, https://timesmachine.nytimes.com/timesmachine/1965/08/28/96716334.pdf.

68. Charles G. Bennett, "Planning Board Loses Power Bid," *New York Times*, August 27, 1965, https://timesmachine.nytimes.com/timesmachine/1965/08/27/101565314.pdf.

69. Joseph Mc C. Leiper, New York City Department of City Planning, "Transportation Policy-Making in New York," October 1966, via TBTA records, unboxed.

70. Transportation Council Off-Street Parking Committee, "A Policy on Off-Street Parking for the City of New York," draft, December 1966, via TBTA records, box 107-4.

71. Robert Moses, "Safety and Our Highways," *Newsday*, September 24, 1966.

72. Automobile Club of New York, "The Automobile in New York City, A Statement," February 1966, via TBTA records, box 107-4.

73. *Long Island Star-Journal*, January 26, 1966, via TBTA records, box 107-3.

74. Auto Club, "Statement by Charles Murphy, Vice President, Before City Council, on Transportation Consolidation," January 27, 1967, via TBTA records, box 110-4.

75. Transportation Council Off-Street Parking Committee, "Policy on Off-Street Parking for the City of New York."

76. Edward Hudson, "The Mayor Plans New Traffic Unit," *New York Times*, December 24, 1972, https://www.nytimes.com/1972/12/24/archives/the-mayor-plans-new-traffic-unit-advocates-use-of-civilians-for.html.

77. "Lindsay's 'Official' Car Gets a Ticket for Parking," *New York Times*, November 18, 1965, https://timesmachine.nytimes.com/timesmachine/1965/11/18/95915096.pdf.

78. "Lindsay Lauds Officer Who Tagged His Car," *New York Times*, November 19, 1965, https://timesmachine.nytimes.com/timesmachine/1965/11/19/95002969.pdf.

79. Editorial board, "New York Program: Traffic," *New York Times*, December 22, 1965, https://timesmachine.nytimes.com/timesmachine/1965/12/22/95921375.pdf.

80. New York State Department of Environmental Conservation, "New York City Metropolitan Area Air Quality Implementation Plan Transportation Controls," April 1973, Ketcham papers.

81. Editorial board, "New York Parking Crisis," *New York Times*, January 20, 1967, https://timesmachine.nytimes.com/timesmachine/1967/01/20/82569151.html.

82. "Auto Club Bids City Reinstate Towing to Clear Midtown," *New York Times*, December 21, 1964, https://www.nytimes.com/1964/12/21/archives/auto-club-bids-city-reinstate-towing-to-clear-midtown.html.

83. Terence Smith, "New Drive Begun on Double Parking in Theater District," *New York Times*, January 29, 1966, https://timesmachine.nytimes.com/timesmachine/1966/01/29/79294469.pdf.

84. Alfred E. Clark, "Towaway Policy Angers Motorists," *New York Times*, September 17, 1966, https://timesmachine.nytimes.com/timesmachine/1966/09/17/121031508.html.

85. "Police Expanding Towaway Drive," *New York Times*, September 16, 1966, https://timesmachine.nytimes.com/timesmachine/1966/09/16/82511191.html.

86. Clark, "Towaway Policy Angers Motorists."

87. "Towaway Drive Will Cover Area South of 72d St.," *New York Times*, December 18, 1966, https://timesmachine.nytimes.com/timesmachine/1966/12/18/90241401.pdf.

88. Editorial board, "Traffic Flows Again," *New York Times*, January 26, 1967, https://timesmachine.nytimes.com/timesmachine/1967/01/26/82578156.html.

89. Alfred E. Clark, "Mayor's Car Is Double-Parked, in Towaway Zone, by a Hydrant," *New York Times*, January 22, 1967, https://timesmachine.nytimes.com/timesmachine/1967/01/22/89658104.pdf.

90. Terence Smith, "Towaway Plan Greeted with Dismay," *New York Times*, January 21, 1967, https://timesmachine.nytimes.com/timesmachine/1967/01/21/82993656.html.

91. Seth S. King, "Mayor Deprives 3 Aides of Parking for 2 Weeks for Illegal Parking," *New York Times*, February 12, 1967, https://timesmachine.nytimes.com/timesmachine/1967/02/12/82580115.pdf.

92. Bernard Weinraub, "Scofflaw Pays for 156 Tickets and Lectures City on Parking," *New York Times*, August 3, 1966, https://timesmachine.nytimes.com/timesmachine/1966/08/03/82867262.html.

93. Editorial board, "Do They Mean It This Time?," *New York Times*, July 19, 1966, https://timesmachine.nytimes.com/timesmachine/1966/07/19/96974743.html.

94. Alfonso A. Narvaez, "City's New Parking Violation Bureau Speeds Hearing of Cases," *New York Times*, January 31, 1971, https://www.nytimes.com/1971/01/31/archives/citys-new-parking-violation-bureau-speeds-hearing-of-cases.html.

95. "Mayor Sets Worth of Parking Agency at 156 Policemen," *New York Times*, May 10, 1971, https://www.nytimes.com/1971/05/10/archives/mayor-sets-worth-of-parking-agency-at-156-policemen.html.

96. "City Enlists Bank and Computer Concern in Its War on Scofflaws," *New York Times*, May 25, 1967, https://timesmachine.nytimes.com/timesmachine/1967/05/25/82160411.html.

97. Joseph C. Ingraham, "City to Ban Meter Parking in Midtown by November," *New York Times*, January 6, 1970, https://www.nytimes.com/1970/01/06/archives/city-to-ban-meter-parking-in-midtown-by-november-midtown-meter.html.

98. Arnold H. Lubasch, "New Strict No-Parking Rules Appear to Speed Traffic in Financial District," *New York Times*, September 22, 1970, https://www.nytimes.com/1970/09/22/archives/new-strict-noparking-rules-appear-to-speed-traffic-in-financial.html.

99. Frank J. Prial, "City to Initiate a Program of Strict Traffic Controls," *New York Times*, June 3, 1973, https://www.nytimes.com/1973/06/03/archives/city-to-initiate-a-program-of-strict-traffic-controls-starting-july.html.

100. Frank J. Prial, "Traffic Plan Set for All Midtown," *New York Times*, June 12, 1973, https://www.nytimes.com/1973/06/12/archives/traffic-plan-set-for-all-midtown-aim-of-new-system-is-to-rid-area.html.

101. Prial, "City to Initiate a Program."

102. Edward Hudson, "Show No Mercy, Mayor Tells the Police in Pressing Midtown Parking Program," *New York Times*, June 28, 1973, https://www.nytimes.com/1973/06/28/archives/show-no-mercy-mayor-tells-the-police-in-pressing-midtown-parking.html.

103. Edward Hudson, "Midtown Traffic Termed 'A Little Better' by Mayor," *New York Times*, July 4, 1973, https://www.nytimes.com/1973/07/04/archives/midtown-traffic-termed-a-little-better-by-mayor-contrast-with.html.

104. Frank J. Prial, "Traffic Plan Wins Initial Approval," *New York Times*, June 13, 1973, https://www.nytimes.com/1973/06/13/archives/traffic-plan-wins-initial-approval-but-lindsays-madison-mall.html.

105. Frank J. Prial, "Illegal Parkers Pose a Burden on the City," *New York Times*, August 5, 1971, https://www.nytimes.com/1971/08/05/archives/illegal-parkers-pose-a-burden-on-the-city-incidence-of-illegal.html.

106. Lawrence Van Gelder, "State Troopers Sent into City as Crime Rises," *New York Times*, July 14, 1977, https://www.nytimes.com/1977/07/14/archives/state-troopers-sent-into-city-as-crime-rises-some-civilians-assist.html.

107. Robert D. McFadden, "100 Policemen Hurt," *New York Times*, July 15, 1977, https://www.nytimes.com/1977/07/15/archives/100-policemen-hurt-thousands-of-false-alarms-add-to-problems.html.

108. Robert D. McFadden, ".44 Killer Wounds 12th and 13th Victims," *New York Times*, August 1, 1977, https://www.nytimes.com/1977/08/01/archives/44-killer-wounds-12th-and-13th-victims-he-strikes-in-brooklyn-for.html.

109. Richard Edmonds, William Federici, and William Sherman, "Parking Ticket Was the Key to Catching Son of Sam," *New York Daily News*, August 12, 1977, https://www.nydailynews.com/new-york/nyc-crime/clues-1-ticket-catch-son-sam-article-1.3370198.

110. Maurice Carroll, "Vast Plaza Project at City Hall Would Raze Tweed Courthouse," *New York Times*, March 24, 1974, https://www.nytimes.com/1974/03/24/archives/vast-plaza-project-at-city-hall-would-raze-tweed-courthouse.html.

111. Carroll, "Vast Plaza Project."

112. "Group Near Columbia Prefers Its Garage to a Public Library," *New York Times*, October 28, 1974, https://www.nytimes.com/1974/10/28/archives/group-near-columbia-prefers-its-garage-to-a-public-library.html; Emily M. Bernstein, "Room for Books or Cars, Not Both," *New York Times*, October 3, 1993, https://www.nytimes.com/1993/10/03/nyregion/neighborhood-report-upper-west-side-room-for-books-or-cars-not-both.html; Janet Allon, "Dormitory Plan: One Minus, Many Pluses," *New York Times*, February 22, 1998, https://www.nytimes.com/1998/02/22/nyregion/neighborhood-report-morningside-heights-dormitory-plan-one-minus-many-pluses.html.

113. "Motorists to Be Allowed to Park at Most of 14,000 Broken Meters," *New York Times*, November 17, 1977, https://www.nytimes.com/1977/11/17/archives/motorists-to-be-allowed-to-park-at-most-of-14000-broken-meters.html.

114. "Carey, Beame Agree on Air-Code Move," *New York Times*, April 20, 1975, https://www.nytimes.com/1975/04/20/archives/carey-beams-agree-on-aircode-move.html.

115. Lee Dembart, "Broad Parking Ban in Manhattan Begins as Mayor Yields to Ruling," *New York Times*, June 16, 1977, https://www.nytimes.com/1977/06/16/archives/broad-parking-ban-in-manhattan-begins-as-mayor-yields-to-ruling-206.html.

116. Editorial board, "Pollution Paralysis," *New York Times*, May 6, 1974, https://www.nytimes.com/1974/05/06/archives/pollution-paralysis.html.

117. Editorial board, "The Case for Tolls," *New York Times*, October 7, 1975, https://www.nytimes.com/1975/10/07/archives/the-case-for-tolls.html.

118. Editorial board, "The Parking Farce, Cntd.," *New York Times*, June 25, 1977.

119. Editorial board, "Parking Farce."

120. Fred Ferretii, "New York Now Says Parking Edict Means Loss of 12,700 Spaces," *New York Times*, June 17, 1977, https://www.nytimes.com/1977/06/17/archives/new-jersey-pages-new-york-now-says-parking-edict-means-loss-of.html.

121. Ross Sandler and David Schoenbrod, "On City Parking Restrictions," letter, *New York Times*, June 25, 1977, https://www.nytimes.com/1977/06/25/archives/letter-on-city-parking-restrictions.html.

122. Frank I. Prial, "New Clean-Air Plan to Curb Auto Fumes Is Submitted by City," *New York Times*, July 7, 1977, https://www.nytimes.com/1977/07/07/archives/new-cleanair-plan-to-curb-auto-fumes-is-submitted-by-city-a.html.

123. John B. Oakes, "Beame's Smoggy View," *New York Times*, July 8, 1977, https://www.nytimes.com/1977/07/08/archives/mayor-beames-smoggy-view.html.

124. Lee Dembart, "New York Wins Clean-Air Accord, Easing Limit on Downtown Parking," *New York Times*, August 19, 1977.

125. New York City Department of City Planning, "Manhattan Core Public Parking Study," December 2011, https://www1.nyc.gov/assets/planning/download/pdf/plans/manhattan-core-public-parking/mncore_study.pdf.

126. Lee Dembart, "Koch, in Inaugural, Asks That Pioneers 'Come East' to City," *New York Times*, January 2, 1978, https://www.nytimes.com/1978/01/02/archives/koch-in-inaugural-asks-that-pioneers-come-east-to-city-key.html.

127. Leslie Maitland, "Justice for the Unjust Parking Tickets," *New York Times*, January 11, 1979, https://www.nytimes.com/1979/01/11/archives/justice-for-the-unjust-parking-tickets-justice-for-all-those-unjust.html.

128. "Koch Makes Example of Scofflaw's Porsche," *New York Times*, June 22, 1979, https://www.nytimes.com/1979/06/22/archives/koch-makes-example-of-scofflaws-porsche.html.

129. Ari L. Goldman, "Bus-Only Lanes to Be Increased to Speed Travel," *New York Times*, June 15, 1982, https://www.nytimes.com/1982/06/15/nyregion/bus-only-lanes-to-be-increased-to-speed-travel.html; "Buses Get Own 5th Ave. Lane in a New Bid to Ease Tie-Ups," *New York Times*, June 16, 1983, https://www.nytimes.com/1983/06/16/nyregion/buses-get-own-5th-ave-lane-in-a-new-bid-to-ease-tie-ups.html.

130. Selwyn Raab, "Accord Reached in Investigation of City Awards," *New York Times*, January 29, 1986, https://www.nytimes.com/1986/01/29/nyregion/accord-reached-in-investigation-of-city-awards.html.

131. Editorial board, "The Manes Nightmare," *New York Times*, January 16, 1986, https://www.nytimes.com/1986/01/16/opinion/the-manes-nightmare.html.

132. Richard J. Meisin, "Manes's Death: A Frantic Call, a Fatal Thrust," *New York Times*, March 15, 1986, https://www.nytimes.com/1986/03/15/nyregion/manes-s-death-a-frantic-call-a-fatal-thrust.html.

133. James Barron, "Tangled Strands: Anatomy of the New York City Scandal," *New York Times*, March 23, 1987, https://www.nytimes.com/1987/03/23/nyregion/tangled-strands-anatomy-of-the-new-york-city-scandal.html.

134. Bruce Schaller, "CITYinFLUX: Understanding and Untangling Traffic and Transportation in NYC," Schaller Consulting, April 2007, http://www.schallerconsult.com/pub/cityinflux.pdf.

135. Morris Kaplan, "A City Aide Admits Parking-Ticket Fix; Will Testify against Two Co-Defendants," *New York Times*, November 27, 1973, https://www.nytimes.com/1973/11/27/archives/a-city-aide-admits-parkingticket-fix-will-testify-against-two.html.

136. Morris Kaplan, "Levy Ticket-Fixing Trial Told of Officials' Payoffs," *New York Times*, December 4, 1973, https://www.nytimes.com/1973/12/04/archives/levy-ticketfixing-trial-told-of-officials-payoffs-cutrate-prices.html.

137. Editorial board, "Free Parking," *New York Times*, March 7, 2008, https://www.nytimes.com/2008/03/07/opinion/07fri4.html.

138. New York City Department of Transportation, "Street Parking Rates," accessed April 10, 2022, https://www1.nyc.gov/html/dot/html/motorist/parking-rates.shtml#rates.

139. New York City Department of Finance, "Violation Codes, Fines, Rules & Regulations," accessed April 10, 2022, https://www1.nyc.gov/site/finance/vehicles/services-violation-codes.page.

140. New York City Department of City Planning, "Manhattan Core Public Parking Study," December 2011, https://www1.nyc.gov/assets/planning/download/pdf/plans/manhattan-core-public-parking/mncore_study.pdf.

16. Our Right to Park: The High Cost of Residential Parking

1. ABC News, "ABC News Special Report: America Under Attack," September 11, 2001.

2. Christopher Gray, "When Streets Were Vehicles for Traffic, Not Parking," *New York Times*, March 17, 1996, https://www.nytimes.com/1996/03/17/realestate/streetscapes-cars-when-streets-were-vehicles-for-traffic-not-parking.html.

3. "Mulrooney Is Assailed on Night Parking Policy," *New York Herald Tribune*, December 10, 1931.

4. "Police to Seize Autos Parked Out All Night," *New York Herald Tribune*, July 12, 1934.

5. "Overnight Parker Fined $5 on His $5 Automobile: Magistrate Burke Continues War on Unsafe Rattletraps," *New York Herald Tribune*, May 13, 1936.

6. "Parking Held Crux of Traffic Puzzle," *New York Times*, February 24, 1937, https://timesmachine.nytimes.com/timesmachine/1937/02/24/99106920.html.

7. "Parking Ban Excepts Few," *New York Times*, December 14, 1938, https://timesmachine.nytimes.com/timesmachine/1938/12/14/98873217.pdf.

8. New York City Department of Transportation, "New York City Mobility Report," October 2016, https://www1.nyc.gov/html/dot/downloads/pdf/mobility-report-2016-screen-optimized.pdf.

9. "Police Lift Ban on Night Parking," *New York Times*, April 4, 1947, https://timesmachine.nytimes.com/timesmachine/1947/04/04/87516618.html.

10. Joseph C. Ingraham, "Overnight Parking Ban Is Official," *New York Times*, April 5, 1947, https://timesmachine.nytimes.com/timesmachine/1947/04/05/87729015.pdf.

11. "Parking Ban Excepts Few."

12. Lee E. Cooper, "Garages Legalized in Apartment Buildings," *New York Times*, June 9, 1939, https://timesmachine.nytimes.com/timesmachine/1939/06/09/93926982.html.

13. "New Parking Curb Adopted by Board," *New York Times*, July 21, 1950, https://timesmachine.nytimes.com/timesmachine/1950/07/21/113166864.pdf.

14. Editorial board, "Requiring Garage Space," *New York Times*, July 3, 1950, https://timesmachine.nytimes.com/timesmachine/1950/07/03/91107698.pdf.

15. Milton Lewis, "Police War on Parking at Projects: Tag Stuyvesant Town, Peter Cooper Village Tenants," *New York Herald Tribune*, September 11, 1957.

16. Alexander Rubin, "Motorists' Dilemma: Garages Full and Overnight Street Parking Forbidden," letter to the editor, *New York Herald Tribune*, March 12, 1947.

17. Ingraham, "Overnight Parking Ban Is Official."

18. Henry Volk, "The Parking Problem: Reader Tells of Cars Lining City Curbs," *New York Herald Tribune*, October 16, 1949.

19. "Uptown Garages Are Found Ample," *New York Times*, July 5, 1949, https://timesmachine.nytimes.com/timesmachine/1949/07/05/96464020.html.

20. Howard Cohn, "No Parking Mon Wed Fri; Alternate Parking Rules Keep Motorists Grimly on the Move," *New York Times,* October 18, 1959, https://www.nytimes.com/1959/10/18/archives/no-parking-mon-wed-fri-alternate-parking-rules-keep-motorists.html.

21. Arthur Gelb, "Parking to Shift from Side to Side of Streets to Allow for Cleaning," *New York Times*, July 20, 1950, https://timesmachine.nytimes.com/timesmachine/1950/07/20/94268305.pdf.

22. Cohn, "No Parking Mon Wed Fri."

23. A. E. Hotchner, "Are You a Traffic Neurotic?," *New York Herald Tribune*, March 22, 1953.

24. "Finding a Spot to Park," *New York Herald Tribune*, November 25, 1954.

25. "New Parking Code Arouses Protests," *New York Times*, November 23, 1954, https://timesmachine.nytimes.com/timesmachine/1954/11/23/84438883.html.

26. R. Bernstein, "Parking Hours Protested," letter, *New York Times*, October 8, 1955, https://timesmachine.nytimes.com/timesmachine/1955/10/08/83780955.pdf.

27. Joseph C. Ingraham, "72-Hour Parking Set for 600,000," *New York Times*, November 22, 1954, https://timesmachine.nytimes.com/timesmachine/1954/11/22/84438263.html.

28. Charles G. Bennett, "City Board Kills Night Parking Fee," *New York Times*, April 22, 1952, https://timesmachine.nytimes.com/timesmachine/1952/04/22/84251952.html.

29. Editorial board, "Overnight Parking Fees," *New York Times*, September 2, 1961, https://timesmachine.nytimes.com/timesmachine/1961/09/02/98542256.html.

30. City Planning Commission and New York City Department of City Planning, "The City of New York Zoning Guidebook," 1961, https://www1.nyc.gov/assets/planning/download/pdf/about/city-planning-history/zoning_handbook_1961.pdf.

31. "Main Points of New Zoning Plan for a More Orderly, Less Cramped City of Future," *New York Times*, February 16, 1959, https://timesmachine.nytimes.com/timesmachine/1959/02/16/83671927.html.

32. Edward Ranzal, "Civilians Prepare to Direct Traffic," *New York Times*, August 21, 1973, https://www.nytimes.com/1973/08/21/archives/civilians-prepare-to-direct-traffic-first-of-force-of-500-will-work.html.

33. "Cars Impeding Fire-Fighting Face Ban," *New York Times*, August 3, 1971, https://timesmachine.nytimes.com/timesmachine/1971/08/03/79146791.pdf.

34. Edward Hudson, "Fire Fatality Laid to Illegal Parkers," *New York Times*, August 26, 1972, https://www.nytimes.com/1972/08/26/archives/fire-fatality-laid-to-illegal-parkers-illegal-parkers-blamed-in.html.

35. "Village vs. Meters," *Village Voice*, August 12, 1971.

36. Frank J. Prial, "Illegal Parkers Pose a Burden on the City," *New York Times*, August 5, 1971, https://www.nytimes.com/1971/08/05/archives/illegal-parkers-pose-a-burden-on-the-city-incidence-of-illegal.html.

37. James Barron, "Car Owners vs. the Odds," *New York Times*, September 19, 1993, https://www.nytimes.com/1993/09/19/nyregion/car-owners-vs-the-odds.html.

38. Ivan Berger, "Coping with Car Stereo Theft," *New York Times*, June 23, 1990, https://www.nytimes.com/1990/06/23/style/consumer-s-world-coping-with-car-stereo-theft.html.

39. Kathleen Brady, "City Car Owners: Joys and Sorrows," *New York Times*, April 19, 1984, www.nytimes.com/1984/04/19/garden/city-car-owners-joys-and-sorrows.html.

40. Bruce Schaller, "CITYinFLUX: Understanding and Untangling Traffic and Transportation in NYC," April 2007.

41. "Community Board 6 Votes 'No' to Queens Boulevard Redesign," *Forest Hills Post*, June 14, 2018, https://foresthillspost.com/community-board-6-votes-no-to-queens-boulevard-redesign.

42. David Meyer, "B82 Select Bus Service—Kneecapped by Marty Golden and Co.—Will Start on Monday," *Streetsblog*, September 26, 2018, https://nyc.streetsblog.org/2018/09/26/b82-select-bus-service-kneecapped-by-marty-golden-and-co-will-start-on-monday/.

43. Gersh Kuntzman, "Cycle of Rage: NIMBY Lawyer Arthur Schwartz Sees Himself as Jane Jacobs Fighting Robert Moses," *Streetsblog*, January 14, 2019, https://nyc.streetsblog.org/2019/01/14/cycle-of-rage-nimby-lawyer-arthur-schwartz-sees-himself-as-jane-jacobs-fighting-robert-moses/.

44. Sewell Chan, "Putting the Park Back in Parking," *New York Times*, September 21, 2007, https://cityroom.blogs.nytimes.com/2007/09/21/putting-the-park-back-in-parking.

45. Howard Yaruss, interview with the author, December 30, 2021.

46. Donald Shoup, interview with the author, January 19, 2022.

47. "Abolish All Free On-Street Parking, UWS Community Board Committee Says," *West Side Rag*, May 31, 2019, https://www.westsiderag.com/2019/05/31/abolish-all-free-on-street-parking-uws-community-board-committee-says.

48. James Barron, "Could New York City Eliminate Free Street Parking?," *New York Times*, November 20, 2019, https://www.nytimes.com/2019/11/20/nyregion/nyc-street-parking.html.

49. Alex Israel, "End 'Free Parking' on the Upper West Side? Community Board Tones Down Language in Resolution," *West Side Rag*, November 14, 2019, https://www.westsiderag.com/2019/11/14/end-free-parking-on-the-upper-west-side-community-board-tones-down-language-in-resolution.

17. Fast Forward: Plans to Fix New York's Bus System

1. Metropolitan Transportation Authority, "Comprehensive Annual Financial Report for the Years Ended December 31, 2012 and 2011," June 21, 2013, http://web.mta.info/mta/investor/pdf/2012/2012-Comprehensive-Annual-Financial-Report.pdf; Metropolitan Transportation Authority, "Subway and Bus Ridership for 2019," https://new.mta.info/agency/new-york-city-transit/subway-bus-ridership-2019.

2. Metropolitan Transportation Authority, "New York City Travel Survey," June 30, 2020, https://new.mta.info/document/28971.

3. Everett A. White, "Surface Transit Facilities" (letter), *New York Times*, May 16, 1947, https://timesmachine.nytimes.com/timesmachine/1947/05/16/88782218.pdf.

4. Peter Kihss, "Transit System Cost 2.1 Billion," *New York Times*, April 13, 1959, https://timesmachine.nytimes.com/timesmachine/1959/04/13/83680991.pdf.

5. Stanley Levey, "City's Buses Turn Loss into Surplus," *New York Times*, August 7, 1957, https://timesmachine.nytimes.com/timesmachine/1957/08/07/90828940.pdf.

6. Leonard Ingalls, "More Cuts Asked in Transit System," *New York Times*, September 10, 1954, https://timesmachine.nytimes.com/timesmachine/1954/09/10/93408902.pdf.

"15c Far Costlier to Surface Lines," *New York Times*, July 25, 1954, https://timesmachine.nytimes.com/timesmachine/1954/07/25/92594633.pdf.

7. "TV Found Factor in Transit Traffic Drop," *New York Times*, October 22, 1953, https://timesmachine.nytimes.com/timesmachine/1953/10/22/83823464.pdf.

8. Benjamin Fischler, "Thoughts of a Bus Rider" (letter), *New York Times*, October 13, 1948, https://timesmachine.nytimes.com/timesmachine/1948/10/13/93797613.pdf.

9. Leo Egan, "City Bus Service Ordered Speeded," *New York Times*, April 8, 1949, https://timesmachine.nytimes.com/timesmachine/1949/04/08/96452893.pdf.

10. Leonard Ingalls, "Private Bus Lines Win 3c Fare Rise Effective Today," *New York Times*, January 1, 1954, https://timesmachine.nytimes.com/timesmachine/1954/01/01/83743475.pdf.

11. Stanley Levey, "Transit Is Facing $4,000,000 Deficit," *New York Times*, January 4, 1955, https://timesmachine.nytimes.com/timesmachine/1955/01/04/83343855.pdf.

12. A. H. Raskin, "$5,000,000 Needed to Replace Buses," *New York Times*, July 27, 1955, https://timesmachine.nytimes.com/timesmachine/1955/07/27/83364394.pdf.

13. Leonard Ingalls, "The Transit Authority: A Balance Sheet for First 18 Months," *New York Times*, December 14, 1954, https://timesmachine.nytimes.com/timesmachine/1954/12/14/96516279.pdf.

14. Editorial board, "Riding in Public Transit," *New York Times*, January 21, 1952, https://timesmachine.nytimes.com/timesmachine/1952/01/21/96492204.pdf; Ralph Katz, "Bus Losses Worry Lines and Unions," *New York Times*, May 12, 1955, https://

timesmachine.nytimes.com/timesmachine/1955/05/12/84146871.pdf; Stanley Levey, "Deficit Is Shown by Transit Body," *New York Times*, July 16, 1958, https://timesmachine.nytimes.com/timesmachine/1958/07/16/91397432.pdf.

15. Stanley Levey, "Autos Aggravate Transit Problem; Kheel Seeks Cure," *New York Times*, May 31, 1955, https://timesmachine.nytimes.com/timesmachine/1955/05/31/79450645.pdf.

16. Stanley Levey, "Kheel Sees Fare at 20c If Riders Keep Diminishing," *New York Times*, June 13, 1955, https://timesmachine.nytimes.com/timesmachine/1955/06/13/80774119.pdf.

17. Ralph Katz, "Profited for Seized Bus Routes Foreseen by Transit Chairman," *New York Times*, April 11, 1962, https://timesmachine.nytimes.com/timesmachine/1962/04/11/86703122.pdf.

18. "Ridership Down for Bus Agency," *New York Times*, September 4, 1974, https://www.nytimes.com/1974/09/04/archives/ridership-down-for-bus-agency-levitt-puts-mabstoa-loss-at-56million.html.

19. Harris Schechtman, interview with the author, April 13, 2022.

20. Tri-State Transportation Commission, "Hub-Bound Travel 1963," August 1966.

21. Port Authority of New York and New Jersey, "History of the Port Authority Bus Terminal," accessed April 9, 2022, https://www.panynj.gov/bus-terminals/en/port-authority/pabt-history-.html.

22. New York Metropolitan Transportation Council, "Hub Bound Travel Data 2019," https://www.nymtc.org/Portals/0/Pdf/Hub%20Bound/2019%20Hub%20Bound/DM_TDS_Hub_Bound_Travel_2019.pdf.

23. Bruce Schaller, "CITYinFLUX: Understanding and Untangling Traffic and Transportation in NYC," April 2007.

24. Nancy Moran, "Private Lines Running Express Buses to the City's Outskirts," *New York Times*, June 11, 1970, https://www.nytimes.com/1970/06/11/archives/private-lines-running-express-buses-to-the-citys-outskirts.html.

25. "Mayor Buses in to Plug Express Lines," *New York Times*, August 17, 1971, https://www.nytimes.com/1971/08/17/archives/mayor-buses-in-to-plug-express-lines.html.

26. "Express Buses Have It All Over the M.T.A.," *New York Times*, November 14, 1981, https://www.nytimes.com/1981/11/14/opinion/l-express-buses-have-it-all-over-the-mta-092639.html.

27. New York Metropolitan Transportation Council, "Hub Bound Travel Data 2019," https://www.nymtc.org/Portals/0/Pdf/Hub%20Bound/2019%20Hub%20Bound/DM_TDS_Hub_Bound_Travel_2019.pdf.

28. "1st and 2d Avenues Will Get Bus Lanes," *New York Times*, January 4, 1970, https://www.nytimes.com/1970/01/04/archives/1st-and-2d-avenues-will-get-bus-lanes.html.

29. Joseph C. Ingraham, "City to Ban Meter Parking in Midtown by November," *New York Times*, January 6, 1970, https://www.nytimes.com/1970/01/06/archives/city-to-ban-meter-parking-in-midtown-by-november-midtown-meter.html.

30. David A. Andelman, "City Is Planning Transition Steps on Traffic Shifts," *New York Times*, July 24, 1980, https://timesmachine.nytimes.com/timesmachine/1980/07/24/112081498.pdf.

31. Ari L. Goldman, "2 Lanes on Madison Ave. to Be Reserved for Buses," *New York Times*, May 26, 1981, https://www.nytimes.com/1981/05/26/nyregion/2-lanes-on-madison-ave-to-be-reserved-for-buses.html.

32. Ari L. Goldman, "Bus-Only Lanes to Be Increased to Speed Travel," *New York Times*, June 15, 1982, https://www.nytimes.com/1982/06/15/nyregion/bus-only-lanes-to-be-increased-to-speed-travel.html.

33. Ari L. Goldman, "Buses Get Own 5th Ave. Lane in a New Bid to Ease Tie-Ups," *New York Times*, June 16, 1983, https://www.nytimes.com/1983/06/16/nyregion/buses-get-own-5th-ave-lane-in-a-new-bid-to-ease-tie-ups.html.

34. Ronald Smothers, "New Traffic Rules on 49th, 50th, and 51st Sts. Studied," *New York Times*, September 27, 1980, https://timesmachine.nytimes.com/timesmachine/1980/09/27/111296036.pdf.

35. Letter from Katharine Hepburn to Sam Schwartz, March 12, 1986, Sam Schwartz papers.

36. Frederic Papert, "On Mass Transit Ease Traffic with a Trolley," letter, *New York Times*, December 3, 1983, https://www.nytimes.com/1983/12/03/opinion/l-letter-on-mass-transit-ease-traffic-with-a-trolley-086532.html.

37. Suzanne Daley, "All Grumman Buses to Be Put off Streets in City Permanently," *New York Times*, February 8, 1984, https://www.nytimes.com/1984/02/08/nyregion/all-grumman-buses-to-be-put-off-streets-in-city-permanently.html.

38. Schechtman interview.

39. Ted Orosz, interview with the author, February 7, 2022.

40. Thomas J. Lueck, "New York's Bus Ridership Surges after Long Decline," *New York Times*, December 22, 1998, https://www.nytimes.com/1998/12/22/nyregion/new-york-s-bus-ridership-surges-after-long-decline.html.

41. Michael Bloomberg, "Untangling Traffic: Bloomberg's Promises," *Streetsblog*, July 11, 2001, https://usa.streetsblog.org/bloombergs-promises/comment-page-1/.

42. Joan Byron, interview with the author, January 24, 2022.

43. Veronica Vanterpool, interview with the author, January 19, 2022.

44. Partnership for New York City, "Growth or Gridlock: The Economic Case for Traffic Relief and Transit Improvement for a Greater New York," December 2006, https://pfnyc.org/wp-content/uploads/2020/02/Growth-or-Gridlock.pdf.

45. Jon Orcutt, interview with the author, October 4, 2021.

46. Thomas J. Lueck, "New York's Bus Ridership Surges after Long Decline," *New York Times*, December 22, 1998, https://www.nytimes.com/1998/12/22/nyregion/new-york-s-bus-ridership-surges-after-long-decline.html.

47. Orosz interview.

48. New York City Department of Transportation and Metropolitan Transportation Authority, "Fordham Road Public Workshop," June 2, 2021, https://www1.nyc.gov/html/dot/downloads/pdf/fordham-rd-major-deegan-expwy-boston-rd-jun2021.pdf.

49. Vanterpool interview.

50. New York City Department of Transportation, "Better Buses Fordham Road/Pelham Parkway," https://www1.nyc.gov/html/brt/html/routes/pelham.shtml.

51. New York City Department of Transportation, "Mayor Bloomberg, DOT Commissioner Sadik-Khan, DDC Commissioner Burney, And MTA Chairman Prendergast Announce Launch of Select Bus Service on Nostrand/Rogers Avenues," November 18, 2013, https://www1.nyc.gov/office-of-the-mayor/news/371-13/mayor-bloomberg-dot-commissioner-sadik-khan-ddc-commissioner-burney-mta-chairman-prendergast/#/0.

52. New York City Department of Transportation, "New York City Mobility Report," August 2019, https://www1.nyc.gov/html/dot/downloads/pdf/mobility-report-print-2019.pdf.

53. Brad Aaron, "Will DOT and the MTA Prioritize Parking over Tens of Thousands of B82 Riders?," *Streetsblog*, April 16, 2018, https://nyc.streetsblog.org/2018/04/16/will-dot-and-the-mta-prioritize-parking-over-tens-of-thousands-of-b82-riders/

54. Gersh Kuntzman, "Eyes on the Street: Great B82 SBS Service Hurt by Cars, Golden, Felder," *Streetsblog*, October 25, 2018, https://nyc.streetsblog.org/2018/10/25/eyes-on-the-street-great-b82-sbs-service-hurt-by-cars-golden-felder/.

55. Bill de Blasio, interview with the author, April 28, 2023.

56. Polly Trottenberg, interview with the author, February 15, 2022.

57. Gersh Kuntzman, "14th Street Landowners Sue City over Car Free Busway," *Streetsblog*, June 21, 2019, https://nyc.streetsblog.org/2019/06/21/breaking-14th-street-landowners-sue-city-over-car-free-busway/.

58. Gersh Kuntzman, "Cycle of Rage: NIMBY Lawyer Arthur Schwartz Sees Himself as Jane Jacobs Fighting Robert Moses," *Streetsblog*, January 14, 2019, https://nyc.streetsblog.org/2019/01/14/cycle-of-rage-nimby-lawyer-arthur-schwartz-sees-himself-as-jane-jacobs-fighting-robert-moses/.

59. "Better Buses 14th Street," New York City Department of Transportation, accessed April 8, 2022, https://www1.nyc.gov/html/brt/html/routes/14th-street.shtml.

60. "Select Bus Service," Metropolitan Transportation Authority, accessed April 8, 2022, http://web.mta.info/mta/planning/sbs/routes.html.

61. "Subway and Bus Ridership for 2019," Metropolitan Transportation Authority, accessed April 8, 2022, https://new.mta.info/agency/new-york-city-transit/subway-bus-ridership-2019.

62. "Bus Performance Dashboard," Metropolitan Transportation Authority, accessed April 8, 2022, http://busdashboard.mta.info/.

63. New York City Department of Transportation, "New York City Mobility Report."

64. Riders Alliance, "Bus Rider Blues: True Stories from 50 New Yorkers," December 7, 2021, https://static1.squarespace.com/static/61033b9bd377817f5bcc6db9/t/61ae65b63220e536ef873dae/1638819290032/Bus+Rider+Blues+2021+-+Riders+Alliance.

65. Sasha Blair-Goldensohn, interview with the author, February 16, 2022.

66. Danny Pearlstein, interview with the author, February 7, 2022.

67. TransitCenter et al., "Turnaround: Fixing New York City's Buses," July 2016, https://transitcenter.org/wp-content/uploads/2016/07/Turnaround_Fixing-NYCs-Buses-20July2016.pdf.

68. David Bragdon, interview with the author, February 22, 2022.

69. Andy Byford, interview with the author, April 1, 2022.

70. Riders Alliance, "Bus Rider Blues."

18. Ban, Charge, or Suffer: The Forever Politics of Congestion Pricing

1. Peter D. Norton, *Fighting Traffic: The Dawn of the Motor Age in the American City* (Cambridge, Mass.: MIT Press, 2008).

2. Samuel I. Schwartz, *No One at the Wheel: Driverless Cars and the Road of the Future* (New York: PublicAffairs, 2018).

3. Tri-State Regional Planning Commission, "Hub Bound Travel Trips Crossing the Manhattan Central Business District Cordon in 1971," February 1973.

4. Charles L. Goldenberg, "Traffic: Ease or Ban" (letter), *New York Times*, February 8, 1971, https://timesmachine.nytimes.com/timesmachine/1971/02/08/91266191.pdf.

5. "Hub Bound Travel Report 2007," New York Metropolitan Transportation Council, rev. June 2009, https://www.nymtc.org/Portals/0/Pdf/Hub%20Bound/Hub_Bound_Travel_Report_2007_Revised_June2009.pdf.

6. William Safire, "Gridlocks and Givebacks," *New York Times,* April 27, 1980, https://timesmachine.nytimes.com/timesmachine/1980/04/27/114074584.pdf.

7. David A. Andelman, "City Is Planning Transition Steps on Traffic Shifts," *New York Times*, July 24, 1980, https://timesmachine.nytimes.com/timesmachine/1980/07/24/112081498.pdf.

8. Glenn Fowler, "Ban on Driver-Only Cars at 4 Bridges Starts Sept. 22nd," *New York Times*, July 23, 1980, https://timesmachine.nytimes.com/timesmachine/1980/07/23/113949059.pdf.

9. Glenn Fowler, "Auto Club Seeking to Bar Curb on Driver-Only Cars," *New York Times*, July 24, 1980, https://timesmachine.nytimes.com/timesmachine/1980/07/24/112081511.pdf.

10. "Stay on Bridge Ban Is Upheld on Appeal," *New York Times*, October 22, 1980, https://timesmachine.nytimes.com/timesmachine/1980/10/22/111302215.pdf.

11. U.S. Department of Transportation ITS Joint Program Office, "Effects of Catastrophic Events on Transportation System Management and Operations New York City September 11, 2001," April 21, 2002.

12. William Vickrey, "Principles of Efficient Congestion Pricing," Columbia University, June 1992, https://www.vtpi.org/vickrey.htm.

13. Randy Kennedy, "Bloomberg May Seek to Continue Ban on One-Occupant Cars Entering Manhattan," *New York Times*, February 20, 2002, https://www.nytimes.com/2002/02/20/nyregion/bloomberg-may-seek-to-continue-ban-on-one-occupant-cars-entering-manhattan.html.

14. Sam Roberts, "July 19, 1911: The Day East River Tolls Melted Away," *New York Times*, July 19, 2011, https://cityroom.blogs.nytimes.com/2011/07/19/july-19-1911-the-day-east-river-tolls-melted-away.

15. "The Brooklyn Bridge: A Schedule of Tolls Reported," *New York Times*, March 13, 1883, https://timesmachine.nytimes.com/timesmachine/1883/03/13/102804778.pdf.

16. "To Abolish Tolls on City Bridges," *New York Times*, July 7, 1911, https://timesmachine.nytimes.com/timesmachine/1911/07/07/104828082.pdf.

17. Edward C. Burks, "Kheel Agrees to Head 'Save Transit Fare' Group," *New York Times*, August 5, 1969, https://timesmachine.nytimes.com/timesmachine/1969/08/05/89015751.pdf.

18. Maxwell Lehman, "For Kheel Toll Plan" (letter), *New York Times*, August 13, 1969, https://timesmachine.nytimes.com/timesmachine/1969/08/13/89018510.pdf.

19. Peter Passell, "2 Theorists of Real-Life Problems Get Nobel," *New York Times*, October 9, 1996, https://www.nytimes.com/1996/10/09/business/2-theorists-of-real-life-problems-get-nobel.html.

20. Tom Wicker, "In the Nation: Subway, Suburb, and Subsidy," *New York Times*, January 15, 1970, https://timesmachine.nytimes.com/timesmachine/1970/01/15/76675155.pdf.

21. Edward C. Burks, "Lindsay Endorses Kheel Toll Plan," *New York Times*, August 21, 1969, https://timesmachine.nytimes.com/timesmachine/1969/08/21/89022768.pdf.

22. "Kheel Fare Plan Derided by Moses," *New York Times*, October 10, 1969, https://timesmachine.nytimes.com/timesmachine/1969/10/10/78546073.pdf.

23. "Smith Fights Plan for Tolls on Free Access into City," *New York Times*, October 11, 1969, https://timesmachine.nytimes.com/timesmachine/1969/10/11/83781911.pdf.

24. Charles G. Bennett, "New Bridge Tolls Studied by City," *New York Times*, September 16, 1966.

25. Emanuel Perlmutter, "Controller Asks Mayor to Drop East River Bridge-Toll Study," *New York Times*, February 8, 1971, https://www.nytimes.com/1971/02/08/archives/controller-asks-mayor-to-drop-east-river-bridgetoll-study.html.

26. Edward Ranzal, "Tolls on Harlem River Bridges Studied," *New York Times*, March 25, 1971, https://www.nytimes.com/1971/03/25/archives/tolls-on-harlem-river-bridges-studied.html.

27. "Auto Club Assails Bridge Toll Plan," *New York Daily News*, August 16, 1976, via TBTA records, box 1129.

28. Arnold H. Lubasch, "Deadline for Tolls on 13 Bridges Is Set," *New York Times*, February 23, 1977, https://www.nytimes.com/1977/02/23/archives/deadline-for-tolls-on-13-bridges-is-set-judge-orders-that-fees-on.html.

29. "Hub Bound Travel Report 2007."

30. Rachel Shapiro, "Bring Back Two-way Tolling on the Verrazano-Narrows Bridge?," *Staten Island Advance*, February 8, 2017, https://www.silive.com/news/2017/02/bringing_back_two-way_tolling.html.

31. Memo from David Gurin to Deputy Mayor Robert Wagner on East River Bridge tolls, December 20, 1982, Gurin papers.

32. David W. Dunlap, "Koch Backs $10-a-Day Fees on Vehicles to Reduce Pollution," *New York Times*, August 4, 1987, https://www.nytimes.com/1987/08/04/nyregion/koch-backs-10-a-day-fees-on-vehicles-to-reduce-pollution.html.

33. Robert O. Boorstin, "U.S. Presses City to Cut Pollutants," *New York Times*, January 1, 1987, https://www.nytimes.com/1987/01/01/nyregion/column-one-clean-air-us-presses-city-to-cut-pollutants.html.

34. "Coalition of New York's Top Business, Labor and Civic Leaders . . . ," *PR Newswire*, August 12, 1987.

35. Ross Sandler, "How the City Can Better Manage the Flow; What Can Be Done about All the Traffic Congestion," *New York Times*, October 11, 1987, https://www.nytimes.com/1987/10/11/weekinreview/region-city-can-better-manage-flow-what-can-be-done-about-all-traffic-congestion.html.

36. Maria Newman, "Mayor Proposes a Fee for Driving into Manhattan," *New York Times*, April 22, 2007, https://www.nytimes.com/2007/04/22/nyregion/23mayorcnd.html.

37. "Hub Bound Travel Report 2008," New York Metropolitan Transportation Council, February 2010, https://www.nymtc.org/Portals/0/Pdf/Hub%20Bound/HUB_Bound_2008_Report.pdf.

38. "Central London Congestion Impacts Monitoring," Transport for London, July 2007, https://content.tfl.gov.uk/fifth-annual-impacts-monitoring-report-2007-07-07.pdf.

39. Sewell Chan, "Driving around Manhattan, You Pay, under One Traffic Idea," *New York Times*, November 11, 2005, https://www.nytimes.com/2005/11/11/nyregion/driving-around-manhattan-you-pay-under-one-traffic-idea.html.

40. Ronald Smothers, "Grumbling, but Still Moving, under New Rush-Hour Tolls," *New York Times*, March 27, 2001, https://www.nytimes.com/2001/03/27/nyregion/grumbling-but-still-moving-under-new-rush-hour-tolls.html.

41. Federal Highway Administration, "Pricing on Toll Facilities," July–September 2003, https://www.fhwa.dot.gov/policy/otps/vpqrrt/sec5.cfm.

42. "Growth or Gridlock," Partnership for New York City, December 2006, https://pfnyc.org/research/growth-or-gridlock-the-economic-case-for-traffic-relief-and-transit-improvement-for-a-greater-new-york/.

43. Ray Rivera, "Congestion Pricing Proposal Races Ahead," *New York Times*, June 7, 2007, https://www.nytimes.com/2007/06/07/nyregion/07cnd-congestion.html.

44. Nicholas Confessore, "G.O.P. Senators Draft Bill to Enact Plan for Manhattan Driving Fee," *New York Times*, July 14, 2007, https://www.nytimes.com/2007/07/14/nyregion/14congest.html.

45. Nicholas Confessore, "State Lawmakers Give Bloomberg Traffic Plan a Cool Reception," *New York Times*, June 8, 2007, https://www.nytimes.com/2007/06/08/nyregion/08cnd-hearing.html.

46. Nicholas Confessore, "Democrats on Traffic Fees: Thumbs Down," *New York Times*, June 13, 2007, https://empirezone.blogs.nytimes.com/2007/06/13/democrats-on-traffic-fees-thumbs-down/.

47. Environmental Protection Agency, "Approval and Promulgation of Implementation Plans and Designation of Areas for Air Quality Planning Purposes; State of New York," Federal Register 67, no 76 (April 19, 2002), https://www.govinfo.gov/content/pkg/FR-2002-04-19/pdf/02-9493.pdf#page=1.

48. Sewell Chan, "Are You Ready to Pay to Park on Your Street?," *New York Times*, June 17, 2007, https://cityroom.blogs.nytimes.com/2007/06/17/are-you-ready-to-pay-to-park-on-your-street/.

49. William Neuman, "Manhattanites Face Driving Fee on the Way Out," *New York Times*, June 30, 2007, https://www.nytimes.com/2007/06/30/nyregion/30congest.html.

50. Sewell Chan, "Congestion Pricing: It's Getting Personal," *New York Times*, July 10, 2007, https://cityroom.blogs.nytimes.com/2007/07/10/congestion-pricing-its-getting-personal/.

51. Sewell Chan, "Reports Give Conflicting Views of Congestion Pricing in City," *New York Times*, March 2, 2006, https://www.nytimes.com/2006/03/02/nyregion/reports-give-conflicting-views-of-congestion-pricing-in-city.html.

52. "Manhattan vs. the Outer Boroughs, *New York Times*, May 24, 2007, https://empirezone.blogs.nytimes.com/2007/05/24/manhattan-vs-the-other-boroughs/.

53. Andy Newman, "Outside Manhattan, Many Oppose Congestion Plan," *New York Times*, June 9, 2007, https://www.nytimes.com/2007/06/09/nyregion/09congestion.html.

54. David Spiel, "I'm Outta Here," *New York Times*, June 10, 2007, https://www.nytimes.com/2007/06/10/opinion/nyregionopinions/10LIspiel.html.

55. Kathy Wylde, interview with the author, March 13, 2022.

56. Danny Hakim, "Silver Challenges Health Benefits Promised in Manhattan Toll Plan," *New York Times*, June 12, 2007, https://www.nytimes.com/2007/06/12/nyregion/12silver.html?searchResultPosition=2.

57. Mark Weprin, interview with the author, March 1, 2022.

58. Editorial board, "Get Moving on Traffic Relief," *New York Times*, May 25, 2007, https://www.nytimes.com/2007/05/25/opinion/25fri2.html.

59. Danny Hakim, "Report Recommends Rejecting Plan on City Traffic," *New York Times*, July 9, 2007, https://www.nytimes.com/2007/07/09/nyregion/09congest.html.

60. Nicholas Confessore and Michael M. Grynbaum, "Skepticism in Albany about Traffic Plan Deadline," *New York Times*, July 13, 2007, https://www.nytimes.com/2007/07/13/nyregion/13congestion.html.

61. Anahad O'Connor and Danny Hakim, "Bloomberg Lashes Out at Lawmakers," *New York Times*, July 17, 2007, https://www.nytimes.com/2007/07/17/nyregion/17cnd-congestion.html.

62. Sewell Chan, "Poll: Opposition to Congestion Pricing Is Growing," *New York Times*, August 30, 2007, https://cityroom.blogs.nytimes.com/2007/08/30/poll-opposition-to-congestion-pricing-is-growing/.

63. Sewell Chan, "Is Manhattan Turning against Congestion Pricing?," *New York Times*, November 19, 2007, https://cityroom.blogs.nytimes.com/2007/11/19/is-manhattan-turning-against-congestion-pricing/.

64. William Neuman, "Panel Passes Congestion Pricing Plan," *New York Times*, January 31, 2008, https://cityroom.blogs.nytimes.com/2008/01/31/panel-passes-congestion-pricing-plan/.

65. Editorial board, "Give It a Green Light; Congestion Pricing Is Right for Right Now," *Newsday*, March 28, 2008.

66. Sewell Chan, "Council Votes 30–20 for Traffic Fees," *New York Times*, March 31, 2008, https://cityroom.blogs.nytimes.com/2008/03/31/council-panel-approves-congestion-pricing-measure/.

67. Jeremy W. Peters, "Mayor Presses for $8 Fee for Drivers to Enter Parts of Manhattan," *New York Times*, April 3, 2008, https://www.nytimes.com/2008/04/03/nyregion/03congest.html.

68. Diane Cardwell and Danny Hakim, "Bloomberg Tactics Were Highhanded on Traffic Plan, Lawmakers Say," *New York Times*, April 8, 2008, https://www.nytimes.com/2008/04/08/nyregion/08bloomberg.html.

69. Editorial board, "It's Up to You, Mr. Silver," *New York Times*, April 2, 2008, https://www.nytimes.com/2008/04/02/opinion/02wed4.html.

70. Nicholas Confessore, "Congestion Pricing Plan Dies in Albany," *New York Times*, April 7, 2008, https://cityroom.blogs.nytimes.com/2008/04/07/congestion-pricing-plan-is-dead-assembly-speaker-says/.

71. Editorial board, "Mr. Silver Does It Again," *New York Times*, April 8, 2022, https://www.nytimes.com/2008/04/08/opinion/08tue2.html.

72. Sam Schwartz, interview with the author, February 20, 2022.

73. Charles Komanoff, interview with the author, October 8, 2021.

74. Alex Matthiessen, interview with the author, March 14, 2022.

75. Emma G. Fitzsimmons, "Transit Group's Next Challenge: Selling a New Version of Congestion Pricing," *New York Times*, February 17, 2015, https://www.nytimes.com/2015/02/18/nyregion/transit-group-would-add-tolls-to-four-new-york-bridges.html.

76. Bill Keller, "Meet Sam Schwartz," *New York Times*, March 5, 2012, https://www.nytimes.com/2012/03/05/opinion/keller-meet-sam-schwartz.html.

77. Community Service Society, "Congestion Pricing: A CSS Analysis," October 24, 2017, https://www.cssny.org/news/entry/congestion-pricing-css-analysis.

78. Emma G. Fitzsimmons, "Group Seeks New Tolls in Manhattan to Pay for Region's Transportation Needs," *New York Times*, February 17, 2015, https://www.nytimes.com/2015/02/17/nyregion/group-seeks-new-tolls-in-manhattan-to-pay-for-regions-transportation-needs.html.

79. MoveNY, "Move QU," February 2015, https://movenewyork.files.wordpress.com/2015/02/move-qu-forward.pdf.

80. "Uber Congestion," *New York Post*, February 17, 2015, https://nypost.com/2015/02/17/uber-congestion/.

81. Fitzsimmons, "Transit Group's Next Challenge."

82. Uday Schultz, "Right Sizing the MTA: Cuts Too Far," Permanent Citizens Advisory Committee, MTA, August 9, 2017, https://pcac.org/right-sizing-the-mta-cuts-too-far-and-the-mtas-budget-efficiencies/.

83. Emma G. Fitzsimmons, "Money Out of Your Pocket: New Yorkers Tell of Subway Delay Woes," *New York Times*, May 31, 2017, https://www.nytimes.com/2017/05/31/nyregion/money-out-of-your-pocket-new-yorkers-tell-of-subway-delay-woes.html.

84. John Raskin, correspondence with the author, April 18, 2022.

85. Shane Goldmacher, "Cynthia Nixon Enters Race for New York Governor," *New York Times*, March 19, 2018, https://www.nytimes.com/2018/03/19/nyregion/cynthia-nixon-new-york-governor-cuomo.html.

86. Cynthia Nixon (@cynthianixon), "Tax the Rich. Fix the Subway," Tweet, September 5, 2018, https://twitter.com/cynthianixon/status/1037348010307420160.

87. Fix NYC Advisory Panel, "Fix NYC Advisory Panel Report," January 2018.

88. Editorial board, "Andrew Cuomo's Vision of New York's Future, and His," *New York Times*, January 3, 2018, https://www.nytimes.com/2018/01/03/opinion/andrew-cuomo-new-york-speech.html.

89. "Subway Performance Dashboard," Metropolitan Transportation Authority, accessed April 8, 2022, http://dashboard.mta.info/.

90. Nikki M. Mascali, "Straphangers Vent Frustrations Using #CuomosMTA," *Metro*, January 9, 2018, https://www.metro.us/straphangers-vent-frustrations-using-cuomosmta/.

91. Winnie Hu and Vivian Wang, "Cuomo's Congestion Pricing for New York City Begins to Take Shape," *New York Times*, January 16, 2018, https://www.nytimes.com/2018/01/16/nyregion/cuomos-congestion-pricing-for-new-york-city-begins-to-take-shape.html.

92. Winnie Hu and Vivian Wang, "Congestion Plan for Manhattan Gets Mixed Reviews," *New York Times*, January 19, 2018, https://www.nytimes.com/2018/01/19/nyregion/mayor-congestion-pricing-cuomo.html.

93. Hu and Wang, "Congestion Plan for Manhattan Gets Mixed Reviews."

94. Andy Byford, correspondence with the author, April 1, 2022.

95. Emma G. Fitzsimmons, "Can Charging Drivers Really Solve the Subway Crisis?," *New York Times*, October 12, 2018, https://www.nytimes.com/2018/10/12/nyregion/congestion-pricing-subway-mta.html.

96. Sarah Maslin Nir, "Data Shows City Drivers Won't Face the Brunt of Congestion Fees," *New York Times*, January 30, 2018, https://www.nytimes.com/2018/01/30/nyregion/congestion-pricing-report.html.

97. Editorial board, "Does Gov. Cuomo Really Want Congestion Pricing to Pass in NY?," *New York Post*, January 31, 2019.

98. David W. Chen, "In Protests, a Hint of the Fight to Come over Congestion Pricing," *New York Times*, January 21, 2018, https://www.nytimes.com/2018/01/21/nyregion/congestion-pricing-protests.html.

99. Emma G. Fitzsimmons, "Cuomo Warns of a 30 Percent Fare Hike If Congestion Pricing Fails," *New York Times*, February 7, 2019, https://www.nytimes.com/2019/02/07/nyregion/congestion-pricing-fare-hike.html.

100. Jesse McKinley and Winnie Hu, "Congestion Pricing in Manhattan, First Such Plan in U.S., Is Close to Approval," *New York Times*, March 25, 2019, https://www.nytimes.com/2019/03/25/nyregion/congestion-pricing-nyc.html.

101. Amy Paulin, interview with the author, March 10, 2022.

102. Melissa DeRosa, interview with the author, May 24, 2023.

103. Andrew Cuomo, interview with the author, April 3, 2023.

104. John Liu, interview with the author, March 14, 2022.

105. "Governor Andrew Cuomo Announces Highlights of the FY 2020 State Budget," State of New York Division of the Budget, Accessed April 8, 2020, https://www.budget.ny.gov/pubs/press/2019/pr-enactfy20.html.

106. "Congestion Pricing Won't Work, New Yorkers Say, Quinnipiac University Poll Finds," Quinnipiac University, accessed April 8, 2022, https://poll.qu.edu/poll-release?releaseid=2612.

107. Ritchie Torres, press conference attended by the author, August 15, 2022.

108. "Finding of No Significant Impact," Metropolitan Transportation Authority, June 27, 2023, https://new.mta.info/project/CBDTP/environmental-assessment.

109. "Siena College Poll Conducted by the Siena College Research Institute," Siena College, April 17, 2024, https://scri.siena.edu/wp-content/uploads/2024/04/Final-SNY0424-Crosstabs.pdf.

19. Two Miles: Bronx Mothers versus the Ghost of Moses

1. Nilka Martell, interview with the author, August 15, 2022.

2. Evan Simpo-Badnarski, "Dolphins Spotted in Bronx River, A Sign of Cleaner Waters," *New York Post*, January 20, 2023, https://nypost.com/2023/01/20/dolphins-spotted-in-bronx-river-a-sign-of-cleaner-waters/.

3. Jill Jonnes, "Saving the Bronx River: An Excerpt from *South Bronx Rising*," Gotham Center for New York City History, https://www.gothamcenter.org/blog/saving-the-bronx-river.

4. Tony Bouza, interview with the author, April 7, 2023.

5. Jonnes, "Saving the Bronx River."

6. Fernando Ferrer, interview with the author, April 6, 2023.

7. Ruben Diaz Jr., interview with the author, April 28, 2022.

8. "Partnership for the Future," Community Board 3, Borough of the Bronx, Spring 1993, https://www.nyc.gov/assets/planning/download/pdf/community/197a-plans/bx3_partnership_197a.pdf.

9. George Pataki, interview with the author, June 10, 2022.

10. Danny Peralta, interview with the author, February 10, 2022.

11. Wanda Salaman, interview with the author, May 23, 2022.

12. Winnie Hu, "Where a Little Girl Met Her Death, the Big Trucks Now Find a Hostile Welcome," *New York Times*, August 9, 1998, https://www.nytimes.com/1998/08/09/nyregion/neighborhood-reports-hunts-point-where-little-girl-met-her-death-big-trucks-now.html.

13. Marina Lakhman, "The Greening of a Highway," *New York Times*, January 3, 1999, https://www.nytimes.com/1999/01/03/nyregion/neighborhood-report-east-tremont-the-greening-of-a-highway.html.

14. Jim O'Grady, "Sheridan's Fork in the Road," *New York Times*, November 11, 2001, https://www.nytimes.com/2001/11/11/nyregion/neighborhood-report-bronx-up-close-sheridan-s-fork-road-either-fix-it-kill-it.html.

15. Ben Fried, "City Abruptly Rejects Sheridan Teardown," *Streetsblog*, June 8, 2012, https://nyc.streetsblog.org/2012/06/08/city-abruptly-rejects-sheridan-teardown-serrano-and-advocates-fight-back/.

16. "The Sheridan Expressway Study," City of New York, December 2013, https://www.nyc.gov/assets/planning/download/pdf/plans-studies/sheridan-hunts-point/final_full_report.pdf.

17. Jimmy Vielkind, "Invoking Robert Moses, Cuomo Unveils His Long Island Agenda," *Politico*, January 5, 2016, https://www.politico.com/states/new-york/albany/story/2016/01/invoking-robert-moses-cuomo-unveils-his-long-island-agenda-029638.

18. Marcos Crespo, interview with the author, April 29, 2022.

19. Andrew M. Cuomo, interview with the author, April 3, 2023.

20. Crespo interview.

21. Diaz interview.

22. Cuomo interview.

23. "Governor Cuomo Announces $1.8 Billion Project to Transform the South Bronx," March 20, 2017, Office of Bronx Borough president, https://bronxboropres.nyc.gov/2017/03/20/governor-cuomo-announces-1-8-billion-project-to-transform-south-bronx/.

24. "Appendix X: Reassessment of Concept 2," New York State Department of Transportation, April 2019, https://www.dot.ny.gov/southbronx/repository/X731.55_FEIS_Appendix_X.pdf.

25. David Meyer, "South Bronx to Cuomo: Don't Cut Off Hunts Point from the Bronx River with Another Highway," *Streetsblog*, March 29, 2018, https://nyc.streetsblog.org/2018/03/29/south-bronx-to-cuomo-dont-cut-off-hunts-point-from-the-bronx-river-with-another-highway/.

26. Diaz interview.

27. Crespo interview.

28. Marilyn Lara, "Community Rallies for a Reversal of State's Sheridan Plan," *Hunts Point Express*, March 5, 2018, https://huntspointexpress.com/2018/05/06/community-rallies-for-a-reversal-of-states-sheridan-plan/.

29. Dariella Rodriguez, interview with the author, April 18, 2023.

30. Tawkiyah Jordan, interview with the author, June 10, 2022.

31. Elena Conte, interview with the author, March 10, 2022.

32. Mychal Johnson, interview with the author, May 20, 2022.

33. Martell interview.

34. Peter Muennig, interview with the author, April 14, 2023.

35. Ritchie Torres, interview with the author, June 20, 2022.

36. Muennig interview.

20. *Deliveristas* and Dining Sheds: Locked-Down New York Unlocks Its Streets

1. New York City Office of the Mayor, "Transcript: Mayor de Blasio Holds Media Availability on COVID-19," March 16, 2020, https://www1.nyc.gov/office-of-the-mayor/news/156-20/transcript-mayor-de-blasio-holds-media-availability-covid-19.

2. New York City Office of the Mayor, "Mayor de Blasio Issues New Guidance to New Yorkers," March 20, 2020, https://www1.nyc.gov/office-of-the-mayor/news/173-20/mayor-de-blasio-issues-new-guidance-new-yorkers.

3. Office of the Special Narcotics Prosecutor for the City of New York, "NYC Overdose Deaths," https://www.snpnyc.org/opioid-crisis/.

4. New York City Department of Transportation, "Cycling in the City," September 2021, https://www1.nyc.gov/html/dot/downloads/pdf/cycling-in-the-city-2021.pdf.

5. "Seven Major Felony Offenses," New York Police Department, https://www1.nyc.gov/assets/nypd/downloads/pdf/analysis_and_planning/historical-crime-data/seven-major-felony-offenses-2000-2021.pdf.

6. Regan Weal, interview with the author, April 19, 2022.

7. Metropolitan Transportation Authority, "Subway and Bus Ridership for 2019," https://new.mta.info/agency/new-york-city-transit/subway-bus-ridership-2019.

8. Louis Ortiz, interview with the author, April 19, 2022.

9. Weal interview.

10. Julianne Cuba, "More Healthcare Workers Are Biking, Showing Urgency for Safe Routes through Central Park," *Streetsblog*, April 13, 2020, https://nyc.streetsblog.org/2020/04/13/healthcare-workers-are-biking-showing-urgency-for-safe-routes-through-central-park/.

11. Polly Trottenberg, interview with the author, February 15, 2022.

12. Jose Martinez, "Citi Bike Races into Upper Manhattan to Help Health Workers," *The City*, April 13, 2020, https://www.thecity.nyc/2020/4/13/21247116/citi-bike-races-into-upper-manhattan-to-help-health-workers.

13. New York City Department of Transportation, "Cycling in the City," September 2021, https://www1.nyc.gov/html/dot/downloads/pdf/cycling-in-the-city-2021.pdf.

14. Citi Bike, "Citi Bike Breaks Single Day Ridership Record during Tropical Storm Recovery," accessed April 13, 2022, https://ride.citibikenyc.com/blog/citi-bike-breaks-single-day-ridership-record-during-tropical-storm-recovery.

15. New York City Department of Transportation, "Cycling in the City," September 2021, https://www1.nyc.gov/html/dot/downloads/pdf/cycling-in-the-city-2021.pdf.

16. Thomas Tracy, Wes Parnell, and Molly Crane-Newman, "Queens Man Charged in DoorDash Delivery Worker's Murder; Victim Died Trying to Protect His E-Bike and Livelihood," *New York Daily News*, May 6, 2021, https://www.nydailynews.com/new-york/manhattan/ny-queens-man-murder-food-delivery-worker-francisco-villalva-vitinio-20210506-3f2ufkjqvvhn3ojxoh4z7sizrm-story.html.

17. Nicholas Williams, Rocco Parascandola, and Clayton Guse, "Surveillance Video Shows Suspect in Fatal Stab of Grubhub Deliveryman Sit with Victim on Manhattan Park Bench," *New York Daily News*, October 17, 2021, https://www.nydailynews.com/new-york/nyc-crime/ny-grubhub-e-bike-robbery-fatal-stabbing-suspect-video-20211017-jhwvyqbr5ncyrhuzleqdwgzqju-story.html.

18. Transportation Alternatives, "Transportation Alternatives Statement after Delivery Truck Driver Kills Two Individuals on the Upper East Side," December 25, 2021, https://www.transalt.org/press-releases/transportation-alternatives-statement-after-delivery-truck-driver-kills-two-individuals-on-the-upper-east-side.

19. Brittany Kriegstein and Clayton Guse, "Hardworking Immigrant DoorDash Deliveryman Fatally Struck on E-Bike by Hit-and-Run Driver in Brooklyn," *New York Daily News*, September 26, 2021, https://www.nydailynews.com/new-york/nyc-crime/ny

-brooklyn-e-bike-rider-fatally-struck-by-hit-and-run-driver-20210926-a7bxxzjggzf4rmxgx4f5zfxc2m-story.html.

20. Sergio Solano, interview with the author, October 14, 2021.

21. Fiifi Frimpong, "Deliveristas March to Demand Protection on the Willis Avenue Bridge and Beyond," *Streetsblog*, June 29, 2021, https://nyc.streetsblog.org/2021/06/29/deliveristas-march-to-demand-protection-on-the-willis-avenue-bridge-and-beyond/.

22. New York City Department of Transportation, "Cycling in the City," https://www.nyc.gov/html/dot/html/bicyclists/cyclinginthecity.shtml.

23. Keith Collins, "Why Bicycle Deaths in New York City Are at a 24-Year High," *New York Times*, March 5, 2024, https://www.nytimes.com/2024/03/05/nyregion/nyc-cyclist-deaths-ebike.html.

24. Nicole Gelinas, "E-nough," *City Journal*, September 21, 2023, https://www.city-journal.org/article/e-bikes-reversing-progress-in-making-ny-streets-safer-for-pedestrians-and-traditional-cyclists.

25. Times Square Alliance, "Pedestrian Counts," accessed April 12, 2022, https://www.timessquarenyc.org/do-business/market-research-data/pedestrian-counts#.VddSEvlVhBc.

26. Bill de Blasio, interview with the author, April 28, 2023.

27. Winnie Hu, "The Pandemic Gave New York Open Streets. Will They Survive?," *New York Times*, August 8, 2021, https://www.nytimes.com/2021/08/09/nyregion/open-streets-jackson-heights.html.

28. Josephine Stratman, "Open Streets Forged a Sense of Community in NYC during the Pandemic. Now They're Tearing One Neighborhood Apart," *New York Daily News*, September 23, 2022, https://www.nydailynews.com/new-york/ny-open-streets-queens-dispute-34th-avenue-jackson-heights-20220923-qpl2gapyo5diphnnowrgmd53h4-story.html.

29. Kenya Mighty, interview with the author, October 31, 2021.

30. David Meyer and Kevin Sheehan, "NYC Gave Up 8,550 Parking Spots for Al Fresco Dining amid COVID, *New York Post*, May 23, 2021, https://nypost.com/2021/05/23/nyc-gave-up-8550-parking-spots-for-outdoor-dining-amid-covid/.

31. De Blasio interview.

32. Majora Carter, interview with the author, March 8, 2022.

33. Carter interview.

34. New York City Department of Transportation, "Citywide Mobility Survey: Transportation Impacts of COVID-19 October 2020 Panel Results," https://www1.nyc.gov/html/dot/downloads/pdf/2020_cms_covid_october_summary_report.pdf.

35. William Dean, interview with the author, May 25, 2020.

36. Griffin Kelly and Melissa Klein, "NYC Protesters Rally in Greenwich Village against Outdoor Dining Sheds," *New York Post*, February 5, 2022, https://nypost.com/2022/02/05/nyc-protesters-rally-in-greenwich-village-against-outdoor-dining/.

37. David Soares, "The Bail Laws Takedown Albany Refused to Hear," *New York Post*, February 19, 2023, https://nypost.com/2023/02/19/albany-county-da-david-soares-new-yorks-bail-laws-are-a-bust/.

38. "Adult Arrests 18 and Over: 2012–2021," New York State Division of Criminal Justice Services, https://www.criminaljustice.ny.gov/crimnet/ojsa/arrests/index.htm.

39. "Seven Major Felony Offenses," New York Police Department, https://www.nyc.gov/assets/nypd/downloads/pdf/analysis_and_planning/historical-crime-data/seven-major-felony-offenses-by-precinct-2000-2022.pdf.

40. De Blasio interview.

41. New York Metropolitan Transportation Council, "Hub Bound Travel Data 2020," https://www.nymtc.org/Portals/0/Pdf/Hub%20Bound/2020%20Hub%20Bound/DM_TDS_Hub_Bound_Travel_2020.pdf.

42. Peter Madonia, interview with the author, February 23, 2022.

43. Christina Goldbaum, "Why the Fight over Parking in New York Is 'Like the Hunger Games,'" *New York Times*, January 5, 2021, https://www.nytimes.com/2021/01/05/nyregion/nyc-residential-parking.html.

44. Clayton Guse, "Some Bronx Car Owners Forced to Sleep in Vehicles While Waiting for Scarce Street Parking Spots: 'It's a Parking War,'" *New York Daily News*, March 26, 2022, https://www.yahoo.com/now/bronx-car-owners-forced-sleep-020000602.html.

45. New York City Taxi and Limousine Commission, "COVID-19 Impact on the NYC For-Hire Industry," accessed April 11, 2022, https://www1.nyc.gov/assets/tlc/downloads/pdf/covid-impact-report.pdf.

46. Caroline Tanner, "Why Yellow Cabs Are (Again) Your Best Bet in New York City," *The Points Guy*, November 4, 2021, https://thepointsguy.com/news/uber-lyft-shortage-taxi/.

47. Kim Mackrael and Preetika Rana," Uber and Lyft Thought Prices Would Normalize by Now. Here's Why They Are Still High," *Wall Street Journal*, October 30, 2021, https://www.wsj.com/articles/uber-and-lyft-thought-prices-would-normalize-by-now-heres-why-they-are-still-high-11635586381.

48. Riders Alliance, "Bus Rider Blues: True Stories from 50 New Yorkers," December 7, 2021, https://static1.squarespace.com/static/61033b9bd377817f5bcc6db9/t/61ae65b63220e536ef873dae/1638819290032/Bus+Rider+Blues+2021+-+Riders+Alliance.

49. "Collisions and Summonses Traffic Data Archive," New York Police Department, https://www.nyc.gov/site/nypd/stats/traffic-data/traffic-data-archive.page.

50. Julianne Cuba, "Reckless Driver Who Killed Baby Apolline Took Driver 'Accountability' Course—But It Didn't Change a Thing," *Streetsblog*, October 6, 2021, https://nyc.streetsblog.org/2021/10/06/reckless-driver-who-killed-baby-apolline-took-driver-accountability-course-but-it-didnt-change-a-thing/.

51. Kayla Levy, "Car-Free Plaza to Replace Road Where Driver Killed Baby," *Patch*, March 16, 2022, https://patch.com/new-york/fortgreene/car-free-plaza-replace-road-where-driver-killed-baby-dot.

52. Transportation Alternatives, "Sen. Schumer, Families for Safe Streets Members, Los Deliveristas Unidos, Next City Council Members Honor 2021 Crash Victims at World Day of Remembrance, Commit to Vision Zero Expansion," press release, November 22, 2021, https://www.transalt.org/press-releases/sen-schumer-families-for-safe-streets-members-los-deliveristas-unidos-next-city-council-members-honor-2021-crash-victims-at-world-day-of-remembrance-commit-to-vision-zero-expansion.

21. Sick Transit: Whither the Subways—and New York?

1. Delilah Goble, interview with the author, March 26, 2023.

2. Jose Martinez, "Widow of Motorman Killed in Subway Arson Fire Still Waiting for Answers," *The City*, June 14, 2020, https://www.thecity.nyc/2020/6/14/21291002/widow-of-motorman-killed-in-subway-arson-fire-still-waiting-for-answers.

3. David Meyer, "Andy Byford: Gov. Andrew Cuomo made my subway-saving job 'intolerable'," *New York Post*, March 7, 2020, https://nypost.com/2020/03/06/andy-byford-gov-andrew-cuomo-made-my-subway-saving-job-intolerable/.

4. Christina Goldbaum, "Who's Your Train Daddy?," *New York Times* February 21, 2020, https://www.nytimes.com/2020/02/21/nyregion/andy-byford-mta-last-day.html?searchResultPosition=19 .

5. "Subway Performance Dashboard," Metropolitan Transportation Authority, accessed April 8, 2022, http://dashboard.mta.info/.

6. "Subway and Bus Ridership for 2019," Metropolitan Transportation Authority, accessed April 8, 2022, https://new.mta.info/agency/new-york-city-transit/subway-bus-ridership-2019.

7. "How NYC Subway Riders Are Coping with Coronavirus Fears," *New York Post*, January 30, 2020, https://nypost.com/2020/01/31/how-nyc-subway-riders-are-coping-with-coronavirus-fears/.

8. Sarah Feinberg, interview with the author, March 23, 2022.

9. "Metropolitan Transportation Authority, New York; Joint Criteria; Note; Transit," S&P Global Ratings, March 24, 2020, https://new.mta.info/document/19536.

10. "Moody's Downgrades MTA, NY's Transportation Revenue Bonds to A2 from A1; Outlook Is Negative," Moody's Investor Service, April 16, 2020, https://new.mta.info/document/19526.

11. "Yield Curves and Indices," Electronic Municipal Market Access, Municipal Securities Rulemaking Board, https://emma.msrb.org/ToolsAndResources/BloombergYieldCurve.

12. Dana Rubinstein, "Why the MTA May Actually Get Its Bailout, Trump's History Notwithstanding," *Politico*, March 23, 2020, https://www.politico.com/states/new-york/city-hall/story/2020/03/23/why-the-mta-might-actually-get-its-bailout-trumps-history-notwithstanding-1268716.

13. Andrew M. Cuomo, interview with the author, April 3, 2023.

14. "A 33-Year-Old Trump Talks NYC Real Estate in 1980," MSNBC, https://www.msnbc.com/documentaries/watch/today-show-1980-with-donald-trump-589527619719.

15. Metropolitan Transportation Authority, "Transit and Bus Committee Meeting," October 2020, https://new.mta.info/document/21321.

16. Subway Fare Evasion, Metropolitan Transportation Authority, accessed May 8, 2024, https://dashboard.mta.info/?subway/fareevasion.

17. Brittany Kriegstein and Leonard Greene, "Delivery Man Fatally Shot While Waiting on a Bus. Family Says He'd Be Alive If NYC Subways Were Running Overnight," *New York Daily News*, May 26, 2020, https://www.nydailynews.com/new-york/ny-manhattan-shooting-subway-shutdown-20200526-f3vhzizr2fdyhjwqhpc2fuvply-story.html.

18. Feinberg, interview.

19. Julia Marsh, David Meyer, and Natalie Musumeci, "MTA's Sarah Feinberg Slams De Blasio Over Latest Subway Crime Spree," *New York Post*, May 14, 2021, https://nypost.com/2021/05/14/mtas-feinberg-slams-de-blasio-over-latest-subway-violence/.

20. Dave Colon, "Gov. Cuomo Restores 24-7 Service on Filthy, Crime-Ridden Subway That He Runs but Doesn't Ride," *Streetsblog NYC*, May 3, 2021.

21. Winnie Hu et al., "Is the Subway More Dangerous? Data Is Mixed," *New York Times*, May 18, 2021, https://www.nytimes.com/2021/05/18/nyregion/mta-subway-crime-stats-rates.html.

22. Jan Lee, correspondence with the author, April 3, 2023.

23. Marsh, Meyer, and Musumeci, "MTA's Sarah Feinberg Slams De Blasio."

24. "Alan Finder, "Chief of Transit Officers Resigns After 21 Months," *New York Times*, January 17, 1992, https://www.nytimes.com/1992/01/17/nyregion/chief-of-transit-officers-resigns-after-21-months.html; The City of New York Adopted Budget Fiscal Year 2024, https://www.nyc.gov/assets/omb/downloads/pdf/erc6-23.pdf.

25. Metropolitan Transportation Authority, "Spring 2022 Customers Count Survey," https://new.mta.info/document/95531.

26. "Mayor Adams and Governor Hochul Announce Major Actions to Keep Subways Safe and Address Transit Crime, Building on Ongoing State and City Collaboration," press release, city of New York, October 22, 2022, https://www.nyc.gov/office-of-the-mayor/news/773-22/mayor-adams-governor-hochul-major-actions-keep-subways-safe-address-transit.

27. Hannah Meyers, correspondence with the author, May 5, 2024.

28. Tina Moore and Matthew Sedacca, "Assault Victim of Jordan Neely Rips NYC for Failing to Address His Mental Health Issues," *New York Post*, May 6, 2023, https://nypost.com/2023/05/06/nyc-failed-to-address-jordan-neelys-mental-health-issues-victim/.

29. Editorial, "The Killing of Richard Henderson Is a Nightmare Shared by Every New Yorker," *New York Post*, January 19, 2024, https://nypost.com/2024/01/19/opinion/the-killing-of-richard-henderson-is-a-nightmare-shared-by-every-new-yorker/.

30. Haley Brown et. al., "Victim of Fatal NYC Subway Shove Was 'Honest and Sincere Person,' Neighbor Says," *New York Post*, March 27, 2024, https://nypost.com/2024/03/27/us-news/victim-of-fatal-nyc-subway-shove-was-honest-and-sincere-person-neighbor-says/.

31. Nolan Hicks et. al., "MTA boss Admits Subway Crime a 'Nightmare' but Vows NYC Won't Go Back to Bad Old Days," *New York Post*, March 27, 2024, https://nypost.com/2024/03/27/us-news/mta-boss-admits-subway-crime-a-nightmare-but-vows-nyc-wont-go-back-to-bad-old-days/.

32. Janno Lieber, interview with the author, December 12, 2023, https://manhattan.institute/event/congestion-pricing-and-challenges-facing-the-mta-janno-lieber.

33. Steve Cuozzo, "REBNY Reports Office Building Visitations Up as It Switches to Monthly Reports," *New York Post*, November 19, 2023, https://nypost.com/2023/11/19/business/rebny-takes-big-step-in-correcting-office-occupancy-misperceptions/.

34. Carl Campanile, "Midtown, Lower Manhattan Foot Traffic Down 33%," *New York Post*, November 5, 2023, https://nypost.com/2023/11/05/metro/midtown-lower-manhattan-still-suffering-from-one-of-worst-post-covid-recovery-rates-in-us-survey/.

35. Kathy Wylde, interview with the author, March 13, 2022.

36. Jessica Murray, interview with the author, April 7, 2022.

37. Eric Goldwyn, Alon Levy, Elif Ensari, and Marco Chitti, "Transit Costs Project: Understanding Transit Infrastructure Costs in American Cities," New York University Marron Institute of Urban Management, February 11, 2023, https://transitcosts.com/wp-content/uploads/TCP_Final_Report.pdf.

38. "Our Subway Open, 150,000 Try It," *New York Times*, October 28, 1904, https://timesmachine.nytimes.com/timesmachine/1904/10/28/118948832.pdf.

BIBLIOGRAPHY

Books

Ballon, Hilary, and Kenneth T. Jackson, eds. *Robert Moses and the Modern City: The Transformation of New York*. New York: W. W. Norton, 2007.

Branford Electric Railway Association. *Brooklyn Streetcars*. Charleston, S.C.: Arcadia, 2008.

Breines, Simon, and William J. Dean. *The Pedestrian Revolution: Streets without Cars*. New York: Random House, 1974.

Buzbee, William W. *Fighting Westway: Environmental Law, Citizen Activism, and the Regulatory War That Transformed New York City*. Ithaca, N.Y.: Cornell University Press, 2014.

Caro, Robert A. *The Power Broker: Robert Moses and the Fall of New York*. New York: Vintage, 1974.

Carson, Rachel. *Silent Spring*. Boston: Houghton Mifflin, 1962.

Chalfant, Henry, and Sacha Jenkins. *Training Days: The Subway Artists Then and Now*. New York: Thames and Hudson, 2014.

Cohen, Lizabeth. *Saving America's Cities: Ed Logue and the Struggle to Renew Urban America in the Suburban Age*. Cambridge and New York: Farrar, Straus and Giroux, 2019.

Corcoran, Sean, and Carlo McCormick. *City as Canvas: New York City Graffiti from the Martin Wong Collection*. New York: Skira Rizzoli, 2013.

Daughen, Joseph R., and Peter Binzen. *The Wreck of the Penn Central*. Boston: Little, Brown, 1971.

Derrick, Peter. *Tunneling to the Future: The Story of the Great Subway Expansion That Saved New York*. New York: New York University Press, 2001.

Doig, Jameson W. *Empire on the Hudson: Entrepreneurial Vision and Political Power at the Port of New York Authority*. New York: Columbia University Press, 2001.

Dwyer, Jim. *Subway Lives: 24 Hours in the Life of the New York City Subway*. New York: Crown, 1991.

Dyja, Thomas. *New York, New York, New York: Four Decades of Success, Excess, and Transformation*. New York: Simon and Schuster, 2021.

Flint, Anthony. *Wrestling with Moses: How Jane Jacobs Took on New York's Master Builder and Transformed the American City*. New York: Random House, 2009.

Freeman, Joshua B. *In Transit: The Transport Workers Union in New York City, 1933–1966*. Philadelphia: Temple University Press, 2001.

Friss, Evan. *On Bicycles: A 200-Year History of Cycling in New York City*. New York: Columbia University Press, 2019.

Gilbert, Gorman. *The Taxicab: An Urban Transportation Survivor*. Chapel Hill: University of North Carolina Press, 1982.

Grabar, Henry. *Paved Paradise: How Parking Explains the World*. New York: Penguin, 2023.

Gratz, Roberta Brandes. *The Battle for Gotham: New York in the Shadow of Robert Moses and Jane Jacobs*. New York: Nation, 2010.

———. *It's a Helluva Town: Joan K. Davidson, the J.M. Kaplan Fund, and the Fight for a Better New York*. New York: Bold Type, 2020.

Higashide, Stephen. *Better Buses, Better Cities: How to Plan, Run, and Win the Fight for Effective Transit*. Washington, D.C.: Island Press, 2019.

Hodges, Graham Russell Gao. *Taxi!: A Social History of the New York City Cabdriver*. Baltimore: Johns Hopkins University Press, 2007.

Hood, Clifton. *722 Miles: The Building of the Subways and How They Transformed New York*. New York: Simon and Schuster, 1993.

Hylan, John Francis. *Autobiography of John Francis Hylan, Mayor of New York*. New York: Rotary Press, 1922.

Jordan, Pete. *In the City of Bikes: The Story of the Amsterdam Cyclist*. New York: HarperPerennial, 2013.

Kanigel, Robert. *Eyes on the Street: The Life of Jane Jacobs*. New York: Alfred A. Knopf, 2016.

Kriegel, Jay L., ed. *John V. Lindsay: 50th Anniversary Commemoration*. McLean, Va.: International, 2015.

Jacobs, Jane. *The Death and Life of Great American Cities*. New York: Vintage, 1961.

———. *The Last Interview and Other Conversations*. Brooklyn: Melville House, 2016.

Jakle, John A., and Keith A. Sculle. *Lots of Parking: Land Use in a Car Culture*. Charlottesville: University of Virginia Press, 2004.

Jonnes, Jill. *Conquering Gotham: The Construction of Penn Station and Its Tunnels*. New York: Viking, 2007.

———. *South Bronx Rising: The Rise, Fall, and Resurrection of an American City*. 2nd ed. New York: Fordham University Press, 2002.

LeFevre, Joel. *Forcing the Hand of Justice: Seeking the Truth about My Brother's Death; My Family's Fight against a Broken System (The NYPD)*. Manitoba: Friesen, 2021.

Lerner, Barron H. *One for the Road: Drunk Driving since 1900*. Baltimore: Johns Hopkins University Press, 2011.

Mahler, Jonathan. *Ladies and Gentlemen, the Bronx Is Burning: 1977; Baseball, Politica, and the Battle for the Soul of a City*. New York: Picador, 2005.

Manshel, Andrew M. *Learning from Bryant Park: Revitalizing Cities, Towns, and Public Spaces*. New Brunswick, N.J.: Rutgers University Press, 2020.

Merrill, Jean. *The Pushcart War*. New York: New York Review of Books, 1964.

Meyers, Stephen L. *Manhattan's Lost Streetcars*. Charleston, S.C.: Arcadia, 2005.

Minton, Anna. *Ground Control: Fear and Happiness in the Twenty-First Century City*. New York: Penguin, 2009.

Mitgang, Herbert. *Once Upon a Time in New York: Jimmy Walker, Franklin Roosevelt, and the Last Great Battle of the Jazz Age*. New York: Free Press, 2000.

Morris, John E. *Subway: The Curiosities, Secrets and Unofficial History of the New York City Transit System*. New York: Black Dog and Leventhal, 2020.

Moscow, Warren. *The Last of the Big-Time Bosses: The Life and Times of Carmine De Sapio and the Rise and Fall of Tammany Hall*. New York: Stein and Day, 1971.

Moss, Jeremiah. *Vanishing New York: How a Great City Lost Its Soul*. New York: Dey Street, 2018.

Newfield, Jack. *The Education of Jack Newfield*. New York: St. Martin's, 1984.

Newfield, Jack, and Wayne Barrett. *City for Sale: Ed Koch and the Betrayal of New York*. New York: Harper and Row, 1988.

Norton, Peter D. *Fighting Traffic: The Dawn of the Motor Age in the American City*. Cambridge, Mass.: MIT Press, 2008.

Plotch, Philip Mark. *Last Subway: The Long Wait for the Next Train in New York City*. Ithaca, N.Y.: Three Hills, 2020.

———. *Politics across the Hudson: The Tappan Zee Megaproject*. New Brunswick, N.J.: Rutgers University Press, 2015.

Raskin, Joseph B. *The Routes Not Taken: A Trip through New York City's Unbuilt Subway System*. New York: Fordham University Press, 2014.

Ravitch, Richard. *So Much to Do: A Full Life of Business, Politics, and Confronting Fiscal Crises*. New York: PublicAffairs, 2014.

Roberts, Sam. *Grand Central: How a Train Station Transformed America*. New York: Grand Central, 2013.

Rockefeller, David. *Memoirs*. New York: Random House, 2002.

Sadik-Khan, Janette. *Streetfight: Handbook for an Urban Revolution*. New York: Viking, 2016.

Sagalyn, Lynne B. *Times Square Roulette: Remaking the City Icon*. Cambridge, Mass.: MIT Press, 2001.

Schwartz, Samuel I. *No One at the Wheel: Driverless Cars and the Road of the Future*. New York: PublicAffairs, 2018.

———. *Street Smart: The Rise of Cities and the Fall of Cars*. New York: PublicAffairs, 2015.

Shoup, Donald. *The High Cost of Free Parking*. New York: Routledge, 2005.

Sparberg, Andrew J. *From a Nickel to a Token: The Journey from Board of Transportation to MTA*. New York: Fordham University Press, 2015.

Vanderbilt, Tom. *Traffic: Why We Drive the Way We Do (And What It Says about Us)*. New York: Random House, 2008.

Wolmar, Christian. *Are Trams Socialist? Why Britain Has No Transport Policy*. London: London Publishing Partnership, 2016.

Manuscript Collections

Carson, Lettie Gay. Papers. Manuscripts and Archives Division. New York Public Library. Astor, Lenox, and Tilden Foundations.

Hayes, Shirley. Papers. New-York Historical Society.

Jacobs, Jane. Papers. John J. Burns Library. Boston College.
Moses, Robert. Papers. Manuscripts and Archives Division. New York Public Library. Astor, Lenox, and Tilden Foundations.
NYPIRG Straphangers Campaign Records. Manuscripts and Archives Division. New York Public Library. Astor, Lenox, and Tilden Foundations.
Regional Plan Association Records. Division of Rare and Manuscript Collections. Cornell University Library.
Transport Workers Union of America Records. WAG 235. Tamiment Library/Robert F. Wagner Labor Archives, New York University.
Triborough Bridge and Tunnel Authority Records, 1946–69. Metropolitan Transportation Authority Bridges and Tunnels Special Archive. New York.

Oral Histories

Hayes, Shirley. "An Oral History Interview Conducted for the GVSHP Preservation Archives." Interview by Josh Berman. Greenwich Village Society for Historic Preservation, 2000. https://media.villagepreservation.org/wp-content/uploads/2020/05/15034903/hayes_transcript.pdf.
Lyons, Edith. "An Oral History Interview Conducted for the GVSHP Preservation Archives." Interview by Vicki Weiner. Greenwich Village Society for Historic Preservation, 1997 and 1998. https://media.villagepreservation.org/wp-content/uploads/2020/05/15034857/lyons_transcript.pdf.
MTA Capital Program 1979–91. Oral History Project. Manuscripts and Archives Division. New York Public Library. Astor, Lenox, and Tilden Foundations.
Downey, Mortimer. Interview by Wendy Feuer, February 15, 2020.
Plavin, David. Interview by Wendy Feuer, July 1, 2021.
Polan, Steven M. Interview by Wendy Feuer, June 1, 2021.
Ravitch, Richard. Interview by Wendy Feuer, June 7, 2021.
Fox, Hetty. "Interview with the Bronx African American History Project." Interview by Mark Naison, Richard Richardson, and Mark C. Smith. BAAHP Digital Archive at Fordham University. https://research.library.fordham.edu/baahp_oralhist/102/.

INDEX

Nicole Gelinas is a senior fellow at the Manhattan Institute, a contributing editor to the Manhattan Institute's *City Journal*, and a regular columnist for the *New York Post*. She is the author of the 2009 book on the global financial crisis, *After the Fall: Saving Capitalism from Wall Street—and Washington*. She and her husband live in Hell's Kitchen.

EMPIRE STATE EDITIONS

SELECT TITLES FROM EMPIRE STATE EDITIONS

Andrew J. Sparberg, *From a Nickel to a Token: The Journey from Board of Transportation to MTA*

New York's Golden Age of Bridges. Paintings by Antonio Masi, Essays by Joan Marans Dim, Foreword by Harold Holzer

Daniel Campo, *The Accidental Playground: Brooklyn Waterfront Narratives of the Undesigned and Unplanned*

John Waldman, *Heartbeats in the Muck: The History, Sea Life, and Environment of New York Harbor, Revised Edition*

John Waldman (ed.), *Still the Same Hawk: Reflections on Nature and New York*

Joseph B. Raskin, *The Routes Not Taken: A Trip Through New York City's Unbuilt Subway System*

Phillip Deery, *Red Apple: Communism and McCarthyism in Cold War New York*

North Brother Island: The Last Unknown Place in New York City. Photographs by Christopher Payne, A History by Randall Mason, Essay by Robert Sullivan

Stephen Miller, *Walking New York: Reflections of American Writers from Walt Whitman to Teju Cole*

Tom Glynn, *Reading Publics: New York City's Public Libraries, 1754–1911*

R. Scott Hanson, *City of Gods: Religious Freedom, Immigration, and Pluralism in Flushing, Queens*. Foreword by Martin E. Marty

Mark Naison and Bob Gumbs, *Before the Fires: An Oral History of African American Life in the Bronx from the 1930s to the 1960s*

Robert Weldon Whalen, *Murder, Inc., and the Moral Life: Gangsters and Gangbusters in La Guardia's New York*

Joanne Witty and Henrik Krogius, *Brooklyn Bridge Park: A Dying Waterfront Transformed*

Sharon Egretta Sutton, *When Ivory Towers Were Black: A Story about Race in America's Cities and Universities*

Pamela Hanlon, *A Wordly Affair: New York, the United Nations, and the Story Behind Their Unlikely Bond*

Britt Haas, *Fighting Authoritarianism: American Youth Activism in the 1930s*

David J. Goodwin, *Left Bank of the Hudson: Jersey City and the Artists of 111 1st Street*. Foreword by DW Gibson

Nandini Bagchee, *Counter Institution: Activist Estates of the Lower East Side*

Susan Celia Greenfield (ed.), *Sacred Shelter: Thirteen Journeys of Homelessness and Healing*

Elizabeth Macaulay-Lewis and Matthew M. McGowan (eds.), *Classical New York: Discovering Greece and Rome in Gotham*

Susan Opotow and Zachary Baron Shemtob (eds.), *New York after 9/11*

Andrew Feffer, *Bad Faith: Teachers, Liberalism, and the Origins of McCarthyism*

Colin Davey with Thomas A. Lesser, *The American Museum of Natural History and How It Got That Way*. Forewords by Neil deGrasse Tyson and Kermit Roosevelt III

Wendy Jean Katz, *Humbug: The Politics of Art Criticism in New York City's Penny Press*

Lolita Buckner Inniss, *The Princeton Fugitive Slave: The Trials of James Collins Johnson*

Mike Jaccarino, *America's Last Great Newspaper War: The Death of Print in a Two-Tabloid Town*

Angel Garcia, *The Kingdom Began in Puerto Rico: Neil Connolly's Priesthood in the South Bronx*

Jim Mackin, *Notable New Yorkers of Manhattan's Upper West Side: Bloomingdale–Morningside Heights*

Matthew Spady, *The Neighborhood Manhattan Forgot: Audubon Park and the Families Who Shaped It*

Marilyn S. Greenwald and Yun Li, *Eunice Hunton Carter: A Lifelong Fight for Social Justice*

Jeffrey A. Kroessler, *Sunnyside Gardens: Planning and Preservation in a Historic Garden Suburb*

Elizabeth Macaulay-Lewis, *Antiquity in Gotham: The Ancient Architecture of New York City*

Ron Howell, *King Al: How Sharpton Took the Throne*

Phil Rosenzweig, *"12 Angry Men": Reginald Rose and the Making of an American Classic*

Jean Arrington with Cynthia S. LaValle, *From Factories to Palaces: Architect Charles B. J. Snyder and the New York City Public Schools*. Foreword by Peg Breen

Boukary Sawadogo, *Africans in Harlem: An Untold New York Story*

Alvin Eng, *Our Laundry, Our Town: My Chinese American Life from Flushing to the Downtown Stage and Beyond*

Stephanie Azzarone, *Heaven on the Hudson: Mansions, Monuments, and Marvels of Riverside Park*

Ron Goldberg, *Boy with the Bullhorn: A Memoir and History of ACT UP New York*. Foreword by Dan Barry

Peter Quinn, *Cross Bronx: A Writing Life*

Mark Bulik, *Ambush at Central Park: When the IRA Came to New York*

Matt Dallos, *In the Adirondacks: Dispatches from the Largest Park in the Lower 48*

Brandon Dean Lamson, *Caged: A Teacher's Journey Through Rikers, or How I Beheaded the Minotaur*

Raj Tawney, *Colorful Palate: Savored Stories from a Mixed Life*

Edward Cahill, *Disorderly Men*

Joseph Heathcott, *Global Queens: An Urban Mosaic*

Francis R. Kowsky with Lucille Gordon, *Hell on Color, Sweet on Song: Jacob Wrey Mould and the Artful Beauty of Central Park*

Jill Jonnes, *South Bronx Rising: The Rise, Fall, and Resurrection of an American City, Third Edition*

Barbara G. Mensch, *A Falling-Off Place: The Transformation of Lower Manhattan*

David J. Goodwin, *Midnight Rambles: H. P. Lovecraft in Gotham*

Felipe Luciano, *Flesh and Spirit: Confessions of a Young Lord*

Maximo G. Martinez, *Sojourners in the Capital of the World: Garifuna Immigrants*

Jennifer Baum, *Just City: Growing Up on the Upper West Side When Housing Was a Human Right*

Davida Siwisa James, *Hamilton Heights and Sugar Hill: Alexander Hamilton's Old Harlem Neighborhood Through the Centuries*

Annik LaFarge, *On the High Line: The Definitive Guide, Third Edition*. Foreword by Rick Dark

Marie Carter, *Mortimer and the Witches: A History of Nineteenth-Century Fortune Tellers*

Alice Sparberg Alexiou, *Devil's Mile: The Rich, Gritty History of the Bowery*. Foreword by Peter Quinn

Carey Kasten and Brenna Moore, *Mutuality in El Barrio: Stories of the Little Sisters of the Assumption Family Health Service*. Foreword by Norma Benítez Sánchez

Kimberly A. Orcutt, *The American Art-Union: Utopia and Skepticism in the Antebellum Era*

Jonathan Butler, *Join the Conspiracy: How a Brooklyn Eccentric Got Lost on the Right, Infiltrated the Left, and Brought Down the Biggest Bombing Network in New York*

Jack Hodgson, *Young Reds in the Big Apple: The New York Young Pioneers of America, 1923–1934*

For a complete list, visit www.fordhampress.com/empire-state-editions.